NEW PERSPECTIVES ON THE CHINESE COMMUNIST REVOLUTION

New Perspectives on the Chinese Communist Revolution brings together the work of a new, international generation of students of Chinese Communist Party (CCP) history. Exploiting new sources made available in China in the 1980s, some chapters in this book bring new events and areas into the study of the CCP. Other chapters provide detailed analyses on the basis of new evidence of long-standing problems in the history of the CCP, such as the rise of Mao Zedong. Yet others are significant because they offer new explanatory frameworks for understanding CCP history, such as the importance of Yan'an as symbolic capital. New issues are brought up, such as the role of women, internal CCP terror, the use of opium sales to sustain the Yan'an economy, and the great difficulty of controlling mass peasant movements once mobilized. The most important contribution of the volume is to show that the old explanations of the CCP's success—peasant support, organizational strength, the supply of administrative services—are incomplete and do not account for the diverse and heterogenous nature of the CCP and the great difficulties it had in building up mass support. This volume makes clear that the question of the CCP's success remains one of the most elusive but also most important that historians of China face today.

NEW PERSPECTIVES ON THE CHINESE COMMUNIST REVOLUTION

Edited by Tony Saich and Hans van de Ven

David E. Apter	John Dunn
Stephen C. Averill	Christina Gilmartin
Gregor Benton	Kathleen Hartford
Lucien Bianco	Warren Sun
Timothy Cheek	Frederick C. Teiwes
Chen Yung-fa	Susanne Weigelin-Schwiedrzik

An East Gate Book

M.E. Sharpe
Armonk, New York
London, England

An East Gate Book

Copyright © 1995 by M. E. Sharpe, Inc.

Library of Congress Cataloging-in-Publication Data

New perspectives on the Chinese Communist revolution / edited by
Tony Saich and Hans J. van de Ven.
P.   cm.
Papers from a conference sponsored by Sinological Institute,
Leiden University and International Institute of Social History,
held January 8–12, 1990 in Leiden and Amsterdam.
Includes bibliographical references and index.
ISBN 1-56324-428-4   —   ISBN 1-56324-429-2 (pbk.)
1. Chung-kuo kung ch´an tang—History—Congresses.
2. Communism—China—History—Congresses.
I. Saich, Tony. II. Van de Ven, Hans J.
JQ1519.A5R57   1994
951.04—dc20   94-26985
CIP

Printed in the United States of America

∞

BM (c)   10   9   8   7   6   5   4   3   2   1
BM (p)   10   9   8   7   6   5   4   3   2   1

Contents

Acknowledgments

The chapters in this book are the result of a conference cosponsored by the Sinological Institute, Leiden University, and the International Institute of Social History, Amsterdam, held between 8 and 12 January 1990. The first two days of the workshop were held in Leiden, and after a day's break to recuperate the International Institute of Social History hosted the final two days, including the public session held on the last afternoon.

First, the staff of both institutions must be thanked for their cooperation in ensuring that the planned program ran smoothly. Financial support was received from the Royal Netherlands Academy of Arts and Sciences (Koninkrijke Nederlandse Akademie van Wetenschappen), the International Institute of Social History (Internationaal Instituut voor Sociale Geschiedenis), the Faculty of Letters of Leiden University, the Foundation for the Advancement of Cultural Relations Between the Royal Netherlands and China (Stichting ter Bevordering van de Culturele Betrekkingen tussen het Koninkrijk der Nederlanden en China), and AKZO nv. Without their various financial contributions, it would have been impossible to bring such an array of scholars to the Netherlands.

In addition to the participants, the following individuals deserve our thanks for their help in organizing the workshop: Dr. Woei-Lien Chong, Professor E. Fischer, Dr. Stefan R. Landsberger, Ms. A. Merens, and Professor E. Zürcher. Special thanks are reserved for Ms. Els Heye, without whose help I would have gone crazy during both the preparations for the conference and the conference itself. She dealt with all manner of technical problems with a reassuring calm and still had time to put together an entertaining social program for the conference participants.

Finally, there was the headache of publication. Two anonymous reviewers provided constructive criticisms that have improved the final product considerably. I would also like to thank Jeff Wasserstrom for his comments on restructuring the manuscript as well as for his helpful remarks on the individual chapters. We would especially like to thank Doug Merwin for his enthusiastic response to our plea for assistance. As usual, he and the staff of M. E. Sharpe offered all possible assistance to enable the volume, in its present form, to see the light of day.

Tony Saich
Leiden, January 1994

Abbreviations

AB	Anti-Bolshevik Corps
BFHQ	*Beifang hongqi* (Northern Red Flag)
CC	Central Committee
CCP	Chinese Communist Party
CEC	Central Executive Committee
Comintern	Communist International
CPSU	Communist Party of the Soviet Union
CYL	Communist Youth League
DTWJ	*Deng Tuo wenji* (Collected Works of Deng Tuo)
ECCI	Executive Committee of the Communist International
ERA	Eighth Route Army
FBIS	Foreign Broadcasting Information Service
GMD	Guomindang (Nationalist Party)
HBLS	*Hebei geming lieshi shiliao* (Biographies of Hebei Revolutionary Martyrs)
HBWS	*Hebei wenshi ziliao xuanji* (Collection of Hebei Historical Materials)
HBYK	*Hebei yuekan* (Hebei Monthly)
NFA	New Fourth Army
NLV	National Liberation Vanguards
PRC	People's Republic of China
SGNBQ	*Kang-Ri zhanzheng shiqi Shaan-Gan-Ning bianqu caizheng jingji shiliao zhaibian* (Selected Historical Documents on the Finance and Economics of the Shaan-Gan-Ning Border Region During the Anti-Japanese War)
SXWS	*Shanxi wenshi ziliao* (Shanxi Historical Materials)
SYL	Socialist Youth League
TJWS	*Tianjin wenshi ziliao xuanji* (Collection of Tianjin Historical Materials)
WSSQDST	*Wusi shiqi de shetuan* (Societies and Associations of the May Fourth Period)
WSZL	*Wenshi ziliao xuanji* (Collection of Historical Materials [National])
XWGZ	*Zhongguo gongchandang xinwen gongzuo wenjian huibian* (Collected Documents of CCP Journalism Activities)
XXZL	*Xinmin xuehui ziliao* (Materials on the New Citizen's Study Society)

| ZGQN | *Zhongguo qingnian* (Chinese Youth) |
| ZYGM | *Zhongyang geming genjudi shiliao xuanbian* (Selected Historical Materials on the Central Revolutionary Base Area) |

The system of transcription for Chinese names and places used in this book is the *Hanyu pinyin* system. This system is now used by the PRC and is increasingly used by scholars outside the PRC. However, for several familiar names the *Hanyu pinyin* system has not been used. These are the following:

Familiar Spelling	*Hanyu pinyin*
Canton	Guangzhou
Chiang Kai-shek	Jiang Jieshi
Sun Yat-sen	Sun Zhongshan
Yangtze River	Changjiang

Contributors

David E. Apter is the Henry J. Heinz II Professor of Comparative Political and Social Development, Yale University.

Stephen C. Averill is associate professor of history, Michigan State University.

Gregor Benton is professor with the Department of East Asian Studies at the University of Leeds.

Lucien Bianco is professor at the École des Hautes Études en Sciences Sociales, Paris.

Timothy Cheek is associate professor of history, Colorado College.

Chen Yung-fa is concurrently Research Fellow of the Institute of Modern History, Academia Sinica, and professor at National Taiwan University.

John Dunn is professor of political science, Cambridge University, and a Fellow of King's College.

Christina Gilmartin is associate professor of history, Northeastern University, and a research fellow at the Fairbank Center, Harvard University.

Kathleen Hartford is professor of political science, University of Massachusetts (Boston), and a research fellow at the Fairbank Center, Harvard University.

Tony Saich is professor of contemporary Chinese politics and administration at the Sinological Institute, Leiden, and a Senior Research Fellow at the International Institute of Social History, Amsterdam.

Warren Sun is a researcher at the Department of Government, University of Sydney.

Frederick C. Teiwes is professor of Chinese politics (Personal Chair) in the Department of Government at the University of Sydney.

Hans J. van de Ven is lecturer at the Faculty of Oriental Studies, Cambridge University.

Susanne Weigelin-Schwiedrzik is professor of modern Chinese studies, Heidelburg University, Germany.

Introduction

No matter what the future may hold for the Chinese Communist Party (CCP)—and it would be simply naive to assume its early demise—the history of Chinese communism remains a most compelling story. Here we have a group of people, a very small group indeed at the time of the CCP's inception in the 1920s, who set out to alter their world in the hope of bringing prosperity and justice. Repeatedly driven to the social and geographic margins of China and not only fearful of their enemies but also on occasion deeply suspicious of one another, in 1949 they conquered the vastnesses of China. While convinced that possession of political power was the sine qua non for a better China, they were not certain about much else and constructed along the way new institutions, styles of operation, values, histories, myths, and vocabularies. The boldness and comprehensiveness of what they set out to achieve, as well as the fundamental nature of the questions they asked about the nature of society, politics, and the shape of the past and future all render the CCP a compelling subject of inquiry, not just for China experts but also for historians and social scientists generally.

This collection of essays presents new perspectives on the history of the CCP between its founding in 1920 and its conquest of China in 1949. The chapters draw on the voluminous primary sources that have become available in the last decade and a half. The authors draw attention to events and places that until now have suffered historiographical neglect or offer revisionist interpretations of the signal events and leading figures of CCP history, in many cases relating them to new theoretical perspectives on culture and local society, including language and gender relations. At the conference on new perspectives on the Chinese communist revolution held in 1990 in Amsterdam and Leiden, where the essays that make up the present volume were first presented, all participants agreed that existing discussions of CCP history could no longer account for the new data and new ideas that have emerged in the last years. The conference became an exciting seminar in which new arguments were explored freely; it was not an event devoted to the stubborn defense of established positions. No single new interpretative framework was produced, so it would not be appropriate to formulate such a framework here. The differences in methodology and perspective adopted by the authors would mean that the result could only be a Procrustean bed.

Taken together, the essays illustrate several important points. The first is that to define the CCP as a Leninist party begs more questions than it answers. For one thing, regional diversity was one of its hallmarks, and this diversity was in constant tension with the notion of the party as a hierarchical, centrally controlled organization. Communist organizations evolved out of local society, adapted themselves to it, and were enmeshed in it.

As a whole the volume also illustrates that a monocausal explanation for the CCP's conquest of China—be it the popular appeal of its socioeconomic program, its organizational strength, or the accidents of history that ran in its favor—is inadequate. Others factors, such as the creation and exploitation of symbolic power and the CCP's provision of new templates for action, should be included in our account of its history. With its myriad centers of power, substantial if decentralized military forces, and strong local traditions, China was not an easy place to make revolution. Unlike their Russian counterparts, Chinese Communists did not and could not have become the masters of their society by means of a coup in one central urban place. Chinese Communists adapted their policies, institutions, and styles of operation to the rich variety of realities they encountered in China. To say that the CCP rose to power on the basis of a peasant revolution is a caricature of a much more complex process.

Before outlining briefly how individual chapters contribute to our understanding of early CCP history, it may be useful to summarize the standard Western account. After the creation of communist groups in several places in 1920, in July 1921 several representatives convened a First Congress in Shanghai with the aid of the Comintern emissaries Maring and Grigori Voitinsky. Despite the strong objection of many Chinese Communists, in 1923 under Comintern pressure the CCP entered into a United Front with the nationalist Guomindang (GMD), which ended in 1927 with Chiang Kai-shek's attempt to expunge the Communists not only from the GMD but also from Chinese politics.

In the following period the CCP fell prone to intense factional struggle. Compelled to survive in mountain country and dependent on guerrilla tactics, its members managed to create soviets in Central and South China of which the Jiangxi Soviet was the most famous. In these soviets, Chinese Communists experimented with military organization as well as the creation of a revolutionary political system and the pursuit of a revolutionary social agenda. Because radical land reform generated strong opposition and because of Chiang Kai-shek's increasingly determined and sophisticated Encirclement campaigns, in October 1934 the Jiangxi Soviet was evacuated. The strategic retreat became known as the Long March.

As communist troops and personnel decamped to the north, Mao Zedong began his ascent to supremacy within the CCP at the Zunyi Conference of 1935, gradually outmaneuvering his rivals Zhang Guotao and Wang Ming. The late 1930s saw the establishment of new CCP bases in the north, the most famous being the Shaan-Gan-Ning Border Region with Yan'an as its capital. The CCP also entered into a second United Front with the GMD dedicated to ousting the Japanese from China. Using the opportunities that the United Front and the Japanese invasion offered, the CCP expanded its military forces, increased its membership, and successfully projected itself to substantial numbers of intellectuals as an enlightened and patriotic party.

Beginning in 1942 a Rectification campaign instilled a common set of norms and styles of operation for cadres and built up Mao Zedong's ideological and political authority. At the same time, the so-called mass line or Yan'an way—decentralized production; close contact between leaders and led; and the incorporation of much of the population into political institutions under CCP control, but not numerical domination—was institutionalized. The basis for victory was laid.

After the Japanese surrender in 1945, the second United Front quickly broke down. Episodic negotiations between the CCP and the GMD were conducted less in good faith and more for public posturing; civil war was inevitable. Victory went to the CCP in part because of incurable GMD factionalism, corruption, and its lack of a social base, as well as urban inflation. By contrast, the CCP had a popular following, and its troops were disciplined and inspired. During the Japanese withdrawal from Manchuria, the CCP received decisive assistance from the Soviet Union to build up its presence in the area, while U.S. support for the GMD declined after the end of World War II. After the CCP secured Manchuria, the conquest of the remainder of mainland China proved surprisingly easy.

This account suggests that only a few places were of importance: Shanghai and Canton before 1927; Jiangxi in the early 1930s; and Yan'an afterward. It also gives the impression that only a limited number of individual Communists mattered: Chen Duxiu and Li Dazhao before 1927; primarily Mao Zedong afterward. A few events are seen as determining the fate of the CCP: the two united fronts; the 1927 crackdown on the CCP by Chiang Kai-shek; the Long March (especially the Zunyi Conference); the Rectification campaign; and the rise of Mao Zedong. In focusing on these great names, signal events, and crucial places, Western historiography has been influenced by the version of CCP history advanced in the People's Republic of China (PRC).

What do the individual chapters have to offer? This volume is divided into three sections, each preceded by a short historiographical essay. Early organizational trends of the CCP form the subject of Part I. My own chapter discusses the text-centeredness of the CCP and the creation of an operational style based on this. Gilmartin's essay breaks new ground in addressing the issue of the role of women in the CCP. She suggests that the CCP constituted a subculture that fitted the hopes of women members for a new place in Chinese society. In practice, Gilmartin argues, women in the CCP were treated by the predominantly male leaders with traditional prejudice and remained second-class members. Weigelin-Schwiedrzik's historiographical essay about recent writings on Li Dazho describes the political use that various factions make of Li today. She suggests that Li is a problematic subject for Chinese historiographers because he pursued policies in the early years of the CCP that did not match the "two-line" model that the 1945 Resolution on CCP History prescribed for mainland historians. The chapter is relevant to the early CCP in that it argues that Li played a far greater role in the CCP in the 1920s than historians both in China and elsewhere have acknowledged.

Regional variables in mobilization are the topic of Part II. The much-praised recent crop of base area studies has already rendered obsolete the Yan'an focus of earlier scholarship and moved the analysis of CCP victory beyond explanations based on peasant nationalism such as that of Chalmers Johnson or the sociopolitical appeal of the mass line, as was argued by Mark Selden. The chapters of Part II examine CCP mobilizational efforts in periods and places not covered by the base area studies that focused on northern China in the late 1930s and early 1940s.

Averill adopts an ecological approach in his study of the Futian incident of 1931. He shows that the CCP and the GMD were hybrid organizations shaped by existing and overlapping local groupings and describes how conflicts of interest, ambiguity of factional affiliation, as well as opportunities for score-settling and advancement created by higher level CCP and GMD programs, resulted in an atmosphere of mutual distrust in which one of the CCP's bitterest counterrevolutionary purges became virtually inevitable. He describes local society in detail and interweaves biography with top-down and bottom-up analyses of CCP institutions. The result is a convincing and chilling exposé of internal CCP conflict. No one can ever again describe local CCP cadres in a depersonalized, amorphous fashion.

Hartford surveys CCP activity in rural Hebei in the period between the founding of the CCP and the establishment of the Jin-Cha-Ji Anti-Japanese Base Area. She makes clear that much CCP activity went on in the area before the base areas were created. She sees amateurism and mismanagement as the main causes for the repeated defeats suffered by Chinese Communists during this time. Clearly, her question of why the CCP, despite this, was able to attract new recruits continuously deserves further attention. Benton's chapter seeks to establish generalizations about the activities of troops left behind in central China in 1934 when the main Red Army forces set off on the Long March. The chapter should be read as a commentary on the author's *Mountain Fires* (Berkeley: University of California Press, 1992). In drawing attention to the New Fourth Army troops, Benton indicates that it is simplistic to think of a southern and northern phase in the CCP's pre-1945 history.

Part II concludes with Bianco's synthesis of recent scholarship on CCP–peasant relations. He shows that the mobilization of the peasantry was no easy task for Chinese Communists and that the peasantry, once mobilized, was often difficult to control. He demonstrates further that peasant support for the CCP was conditional, so CCP peasant activists had to develop a careful appreciation of the local socioeconomic environment and adjust their actions accordingly.

Leading off Part III—Toward Victory—is Apter's new reading of the Yan'an period. Apter analyzes the construction of symbolic capital by Mao Zedong, building upon discourse theories advanced by, among others, Bourdieu. In his account, Mao Zedong appears as a master narrator able to convince his audience that China was on an odyssey to a utopian future. CCP victory and Mao's own dominance in the CCP were, according to the new narrative, interrelated, and both were essential to the odyssey's successful completion. Apter describes the Rectification campaign of 1942–44 as a process of "exegetical bonding" in which Yan'anites developed a sense of being the chosen people by studying and discussing Rectification texts.

Cheek's chapter describes how the CCP attracted intellectuals from urban centers. Eschewing any simplifications about ideological commitments of intellectuals or false CCP promises, Cheek concentrates his inquiry on the attitudes and activities of those who populated CCP propaganda institutions in the Jin-Cha-Ji Base Area. He concludes that intellectuals saw service in these institutions as an "honorable vocation." He also suggests that there was no basic conflict between carrying out the CCP's propaganda work and engaging in elite cultural activities.

Apter's chapter should be read in conjunction with those of Ch'en, Saich, and Teiwes. Ch'en's article makes the case that opium traffic was of great significance to the Yan'an economy. It is a warning to anyone ignoring basic economic realities in the study of revolution. Even if further research is required to confirm Ch'en's data, our understanding of Yan'an's success will need revision. Yan'an economic policies and the behavior of Chinese Communists in Yan'an can no longer be romanticized.

Saich examines the gestation of the 1945 Resolution on History, with its Maoist interpretation of the CCP past. Saich shows the centrality of constructing that interpretation to the Rectification campaign, and also demonstrates the influence of Liu Shaoqi in particlular but also of others in the Maoist leadership. In his account, while Chen Boda and Ai Siqi do not figure very largely, Ren Bishi emerges as an important figure.

Teiwes describes in detail the formation of the Maoist leadership, paying close attention to Mao's relationship with other leaders such as Wang Jiaxiang, Zhou Enlai, and Liu Shaoqi, as well as their reasons for supporting Mao. If the broad outline of the story was already known, Teiwes's account painstakingly fleshes out the details and illustrates that the newly available sources enhance our understanding of elite strife in the CCP considerably.

In his concluding essay, John Dunn places the scholarship brought together in this volume in a wider international and theoretical perspective. He notes that modern revolutions such as the Chinese one unite two very different components: a passage of relatively decisive social and political destruction and a passage, seldom or never as decisive and usually far less rapid, of social, economic and political re-creation. The latter question would be the topic of a separate volume. On the first question, he points out that the essays contribute much to our understanding of the triumph of the CCP but leave relatively untouched the parallel issue of what this victorious party triumphed over.

Even if the conference participants shared the conviction that new things could and should be said about the Chinese Communist Party, the above review will have made clear that they also address issues that were central in earlier studies. The rise of Mao Zedong, CCP mobilizational strategies, and CCP institutional arrangements provide examples of this. The mounting evidence of local opposition to the CCP, organizational weakness, and fragmentation ensures the continuing validity of asking what gave the CCP the strength to survive, especially in the first two decades of its existence. In this respect, these chapters illustrate that academic progress is a matter not just of breaking paradigms but also of the steady accumulation of knowledge.

The conference, held in early 1990, brought together scholars from many countries, but the political situation in China made it impossible for PRC scholars to attend. The chapters, however, bear testimony to the rich fruits that Chinese scholarship produced in the 1980s. Through the activities of Chinese historians a significant amount of archival material—CCP documents, periodicals, handbooks—has become available. The present work would have been impossible without it.

All authors have also benefited greatly from direct personal contact with PRC historians. Their detailed knowledge sets a standard to which outsiders can only aspire. The opportunity to visit the places where the historical events described in the chapters took place was not only a pleasure but also essential in some cases, such as Averill's. Interviews with surviving participants, or their relatives, were similarly informative in developing a sense of the personalities involved in the CCP's history. Apter's essay depended on having the opportunity to interview remaining Yan'anites.

In the last decade, many CCP survivors have published their memoirs. At the conference their usefulness was a topic of debate. Some chapters, by Hartford, Benton, Teiwes, and Cheek, for example, draw heavily on them. Obviously their use is not straightforward. Only the survivors are in a position to produce memoirs, which can be opportunities for self-justification and the settling of old scores. Even if current memoirs are more frank than any of those published previously in the PRC, current political purposes, such as the re-evaluation of Mao Zedong or the building up of the present leadership's legitimacy, do influence them.

At the same time, it would be foolish to put the memoirs aside entirely. When used to fill in local color and personal details in a story that is known from other sources, the memoir literature can be plumbed with some confidence. For those interested in the perceptions and attitudes of CCP members, memoirs are a useful point of departure. Sometimes they record events, describe personalities, or detail interactions for which there is no other documentation. Great caution is necessary, of course, when this is the case. The value of memoirs ultimately depends on how the historian uses them.

Foreign historians have also benefited from the articles and books written in the last decade by scholars in the PRC. Studies of the CCP in China cannot ignore political realities. The Resolution on Some Historical Questions adopted in the early 1980s sets boundaries that are difficult to cross, certainly in public. In addition, like other historians, those in the PRC are influenced by their own times and concerns, including the rectification of what they believe to be the gross injustices of previous historical accounts. Only a few experts in the West may be interested in these.

With respect to the early CCP, for example, several PRC historians have argued recently that the official theory that Chen Duxiu's "rightism" and "defeatism" were responsible for the debacle of 1927 is inaccurate and that much of the blame should be placed on the leftist influences of the Comintern, and implicitly the CCP's Canton branch, which included Peng Pai, Zhou Enlai, and Mao Zedong. While attempts were made to push through a re-evaluation of Chen Duxiu, and perhaps even a rehabilitation, in the end this was thwarted by political leaders, no doubt fearful of the political fallout that inevitably would have resulted. There are other "hot issues" such as Mao Zedong's own role in the Jiangxi Soviet and the proceedings of the Zunyi Conference. Chinese scholarship on all these issues is important, and the authors whose work is assembled here have made much use of it. Yet we have not sought to include Chinese essays on these topics, in part because no papers represented them at the conference, but also because our purpose was to move away from a historiography that focuses on some main events, leaders, and places.

This volume, as mentioned, is not dedicated to the defense of a single new interpretation of CCP history; one of its values is that it suggests new subjects for inquiry and new approaches to them. An example is the connection between Chinese communism and instances of revolution elsewhere. In the past, analyses have focused on the impact in China of the October Revolution, Comintern leaders, especially Stalin, or Comintern agents such as Maring and Otto Braun. Several essays in this volume indicate that it is also important to see Russian communism and revolutionary experience as a module imitated and exploited by Chinese Communists.

To take this one step further, I would like to suggest that it may be useful to produce a general history of modern revolutions that shows their interconnectedness. The Chinese context cannot be omitted from any serious account of the origins of the CCP and the revolution with which it sought to associate itself. Nor, as is still too often the case, should we ignore the utopian and communalist aspirations that can be found in the Chinese past, or the activities of those that sought their realization. But China-centeredness can be carried too far. The CCP was also the product of the spread of revolutions and of communism, in which one episode of revolution fed on others. In our accounts of the CCP, its indebtedness to a tradition of revolutions must have at least some space.

For the China field, this would be especially important in providing an antidote to culturalist explanations of some CCP features. It seems to me, for example, fundamentally mistaken to interpret the personality cult of Mao Zedong as the result of the continuing influence of Chinese feudalism, as PRC historians do, or of Chinese political and cultural traditions, as some Western scholars assert. Personality cults are common to many revolutionary and also militarist regimes and seem more modern than traditional. Can one imagine the Kangxi emperor holding mass peasant rallies? To understand the personality cult of Mao, would it not be more helpful to examine the political environments that produced Stalin, Hitler, and Nasser than to compare Mao with China's past emperors?

Similarly, the reading and discussion of texts may have been features of dynastic China, and, on occasion, even villagers were exposed to the state orthodoxy through village lectures. But again the CCP shares its text-centeredness with other modern revolutions. To legitimize political action on the basis of texts—be it a constitution, the works of ideological masters, or the resolutions of a congress—is a clear departure from regarding monarchical utterances (not of a specific person, as was the case with Mao Zedong) as sacred and binding. The use of these texts to create a sense of cohesion again is a phenomenon found in many countries and cannot be regarded as generic to Chinese culture, although that culture naturally did shape the approach of Chinese Communists to texts as well. As in other communist revolutions, in China the print media, language reform, educational institutions, the performing arts and, after 1949, archeology, museums, and films have all featured in the attempt to create a new sense of identity and to set new goals for the future, with mixed results.

Questions that arise here are how to distinguish between communist revolutionary traditions and nationalism, and why, after seizing power, communist parties have been less successful over time than nationalism in evoking powerful sentiments of collective destiny. On taking power communist regimes quite consciously imitated nationalist strategies in nurturing national pride. One of the reasons why over time the claims of communist regimes to be the inevitable outcome of national pasts and the worthy rulers of the country acquired a hollow ring was because these claims were incongruous. Not only did communism anticipate the withering away of nations, but communist states also portrayed the national past as something riddled with evil. Nationalist histories, of course, also have their "dark pages." But they depict shameful episodes in the national past as already long since overcome; the overcoming itself becomes part of the national essence. For Communists the dark pages of history remained in the present: the enemy within had to be fought, and bad habits broken. Other more prosaic reasons have also played their role. Communist states have not been successful economically for a variety of reasons, not all connected to the shortcomings of the command economy. Their lack of access to world markets and capital markets was a problem that West European nations did not face after World War II.

This is not to deny that communist parties have been capable of generating high passion and high hatred and to move people to the extremes of heroism and brutality, especially, but not only, during their revolutionary phase. How communist parties achieved and exploited the energies that were released are topics that require further study. We now know much about the stage of social, political, and economic conditions on which the drama of a communist revolution was played out. How the actors were moved to take up their roles is not yet all that clear.

A linguistic and anthropological approach seems required to understand that. Notions such as class warfare and the idea that communist leadership, despite being threatened by devious internal and external enemies, was leading the world to an imminent and just outcome to history could provide powerful motivation. Once hopes, dissatisfactions, and conflicts were expressed in the terms of communism, traditional bonds—already frayed—were seemingly sundered, and concepts of justness evaporated. Making revolution assumed an immediacy and importance that overrode all else. The road back to the village, or the study, was blocked after perceptions of normality were inverted, local strife was expressed in the passionate terms of communism, and the belief in an early realization of a better world became accepted. A *Zeitgeist* took shape in which radical action and violence became routine. Some performed acts of heroism; but repulsive behavior too could be cloaked in the mantle of revolution.

It is the concrete institutionalized processes producing this *Zeitgeist* that lend themselves most easily to analysis. In the 1920s communist texts began to make sense to a few intellectuals. Typically they studied in deeply divided intellectual communities, where, on the one hand, a sense of responsibility for the nation was instilled, but, on the other, few dignified and worthwhile careers seemed available. Meeting in small groups, the notion of being bound by a special mission developed, especially when it appeared that the large masses of the country and even many of its elites were unaware of or unconcerned about the fate of their society.

In the same way that the Taiping ideology could work its effect only in the deeply divided and contentious social reality of South China, communism generated a revolution in China only when it meshed with the social and political dislocations of this century. This first happened in the late 1920s in many urban centers but also in the countryside of Guangdong and Hunan. It was there that conspiratorial organizational practices, the depiction of the world in terms of oppressors and oppressed, the communist legitimation for the overthrow of existing political structures, and the committing of violent acts including those against one's own neighbors made their impact first. It was also there that the dramatic roles that communism provided became prescriptive and found enactment. In this volume Averill's chapter shows how complicated this process was.

The CCP's victory resulted in part from the impact of the new way of looking at the world, the symbolic structures, and templates for radical action that communism provided. At the same time, the CCP somehow had to mobilize constructively the passions released for its own purposes and exploit them to enhance its own prestige. The essays in Parts II and III in this volume, especially Bianco's chapter, illustrate that these were by no means simple tasks and certainly not consistently achieved. Apter's chapter on the construction of symbolic capital by Mao Zedong in Yan'an illustrates that what he terms "exegetical bonding" was one way in which the CCP accomplished them. In addition one may point to party committees, CCP-run schools, theatrical plays, nurseries, media, and economic organizations, and, on the darker side, internal surveillance and secret intelligence organizations. The military was also a highly suitable arena in which to foster a sense of sharing in a heroic mission that the CCP leadership could direct and exploit.

Further study of early CCP history promises to continue to be rewarding. New sources are accumulating, our knowledge of CCP institutions is expanding, and new geographic areas of CCP activity are being brought into our view. Radically new perspectives on how the CCP operated and achieved its success are emerging. These chapters are brought together here in the hope of laying some of the groundwork for further study of the CCP.

Hans J. van de Ven
July 1993

NEW PERSPECTIVES ON THE CHINESE COMMUNIST REVOLUTION

Part I

EARLY ORGANIZATIONAL TRENDS

Academic study of the early CCP began in the 1950s and 1960s after the CCP had established its rule over the whole of China. The questions that figured prominently at the time were the nature of Chinese communism and its relation to China's past culture; the attraction of communism for Chinese intellectuals; the history of the first United Front of the CCP with the GMD; and the link between the CCP and Moscow. The most influential products of this period were Benjamin Schwartz's *Communism and the Rise of Mao* (1951), Maurice Meisner's *Li Ta-chao and the Origins of Chinese Marxism* (1967), Alan Whiting's *Soviet Policies in China, 1917–1924* (1954), and Conrad Brandt's *Stalin's Failure in China, 1924–1927* (1952).

According to Schwartz and Meisner, Chinese intellectuals were attracted not so much to Marxism as to Leninism. The messianic message of Leninism, especially as symbolized by the October Revolution, promised a rapid transformation of the world in which its profound contemporary inequities would be overcome. Leninism also provided a seemingly practical way of realizing this transformation. Furthermore, not only did it suggest an explanation for China's lack of economic development and national strength, but also it was interpreted to mean that China's backwardness destined it to an important role in the communist revolution and consequently in world history. Thus Leninism was also seen as catering to wounded national pride.

Schwartz, Meisner, and Stuart Schram argued that Chinese communism was different from Russian communism in doctrinal terms. Schwartz systematically set out Mao Zedong's views on peasant revolution, stressing their radical departure from the communist orthodoxy that holds that only the industrial proletariat can be the motive force of history and lead the revolution. Meisner argued that in Li Dazhao's thought, which emphasized voluntarism, populism, and nationalism, one can already discern many of the essential elements of Mao Zedong's views and Chinese communism in general. In *The Political Thought of Mao Tse-tung* (1969), Schram closely examined the evolution of Mao's thought. He illustrated its roots in China's past, especially its great popular novels and reformist thinking, and made clear how Mao reflected on Chinese society. At a time when in the West Communists everywhere were portrayed as holding identical views and as under the sway of Moscow, these views, emphasizing the Chineseness of Chinese communism, were pathbreaking.

The Comintern and especially Stalin were heavily criticized by early Western historians of the CCP. Whiting focused on the conflicting demands on policy-makers in Moscow of promoting the world revolution and safeguarding the interests of the new communist state. He concluded that the latter usually won out. Brandt argued that in 1926 and 1927, Stalin persisted in following a China policy that cost Chinese Communists the victory in their battle for power with the GMD. While Stalin was fighting Trotsky for supreme leadership in the Soviet Union, his principal interest in China was not to see the revolution succeed but to win the dispute with his rival. He consequently persisted in prescribing for the CCP an impossible and fatal policy. He insisted that it continue the United Front with the GMD and endorsed the creation of an independent CCP military force only after it was much too late.

These studies on the early CCP remained unchallenged until the late 1980s, when new sources became available in China. Arif Dirlik, who published *The Origins of Chinese Communism* in 1989, showed that Chinese intellectuals were attracted not just to Leninism but to a wide range of radical thought, especially anarchism. In Dirlik's view, the founding of the CCP was the result not of the symbolic impact of the October Revolution but of the activities of Comintern agents and the rise of a Chinese working class. In *From Friend to Comrade*, van de Ven emphasized the indigenous roots of the CCP, its early regionalism, and the diffuseness of its power structure. He furthermore argued that the CCP's defeat in 1927 was the result neither of Stalin's intervention nor of Chen Duxiu's "defeatist" policies. At the time, the CCP did not have the urban or rural foundations that could have ensured it victory, and neither did it have the capacity to sustain a large military force. The realization that such a force was needed was only just emerging.

An important discovery for the study of the early CCP has been the Sneevliet Archive, held at the International Institute of Social History, Amsterdam. The documents of the archive are brought together by Saich in *The Origins of the First United Front in China: The Role of Sneevliet (Alias Maring)*(1991). They illustrate the complex relationship between the early CCP and the Comintern. The latter was always important, but its authority was not always accepted nor were its policies adopted without challenge. The materials illustrate the difficulties faced by Comintern agents, operating in an alien society, having to rely on a few informants, and involved in internal CCP conflicts. Chinese Communists at times disregarded the advice of Comintern agents or even traveled to Moscow to advocate their own views. Bewildered Comintern leaders were reduced to adopting resolutions designed to appease both sides.

The main thrust of recent studies of early ideological developments has been to downplay the creativity of early CCP ideologues. Dirlik, for example, has written that once Leninism was adopted as an organizational principle, in the CCP "clichés of Bolshevism substituted for independent analysis" (268–70). The strongest advocate of decoding ideological debate in terms of its roots in political struggle is Werner Meissner, who discussed the ideological developments of mainly the 1930s in *Philosophy and Politics in China* (1990). Michael Luk, in *The Origins of Chinese Bolshevism* (1990), on the other hand, analyzed ideological developments in the early CCP as the development of a distinct system of thought, not as simply a Russian import, with many Chinese Communists seen as instinctive Leninists.

The three chapters collected here seek to develop our understanding of the early CCP further. As mentioned in the Introduction, van de Ven's chapter attempts to analyze the early CCP as a text-based political party. He takes the reflections of Chinese Communists seriously, but also seeks to take account of the fact that they were never written as part of a purely theoretical debate. Gilmartin makes the case that the CCP constituted a subculture for progressive women seeking a new life-style and a political role. Furthermore, she argues that the patriarchal attitudes of male CCP members led to the exclusion of female leaders from the formal power structure. Weigelin-Schwiedrzik reviews current Chinese discussions of the role of Li Dazhao in the early CCP. Li's role has long remained undiscussed in China and in the West. While the principal focus of the chapter is on historiographical issues in current PRC writings on Li, it also suggests that Li played a crucial role in North China in building up communist activity, in creating a mass movement together with the GMD, in seeking a "revolution in the capital" in 1925, and in actively leading Beijing protests in 1926. Our understanding of the nature of Li's Marxism and his connections with the regime of Yuan Shikai as well as the Progress Party are also enhanced.

Chapter 1

The Emergence of the Text-Centered Party

Hans J. van de Ven

Texts were, and are, fundamental to the Chinese Communist Party (CCP) as an organization. A substantial part of the activities of party members was consumed by the writing, reading, discussion, and dissemination of texts. Involvement with a specific genre of texts, those of Marxism-Leninism, helped set CCP members apart from the rest of Chinese society and fostered a sense of privileged insight and participation in a special mission. Marxism-Leninism constituted a language with the aura of a secret code, requiring initiation. Even if CCP texts asserted a radical secularity, in some ways the CCP was like a religious sect founded on sacred texts.

For the CCP to be effective in the pursuit of its goals, firstly, the acquisition of power, the membership had to be cohesive as well as willing to sacrifice much, travel far, and follow central directives. The focus on certain special texts helped create the sense of community, the practices, and the language that enabled members from different areas and social backgrounds to cooperate and formulate shared attitudes and goals. On the basis of these texts, a CCP political culture was built that combated the divisions among the membership of region, education, and belief.

It was in the 1920s that Chinese Communists laid the foundation for a text-centered party. The spread of print media in the late nineteenth and early twentieth century made the emergence of such a party possible. The broadening of the political realm and the creation of political parties in the same period also paved the way. In shaping the CCP the model set by the Bolsheviks was particularly important.

The focus of this chapter is not the general nature of the CCP as a text-centered party. It also does not seek to describe how members responded to texts and how this shaped the CCP—subjects that are important in chapter 8. Instead the present aims are more mundane. I describe the rise of the CCP's internal propaganda institutions whose tasks were to focus the membership on texts and control their interpretation. I also discuss the specific ideological debates up until 1927 that made the interpretation of texts a central leadership issue and that linked the allocation of power to prestige in the ideological realm, even if leadership was never a matter of ideology alone.

Lenin's Views of the Party Organ

Karl Marx himself did not claim that propaganda was central to revolution. For Marx it was social praxis that mattered: revolutions resulted from changes in the relations of production. Class warfare, according to Marx, was articulated in ideological terms, but ideas in themselves could not arouse such warfare.[1] It was Lenin who first articulated clear ideas about how a party journal not only promoted but was essential to the creation of a revolution. Lenin lived at a time when mass periodicals had become current and when revolutionaries made frequent use of them.

When Lenin wrote *What Is to Be Done?* in 1902 to set out his ideas about party organization, especially the role of the party organ, he did not argue that the principal purpose of a party publication was to bring "political class consciousness" to the working class. As is well known, Lenin believed that such consciousness "can be brought to the workers *only from without*."[2] Censorship and political repression made it impossible to achieve this goal through the publication of mass periodicals. Instead, Lenin argued, Social Democrats—as the party of Russian Communists was known before the schism between Bolsheviks and Mensheviks in 1903[3]—themselves "must go among all classes of the population; they must dispatch units of their army *in all directions*."[4] For this it was essential for the Social Democrats to have a small, centralized, and disciplined organization, operating secretly throughout Russia.[5] The party organ was Lenin's means to create such an organization.

A party organ was essential for the party leadership to inject a common purpose into the actions of scattered revolutionary groups. It was to function as a "guideline" providing direction to the individual actions of bricklayers: without it no house could be built.[6] Involvement in the nationwide party organ—writing articles, compiling reports, distributing issues, etc.—provided an organizational focus for all party members and promoted their contact with the revolutionary elements of the population. One of Lenin's aims was to counter the parochialism of the myriad revolutionary groups in Russia that had caused past revolutionary efforts to remain futile, despite widespread working-class discontent.[7]

In Lenin's view, the leadership had to control the contents of the party organ. Only in this way could it ensure that the membership pursued a joint strategy effectively and that the party did not fragment because of divisive debates. The production and dissemination of texts, therefore, was to be firmly in the hands of the seasoned revolutionaries who made up the leadership.

A crucial task of the party organ was the defense of Marxist dogma. Lenin's phrase "without revolutionary theory, there can be no revolutionary movement" has become famous.[8] The dictatorship of the proletariat, class struggle, the concept of pauperization, and the opposition between socialism and liberalism were, according to Lenin, the most fundamental dogmas.[9] He held deviations from doctrine responsible for the lack of success of the communist movement, lashing out, for example, against the restriction by Social Democrats of their activities for improving the economic welfare of workers, their participation in bourgeois political institutions, and their support for spontaneous local labor unrest.[10] The justification of policy as correctly applied doctrine was a central feature of the party organ.

Not only was Lenin's concept of the party influential, but the same is also true for his rhetorical style, which was direct, blunt, and combative, and designed to polarize. He chided and ridiculed his opponents mercilessly. Lenin frequently used the device of labeling the ideas of those he wished to attack as an "ism" and then expounded how the "ism" violated dogma. He suggested that loss of doctrinal purity led to lack of resolve and courage. Lenin invoked Marx constantly and represented himself as the one Communist who was loyal to his ideas. In his climb to the top leadership, he made ideological insight and the defense of the dogma the principal issues. A further feature of Lenin's style was a down-to-earth tone, combined with emotional intensity. The overall impact was to indicate that great changes were within reach, but that grave dangers remained and immediate and courageous action was required.

Lenin's ideas about party organization evolved after 1902, as did the practice of the Bolsheviks and other Communists. In *What Is to Be Done?* Lenin spoke of only one party journal. The CCP and Russian Communists divided the functions outlined by Lenin for one party organ among several journals. While Lenin envisioned a party oriented and based mainly on a party organ, bureaucratic structures, armies, and security networks became important elements of party organization as well. In addition, the agitational role of propaganda was given far more prominence. Yet the text-centeredness of communist parties has always remained.

The Chinese Background

The Leninist party was a vehicle well suited to mobilize those with a commitment to a new, purer life and dedicated to the transformation of their society. As an organization it offered an alternative community that could attract those dissatisfied with current social arrangements, as chapter 2 in this volume suggests, and the dedication to a grand cause gave meaning to their activities. Young Chinese intellectuals in the 1920s accepted the demands of party membership for many reasons, including the perceived backwardness of China, the brutalization of politics that typified the warlord decade, and the failure of liberal alternatives. The new schools that had emerged in the previous two decades had generated a large group of youths with a strong sense of responsibility for China's future. Sizable numbers of them found it difficult to envisage honorable careers to discharge that responsibility, with the government of the time seen as corrupt and with professions viewed as serving only selfish ambitions.

The concern of this section, however, is not the motivation of the earliest Communists, but how study societies prepared them for membership in the CCP. Recent scholarship by Arif Dirlik, Vera Schwarcz, John Leung, and others have described the study societies of the New Culture movement beginning in 1915 and the CCP's roots in them.[11] The New Citizen Study Society was founded in April 1918 by Mao Zedong and other Hunanese, many of whom became leading figures in the CCP. I will use it as a typical case.

The society's constitution stated that "the aim of the society is the renewal of learning, the steeling of character, and the improvement of the minds of the people and their customs."[12] As the quotation suggests, members thought of the renewal of the self and the world as connected processes and held that cultural change was the basis for all change. They also believed that the individual was not able to achieve change on his or her own. "One-man wars," wrote Mao, "use a great deal of energy but achieve no result."[13] A 1920 report of the society stressed the importance of regular discussion and meetings, and following words with cooperative action:

> many people talk about reform, but it is no more than a vague goal. . . . What it
> might mean on an individual level, some have discussed this a little bit; but for
> the association or communally, there has been very little.[14]

Correspondence was important in the efforts of the society to evolve common attitudes and common goals. All members were to report at least once a year—many wrote more frequently—"on themselves and the areas where they live as well as on the fruits of their studies" in order to "assist each other."[15] The letters were distributed among the membership in three volumes in 1921, probably edited by Mao Zedong.[16] Its purpose was to elucidate "methods by which to associate with like-minded people, discuss learning and study, develop oneself, and change the world."[17]

In their letters, society members often attempted to justify a specific course of action, with the society treated as a legitimizing agency. This was true, for example, for those who decided to leave China to go abroad, such as Cai Hesen; it was also true for Mao Zedong, who decided not to go abroad.[18] The third and last volume of the collection ended with a series of letters mainly by Mao Zedong and Cai Hesen concerning the appropriateness of a "Russian-style" revolution in China. Writing from France, where the issue had been discussed in July 1920 at a meeting of New Citizen Study Society members there, Cai had commended the idea to Mao, and his letters had contained elementary explanations of Leninist party organization and the Comintern in Moscow. A meeting of New

Citizen Study Society members in Changsha during the first days of 1921 discussed whether the society should adopt Marxism-Leninism as its "common goal," which it did after a debate in which Mao played a leading role.[19]

New Citizen Study Society members produced a great many periodicals. Mao Zedong himself edited the *Xiang River Review*, which published his first important article, "The Great Unity of the People" (*Minzhong de dalianhe*).[20] He and others were also involved in running a bookstore, the Cultural Book Club (Wenhua shushe), which distributed translations of popular Western philosophers, political thinkers, and literary authors. It also sold popular student magazines such as *New Youth* (Xin qingnian). The aim was to spread the "new learning" (*xin zhishi*) and new cultural values.

CCP historiography has cast the CCP as the product and inheritor of the New Culture movement, especially the May Fourth demonstrations of 1919. This account obscures the links of the CCP with earlier Chinese traditions of protest, specifically late Qing reformism. The New Citizen Study Society took its title from Liang Qichao's "Xinminshuo" (On the Renewal of the People), published in 1903, and Liang's periodical *The New Citizen Journal* (Xinmin congbao), which he began in Tokyo in 1902.[21] Qing reformists set up study societies, and similar to students sending circular telegrams denouncing warlord actions, they issued remonstrating memorials.[22] Qing reformist notions, such as Yan Fu's assertion that cultural renewal was essential for China's regeneration, that despotism was responsible for backwardness, and that national regeneration depended on the ability to develop cooperative associations, were all taken up by New Citizen Study Society members. In the choice of the name of their society, they alluded to the reformists' principled protest, search for new ideas, and activist stance, it seems, out of a certain respect and to derive dignity for their own actions.

The decision of New Citizen Study Society members to choose Qing reformists as their precursors is remarkable: they could have presented themselves as following in the footsteps of Sun Yat-sen and the GMD. Their refusal probably derives from Liang Qichao's active opposition to the 21 Demands of the Japanese, his campaign to reactivate the National Assembly, and his leadership in the movement opposing Yuan Shikai's monarchical movement.[23] Sun Yat-sen did not issue a sustained cultural or political criticism of Yuan, while Liang defended constitutionalism and new learning.[24] Chinese Communists in the early 1920s expressed suspicion of Sun's militaristic tendencies as well as what they saw as "backward" organizational practices.[25]

The New Citizen Study Society and party cells shared several important features. Texts were central to both; personal relations were intense; and members of both projected themselves as the vanguard of a new world. Like Chinese Communists, members of the New Citizen Study Society viewed their organization as possessing authority in matters of thought and personal attitudes.

The differences must be brought out as well. CCP members emphasized the primacy of politics whereas the New Citizen Study Society was dedicated to the transformation of Chinese culture. Its members presented their letters and essays as part of an open-ended search for the way toward a new China. They did not envisage their society as a sharply defined hierarchical structure, controlled by a leadership that wielded the party as a tool.

Laying the Foundation for a CCP Party Press

Central institutions in control of CCP publications were essential to the text-centered party as conceptualized by Lenin. Their creation formed an important step in the CCP's move away from study society traditions. Chinese Communists eventually would be asked to read specific texts, make certain dogmas their own, and adopt views stipulated in documents sent to them by a faraway leadership with whom they had no personal contact. Instead of a personal quest for enlightenment conducted with the assistance of like-minded friends, for conscientious CCP members—not all—the reading of texts involved the judgment as to what extent their own personalities and attitudes conformed to the ideals formulated in the texts. That judgment was arrived at in long and often painful self-criticism sessions conducted by CCP cells.[26] Rather than personal friendships, the party stood central.

The institutions that later made this approach to texts possible were slow to emerge. When Chinese Communists began to produce publications, they treated them like those of study societies. Propaganda was the dissemination of communist ideas outside the CCP. Early pamphlets opposed the Washington Conference of 1922. Articles sent by the Comintern were translated, and essays by Chen Duxiu, Li Hanjun, and others were distributed.[27] Chen Duxiu reported that the "People's Press" (Renmin chubanshe) had been established and had published translations of Marx's *Communist Manifesto* and *Wages, Labor, and Capital* (Lohn, Arbeit, und Kapital); five volumes of translations of Lenin's writings; Bukharin's *A Plan for a Communist Party* and *Resolutions and Declarations of the Comintern.*[28]

At the local level, Beijing Communists distributed pamphlets such as *The Russian Revolution and Class Struggle* and published *The Workers' Weekly* (Gongren zhoukan) and *The Voice of Humanity* (Rensheng), both shut down by local authorities before the First Congress. In Shanghai, two periodicals were published, including *The Salesclerk* (Huoyou) and an illustrated magazine for workers. On the morning of New Year's Day 1922, Shanghai Communists, with the aid of Chinese and Korean Socialist Youth League members, distributed on the streets of Shanghai sixty thousand New Year's cards, with a stanza celebrating communism inside.[29] In the afternoon they handed out twenty thousand leaflets at popular gathering places. Beijing Communists published *The Beijing Weekly* (Beijing zhoukan) for railroad workers. They also set up a reading room and schools. Similar activities were undertaken in Guangdong Province, Changsha, and Hankou.[30]

The first efforts to create centrally controlled propaganda institutions aimed at CCP members were part of a general trend toward centralization. Internal conflict encouraged the evolution of central institutions capable of reaching decisions without throwing the CCP into chaos. Before the Third Congress of June 1923, clashes had occurred between Chen Duxiu and Communists in Guangdong, as well as between Chen Duxiu and Zhang Guotao, who was in charge of the labor movement. At the Third Congress itself a dramatic confrontation took place over the bloc-within policy.[31]

The return to China of men like Cai Hesen also promoted centralization. They had been exposed to the practices of political parties in Europe and some had visited Moscow. Cai Hesen, who was expelled from France and did not travel to Moscow, was elected to the CCP Central Executive Committee at the Second Congress of 1922 with responsibility for propaganda and was the editor of *The Guide Weekly* (Xiangdao zhoubao)—the CCP's official organ, comparable to the *People's Daily* of today.[32] Its title was a reference to Lenin's metaphor for the party organ as a "guideline" for bricklayers.

On 15 October 1923, the CCP issued regulations governing propaganda. They were first made known in the form of a letter to all regional and local committees as well as all CCP cells.[33] In November, the regulations were endorsed by the Central Executive Committee. They created an Education and Propaganda Committee (Jiaoyu xuanchuan weiyuanhui) whose members were to be appointed by the Central Executive Committee of the CCP and the Socialist Youth League.[34] The reason for the arrangement was probably that the lines between the two organizations were still blurred. In May 1924, the Central Executive Committee published a resolution setting out criteria to separate the two.[35]

"The task of the Education and Propaganda Committee," the November regulations stated, "is to research and carry out political and ideological education within the two organizations and agitation outside of them."[36] At the central level, the committee was to administer editorial, correspondence, information, and printing departments, as well as a library.[37] The members of the committee were Cai Hesen, Qu Qiubai, Peng Shuzhi, Yun Daiying, and Gao Junyu.[38] All were leading early CCP propagandists.

The central Propaganda and Education Committee headed a hierarchy linked to local committees. Each local committee—the lowest level of the CCP organizational hierarchy—was to elect one member to take charge of local propaganda affairs. This person was to receive orders from and report to both the local committee and the Central Education and Propaganda Committee.[39] Under the leadership of the propaganda officer, meetings of local CCP committees had to discuss central directives and topics drawn from CCP and League publications. The officer also had to organize study sessions open to CCP and Socialist Youth League members and file monthly reports. These reports were to comment on the contents of local discussions, membership numbers, attendance at meetings, the reading material that was used, as well as the local response to the material sent by the Central Education and Propaganda Committee, and finally, points of doubt about central texts expressed by participants.[40] The October propaganda regulations insisted that members send two copies of anything they published of a political nature to the Education and Propaganda Committee.[41]

In November 1923, the Central Executive Committee also adopted a statement of CCP positions on several issues, which CCP members were instructed to follow in public.[42] CCP propaganda was to be aimed principally "against English and American imperialism and the Zhili Clique."[43] The Zhili Clique was headed by the warlord Wu Peifu, who had presided over the suppression of a strike by Beijing-Hankou Railroad Workers that had begun on 7 February 1923. The union had been organized by the CCP's Labor Secretariat led by Zhang Guotao. CCP propaganda also was to emphasize the need for the GMD to carry out reorganization and was to oppose the "Research Clique," consisting of constitutionalists like Liang Qichao. The arguments to be used were that a constitution was impotent if "the masses" did not possess political power and that constitutionalists were unpatriotic and compromised with those in power.[44] CCP propaganda was furthermore to attack the "Eastern Culture Clique," probably referring to people like Liang Shuming, who argued that Eastern culture, emphasizing harmony, provided a basis for a modern nation without the individualism and violence of Western culture.[45]

One of the most important activities of the Education and Propaganda Committee was the publication of the *Party Journal* (Dangbao), defined as "the organ for the discussion of internal CCP issues and the publication of official resolutions, reports, and so on."[46] The *Party Journal* was the CCP's first internal periodical, and the issues that are extant—numbers one, three, and four—suggest that its editors did what the regulations stipulated. A 1924 Central Executive Committee document stated that all CCP members were to receive a copy of the *Party Journal* free.[47] The *Party Journal* symbolized a sharp distinction between "internal" and "public" that was central to Lenin's conception of the party, and crucial for texts to function as its base.

The *Party Journal*'s pages published the resolutions of Central Executive Committee meetings, as well as reports of representatives of CCP regional units to these meetings.[48] The resolutions of the Central Executive Committee meetings contained detailed exposes of CCP experiences throughout China and concrete discussions of problems. They not only provided policy guidance but also set out organizational procedures. In the resolutions information can be found on United Front activities, the labor and peasant movements, youth activities, and regional affairs of CCP branches.

The *Party Journal* also contained discussions of sensitive topics. The first article of the first issue, published on 30 November 1923, carried the title "The Reasons for the Existence of the Chinese Communist Party." It sought to counter the argument that there was no real need for a CCP at the present stage of the revolution in China.[49] Opponents of Maring's bloc-within policy feared that it would lead to the dissolution of the CCP in the GMD and that Maring saw no real need for the CCP.[50] The article wrote in defense of the CCP:

> Each political party reflects a class. No matter how immature the Chinese proletariat, nobody can deny its existence, or the existence of the party which represents it. . . . The national revolution in colonial and semicolonial countries, and especially the national revolution in the international colony that China is, cannot succeed unless it is linked with the oppressed peoples of the world, is combined with the revolution of all oppressed classes, and is supported by the world's proletariat.[51]

The vast changes in CCP organization and propaganda institutions envisaged in CCP documents did not become reality overnight. The May 1924 report of the Central Bureau—the proto-Politburo—to the Central Executive Committee made clear that the CCP's propaganda apparatus remained understaffed and therefore weak.[52] The Fourth Congress of the CCP of January 1925 passed a resolution on propaganda that evaluated the activities of the Propaganda and Education Committee:

> There has been very little internal political education. . . . As a result, members of our party have published strange discussions in GMD organs which criticize our party or even more unsatisfactorily, which misinterpret our policies.[53]

Nonetheless an important change had taken place. Centrally controlled propaganda institutions were seen as essential to the integration of the CCP and the creation of a cohesive body of revolutionaries. The training of revolutionaries had been assigned a prime responsibility of the party's propaganda apparatus. The resolution on propaganda of the May 1924 Central Executive Committee mentioned that "internal party education is very important."[54] The January 1925 Resolution on Propaganda again stated that "the *Party Journal* is the most important organ for our secret organization to educate party members."[55] Internal propaganda under central control was seen as decisively important to the future of the CCP.

Ideological Debate

Chinese Communists began to apply the theory of Marxism-Leninism to China and to justify policy in its terms when they clashed over the usefulness of the United Front with the GMD, which became official CCP policy in 1923. The issue generated debate in the CCP about a whole range of topics, including the nature of the CCP, its base in China, the stage the revolutionary process had reached, the CCP's proper role in it, and the meaning of previous political events, especially the 1911 Revolution. The further Chinese Communists developed their own ideological standpoints and their own definitions of the Chinese situation, the more they adopted Leninist rhetoric, emphasized the importance of upholding dogma, and sought to demonstrate that their actions were based upon it. The debate was the first step in the replacement of the New Culture discourse with a communist one.

Even if ideological debates revolved around issues of policy, they still had the nature of an intellectual exercise aimed at collectively working out the nature of Chinese society and its class relations to determine the CCP's appropriate policies. Ideology was not yet the arena in which political capital was made or lost. Chen Duxiu was able to maintain his position, even though the ideological analysis that he used in 1923 to defend the United Front was immediately challenged and rapidly abandoned.

The conflicting views about the United Front that existed among Chinese Communists between 1923 and 1925 are discussed below at some length not only to illustrate the growing role of ideology in the production of CCP texts. In the discussion about the United Front, many notions advanced about the nature of Chinese society and revolution that proved influential have previously received little attention. In addition, Maring's conception of the United Front was so rapidly modified that it cannot be seen as the fatal policy imprisoning the CCP as has been believed until now. Moreover, the discussions, as well as the build-up of an internal propaganda system, show that by 1923 communist texts and what they stood for had begun to mold Chinese communism.

In an article written in April 1923 bearing the title "The Bourgeois Revolution and the Revolutionary Bourgeoisie," Chen Duxiu attempted to set out an ideological justification for the bloc-within policy, which he defended at the Third Congress of June 1923.[56] Chen's article had the dual purpose of justifying to CCP members the need to support the GMD in a United Front and steering the Front in a direction agreeable to the CCP. He sought to accomplish the first objective by fitting the Chinese revolution into Marxist historiographic terms and stated that a bourgeois democratic revolution was the current item on China's historical agenda.

Foreshadowing later CCP orthodoxy, Chen argued that beginning in the Qin and Han dynasties, China had been a "feudal patriarchal society" in which agriculture and handicraft industries were "developed and tended toward further progress, but new economic forces (such as capitalist large-scale industries) were very weak."[57] Western expansion during the Ming dynasty had sown the seeds for unprecedented change. The Opium War had meant an attack by Western capitalism on China's imperial institutions as well as its "feudal patriarchal moral ideology."[58] The pressure of international capitalism had broken open China's borders, and while it had oppressed internal economic development it had also "forced [us] into the period of transition between feudal patriarchalism and bourgeois democracy, with calls for 'wealth and power,' 'reform,' 'self-strengthening,' and 'change the laws' spreading throughout the country."[59] These slogans were all current in the last decades of the Qing dynasty.

The 1911 Revolution, according to Chen, had been a conflict between Han Chinese and Manchus only on the surface—a fairly common view at the time. The revolution had been carried out by constitutionalists and revolutionaries who had shared the hope of changing the dynastic political order and stimulating commerce and industry. It had failed "because the immature bourgeoisie had not developed to the extent that it had clearly separated from the feudal bureaucratic class."[60] As a result, midway through the revolution, China's bourgeoisie had sued for peace and stability, "not realizing that the victory of the democratic Revolutionary Party was the victory of their own class."[61] (The Revolutionary Party was the precursor of the GMD.) Military and political power had consequently fallen to "evildoers of the imperial administration, the Beiyang Military Clique," of which Yuan Shikai had been the head. "Knowing that the success of the Chinese bourgeois democratic revolution was disadvantageous for them," Chen argued, "the English, American, and Japanese imperialists used all their power to assist the Beiyang Clique to suppress the revolution."[62] The explanation of warlordism and its domestic base were central themes in early CCP ideological debate and propaganda.

Chen Duxiu argued that, at the present stage, China needed to carry through a bourgeois democratic revolution against "imperialism" and "feudalism." The latter referred specifically to warlords, but also more generally to anything and anybody associated with China's "backwardness." Chen stated that "in China at present the economic situation is such that the warlord class has already become differentiated from the bourgeoisie, but the differentiation between the bourgeoisie and the proletariat has not yet achieved a level of sharp separation."[63] This was the ground on which he justified the United Front with the GMD.

Chen sought to influence the GMD's agenda by setting out what he thought the GMD should do. Chen played down the significance of Sun Yat-sen, stating that "revolutions were not miracles worked by one or two great heroes."[64] According to Chen, the GMD needed to build up a social base.[65] He argued that in a semi-colony such as China, with its fragile bourgeois economy, the bourgeoisie tended to split into three groups. One included overseas Chinese merchants and the owners of newly formed companies along the Yangtze River. These were revolutionary because imperialism and warlordism prevented them from expanding their economic activities. Those members of the bourgeoisie who depended for their livelihoods on foreigners or warlords were by nature antirevolutionary. Chen singled out the "bureaucratic bourgeoisie" (guanliao zichan jieji) who exploited official position as the most dangerous of these. The third group consisted of those with small enterprises or workshops who had no plans for expansion and therefore were not concerned with imperialism or warlordism. The GMD's policy, Chen advised, should be to base itself on the "revolutionary bourgeoisie," adopting policies aimed against warlordism and imperialism to improve their economic situation. While the GMD should seek to establish cooperation with the "neutral bourgeoisie," it should firmly exclude the anti-revolutionary bourgeoisie and aim its activities against them.[66]

Even if Chen Duxiu put his name to "The Bourgeois Revolution," this does not mean that he produced it on his own. It is not possible to trace the origins of Chen's views, but similar ideas had been formulated already. A January 1923 Comintern Executive Resolution had stated, for example, that the "independent workers' movement is weak," and that in China the proletariat was still "insufficiently differentiated."[67] The same resolution had described the GMD as "the only serious national-revolutionary group in China" and that it consisted of various groups and classes.[68]

The aspect of "The Bourgeois Revolution" that proved most controversial was the limited role it assigned to the CCP. Chen stated, "The current mission of the GMD . . . should be: to lead the revolutionary bourgeoisie, unite with the revolutionary proletariat, and realize the bourgeois democratic revolution."[69] He also wrote that "the victory of democratic revolution would indeed be the victory of the bourgeoisie," but that the "immature proletariat" would gain opportunities to expand its activities and its influence, and therefore should cooperate.[70] It should be stressed that the article was written with a GMD audience in mind and thus did not necessarily reflect Chen Duxiu's true views, even if many CCP members at the time and later PRC historians of the CCP have assumed that it did.

In a May 1923 article titled "The Chinese Revolutionary Movement and the International Situation," Cai Hesen sought to introduce a formulation creating a greater place for the CCP in the United Front, arguing that the GMD could not lead the revolution in China.[71] He did this by suggesting that Chen's analysis had been doctrinally deficient. Whereas Chen had focused on the domestic situation, Cai Hesen analyzed the place of the CCP from the perspective of Lenin's theory of imperialism. Following orthodoxy, he maintained that China's revolution would not be a bourgeois one—as had been carried out by the European bourgeoisies—but a national one. The latter was different in that it was to take place in Asian and colonial countries and consisted of uprisings of various segments of the population against imperialist powers and their domestic supporters. National revolutions were seen as the triggers of the worldwide revolution leading to the destruction of capitalism everywhere. Like Chen Duxiu, Cai made the point that the Chinese bourgeoisie had to be weak because foreign capitalists would not allow it to grow powerful.

The failure of the 1911 Revolution, according to Cai, was not simply the result of the low level of development achieved by the bourgeoisie, as Chen had argued. He stated that the GMD—ignoring the constitutionalists, as CCP historiography often does—acted on the basis of "erroneous views" and thereby blocked the consummation of the revolution. The GMD had been unable to see the links between Chinese and international developments and had mistakenly expected assistance from foreign countries. "Because the GMD has broadcast such views," Cai argued, "it has constantly drawn in its head and shrunk like a coward from coming out to lead the anti-imperialist mass movements which have spread like wildfire throughout the country."[72] The GMD had impeded the national revolution because it feared being branded procommunist or radical by foreign capitalists.[73]

This view of the GMD made it difficult for Cai to accept the party as the leader of the United Front, and at the Third CCP Congress of June 1923 the issue of which party was to lead the Front became a central point of conflict. Cai Hesen and Zhang Guotao appear to have submitted something like a draft resolution to the congress, stating that the CCP should at least participate in the leadership of the United Front, if not simply lead it:

> 2. The 3 congress acknowledges Chinese proletariat occupies the important position in the national movement. In other words, the Chinese proletariat in the future revolution will be at least one of factors in its leading.[74]

Cai and Zhang Guotao's views were, it should be noted, consistent with Lenin's. In *What Is to Be Done?* Lenin had argued that the proletariat should be the vanguard of the revolution and control its course, but that the revolution itself should involve several strata of the population.[75] However, the declaration of the Third Congress, pushed by Maring,[76] stated that "the Chinese GMD must be the central force in the national revolution, and even more, it must occupy the leadership position in it."[77] It is important to note this, not in order to demonstrate that the resolution violated Leninist doctrine, but to suggest that Cai Hesen and Zhang Guotao acted at the Third Congress probably aware of the doctrinal justification that they could muster for their position.

Internal CCP opposition to the formulations of the Third Congress on CCP–GMD relations was strong and eventually prevailed. In December 1923 the newly formed Central Executive Committee of the CCP met for the first time. The committee endorsed an expanded CCP role in the national revolution, and in February 1924 the Central Executive Committee adopted a resolution declaring that the CCP was to take over the GMD from within as the national revolution progressed. In January 1925, the Resolution on Propaganda of the Fourth CCP Congress declared that, until the May 1924 meeting of the Central Executive Committee, party periodicals "excessively emphasized the power of the bourgeoisie because the text of the Third Congress resolution on national movement lacked clarity and also in order to combat immature leftism."[78]

Within China, besides Cai Hesen and Zhang Guotao, Deng Zhongxia supported a more active role for the CCP in the national revolution. Deng Zhongxia and Zhang Guotao had established an evening school for Tangshan railroad workers while both were students in Beijing.[79] In December 1923 Deng published two articles that unambiguously endorsed the standpoint that the CCP was to lead the national revolution. The articles were printed in *China Youth*, published by the Chinese Socialist Youth League.

In the first article, titled "On The Workers' Movement," Deng wrote that "experience has shown . . . that for the success of the revolution in China at present one must have a joint rising of allied classes." He argued that "the masses of workers are in the position of being the main force, in the democratic revolution as well as the social revolution."[80] Deng referred to both the Hong Kong Seamen's Strike of January–March 1922 and the 7 February strike of 1923 as evidence for his claim that the proletariat was "the most courageous vanguard in the armies of the revolution."[81] The article criticized pessimism about the Chinese labor movement, writing that "unfortunately following the defeat of the 7 February strike, some experts in social movements naturally began to waver, and their regard and enthusiasm for the workers' movement declined."[82] The second article made the same points.[83]

Strong opposition to the resolutions of the Third Congress also existed among Chinese Communists outside China. According to a recent article by the Chinese historian Jin Zaiji, following the arrival in Moscow of the congress' resolutions and Chen Duxiu's "The Bourgeois Revolution," Chinese Communists studying there convened a meeting in December that was critical of the Third Congress. Jin argues that Luo Yinong, together with Peng Shuzhi, the vice secretary of the branch, and officers of the Comintern, advanced the idea that the national revolution in China could succeed only if it took place under the leadership of the proletariat, and in alliance with the peasantry.[84]

There is positive evidence for Jin's assertions: Peng Shuzhi stated in a still-extant letter that the Third Congress had mishandled the "issue of the leadership position of the proletariat in the national revolution . . . our comrades underestimated the force of the proletariat in the national revolution."[85] Peng's letter furthermore mentioned that the Moscow branch again convened a meeting in July 1924 that deputed him to travel to China, presumably to represent its views there.[86] In the letter, Peng asserted that he had played a large role in convincing CCP members that the proletariat ought to be the leading element in the national revolution. He also stated that Chen Duxiu had come to agree with the viewpoint,[87] something that is probable, given Chen Duxiu's articles following the Third Congress and formal CCP policies in favor of greater CCP independence outside the Guangdong area.[88] The Fourth Congress elected Peng to the Central Bureau and placed him in charge of the Propaganda Department.[89]

Articles published by Peng Shuzhi after his return to China show that even though he did not support the Third Congress interpretation of the United Front, he did not agree with Cai Hesen, Deng Zhongxia, and Zhang Guotao. He did not share their optimism about the Chinese labor movement. In the letter to the Moscow branch, Peng reported that at the Fourth Congress "some comrades still suffered from infantile leftism" and maintained that "industrial workers should not be made to join the GMD."[90] Peng did not support Cai Hesen's and Zhang Guotao's view that the CCP should independently head the labor movement and that this could produce victory in the national revolution. He wanted a continuation of the United Front, but under CCP leadership.

As with the articles of other CCP members, the analysis of the 1911 Revolution figured prominently in Peng's writings. In an October 1924 article entitled "The Causes and Consequences of the 1911 Revolution," Peng argued, as had other CCP members before him, that the 1911 Revolution had resulted from imperialist encroachment on a feudal economic system that had caused the bankruptcy of small producers and handicraft workers. According to Peng, the standard by which to judge whether the 1911 Revolution had been a revolution was whether it had produced a reorganization of the forces of production and consequently a new political order. This had not been the case.

The revolution had failed not only because economic conditions had not been ripe. "The GMD," he argued, "representing the principal men of the 1911 Revolution, also must bear responsibility."[91] Its error had been blindness to who its real enemies and supporters were and its lack of knowledge about the organization of a revolution.[92] The barely concealed message was the necessity of GMD reorganization, the creation of a social base before engaging in military adventures, and alliance with the CCP rather than others. This analysis was of course intended to buttress a more aggressive role for the CCP in the United Front.

In contrast to Chen Duxiu, Peng sought to build up a positive image of Sun Yat-sen. GMD members had pressed Sun after 1911 to desist from further revolution. He had agreed to the United Front and GMD reorganization because he had realized that a new revolutionary movement was emerging, in which the CCP was to play a role.[93]

Peng Shuzhi's rise to a position of considerable power in the CCP after 1925 has long been a puzzle. The paragraphs above suggest that, in the same way as the later twenty-eight Bolsheviks and Wang Ming, his position depended on his status as a Moscow deputy and expert in ideology and communist organization. He was disliked by many CCP members in China, especially Qu Qiubai, who, as we shall see, claimed superior ideological insight for themselves. Held responsible for the debacles of 1926 and 1927, Peng was expelled from the CCP and began a career as a Trotskyite.

On the eve of the May Thirtieth movement (1925) that would reshape China's political map, the CCP had changed fundamentally since its founding. Internal propaganda institutions delivered centrally endorsed texts to CCP members who were supposed to discuss them in cells. An internal publication had been set up, delineating CCP members from outsiders. The United Front with the GMD had produced wide-ranging debates, with the participants using Marxist-Leninist rhetoric to articulate their views and develop new accounts of Chinese history and the country's present malaise. Ideology played a role in the justification of policy and in the allocation of power.

Qu Qiubai as Lenin

The text-centered party became a reality not just when Marxist-Leninist texts assumed a central role in the integration of the membership and when policy became justified in ideological terms. Ideological texts came "alive" in the CCP especially after the rhetoric of these texts—its language, dogmas, norms, histories, and legends—became an instrument in struggles for power within the CCP, welding together organization, leadership, and the production of texts. This happened in the CCP after 1925, when leadership conflict became serious.

Before the May Thirtieth movement ideological debates in the CCP had little immediate political relevance for China as a whole. The party was still small—it had fewer than a thousand members—and had little influence. After 1925 the CCP's membership expanded rapidly, nominally approaching sixty thousand two years later. The CCP's political significance also increased tremendously. It was involved in large-scale mass demonstrations in cities like Shanghai, and in the South China countryside, especially in Guangdong Province, it helped create a widespread peasant movement that threatened the local order. It was a partner in an alliance on the verge of taking power. At a time of very rapid and therefore confusing change, conflicts within the CCP about the changes and their implication for policy assumed a far greater significance. The outcome of the conflicts now were seen by Chinese Communists as affecting the fate of China and the lives of substantial numbers of people. Within the CCP real power was at stake.

In 1926 Qu Qiubai began a campaign against the leadership of Chen Duxiu that took its cue from Lenin. As Qu's campaign progressed, the Marxist-Leninist mode of discourse in the CCP became entrenched. Qu skillfully exploited the symbols, legends, and norms embedded in Marxist-Leninist texts to attack Chen Duxiu's policies and build up his own political capital. If before 1925 Chen Duxiu was able to maintain his position despite a lack of ideological prestige, afterward this was no longer possible. Control over the production and dissemination of texts formulated in the rhetoric of Marxism-Leninism became a crucial matter in the CCP.

All those involved in the conflict chose to make their case through texts using Marxist-Leninist discourse. Matters of doctrine, besides policy issues and personal ambition, were of course divisive in themselves. But the fact that one single mode of discourse became entrenched also prevented the breakup of the CCP, which could easily have happened.

In July 1926 Chen Duxiu published "On the Northern Expedition of the National Government," an article that has been held up in China as typical of Chen's "defeatism" and "rightist deviationism." In it Chen argued that the Northern Expedition—a military drive launched in July 1926 by the GMD's Canton government that reunified China in 1928—was a defensive military operation to protect the government from the southward campaign of Wu Peifu, the northern warlord.[94] "It cannot," he wrote, "represent the entire meaning of China's national revolution."[95] This entailed the overthrow of imperialism and warlordism in an uprising of all revolutionary classes.

Chen was not optimistic about the possibilities for the CCP in the Northern Expedition; he advocated the strengthening of the GMD's left wing, which could become a powerful political force only if the CCP desisted from efforts to control the GMD from within.[96] He appears to have favored a loosening of the United Front, or even its end.[97]

Qu Qiubai's vision of the Northern Expedition could not have been more opposed. In early August 1926, Qu wrote an article called "The Significance of the Revolutionary Struggle of the Northern Expedition," which, according to Chen Tiejian, Qu's biographer, was refused by *The Guide Weekly*, thus illustrating the importance that control over the dissemination of texts had assumed.[98] In the article, Qu claimed that "the future of the revolution has now arrived at a new stage" characterized by "the struggle between the proletariat and the bourgeoisie for the leadership of the revolution."[99] He stated that China's peasantry, the industrial proletariat, and the petty bourgeoisie constituted the "revolutionary common people" who were to establish "the dictatorship of the common people."[100] For Qu, then, the Northern Expedition was a revolutionary movement that provided the CCP with an opportunity to seize power.

In the spring of 1927, Qu produced two works, one a collection of his writings since 1923 and one a long pamphlet entitled *Controversial Issues in the Chinese Revolution*, written in February 1927. Qu distributed these documents among those attending the CCP's Fifth Congress in April.[101] Qu's aim in producing the two works was to justify in ideological terms the understanding of the Northern Expedition that he had articulated in his August 1926 article. Here I would like to draw attention not just to the contents of Qu Qiubai's arguments but also to the way he made them. His rhetorical style was modeled on Lenin's.

Qu Qiubai's ideological analysis of the Chinese situation ran as follows. His point of departure was that imperialism had hindered the development of a Chinese bourgeoisie. It had produced a "bureaucratic comprador class" (*guanliao maiban jieji*) originating from landlords. Bureaucratic compradors had depended on imperialism, and frequently their government jobs, to set up their own enterprises and industries. In addition China had a "national bourgeoisie" (*minzu zichan jieji*) that had sprung from "landowners and local bullies." The commercialization that had accompanied imperialism had affected them, but not to the same degree as compradors. They were commercializing domestic agricultural production and handicraft industry, gradually achieving national scales.[102]

According to Qu, the participants in the Chinese revolution included the proletariat, the national bourgeoisie, the petty bourgeoisie of shopowners and artisans, as well as the peasantry, whose participation was crucial. Led by the proletariat, the revolution was to result in "the overthrow of warlords, that is the regime of the bureaucratic, comprador, and landholding classes, who are the representatives of imperialism."[103] It was not a proletarian revolution but "for the greatest part a bourgeois nationalist revolution,"[104] and was to lead to a "nationalist dictatorship of workers, peasants, and common people."[105] Its aim was the abolition of imperialist privileges in China.[106]

The national bourgeoisie, Qu maintained, was revolutionary only up to a point. It competed with and was oppressed by imperialism, but did not want to overthrow it. The national bourgeoisie sought to strengthen its political power to combat elements of imperialism that hindered its development, such as the lack of tariff autonomy.[107] After the May Thirtieth movement, the Shanghai Chamber of Commerce and other such elite organizations signaled the political arrival of the national bourgeoisie. While seeking "national reforms," Qu wrote, the national bourgeoisie "only hopes to reach an accommodation with imperialism and the comprador and land-owning classes and will sacrifice the interests of the workers and peasant classes."[108] The March Twentieth incident of 1926, when Chiang Kai-shek had curtailed communist activity in Guangdong, had begun this period. Afterward, the national bourgeoisie fought the proletariat for the leadership of the revolution in order "to establish its qualifications for an accommodation with imperialism and the landholding class."[109]

This analysis of the class makeup of Chinese society formed the basis for Qu Qiubai's ideological justification for an aggressive CCP policy in the Northern Expedition with the ultimate aim of seizing national power. While neither Chen Duxiu nor Peng Shuzhi expected the CCP to emerge victoriously from the Northern Expedition, Qu stated that "even if the Chinese revolution is a national revolution of a bourgeois nature, it cannot be victorious if [it is] not led by the proletariat."[110]

Qu imitated Lenin's style of argumentation in making his points. In *Controversial Issues*, he presented himself as the defender of Marxist-Leninist doctrine against heresies that had arisen in the party. He attacked them in much the same way as Lenin: he labeled the views of his opponents an "ism" and ridiculed them. He asserted that his opponents were unable to interpret China's situation correctly in terms of Marxism-Leninism and that miscomprehension had produced feebleness, arrogance, and aloofness. Qu's mode of attack underscores the fading of New Culture styles of discourse and the deepening of the communist style.

The opening sentence of Qu's preface to his collection of earlier essays stressed the importance of theoretical work. Clearly echoing Lenin's dictum about the importance of theory, Qu stated that "revolutionary theory must never be divorced from revolutionary practice."[111] He claimed that he had worked hard for this goal, but loyally under Chen Duxiu's guidance.[112] This allowed him to suggest that he had been a faithful party member learning at the feet of the great Chen Duxiu, and at the same time that whatever errors he had made were not his responsibility.

Qu felt it nevertheless necessary to make it clear that he had always believed that the CCP was to lead the national revolution in China. In a postscript to the second chapter of *Controversial Issues*, bearing the title "On the Party Program of the Third Congress," Qu Qiubai admitted that "the program was drafted by me."[113] It was, it will be remembered, the Third Congress that had endorsed the bloc-within policy. The program stated that because of imperialism and feudalism "the bourgeoisie was not able to grow sufficiently and therefore the proletariat naturally also was unable to do so."[114] "The proletariat," it declared, "was scattered"[115] and "immature."[116] Even so, China would move toward a national revolution, but "this revolution will be bourgeois in nature." The proletariat, and by implication the CCP, was—merely—"to participate."[117]

Qu attempted to distance himself from the Third Congress program by arguing that "it was reprinted only after Comrade [Chen] Duxiu had revised it." He provided three examples. According to Qu, his formulation that "in this revolution, the proletariat is the single most true, advanced, and fundamental force" had been altered into "the proletariat is indeed a real, most fundamental, and powerful element."[118] According to Qu, Chen Duxiu had revised his draft, removing the idea that the CCP was to possess the leading role in the national revolution.

In suggesting that Chen Duxiu was the man crucially responsible for the CCP's ideological line and that Chen's "ideological errors" dated back some time, Qu played on the dissatisfaction with Chen Duxiu that had spread among party members. This was especially strong among Chinese Communists active in Guangdong after the March Twentieth incident of 1926, when Chiang Kai-shek had imposed martial law and restricted the activities of CCP members and Russians in the GMD. After the escalation of peasant movements in the fall of 1926, many believed that the CCP might have been able to defeat Chiang Kai-shek and that it had been an error to give in to him after the incident.[119]

The fifth and most combative chapter of *Controversial Issues* was called "Internal Problems of the CCP During the Chinese Revolution." The chapter suggested that the CCP was controlled by a faction that had led the party astray because it had not applied Marxism-Leninism to China correctly and acted like a clique in the imperial bureaucracy. Qu Qiubai felt compelled to speak out, he stated, because of an overriding commitment to the doctrine.[120] Qu identified "Peng Shuzhi-ism" as the ideological deviation that had perverted policy and leadership practices. A measure of personal envy may have played a role here, since Peng had replaced Qu as the CCP's chief ideologue after the former's return to China. But it was also Peng who had sought to spell out the ideological justification for the CCP's declared policies, and he therefore formed the best subject for the type of attack that Qu mounted—the weapons determined the enemy. Given that Qu Qiubai accused Chen Duxiu of changing his "correct" Third Congress draft, it is obvious that Chen was also a target, and clearly the more important one.

According to Qu, Peng did not understand the nature of class relations in Chinese society and therefore failed to understand China's revolution. In *Controversial Issues*, Qu provided a detailed analysis, running to several dozen pages, of China's economic development, the class composition of its society, and how that had determined China's revolutionary history. Qu did so, he stated, to explain why the Chinese revolution had followed the course it did, as well as to demonstrate the shortcomings in Peng Shuzhi's view that—and here Qu quoted from Peng's articles, something that, like Lenin, he often did—" 'In this deformed and confused China, naturally there was this deformed and confused Revolutionary Party, and naturally there were these deformed and confused revolutionary policies.' "[121]

In caricaturing Peng's views in this fashion, Qu painted him as lazy in theoretical analysis, and therefore unable to grasp how its revolution had been shaped by the relations of production in China and its consequent class relationships. Disaster was inevitable. According to Qu, the root cause of Peng's errors was his "mechanistic understanding" of Marxism-Leninism.[122] Qu quoted Peng's slogan of "first propaganda, then organization, and finally armed uprising"—used by Peng to criticize the GMD's tendency to stress military activity[123]—as evidence that Peng prosecuted revolution according to "formulas."[124]

Qu Qiubai was a highly skilled propagandist: he wrote with flair, knew the doctrine, and ably exploited Marxism-Leninism for effect. Qu should not be regarded merely as parroting Stalin to seek power. He had opposed the CCP leadership consistently since the beginning of the Northern Expedition and well before Stalin's famed intervention, which he welcomed and exploited. Qu's writings evolved out of CCP polemics going back to the Third Congress and responded to conflicts between CCP members in Guangdong and Chen Duxiu about policies toward the GMD and toward mass movements that had arisen after the outbreak of the May Thirtieth movement.[125]

Qu Qiubai's campaign succeeded. Much of his criticism found its way into the resolutions of the 7 August emergency conference of the CCP (1927). The meeting elected Qu as CCP general secretary, but he did not last a year in the position. Chen Tiejian, Qu's biographer, argues that Qu was not able to combine his qualities as a CCP propagandist and theorist with those of a leader. Qu, according to Chen, was unable to remain steadfast when political struggles heated up.[126] Chen Tiejian's analysis seems correct. Qu lacked the strength of character to provide leadership in moments of crisis. Even though he tried to imitate him, Qu Qiubai was no Lenin.

As CCP historians now argue,[127] the debates in the 1920s influenced the concept of "new democracy," which Mao assigned a central place in his theoretical essays of 1939 and after. Besides taking over many of the ideas first suggested in the 1920s concerning the nature of modern Chinese history, class relations, the 1911 Revolution, and the leadership of Chen Duxiu, Mao also built on the notion that the national bourgeoisie possessed a dual nature in many of his writings, including "The Role of the Chinese Communist Party in the National War" and "On New Democracy."[128] Its immediate progenitor was of course Qu Qiubai, but one can also see seeds in the Comintern's and Chen Duxiu's divisions of the GMD. Mao also developed further the strategy formulated in the 1920s that in China the revolution would be conducted under the leadership of the CCP but in combination with the peasantry and the national bourgeoisie and aimed at the eradication of feudalism and imperialism. Like Qu Qiubai, Mao did not argue that the result would be the dictatorship of the proletariat; it would be a joint dictatorship of all revolutionary classes.

Qu Qiubai's attack on Chen Duxiu's leadership illustrates that by 1927 the production of Marxist-Leninist texts had become a highly serious business. While power depended on many things, it was through texts that power was displayed. Texts could assume this importance not just because the CCP was devoted to the realization of a set of ideological goals. Many groups striving for the realization of a belief allow differences of opinion. However in the early CCP the organization was made to cohere by internal propaganda institutions that linked membership closely with Marxist-Leninist texts.

The May Fourth movement played no role in early CCP debates, despite the cliché that the movement led to the founding of the CCP. Only in the late 1930s did the CCP cast itself as the inheritor of the May Fourth movement. In the 1920s the discussions of Chinese Communists focused on the nature of the 1911 Revolution, the GMD, and the class makeup of Chinese society. The May Fourth movement has received little attention probably because the founding of the CCP grew out of the perception that the movement, limited to students and stressing cultural change, had failed. In addition, in the 1930s the CCP sought to bolster its standing among patriotic intellectuals. No better way existed to do so than to present the CCP as the product of the May Fourth movement. In the 1920s Chinese Communists strove to distance themselves from their intellectual roots.

In the discussion above, I have attempted to sketch the emergence of the CCP as a party founded on Marxist-Leninist texts and some consequences for its organization and operation. Marxist-Leninist texts formed the basis of the CCP's political culture, characterized by the use of a special language, familiar to party members but to few others. Conflicts were articulated in doctrinal terms. Opponents were denounced for being "deviationist" in one way or another. Membership meant initiation into this culture.

This political culture was very much shaped by the example provided by Russian Communists. It is true that by the late 1920s, Chinese communism, as opposed to Marxism or Leninism, began to have meaning. It is also true that in important ways the CCP was rooted in the Chinese past and its rise must be placed in the context of China's own traditions of protest and political action. Yet this should not obscure the fact that the communist past molded Chinese communism and CCP practices. Qu Qiubai's campaign against Chen Duxiu cannot be understood without reference to Lenin.

The internalization of Marxism-Leninism meant the fading of New Culture styles of argumentation and debate. Marxism-Leninism imposed categories, prescribed courses of action, endorsed norms, and suggested forms of organization. Yet while communist styles of argument enveloped CCP members, it did not imprison them. Marxism-Leninism enabled them to develop a new understanding of China, construct new organizations, and pursue new programs. As they debated the issue of who was to lead the national revolution in the terms of the doctrine, Chinese Communists generated a new "account" of China's past weaknesses, which they used to suggest that they were the ones to salvage the nation in a revolutionary process that was sweeping the globe. In the new rendering, they depicted all other political actors as responsible for China's sorry state and used Marxism-Leninism to draw a sharp line between themselves and other political actors and between themselves and the past. They also employed it to justify their decision to enter China's well-populated political arena and seek power, arguing that they were part of a new world and were the agents of its realization in China.

Marxism-Leninism and Chinese communist interpretations of the Chinese situation allowed the linkage of disparate experiences to a central narrative of communist revolution. This made it possible for the CCP to bring into one organization women seeking a new life-style, Guangdong peasants seeking land and an end to harsh taxation, industrial workers in Shanghai desiring better working conditions and an increase in their remuneration, and intellectuals seeking to change Chinese politics and society. Fights at different levels of society and in different geographic areas could all be apprehended as part of a larger, comprehensive struggle. While we cannot know what went on in the minds of the guerrillas as they roamed through the hills, the linkage to a wider struggle that the narrative provided must have strengthened the resolve of many. The CCP has sustained itself over many decades, several times rising from the dead. The text-based nature of the CCP is one of the many factors that account for this.

Notes

1. Anthony Giddens, *Capitalism and Modern Social Theory* (Cambridge: Cambridge University Press, 1971), 40–45.

2. Lenin, *What Is to Be Done?* tr. Joe Fineberg and G. Hanna, intr. Robert Service (Harmondsworth: Penguin Books, 1988), 143. Lenin's italics.

3. Leonard Schapiro, *The Communist Party of the Soviet Union* (New York: Vintage Books, 1960), 36–53.

4. Lenin, *What Is to Be Done?* 144. Lenin's italics.

5. Ibid., 173–212.

6. Ibid., 221–23.

7. Ibid., 203–12.

8. Ibid., 91.

9. Ibid., 75.

10. Ibid., 75–90 and 100–130.

11. Arif Dirlik, *The Origins of Chinese Communism* (Oxford: Oxford University Press, 1989), 149–216; John Leung, "The Chinese Work-Study Movement: The Social

and Political Experience of Chinese Students and Student-Workers in France, 1913–1925" (Ph.D. dissertation, Brown University, 1982), 196–222; Vera Schwarcz, *The Chinese Enlightenment: Intellectuals and the Legacy of the May Fourth Movement of 1919* (Berkeley: University of California Press, 1986), 128–44.

12. "Xinmin xuehui huiwu baogao (diyihao): minguo jiunian dongkan" (Report of the New Citizen Study Society [Number One]: Published in the Winter of 1920) in Zhang Yunhou et al., eds., *Wusi shiqi de shetuan* (Societies and Associations of the May Fourth Period, *WSSQDST*) (Beijing: Sanlian Press), 1: 575–76.

13. "Mao Zedong gei Tao Yi" (Letter from Mao Zedong to Tao Yi), in Museum of the Chinese Revolution and Hunan Provincial Museum, eds., *Xinmin xuehui ziliao* (Sources for the New Citizen Study Society, *XXZL*) (Beijing: People's Press, 1980), 59–60. The letter is dated February 1920.

14. Ibid., 59.

15. "Xinmin xuehui huiwu baogao (diyihao)," 576.

16. For the three volumes, see *XXZL*, 42–163. For Mao's involvement, see "Chuban Xinmin xuehui huiyuan tongxinji' qishi" (Announcement Regarding "Collection of Correspondence of Members of the New Citizen Study Society"), in *XXZL*, 42. It is not entirely clear when the collection was distributed. Containing letters up until November 1920, it may be that the first two volumes were distributed at the New Year's Conference of the New Citizen Study Society, and that the third volume contained the letters by Cai Hesen about party organization and the Comintern, and may have been distributed after the conference, in order to convince all members of the correctness of the decision to devote the New Citizen Study Society to the realization of a Bolshevik revolution.

17. "Fakan de yisi ji tiaoli" (The Purpose and Principles of the Publication [of New Citizen Study Society] Correspondence) in *XXZL*, 42. See also Mao's letter to Tao Yi, in *XXZL*, 61.

18. Cai Hesen wrote several letters about his reasons for going to France. See *XXZL*, 46–57. For Mao Zedong, see "Mao Zedong gei Zhou Shizhao" (Letter from Mao Zedong to Zhou Shizhao) in *XXZL*, 62–65. Dated 14 March 1920.

19. "Xinmin xuehui huiwu baogao: (dierhao)" (Report of New Citizen Study Society Affairs: [Number Two]) in *WSSQDST*, 1: 592–94.

20. The text can be found in Institute of Modern History of the Chinese Academy of Social Sciences and Party History Section of the Museum of the Chinese Revolution, eds., *"Yida qianhou": Zhongguo gongchandang diyici daibiao dahui qianhou ziliao xuanbian* ("Around the Time of the First Congress": Selected Sources for the Period of the First National Congress of the CCP) (Beijing: People's Press, 1980), 1: 82–95. Published in three installments between 21 July and 4 August 1919. For a translation, see *China Quarterly*, no. 49 (1972): 82–95.

21. Liang Qichao, "Xinminshuo" (On the Renewal of the People), in *Yinbingshi congshu* (Writings from the Ice Cream Parlor) (Shanghai: Commercial Press, 1916–17), 1: 1–255. Andrew Nathan, *Chinese Democracy* (Berkeley: University of California Press, 1986), 55.

22. Chang Hao, "Intellectual Change and the Reform Movement," in John Fairbank and K. C. Liu, eds., *The Cambridge History of China* (Cambridge: Cambridge University Press), 11: 290–318.

23. Zhang Pengyuan (Chang P'eng-yuan), *Liang Qichao yu minguo zhengzhi* (Liang Qichao and Republican Politics) (Taibei: Shihuo Press, 1982), 64–104.

24. Ibid., 152–84.

25. "Chen Duxiu zhi Wu Tingkang de xin" (Letter from Chen Duxiu to Voitinsky, dated 6 April 1922) in Shi Guang et al., eds., *"Erda" he "Sanda": Zhongguo gongchandang dier, sanci daibiao dahui ziliao xuanbian* (The Second and Third Congresses: Selected

Sources for the Second and Third National Congresses of the CCP, *EDHSED)* (Beijing: Chinese Academy of Social Sciences Press, 1985), 36. See also "Chen Duxiu zhi Wu Tingkang de xin" (Letter from Chen Duxiu to Voitinsky), in *EDHSD*, 55. Dated 30 June 1922.

26. See, for example, Chang Jung, *Wild Swans* (New York: Simon and Schuster, 1991), 151–69.

27. "Chen Duxiu gei gongchan guoji de baogao" (Report from Chen Duxiu to the Comintern), in *EDHSD*, 56. Dated 30 June 1922.

28. Ibid., 57–58.

29. Ibid., 57.

30. Ibid., 60–61.

31. Hans J. van de Ven, *From Friend to Comrade: The Founding of the Chinese Communist Party, 1920–1927* (Berkeley: University of California Press, 1991), chap. 3.

32. "Cai Hesen tongzhi shengping nianbiao" (Chronology of Comrade Cai Hesen's Life), in Cai Hesen, *Cai Hesen wenji* (Collected Works of Cai Hesen) (Beijing: People's Press, 1980), 820–41.

33. "Zhongying (ji zhongyang) zhi gequ, difang, he xiaozu tongzhi xin—banfa jiaoyu xuanchuan weiyuanhui zuzhifa" (Letter from Zhongying [i.e. the Central Committee] to the Comrades of All Regional and Local Committees as Well as of Small Groups—Proclamation of Organizational Regulations for the Education and Propaganda Committee), in Institute of Journalism, Chinese Academy of Social Science, ed., *Zhongguo gongchandang xinwen gongzuo wenjian huibian* (Collected Documents of CCP Journalism Activities, *XWGZ*) (Beijing: Xinhua Book Company, 1980), 6–11. Dated 15 October 1923.

34. Ibid., 6.

35. "S. Y. gongzuo yu C. P. guanxi jueyian" (Resolution on the Relationship of the S. Y. [Socialist Youth League] and the C. P. [Communist Party]), in "Zhongguo gongchandang kuoda zhixing weiyuanhui huiyi wenjian" (Documents of the Enlarged Central Executive Committee of the CCP), in *EDHSD*, 275–77.

36. "Zhongying (ji zhongyang) zhi gequ, difang, he xiaozu tongzhi xin," *XWGZ*, 7.

37. Ibid.

38. Wang Jianying, ed., *Zhongguo gongchandang zuzhishi ziliao huibian* (Collected Materials on the Organizational History of the CCP) (Beijing: Red Flag Press, 1982), 19.

39. "Zhongying (ji zhongyang) zhi gequ, difang, he xiaozu tongzhi xin," *XWGZ*, 9.

40. Ibid., 10.

41. Ibid.

42. "Jiaoyu xuanchan wenti jueyian" (Resolution on Educational and Propaganda Issues), in "Zhongguo gongchandang diyici zhongyang zhixing weiyuanhui wenjian" (Documents of the First Central Executive Committee Meeting of the CCP), *EDHSD*, 246–49. Dated 24 and 25 November 1923. The first and the second CCP constitutions of June 1922 and July 1923, respectively, also bound CCP members to adhere in public to CCP policies. See *EDHSD*, 90 and 192.

43. "Jiaoyu xuanchan wenti jueyian," ibid., 247.

44. Ibid., 246.

45. Ibid., 248.

46. "Zhongying (ji zhongyang) zhi gequ, difang, he xiaozu tongzhi xin," *XWGZ*, 7.

47. "Gedifang fenpei ji tuixiao zhongyang jiguanbao banfa: (yijiuersinian, jiuyue ershiwuri)" (Methods for the Distribution and Sale of Central Organs [25 September 1924]), *XWGZ*, 15.

48. For an introduction to the *Party Journal*, see Hans van de Ven, "*Dangbao*: The CCP's First Internal Publication," in *CCP Research Newsletter* 5 (Spring 1990), 8–24. In

addition to the four issues discussed in the article, I have now found a reference to a fifth issue. Peng Shuzhi states that he published an article with the title "Some Basic Concepts which We Should Possess about the GMD" in the fifth issue of the *Party Journal*. See Peng Shuzhi, "Guanyu dang de disici quanguo daibiao dahui" (Concerning the Fourth National Congress of the CCP), in *Zhonggong dangshi ziliao* (Sources for CCP History) no. 3 (1982): 17. Copies of the four issues can be found at the International Institute of Social History in Amsterdam.

49. "Zhongguo gongchandang cunzai de liyou," in *Dangbao*, no. 1, 30 November 1923, 1. Reprinted in *EDHSD*, 424–25.

50. Chang Kuo-t'ao, The Rise of the Chinese Communist Party, 1921–1927 (Lawrence: Kansas University Press, 1971), 1: 301; Maring, "Fuer Genosse Sinoview/Bucharin/ Radek" (Letter to Zinoviev, Bukharin, and Radek), Sneevliet Archive, 231; "Discussion on the Relation between the CPC and Kuomintang," Sneevliet Archive, 271. The Sneevliet Archive is held at the International Institute of Social History in Amsterdam. The documents are brought together and translated in Tony Saich, *The Origins of the First United Front in China: The Role of Sneevliet (Alias Maring)* (Leiden: Brill, 1991).

51. "Zhongguo gongchandang cunzai de liyou," in *Dangbao*, No.1, 30 November 1923, 1. Reprinted in *EDHSD*, 424.

52. "Zhongyangju baogao" (Report of the Central Bureau) in "Zhongguo gongchandang kuoda zhixing weiyuanhui" (Enlarged Central Executive Committee of the CCP), *EDHSD*, 282. The meeting was held 10 to 15 May 1924.

53. "Duiyu xuanchuan gongzuo zhi yijuean" (Resolution Concerning Propaganda Work), *XWGZ*, 19.

54. "Dangnei zuzhi ji xuanchuan gongzuo jiaoyu wenti yijuean" (Resolution Concerning Internal Party Organization and Issues of Propaganda Work and Education), in "Zhongguo gongchandang kuoda zhixing weiyuanhui huiyi wenjian," *EDHSD*, 280.

55. "Duiyu xuanchuan gongzuo zhi yijuean," *XWGZ*, 20.

56. Chen Duxiu, "Zichanjieji de geming yu geming de zichanjieji" (The Bourgeois Revolution and the Revolutionary Bourgeois), in The Secretariat of the CCP CC, ed., *Liuda yiqian: dang de lishi cailiao* (Before the Sixth Party Congress: Materials for Party History) (Beijing: People's Press, 1952), 56–59. First published in *The Guide Weekly*, no. 22 (18 April 1923).

57. Ibid., 56.

58. Ibid.

59. Ibid.

60. Ibid., 57.

61. Ibid.

62. Ibid.

63. Ibid., 59.

64. Ibid., 57.

65. Ibid.

66. Ibid., 58.

67. "ECCI Resolution on the Relations Between the Chinese Communist Party and the Kuomintang" (12 January 1923), in Jane Degras, *The Communist International: 1919–1943: Documents* (London: Oxford University Press, 1983), 2: 6.

68. Ibid., 5.

69. Chen Duxiu, "Zichanjieji de geming," *Liuda yiqian*, 59.

70. Ibid., 59.

71. Cai Hesen, "Zhongguo geming yundong yu guoji guanxi" (The Chinese Revolutionary Movement and the International Situation), *Liuda yiqian*, 61–64. First published in *The Guide Weekly*, no. 22 (2 May 1923).

72. Ibid., 64.

73. Ibid.

74. This is a direct quote from a document in English in the Sneevliet Archives. "Thesis on the Relation between National Movement and Komintan [*sic*]," Sneevliet Archive, 278. In his memoirs, Zhang Guotao states that the "revised version of my proposal was put to a vote." He does not elaborate what kind of proposal it was, but his remarks conform to the document from the Sneevliet Archive quoted in the text. See Chang Kuo-t'ao, *Rise of the Chinese Communist Party*, 1: 310.

75. Lenin, *What Is to Be Done?*, 143–47.

76. Maring, "Discussion on the Relation between the CPC and the Kuomintang," Sneevliet Archive, 271; Chang Kuo-t'ao, *Rise of the Chinese Communist Party*, 1: 306–10.

77. "Zhongguo gongchandang disanci daibiao dahui xuanyan" (Manifesto of the Third Congress of the Chinese Communist Party), *Liuda yiqian*, 65. Dated June 1923.

78. "Duiyu xuanchuan gongzuo jueyian," *XWGZ*, 18.

79. Xiao Chaoran, ed., *Zhonggong dangshi jianming cidian* (A Concise Dictionary of CCP History) (Beijing: Liberation Army Press, 1987), 613 and 760. See also Chang Kuo-t'ao, *Rise of the Chinese Communist Party*, 1: 50–51.

80. Deng Zhongxia, "Lun gongren yundong" (On the Workers' Movement), in *Liuda yiqian*, 86. First published in *Zhongguo qingnian* (China Youth), no. 7 (15 December 1923).

81. Ibid., 86.

82. Ibid., 87.

83. "Zhongguo gongren zhuangkuang ji women yundong zhi fangzhen" (The Situation of Chinese Workers and the Policy of Our Movement), in *Liuda yiqian*, 88–90. First published in *China Youth*, no. 10 (6 December 1923).

84. Jin Zaiji, "Lun Luo Yinong dui Chen Duxiu de youqing jihuizhuyi de dizhi he fandui" (On Luo Yinong's Resistance and Opposition to Chen Duxiu's Rightist Opportunism), in *Dang de wenxian* (Party Documents), no. 2 (April 1989): 70.

85. "Guanyu dang de disici quanguo daibiao dahui—Peng Shuzhi gei Zhonggong lü Mo zhibu quanti tongzhi de xin" (Concerning the Fourth National Congress of the CCP: A Letter from Peng Shuzhi to all Comrades of the CCP's Moscow Branch), *Zhonggong dangshi ziliao* (Sources for CCP History), no. 3 (1982): 16–22. The letter is dated 2 February 1925.

86. Peng Shuzhi, "Guanyu dang de disici quanguo daibiao dahui," 17.

87. Ibid.

88. See Chen Duxiu, "Women de huida" (Our Response), in *Liuda yiqian*, 170–75. First published in *The Guide Weekly*, no. 83 (17 September 1924); "Lun guomin zhengfu zhi beifa" (On the Northern Expedition of the Nationalist Government), in ibid., 531–32. First published in *The Guide Weekly*, no. 161 (7 July 1926); for formal CCP policy, see the Central Executive Committee Resolutions of February and May 1924 (*EDHSD*, 263–66 and 268–70); for the resolutions of the Fourth CCP Congress, see the Central Committee Archives, ed., *Zhonggong zhongyang wenjian xuanji* (Selected Documents of the CC of the CCP) (Beijing: Central Party School Press, 1982–), 2: 271–80; for those of the October 1925 Central Executive Committee Meeting, see ibid., 396–406.

89. Peng Shuzhi, "Guanyu dang de quanguo daibiao dahui," 19.

90. Ibid.

91. Peng Shuzhi, "Xinhai geming yuanyin yu jieguo" (The Causes and Results of the 1911 Revolution), in *Liuda yiqian*, 190. First published in *The Guide Weekly*, no. 86 (8 October 1924).

92. Ibid.

93. Peng Shuzhi, "Guomindang youpai fan geming de jingji beijing" (The Economic Background to the Counter-Revolution of the GMD Right-wing Clique) in *Liuda yiqian*, 164–66. First published in *The Guide Weekly*, no. 82 (10 September 1924).

94. Chen Duxiu, "Lun guomin zhengfu zhi beifa," 531–33.

95. Ibid., 531.

96. This position was set out in letters from the Central Bureau in Shanghai to the Guangdong Regional Committee. See Guangdong Provincial Archives and Office of the Party History Research Committee of the Guangdong Provincial Committee, eds., *Guangdongqu dang, tuan yanjiu shiliao* (Source Materials for Research on the History of the Party and the Socialist Youth League in the Guangdong Region) (Canton: Guangdong People's Press, 1983), 411–91. See also Chen Duxiu, "Zhengzhi baogao" (Political Report) in "Zhongyang tebie huiyi" (The Special Central Executive Committee Meeting), in Central Committee Archives, ed., *Zhonggong zhongyang wenjian xuanji*, 2: 381–89. Dated 13 December 1926.

97. This is suggested in "Gei Jiang Jieshi de yifeng xin" (Letter to Chiang Kai-shek), in Chen Duxiu, *Chen Duxiu wenzhang xuanbian* (Selected Articles) (Beijing: Sanlian Bookstore, 1984), 3: 226–32. First published in *The Guide Weekly*, no. 157 (4 June 1926); "Zhongguo gongchandang wei shiju yu ji Guomindang lianhe zhanxian zhi Zhongguo Guomindang shu" (Letter from the CCP to the GMD on the Present Situation and the Joint United Front with the GMD), in Central Committee Archives, ed., *Zhonggong zhongyang wenjian xuanji*, 2: 97–99. See also Xiang Qing, "Gongchan guoji, Sulian, he Zhongshanjian shijian" (The Comintern, the Soviet Union, and the Naval Vessel Zhongshan Incident), in *Dangshi ziliao* (Sources of Party History), no. 3 (1982): 106–9.

98. Chen Tiejian, *Qu Qiubai zhuan* (Biography of Qu Qiubai) (Shanghai: Shanghai People's Press), 251–52; Qu Qiubai, "Beifa de geming zhanzheng zhi yiyi" (The Significance of the Revolutionary Struggle of the Northern Expedition), in Qu Qiubai, *Qu Qiubai xuanji* (Selected Works) (Beijing: People's Press, 1985), 289–96.

99. Ibid., 294.

100. Ibid.

101. Chen Tiejian, *Qu Qiubai zhuan*, 273. For the text of the pamphlet, see *Liuda yiqian*, 670–736.

102. Ibid, 673–85.

103. Ibid., 695.

104. Ibid.

105. Ibid., 716.

106. Ibid.

107. Ibid., 686–87.

108. Ibid., 702.

109. Ibid., 699.

110. Ibid.

111. "Qu Qiubai lunwenji zixu" (Author's Preface to the Collected Essays of Qu Qiubai), in *Qu Qiubai xuanji*, 310.

112. Ibid., 311.

113. Qu Qiubai, "Zhongguo gemingzhong zhi zhenglun wenti" (Controversial Issues in the Chinese Revolution), in *Liuda yiqian*, 698.

114. "Zhongguo gongchandang danggang cao'an" (CCP Draft Program), in "Zhongguo gongchandang disanci quanguo daibiao dahui jueyian ji xuanyan" (Resolutions and Manifesto of the Third National Congress of the CCP), *EDHSD*, 177. Dated June 1923.

115. Ibid., 176.

116. Ibid., 177.

117. Ibid., 178.

118. Qu Qiubai, "Zhongguo gemingzhong zhi zhenglun wenti," 698. Qu quotes the Third Congress Party Program correctly, see *EDHSD*, 177.

119. The conflict between Chen Duxiu and CCP members active in Guangdong is set out in van de Ven, *From Friend to Comrade*, chap. 5.

120. Qu Qiubai, "Zhongguo gemingzhong zhi zhenglun wenti," 718.

121. Ibid., 672.

122. Ibid., 723.

123. Ibid., 722 and 723. For Peng's exact phrase and his use of it, see Peng Shuzhi, "Xinhai geming de yuanyin yu jieguo," 190.

124. Qu Qiubai, "Zhongguo gemingzhong zhi zhenglun wenti," 723–24.

125. Hans van de Ven, *From Friend to Comrade*, chap. 5.

126. Chen Tiejian, *Qu Qiubai zhuan*, 292.

127. See, for example, Xiao Chaoran, *Zhonggong dangshi jianming cidian*, 1140–41.

128. Mao Zedong, *Selected Works* (Beijing: Foreign Languages Press, 1965), 2: 195–212 and 339–84. Dated October 1938 and January 1940.

Chapter 2

The Politics of Gender in the Making of the Party

Christina Gilmartin

The founders of the CCP in the early 1920s were committed to the revolutionary questioning of many aspects of their own culture, including male-female relations, the patriarchal family structure, and the social and legal status of women. However, at the same time that they formulated a radical program on gender transformation that challenged the dominant culture, they reproduced and reinscribed central aspects of the existing gender system from the larger society within their own revolutionary party organization. This contradiction was further mirrored in the radical egalitarian fashion in which Communists conducted their personal lives, while at the same time replicating certain traditional aspects of gender hierarchy.

Western scholars of the CCP have given little consideration to gender issues in the communist revolutionary process. This oversight is all the more noticeable in view of the growth of women's studies scholarship during the last decade. Even recent path-breaking works on party history, such as Arif Dirlik's *The Origins of Chinese Communism*, have surprisingly little to say on this subject.[1] The general impression conveyed in party histories is that women have had little to do with the making of the CCP and its revolutionary programs. This chapter aims to show that gender is an important category of analysis that should be incorporated, in the broadest possible manner, into general studies of the party. Among other things, this examination of the role of gender during the formative years of the CCP provides important perspectives on issues of general concern to historians and political scientists, such as the development of the party as an institution, the meaning of the party to its early members, and the process through which leaders gained power and legitimized their exercise of authority.

Radical Gender Discourses

The significant emphasis that early CCP members, particularly those in the Shanghai organization, placed on the issue of women's liberation in their writings is not generally recognized by Western or Chinese scholars. From the very inception of the CCP in 1920, its adherents produced a voluminous literature that posed a fundamental challenge to the dominant culture and advocated a social transformation of values and human relationships.[2] An examination of this discourse reveals much about the origins of the party, particularly its sinification of Marxism, its links to the reformist-revolutionary political culture that had evolved in China over the past few decades, and its assimilation of new cultural values and behaviors.

The gender ideology of the early CCP was not adopted ready-made from European socialist and communist parties, nor was it created ex nihilo. Rather, it was synthesized from several sources, the most important of which were May Fourth feminism and the Marxist critique of the family that was based primarily on the writings of Friedrich Engels. These two currents mingled in the Chinese communist movement as part of a single historical trend and enshrined the ideal of women's emancipation within the movement itself.

Although a complete Chinese translation of Friedrich Engels's *Origin of the Family, Private Property and the State* did not appear until 1929, the gist of his argument was conveyed in partial translations and summaries and echoed in the translations of August Bebel's writings.[3] Chinese communist writers placed much emphasis on Engels's materialist theory, which attributed the historic defeat of women as independent and autonomous beings to the emergence of significant holdings of private property and the advent of class society.[4] The enchantment of Chinese Communists with this Engelsian analysis developed in part because it denaturalized Chinese patriarchal power and opened up the possibility of its demise at some time in the foreseeable future.

Engels's materialist analysis of the family as the prime locus of female oppression resonated well with the antifamily orientation of many Chinese Communists. They found in this materialist interpretation a theoretical framework for their May Fourth critique of the family as a despotic institution that perpetuated the odious practices of footbinding, concubinage, arranged marriages, women's illiteracy, seclusion, and female submission to male authority. Thus, Engels's theory not only justified the continuing condemnation of the family in Chinese communist writings, but also facilitated the retention of other May Fourth feminist issues in the communist gender discourse, at least until 1927. A brief review of a few representative titles by Communists exemplifies this phenomenon: "Sadness about the Sin of the Marriage System," "The Event of Ms. Xi Shangzhen's Suicide in the Office of the Commercial Press," "Women's Consciousness," "The Relationship between Love and Virginity," "An Admonition to New Gentlemen Who Denigrate Social Contact between Men and Women," "Social Contact between Men and Women and Old Ethics," "The Tragedy of the Old Style of Marriage," "The Issue of a Love Triangle," "A Discussion of the Co-Educational School Issue," "The Problem of Preventing Women Students from Getting a Divorce," and "How to Solve the Dilemma of Social Contact between Men and Women."[5]

The relationship between May Fourth and Marxist ideas about women's emancipation seemed so compatible in certain respects that it facilitated the acceptance of some Engelsian theories among influential noncommunist intellectuals. Consider, for example, the pervasiveness of the contention that women's economic independence was the decisive determinant of genuine gender equality. At roughly the same time that Communists like Li Hanjun, Mao Dun (pseudonym of Shen Yanbing), Chen Wangdao, and Shen Zemin were writing about the importance of women's acquiring the education and job skills to become self-supporting, well-published non-Marxist writers like Lu Xun, Hu Shi, Chen Youqin, Gao Xian, Li Xiaofeng, and Wu Yu were making the same point. Lu Xun's memorable speech "What Happens to Nora after She Leaves Home" to the women students at Beijing Women's Higher Normal Institute and his poignant story "Regret for the Past" contained graphic accounts of the probable fate that awaited those Chinese women who tried to escape the control of their families without having acquired the capability or means to support themselves. For Lu Xun, the outcome was patently clear: such women would either become irreparably debased or have to resubmit to their family's controls.[6]

Another Engelsian idea that received great attention in the early Chinese communist movement was the comparison of the institution of marriage with prostitution. The notion that the difference between a wife and a streetwalker was only the length of time that her sexual services were secured seemed to capture the inhumanity of the arranged marriage system and strip it of any lingering legitimacy for radical intellectuals. Shen Zemin, the younger brother of the well-known writer Mao Dun, published one of the most impassioned indictments of the marriage system that adhered to this mode of interpretation. He charged:

> The present system has a tendency to turn women into prostitutes. This is because the system is alive and expanding, purposely and incessantly swallowing innocent people into its bloody mouth. The present number of people who have fallen victims will increase. In such a social reality, this system noiselessly forces upper class women to sell unconsciously their most precious "sex." It forces working class women who can barely subsist to turn directly into prostitutes. . . .
>
> Money, of course, is not the only reason why women degenerate into this deplorable status, as women do not necessarily always demand money. Women have their own reasons for exchanging their only possession—their sexual services. In order to avoid the isolation of remaining single, or to fulfill a desire to become a mother, or to have their vanity indulged, women often marry men they do not love. Emotionally their predicament is similar to the experiences of prostitutes, for they have to painfully submit to their husbands and put up with fondling caresses in the absence of love.[7]

The natural progression of this argument led Shen and other Communists of his era to call for the abolition of marriage. They believed that family-controlled marriages served only family interests and often resulted in unhappy unions for the individuals involved. In this respect, they were revealing certain anarchist inclinations. Such traits, for example, can be identified in the writings of Shi Cuntong, who was more candid than most budding Communists in acknowledging his anarchist inclinations. In several articles on marriage that he published in May 1920, when he joined the Shanghai Marxist Research Society, he argued that marriage was the main instrument shackling individuals to the family system. Moreover, in Shi's view, marriage essentially required the subordination of one individual's emotions and sexuality to those of another person—a situation that no one should be forced to tolerate.[8]

As Arif Dirlik has noted, Chen Duxiu was one of the few early members of the party who was not influenced by anarchist ideas.[9] But even though he did not call for the dissolution of the family, Chen Duxiu was well known for his critique of the family's virtual enslavement of women.[10] During the May Fourth era, he played a major role in rendering the issue of women's emancipation into a central item of discourse among Chinese intellectuals in his role as editor and writer for the influential journal *New Youth*.[11] After his conversion to communism in early 1920, Chen Duxiu no longer expounded at length on May Fourth feminist ideas in his writings. Rather, beginning in May 1920, he focused his attention on the exploitation of women workers, publishing an article on the procurement process of Hunanese women workers by the Shanghai Cotton Mills in a special edition of *New Youth* devoted to factory conditions. Nine months later, he founded the communist periodical *Labor and Women* (Laodong yu funü) in Canton and contributed several articles that explored the connections between class and gender exploitation. Even after this journal folded a few months later, Chen continued to publish on the topic.[12]

To be sure, Chen Duxiu did not completely abandon his May Fourth feminist perspective when he became a Communist. A close reading of his works reveals a continuing commitment to certain May Fourth issues, such as the importance of women's attaining a sense of personhood and dignity (*renge*), the need for women's education, and the value of developing co-educational schools.[13] Perhaps the strongest legacy of his May Fourth feminist orientation was his lack of hostility to women's rights and suffrage groups. Rather he looked upon these groups as natural allies of the party and encouraged Communists to work with some of them.[14] In this endeavor, Chen was supported by Li Dazhao, with the result that a greater compatibility was created in the early CCP between Marxism and feminism than was generally true in other communist and socialist parties of that era.[15]

This communist discourse on gender issues demonstrated that the liberation of women was a matter of relatively high priority for the CCP. Yet it must be acknowledged that, in certain respects, it had more symbolic than actual import.

Like the feminist press of the May Fourth era, this communist discourse was entirely male produced.[16] Thus, to a certain degree, communist male feminists were carrying on a tradition in Chinese political culture that had first appeared during the tumultuous 1890s, when the threat of colonization loomed large. At that time, strains of indigenous feminist thought, present in China for many centuries, were invigorated by Western feminist ideas and emerged as a distinct political creed.[17] What is most significant about the birth of modern feminism in China is that it was shaped through encounters with imperialism. While male revolutionaries and reformers showed tremendous interest in specific issues regarding the subordination of women, such as footbinding and education, on an abstract level they inextricably linked China's national weakness in the world to the low status of its women. According to these reformist and revolutionary paradigms, the emancipation of Chinese women was central to the restoration of national strength and the achievement of modernity.

This sense of urgency about women's emancipation that pervaded the writings of many male Communists in the early 1920s was largely attributable to the nationalist origins of modern Chinese feminism. Nonetheless, this was not the only motivating force behind the communist gender discourse. Equally significant was the role that these writings played in guiding male Communists through a problematic new social reality in gender relations.[18] The breakdown of restrictions on heterosocial interaction during the May Fourth era, the introduction of co-education, the appearance of free-choice marriages and consensual unions, the growing public knowledge of birth control (especially after the speaking tour of Margaret Sanger in 1922), the expansion of prostitution, and the concern about venereal disease reflected an increasing sexualization of urban society that was especially pronounced in the Western enclaves of Shanghai and other large urban centers.

The sexual revolution in China had an impact not just on the ideological views of Chinese communist males but also on their lives, particularly in the changing patterns of heterosocial interaction, free-choice marriages, and consensual unions. For many Communists, the issue of marriage was particularly agonizing. Chen Duxiu, for instance, was very unhappy with his arranged marriage to Gao Dazhong, an illiterate rural woman three years his elder.[19] Their constant bickering left deep grudges. At first, he sought relief in writing, and he published an essay denouncing the marriage system in China in 1904.[20] As Lee Feigon has noted in his authoritative biography of Chen Duxiu, in 1910 he not only left her, but also took the highly unconventional step of entering into a consensual union with his wife's younger sister. A graduate of Beijing Women's Normal Institute, Gao Junman was willing to endure public censure and even the rebuke of her parents because of her strong commitment to becoming a "new woman" who defied social conventions and lived her own life. She became absorbed in the Bohemian culture of the 1910s and was an enthusiastic adherent of the New Culture movement.[21]

The scandal of this action continued to haunt the couple long after they began to live together. Chen Gongbo, a founding member of the CCP, remembered that Chen Duxiu was hounded by conservative critics in Canton when he was serving as education minister in the warlord government of Chen Jiongming in 1920 and 1921. Rumors of his immoral conduct with women abounded and fueled calls in the newspapers for his resignation.[22] Also at issue here was Chen's advocacy of gender change in the school system. The appointment of Yuan Zhenying, a well-known radical, as the principal of the First Middle School provoked much opposition, especially when Yuan integrated New Culture movement ideas into the curriculum and made the school co-educational. Particularly objectionable to the city's established elite was the practice of having boys and girls sit at the same desks.[23]

Chen was not the only Communist who left an arranged marriage. But some, like Gao Junyu and Chen Wangdao, chose to go one step further and do it in a more "modern" way by seeking to divorce their illiterate rural wives. In Chen Wangdao's case, this decision proved tragic, for his wife found the prospect of being a divorcée in a rural community so humiliating that she committed suicide. Understandably, many Communists never formalized their separations from their first wives, particularly when children were involved.

Most Communists wrestled with various methods of handling their arranged marriages in private, but on occasion scandals resulting from their unconventional practices reached the newspapers. One of the most infamous cases in Shanghai involved Zhou Fuhai, who had been appointed acting secretary to Chen Duxiu at the First Party Congress. News of his love affair with the daughter of the chief secretary of the Shanghai General Chamber of Commerce was printed in the *Shanghai Eastern Times*. According to Zhang Guotao, the paper reported that a young Hunanese man, "who claimed to be the most progressive disciple of socialism in China . . . already had a wife in his home village and was said to be a father."[24] When the chief secretary of the Shanghai General Chamber of Commerce threatened to sue Zhou for seducing his daughter, Zhang Guotao hastened to explain the new morality that was common in the party at that time:

> I could see how furious Yang was, and I tried to calm him. If Chou Fo-hai [Zhou Fuhai] was really married, I said, and had hidden the fact while carrying on a love affair with another girl, then that, of course, was not right. But, I added, there were many young men these days with old-fashioned wives at home, whose marriages were arranged by their parents. Even though they loathed their wives, the old moral code enslaved them and they could not get a divorce. So, many of them sought love away from home and perhaps even married again.[25]

These examples demonstrate that the gender discourse in the early party not only was nationalist inspired but also affirmed an experimentation in radical sexual politics. For the first generation of Communists, challenging the existing sexual codes was connected to their overall rebellion against Chinese traditional norms. To be sure, not every male Communist rejected the traditional marriage practices. Nonetheless this new political organization quickly gained a reputation as a haven for those wishing to lead unconventional lives.

Programmatic Development and Female Recruitment

Soon after the First Party Congress in July 1921, the transition from discourse to programmatic development commenced in Shanghai. While the male founders of the party may have felt little remorse about dominating the communist publications on women's issues, they quickly realized that women were needed to develop a women's program. Gender segregation in most areas of Chinese life necessitated the use of women organizers to work directly with women students, workers, and activists. During the first four years of the party's development, a few women organizers were given tremendous latitude by the party founders to build a women's program. They constructed a women's program that attracted a significant core of women cadres to the party, while at the same time creating a solid organizational framework for the large-scale mobilization of women in the national revolution (1925–27).

Significantly, the first women's organizers of the CCP were not members. In fact, only Miao Boying and Liu Qingyang held membership status at the time of the First Party Congress. As they were in Beijing and France at the time, Chen Duxiu delegated the responsibility of commencing the communist women's program to his spouse, Gao Junman, and to Wang Huiwu, the wife of Li Da, who had just been elected to the Central Bureau, the highest leadership body in the communist organization. These two women had developed a close working relationship while living in the same house, no. 6 Yuyang Lane in the French Concession, an abode that had previously served as a headquarters for Shanghai radicals and which Chen Duxiu had taken over from Dai Jitao late in the summer of 1920 for the newly established communist organization. Wang Huiwu, the younger of the two, proved the more able administrator and leader and soon emerged as the unofficial head of the women's program.

Wang Huiwu and Gao Junman were responsible for developing an alliance with the Shanghai Women's Circle (Shanghai nujie lianhehui), setting up a women's journal entitled *The Women's Voice* (Funü sheng), and founding the Shanghai Pingmin Girls' School. Their work was overseen by Li Da, who monitored the journal and assumed the title of the official principal of the school, which opened its doors shortly after the Lunar New Year in 1922. But Wang Huiwu, with the aid of Gao Junman and Wang Jianhong, actually ran the school and the journal. Thus, these women were provided with a unique opportunity to build their own institutions within a Chinese political party.

The early history of the communist women's program shows little tension between class and gender issues at a programmatic level. In many respects,

Wang Huiwu and Gao Junman strove to encourage cross-class collaboration among women through the school and the journal. To this end, the curriculum was designed to attract "common" (*pingmin*) women from the lower classes as well as graduates of middle schools who needed further preparation for entrance to university. In a similar vein, *The Women's Voice* carried articles on a variety of topics, such as women's education, factory conditions endured by women workers and their strikes, women's literature, and birth control. Through their writings in the journal, Wang Huiwu, Gao Junman, and Wang Jianhong sought to convince women students and intellectuals to become active in a new women's movement that would involve women from several classes.[26]

After Xiang Jingyu took over leadership of the newly created communist Women's Bureau, a body that was set up at the Second Party Congress (July 1922) in accordance with a decree of the Comintern, the earlier orientation of the communist women's program was basically reaffirmed. Contrary to the general assertion in Western scholarship that Xiang Jingyu devoted most of her energies to labor organizing, the main thrust of the Women's Bureau program under her guidance was to form tactical alliances with the various groups of the independent women's movement and attract women students in order to develop a core of women organizers for the national revolution.[27] To this end, Xiang Jingyu accepted a post as one of the main editors of the *Women's Weekly* (*Funü zhoubao*), an eight-page weekly supplement of the GMD-run newspaper in Shanghai, *Republic Daily* (*Minguo ribao*). After the GMD's First Congress in 1924, Xiang became the head of the GMD Shanghai Women's Movement Committee, a role that allowed her to shape the programmatic development of the GMD Women's Department. She also became a founding member of the Guangdong Women's Rights Alliance.

To be sure, Xiang Jingyu did not completely embrace female intellectuals. In fact, from time to time she expressed her concern over the narrowness of their vision and their lack of interest in the plight of Chinese women workers. In her harshest indictment of women's rights and suffrage groups during her three-year tenure as head of the Women's Bureau, she described them as made up of "the cream of women intellectuals," who were used to lives of leisure and were totally dependent on the support of men—fathers, husbands, and sons. Moreover, she wondered whether their involvement in the women's movement amounted to anything more than a passing fancy.[28] However, despite these concerns, Xiang believed that these women had much to offer the cause of women's liberation. To this end, she continually encouraged them to rise above these limitations and focus their energies on bringing about women's emancipation. Most importantly, she believed that women had to be incorporated into the revolutionary process as agents of their own emancipation.

Much more could be said about Xiang's development of the communist Women's Bureau between 1922 and 1925. However, for the purposes of this study, it is more useful to examine the backgrounds and political experiences of the women who were recruited to the party during Xiang's tenure at this bureau. By making these women more visible, we are able to gain insights into how the first generation of women Communists saw the party and how they participated in the development of the organization.

Between 1921 and May 1925, approximately one hundred women were recruited into the CCP.[29] As is common in revolutionary movements in other parts of the world, these early women Communists for the most part did not come from the ranks of the dispossessed, but from gentry, intellectual, or commercial families, though the economic circumstances of these families varied enormously. Among those from prosperous families were Xiang Jingyu, whose father was a prominent businessman and head of the Chamber of Commerce in Xupu, a small town in western Hunan; Yang Zhihua, who was the daughter of a silk merchant and small landlord in Zhejiang; and Yang Zilie, who grew up in an extended multigenerational compound in Hubei that was reminiscent of gentry life as portrayed in the novel *Dream of the Red Chamber*. Also from a financially well-off family was Liu Qingyang, whose Muslim (Hui) father rose from poverty to modest prosperity by operating a mutton market in Tianjin and whose brothers became influential in North China newspaper circles.

Many women from impoverished families were related to China's former ruling elite. Wang Huiwu's father could not secure an adequate income from the local school he ran in Jiaxing, Zhejiang, although he was well-educated, having attained a *xiucai* degree in the imperial examination system during the late Qing period. Zhong Fuguang's father was an impoverished Sichuan landlord, and Cai Chang could claim descent from the illustrious Qing dynasty official Zeng Guofan, although she too grew up in straitened circumstances.

Thus, it was the schools that proved to have the greatest impact on these women's early political socialization. These schools not only removed these women from the direct control of their families but also allowed them a unique opportunity to experience a strong sense of community with other young women and exposed them to a host of new ideas. These schools conditioned women's early political orientation because they engendered feminist and nationalist consciousness and provided certain participatory skills, particularly during the May Fourth protests. The school experiences of Xiang Jingyu illuminate the dedication and idealism that were fostered in these educational environments with the explicit aim of encouraging young Chinese women to identify their quest for an education with patriotic goals. Soon after beginning her public schooling at the age of sixteen, Xiang made a solemn pledge with six other students at the Changde Girls' Normal School to devote herself to intensive study in order to achieve equality between the sexes and save the country through education. When she transferred to Zhounan School in 1914, she decided to mark the occasion by discarding the name Junxian (beautiful and virtuous) that had been given to her at birth because it extolled traditional values that she no longer respected. She adopted instead the name Jingyu, which conveyed the image of alertness, because she wanted to express her belief that women needed to wake themselves up and end their somnambulance. At the time, she wrote passionately in her school diary about the need for women to begin assuming responsibility for ending the sad state of national affairs.[30]

Such nationalist and feminist ideals were becoming increasingly common in girls' schools during the late 1910s and intensified with the outbreak of the anti-imperialist May Fourth protests in 1919. In addition to participating in local demonstrations and boycotts of Japanese goods, many women students began to rebel against school authorities for upholding traditional values about female decorum. Yang Zilie and five other students at the Hubei Provincial Girls' Normal School in Wuchang bobbed their hair to signal their emancipation from traditional bondage.[31] Wang Yizhi and her schoolmates at the No. 2 Hunan Provincial Girls' Normal School mobilized the student body to do away with the moral ethics course (*xiushen ke*), which extolled the Confucian virtues of female chastity and subservience to male authority.[32]

Their transition from May Fourth activists to Communists was quite similar to that of early male Communists in the party. For some, participation in study groups such as the New Citizen Study Society, the Awakening Society, and the Work-Study Mutual Aid societies was crucial. For others, the influence of communist teachers or closer relatives proved decisive. These women were also influenced by the same Marxist ideological currents that prompted their male counterparts to join the CCP. However, an equally compelling reason was their perception that the CCP was a vigorous proponent of women's equality that provided the possibility of an alternative life-style for those resisting conventional gender roles. In short, the party loomed as a viable answer to the question posed by Lu Xun in his famous lecture at Beijing Women's Normal University: "What happens after [Ibsen's] Nora leaves home?"[33] Because few career opportunities were open to these women and higher education was even more difficult to obtain, they looked to the party as a sanctuary of like-minded people who would support their rejection of an arranged marriage and their determination to create new gender roles.

The importance of May Fourth as a motivating political force for the first generation of women Communists not only marked them as a distinct group of women in the party but also distinguished them somewhat from early communist males, who were more evenly spread over several student generations. Many male Communists, such as Chen Duxiu, had gained valuable political experience during the 1911 Revolution. In his study of 102 early communist leaders, C. Martin Wilbur has identified twelve communist male "elders" who ranged in age between thirty-five and fifty-three in 1927 (most of whom were quite prestigious), while I can identify only one early communist woman, Chen Junqi (1885–1927), in this age bracket, and she never became an important leader.[34]

This discrepancy seems to reflect a different historical pattern of political involvement between men and women. Of the relatively small number of women who participated in the 1911 Revolution, most had withdrawn from politics shortly afterward, either because of childrearing responsibilities or because of their disenchantment with political parties after the GMD's refusal to support a women's suffrage clause in the provisional constitution of 1912 and its refusal to retain an equal rights plank in the party program of 1912. After the break of student protests in 1919, a few of these women found their way back into politics, but as leaders of women's groups rather than as active members of political parties. Notably, Huang Zonghan, the widow of GMD veteran leader Huang Xing, formed the Shanghai Women's Circle, and Wang Changguo founded the Hunan Women's Circle, which stunned the nation in 1921 by actually engineering her election to the Hunan provincial assembly.

Radicalized during the May Fourth protests, these first communist women saw themselves as pioneers in the cause of bringing about social and political change in China. Moreover, they were attracted by the party's supportive environment in a largely hostile society. Thus, to these women concerned with challenging traditional gender relationships and providing alternative role models, the party appeared more as a subculture than as a political institution. Rejecting traditional family-arranged marriages, many entered into free-choice marriages or consensual unions and explicitly refused to have a wedding ceremony. Others experimented with casual affairs. The experimentation in social relationships and the redefinition of gender roles in this communist subculture increased these women's sense of dignity and constituted a powerful incentive for their political involvement. To be sure, venturing into politics was a big step, particularly in a country where until recently the realm of politics had been a strictly male domain and women had been denied formal access to political roles. Thus the entry of these women into the CCP put them on the cutting edge of social change.

Women's Status in the Power Apparatus

At the same time, however, the radical egalitarian spirit that pervaded the subculture masked the formation of distinctly unequal gender relationships within the emerging power structures of the party. For young communist women, their personal lives were an important part of their political activities. As a result, they seemed largely unaware of the reintegration of patriarchal attitudes and patterns of political behavior into the communist polity.

The pattern of depriving women of appropriate political status was apparent from the beginning. Both Gao Junman and Wang Huiwu possessed credentials that justified their selection as women's organizers. Although Gao Junman had never shown much interest in politics, she was a graduate of the Beijing Women's Normal Higher Institute and a strong proponent of the new literature movement. Wang Huiwu, younger than Gao, had been radicalized during the May Fourth student protests and had published her articles on women's issues in widely read journals. She had also already proved effective as a logistics organizer for the First Party Congress. Nevertheless, it must be acknowledged that the main credentials of these two for starting up the communist women's program were their relationships with important male leaders. Moreover, Gao Junman and Wang Huiwu were not party members.

Similarly, there is no record of Xiang Jingyu's having undergone a formal admission procedure when she arrived in Shanghai from France at the beginning of 1922. Although party historians assert that Xiang became a member at that time, they have been unable to identify anyone who might have introduced her to the party, whereas it is well known that her husband, Cai Hesen, was formally proposed for membership by Chen Duxiu and Chen Gongpei.[35]

Although the evidence is limited and sketchy, in light of later developments the nebulous status of these first two organizers of the women's program seems to indicate the existence of strongly felt, unarticulated patriarchal attitudes about the incompatibility of women's holding political power. As such, their experiences constituted the beginning of an informal power structure at the center of communist power.

More importantly, the formal establishment of the Women's Bureau at the Second Party Congress (July 1922) proved largely ineffectual in promoting women in other areas of the party hierarchy, so women found it difficult to assume positions outside the Women's Bureau. By the Fourth Party Congress (January 1925), the emergence of inequalities of power organized along a gender axis was a permanent reality in the party. Since the majority of female recruits came from girls' middle and normal schools, it seems significant that women commanded so few leadership positions in the Socialist Youth League (SYL). Nor were women able to gain official delegate status at the first four party congresses, although at least a few of them were present at the meetings in an informal capacity associated with their relationships to important male Communists.[36] Thus, women could express their opinions but could not vote.

It might well be argued that the Women's Bureau was not an effective vehicle in easing women into the communist bureaucracy because it was imposed from outside by the Comintern.[37] In fact, if we are to accept the opinion of Chen Gongbo, one of the congress's participants, few people in the party at that time were willing to establish this bureau without the directive. This seems curious in view of the initial achievements of Wang Huiwu and Gao Junman and since so many members of the party had expressed their concern in writing for improving women's status and transforming traditional norms. If true, it indicates that the unarticulated assumptions against women holding formal positions of power were indeed quite strong in the early party.

Regardless of the validity of Chen Gongbo's assertion, the establishment of this bureau did have some positive impact on women's status in the Shanghai party. Within a very short time, women were given formal membership status and were appointed to responsible positions. Wang Yizhi, a student at the Shanghai Pingmin Girls' School, in August 1922 became the first woman to be formally admitted to the Shanghai communist organization. In the same month, Xiang Jingyu was selected as head of the Women's Bureau.

The naming of Xiang Jingyu as head of the Women's Bureau marked the first explicit female leadership appointment by a communist body. It also propelled her to the pinnacle of the inner party power structure. She brought a wealth of experience and insight to the position. Yet even though she was already known in her own right as an astute and experienced political activist, it is highly unlikely that Xiang would have been appointed to the post if she had not been married to a high-ranking Communist. As it was, Cai Hesen, whom she had married in 1920 while studying in France, was elected to the Central Executive Committee (CEC) at the Second Party Congress in 1922.

The experiences of the most talented and influential woman of the period, Xiang Jingyu, illustrate the barriers that women faced in assuming official positions in the political hierarchy. For years hagiographic biographies have claimed that she was an elected official of the CEC from 1922 until 1927. The All-China Women's Federation has been particularly interested in promoting this image of Xiang Jingyu in its publications. However, most of the evidence in support of her election as a member or even an alternate is quite suspect and has not been confirmed by recent studies.[38]

The ambiguity over Xiang Jingyu's status in the party hierarchy stems largely from a confusion between her full participation and limited institutional status. The memoirs of various high-ranking Communists make it clear that Xiang attended CEC meetings and was in charge of much of the organizational work related to that body. Luo Zhanglong, who was elected to the CEC at the Third Party Congress and was an alternate at the Fourth Party Congress, was impressed by Xiang Jingyu's political skills and recalled that she had managed and arranged all matters concerned with the CEC.[39] Thus, while Xiang Jingyu was not an officially elected member of CEC, in fact she served on this body in an unofficial capacity. In this way, Xiang Jingyu carried on a tradition inherited from Gao Junman, the wife of Chen Duxiu, and Wang Huiwu, the wife of Li Da, who had been the first members of an informal political power structure.

During the next few years Xiang Jingyu developed the communist Women's Bureau into a strong, vibrant institution within the party. It is doubtful that any other early communist woman could have exerted a strong enough leadership role in the higher echelons of the party to persevere against the largely unarticulated assumptions that communist men held about sharing power and prestige in the party with women. When Xiang drafted her resolution on the women's movement for the Third Party Congress in 1923, she strove to combat the deep-seated contempt some male members felt toward the women's movement. She argued that this movement was important politically despite its history of strong divisions and lack of action. She warned her comrades that if the CCP were to have any impact on invigorating and influencing these women's groups, Communists could not show disdain toward "Madames" (*taitai*), "young misses" (*xiaojie*), and women politicians and should not scare them away by stressing the theory of class struggle.[40] Xiang was also critical of her male comrades for failing to encourage female recruitment, with the result that communist organizations in places such as Canton had few, if any, women members. It was only after Xiang agitated for the adoption of a resolution at the Fourth Party Congress (January 1925) placing a special priority on recruiting women that a breakthrough was achieved in these places.[41]

Although Xiang Jingyu proved an effective and assertive head of the Women's Bureau, her position was never secure. When her relationship with Cai Hesen began to deteriorate because of her involvement in an affair with Peng Shuzhi, she lost her unofficial standing on the CEC and her command of the communist Women's Bureau. Despite the centrality of her role in the effort to invigorate the GMD and to form an alliance of women's groups for the national revolution, she was sent to the Soviet Union, as was Cai Hesen. Upon her return to China in the spring of 1927, she was unable to resume the important leadership positions that she had held in the past. Had she continued her relationship with Peng Shuzhi, she might have been able to assume positions commensurate with his high political status. But as an unattached female, she lost her access to the world of high politics in the CCP.

Patriarchal Preferences and Female Complicity

In probing for the reasons why communist men tolerated such a discrepancy between their writings about women's equality and the reproduction of an unequal power hierarchy in the party, we find that their political identities were greatly influenced by patriarchal conceptions of power. Despite their ardent espousal of the cause of women's emancipation, these early male Communists assumed that they should be the power holders, without realizing their virtual monopoly became a means to define their self-importance through exclusiveness. It seemed only too natural to them that men should hold the reins of power and serve as theoreticians and policymakers while women filled less important roles.

Although these patriarchal attitudes remained largely unarticulated, occasionally they were vocalized. Peng Shuzhi, for example, once objected to a woman's wielding formal power on behalf of the party because her behavior violated his sense of what was appropriate. He was upset with Chen Duxiu's decision to send Liu Qingyang to the Comintern's Fifth Congress in Moscow (1924). She was much too outspoken and strident for his tastes. Moreover, in his estimation she was culturally deficient and politically uncouth. Definitely the wrong choice of delegate to an international communist meeting from Peng Shuzhi's point of view. And yet Liu Qingyang was one of the most articulate, experienced, and well-educated women in the communist movement. She had first found her way into politics by serving as a leader of the May Fourth protest in Tianjin while a teacher at a well-known women's normal school. Later she studied in Europe, where she joined the CCP in 1921 and upon her return to China assumed several positions, including the editorship of a Tianjin women's newspaper. She was hardly a culturally deficient woman. No doubt if she had not spoken up at the Comintern meetings, had sat docilely on the train to and from Moscow, and had only spoken when addressed, Peng Shuzhi would have tolerated—even welcomed—her presence. As it was, she "harassed" him continually by her attempts to engage him in conversation.[42]

Most male Communists, it seems, retained some traditional expectations of gender roles despite their support for the cause of women's emancipation. These traditional expectations were most clearly revealed in the division of labor within their families. They assumed that their wives would perform domestic duties and shoulder the responsibilities of childrearing while they maintained a high level of political activity. Li Dazhao entered into an arranged marriage with Zhao Renlan, a self-sacrificing, illiterate woman who attended to their children and the menial work around the house so that her husband could devote the maximum time to his studies and to his public life as a party leader and teacher. She made it possible for him to pursue his ideals while her life was weighed down with household drudgery. Although he may have indeed loved her dearly, as one biographer maintains, he displayed little interest in relieving her of some of her household responsibilities so that she might gain time for intellectual development or public activities.[43]

While Li Dazhao failed to subject the traditional division of gender roles in his family to a penetrating critique, Chen Duxiu was known for his radical sexual politics. Yet on closer scrutiny, it becomes apparent that Chen's radicalness in this regard masked the self-serving nature of his actions. Although Gao Junman's claim that Chen often bragged that he had slept with women from every province except Gansu most likely exaggerates his promiscuity, the evidence of Chen's womanizing is too strong to dismiss.[44] Like many other intellectuals of the 1910s, Chen reportedly frequented the red·light district in Beijing (Bada Hutong) and was known to have had affairs before he settled into a permanent relationship toward the end of his life with Pan Lanzhen, a young Shanghai worker twenty years his junior.[45] Not only is it difficult to argue that Chen's sexual practices were based on a genuine desire to build an equal relationship with a woman, but it seems that he often expected women to cater to his wishes. Many years later, while writing his autobiography, Chen still recalled the anger he felt toward his first wife, Gao Dazhong, because she refused to give him her gold bracelet to cover his traveling expenses to study in Japan. No doubt Chen believed that the importance of his studies more than justified his wife's giving up a major portion of her dowry.[46] Thus, Chen Duxiu seemed in some ways very traditional in his relationships with women.

Chen seemed equally blind to the influence of traditional notions of power on his role as party chief. At the time of the founding of the CCP, Chen had wanted to avoid the mistake of Sun Yat-sen, who had proved to be an altogether dominating leader of the GMD.[47] Nevertheless, Chen set an authoritarian tone in the fledgling party that was difficult to counter because of his tremendous stature as an intellectual and communist politician.[48] This patriarchal style, in turn, supported the perseverance of other traditional notions of power, including those affecting gender relations, and militated against a serious critique of existing power relations in the early party. As a result, a somewhat modified type of court politics reminiscent of the imperial period emerged at the center of the CCP. A central characteristic of this type of court politics was the development of an informal power structure for women premised on the notion that women did not require access to formal decision-making positions.

Although male Communists played a major role in reproducing a gender hierarchy within the party, women also participated in defining their second-class status. In other words, the social expectations of communist men were critical in shaping these women's political identities, but the self-images of the women themselves were also operative in their acceptance of secondary political status, which clearly distinguished them from their male counterparts.

While communist ideals about the importance of women's emancipation helped motivate women to join the party, traditional representations of women continued to shape their political identities. As a result, communist women gravitated toward the roles of organizers and managers—roles that seemed compatible with their self-images of their strengths. Many of their duties, which were often taken for granted and not highly valued, can thus be seen as an extension of women's traditional roles as housekeepers and mothers. For instance, Wang Huiwu took logistical responsibility for the First Party Congress, including the procuring of a site. When the meeting was discovered by Shanghai International Settlement police, she again was commissioned to find a haven for the deliberations and this time she utilized contacts in her hometown area in South Lake, Zhejiang. Xiang Jingyu also managed many of the day-to-day details of the CEC between 1922 and 1925, largely because she was seen as more capable than the male members in such matters. By agreeing to perform tasks that men were not performing, these women participated in setting the historical boundaries of female behavior and experience in the CCP. In so doing, they were participating in the construction of gendered political identities that would have a long-term impact in the making of a communist state.

Women retained traditional ideological traits that shaped their political behavior not only because of historical influences. Most women revolutionaries at that time could not break through the psychological and tangible barriers to their assuming more egalitarian political roles in the party. They did not seem to question the extent to which they assumed childrearing responsibilities, which they saw as an extension of their biologically determined reproductive roles.

While they looked forward to the day when a socialist state would relieve them of some of their responsibilities through the establishment of day-care centers and canteens, they adhered to the sanctity of *muxing*, or maternal instincts, and thus failed to agitate for a redivision of household responsibilities with their husbands. Thus women's political identities were to some extent shaped by a traditional household ideology that both inhibited women's ability to assert their independence and encouraged their assumption of roles as nurturers, supporters, and organizers—roles compatible with their mothering experiences.

Because these women Communists assumed a greater role in household affairs, particularly childrearing, they had less time to pursue careers in the party and their self-images as revolutionary women were adversely affected. While communist men felt relatively little infringement upon their political careers by the addition of children, communist women had to recast their lives. These female revolutionaries often were able to ameliorate their burden in some measure by hiring nannies (*baomu*), yet it was still the female revolutionary who had to oversee these nannies and fill in their absences. Suddenly the managing of the household became a major affair in the lives of communist women. For some it became a real political feat to carry on with their political lives after having children. For example, Luo Zhanglong, an early male member of the party, has attributed Yang Kaihui's outstanding ability to juggle the rearing of two children with her numerous political tasks to her unusually good health.[49] Yet it is significant that she did not hold any specific positions in the party but served as an all-purpose organizer.

The real constraints imposed upon the lives of these revolutionary mothers militated against their developing stronger qualities of self-assertion and independence in the realm of politics—attributes that were essential to their assumption of leadership roles. It is significant that those women who did become important leaders in the Women's Bureau and the mass mobilization of women for the national revolution either sent their children off to relatives to rear, such as Xiang Jingyu and Yang Zhihua, or did not have children, such as Deng Yingchao and Liu Qingyang.[50] They were in a position to devote all their time to developing those values and skills that enabled them to feel self-confident as decision-makers and authority figures.

Concluding Comments

From the beginnings of the communist movement, male members recognized the need for radical gender reform and placed much emphasis on this issue in their writings. Their strongly felt egalitarian impulses also manifested themselves in the communist subcultures of the larger cities. Their personal lives were seen as an integral part of their political convictions. This characteristic had tremendous appeal for the first generation of women Communists, for whom the party functioned more as a subculture than a modern political institution. This subculture came into being at a time when family reform was at the top of the revolutionary agenda, and it was intended to serve as an alternative to the traditional "oppressive" family system, that is, an egalitarian surrogate family.

In sharp contrast to this subculture, the founders of the party constructed a political organization that was fundamentally patriarchal. While these young Communist males were eager to do away with the most brutal forms of gender oppression, many of which had affected them as young men, they were not willing to relinquish decision-making power. Thus, an important unstated precondition for promotion within the party hierarchy outside the Women's Bureau was gender. In this respect, male Communists were drawing a distinction between gender reform in society and in the polity. As they reproduced certain aspects of the existing gender system within the party, they revealed their fundamentally patriarchal approach to the issue of women's emancipation. At the core of their ideology was the conviction that men were the ultimate arbiters of women's issues. Full female agency was a prospect that they could not completely accept.

Long before Mao Zedong assumed control of the CCP, these patriarchal practices were entrenched in the party's organizational principles, structures, and expected leadership roles. Despite differences in personality and the conditions facing the organization during their tenures as party heads, Chen Duxiu and Mao Zedong both exhibited strong patriarchal traits in their styles of leadership. It may well have been impossible to do otherwise. In any event, a patriarchal style of leadership resonated well in the political culture of this new party.

With the establishment of the communist state, women proved somewhat successful in carving out new roles in economic and social sectors of the public realm. However, they still encountered immense difficulties in the political sectors, particularly in the realm of high politics. Despite the ardent advocacy of gender equality, a male-dominated power hierarchy has continued to prosper, including a fairly distinct sexual division of labor in political life that extends from top to bottom of the party and government. Ultimately, the persistence of an informal power system in which women participate by virtue of their marriages to high-level leaders of the CCP and government has aroused tremendous resentment against women in the political realm. Thus, while it can be shown that the Chinese communist revolution has brought many positive changes for women, the party has remained an essentially male-dominated organization.

Notes

This article is based on research funded by the Committee on Scholarly Communication with the People's Republic of China. Much of the writing was funded by a fellowship from the American Council of Learned Societies. I am also grateful to the participants of the International Conference on New Perspectives on the Chinese Communist Revolution for their helpful responses to my paper and to Gail Hershatter, Carma Hinton, Emily Honig, Hans van de Ven, and Marilyn Young for their perceptive written comments on earlier drafts of this manuscript.

1. Arif Dirlik, *The Origins of Chinese Communism* (New York: Oxford University Press, 1989).

2. The commencement of the Chinese communist movement can be dated as either March 1920 or August 1920, depending on whether the establishment of the Society for the Study of Marxist Theory in Beijing under Li Dazhao or the formation of the Shanghai communist nucleus under Chen Duxiu is used as one's starting point. For a complete discussion of the origins of the communist movement in China, see Tony Saich, "Through the Past Darkly: Some New Sources on the Founding of the Chinese Communist Party," *International Review of Social History*, 30, part 2 (1985): 167–82; and Dirlik, *The Origins of Chinese Communism*. A useful Chinese primary source is Contemporary History Research Group of the Chinese Academy of Social Sciences and the Party History Research Group of the Museum of the Chinese Revolution, ed., *"Yida" Qianhou. Zhongguo gongchandang diyici daibiao dahui qianhou ziliao xuanbian* (Around the Time of the First Party Congress: Selected Sources for the Period of the First National Congress of the CCP) (Beijing: People's Press, 1980–), 3 vols.

3. The first partial translation of Engels's work appeared in *Tianyi bao* (Natural Justice) in 1907. During the May Fourth era, Yun Daiying translated sections of this work. See Yun Daiying, "Yingzhe ershi lun jiating de qiyuan," (Engels on the Origin of the Family), *Dongfang zazhi* (Eastern Miscellany), 17, nos. 19 and 20.

The date of 1929 for the first complete translation of this work is given by Laszlo Ladany, *The Communist Party of China and Marxism 1921–1985* (Hoover: Stanford University Press, 1985), 4.

For a discussion of the overlap between the ideas of August Bebel and Friedrich Engels, see Alfred G. Meyer, "Marxism and the Women's Movement," in Dorothy Atkinson, Alexander Dallin, and Gail Warshofsky Lapidus, eds., *Women in Russia* (Stanford: Stanford University Press, 1977), 96–99.

4. See, for instance, [Li] Hanjun, "Nüzi zenyang cai neng dedao jingji duli?" (How Can Women Achieve Economic Independence), *Fünu pinglun* (Women's Critic), no. 3 (17 August 1921): 3–4.

5. Xiaofeng (pseud. Chen Wangdao), "Hun zhidu zui'e beigan," (Sadness about the Sin of the Marriage System), *Juewu* (Awakening), 24 June 1921; Chen Wangdao, "Xi Shangzhen nüshi zai Shangbaoguanli shangdiao shijian" (The Event of Ms. Xi Shangzhen's Suicide in the Office of the Commercial Press), *Fünü pinglun*, no. 59 (20 September 1922); Bing (pseud. Mao Dun), "Nüxing de zijue" (Women's Consciousness), *Fünü pinglun*, no. 1 (3 August 1921); Pei Wei (pseud. Mao Dun), "Lian'ai yu zhenjie de guanxi" (The Relationship between Love and Virginity), *Fünü pinglun*, no. 5 (31 August 1921); Heming (pseud. Li Da), "Gaodi hui nannü shejiao de xinxiang yuan" (An Admonition to New Gentlemen Who Denigrate Social Contact Between Men and Women), *Fünü pinglun*, no. 7 (14 September 1921); [Shao] Lizi, "Nannü shejiao yu jiu lijiao" (Social Contact Between Men and Women and Old Ethics), *Fünü pinglun*, no. 7 (14 September 1921); [Shao] Lizi, "Jiushi hunzhi de beiju" (The Tragedy of the Old Style of Marriage), *Minguo ribao* (Republic Daily), 13 September 1921; Shen Zemin, "Sanjiao lian'ai de wenti" (The Issue of a Love Triangle), *Fünü zhoubao* (Women's Weekly), no. 80 (29 March 1925); [Shen] Xuanlu, "Taolun nannü tongxiao wenti" (A Discussion of the Co-Educational School Issue), *Laodong yu fünü* (Labor and Women), no. 4 (6 March 1921); [Xiao] Chunü, "Qudi nüxuesheng lihun wenti" (The Problem of Preventing Women Students from Getting a Divorce), *Juewu*, 18–19 October 1924; [Li] Hanjun, "Nannü shejiao yinggai zenyang jiejue?" (How to Solve the Dilemma of Social Contact Between Men and Women), *Fünü pinglun*, no. 7 (14 September 1921).

6. "Regret for the Past" depicts the death of a "new woman" named Shijun who had left her family and moved in with her lover, only to find herself without any means of

support after the romance failed. For illustrative writings by other writers of this era, see Hu Shi, "Nüzi wenti de kaiduan" (The Starting Point of the Woman Question), *Funü zazhi* (Women's Magazine), 8, no. 1 (October 1922): 126; Chen Youqin, "Nüzi jingji duli zhi jichu" (The Basis of Women's Economic Independence), *Funü zazhi*, 10, no. 1 (January 1924): 55; Gao Xian, "Lian'ai duli" (Independent Love) in Meisheng, ed., *Zhongguo funü wenti taolunji* (Collection of Discussions on the Chinese Women's Question), 4: 56–71; Y.D. [pseud. Li Xiaofeng], "Zhiye yu funü" (Occupations and Women), *Funü zazhi*, 7, no. 11 (November 1921):8–11.

Wu Yu was cited as being a prominent proponent for the importance of women's achieving economic independence in order to secure their full autonomy in society and in marriage. See *Zhongguo funü yundongshi* (History of the Chinese Women's Movement) (Beijing: n. p., 1929), 99.

Lu Xun was the most eminent May Fourth writer to advocate women's economic independence; Hu Shi was a Western-educated intellectual who was the most prominent promoter of pragmatism in China; Chen Youqin was an eminent scholar of classical literature; Gao Xian was a graduate of Tokyo University who worked at Commercial Press; Li Xiaofeng was a founder of the New Tide Society in Beijing and published extensively under the pseudonym of Y. D. in Shanghai feminist periodicals; and Wu Yu was the leading intellectual iconoclast critic of the notion of feudalism.

7. [Shen] Zemin, "Nüzi jinri de diwei" (The Position of Women Today), *Funü pinglun*, no. 27 (8 January 1922): 1–2.

8. Shi Cuntong's views on marriage were contained in a series of articles he published in *Juewu* in May 1920. They were: [Shao] Lizi and [Shi] Cuntong, " 'Feichu hunzhi' taolun zhong de liangfengxia" (Two Letters Pertaining to the Discussion on "The Abolition of Marriage"), 15 May; [Shi] Cuntong, " 'Wuru nüzi renge' de jieshi" (An Explanation of "Humiliating Women's Personality"), 15 May; [Shi] Cuntong, "Jiejue hunyin wenti de yijian" (Opinions on How to Solve the Issue of Marriage), 17 May; [Shi] Cuntong, "Bianlun de taidu he feichu hunzhi" (Attitudes on Discussing and Abolishing the Marriage System), 21 May; [Shao] Lizi and [Shi] Cuntong, "Feichu hunzhi wenti de taolun" (A Discussion on the Issue of Abolishing the Marriage System), 23 May; [Shi] Cuntong, "Feichu hunzhi wenti de bianlun" (The Debate over the Issue of Abolishing Marriage), 25 May.

Shi Cuntong's remarks on his early party activities and his anarchist tendencies can be found in Shi Fuliang [Shi Cuntong], "Zhongguo gongchandang di chengli shiqi de jige wenti" (Some Questions Concerning the Period of the Founding of CCP), in *"Yida" qianhou*, 2: 33–34.

9. Dirlik, *Origins of Chinese Communism*, 179.

10. As early as 1904, Chen published an indictment of the arranged marriage system. See Chen Duxiu, "Esu pian" (An Essay on an Evil Custom), *Anhui suhuabao* (Anhui Vernacular Journal), no. 3 (15 May 1904); reprinted in *Chen Duxiu wenzhang xianbian* (Selected Articles of Chen Duxiu) (Beijing: Sanlian Bookstore, 1984), 1: 25–36.

11. Chen Dongyuan, *Zhongguo funü shenghuo shi* (History of the Life of Chinese Women) (Taibei: Taiwan Shangwu Yinshuguan, 1975), 336–37.

12. For some of these important articles on women's issues, see Chen Duxiu, "Shanghai housheng shachang Hunan nügong wenti" (The Issue of Hunanese Women Workers in the Shanghai Housheng Textile Factory), *Xin qingnian* (New Youth), 7, no. 6 (1 May 1920); Chen Duxiu, [Shen] Xuanlu, and Chen Gongbo, "Lifa gonghui chengli yanshuoci" (An Address to the Inaugural Conference of Hairdressers' Union), *Laodong yu funü*, no. 1 (13 February 1921); Chen Duxiu, "Women weishenma yao tichang laodong yundong yu funü yundong" (Why We Promote the Labor Movement and the Women's Movement), *Laodong yu funü*, no. 2 (20 February 1921); Chen Duxiu, "Zhu Shanghai sisha nügong xiehui chenggong" (To the Success of the Shanghai Women's Silk and Textile Union),

Xiangdao zhoubao (The Guide Weekly), no. 52 (20 January 1924); and Chen Duxiu, "Shanghai sichang nügong dabagong" (The General Strike by Shanghai Women Silk Workers), *Xiangdao zhoubao*, no. 70 (18–25 June 1924).

13. Such ideas can be found in the following essays: Chen Duxiu, "Funü wenti yu shehuizhuyi" (The Woman Question and Socialism), *Guangdong chunbao* (Guangdong Masses), 31 January 1921; Chen Duxiu, "Pingmin jiaoyu" (Universal Education), *Funü sheng* (The Women's Voice), no. 6 (5 March 1922): 1; and Chen Duxiu, "Shehui zhuyi duiyu jiaoyu he funü erfangmian de guanxi" (The Relationship of Socialism to the Two Issues of Education and Women), *Juewu*, 23 April 1922.

14. Such ideas are expressed in several articles and official communist documents disseminated under Chen's name. See, for example, Chen Duxiu, "Funü wenti yu shehui zhuyi" (The Woman Question and Socialism) and "Zhongguo gongchandang zhongyangju tonggao" (Circular of the Central Bureau of the CCP), *Zhongguo dangshi cankao ziliao* (Reference Materials on CCP History), 2: 202.

15. For a representative article of Li Dazhao's viewpoints on this issue, see Shou Chang [pseud. Li Dazhao], "Xiandai de nüquan yundong" (The Contemporary Women's Movement), *Funü pinglun*, no. 25 (18 January 1922): 2.

16. According to Perry Link, the editor of *Funü shibao* estimated that less than 10 percent of his magazine's readership was female. Perry Link, *Mandarin Ducks and Butterflies* (Berkeley: University of California Press, 1981), 250. Jacqueline Nivard reports that most writers and readers for *Funü zazhi* (The Women's Magazine) were also male. Jacqueline Nivard, "Histoire d'une revue féminine chinoise: *Funü zazhi*, 1915–1931" (The History of a Chinese Feminist Journal: Funü zazhi, 1915–1931) (Ph.D. dissertation, Paris, l'EHESS, 1983).

17. Certain feminist ideas had in fact been present in China for many centuries. Hsiung Ping-chen has put forward an interesting hypothesis on the origins of indigenous feminist ideas in China in her unpublished paper, "The Relationship Between Women and Children in Early Modern China," presented at the seventh annual convention of the National Women's Studies Association in Seattle, Washington, June 1985. Another insightful view on the emergence of feminist ideas in Qing China can be found in Paul Ropp, "The Seeds of Change: Reflections on the Condition of Women in the Early and Mid Ch'ing," *Signs*, no. 1 (1976): 5–23.

18. For a discussion of the role of ideology in providing a roadmap to changing social realities, see Clifford Geertz, "Ideology as a Cultural System," in *The Interpretations of Cultures* (New York: Basic Books, 1973), 218.

19. Wang Guangyuan, ed., *Chen Duxiu nianpu* (Chronology of Chen Duxiu) (Sichuan: Chongqing Press, 1987), 4.

20. Chen Duxiu, "Esu pian."

21. Lee Feigon, *Chen Duxiu: Founder of the Chinese Communist Party* (Princeton: Princeton University Press, 1983), 53.

22. Chen Gongbo, "Huiyi" (Memoirs), in *"Yida" qianhou*, 2: 427.

23. Tang Dongqing, "Tang Dongqing de huiyi" (Memoirs of Tang Dongqing), in *"Yida" qianhou*, 2: 458.

24. Chang Kuo-t'ao [Zhang Guotao], *The Rise of the Chinese Communist Party, 1921–1927* (Lawrence: University Press of Kansas, 1971), 1: 156–57.

25. Ibid., 157.

26. See, for example, [Wang] Jianhong, "Nüquan yundong ying yidao disi jieji" (The Women's Movement Should Be Moved to the Fourth Class), *Funü sheng*, no. 1 (13 December 1921): 1–2; [Gao] Junmei (Gao Junman), "Funü yu laodong" (Women and Labor), *Funü sheng*, no. 2 (21 December 1921): 1; and [Wang] Huiwu, "Zhongguo funü yundong de xin quxiang" (A New Tendency of the Chinese Women's Movement), *Funü sheng*, no. 3 (12 January 1922): 1.

27. The portrayal of Xiang Jingyu as primarily a labor organizer is found in almost all the relevant literature. See, for example, Suzette Leith, "Chinese Women in the Early Communist Movement," in Marilyn Young, ed., *Women in China* (Ann Arbor: University of Michigan Press, 1973), 56–57.

28. Xu Rihui, *Xiang Jingyu wenji* (Collected Writings of Xiang Jingyu) (Changsha: Hunan People's Press, 1980), 90.

29. Approximately 10 percent of the total membership of 994 at the Fourth Party Congress (January 1925) was female. By December 1926 there were 1,892 women members of the CCP. Wang Jianying, *Zhongguo gongchangdang zuzhi zi liao huibian* (Collected Materials on the Organizational History of the CCP)(Beijing: Red Flag Press, 1983), 8, 17, 30, and 33.

30. Ibid., 2.

31. Yang Zilie, *Zhang Guotao furen huiyilu* (Memoirs of Mrs. Zhang Guotao) (Hong Kong: Center for Research on Chinese Problems, 1970), 86.

32. Wang Yizhi, "Wusi shidai de yige nüzhong" (A Women's School in the May Fourth Era), *Wusi yundong huiyilu* (Memoirs of the May Fourth Movement), 518.

33. Yang Xianyi and Gladys Yang, trans., *Lu Xun Selected Works*, 2: 85–92.

34. C. Wilbur Martin, "The Influence of the Past," in John Wilson Lewis, ed., *Party Leadership and Revolutionary Power in China* (Cambridge: Cambridge University Press, 1970), 47.

35. Interview with Cai Bo, son of Cai Hesen and Xiang Jingyu, 23 July 1983 in Beijing, and with Dai Xugong, biographer of Xiang Jingyu, in March 1983 in Wuhan. For Cai Hesen's introducers, see Dai Xugong, *Xiang Jingyu zhuan* (A Biography of Xiang Jingyu) (Beijing: People's Press, 1981), 75.

36. There is a great deal of ambiguity about Xiang Jingyu's status at these congresses. Her son, Cai Bo, reported that party historians are divided on this question. The most authoritative scholars, however, do not list her as a delegate, with the possible exception of the Third Party Congress. Interview with Cai Bo in Beijing on 23 July 1983.

37. Ch'en Kung-po [Chen Gongbo], *The Communist Movement in China* (New York: Octagon Books, 1966), 129.

The role of the Comintern in the establishment of this Women's Bureau is discussed in the resolution on the women's program passed at the Second Congress. See "Zhongguo gongchandang dierci quanguo daibiao dahui guanyu funü yundong de jueyi" (Resolution of the CCP's Second National Congress on the Women's Movement), in All-China Women's Federation Research Department on the History of the Women's Movement, ed., *Zhongguo funü yundong lishi ziliao, 1921–1927* (Historical Materials on the Chinese Women's Movement, 1921–1927) (Beijing: People's Press, 1986), 29–30.

38. For the Third Party Congress, see, for example, Wang Jianying, *Zhongguo gongchandang zuzhi ziliao huibian*, 18; Guangdong Museum of Revolutionary History, ed., *Zhonggong "sanda" ziliao* (Materials on the CCP's "Third Congress") (Canton: Guangdong People's Press, 1985), 99; and the account of the Comintern representative Maring (Sneevliet) in Tony Saich, *The Origins of the First United Front in China: The Role of Sneevliet (Alias Maring)* (Leiden: Brill, 1991), 223–24.

39. "Luo Zhanglong tan Zhonggong 'sanda' de qianhou qingkuang" (Luo Zhanglong Discusses the Situation Around the Time of the CCP's "Third Congress"), in *Zhonggong "sanda" ziliao*, 181.

40. "Zhongguo gongchandang disanci quanguo daibiao dahui guanyu funü yundong jueyian," in *Zhongguo funü yundong lishi ziliao*, 68–69.

41. "Zhongguo gongchandang disici quanguo daibiao dahui duiyu funü yundong zhi jueyian" (Resolution of the CCP's Fourth National Congress on the Women's Movement), in *Zhongguo funü yundong lishi ziliao, 1921–1927*, 279–81.

42. Claude Cadart and Cheng Yingxiang, *Memoires de Peng Shuzhi: L'Envol du communisme en Chine* (The Memoirs of Peng Shuzhi: The Origins of Communism in China) (Paris: Gallimard, 1983), 367–68.

43. Zhao Zhangan et al., *Lao gemingjia de lian'ai, hunyin and jiating shenghuo* (Love, Marriage and Family Life of Veteran Revolutionary Families) (Beijing: Workers' Press, 1985), 30–36.

44. Feigon, *Chen Duxiu*, 53.

45. Hu Shih, for instance, frequented brothels as a way of dealing with an unhappy marriage. For sources on Chen's promiscuous behavior, see Pu Qingquan, "Wo suo zhidao de Chen Duxiu" (What I Know about Chen Duxiu), in *Chen Duxiu pinglun xuanbian* (Selected Critical Essays on Chen Duxiu) (Henan: Henan People's Press, 1982), 369; Li Da, *Yida qianhou*, 2: 3; and Wang Huiwu, *Yida qianhou*, 2: 76–77.

46. Wang Guanyuan, *Chen Duxiu nianpu*, 6–23.

47. Feigon, *Chen Duxiu*, 153.

48. Numerous sources confirm the severity of Chen Duxiu's temper and the extent to which he expected conformity. See, for example, Li Da's and Wang Huiwu's reminiscences in *"Yida" qianhou*, 2: 16, 54, and 76–78; and Bao Huiseng, *Bao Huiseng huiyilu* (The Memoirs of Bao Huiseng) (Beijing: People's Press, 1983) 368–69; and Li Weihan, "Guanyu baqi huiyi de yixie huiyi" (Some Memories about the 7 August Conference), in Li Weihan, *Huiyi yu yanjiu* (Reminiscences and Research) (Beijing: CCP Party History Materials Press, 1986), 1: 157–58.

49. "Luo Zhanglong tan Zhonggong 'sanda' de qianhou qingkuang," 180–81.

50. Although Deng Yingchao experienced one difficult pregnancy in 1927, she never had any children. Liu Qingyang started a family after she withdrew from politics in 1927; she was already in her late thirties.

Chapter 3

What Is Wrong with Li Dazhao?

Susanne Weigelin-Schwiedrzik

On 28 October 1989, the CCP CC convened in Beijing's Huairen Hall to commemorate the one hundredth birthday of Li Dazhao. General Secretary Jiang Zemin and then–State President Yang Shangkun, together with members of the Politburo's Standing Committee, participated in a meeting headed by Peng Zhen.[1] Jiang Zemin delivered a speech in which he highly praised Li Dazhao's political merits. He defined Li as a "forerunner of the Chinese communist movement, a brilliant Marxist" and "outstanding proletarian revolutionary, one of the founders of the [C]CP" who had been among the first to understand that intellectuals had to come together with the working class in order to transform China according to a program of socialism, not capitalism. According to Jiang, commemorating Li Dazhao meant learning from him how to stick to the basics of Marxism-Leninism in theoretical, political, and moral matters.[2]

The next day a symposium on Li Dazhao at the Great Hall of the People in Beijing was opened by Hu Sheng,[3] with Hu himself delivering a short inaugural address and Hu Qiaomu presenting a more detailed speech under the title "Commemorating the Great Forerunner of the Chinese Communist Movement Li Dazhao."[4] Hu Sheng stressed that Li Dazhao should be regarded as the first Marxist in the colonialized world who had begun to transform his original "bourgeois democratic standpoint" into a Marxist conviction even before the May Fourth movement.[5] Hu Qiaomu's report was published in the newspapers under the title "the glorious revolutionary tradition of Beijing University is unshakable."[6]

The symposium lasted from 29 October until 1 November, with sixty-seven papers presented by scholars from mainland China, Japan, Mongolia, Czechoslovakia, and the Soviet Union.[7] Discussion focused on the question of how to evaluate the historical merits of Li Dazhao, in other words, how to understand the process of his becoming a Marxist. Therefore, most papers covered Li Dazhao's thought before 1919, his first discussions of Marxism and the October Revolution as well as the question of when finally Li Dazhao can be regarded as having metamorphosed into an orthodox Marxist.[8]

In his speech during the closing meeting of the symposium, Wang Xuezhen as president of the Chinese Society for Research on Li Dazhao summarized activities to commemorate Li Dazhao since his death in 1927. According to Wang, while comrades from the Beijing party organization had risked their lives to prepare a first volume of Li Dazhao's essays, which was finally published in 1935 with a foreword by Lu Xun,[9] the broad propaganda of Li Dazhao as a model hero had not begun until the end of the 1950s and was unfortunately interrupted by the "ten years of chaos" (1966–76), but had continued successfully since 1979. The climax of these activities came when the CC inaugurated a memorial yard for Li Dazhao in 1983[10] and in the 1989 activities to commemorate the one hundredth anniversary of his birth.[11]

According to this summary of the 1989 commemoration festivities, nothing is wrong, or has ever been wrong, with Li Dazhao. He has always been regarded as an outstanding Communist; more than six hundred articles have been published since 1949, twenty books have come out, and the two volumes of his essays, *Li Dazhao wenji*, can be bought in bookstores all over China.

However, if we look a little more closely at recent and earlier activities as well as publications on Li, the picture becomes disturbed. Why is Li commemorated as a forerunner of the communist movement rather than as one of the "martyrs" who was killed in 1927 by warlord troops in Beijing on the grounds of being a political criminal? Why was a memorial yard built for him only in 1983, when many other "martyrs" had received this honor much earlier? Why did discussion focus on his thought and activities before the founding of the CCP, and why are there hardly any publications to be found on his activities as one of the leaders of the communist movement in North China? And—last but not least—why has Li Dazhao, who has been praised as a model of loyalty, unshakability, and morality, appeared significantly less in mainland publications than Chen Duxiu, who has been treated as a symbol of the bad in Chinese communist historiography ever since it came into being?

A Comparison of Hu Qiaomu's and Jiang Zemin's Speeches: Li Dazhao as a Model for Intellectuals or for Cadres?

While the *Renmin ribao* report exclusively summarizes those passages of Hu Qiaomu's speech dealing with Li Dazhao's relationship to Beijing University,[12] the *Guangming ribao* summary focuses on those sections where Hu Qiaomu discusses the role of intellectuals in the Chinese revolution.[13] The *Zhonggong dangshi yanjiu* full version of the speech finally reveals that Hu's address to the Li Dazhao symposium was in fact aimed at re-evaluating the role of those intellectuals who had received a traditional education before turning to the revolution of 1911, the New Culture movement, and the CCP. In contrast to earlier interpretations of this kind of intellectual development, Hu Qiaomu places Li Dazhao within the continuum of those "outstanding Chinese intellectuals who have since antiquity adhered to the tradition of showing concern for the fate of the country."[14]

Hu did not argue, as was the case with earlier interpretations, that a break with Chinese tradition enabled Li Dazhao finally to become the first Chinese Marxist, but that patriotism as the modern version of the Chinese intellectuals' concern for their country, combined with Li's feeling of solicitude for the "broad masses of the Chinese people," made him different from the mainstream of intellectuals in the early twentieth century. Since Li conceived of himself as a spokesman of the masses from the very beginning of his political career, he avoided making the mistake of understanding individualism as an alternative to the Confucian Li (rites) and therefore became an optimist while other intellectuals tended toward pessimism during the period 1912–19. When Li began to move toward Marxism-Leninism, Hu stressed that one has to see his patriotism and not, as the conventional wisdom has it, his democratic outlook. "Starting out from a patriotic standpoint, advancing through democratization and walking forward toward communism was the common path taken by many progressive elements at the time. However, the question remains: Why was it Li Dazhao and not somebody else who was the first to abandon the capitalist program and turn toward the socialist program of building the country?"[15] Theoretically, according to Hu Qiaomu, Li Dazhao's thought shows signs of spontaneous materialist and dialectic thinking as Li was, on the one hand, interested in the reality of things and, on the other hand, by observing reality, he acknowledged that the world was full of contradictions. Politically, Li's inclination toward the "broad masses" had made him, although a democrat himself, suspicious of the bourgeois democratic republic. According to Hu, this kind of doubt was the bridge that had to be crossed before accepting that communism was a better solution than both bourgeois democracy and feudal bureaucracy. As Li was looking for something superior to both "feudalism" and "capitalism," he was the first Chinese intellectual to understand that the 1917 October Revolution was the model that would enable China to shake off the handicap of lagging behind world history and jump up to the front of the most advanced nations in the world.[16]

Li Dazhao took his final step toward Marxism-Leninism, Hu Qiaomu goes on to say, as a scholar who spent his life in the search for truth, and who, even after becoming an active revolutionary, did not give up his scholarly identity but continued to write essays analyzing Chinese society.[17]

Only after these comments does Hu Qiaomu turn to discuss the "revolutionary tradition" of Beijing University: a tradition of antifeudal, anti-imperialist struggle followed by outstanding contributions to the development of socialist China since 1949 in the field of science and technology.[18]

Leaving aside the fact that Renmin ribao, as the CCP's central organ, uses these final paragraphs to summarize the contents of Hu Qiaomu's whole speech,[19] we must take a closer look at Jiang Zemin's message[20] in order to find out more about the basic positions being taken in the 1989 discussion about Li Dazhao. Jiang Zemin's speech, clearly not directed toward a scholarly audience, is much more conventional and shallow than Hu Qiaomu's. Nevertheless, two common points of interest can be found. First, like Hu, Jiang is keen to point out that Li Dazhao was "a great patriot" who turned to communism after having passed through bourgeois democracy. Unlike Hu, he does not point to any roots in the Chinese tradition, but sticks to the conventional vision of Li Dazhao as one of the intellectuals who had begun by hoping to find a solution for China's problems among the models in the Western capitalist world, but who had learned through practice that "the capitalist program for building the country did not work in China."[21]

Secondly, Jiang Zemin also wants to draw attention to Li's close connection to "the masses of the people," but again unlike Hu, Jiang mentions Li's concern for the masses only in the context of his Marxist world view and not as part of his roots in the Chinese tradition. For Jiang, Li is mainly an "outstanding soldier," while for Hu he is a communist intellectual; for Jiang, Li is the forerunner of the new, while for Hu he is the link between China's past and future. For Jiang, Li is the model for communist cadres to learn from, but for Hu, he is the model for intellectuals to find their orientation.

**Academic Discussion on the Pre-Marxist Li Dazhao:
Continuity or Break?**

After more than ten years of internal critique and public silence about Li Dazhao, in 1979 historiographers used the ninetieth anniversary of his birth to reintegrate Li Dazhao into political and scholarly debate.[22] Li Xin delivered a speech called "Conduct Research on Li Dazhao, and Study Li Dazhao" avoiding most of the common definitions regarding the how and when of Li's turning toward Marxism-Leninism, but sticking to the conventional formula used since the first post-1949 publications on Li Dazhao that Li had started out as a "radical democrat" before becoming a Marxist.[23] However, especially since the mid-1980s this formula (*tifa*) has been questioned by some scholars, with the obvious result that Hu Qiaomu was willing to use their findings to present his ideas on Li.[24]

Li Dazhao's attitude toward Yuan Shikai is the main problem to be addressed in trying to discover what position Li held before he began to praise the October Revolution. This topic has not appeared in textbooks and articles on Li Dazhao but more recently has attracted the interest of some historiographers. An article by Yang Hongzhang concedes that Li had supported Yuan Shikai after the 1911 Revolution and only in 1914 had begun to think of Yuan as a despot who was interested only in monopolizing power.[25] When Yuan's intrigues to re-establish the imperial system were finally published in 1915, Li Dazhao became a radical critic of Yuan, referring to him in his article "Politics and the Respectability of the People's Civilization" as "the enemy of the nation."[26] Zhu Chengjia suggests in his article on Li Dazhao and Yuan Shikai that Li Dazhao moved away from Yuan Shikai at an even later date. In Zhu's view, Li recognized the problems of the republic quite early, but he did not see Yuan Shikai as responsible for its faults; on the contrary, Li still invested hope in his being the one and only politician who could rise above the quarrels beginning between different parties and use his moral prestige to solve the problems that confronted China. The reason why Li Dazhao supported Yuan until 1915 or even 1916 is to be found in his insistence that China remain a unified country under a centralized leadership. For Li, China's unification was more important than anything else, and democratization was, in this context, of only secondary importance.[27] While Zhu Chengjia stresses the weak points of Li Dazhao's thinking as inhibiting him from advancing faster from his false standpoints to a correct analysis of Chinese society, Yang Hongzhang describes Li's support for Yuan more positively as part of his democratic outlook. For Yang, the democrat Li had his doubts about Yuan Shikai from the very beginning, but nevertheless he hoped that the imperfect democratic system could be developed into an ideal form of political organization. Only after having found out that Yuan was not interested in improving the system did Li change and begin to criticize and even fight against Yuan Shikai.[28]

Here again we find Yang Hongzhang trying to interpret Li Dazhao as an avant-garde thinker, while Zhu Chengjia is mainly interested in portraying him as a representative of China's bourgeoisie: a bourgeoisie that in China was linked to traditional forces—quite unlike the revolutionary force that it had been in early European bourgeois society.[29] His argument closely resembles the views of Liu Guisheng about the roots of Li Dazhao's thought in ancient Chinese philosophy and political theory. Liu Guisheng makes the point that Li was mostly influenced by Wang Fuzhi and Zhuang Zi, but also by Tan Sitong, Yan Fu, and Liang Qichao. "This system [of thought], when viewed through contemporary eyes, in Chinese terms follows on from the late Qing's combination of Han and Song learning . . . while in Western terms it follows on from nineteenth-century English utilitarianism rather than from eighteenth-century French Enlightenment."[30]

In the context of Liu Guisheng's interpretation, Li is viewed as politically tending toward constitutionalism and ideologically belonging to the elite-oriented group of reformers with "deep roots in Chinese traditional thinking."[31] According to Liu Guisheng and others, this was Li's starting point and is what makes Hu Qiaomu and Jiang Zemin change the original formula to state that Li's point of departure was "patriotism." What is not mentioned in any of the articles I have been able to consult is the fact that Li's inclination toward constitutionalism has to be seen in the context of his connections with Tan Hualong and the Jinbudang (Progressive Party). Meisner, in his study of Li Dazhao, seems to infer that Li Dazhao needed Tan Hualong economically, while Liu Guisheng's interpretation of Li's early thought hints at the possibility that the Jinbudang had influenced Li much more deeply.[32]

Authors such as Zhang Jingru, who, since the late 1950s, have written articles about how Li Dazhao was influenced by the theory of evolution before turning toward Marxism, apparently found it hard to argue against those who find proof for Li's nondemocratic thinking after 1911. This is why they focus on the last years before the May Fourth movement (1919) to try to show that by then Li had become a radical democrat or even an "intellectual with communist inclinations" (*juyou chubu gongchanzhuyi sixiang de zhishi fenzi*). In his paper for the Li Dazhao symposium, Zhang Jingru tried hard to prove that Li should be defended against those who say,

> Right from its first introduction into China Marxism was not of an orthodox kind but had been transformed by Confucian thought. . . . However, in fact, Li Dazhao and other progressive elements from the very beginning of their propagation of Marxism tended toward truthfulness to the original meaning, [which means that] they did not revise Marxism with the help of Confucian thought. They could do this because they had gone through the purification of democratization and had led a relatively thorough struggle against feudalism (before changing into Marxists).[33]

One proof for Li Dazhao's change of ideas in the period just before 1919 was his contribution to the discussion on the differences between Western and Eastern civilizations. In this discussion, according to Tan Shuangquan, Li described traditional Chinese society as stagnant and thus China as among those nations to be defeated by the Western nonstagnant (i.e., progressing) civilization.[34] However, although Li proclaimed learning from the West as a remedy for the "stagnant" society, he did not go to the extreme of propagating total Westernization. He stood for a "third kind of new civilization" combining Western and Eastern traditions on the basis of correcting the shortcomings of one civilization with the relevant strong points of the other.[35] In contrast to Zhang Shizhao, Li based his proposal to combine the best of East and West on his strong repulsion of Confucianism as well as on a basically correct Marxist understanding of the relationship between Confucian morale and the feudal economic basis. "Li Dazhao's analysis of feudal morale shows that he had, in principle, moved away ideologically from the theory of evolution toward historical materialism, i.e., Marxism."[36]

By showing how Li Dazhao participated in the discussions on the differences between Eastern and Western civilizations during the period of the New Culture movement, Tan is able to make use of Li Dazhao in two ways. On the one hand, he can remove the stain on Li Dazhao's copybook caused by those interpretations that stress his close connections to Chinese tradition and by so doing divert the suspicion that Chinese Marxism was shaped by traditional Chinese thinking. On the other hand, he can reintegrate Li Dazhao into the group of intellectuals who believed in the theory of evolution and who stood for democracy. Only after having gone through all this can he make the additional argument that "[Li

Dazhao's] third kind of civilization is socialist civilization."[37] This means that Li Dazhao can be claimed as the founding father of the 1989 CCP leadership that wants to find a solution between the "total Westernization" that they claim was propagated by Zhao Ziyang and some form of cultural conservatism that is only interested in preserving the Chinese essence and that therefore repudiates any kind of modernization.

Zhang Hua's contributions to the discussion on continuity and break in Li Dazhao's thinking were written before the June Fourth incident (1989) and have quite a different tone.[38] In his articles on Li Dazhao and the ideal of Young China (*Shaonian Zhongguo*), he attempts to show that the process of accepting Marxism cannot be characterized as marking a total break with earlier ideas provoked by ideological debates between Marxists and anti-Marxists. Zhang points out that the kind of Marxism that was finally accepted by Chinese intellectuals after May Fourth was a combination of several socialist theories. To provide an example of this process, Zhang presents his research on Li Dazhao's relation to the *Shaonian Zhongguo* group. According to Zhang, this group was inclined toward utopian socialism, which "seems to be the starting point for the propagation of Marxism in China."[39] In this phase, Marxism was no more than an instrument for the abstract repudiation of both feudalism and capitalism. But as Li Dazhao did not know enough about the relationship between capitalism and socialism, he tended toward utopian socialism, which led him back to a peasant ideology. And this, in Zhang's view, represents exactly the utopian socialists' incorrect understanding of the relationship between economic base and ideological superstructure that "has long impeded people's scientific understanding of the socialist way in China." [40]

Zhang Hua goes on to say that Li Dazhao not only abstractly searched for an alternative, but he also pragmatically longed for a solution by simply negating the then existing society in China. This kind of simplistic negation is the basis for Li's revolutionary enthusiasm as well as the reason why his understanding of Marxism was strongly shaped by traditional Chinese ethics. As Li and others "longed more for the purity of an ideal society rather than being knowledgeable about the complexity of building socialism in an economically underdeveloped country . . . the socialism the May Fourth intellectuals desired did not accord with reality," [41] and thus they propagated, for example, the necessity of eliminating the difference between mental and physical labor as a main aim of socialism. Later, such a view would have far-reaching consequences. "If we go back to history, we come across an interesting phenomenon: there is no echo at all in contemporary China regarding the ideal of 'Young China.' But, in fact, it seems of utmost importance to engage in research on the specifics of Chinese Marxism in the May Fourth era in order to find their origins when summarizing left-opportunist mistakes."[42]

Zhang Hua's article seems to belong to a group of publications in which members of the youngest generation of party historiographers were trying to occupy a field that had until then been held by representatives of the conservative or orthodox factions of the CCP. Especially in the first half of 1989, they published articles on many aspects of party history challenging the hagiography that was intended to legitimize the "generation of old revolutionaries' " claim for power. Since Mao Zedong admitted that his understanding of Marxism had been strongly influenced by Li Dazhao, Zhang Hua can write on the utopianism of early Chinese Marxism taking Li Dazhao as his example while in fact criticizing the roots of *Mao Zedong sixiang* (Mao Zedong Thought). However, Zhang also shows how "dangerous" it can be to divert from the conventional view that Li Dazhao became a Marxist on the basis of being a radical democrat. His argument leads directly to the phenomenon Zhang Jingru was trying to criticize in his contribution to the Li Dazhao symposium.[43] If Li Dazhao's Marxism was not the result of a break with Chinese tradition but was, on the contrary, shaped by this tradition, then Li can be used to prove that Chinese Marxism was "revised" by Confucianism from the very beginning of its propagation in China.

Comparing the different standpoints on the question of continuity and change in Li Dazhao's early thought, we find two different arguments for continuity juxtaposed by one that sticks to the conventional way of conceiving the problem. While Hu Qiaomu, in line with historiographers such as Liu Guisheng and Zhu Chengjia, sees the continuity of traditional thinking in Li's approach to political and theoretical problems in the pre–May Fourth era, Zhang Hua identifies the continuity of peasant ideology in the utopian thinking of Li Dazhao and other intellectuals participating in the New Culture movement. For Hu Qiaomu continuity is an additional argument for the good quality of Li Dazhao's thought, while Zhang Hua singles out this continuity as the precondition for later "left-opportunist" mistakes within the CCP. One of the reasons why both of them argue for continuity but in so doing come to totally different evaluations is that they refer to different aspects of traditional Chinese thought. When Hu Qiaomu praises Li for his roots in tradition, he does not mention those aspects whose continuation lead Zhang Hua to criticize Li. However, no matter how different their arguments for continuity in Li's thought are, they are both opposed to Jiang Zemin's use of those historiographers' interpretations that stress aspects of a break in the development of Li's thought.

On the other hand, we find common interests in the otherwise contradictory standpoints between Hu Qiaomu, on the one side, and Jiang Zemin, who takes his arguments from more conservative historiographers such as Zhang Jingru, on the other. Hu and Jiang both want to establish Li Dazhao as the founder of Chinese socialism. Either by interpreting Li as the model for how Chinese traditional thought can be combined with Marxism (Hu Qiaomu) or by taking him as a model for how the critique of both feudalism and capitalism can lead to Marxism (Jiang Zemin), Li can be shown to have been engaged in a constant search for a Chinese solution, and in a search for something superior both to conservatism and total Westernization. They are united against their common enemy, in this case again represented by Zhang Hua, who conceives of this kind of Chinese socialism as the root of all further mistakes.

What Is So Good about Li Dazhao's Marxism?

Like Zhang Hua, Wang Huilin published an article containing new ideas on Li Dazhao shortly before the June Fourth incident.[44] He discusses Li's article "Populism" interpreting it as the only proof of Chinese Marxists being concerned with the relationship between proletarian dictatorship and democracy.[45] According to the *Dangshi yanjiu tongxun* interpretation of Wang's article, it is Wang's aim to show that most Chinese Marxists followed Lenin in saying that in the process of building socialism with the necessity of suppressing the bourgeoisie, democracy will diminish just as the state will vanish.[46] Only Li Dazhao believed proletarian dictatorship to be the highest form of democracy, which is why socialism should lead to an unfolding of democracy and not to its disappearance. Li Dazhao stressed the necessity of combining socialism and democracy, according to Wang, because he believed that both socialism and democracy sprang from the same origin.

Wang Huilin tries hard to prove Li Dazhao's interest in socialist democracy because he wants to convince his readers that democracy should not be criticized simplistically as having a bourgeois class character (*jiejixing*), but that it is also of interest for all the people (*quanminxing*). He obviously wants to remind the CCP leadership of some form of democratic tradition within the party thus trying to prevent democratic elements from being forced to remain outside the CCP.

In contrast to this somewhat contrived attempt to claim Li Dazhao's Marxism for reformist factions within the CCP, Peng Ming in his article on Li Dazhao and the propagation of Marxism-Leninism characterizes Li's Marxism quite conventionally in four points.[47] Li's Marxism was anti-imperialist, but not blindly nationalistic, as Li aimed at connecting Chinese history with world history. Li's Marxism was also characterized as reflecting the necessity for intellectuals to seek support from the masses, especially from the peasant masses. Li Dazhao was supposed to have taught his readers how to differentiate between old and new forms of democracy. Referring to the exact same article as Wang Huilin, Peng Ming goes on to say that Li had prepared the basis for Mao Zedong's theory of New Democracy by demanding that socialism implement a real and higher form of democracy than the "false democratic system" produced by the bourgeoisie.[48] This interpretation is, of course, an indirect repudiation of Wang Huilin's point. Not only Li Dazhao should be praised for including the demand for unfolding democracy into his theory, but also Mao. There is nothing new to be learned from Wang's re-evaluation of Li Dazhao!

Li Dazhao in the 1920s: The Model Revolutionary?

According to the summary of the discussions during the Li Dazhao symposium, the questions of Li's contribution to building the CCP and organizing its political activities in the 1920s were discussed under the topics of "correctly understanding and evaluating Li Dazhao's contribution to the Chinese communist move-ment" and "Li Dazhao's ideas on building the party."[49] However, none of the papers dealing with these questions were published after the symposium, and with few exceptions no articles on these topics appeared in magazines and news-papers.

In June 1989, though, one small booklet by the Research Department on Party History of the CCP Beijing Party Committee appeared that is concerned exclu-sively with Li Dazhao's political activities after the establishment of the CCP organization in Beijing.[50] The authors outline Li's contributions to the establish-ment of the First United Front between the GMD and CCP,[51] its preservation in the face of attacks by right-wing GMD politicians,[52] and to ensuring that the development of the party and the mass movement guaranteed the CCP's inde-pendence within the United Front.[53] On the one hand, Li's close links to GMD politicians, especially his cordial relationship with Sun Yat-sen, is described as being of great importance in bringing the two parties together;[54] on the other hand, Li is described as having been active in persuading the CCP of the neces-sity for cooperation with the GMD through his repudiation of Zhang Guotao's so-called left opportunism that was put forward during the Third Party Con-gress.[55]

While such information had already been vaguely revealed in publications of the 1950s and 1960s,[56] the fact that Li Dazhao was sent to participate in the Comintern's Fifth Congress in Moscow had previously been disclosed only in book-length biographies on Li Dazhao.[57] Even in the 1950s, when the CCP's relationship to the Soviet Union was still quite close, authors writing on Li Dazhao must have felt uneasy about dwelling too much on Li Dazhao's contacts with the Comintern; they must have felt strong reservations about disclosing the fact that, before he was killed by the Beijing authorities, Li was taken into custody while hiding in a building on the compound of the Soviet embassy. This piece of information, which would normally qualify Li to be a "martyr," is found only in a minority of party history textbooks published in the 1950s, 1960s, and 1970s.[58]

The mass movement in North China led by the CCP and the GMD is one of the topics covered by the Research Department on Party History of the Beijing Party Committee that does not normally appear in textbooks or articles on party history. However, as an official assessment has not been made, the authors simply provide a description of the main party and mass activities and do not attempt any kind of evaluation. They confine themselves to hinting that Li Dazhao was not a member of Chen Duxiu's faction but showed concern for arousing the masses.

Of special interest in this context is the so-called revolution in the capital (*shoudu geming*), which is described at considerable length as the Beijing party organization's attempt to overthrow political power at the center in 1925.[59] As a sign of political enthusiasm, the mass movement is characterized as making a positive contribution toward removing the warlord regime. However, the authors display reserve when discussing the theoretical justification for this, as it seems to conform more with the "Russian model" of proletarian revolution than with the particular Chinese path to revolution as usually praised by Li Dazhao.

Finally, the massacre of 18 March 1926 is mentioned not only to show how actively Li participated in the movement but also to make clear that Li was not afraid of being directly, even physically, confronted by the enemy.[60] Only after having established Li as a hero do the authors establish his qualifications as a "martyr" by detailing Li Dazhao's last days.[61] Even though Li knew that he was in danger, he had chosen to send the best comrades to the South, where the revolutionary movement was developing with fewer problems while he remained in Beijing hiding in the embassy compound to lead the CCP's underground work.

What Is Wrong with Li Dazhao?

The fact that the Beijing party committee's Research Department on Party History was the first to present this detailed account of Li Dazhao's activities as one of the party leaders partly explains why this aspect of Li Dazhao's life is seldom referred to and why, until now, it has never aroused any discussion. It took the CCP CC over twenty-six years after Li Dazhao's execution to agree on an official evaluation of his contribution to the Chinese revolution. Without this official evaluation party historiographers simply had no right to conduct research on, and write about, Li Dazhao, especially on Li Dazhao as a leader of the Chinese communist movement. However, even with an official evaluation, the problem is still not totally resolved. The text written for inscription on the stele in Li Dazhao's memorial yard mentions only vaguely Li's activities in Beijing, avoiding an overall impression of him as a heroic and unshakable fighter against imperialism and feudalism. The text does not say anything about the "revolution in the capital," about Li Dazhao's cooperation with the Comintern, or his having been arrested while hiding in the compound of the Soviet embassy.[62]

The problem the inscription is trying to avoid, and the booklet on Li Dazhao is forced to circumvent by refraining from any kind of evaluation, is that Li Dazhao cannot be integrated into the "two-line struggle" paradigm that still dominates appraisal of party activities. He is not an urbanized intellectual like Chen Duxiu, he is not the representative of the Comintern like Wang Ming, he is not one of the students who returned from France like Zhou Enlai, and he does not belong to the Mao Zedong group. Therefore, he can be neither criticized for belonging to any faction of opportunists nor praised for being a member of Mao's entourage.

Even though Li must have cooperated closely with Chen Duxiu, to my knowledge, no publication links Li to Chen Duxiu's so-called right opportunism.[63] The proof of his adhering to the "correct line" of independence during the United

Front is his enthusiastic organization of the mass movement in Beijing. Yet this kind of enthusiasm does not conform with the party's later decision that the main task of the 1924–27 period of party history was the military fight against the Northern warlords led by the United Front of the GMD and the CCP. Does this mean that Li Dazhao was a "leftist"? In order to prevent readers from drawing this kind of conclusion, articles describe Li as one of the most important representatives of the United Front policy playing a decisive role in the GMD's First Party Congress as well as in the CCP's Third Congress, where Li defended the United Front against attacks from the left as formulated by Zhang Guotao.

If Li Dazhao is said to have been neither a rightist nor a leftist, if he managed to organize mass movements while keeping close contacts with the GMD as part of the United Front policy, if he not only was interested in the workers' and students' political activities but also was among the first to understand the importance of organizing peasants and of building an army, then Li can be praised for possessing all those qualities normally attributed to Mao Zedong.

And this is the second reason that Li Dazhao's party activities have to be omitted from discussion. Party historiography allows only Mao Zedong as the charismatic leader to take his position outside, or even above, the party's two-line struggle. All other members of the party leadership have to belong either to the group of "opportunists" or to Mao's entourage. Within this framework, the most outstanding representatives of the many "opportunist" lines can be described in terms of all their "incorrect" theoretical contributions, but only the members of the entourage can be referred to by name along with one or two activities that they have organized under the leadership of the correct line. While Mao Zedong was still alive and party historiography had to perpetuate his charisma, writing on Li Dazhao was constantly curtailed by the threat of harming the reputation of the charismatic leader. Only if Li is praised exclusively for his contributions in the pre-1921 period can he coexist with Mao and therefore be integrated into a Mao-centered party historiography.[64]

When in 1979 Li Xin wrote his article about Li Dazhao calling upon party historiographers to be "truthful to the facts, and to stick to the truth without reservation" he used the chance offered in the late 1970s to reintegrate Li Dazhao into party history.[65] His article is, to my knowledge, the first detailed description of both aspects of Li's life to be published nationwide since 1957.[66] But by referring to "reservation," Li Xin seems to hint at the possibility of depicting Li as a new leader of the communist movement in China. Therefore he continues by defining the limits of praise for Li as follows: "But we are not feudal historiographers, we are proletarian historians . . . we must regard our respected Li Dazhao as a good friend of the people, a loyal servant and soldier, and we should not make him out to be a saint or a god. He is of outstanding morality, and his articles are very good, his contributions great, but he is also not without shortcomings and mistakes."[67] Li Xin does not want Li Dazhao to replace Mao Zedong in the process of de-Maoification, he only wants to contribute to de-Maoification by giving Li Dazhao more space in party historiography. Since, at the time, the victory of the Chinese revolution was still accepted as the main proof of the correctness of Mao Zedong's revolutionary strategy, Li Xin's manner of presenting Li Dazhao quite naturally led back to writing about him as one of the earliest Marxists in China, thus claiming for him a position among those who collectively created Mao Zedong Thought.

The relationship between Mao Zedong as a member of the second generation of "revolutionaries" and Li Dazhao as a member of the first generation is another reason for the propaganda machinery not to have made full use of Li Dazhao as a "model Communist" before the late 1970s. The conflict between those Communists who had built the party in the early 1920s and those who took over power after 1927 can be disguised as exclusively an inner-party struggle with Chen Duxiu's right opportunism as long as Li Dazhao's role in party history is minimized by acknowledging his merits in the dissemination of Marxist thought between 1919 and 1922. Those who claim to be the "old generation of revolutionaries" had been youngsters when the party was founded in 1921. Nevertheless, they legitimize their power monopoly in the CCP by describing themselves as the founding generation. That is why they have to stress the political side of the conflict with the even older generation of politicians such as Li Dazhao and Chen Duxiu by reducing it to the struggle against Chen Duxiu, whose political line can be shown to be wrong by holding it responsible for the defeat of the Great Revolution (1925–27).

This explains why there are so many articles on Chen Duxiu.[68] In contrast to Li Dazhao, he fits into the "two-line struggle" paradigm, and unlike Li the discussion of his "mistakes" can be used by both sides in inner-party struggle. While the older generation of revolutionaries insists that Chen was responsible for the defeat of the Great Revolution, the younger generation takes a detour by finding many other reasons for the defeat before they are able to "rehabilitate" Chen Duxiu and redefine the relationship between capitalism and socialism in China.

Unlike Chen's, Li Dazhao's party activities cannot easily be used by the older generation of revolutionaries to insist on their view of party history; at the same time, the younger generation does not pay too much attention to him as his essays can hardly be used to promote their ideas. This is why Li Dazhao's party activities were again left undiscussed in the period of preparation for the commemoration of the one hundredth anniversary of his birth, while Li's contribution to the formulation of Chinese Marxism could be dwelled upon by discussing the question of whether the CCP's decision to lead China directly into a socialist revolution was correct or not. The discussions mentioned above on continuity and breaks in Li Dazhao's thought as well as on the evaluation of his propagation of Marxism have to be seen in this context.

Yet all the above-mentioned reasons still do not appear to justify why Li Dazhao cannot be appraised like most other "martyrs" of the Chinese communist movement, why it took so long to erect a stele for him and why since the late 1950s he has not been propagated as a hero for Chinese youth to learn from. The reason for this astonishing phenomenon seems to be that Li Dazhao's connections with the Soviet Union and the Comintern are viewed as having been quite strong. Suspicions that he "leaned too far toward the Soviet Union" are aroused not only by the fact that he was arrested in the Soviet embassy but also because Soviet China studies propagated Li as a model for Sino-Soviet friendship. Especially in the context of the militant "antirevisionism" of the CCP under Mao's leadership in the early 1960s, Li Dazhao's hiding in the Soviet embassy came close, in the eyes of some, to betraying his country as well as the Chinese communist movement. Despite his other qualities, Li's apparent pro-Soviet communism stance would have meant that propagating him as a "martyr" and hero would have strengthened the pro-Soviet faction in the CCP. Neither Mao, the charismatic leader, nor the other anti-Soviet factions in the CCP could support this.

Should the CCP regain interest in promoting Li Dazhao in the context of party history, other, new arguments have to be found to support the research. One article written by Li Yunchang that was published to commemorate the one hundredth anniversary of Li Dazhao's birth provides us with a clue.[69] In an overall evaluation, Li Yunchang praises Li Dazhao for playing the precursor's role in nearly every aspect of the Chinese communist movement, not only in disseminating Marxist thought but also in initiating or leading the workers', peasants', and the women's movement in North China. According to Li Yunchang, Li Dazhao should be seen as the first leader of the workers' movement, the first member of the party leadership who paid attention to the situation in the villages and to the necessity of armed revolution.

This praise for Li Dazhao as the direct leader of the revolution in North China has far-reaching consequences for the whole of party history:

> During the May Fourth era, the center of the Chinese revolution was in Beijing; during the Great Revolution and the period of the Rural Revolution the center was in the south; after the troops of the Long March had reached Shaanbei the center of the Chinese revolution moved again from the South to the North. Finally the revolution achieved victory with North China as its base. The reason for this is that the North had the revolutionary foundations laid down by Li Dazhao, the party organization of the North, armed forces in the countryside and masses that had long been trained by the party. This is an amazing fact the historical meaning of which is, at the same time, great and deep.[70]

Li Yunchang breaks at least two taboos in his article. On the one hand, he is not shy about praising Li Dazhao even to the point that Li seems to be of much greater importance than Mao Zedong himself. On the other hand, he openly speaks about the north-south conflict in the party. There are at least two explanations for this. As with the pamphlet published by the Research Department of the Beijing party committee,[71] Li cannot diverge from the CC's official evaluation in the inscription on the stele in Li Dazhao's memorial yard.[72] However, both the Beijing party committee and Li Yunchang can resurrect Li Dazhao as a local or regional hero. In this way, they can circumvent the center's assessment of Li Dazhao and speak up as the responsible party organization in claiming justice for Li. At the same time, they can portray Li as the one leader of the CCP who laid the foundations in North China that later turned out to be of utmost importance for victory throughout the whole country.

Until the early 1980s, party history focused on a single center that moved from one part of China to the other. This center, in turn, formed the focus of attention for the whole movement, with the party leader constituting the key element. This kind of party historiography forced the pre-1949 decentralized movement to conform to the centralized pattern of the post-1949 state, therefore textbooks on party history that concede the coexistence of several liberated areas of the equivalent importance at the same time are difficult to find. The prerequisites of a centralized state force a hierarchical order of ranking. One further consequence of this kind of historiography is that whatever does not belong to the "center" cannot become part of the story. This explains why "the mass movement" in North China cannot be mentioned after the "center" is said to have moved south. In this kind of highly centralized historiography, conflicts between the center and the periphery do not exist as they are both integrated within the framework of democratic centralism.

Li Yunchang's article and the Beijing party committee's pamphlet on Li Dazhao, in this sense, mark the beginning of a rewriting of CCP history. But, at the same time, both Li and the Beijing party committee remain within the framework of party historiography as laid down in the 1945 "Resolution on Some Historical Questions."[73] They simply call for a reshuffling of the contributions of the different centers in party history rather than trying to write CCP history as the history of a decentralized movement.

Notes

1. "Shoudu longzhong jinian Li Dazhao dansheng 100 zhounian" (The Capital Solemnly Commemorates Li Dazhao's 100th Birthday), *Zhonggong dangshi tongxun* (Bulletin on CCP History), no. 22 (25 November 1989): 1.
2. "Zai Li Dazhao danchen yibai zhounian jinian dahui shang Jiang Zemin zongshuji de jianghua" (28 October 1989) (General Secretary Jiang Zemin's Speech at the Meeting to Commemorate Li Dazhao's 100th Birthday), *Renmin ribao* (People's Daily), 29 October 1989, 1.
3. "Jinian Li Dazhao danchen 100 zhounian xueshu taolunhui jishi" (Report on the Academic Symposium in Commemoration of Li Dazhao's 100th Birthday), *Zhonggong dangshi tongxun*, no. 22 (25 November 1989): 2.
4. "Li Dazhao yanjiu xueshu taolunhui zai Beijing kaimu" (An Academic Symposium on Research about Li Dazhao Opens in Beijing), *Guangming ribao* (Guangming Daily), 30 October 1989, 1.

5. Ibid.; for the speech itself see: Hu Sheng, "Jinian Li Dazhao" (In Commemoration of Li Dazhao), *Zhonggong dangshi yanjiu* (Research on CCP History), no. 1 (1990): 7–9.

6. "Hu Qiaomu zai Li Dazhao yanjiu xueshu taolunhui shang shuo Beijing daxue guangrong geming chuantong bu ke dongyao" (During the Academic Symposium on Research about Li Dazhao Hu Qiaomu Said that Beijing University's Glorious Revolutionary Tradition Was Unshakable), *Renmin ribao*, 30 October 1989, 4.

7. According to a report in *Zhonggong dangshi tongxun*, scholars from the United States and Hong Kong had also been invited to participate in the meeting. See "Jinian Li Dazhao xueshu huodong zheng zhuajin choubei" (Preparations for Academic Activities in Commemoration of Li Dazhao Are In Progress), *Zhonggong dangshi tongxun*, no. 11 (6 June 1989): 1.

8. "Jinian Li Dazhao dansheng 100 zhounian Li Dazhao yanjiu xueshu taolunhui zongshu" (Commemorating Li Dazhao's 100th Birthday: Summary of the Academic Symposium on Research about Li Dazhao), *Zhonggong dangshi tongxun*, no. 23 (12 December 1989): 2.

9. Li Dazhao, *Shouchang wenji* (Collected Essays of Shouchang [Li Dazhao]), *Minguo congshu* (Series on the Republican Period), no. 92 (Shanghai: Shanghai Bookstore, n.d.; reprint of the 1949 Beixin Book Company edition of *Shouchang wenji*).

10. For the inscription on the stele erected in Li Dazhao's memorial yard see "Li Dazhao lieshi beiwen" (Epitaph for the Martyr Li Dazhao), *Li Dazhao wenji* (Collected Works of Li Dazhao), (Beijing: People's Press, 1983), 3–6. In 1933, the Beiping (Beijing) party organization had already made one stele for Li Dazhao, but as it could not be openly erected it was buried together with Li Dazhao's coffin. "Yi kuai shibei de youlai" (Where a Stone Stele Came From), *Zhonggong dangshi tongxun*, no. 23 (12 October 1989): 3; and "Li Dazhao lieshi beiwen."

11. "Zai Li Dazhao dansheng 100 zhounian jinian dahui shang de jianghua (zhaiyao)" (Speeches Delivered to the Meeting in Commemoration of Li Dazhao's 100th Birthday [Abstracts]), *Zhonggong dangshi tongxun*, no. 23 (25 November 1989): 1.

12. "Hu Qiaomu zai Li Dazhao yanjiu xueshu taolunhui shang shuo."

13. "Li Dazhao yanjiu xueshu taolunhui," 1.

14. Hu Qiaomu, "Jinian Zhongguo gongchanzhuyi yundong de weida xianqu Li Dazhao" (Commemorate the Great Forerunner of the Chinese Communist Movement Li Dazhao), *Zhonggong dangshi yanjiu*, no. 1 (1990): 1.

15. Ibid., 2.

16. Ibid., 3.

17. Ibid., 4.

18. Ibid., 5–6.

19. "Hu Qiaomu zai Li Dazhao yanjiu xueshu taolunhui shang shuo," 4.

20. "Zai Li Dazhao danchen 100 zhounian dahui shang," 1.

21. Ibid.

22. Interview sources state that since the early 1960s, Li Dazhao had been suspected of tending toward revisionism because of his close connections to the Comintern. During the Cultural Revolution, internally he was accused of having been a traitor. In party history textbooks of the early 1960s, Li Dazhao was still mentioned, whereas party history textbooks compiled during the first years of the Cultural Revolution do not say anything about Li. To my knowledge the Canton party history of 1974 was the first to mention him again. See *Zhongguo gongchandang liangtiao luxian douzheng shi jiangyi (xiugaigao)* (Lectures on the History of the Two-Line Struggle of the CCP [Revised Edition]), internal publication, 1974, 7 and 9.

23. Li Xin, "Yanjiu Li Dazhao, xuexi Li Dazhao," (Conduct Research on Li Dazhao, and Study Li Dazhao), *Guangming ribao*, 31 October 1989, 3.

24. Hu Qiaomu, "Jinian Zhongguo gongchanzhuyi yundong," 1–7.

25. Yang Hongzhang, "Zaoqi Li Dazhao dui beiyang junfa zhengfu taidu de yanbian" (The Early Li Dazhao's Change of Attitude Toward the Government of the Northern Warlords), *Jindaishi yanjiu* (Research on Modern History), no. 4 (1988): 305–9.

26. Li Dazhao, "Minyi yu zhengzhi" (Politics and the Respectability of the People's Civilization), *Li Dazhao xuanji* (Selected Works of Li Dazhao) (Beijing: People's Press, 1959 and 1978), 36–57.

27. Zhu Chengjia, "Li Dazhao dui Yuan Shikai de renshi guocheng" (Li Dazhao's Process of Recognizing Yuan Shikai), *Lishi yanjiu* (Historical Research), no. 6 (1983): 12–21.

28. Yang Hongzhang, "Zaoqi Li Dazhao dui beiyang junfa," 307.

29. Zhu Chengjia, "Li Dazhao dui Yuan Shikai," 20–21.

30. Ibid.

31. Liu Guisheng, "Tan Li Dazhao zaoqi sixiang" (A Discussion of the Early Thought of Li Dazhao), *Zhonggong dangshi tongxun*, no. 20 (25 October 1989): 3.

32. Indeed Meisner only seems to see a financial reason for Li's contacts with Tan (Maurice Meisner, *Li Ta-chao and the Origins of Chinese Marxism* [Cambridge: Harvard University Press, 1967], 14–15 and 28–30).

33. "Zhang Jingru zai Beijing jinian Li Dazhao danchen 100 zhounian xueshu taolunhui de fayan zhaiyao" (Summary of Zhang Jingru's Speech to the Academic Symposium in Commemoration of Li Dazhao's 100th Birthday), *Zhonggong dangshi tongxun*, no. 20 (25 October 1989): 3.

34. Tan Shuangquan, "Li Dazhao yu 'wu si' qianhou dong xi wenhua lunzhan" (Li Dazhao and the Polemic on East and West Around the Time of "May Fourth"), *Zhonggong dangshi yanjiu*, no. 6 (1989): 24–30.

35. Ibid., 26.

36. Ibid., 27.

37. Ibid., 28.

38. Zhang Hua, "Li Dazhao yu 'Shaonian Zhongguo' de lixiang" (Li Dazhao and the Ideal of "Young China"), *Jindaishi yanjiu*, no. 5 (1989): 177–90; for a more outspoken summary of the text see Zhang Hua, " 'Shaonian Zhongguo' zhi lixiang yu Makesizhuyi de chuanbo" (The Ideal of "Young China" and the Dissemination of Marxism), *Zhonggong dangshi tongxun*, no. 9 (10 May 1989): 7.

39. Zhang Hua, " 'Shaonian zhongguo' zhi lixiang yu makesizhuyi de chuanbo," 7.

40. Ibid.

41. Ibid.

42. Ibid. Meisner talks about the "Young China" group and Li Dazhao's influence on it, but he looks at the group more in terms of Li's nascent internationalism than in terms of Li finding a solution to the question of Chinese socialism. See Meisner, *Li Ta-chao*, 182–83.

43. "Zhang Jingru zai Beijing jinian Li Dazhao," 3.

44. Wang Huilin, "Li Dazhao de 'pingmin zhuyi' yu 'gongren zhengzhi' " (Li Dazhao's "Populism" and "Workers' Politics"), *Zhonggong dangshi yanjiu*, no. 6 (1989): 18–23.

45. Li Dazhao, "Pingmin zhuyi" (Populism), in *Li Dazhao xuanji*, 407–27.

46. "Li Dazhao pingmin zhuyi lilun: yi fen duyou de minzhu lilun yichan" (Li Dazhao's Theory of Populism: An Extraordinary Theoretical Heredity for Democratism), *Zhonggong dangshi tongxun*, no. 10 (25 May 1989): 4.

47. Peng Ming, "Li Dazhao he Makesizhuyi zai Zhongguo de chuanbo—jinian Li Dazhao tongzhi danchen 100 zhounian" (Li Dazhao and the Dissemination of Marxism in China—In Commemoration of Comrade Li Dazhao's 100th Birthday), *Renmin ribao*, 27 October 1989, 6.

48. Li Dazhao, "Pingmin zhuyi," 407–27.
49. "Jinian Li Dazhao dansheng 100 zhounian Li Dazhao yanjiu xueshu taolunhui," 2.
50. Research Department on Party History of the CCP Beijing Party Committee, *Li Dazhao yu diyici guo-gong hezuo* (Li Dazhao and the First Cooperation between the GMD and CCP) (Beijing: Beijing Press, 1989).
51. Ibid., 23–25 and 31–38.
52. Ibid., 88–101.
53. Ibid., 50–83 and 102–37.
54. Ibid., 22–23.
55. Ibid., 28–29.
56. The most detailed description of Li Dazhao is in Li Xin, Peng Ming, Sun Sibai, Cai Changsi and Chen Xulu, eds., *Zhongguo xinminzhuyi geming shiqi tongshi* (General History of the Period of the New Democratic Revolution in China) (Beijing: People's Press, 1962 and 1980), vol. 1. On Li Dazhao, see 53–56, 57, 64, 77–78, 80–82, 98, 150, 183, 256–57, and 322–23.
57. Ibid., 43–49. One biography of Li Dazhao is Wang Chaozhu, *Li Dazhao* (Beijing: China Youth Press, 1989).
58. Ibid., 170–73. In Hu Hua, *Zhongguo xin minzhuzhuyi geming shi* (History of the New Democratic Revolution in China) (Beijing: East China People's Press, 1950 and 1951), Li Dazhao is said to have been killed by Zhang Zuolin, but the fact that he was arrested in the Soviet embassy is not mentioned. Li Xin in "Xin minzhuzhuyi geming shiqi tongshi" mentions that Li was hiding in the Soviet embassy when arrested (322). Other party history textbooks of the 1950s and 1960s, to my knowledge, rarely even mention Li's having been killed by the Beijing authorities. See, for example, Xu Yuandong, Ma Qingbo, Cong Xiaonan and Jiang Jue, eds., *Zhongguo gongchandang lishi jianghua* (Lectures on the History of the CCP) (Beijing: China Youth Press, 1962 and 1981). Li is mentioned on pp. 13, 15, and 16–17, but not a word is written about his death.
59. The Research Department on Party History of the CCP Beijing Party Committee, *Li Dazhao yu diyici guo-gong hezuo*, 102–18.
60. Ibid., 123–37.
61. Ibid., 164–89.
62. "Li Dazhao lieshi beiwen"; and *Li Dazhao wenji*, 3–6.
63. Chen Duxiu is mentioned in most of the articles on Li Dazhao while Li Dazhao is rarely mentioned in articles on Chen Duxiu.
64. For a more detailed discussion of party historiography in the PRC see Susanne Weigelin-Schwiedrzik, *Parteigeschichtsschreibung in der VR China: Typen, Methoden, Themen und Funktionen* (Party Historiography in the PRC: Forms, Methods, Themes and Functions) (Wiesbaden: Harrassowitz, 1984); and Susanne Weigelin-Schwiedrzik, "Party Historiography in the People's Republic of China," *Australian Journal of Chinese Affairs*, no. 17 (1987): 77–94; and "Party Historiography," *Chinese Law and Government* (Fall 1986). ·
65. Li Xin, "Yanjiu Li Dazhao, xuexi Li Dazhao," 3.
66. See Liu Nongchao, "Li Dazhao lieshi guangrong geming de yi sheng" (The Glorious Revolutionary Life of the Martyr Li Dazhao), *Zhongguo qingnian bao* (China Youth Daily), 27 April 1957, 4. The article does not mention the "revolution in the capital," but the massacre of 18 March 1927 is described. Liu talks about Li being arrested and killed by the "old warlords in the North," but the fact that he was arrested in the Soviet embassy is not disclosed.
67. Li Xin, "Yanjiu Li Dazhao, xuexi Li Dazhao," 3.
68. For a summary of the discussion on Chen Duxiu as conducted until the early 1980s, see Weigelin-Schwiedrzik, "Party Historiography in the PRC," 87–88; since the

mid-1980s discussions on Chen Duxiu have intensified. For some new aspects of discussions on Chen Duxiu, see Luo Xiangfeng, "Chen Duxiu zai xin wenhua yundong zhong de zuoyong" (Chen Duxiu's Role in the New Culture Movement), *Guizhou minzu xueyuan xuebao* (Guizhou Minorities Institute Journal), no. 1 (1987): 69–74 and 85, reprinted in "Fuyin baokan ziliao" (Reprinted Materials from Journals), *Zhongguo xiandaishi* (Chinese Contemporary History), no. 4 (1987): 187–93; Jia Ling, "Shilun Chen Duxiu zai jiandang de lishi zuoyong" (A Discussion of Chen Duxiu's Historical Role in Building the Party), *Yunnan shifan daxue xuebao* (Journal of the Yunnan Normal College), no. 1, 92–97 and 102, reprinted in ibid., no. 1 (1987): 182–88; Tang Baolin, "Lun da geming shiqi Chen Duxiu yu gongchan guoji de guanxi" (A Discussion of the Relationship Between Chen Duxiu and the Comintern During the Period of the Great Revolution), *Zhonggong dangshi yanjiu*, no. 4 (1988): 6–11; Wang Guangyuan, "Chen Duxiu he Sun Zhongshan" (Chen Duxiu and Sun Yat-sen), *Beijing dang'an shiliao* (Historical materials from the Beijing archives), no. 4 (1986): 78–92, reprinted in ibid., no. 2 (1987): 166–70; Wang Xueqin, "Chen Duxiu yu Zhongshan shijian" (Chen Duxiu and the Zhongshan Incident), *Fudan xuebao* (Journal of Fudan University), no. 5 (1988): 85–89, reprinted in ibid., no. 12 (1988): 205–9; Shi Yefu, "Qiantan gongchan guoji he da geming de shibai" (A Superficial Discussion of the Comintern and the Defeat of the Great Revolution), *Beifang luncong* (Northern Discussion Journal), no. 1 (1987): 34–37, reprinted in ibid., no. 2 (1987): 11–14; Tian Shizu, "Ping Chen Duxiu dui kangzhan qiantu de fenxi" (Evaluation of Chen Duxiu's Analysis of the Perspectives in the Anti-Japanese War), *Anhui jiaoyu xueyuan xuebao* (Journal of the Anhui Teachers' Training College), no. 3 (1987): 25–29, reprinted in ibid., no. 1 (1988): 179–83; Ren Zhenhe, "Lun Chen Duxiu chu yu hou de tuopai wenti" (On the Problem of Chen Duxiu's Trotskyism after his Release from Prison), *Dangshi yanjiu* (Research on Party History), no. 1 (1985): 66–70.

69. Li Yunchang, "Zhongguo geming de weida xianqu—jinian Li Dazhao danchen 100 zhounian" (The Great Forerunner of the Chinese Revolution—In Commemoration of Li Dazhao's 100th Birthday), *Renmin ribao*, 2 November, 1989, 6.

70. Ibid.

71. Research Department on Party History or the CCP Beijing Party Committee, *Li Dazhao yu diyici guo-gong hezuo.*

72. "Li Dazhao lieshi beiwen"; and *Li Dazhao wenji*, 3–6.

73. "Guanyu ruogan lishi wenti de jueyi" (April 1945) (CCP CC Resolution on Some Historical Questions), *Mao Zedong xuanji* (Selected Works of Mao Zedong), 3 (Beijing: People's Press, 1953), 3: 975ff. For an analysis of this resolution, see Chapter 11 by Saich in this volume.

Part II

REGIONAL VARIATIONS

Much of the research on the Chinese communist movement between its suppression by the GMD in 1927 and the arrival in Northwest China of the Long March survivors in 1936 has been driven by the outcome of subsequent events. Mao Zedong's assumption of supreme power within the CCP and the party's own seizure of power in 1949 caused research to focus on the party center and Mao himself in an attempt to understand better the post-1949 rulers of China. The spotlight, to use the phrase of Benton and Hartford (see chapters 5 and 6 in this volume), tracked Mao from Ruijin in Jiangxi along the course of the Long March to his place of rest in what became the Shaan-Gan-Ning Border Region. Good examples of this earlier research are provided in the work of Hsiao Tso-liang, *Power Relations within the Chinese Communist Movement, 1930–34* (1961); John E. Rue, *Mao Tse-tung in Opposition, 1927–1935* (1966); and Benjamin I. Schwartz, *Chinese Communism and the Rise of Mao* (1951).

These works are essentially the history of the victors. Newly available sources enable us to amend this history in significant ways. For example, while the Zunyi Conference (January 1935) clearly marked a significant step in Mao's rise to power, we now know that Mao did not become chairman of the Military Council or of the Politburo, as some historians have suggested. In fact, he was appointed one of the five top leaders of the party and had the right to be involved in all party and army decisions. Similarly, in the early 1930s, the actual differences between Mao and Wang Ming were not so sharp as later official CCP accounts would suggest, and there was even a degree of mutual respect between the two men. Mao was considered favorably by the Wang Ming leadership and was praised in Wang's appendix to the *Two Lines*. Further, while there may have been conflict by the fifth plenum (January 1934), Mao was not dropped from the Politburo as some studies have suggested. This newly available information contradicts the standard view that Wang Ming's rise was detrimental to Mao Zedong.

More importantly, the newly available sources enable researchers to open up other areas and topics for investigation, giving us a much more rounded picture of the communist movement during this period of time. The chapters in this section are essentially works of excavation, retrieving for us forgotten, or deliberately ignored, episodes in that history. They de-center the previous Mao-centered approach to the study of party history. Hartford shows that one cannot just accept the prevailing view that virtually nothing of great importance for party history happened in the northern cities after 1937 and that nothing of any importance occurred in rural areas of North China until the Japanese invasion of 1937. Although the story she tells is full of incompetence and setbacks, the revolutionary movement remained alive in the area, providing bases that could be reactivated and built on at a later stage. Benton retrieves a group that was effectively ignored by PRC historians until after Mao Zedong's death: the troops that were left behind by the Long Marchers and who "re-emerged" later as the New Fourth Army. He provides a compelling account of what enabled these men and women to endure unbelievable hardships and remain committed to the communist cause.

The chapter by Averill covers the Futian incident of 1930, yet barely mentions Mao. Standard accounts interpret the Futian incident in terms of inner-party factionalism, with Mao accusing his opponents of being members of a national secret organization known as the "AB Corps" (Anti-Bolshevik Corps) and of being guilty of "liquidationist" tendencies. In response to the ensuing purge, a local Red Army battalion rebelled against Mao and was subsequently massacred at Futian. Most scholars consider the most important result an increase in Mao's influence. By contrast, Averill's chapter turns the spotlight away from the role of key central figures and their competing policy programs, and focuses our attention on the socioeconomic conditions of the local environment. In so doing, he reminds us that the revolution was fought by real people whose responses were often conditioned by the local context within which they functioned.

Several similar themes arise in the chapters: the paramount need to survive against extremely unfavorable odds; the role that luck played in maintaining or breaking the local movements; and the varied backgrounds of the recruits to the communist movement. The need to survive often forced the local communist movements into alliances with social groups that were distinctly unproletarian in their outlook, and this caused policy compromise that could appear to those in the party center as betrayal of revolutionary principle. The chapters also highlight that the communist movement contained many different tendencies and traditions. Benton points out that the strong "feudal flavor" of communism in the Three-Year War contrasted markedly with the "bureaucratic-centralist" character of the party in the north.

Much recent research, best exemplified here by Bianco's chapter, presents an infinitely more complex picture of the party's policies and its relationship to different forces in the Chinese countryside.[1] This research reveals the extent to which the CCP had difficulty in mobilizing support within society. This was just as true for the rural areas as for urban China in the earlier period. The CCP was successful in putting down local roots where it showed flexibility in adapting policy to local circumstances, where initially it was good at micropolitics. By contrast, attempts to transform local environments to conform with predetermined ideological predispositions were unsuccessful. Even if not reported to their party superiors, judicious compromise often kept the local movements alive. Nothing could be taken for granted. As Bianco shows, recent research on rural China shows that in the rural base areas, the CCP had difficulty not only in mobilizing the peasantry but, after the peasantry was mobilized, in maintaining the momentum or keeping it under control. Indeed, he shows that the CCP was in the difficult position of trying to initiate a peasant movement without peasants.

Note

1. Of particular importance are Chen Yung-fa, *Making Revolution: The Communist Movement in Eastern and Central China, 1937–1945* (1986); Kathleen Hartford, "Step by Step: Reform, Resistance, and Revolution in the Chin-Ch'a-Chi Border Region, 1937–1945" (1980); and David Mark Paulson, "War and Revolution in North China: The Shandong Base Area 1937–1945" (1982).

Chapter 4

The Origins of the Futian Incident

Stephen C. Averill

One day early in December 1930, an officer of the Twentieth Red Army stationed in the small central Jiangxi town of Donggu led his men into the somewhat larger town of Futian several miles away, where they released from prison a group of long-time communist cadres who had been arrested by a representative of Mao Zedong named Li Shaojiu and accused of belonging to an anticommunist group called the AB Corps (AB *tuan*).

This small and in itself rather insignificant action played a pivotal role in encouraging a much larger and more violent movement to "suppress counterrevolutionaries" (*sufan*) within the CCP. Within days the freed party cadres and their erstwhile captors were accusing each other of self-serving betrayal of the revolution; within weeks accusations had given way to widespread purges that left thousands dead; and by the end of 1931 the Futian incident and its violent aftermath had required the direct intervention of national party leaders such as Zhou Enlai for its resolution.

What caused this disruptive struggle within the communist movement? At the time, Mao Zedong and most other CCP members accepted the notion that the root cause of the incident had in fact been a counterrevolutionary conspiracy led by the AB Corps against which the violence that followed had been a regrettable but inevitable necessity. This view remained intact in CCP historiography until the late 1970s.

By contrast, most non-Communist scholars have seen the incident primarily as an expression of intraparty political factionalism. More specifically, they have regarded it as simply the most violent local manifestation of conflict between urban-oriented followers of the CCP's national leader, Li Lisan, and a rural-oriented faction led by Mao Zedong, Zhu De, and others. The incident's most important result, in this view, was to increase Mao's influence and cause acceptance of the "Maoist" rural guerrilla strategy that was to play a major role in the survival and ultimate victory of the communist forces.

Advocates of both views can find support in the available documentary evidence. Equally important, despite their differences, both views share a general approach to the study of the Chinese revolution—common among both Chinese and Western scholars—that stresses the central role of party policies and personalities rather than socioeconomic conditions or other factors in the revolution's success.

To be sure, several existing accounts of the Futian incident themselves acknowledge that the maneuvers of high-level party leaders and the clash of national policies did not take place in a vacuum, but rather in specific social and political environments populated with peasants, bandits, and local party cadres. As a rule, however, these environments and their inhabitants are treated as stage sets and props, passive and peripheral wooden witnesses to the dramas being acted out by the famous stars in their midst.

Such a "star-centered," party-oriented approach is not, however, the only angle from which it is possible—or, in my mind, desirable—to view the Futian incident. This chapter moves beyond the rather circumscribed view of revolutionary politics implied in most existing accounts of the incident and places local context much closer to the center of analysis. More specifically, I shall argue that, far from constituting simply an incidental backdrop against which were played out important clashes of personality and political principle that were inspired, scripted, and directed by the highest-level CCP leaders, the complex society of the Jiangxi hill country, the local revolutionary movement it had nurtured, and the actions of the movement's opponents all also played significant parts in defining the issues and shaping the way in which the Futian incident unfolded.

The Establishment of the Central Jiangxi Base Areas

Some distance south of Nanchang a traveler along the Gan River leaves the broad and prosperous plains of northern Jiangxi and enters the highland country that predominates in the central and southern parts of the province. Barren ocher hummocks and low ridges to the west and rugged, heavily vegetated mountains to the east rise to flank the narrowing plain and the broad, mud-colored river that runs through it. At intervals, breaks in the high terrain mark the entrance of tributaries into the main stream, and at or near these spots the traveler often finds substantial towns and cities, situated strategically astride both the main Gan Valley communications and trade routes and the subsidiary routes feeding the hinterland.

One of the largest of these riverine settlements is Ji'an, a bustling commercial entrepot and administrative-cultural center of about fifty thousand people located halfway between Nanchang and the southern Jiangxi city of Ganzhou. Once an important prefectural capital, Ji'an was in the 1920s the seat of an important county of the same name and the site of several prestigious schools that drew most of their students and faculties from a hinterland that still roughly encompassed the ten counties of the former Ji'an prefecture.[1] In the 1920s, the city also developed into one of Jiangxi's most notable centers of radical politics. After the violent breakup of the GMD-CCP United Front in mid-1927, the region remained a center of communist-led revolutionary activity, which now took the form of rural base-building and guerrilla warfare.

Several such base areas developed within the Ji'an region. Well west of the city, where several tributaries of the Gan originate in the mountainous country along the Hunan border, the famous Jinggangshan base area emerged. East of the Gan, somewhat closer to the city on the edge of a broad, crescent-shaped arc of high mountains that sprawls across central Jiangxi almost to the Fujian border, developed another base area—almost as well-known as Jinggangshan, and sometimes in fact referred to as the "Eastern Jinggangshan"—centered on the town of Donggu. Between these two, in an expanse of arid red hills that build up to low mountains in northwest Ji'an county, lay a third smaller base area centered on several market towns in Yanfu district. Lines drawn on a map connecting these three base areas formed a rough triangle, with the city of Ji'an enclosed within.

These three bases developed at least semi-independently of one another. Jinggangshan in particular, because of its greater distance from Ji'an and its function as the home of the Fourth (Zhu De–Mao Zedong) Red Army between late 1927 and early 1929, had a character rather distinct from the other two bases and deserves a separate detailed analysis that is unfortunately impossible here. Instead, we shall focus on the Donggu and Yanfu bases, especially aspects of their development that are relevant to the Futian incident.[2]

To understand the growth of the Ji'an region's rural base areas, however, we must first focus our attention on the schools of Ji'an city and the smaller towns and cities of the region, for it was from them that the first revolutionary sentiments percolated into the countryside. In the late 1910s and early 1920s, as these schools became centers of nationalist and reform-oriented political agitation and organization, sojourning intellectuals energized by their experiences in them began to join radical parties such as the GMD and the CCP, and eventually to spread their branches to surrounding rural counties.

Their sympathetic faculties helped make Ji'an's Yangming Middle and the Seventh Normal Schools particularly active radical hotbeds. Prominent among them were two middle-aged natives of Anfu County (just west of Ji'an) named Li Songfeng and Zhou Lisheng. Zhou was a former Alliance Society (Tongmeng Hui) member, and Li probably had a similar background. Though both men later became well-known anticommunists, during the mid-1920s, when the parties were allied and distinctions between them often not clearly drawn, their efforts to encourage political activism in their schools substantially aided the regional growth of both parties.

It is important in light of later events to emphasize the early connections that existed among Communists and non-Communists in radical communities in Ji'an and elsewhere. As members of the United Front–era GMD, they all interacted frequently at rallies, meetings, and mass movement organizing activities. Although GMD members often knew which fellow party members were also Communists, this was by no means always the case, and identification was complicated by the existence of many so-called left GMD members whose views on social issues and mass movements often differed little from those of the CCP.

Perhaps even more important was the fact that—apart from the few "old revolutionaries" still involved in the movement—almost all the radicals had been raised in the same elite political culture. Though there may have been some difference in age and family background between young radicals who joined the CCP and those who eventually became right-wing GMD members (with the latter slightly older, somewhat wealthier and more urban in origin than the former), it was still true that most members of both groups were young, well-educated scions of elite families who had been through similar social and political experiences.[3]

The bulk of the young CCP-GMD members in the Ji'an region had, in fact, belonged to the social group that communist observers later variously termed the "new gentry" (*xin shenshi*), "new despotic gentry" (*xin haoshen*), or "rural intellectuals" (*xiangcun zhishi fenzi*). As these terms and the brief glosses occasionally accompanying them in texts suggest, this group consisted predominantly of young graduates of Western-style upper elementary or middle schools living outside big cities, in relatively rural localities such as county seats, market towns, or even villages. Similar to the "old" imperial-era gentry in level of education and largely rural domicile, the "new gentry" were distinguished from them, among other things, by their Western-style education and interest in the "New Culture."[4]

Much of the extensive political conflict afflicting rural Jiangxi during the early twentieth century had involved rivalry for local power and influence among groups of "old" and "new" gentry. A great many early adherents of both the CCP and the GMD had come of political age as "new gentry" participants in these factional struggles during their early school years and had then graduated to similar forms of more intense and sophisticated political activity in higher-level schools in Ji'an, Nanchang, or other cities. As natives of the same region, students of the same teachers, graduates of the same schools, members of the same study societies and associations, and firm believers in the same nationalist and anti-imperialist ideals, they possessed a substantial body of common interests and experiences.

Through the efforts of United Front adherents, Ji'an city and its multicounty rural hinterland developed into one of Jiangxi's most prominent centers of radical party, labor union, and peasant association strength. In 1927, however, this strong and expanding revolutionary movement—like those throughout China—was torn apart by the growing political and military conflict between the CCP and right-wing members of the GMD that accompanied the unraveling of the

United Front. The uncomfortable co-location in Nanchang of the right-wing military and political headquarters of Chiang Kai-shek and the communist-dominated Jiangxi GMD and mass movement organs spawned a particularly vicious form of political trench warfare that soon affected party branches and mass movements throughout the province.

The Ji'an region was especially affected by this intensifying conflict, in part because the size and strategic location of its revolutionary organs made them major prizes, but more significantly because of the importance of regional natives in both the left- and right-wing segments of the province's revolutionary movement. Several Communists from Ji'an and nearby counties had risen to high positions of authority in both the Jiangxi CCP and GMD hierarchies, as had at least one "old revolutionary" with former Tongmeng hui ties. As a result of the favoritism they practiced, at least in the hostile view of one ex-Communist writing later, the provincial party and mass movement organs had all filled up with natives of the Ji'an region.[5]

The right-wing provincial analogue to the influential Ji'an region Communists was the group known as the AB Corps, whose secret organizations communist leaders were still searching for several years later during the Futian incident. We will have more to say about the AB Corps in due course, but for now let us confine ourselves to a brief discussion of what is known of the group's origin and early activities.

The primary leader of the AB Corps was Duan Xipeng, from Yongxin County in the Ji'an region.[6] In Canton in 1925 Duan and some friends set up a small organization—known first as the Youth Work Corps (Qingnian gongzuo tuan) and then as the Communist-Suppression Corps (Changong tuan)—which appears to have been the precursor of the AB Corps. After the Northern Expedition began in 1926, Duan and other right-wing Jiangxi natives returned home to try to reorganize the CCP-dominated provincial GMD organization. Some of these returnees, like Duan, were from the Ji'an region, and they soon contacted former schoolmates, neighbors, and relatives from the region to help them gain political power. Among those who joined them were Li Songfeng and Zhou Lisheng, whose important roles as reformist Ji'an educators have already been noted.

In late 1926, this informal group became known as the AB Corps. The meaning of "AB" in the group's name is a matter of dispute: it was often popularly supposed to stand for "Anti-Bolshevik," an explanation that certainly conveyed accurately the group's attitude, but it is more likely that the term refers to the two levels (the "A" or provincial level and the "B" or local level) on which the group operated.[7]

During the first half of 1927, the AB Corps and the CCP struggled fiercely for control of political institutions in Jiangxi. Both sides dispatched numerous "special emissaries" (*tepai yuan*) to bring the weight of provincial authority to bear on local party branches and mass movements, mobilized gangs to intimidate and beat their opponents, and ultimately began a sort of mutual guerrilla warfare in the rural areas of the province that antedated the final collapse of the United Front by several months.

The Ji'an region was deeply affected by this combat. Although the strength of the region's mass movements made the initial battles inconclusive, during the summer of 1927 Jiangxi's garrison commander, General Zhu Peide, turned solidly against the Communists, and his Ji'an subordinates allowed police and elite militias freely to attack party and mass movement strongholds. Soon the mass movements were disbanded, many well-known local CCP leaders killed or arrested, and the surviving party members driven into hiding.

Although severely shaken by this disaster, the region's Communists soon began to rebuild their shattered movement. Within weeks the party's apparatus in Ji'an city resumed work, though it remained perilously subject to exposure and destruction. Rural cadres also launched several unconnected and originally quite defensive efforts to recruit new followings and—critically important under the circumstances—armed forces able to resist further enemy attacks. Like seeds carried on the wind, many of these efforts fell on unsuitable soil, but enough grew for the movement to survive and ultimately to prosper.

These base-building efforts, especially the formation of guerrilla units composed of loose coalitions of communist cadres, elite power holders, bandit chiefs, and heads of sworn brotherhoods, helped foster the political and institutional environment in which the Futian incident occurred. It is therefore desirable to outline briefly how the base areas centered on Donggu and Yanfu developed between 1927 and 1929.

The Donggu base began in late 1927, when a few CCP members who had returned to their homes in this mountainous and isolated border area founded a new party branch and created several small guerrilla bands from remnants of mass movement organs formed earlier in the border region.[8] To remedy the military weakness of these forces and help re-establish some local credibility after their recent defeats, the CCP cadres also sought help from the Three Dots Society (Sandian hui), a Triad sworn brotherhood long active in both the commercial centers and rural areas of southern Jiangxi. One of the most important bands in the entire region operated in the five-county border area around Donggu, led by Duan Qifeng, a former farm laborer and martial arts master who wielded broad influence among Three Dots bands throughout the region. Using kinship ties and extensive negotiations, CCP cadres were able to contact Duan and persuade him and his band to join the revolution.

The newly enlarged guerrilla band then attacked and redistributed the property of a well-known nearby elite power holder, a decisive action that attracted considerable local attention and encouraged other local Three Dots and militia bands to join them. Shortly thereafter, the Donggu guerrillas merged with another small CCP-led guerrilla detachment into a new unit known as the Seventh Column. This unit succeeded in clearing away most of the remaining local power holders and militias that could pose a serious threat to the embryonic Donggu base area.

Across the Gan River in northwestern Ji'an other Communists escaping the "white terror" used similar methods to carve out the core of what became the Yanfu base area in another of the region's former centers of communist and peasant movement activity.[9] Only incomplete information is available on the founders of the Yanfu and Donggu bases, but as a group the leaders of the Yanfu base appear to have been from wealthier backgrounds than their Donggu counterparts. In his reminiscences, Ji'an party leader Zeng Shan explicitly contrasted the two base areas in this regard, noting, "In the Yanfu area, many of those who participated in the revolution were young students. Quite a few [*bu shao*] of the families of these young intellectual party members had money and a great deal of land."[10]

At any rate, as in Donggu the Yanfu Communists sought to obtain military resources, in this case by allying with a small armed band led by a former army officer to attack opium caravans, wealthy families, and militia forces in the area to obtain funds and weapons.[11] Soon this force joined with another nearby guerrilla unit to form the Ninth Column, which continued to raid caravans and local elites.

In March 1928, the CCP's West Jiangxi Special Committee ordered the Ninth Column to cross the Gan River to Donggu to cooperate with the Seventh Column and other guerrillas there to fight elite-led militia forces and attack market towns and county seats throughout the region. In September 1928, while the two columns rested near Yanfu in Jishui County after hard campaigning on both sides of the Gan, a Special Committee representative named Li Wenlin directed their amalgamation into the Second Independent Regiment of the Jiangxi Red Army.

Li was a twenty-eight-year-old intellectual from a prosperous peasant family in northern Jishui County, near Yanfu. He had returned from Nanchang after the CCP-GMD split to become a founder and early leader of the Ninth Column before transferring to work for the Special Committee. Later to emerge as one of the most prominent regional communist leaders and a major protagonist in the factional disputes culminating in the Futian incident, Li became commander and political commissar of the new unit, while erstwhile Three Dots Society leader Duan Qifeng, now a party member, became executive officer, and another officer became chief of staff.[12]

The Second Regiment ranged widely through central and southern Jiangxi attacking militias, expropriating elites, and ransacking market towns. Under its protection, more local guerrillas formed in the Donggu and Yanfu base areas, numerous other small guerrilla forces (many also with brotherhoods or bandit gangs at their core) popped up elsewhere in the central Jiangxi hill country, and party members around the region launched scattered small-scale peasant uprisings, which added to the accumulating social ferment. Because these proliferating local forces were difficult to control, by late 1928 CCP leaders began amalgamating them into new main force regiments, three of which (the Third, Fourth, and Fifth Independent Regiments) were formed between then and early

1930. Experienced political and military cadres from the Second Regiment such as Duan Qifeng and Li Wenlin played an important role in the creation and staffing of the new units.

In the same period, the Donggu and Yanfu bases also expanded and consolidated the areas under their control. By late 1929, the core of each base included portions of several counties and several tens of thousands of people, mostly peasants still "engaged in production." Among these peasants party leaders formed local Red Guard detachments (*chiwei dui*) to defend their villages against anticommunist militias from outside the base areas. The Red Guards also provided reservoirs of manpower to replace Red Army battle losses or to be formed into more new main force units.

During this initial mobilization and militarization process, party cadres invoked a variety of socioeconomic grievances to obtain peasant participation, but the situation was still too fluid to allow them to introduce fundamental reforms. Thus, while CCP leaders championed rent- and debt-relief for peasants, fined and expropriated individual "local despots," and led peasants to storm transit tax stations, before the end of 1929 they generally had neither the resources nor the security from likely enemy attack necessary to implement widespread land redistribution.

Although communist strength grew steadily throughout the region, it was the Donggu base—probably because of its central location—that eventually came to be viewed by both friends and enemies alike as the primary core of revolutionary activity in central Jiangxi. By late 1929, it was primarily to this base that Red Army units came for rest between campaigns, refugees from failed uprisings or enemy militia raids came for emergency shelter, and CCP representatives from places throughout central and southern Jiangxi came to seek support for new uprisings or political training for recently recruited party members.

Government Opposition and the AB Corps

Far more than is generally recognized in Western accounts of this period, the expansion of communist base areas in Jiangxi met determined resistance from a variety of military and political opponents.[13] Individually, these opponents differed considerably in the extent of their threat to the base areas, and many of them devoted as much of their energy to fighting among themselves as to defeating the CCP; taken together, however, they nonetheless constituted a serious danger to the revolutionary movement and fostered an atmosphere of fear and tension that contributed significantly to the Futian incident.

On the military front, opponents of the Communists ranged from the regular divisions of the Yunnan and Hunan armies deployed in Jiangxi to various paramilitary forces. The large and well-armed regular army units were often misused by being dispersed as garrison forces, or sent lumbering around the countryside in ineffective pursuit of the mobile Red Army units. When they had an immovable territorial target such as the base areas, however, army units could cause great destruction, as they proved in several "bandit suppression" campaigns against Donggu, Yanfu, and other Ji'an region bases.

The paramilitary forces, ranging from well-armed, officially sponsored regional forces that differed from regular troops only in their greater ease of deployment down to elite-raised local militias and lineage braves, proved themselves even more dangerous and persistent enemies of the base areas. Many local militias expelled from their homes in the emerging communist areas simply relocated to nearby government-controlled towns or cities, from whence they waged their own guerrilla war against the communist bases. As the communist threat grew, officials and coalitions of refugee elites combined some of these units into large, highly militarized regional forces that served as functional counterparts of communist forces such as the Seventh and Ninth Columns.

This military struggle was conducted in, and affected by, a complex political environment, in which numerous rival political parties, factions, and groups of nonaffiliated but politically active urban and rural elites simultaneously fought against the Communists and one another. Before describing the challenge that these political actors posed to the Communists, it is necessary to delineate the broader political context in which they operated.

The years 1927–30 were a period of great political fluidity in China, during which rival groups competed to shape and control the political institutions and forms of political interaction that would prevail after the Northern Expedition and the collapse of the United Front. Nationally, Chiang Kai-shek fought powerful warlords and other party leaders for control of the country and the GMD. In Jiangxi, garrison commander Zhu Peide fought to remain independent from both Chiang Kai-shek and the Guangxi warlords, while also trying to manage numerous feuding parties and their factions. And at the county level and below, officials, party members, and local elites squared off against one another in a bewildering array of factional feuds and other political conflicts.

Competition among rival political parties at both provincial and local levels deeply affected the CCP, as did the local-level activities of unaffiliated but politically active and influential elites. Because of the direct or indirect effects these political conflicts had on the Futian incident, it is worth discussing them at some length.

Let us begin with the rival parties.[14] Paramount among these, of course, was the GMD, which even after casting out the Communists was more a loose congerie of competing factions than a unitary political organization. The most important GMD factions in Jiangxi during this period were the Reorganization Clique (Gaizu pai), as the followers of Wang Jingwei were known, and the AB Corps, whose members were close to Chiang Kai-shek. Also active in Jiangxi for much of this period was the Third Party (Disan dang), an independent political organization composed mostly of former CCP or left-wing GMD members.

Relations among these major groups were complex, changeable, and only sporadically revealed in contemporary sources. In general, however, the main pattern was for the Reorganization Clique (often loosely allied with the smaller and weaker Third Party) and Zhu Peide to cooperate against efforts by the AB Corps (often allied with other small cliques) to expand the influence of Chiang Kai-shek's wing of the GMD.

Duan Xipeng and some other major AB Corps leaders had left Jiangxi in 1927 to take posts in Chiang Kai-shek's entourage in Nanjing. Most thereafter spent little time in Jiangxi, and their absence is frequently noted by scholars who accept statements of some of these AB Corps leaders that the organization in fact ceased to exist after 1927. It is also a fact that after Duan and his associates left, the influence of the AB Corps in Jiangxi temporarily declined, and that of the Reorganization Clique and Third Party rose.

Nevertheless, comments in contemporary CCP and noncommunist sources make it clear that the AB Corps remained in existence and continued to compete for political power in Jiangxi.[15] From mid-1928 on, the AB Corps made strong efforts to regain control of the Jiangxi GMD and to spread its influence among the province's well-educated and politically aware population. Government and GMD organs at all levels, major newspapers, schools, and mass organizations such as labor unions all became objects of intense competition among the AB Corps and its rivals.

The struggle was inconclusive for a time, but after Zhu's replacement by Hunanese general Lu Diping late in the summer of 1929 led to reduced patronage for the Reorganization Clique and the Third Party, several of their leaders left the province, and both groups began to decline. By early 1930 the AB Corps had managed to seize control of provincial-level politics, a position that it maintained well into 1931.[16]

While these rivals battled to control the provincial party, diverse other conflicts occurred among elites at and below the county level.[17] Some of these reflected traditional rivalries between urban and rural elites, competing marketing areas, Hakkas and non-Hakkas, or rival lineages. Others manifested more recent conflicts (often with strong generational cleavages) between so-called old and new cliques over diffusion of Western culture. Virtually all these antagonisms were reinforced by personality conflicts among individuals or families of elite power holders heading competing networks of elite or peasant followers.

To these divisions, many of them deeply and enduringly incised in the bedrock of local social structures and geographical features, the spread of new urban-oriented parties such as the GMD and the CCP during the 1920s added yet another dimension. With links both to higher-level party institutions and to more parochial local groupings, branches of the new parties became hybrid organizations exhibiting the influence of both. From higher-level party organs came an unprecedented impetus (analogous to what is commonly called "state-building") toward greater density and intensity of political organization and activity. From the immediate surroundings came equally intense pressure to incorporate or adapt to traditional forms of political interaction.

However much they might try to adapt, the new party organs were obviously still alternative—and thus potentially rival—loci of political power to such established groups as county bureaucracies or incumbent elite power holders. Conflicts between party and officials, or between party and local notables, were common throughout the 1920s.

To these local conflicts, the provincewide struggle among the AB Corps and its rivals added yet another complicating overlay. Because the issues and dynamics of provincial and local politics differed, the AB Corps' increased provincial power did not automatically translate into local gains everywhere.[18] Still, its enhanced provincial power clearly improved its overall position in many of Jiangxi's smaller cities and rural counties, including those in the Ji'an region.

As previously noted, many major AB Corps leaders were natives of counties in the Ji'an region (particularly Yongxin and Anfu counties west of the Gan River) and had taken part in the region's educational affairs and early party organization efforts. It is therefore not surprising that the clique retained considerable influence after 1927 among schools and newspapers in Ji'an city and among GMD branch committees, local militias, and schools in many of the surrounding rural counties.

At the same time, however, the Reorganization Clique/Third Party had also been very active in the Ji'an region. The Ji'an-area Third Party appears to have been more of a force than in most other parts of Jiangxi. It established a regional party office and controlled a major newspaper in Ji'an city and sought persistently to re-establish under its control labor, peasant, and youth organizations similar to those popular under the United Front. As elsewhere, however, by 1930 the Ji'an Third Party appears to have been largely absorbed by the Reorganization Clique, and together they competed with the AB Corps for control of the region's party committees, police and militia detachments, and schools. The circumstances of these struggles varied from place to place, but in general it appears that the AB Corps' main strength lay in county party committees, and that of the Reorganization Clique/Third Party in local militia forces.

As long as Zhu Peide's forces were in the Ji'an region, their officers effectively aided the Reorganization Clique/Third Party, but once they were replaced by Lu Diping's more sympathetic Hunanese subordinates, AB Corps adherents openly attacked schools, militias, and party organs dominated by their rivals. By early 1930, the AB Corps had clearly become the dominant noncommunist force in most of the Ji'an region's shrinking "white" (i.e., nonsoviet) areas.[19]

The extensive coverage given to these struggles in contemporary CCP documents indicates that they were of much more than casual interest to local communist cadres. There were several closely related reasons for this interest, including the significant overlap in social and political background that existed between CCP cadres and their noncommunist counterparts, and the continuing ambivalence of some CCP members' feelings about the role of urban work in the revolutionary struggle. But the most important reason for the intense interest was the simple fact that in urban and rural areas alike the Communists and non-Communists were competing intensely for many of the same constituencies and resources.

In large measure, this competition reflected the lingering influence on both Communists and non-Communists of earlier United Front efforts at mass mobilization, when young activists who then or later joined the CCP, "left GMD" factions such as the Reorganization Clique or the Third Party, and "right GMD" factions such as the AB Corps had all participated in efforts to organize students, workers, and peasants.

After 1927, all these groups used similar tactics to appeal to the same social groups. For example, when discussing work in cities such as Nanchang and Ji'an, CCP documents often noted with concern the efforts activists from the Third Party and Reorganization Clique were making to revive and control unions. Likewise, both these groups and the AB Corps also sought persistently to influence schools (both staff and students) and young people in cities, county seats, and market towns throughout the Ji'an region.[20]

Because labor, educational circles, and youth were all constituencies to which communist leaders had long devoted special attention, they felt threatened when other politicians tried to gain influence among them, especially when (as often happened) these efforts seemed specifically designed to subvert the CCP. Thus party documents complained in mid-1929 that the Third Party had taken advantage of the similarity between its activities and those of the Communists to infiltrate Ji'an CCP and CYL organs. Another reported efforts by the Reorganization Clique to get former Communists to seek readmission to the CCP so that the clique could use the CCP's name to "capture the working masses." And a third noted in early 1930 that the Ji'an region AB Corps falsely used the name of the CCP to deceive young students into entering their own organizations.[21]

Many such incidents occurred in Ji'an city and other urban areas, where unions, schools, and the strongholds of many noncommunist political groups were concentrated, and where the CCP's position had become increasingly tenuous since 1927. In more rural settings as well, however, noncommunist competition for control of population and resources also gradually developed. In part, this was competition for the support of hitherto nonaligned elites living in market towns or villages. As already noted, many early CCP and GMD adherents had come of political age as "new gentry" participants in local factional struggles, and they all therefore had a close personal understanding of the importance of this group in securing political control over the countryside. GMD factions, Third Party, and CCP activists alike realized that the young schoolteachers and other reform-minded new gentry members living in the countryside constituted one of their best and most sophisticated potential sources of new cadres, and they competed fiercely to win them over.[22]

In addition to competing for rural intellectuals, noncommunist political groups in these rural counties also fought among themselves and with the CCP to control militia detachments. AB Corps and Reorganization Clique adherents were particularly effective in their efforts to control these forces and use them in their mutual political (and sometimes military) struggles.[23] At the same time, the effectiveness of the militia opposition, their concentration near and frequent forays into the soviet areas, and their abundant supply of modern rifles, all combined to make militia units attractive and convenient targets for communist subversion. In their efforts to infiltrate these militias, communist cadres were thus competing for resources with their AB Corps and Reorganization Clique counterparts.[24]

In sum, between 1927 and 1930 both communist and noncommunist elites in the Ji'an region, as elsewhere in China, competed to take personal and collective advantage of the opportunities presented by the victorious Nationalist Revolution and the dissolving United Front. It is common (and perfectly accurate) to stress the contrast between the ways in which the increasingly rural and radical communist-led revolution and the increasingly urban and conservative GMD regime went about exploiting these opportunities. But it is also important to point out the extent to which, especially at the local level, adherents of both parties remained part of the same social and political universe, competed for overlapping constituencies and resources, and drew upon similar political repertoires to build their followings.

Such similarities and overlaps are particularly important to note in this chapter because they provided a plausible general context and specific circumstantial evidence to support the accusations of counterrevolutionary behavior that were so prevalent at the time of the Futian incident. In a general environment in which party identities were ambiguous and party memberships transient, factional affiliations were complex and intertwined, and the nature of the political system that would ultimately emerge in postwarlord period China was still profoundly uncertain, it was certainly reasonable to suspect that some CCP and GMD cadres with similar family circumstances, old-school ties, and common political experiences might continue to interact with one another as friends even while their parties were enemies.

This possibility was made even more likely by the specific circumstances of both communist and noncommunist political activity. Communist base-building methods that emphasized cooperating with bandits and other armed power holders, infiltrating local militias, adapting to existing social circumstances, and reaching out to reformist elites all maximized cadres' interaction with untrustworthy social elements and fairly invited the compromise of revolutionary ideals. A few successful attempts by noncommunists to undermine and discredit the CCP via propaganda, misinformation, and double agents gave credence to cadres' fears that more such attempts might be expected, while the strong geographical association of the AB Corps with the Ji'an region and the clique's visible upsurge in political influence in the area following the transfer of Zhu Peide together provided a concrete focus for their fears.

Important as these broad situational factors were in creating an environment favorable for the Futian incident to develop, however, they were not the whole story. Other more proximate influences were involved as well, influences stemming from the confluence between late 1929 and late 1930 of intensified military and political struggles, deepened socioeconomic reforms in the base areas, and heightened factional strife and policy conflicts within the national and regional party leaderships. It is to an examination of these issues that we now turn our attention.

Deepening the Revolution

The intensity of military and political activity in the Ji'an region increased dramatically during the fall and winter of 1929–30 because of major campaigns to control Ji'an city launched nearly simultaneously by the Communists and their enemies. Ji'an's existing importance as a regional cultural and economic center grew after 1927 as it became the headquarters for military communist-suppression efforts, a control point for enforcing an economic blockade on the base areas, and the main destination for émigré elites and militia units fleeing the communist-controlled areas. Ji'an's already strategic location on the Gan River north-south trade and communications route was likewise enhanced by its position blocking free east-west access between the separate communist bases growing on both sides of the river.

In November 1929, the CCP's West Jiangxi Special Committee announced a campaign to "seize Ji'an," impelled by persistent peasant complaints about the economic difficulties and insecurity caused by the Ji'an-centered blockade and militia activity. Over the next several months, party leaders mobilized thousands of peasants and dozens of Red Guard, guerrilla, and Red Army units from bases on both sides of the river to launch a total of eight unsuccessful attacks on the city.

At about the same time, new Hunanese military commanders in Ji'an combined with local elites in a multifaceted "bandit suppression" campaign to roll back the communist-controlled areas that had crept to within a few miles of the city. This campaign began with successful efforts to root out the skeletal underground CCP organization remaining in Ji'an city, shifted to very destructive attacks on communist areas north and west of the city, and finally made serious inroads into the Donggu base and other communist areas east of the Gan River.

The conjunction of these campaigns subjected the Ji'an region to months of very intense military and political struggle that caused severe short-term damage to the Communists. They both failed in their announced aim of capturing Ji'an and also suffered heavy casualties, shrinkage in the territory and population under their control, and severe disruption in some of their political and economic activities. The intense pressure applied by enemy forces and political activists further increased the tensions, acrimonies, and suspicions already engendered within the base areas by the recent implementation of land reform and other fundamental socioeconomic changes.

The enemy attack began with the exposure in Ji'an city of the CCP West Jiangxi Special Committee and CYL organs. One of many similar exposures of the party's underground apparatus in Jiangxi cities occurring after 1927, the breakup of the Ji'an organization led to the death or flight of many cadres. Even worse, the captured CYL committee secretary changed sides and betrayed other cadres, disrupting contact with higher party levels and increasing fear and suspicion among surviving cadres.[25]

In a related development, enemy forces also had some success in using apostate Communists to subvert and infiltrate CCP organs. The Third Party was particularly well placed to mount this sort of subversion because of its many former communist members and its continued interest in mass movement constituencies, but the Reorganization Clique and the AB Corps were likewise involved. One notable site of such activity, according to an April 1930 CCP document, was Li Wenlin's home county of Jishui, where the AB Corps borrowed the name of the CCP in order to mobilize youth, and even went so far as to forge letters and reports using Li Wenlin's own name.[26]

Along with attacking the Communist Party apparatus, the Hunanese encouraged local elites to sow dissension among and wrest control of the peasant population from the CCP. They did this by spreading rumors and misinformation, and by attacking party policies such as those giving greater equality to women or reducing the influence of lineages. Probably the most widespread and effective tactic, however, was to counterorganize the peasantry into paramilitary groups, one of whose main functions was to deny the Communists access to as many peasants as possible.

Both urban and rural groups were formed. As the names of the groups indicate, most urban recruits into the Refugee Units (Nanmin tuan), Fresh Start Units (Zixin tuan), and Guard Detachments (Shouwang dui) came from the refugees and apostate Communists living in the cities.[27] In rural areas, by contrast, the new paramilitary forces, also often called Guard Detachments, appear to have come from peasants living in villages on the fringes of, or within, communist base areas. Some communist documents speak of "rich peasants," "despotic gentry," and the AB Corps coercing villagers into organizing these forces, while others describe peasants who were "deceived" into forming them, or who sought to use them to attack controversial communist policies concerning greater sexual equality for women.[28]

These accounts suggest that while the main impetus for forming rural Guard Detachments came from local elites, their growth was also fueled by local social divisions, intervillage rivalries, and reactions to communist social programs. The Guard Detachments thus resembled elite-led "protective" forces such as the Red

Spears of Henan and Anhui. In fact, in 1928–29 anticommunist Red Spear societies did appear in parts of Jishui County inhabited by people of Henan origin, and in 1929–30 the same area produced elite-led Red and Yellow Study Societies (Honghuang xuehui), groups that one source described (in terms reminiscent of accounts of North China Red Spears) as "a kind of superstitious organization that uses magic potions to drug peasants [to get them] to come to kill the masses and the Red Army in the Red territories."[29]

While Red Spear societies were largely spontaneous and atomistic local responses to worsening social unrest, the Guard Detachments were closely linked to an organized elite-led anticommunist movement with quite clear political content. Taken in conjunction with other efforts by groups like the AB Corps to subvert and destroy CCP party apparatus, such forces were clearly part of a planned, multifaceted attempt to root out communist influence in the central Jiangxi countryside.

This attempt achieved what must have been for the Communists a sobering amount of success. Attacks by urban refugee militias and rural Guard Detachments wrested considerable territory from communist control, killed thousands of Communists and their supporters, induced many villages to end their support for the revolutionaries, and sent a new wave of refugees (communist supporters this time) from the captured territories pouring into the remaining base areas.[30]

The situation was worsened because of the weakening of CCP organs by enemy destruction and subversion and the debilitating effects of the party's own internal conflicts (discussed below). Party documents note that "defeatism" and "flightism" were distressingly common among cadres whose organizations came under attack, and that guerrilla units and cadres in neighboring areas sometimes made excuses to avoid helping threatened comrades elsewhere.[31]

Affected most seriously by the enemy attacks were Yanfu and other scattered base areas north and northwest of Ji'an city, most of which lay in the administrative subregion that the CCP called the North Route (Beilu). In this subregion the deterioration of party affairs and shrinkage of base areas was particularly notable.[32] Somewhat less serious damage apparently occurred almost everywhere else in the region, including the West Route (Xilu) region centered on Jinggangshan, the Central Route (Zhonglu) region centered on Donggu and southern Jishui County, and southern Jiangxi areas such as Xingguo County.[33]

Both these enemy-induced setbacks and the Communists' failure to capture Ji'an heightened controversies that had already been developing within the revolutionary movement over military strategy and the relationship between party and military and local and regional interests.

As already noted, most of the military forces that built the communist bases first emerged from alliances among remnants of earlier peasant associations and the gangs and brotherhoods endemic in the Jiangxi hills. To support these local forces, the main Red Army led by Mao Zedong and Zhu De roved widely through central and southern Jiangxi after leaving Jinggangshan in January 1929, distracting government troops and wreaking conspicuous havoc upon elite-led militias that threatened the growing communist guerrillas. Although this mixture of local guerrilla forces and Red Army main force units allowed rapid expansion of the base areas, it also led to many communication, coordination, and control problems within the revolutionary movement.[34]

Relationships between local party cadres (mostly intellectuals) and the bandit/brotherhood leaders (mostly peasants) whose bands formed the core of many early guerrilla units were often marked by well-justified feelings of mutual suspicion. Party cadres were appalled by the bandits' low political consciousness and unreliability, while bandits resented the contempt with which they were treated and the disproportion between their large military contribution to the revolution and their small voice in strategy and policy-making. On several occasions this mutual suspicion degenerated into outright hostility and violence.[35]

Deeply rooted localist attitudes, social distinctions, and kinship patterns also frequently made it difficult for cadres and guerrillas from different areas to cooperate. As one cadre complained in 1930,

> the guerrilla and Red Guard detachments in various places are extremely numerous, but at the same time their localist flavor is extremely deep. They each have their own corner to protect, and frequently their crossing of borders to attack local tyrants gives rise to disputes (that is, when [detachments] from place A go to place B to seize local tyrants, the Red Guard detachments of place B rise up to oppose them).[36]

Under such conditions, the growth of guerrilla units sometimes simply provided new vehicles and strategies for the revival of old enmities between areas, as apparently occurred between the heavily Hakka area around Donggu and contiguous areas of southern Jishui County heavily populated by people of Henan origin.[37]

To help ameliorate these sorts of problems, the party tried to control expanding local guerrilla units by dispatching experienced cadres (often including personnel from main force Red Army units) to help raise the political consciousness, military expertise, and discipline of guerrilla units, or by sending the guerrillas for training in major and relatively secure base areas such as Donggu. At the same time, the party tried to amalgamate some local guerrillas into larger, better armed, and more mobile units, and to tie their leaders into a hierarchical command structure responsive to higher levels.

The need for even more control became apparent during the campaign to seize Ji'an, when party leaders found it hard to mobilize and coordinate guerrillas from different places.[38] But attempts to remedy these deficiencies by establishing a regional military headquarters and accelerating the process of establishing main force units met with considerable local resistance.

Part of this resistance stemmed precisely from the fact that the amalgamation process uprooted many politically unsophisticated and largely independent guerrilla leaders from their familiar and highly supportive local "nests" and brought them far more thoroughly under the control of higher level authorities. With these personal concerns and consequences clearly in mind, many local leaders greeted the process of military consolidation with much grumbling and not a little outright opposition.

Resistance also stemmed, however, from more general fears of the danger to local bases posed by the creation of new main force units. Because they served as quick strike forces and needed great mobility to avoid government forces, Red Army regional main force units kept in nearly constant motion. Vital as this may have been for the long-term growth of the revolution, from the perspective of local leaders, taking weapons and troops to form such new armies denuded localities of resources needed to defend against dangerous anticommunist militia forces, without at the same time providing reliable replacements.[39] It also suggested the worrisome possibility (which became a reality in 1934) that one day the Red Army might leave and not return. Viewed in this way, ill-armed Red Guards and guerrillas with strong ties to an area could seem to provide more security than stronger but less available Red Army units.

These feelings were deepened by resentment against the involvement of the Fourth Red Army of Mao Zedong and Zhu De in many of the efforts to expand main force units. Some of this resentment doubtless resulted, as past scholars have suggested, from Mao's use of the Fourth Army as a tool to concentrate power in his own hands, but much appears to have been a more general distrust of the Fourth Army as a particularly peripatetic "guest army" whose large number of Hunanese personnel gave it a foreign flavor to local Jiangxi cadres.

Although it is impossible to know the extent to which local cadres moved beyond argument to active resistance against the amalgamation process, some such resistance clearly occurred in both the West and North Route subregions, whose leaderships were generally known for their "closed door" policy toward outside orders, and where heavy losses at the hands of the enemy's Guard Detachments underlined the need for strong local defenses.[40]

Attempts to implement fundamental socioeconomic reforms aroused even more tension within the base areas than did attempts at military consolidation. Land reform was clearly one important reform with tremendous potential for conflict. After the CCP-GMD split, the initial insecurity and small size of the communist areas, the inherent complexity of the land reform process, and the CCP's need to emphasize moderate policies to build the broadest possible coalition of forces to support the revolution all combined to encourage party cadres to confine themselves to mild reforms such as tax remission and rent and interest reduction.

As the base areas expanded, however, thoroughgoing land redistribution became the core of increasingly radical communist policies. Beginning in most places in late 1929 or early 1930, the initial land redistributions were often hasty and confused affairs that produced much individual animosity, divided communities within and among themselves, and generally consumed more human energy in destructive conflict than was released in productive enthusiasm. Different areas based redistribution on varying geographical or population units, disagreed over whether to grant land to landlords, rich peasants, or their families, varied in how they accounted for differences in land quality and household labor power, and generally exhibited an exasperating diversity in the progress and pace of redistribution.[41]

Nevertheless, by the spring of 1930 a majority of the villages in communist-controlled central Jiangxi had at least begun the process of fundamental land reform, and by October of that year about 70 percent of the paddy and mountain land in these areas had been distributed.[42]

During the same period, party leaders took advantage of the impetus developed by land reform to implement other significant political, social, and economic activities. Soviet governments and other administrative bodies, for example, multiplied rapidly, as did many mass movement organs. Party cadres also expanded efforts to reform existing patterns of social interaction such as male-female relations, lineage structures, and ancestor worship. Party officials likewise took several steps to keep the base area economies functioning efficiently despite the disruption caused by the government blockade and the land reform campaigns. Among these steps were establishing financial institutions and small handicrafts enterprises, levying new taxes, assuming the management of certain important markets, and prohibiting rice exports from the base areas.

Taken together, these actions amounted to a comprehensive and fundamental attack on the existing socioeconomic order, and they provoked confusion, doubt, and resistance in some individuals and groups even as they roused enthusiasm in others. Part of the unhappiness stemmed from dissatisfaction with the aims or results of certain radical reforms. For example, prohibition of rice exports, combined with the effects of the government's blockade of the base areas, caused a troublesome "scissors crisis" in which prices of imports rose sharply while the price of grain sold to pay for them remained low. Likewise, communist policies relating to marriage, divorce, and other aspects of male-female relations upset many conservative (especially male) peasants who feared the social tensions and possible immorality that might result from them.[43]

Much of the most determined resistance, however, came from people occupying the shifting, marginal, and transitional social zone between those who were undeniably peasants and those who were indubitably elites. These people, whom cadres sometimes called "the intermediate class" and sometimes "the rich peasants and small landlords," were, as the vagueness and ambivalence of these terms suggests, a lumpy, heterogeneous group who could not be poured smoothly into the standard categories of Marxist social analysis. As I have argued elsewhere, they were a complex group, some of whom were rising ambitiously out of the peasantry and others fighting bitterly to avoid falling back into it. Their attitudes toward the revolution likewise varied: those on the way up jealously guarded their hard-won achievements and opposed reforms that might deprive them of them, while those on the way down were more open to reforms as a means of somehow shoring up their deteriorating position.[44]

Many in the former category became among the most determined opponents of the revolutionary movement and led lineage braves or militiamen to attack Red Guards and defend hilltop fortresses scattered around the base areas. Others feigned surface compliance but used their relative status, wealth, or ability to achieve positions of authority within the newly established soviet government organs, land reform teams, and the CCP itself, which they then used to subvert the reforms or preserve as many of their own possessions and perquisites as possible.

Lower elites threatened with downward mobility generally had more ambivalent attitudes toward the revolution, and some of them even embraced it enthusiastically. Like the *arriviste* lower elites, many of this type also tried to enter revolutionary organs, but they were more concerned with using these positions for their own purposes than with subverting and destroying the movement as a whole.

Others, however, especially well-educated young scions of such households, saw in the revolution both an attractive avenue for rapid personal advancement and an important opportunity for implementing reforms that might make rural Jiangxi a better place. It is worth noting in this regard that a significant number of early Jiangxi CCP members were from declining lower elite families, and that many others with this sort of background continued to join the movement after it began to expand in rural Jiangxi.[45]

During the initial post-1927 struggles, when the tasks of establishing base areas and recruiting military forces (however unsavory their origins) willing and able to defend them seemed more pressing than initiating social and economic changes, these local CCP cadres of elite origin appear to have been determined, energetic, and effective participants in the revolutionary movement. As the trend turned to radical reform, however, some of these cadres became increasingly concerned about the implications for their own power. As Red Guards and guerrilla units were reorganized and centralized and a new administrative hierarchy developed, the personalistic power and influence the founders of the local base areas had built up became increasingly restricted. As land policy moved beyond rent and debt reduction to encompass full-scale land redistribution, the familial wealth and social position of many of these cadres and their relatives was also directly threatened.

These personal concerns were interwoven with and strengthened by broader worries about the risks the reforms posed to the continued viability of the movement as a whole. By restricting and antagonizing the bandits and brotherhoods who had provided much of the movement's early military strength just when enemy militias were becoming increasingly threatening and government armies were massing for a major "bandit suppression" campaign, the military reforms appeared dangerous and counterproductive. So also did land reform and social reforms relating to women. The former alienated the bulk of the movement's most powerful supporters, while the latter alienated many of the able-bodied male peasants who were its vital rank-and-file participants; both distracted and polarized the population and created unrest in the revolution's most secure rear areas.

This growing opposition from a substantial number of elite party cadres, coupled with equally evident resistance from other elites and (especially on certain social issues) some base area peasants, clearly hindered the reforms and contributed to internal clashes that rocked the revolutionary movement.

One of the most serious of these was the case of the "Four Great Party Officials" (Si da dangguan), powerful local cadres who were accused of prolonged resistance to, and defiance of, party policy and directives, and who were eventually executed in February 1930. Little is known about them, but at least two (and probably all four) had been founders of the Yanfu base area, where, as noted earlier, the early party leaders were known for their wealthy elite backgrounds. The power and authority of the four had evidently grown in tandem with the growth of the base area itself.[46]

By late 1929, however, their power and the base area both faced serious challenges. Enemy attacks hit the Yanfu area hard,[47] efforts to expand the Red Army increased demands to field local military units (such as the Independent Third Regiment recently formed from Yanfu area guerrillas) for use outside the base in coordinated regional attacks upon Ji'an,[48] and the call for thorough land redistribution directly threatened the wealth of the cadres' families.

Under these conditions, the "Four Great Party Officials" and like-minded local party members strongly resisted the reforms. They insisted that party members' land should not be confiscated and that rent and debt payments should continue to be made to them. They also used "feudal relations" to gain local peasant support, formed new guerrilla bands personally loyal to them, took control of the locally raised Independent Third Regiment, and recruited rowdies into the party to harass local CCP branches. Only after months of determined effort were higher authorities able to seize and execute the four.[49]

The case of the "Four Great Party Officials" is an extreme example of how far local party leaders might go to preserve the power they had built up with such effort. Nevertheless, the party's use of them as exemplars, symbolic representatives of a larger group sharing similar attitudes, indicates that they had only slightly less visible or effective counterparts in the region. Threatened simultaneously by enemy attacks from outside and party and peasant attacks from inside the base areas, many local cadres of elite origin felt besieged on all sides. They reacted by clinging tightly to whatever power bases they had managed to construct.

In broader terms, the reaction of elite cadres to policies that seemed to undo their past accomplishments was a sign of a more general crisis in the revolutionary struggle that had developed by early 1930. The arrival of the enthusiastically anticommunist Hunan army; the increasingly sophisticated competition posed to CCP control of rural elites and peasants by the AB Corps and other noncommunist rivals; the difficulties caused by bandit/sworn brotherhood coalitions and localist feelings in party efforts to consolidate and upgrade the base areas' military forces; and the tensions induced by attempts to institute major socioeconomic reforms—all these contributed to deep uncertainty and internal conflict over the revolution's proper future course. It was in this context that the final political struggles broke out that led to the Futian incident.

Intraparty Strife

The conflicts that rocked the Jiangxi party in 1930 have been well described by earlier scholars, so a summary account will suffice here.[50] On 7 February, after the Fourth Red Army's return from a foray into Fujian, Mao and army representatives met regional party leaders at Pitou in Ji'an County. Among other things, this conference agreed to set up a new regional party organ (the Southwest Jiangxi Special Committee) and a regional soviet government (established the following month), adopted comprehensive land reform strategy, and intensified efforts to expand the Red Army. Intense arguments occurred over all these issues, but in the end the policies favored by Mao and his associates won out over those espoused by important regional leaders such as Li Wenlin.

Shortly after the Pitou Conference, however, national CCP leader Li Lisan began implementing a new nationwide strategy calling for Red Army attacks on major Chinese cities, new party organs called action committees, and land distribution according to labor power instead of per capita allotments. After attending a conference of delegates from the soviet areas in Shanghai in May, Li Wenlin brought orders to implement these policies back to the Ji'an region, and similar orders went out to the various Red Army units in the area. At about the same time, several party and military organs began to report the discovery of AB Corps "nests" in specific localities and organizations around the base areas.[51]

That summer, Red Army main forces left to attack Nanchang, Changsha and Wuhan, while new armies were created to defend the bases and continue fruitless assaults on Ji'an. One of these armies was the Twentieth Red Army, formed from local Ji'an region guerrillas.[52] Meanwhile, at a congress of the Southwest Jiangxi Special Committee, Li Wenlin and allies seized power and implemented the full range of "Li Lisan line" political and economic programs. They also launched searches for AB Corps adherents in the Southwest Jiangxi Soviet government and the Red Army school, and issued a general resolution calling for heightened anti–AB Corps activity.[53]

In the fall, Mao and the Red Army main forces returned to central Jiangxi following their failure to seize Yangtze Valley cities. Although assaults on major cities had failed, they finally captured Ji'an in October and held it for over a month. More conferences were held to try to iron out continuing disagreements on military and political issues, especially the question of the proper strategy for defending the soviet areas against a predicted massive enemy suppression campaign. Once again, Li Wenlin led strenuous but unsuccessful opposition to policies Mao favored. Ultimately, most Red Army forces withdrew deep into the base areas to await the enemy attack. As the assault neared, large-scale purges of suspected AB Corps elements occurred in the Red Army, Li Wenlin and other party officials were arrested, and shortly thereafter the Futian incident occurred.

Other scholars have viewed these events primarily as part of an ongoing epic struggle over power and policy between Mao Zedong and a succession of opponents in the national party leadership. Certainly this struggle was real and significant, and analysis of it reveals much about the rise of Mao. But to interpret these disputes simply as aspects of a national struggle is to miss the extent to which they were also important local conflicts whose dynamics had as much to do with the particular circumstances in central Jiangxi as they did with the dictates of national party policy.

These local circumstances also included conflicts over power and personality similar in type if not in scale to those involved at the national level. For example, though scanty primary sources and the delicacy with which PRC scholars still discuss intraparty interpersonal relations makes it impossible to provide details, it is nonetheless evident that the disputes between Mao and Li Wenlin went beyond policy questions to include a power struggle between the two that doubtless generated considerable personal animosity.

Personality issues were likewise involved in the animosity that developed between many Jiangxi cadres and Li Shaojiu, Mao's emissary whose arrests started the Futian incident in December 1930. Li had joined the Nanchang Uprising in 1927, worked underground in Hunan, and then been captured and worked for the GMD briefly before rejoining the CCP in the Ji'an region in March 1928. While serving with the Independent Second Regiment, he clashed with Li Wenlin and other local Jiangxi leaders. Later, after the Second and other Ji'an-raised regiments were amalgamated into the Third Red Army, Li became a commissar in one of the new army's units. There he fought with the unit commander and aroused such anger among North Route party leaders that they petitioned higher authorities to remove him from office. All accounts agree that he was an assertive, abrasive individual.[54]

Mao and Li Shaojiu were also both Hunanese, and whatever effect their individual personal abrasiveness may have had on partisan infighting appears to have been compounded considerably by the deeper factional frictions resulting from numerous recently arrived Hunanese outsiders backed by Red Army guns imposing their will on local Jiangxi cadres who were trying to maintain and extend the painfully won gains of their own long struggle. These points indicate that any examination of the personal and factional impact of the intraparty clashes preceding the Futian incident must look down as well as up the political hierarchy from Mao and pay at least as much attention to the complexities and consequences of Mao's interactions with local party leaders in Jiangxi as to the stormy course of his relationship with the party center in Shanghai.

Looked at from a local Jiangxi perspective, many aspects of the Li Lisan line fit in well with the reported predilections of leaders such as Li Wenlin. Attacks on cities such as Nanchang shifted the "guest" Red Army forces of Zhu De and Mao Zedong out of the base areas and weakened their influence there; the formation of action committees provided new organizational venues to bypass or seize power from the more radical supporters of Mao who had achieved dominance at the 7 February Pitou Conference; and Li Lisan's policy of distributing land on the basis of labor power rather than per capita allotments favored rich peasants and other marginal elites over the mass of the peasantry.[55]

As noted previously, issues of military control, political organization, and socioeconomic reform had already been under contentious discussion in the Jiangxi base areas for some time before the factional struggles of 1930 transpired. Militarily, attempts to expand the Red Army and centralize its direction had begun—and had met local resistance—even before the Zhu-Mao Army returned from Fujian or the Li Lisan line was launched. Likewise, the campaign to capture Ji'an started months before Li Lisan made the seizure of cities the centerpiece of his policy. Economically, land reform strategies had already become controversial, and some party leaders of elite origin had already begun following what amounted to a "rich peasant line" well before Li Lisan's land law appeared. Politically, attempts to consolidate and coordinate party organs, to form soviets, and to establish an effective centralized political chain of command were also already well under way before 1930.

The extension of the Li Lisan line to the central Jiangxi base areas and Mao's countermeasures thus appear to have been more overlays on and intensifiers of pre-existing patterns of interaction than the central defining elements of political activity in the Jiangxi bases that much previous scholarship has implied. The externally imposed Li Lisan line provided protection and justification for the locally generated attitudes and factional alignments of some Ji'an region party leaders, as the policies of Mao and his associates provided for those of others. Local leaders whose views on the future course of the revolution were already diverging were thus further polarized, and the animosities among them further inflamed, by the addition of the larger feud between Li Lisan and Mao.

The Futian Incident and Its Aftermath

News of the repudiation of Li Lisan's leadership and policies had already reached the central Jiangxi base areas by the time the Futian incident began to unfold in early December 1930. Before discussing these dramatic events, we should remind ourselves briefly of the state of affairs that then obtained and the atmosphere that then prevailed in the central Jiangxi base areas.

By 1930, the Donggu base area in which the town of Futian lay had grown from a welter of tiny, scattered nodes of communist activity to become the most important base in central Jiangxi. Though distinctive in its importance, Donggu was typical of all these bases in the manner in which it had been built by a diverse coalition of young local intellectuals allied with bandits and other local power holders. Between 1927 and 1930 such coalitions in Donggu and elsewhere had first directed an extensive and multitiered militarization process that built the base areas and then undertaken a major program of reforms intended to transform their social and economic foundations. But these activities had also generated opposition from influential rural elites and party cadres worried about the pace and extent of change and had led to increasingly severe disagreements over control, coordination, and the ultimate goals of the revolutionary movement both within local coalitions and between them and leaders of the main "guest" Red Armies in central Jiangxi.

These problems had been compounded by activities of noncommunist groups such as the AB Corps, whose members had much background in common with the CCP cadres and who had sought to win over both party members and still-uncommitted "new gentry" through means that included misinformation and occasional use of apostate communist double agents. From the Communists' viewpoint, these activities had been disconcertingly effective, as evidenced among other things by the exposure and near-eradication of the party's organs in Ji'an city and the successful misleading of Jishui students by impostors using CCP leader Li Wenlin's name.

By 1930, the sources and manifestations of opposition both outside and inside the revolutionary movement had already begun to appear dangerously coincidental to some party leaders. In a situation where party affiliations in general were ambiguous and easily changeable, where the CCP in particular had already suffered repeated betrayals and exposures of its underground organs, and where noncommunist politicians were openly intriguing against the CCP and its leaders, party leaders could easily imagine infiltration and subversion to be a definite prospect. Likewise, when elites and party members within the base areas resisted military reorganization or land reform, one could easily imagine that their internal opposition had external inspiration.

Encouraging such thoughts were suspicious circumstances that seemed to associate numerous Ji'an region revolutionary leaders with the newly resurgent AB Corps. As noted, Ji'an city schools attended by several early CCP organizers had been home to AB Corps activists since before 1927, and many AB Corps founders and local CCP organizers came from regional counties such as Yongxin, Anfu, and Ji'an. These same counties were also contiguous to or part of the CCP's problem-ridden West and North Routes. Parts of the North Route in particular had been reoccupied by Guard Detachments (many reputedly led by AB Corps elements) during the suppression campaign of 1929–30, and local party leaders (who were largely of elite/landlord origin) had not acquitted themselves well at the time. These leaders included infamous opponents of revolutionary reform such as the "Four Great Party Officials" and another well-known purged party official named Jiang Hanbo.[56] Li Wenlin, the important early Jishui party leader whose name had been invoked by AB Corps agitators posing as CCP members, had also helped found the route's Yanfu base area.

By 1930, Li and other cadres and troops with ties to this troublesome and increasingly suspicious area were scattered widely in party and army units throughout the Ji'an region. From these positions, those among them who might be AB Corps infiltrators could easily proselytize or contact other corps members of similar background from Donggu or elsewhere. Certainly this was the disturbing fear that many CCP leaders had formed by the early spring of 1930, when reports of AB Corps networks inside the base areas began to surface just as the Hunan Army's suppression campaign was at its height.

At about the same time, the national imposition of the Li Lisan line conjoined with the sources of local intraparty dissension noted above to produce increased conflict within the base areas that manifested itself in fierce arguments at a series of meetings held during 1930. The topics (and doubtless the precise factional alignments) involved in these conflicts varied somewhat from meeting to meeting, but all found Mao and his military and political associates struggling with and eventually prevailing over an embattled and increasingly disgruntled minority that included Li Wenlin and other prominent local Jiangxi cadres whose career trajectories, like Li's, had intersected often and openly with sites and sources of potential AB Corps subversion.

If a final catalytic agent was needed to facilitate a violent chain reaction of events in this already volatile environment, it was provided by the imminent prospect of a large government communist-suppression campaign. The Red Army's summer assaults on Yangtze Valley cities had convinced Chiang Kai-shek of the depth of the communist threat, and the end of fighting in North China made it possible in the autumn to mass large forces to attack the Jiangxi bases. Communist leaders at all levels were extremely worried by the prospect of such a major assault striking the dissent-ridden base areas while the Red Army was still seriously debilitated by its heavy summer losses and uncertain of its local support. This widely shared fear not only increased the general sense of crisis in the base areas but also seems to have constituted a major psychological force behind the paranoid persecutions that were soon to begin.

The first large-scale attempt to root out supposed AB Corps subversion in the base areas, an effort that was arguably also the opening act of the extended series of maneuvers and actions that is known as the Futian incident, took the form of a massive purge of the main Red Army forces in early November 1930. As noted above, scattered if slowly growing efforts to suppress AB Corps infiltrators had already begun several months earlier, but the November purges seem to have been far larger and more dramatic. More than four thousand members of several armies (including both the old Fourth Army, with which Mao had long been associated, and the Third Army, in which Li Wenlin and many local Jiangxi

cadres had worked) are said to have come under suspicion in these investigations, and nearly half of them, including "a few dozen" alleged high-ranking AB
Corps leaders, seem eventually to have been executed.[57]

Among those who were touched by this purge was Li Wenlin, who was briefly
arrested, questioned, and then released. As noted, Li had earlier clashed repeatedly
with Mao Zedong, who dominated the Red Army's General Front Committee at the
time. It may therefore very well be the case, as recent work by Chen Yung-fa asserts,
that Mao's desire to destroy his factional opponents and their supporters was a major
factor both Li's in arrest and the Red Army purges as a whole.[58]

At any rate, coerced confessions of some souls less fortunate than Li incrimi-
nated several party and Twentieth Army cadres then in or near Futian, and in
early December Li Shaojiu was sent with orders from the General Front Committee to supervise their arrest. Within several days, Li and some cooperative
party and army cadres in the area (including two long-time allies of Mao) had
arrested as many as eighty or ninety AB Corps suspects, coerced confessions
from some, and executed about half of them. One who narrowly escaped was a
Twentieth Army officer named Liu Di, whom Li Shaojiu had seized and then
released because they were from the same native place in Hunan. This move
soon backfired when Liu, deciding that this was only a temporary reprieve,
counterattacked by seizing Donggu and Futian and releasing the prisoners, while
Li Shaojiu and several other erstwhile purge leaders escaped in the confusion.
Realizing that the affair was far from over, the freed cadres and their rescuers led
the Twentieth Army out of the Donggu area to relative safety across the Gan
River.[59]

West of the Gan, the escapees reconstituted important political committees
they had formerly helped lead in the Donggu base, established close relations
with leaders of the party's West Route subregion in Yongxin, and cooperated
with local forces in military and mass mobilization activities. Once established,
the escaped cadres launched a campaign to clear their names, sending a representative to appeal to the CCP's central leaders in Shanghai, and dispatching vitriolic written resolutions and appeals directed to party and army leaders east of the
Gan River. In these messages, among many other things, they reviled Mao as a
would-be "party emperor" and called upon CCP leaders such as Zhu De, Peng
Dehuai, and Huang Gonglue to join them in opposing him.

These leaders responded by endorsing Mao and his policies and denounced
the escaped "rebels" as landlords, rich peasants, and counterrevolutionaries. The
Mao-dominated General Front Committee soon weighed in with its own lengthy
polemical evaluation of the Futian incident and the subsequent actions of those
involved. During the same period in December and January, Red Army forces
were busy fighting the battles that eventually defeated the government's First
Encirclement Campaign, their efforts reportedly complicated by the lack of cooperation they met for a time from a Donggu-area population made angry and
confused by the cadre killings at Futian and elsewhere.

With things at this bitter impasse, Xiang Ying, the head of the newly established Central Bureau for the Soviet Areas (Suqu zhongyang ju) arrived in southern Jiangxi in early January 1931 and attempted, with limited success, to resolve
the situation. Because Xiang was uncertain where truth lay in this murky matter
and was apparently also under strong political pressure from Mao and his colleagues, the Central Bureau issued several conciliatory but ultimately unsatisfac-
tory statements in January and February that deplored excesses in the work of
"suppressing counterrevolutionaries," declared that participants in the Futian incident may not themselves have been counterrevolutionaries, but still affirmed
that their actions had aided the enemy.[60]

In February, Xiang also dispatched a Jiangxi cadre named Zeng Bingchun to
persuade the escapees to return east of the Gan River. Zeng was well suited to
the task: One of the founders of the Donggu base area, he had held many
positions in base area party and military organs, had helped organize the Twentieth Army in mid-1930, and had served briefly as its first commander. He had
reportedly escaped involvement in the Futian incident because he was then at
home recuperating from an injury.[61]

Zeng did convince several of the Futian incident participants and a West
Route party leader to cross the Gan River in March to seek reconciliation with
their opponents at a Central Bureau meeting in Ningdu County. The Twentieth
Army, however, remained west of the river, where it conducted joint military
operations with regional Red Army units and the Seventh Red Army (newly
arrived from Guangxi) during the spring and early summer of 1931. Zeng himself stayed behind to help coordinate these operations.[62]

Zeng's mission and the softened rhetoric emanating from the Central Bureau
under Xiang Ying's leadership may well have persuaded the alienated cadres
journeying toward Ningdu that the events of the previous several months had
been a temporary aberration, a bad dream that would soon be behind them as
they were welcomed back into the revolutionary mainstream. If so, they were
sadly and, in the end, fatally mistaken. Not long after the cadres arrived in
Ningdu, they were arrested on renewed charges of being AB Corps supporters,
tried, and eventually executed.

Details of the circumstances surrounding these killings and the dramatic
broadening and deepening of the violence-laden movement to "suppress counterrevolutionaries" that subsequently developed are much too complex to be
recounted here in full. In brief, however, it appears that the west bank returnees
had the misfortune to time their arrival to coincide roughly with the first manifestations of a more aggressive line toward the problem of the AB Corps and
other "counterrevolutionaries" being articulated by the national CCP's newly
installed Fourth Plenum leadership group controlled by Wang Ming and other
so-called returned Bolsheviks. In March and April 1931, the Fourth Plenum
issued documents criticizing past suppression activities and re-evaluating the
Futian incident, and sent a delegation to the Central Bureau to convey the new

and harsher line personally to Jiangxi cadres. For several months thereafter, an expanded and unprecedentedly violent wave of purges spread to virtually all parts of the base areas, sweeping away in the process almost all of the base area founders as well as many of the revolutionary movement's ordinary followers.[63]

Recent PRC party historians' accounts discussing this period assign responsibility for its excesses primarily to the mistaken "ultraleft" line of the Wang Ming leadership that was later overturned by Mao Zedong, though some hint at the possibility that Mao himself may have been implicated in the renewed persecution of supposed counterrevolutionaries.[64] In fact, close examination of even the incomplete evidence currently available makes it clear that Mao was at least a willing participant in, if not an active promoter of, the deepening purges. Even before the delegation of the Fourth Plenum arrived in Jiangxi, Mao had already become a dominant force in the Central Bureau, as well as maintaining the strong position he had previously obtained in the Red Army's leadership. After the delegation arrived, Mao appears to have cooperated closely with it during the spring and summer of 1931—the most intense period of the purges—until a realignment of political forces during the autumn began the gradual eclipse of his power.[65]

The question of specifically who presided over the fierce wave of "counterrevolutionary suppression" that spread through the soviet areas during the latter half of 1931 is rendered considerably less important, however, by the fact that the purges soon became so widespread, decentralized, and paranoid that for a time they were largely beyond the control of any of the top leaders. When laxly supervised local cadres working in tense circumstances were urged to find, judge, and punish hidden members of opposition groups plausibly felt to exist in the base areas, and when the background of members of these groups was similar to those of many base area elites—both in and out of the party and government—who had recently argued over socioeconomic reforms and other serious issues, then it is easy to see in retrospect that a torch was being touched to very dry tinder.

The prairie fire that resulted was of a different sort from the revolutionary blaze usually envisaged by communist leaders. If AB Corps agents had indeed truly infiltrated revolutionary organs, then they must certainly have been smoked out and killed, but so were a great many loyal party members, along with other local elites whose bad class backgrounds, work experience, or outspoken opinions alone had made them suspect. Lacking firm guidelines or supervision, cadres could easily superimpose the concrete actions of their own factional opponents or other critics onto vague profiles of AB Corps conduct and find that the images somehow coincided.

Not all the killing was instigated by local party and government cadres, however. In actions that both reflected and contributed still further to the growing inclusiveness of the purge, many campaigns to suppress counterrevolutionaries were conducted within the Red Army, campaigns whose scale and organized quality leave little doubt that they were approved or directed by high leaders such as Mao. One of these involved the Seventh Red Army, newly arrived from Guangxi, but the most notable activity was directed against the Twentieth Army, the unit involved in the Futian incident.[66] Although this force had remained safely west of the Gan River when many Futian incident cadres returned to meet their deaths earlier in 1931, in July Zeng Bingchun finally led the unit back across the river to rejoin the main Red Army forces. In Yudu County, however, the army was suddenly disarmed, all officers at the platoon level or above (including Zeng Bingchun himself) were arrested, and many of them killed, and the ordinary soldiers were dispersed into several other communist armies. The tainted Twentieth Army unit designation was abolished.[67]

By early autumn 1931, the impetus of the purge began to wane, but it was not until after Zhou Enlai arrived in Jiangxi in December as a representative of the party's central leadership that the campaign to purge counterrevolutionaries really began to wind down. Some executions continued well into the following year; as late as 30 May 1932, for example, a group of the last remaining Futian incident participants and other prominent Jiangxi cadres finally met their end.

It is impossible to say precisely how many thousands of people died in the purges, but they included virtually all of the region's early revolutionary leaders and a large percentage of even low-ranking cadres. One PRC study of the purges, for example, admitted that "over 90 percent of the cadres in the southwestern Jiangxi area were killed, detained, or stopped work."[68] Biographies in another recent work on the Donggu base area provide similarly bleak data: Of nineteen people from the region profiled (including almost all of the base area's founders), twelve were executed as counterrevolutionaries during this period, five were killed by the enemy (most of them before 1931), another died of illness, and the sole survivor stayed alive only by leaving the base areas and quitting the revolution.[69]

Among those executed were Li Wenlin, who was arrested in July 1931—ironically while serving at the head of a committee to suppress counterrevolutionaries—jailed for almost a year, and killed in May 1932; Zeng Bingchun, arrested when the Twentieth Army was disbanded and also executed in May 1932; and Duan Qifeng, the one-time Three Dots Society leader and early Donggu guerrilla leader, who survived longer than most by returning to life as a bandit until he was caught and killed in 1933.[70]

Concluding Remarks

Contemporary documents reveal little of what participants really thought about these traumatic affairs then, and the ravages of revolutionary struggle and of time itself have ensured that few survivors remain to convey much to us now.

The meager light available from these dim and distant events has been further occluded and filtered by passage through a thick haze of intervening events and interpretations. Party orthodoxy from 1945 to 1978 stressed the reality and depth of the counterrevolutionary threat and the justifiable need to suppress it, affirming in the process the general correctness of Mao Zedong's policies while maintaining discreet silence about the amount of killing that occurred and the specifics of Mao's involvement in it. Most early noncommunist accounts, seeking to trace Mao's rise to national prominence, focused on the political implications of these events as part of a process of personal power-building and high-level factional struggle only coincidentally connected to local circumstances of any sort. And most post-Mao accounts, spurred by the Cultural Revolution's recent demonstration of the remarkable compatibility of moral purpose and mindless persecution to re-examine and "reverse the verdicts" on similar injustices in the party's past, have strongly denied that there was ever any credible threat from the AB Corps or other groups, but have not advanced any comprehensive alternative explanation for the purges.

Each of these interpretations has in its own way absorbed, polarized, and refracted the pale glimmer of information that now survives to illuminate the complex events and processes surrounding the Futian incident. The result has been a series of partial portraits, each effectively highlighting certain features but only at the cost of casting others into shadow.

The Futian incident cannot be understood simply as a counterrevolutionary conspiracy masterminded by a ramified AB Corps organization. There is no reason whatsoever to think that there were ever elaborate, multitiered secret AB Corps networks plotting the destruction of the revolution such as was alleged by party cadres (both Maoist and non-Maoist) in the perfervid and paranoid atmosphere that prevailed in the months before and especially after the Futian incident. To this extent, I support the revisionist view endorsed by CCP elder Xiao Ke, himself involved in these events as a young man, who concluded in 1982 that

> We comrades who participated in this movement, regardless of whether we were the executors or the victims, all remember that at that time, although many AB Corps and Social Democratic Party [suspects] were attacked, aside from oral confessions there was really no evidence of any sort in hand to prove the existence of these two organizations. Today, 50 years later, after acquainting ourselves thoroughly with the various [available] materials, we still cannot find any concrete evidence proving the existence of these two organizations in the soviet areas at that time.[71]

In their concern to underline the baseless injustice of the charges against party members during this period, however, many revisionist PRC historians have gone beyond the careful ambiguity of Xiao's phrase "at that time" to insist explicitly that the AB Corps did not exist after the spring of 1927.

This view, I am convinced, is incorrect. Its chief leaders may have left Jiangxi, and the group may never have had the hierarchies and networks "discovered" during the purges and reified by Maoist historiography, but there is ample evidence that the AB Corps existed well into the 1930s as a subgroup of the GMD just as real and functional—and every bit as informal and amorphous—as other well-known factions such as the Reorganization Clique and the CC (Ch'en brothers—Guofu and Lifu) Clique. Its members may have interacted more as loosely knit, overlapping clusters of mutual friends, classmates, and hometown associates than as people tightly bound by ideology and organization, but in this they were no different from other contemporary Chinese political groups—including the CCP. Indeed, as shown above, the AB Corps, other noncommunist groups, and the CCP all overlapped considerably in background and experience, and all were engaged in an active, ongoing, mutual competition to build local political power. In sum, credible fears and considerable hard experience did help motivate the work of "counterrevolutionary suppression," whatever irrationality and injustice may have attended its execution.

Similarly nuanced evaluation is required of interpretations stressing that the Futian incident was caused primarily by feuding between supporters of Mao and Li Lisan, and that it is thus best understood as another step in Mao's gradual climb into power within the national communist movement. As indicated, serious intraparty strife did occur in the region, supporters of Mao and Li were deeply involved in it, and the animosities thus generated did much to build up stress along the fault lines within the revolutionary movement that were to rupture so violently during the Futian incident itself. Yet, as we have noted, the main lines of fissure within the movement were already apparent well before the tumultuous struggles of 1930, and they were incised far more deeply into the bedrock of socioeconomic structure and process in the region than the personal power struggles of ambitious individuals could obscure or transform.

In sum, though political intrigue, personality conflict, and collective paranoia all figured prominently in the Futian incident and its attendant events, these factors by themselves cannot fully explain the internecine violence that rocked the Jiangxi countryside of this period. We must add as well some recognition and understanding of the impact on these events of larger social and political processes, whereby an urban-oriented, elite-centered political movement fought against constant resistance first to adapt itself to the harsh imperatives of a rural environment, and then to transform both that environment and itself in fundamental ways. It is this awareness of social process, and of the explosive stresses built up in this difficult but vital transition in the revolutionary movement, that has been missing in most accounts of this period in CCP history, and that I have sought to convey here.

Notes

1. *Ji'an xianzhi* (Gazetteer of Ji'an County), 1941 edition, *juan* 9, 3b–12a.
2. I have described the Jinggangshan base area in a paper entitled "Revolution and Society in South China: Jinggangshan and the Jiangxi Revolutionary Movement," pre-

sented at the annual meeting of the American Historical Association, San Francisco, December 1989.

3. Based on a survey of backgrounds of several dozen early Jiangxi CCP members and nearly 100 Jiangxi right-wing GMD members reported in Stephen Averill, "Revolution in the Highlands: The Rise of the Communist Movement in Jiangxi Province" (Ph.D dissertation, Cornell University, 1982), 86–94 and 107–13.

4. The Jiangxi Provincial Archives and the Teaching and Research Department on Party History of the Party School of the Jiangxi Provincial Party Committee, ed., *Zhongyang geming genjudi shiliao xuanbian* (A Selection of Historical Materials on the Central Revolutionary Base Area, *ZYGM*) 3 vols. (Nanchang: Jiangxi People's Publishing House, 1983), 1: 3 and 135–36; Stephen Averill, "Local Elites and Communist Revolution in the Jiangxi Hill Country," in Joseph Esherick and Mary Rankin, eds., *Chinese Local Elites and Structures of Dominance* (Berkeley and Los Angeles: University of California Press, 1990), 282–304.

5. Yuan Xuehuang, "Jiangxi gongchandang de lishi guan" (View of the History of the Jiangxi Communist Party), *Shehui xinwen* (The Society Mercury), 1, no. 8 (25 October 1932): 179.

6. Qin Xianci, "Duan Xipeng (1898–1948) xiaozhuan" (A Brief Biography of Duan Xipeng [1898–1948]), *Zhuanji wenxue* (Biographical Literature), no. 178 (March 1977): 15 and 67.

7. Xiao Cen, "AB tuan zai Jiangxi" (The AB Corps in Jiangxi), *Shehui xinwen*, 3, no. 8 (24 April 1933): 116; Hong Gui, "Minguo shiliu nian Jiangxi sier shibian huiyi" (Reminiscences of the 2 April 1927 Incident in Jiangxi), *Jiangxi wenxian* (Documents on Jiangxi), no. 13 (April 1967): 9–10.

8. The following account of the Donggu base area is based primarily on Zhong Ping, " 'Ci shi dong Jinggang'—Donggu diqu di chuqi geming douzheng" ("This Is the Eastern Jinggang"—the Early Period of Revolutionary Struggle in the Donggu Area), *Jiangxi wenshi ziliao xuanji* (Selected Historical Accounts of Jiangxi), no. 7 (1981): 53–67; Huang Muxian, "Jiangxi gongnong hongjun diqi, dijiu zongdui de chuangjian" (The Founding of the Jiangxi Worker-Peasant Red Army's 7th and 9th Columns), *Jiangxi shehui kexue* (Jiangxi Social Sciences), no. 1 (1981): 59–62; Chen Ronghua, "Luetan Donggu shan geming genjudi de chuangjian" (A Brief Discussion of the Founding of the Donggu Mountain Revolutionary Base Area), *Jiangxi daxue xuebao* (Journal of Jiangxi University), no. 3 (1979): 27–35.

9. One cause of the Yanfu area's early revolutionary activity was that it was the home of Luo Shibing, one of the first Ji'an natives to join the CCP and a one-time secretary of the provincial party committee. Civil Administration Office of Jiangxi Province, *Bixue danxin* (Loyalty until Death) (Nanchang: Jiangxi People's Press, 1980), 175–82.

10. Zeng Shan, "Huiyi Ganxinan Suweiai shiji" (Recollection of the Southwest Jiangxi Soviet Period), *Jiangxi wenshi ziliao xuanji*, no. 1 (1980): 4.

11. The following account of the Yanfu base is drawn primarily from Huang Muxian, "Jiangxi gongnong hongjun diqi," 60–61; Xie Yi, "Jiangxi gongfei gaikuang" (The General Condition of the Communist Bandits in Jiangxi), *Changong banyue kan* (Communist Suppression Bi-monthly), nos. 24–25 (August 1932): 43–44.

12. Party History Office of the Jishui County Party Committee, "Guanyu Li Wenlin bei cuosha de qingkuang diaocha" (An Investigation into the Circumstances of the Mistaken Killing of Li Wenlin), *Jiangxi dangshi ziliao* (Materials on Jiangxi Party History), no. 1 (1987): 321 and 324–25; Shen Qinghong and Liu Danian, "Donggu geming genjudi he Ganxinan geming genjudi de chuangjianzhe—Li Wenlin" (A Founder of the Donggu and Southwest Jiangxi Revolutionary Base Areas—Li Wenlin), *Jiangxi dangshi ziliao*,

no. 10 (1989): 185–88. Little biographical material was available on Li Wenlin before the appearance of these articles. Most Western sources, based largely on Zhu De's account to Agnes Smedley (in *The Great Road: The Life and Times of Chu Teh* [New York: Monthly Review Press, 1956], 239, 280, and 286–87), have described Li as the son of a large landlord from the Donggu-Xingguo (Tungku-Hsingkuo) area. Instead, these articles note, Li's father (who died of illness in 1927) and his family of ten lived over 240 *li* from Donggu, and supported themselves on thirty-odd *mu* of arable land and a patch of camphor trees, which they managed with the aid of a single part-time laborer called in during the busy season.

13. Much of the description of anticommunist military and political activity that follows is drawn from comments in contemporary documents contained in *ZYGM*, especially vol. 1.

14. Much of the description of political parties that follows is drawn from comments in documents in *ZYGM*, especially vol. 1; and Chen Yichen, "AB tuan yu gaizupai zai Jiangxi huodong de jianwen" (Information about the Activities in Jiangxi of the AB Corps and the Reorganization Clique), *Jiangxi wenshi ziliao xuanji*, no. 9 (1982): 130–41.

15. The AB Corps is mentioned in many issues of the noncommunist journal *Shehui xinwen*; it is also mentioned prominently in Lu Ping, "Jiangxi tongxun" (Report from Jiangxi), *Geming xingdong* (Revolutionary Activities), no. 1 (1 September 1930): 26–29. *Geming xingdong* was a short-lived Third Party journal.

16. Chen Yichen, "AB tuan yu gaizupai," 135–39.

17. The following comments about local elite factionalism are based upon information contained in my still-unfinished book manuscript on the origins of the Jiangxi communist movement.

18. For continued activity by other parties, see Hu Guokang *Duidi douzheng jingyan huiyilu* (Recollections of My Experiences Struggling Against the Enemy) (Taiwan: Guangming Publishing Company, 1963), 24–25 and passim; *ZYGM*, 1: 185–86.

19. For details of the competition between the AB Corps, Reorganization Clique and Third Party in the Ji'an region, see *ZYGM*, 1: 73–76, 95, 118, 134–36, 185–88, and 222.

20. Ibid., 1: 74–76, 102–5, and 187; 2: 82–83.

21. Ibid., 1: 75–76, 96, 138–39, and 187–88.

22. Averill, "Local Elites and Communist Revolution"; *ZYGM*, 1: 3, 135–36, 187–88, 348, and 355.

23. *ZYGM*, 1: 94–95 and 185.

24. Chen Qihan, "Xingguo de chuqi geming douzheng" (The First Period of Revolutionary Struggle in Xingguo), in Solicitation and Editorial Committee for "Thirty Years of the Chinese People's Liberation Army," ed., *Xinghuo liaoyuan* (A Single Spark Can Start a Prairie Fire) (Beijing: People's Liberation Army Press, 1959), 1: 410.

25. *ZYGM*, 1: 554–55, 564–65, and 588–89.

26. Ibid., 187–88.

27. Ibid., 222–23 and 229.

28. Ibid., 1: 224–25, 229, and 255; 2: 268 and 495–96; 3: 93.

29. Elizabeth J. Perry, *Rebels and Revolutionaries in North China, 1845–1945* (Stanford: Stanford University Press, 1980), chap. 5; *ZYGM*, 1: 194 and 346–47; 2: 205, 268, and 495–96.

30. *ZYGM*, 1: 224–25, 254–55, and 346; and 2: 175 and 495–96.

31. Ibid., 1: 224, 255–56, and 346; and 2: 175 and 495–96.

32. For sources see notes 30 and 31. For areas covered by the North Route and other subregions, see *ZYGM*, 2: 183–84.

33. *ZYGM*, 2: 175.

34. For the Zhu-Mao Red Army's movements and their effects, see Jiangxi People's

Press, comp., *Guanshan chenchen cang—Zhongyang geming genjudi de douzheng* (The Pass and the Lines of Hills Are Green—The Struggle for the Central Revolutionary Base Area), 3 vols. (Nanchang: Jiangxi People's Press, 1978), vol. 1.

35. Examples of violence include the killing of the Jinggangshan bandit leaders Yuan Wencai and Wang Zuo, about which I have written in "Revolution and Society in South China." Among the Chinese sources on Yuan and Wang are their biographies in Research Committee on People in CCP History, ed., *Zhonggong dangshi renwu zhuan* (Biographies of People in CCP History) (Xi'an: Shaanxi People's Press, 1981, 1983), 2: 285–311 (Yuan), 7: 171–85 (Wang). For other examples of violence, see *ZYGM*, 2: 427; and Huang Muxian, "Jiangxi gongnong hongjun diqi," 62.

36. *ZYGM*, 1:399.

37. Ibid. These areas of southern Jishui had produced many Red Spear societies and Red and Yellow Study Society branches that fought with communist guerrilla units formed in the Donggu area.

38. The Editing and Writing Group for "The History of the Struggle for the Hunan-Jiangxi Revolutionary Base Area," *Xiang-Gan geming genjudi de douzheng shi* (The History of the Struggle for the Hunan-Jiangxi Revolutionary Base Area) (Nanchang: Jiangxi People's Press, 1982), 30–35; *ZYGM*, 1: 573.

39. *ZYGM*, 1: 418–19; and 3: 94.

40. Ibid., 3: 94.

41. See the discussion and sources cited in Stephen Averill, "Party, Society, and Local Elite in the Jiangxi Communist Movement," *Journal of Asian Studies* vol. 46, no. 2 (May 1987): 293.

42. *ZYGM*, 3: 111. For land reform in Jiangxi the best English source is still Hsiao Tso-liang, *The Land Revolution in China, 1930–1934: A Study of Documents* (Seattle: University of Washington Press, 1969). Some Chinese sources include Mao Zedong, *Nongcun diaocha* (Rural Investigations) (Shanghai: Xinhua Bookstore, 1949), 54–60 and 88–99; The Contemporary China Economic History Group of the Economics Institute of the Chinese Academy of Social Sciences, ed., *Diyi, erci guonei geming zhanzheng shiqi tudi douzheng shiliao xuanbian* (A Collection of Materials on the Land Struggle During the Period of the First and Second Revolutionary Wars) (Beijing: People's Press, 1981); *ZYGM*, 3: 361–537 and passim.

43. *ZYGM*, 1: 254–55, 329–30, and 356–57; and 3: 558–62.

44. For a more extensive discussion of this liminal stratum of the local elite and its involvement in the revolutionary movement, see Averill, "Local Elites and Communist Revolution."

45. Ibid.

46. The "Four Great Party Officials" were Guo Shijun, Luo Wan, Liu Xiuqi, and Guo Xiangxian. The main (though still sketchy) sources of information about them are contemporary CCP documents. See *ZYGM*, 1: 191–92 and 256; *Jiangxi dangshi ziliao*, 7 (1988): 29–30.

47. The height of the attack on the North Route apparently came in March 1930, after the "Four Great Party Officials" had already been executed, but the campaign started earlier. *ZYGM*, 1: 254–55.

48. *ZYGM*, 1: 193; *Jiangxi dangshi ziliao*, 7 (1988): 29–30. The Independent Third Regiment was formed in October 1929, with the Third Column of Yanfu area guerrillas at its core. In January 1930 the Third Regiment, three other independent regiments raised in central Jiangxi, and some Jinggangshan area militia were amalgamated to form the Red Sixth Army. Zhang Tinggui and Yuan Wei, *Zhongguo gongnong hongjun shilue* (A Brief History of the Chinese Worker-Peasant Red Army) (Beijing: n.p., 1987), 53–54; *ZYGM*, 1: 339–40.

49. *ZYGM*, 1: 192; *Jiangxi dangshi ziliao*, 7 (1988): 30–31. It is likely that the inclusion of

the Independent Third Regiment in the Red Sixth Army (see previous note) in January 1930 reduced the party officials' military power in the Yanfu area and facilitated party authorities' efforts to gain control of the situation.

50. Hsiao Tso-liang, *Power Relations within the Chinese Communist Movement, 1930–1934* (Seattle: University of Washington Press, 1961); John Rue, *Mao Tse-tung in Opposition 1927–1935* (Stanford: Stanford University Press, 1966). The following summary draws upon these works and upon Kong Yongsong et al., *Zhongyang geming genjudi shiyao* (A History of the Central Revolutionary Base Area) (Nanchang: Jiangxi People's Press, 1985).

51. On reports of AB Corps networks and campaigns against them in 1930, see Guo Qi and Dong Xia, "Jiangxi suqu chuqi de sufan yu Futian shibian" (The Futian incident and the Suppression of Counterrevolutionaries During the Early Period of the Jiangxi Soviet Areas), *Dangshi yanjiu ziliao* (Research Materials on Party History), no. 5 (1982): 7.

52. *ZYGM*, 1: 239–40.

53. Guo Qi and Dong Xia, "Jiangxi suqu chuqi de sufan," 7.

54. *ZYGM*, 1: 237–38; "Xiao Ke tongzhi tan zhongyang suqu chuqi de sufan yundong" (Comrade Xiao Ke Discusses the Movement to Suppress Counterrevolutionaries During the Early Period of the Central Soviet Area), *Dangshi yanjiu ziliao*, no. 5 (1982): 4; *Jiangxi dangshi ziliao*, 10 (1989): 197.

55. Hsiao Tso-liang, *The Land Revolution*, 1–76; Rue, *Mao Tse-tung in Opposition*, 218–31.

56. For information on Jiang Hanbo's activities, see *ZYGM*, 1: 571–76; and 2: 176–77; *Jiangxi dangshi ziliao*, 7 (1988): 49–54.

57. Wen Hong, "Guanyu Futian shibian ji Jiangxi suqu de sufan wenti" (Concerning the Futian incident and the Problem of the Suppression of Counterrevolutionaries in the Jiangxi Soviet Areas), *Jiangxi wenshi ziliao*, no. 9 (1982): 109–10; Guo Qi and Dong Xia, "Jiangxi suqu chuqi de sufan," 7.

58. Chen Yung-fa, "Zhonggong zaoqi sufan de jiantao: AB tuan an" (A Review of the Suppression of Counterrevolutionaries in the Early Period of Chinese Communism: The Case of the AB Corps), *Jindaishi yanjiusuo jikan* (Journal of the Institute of Modern History), no. 17, Part I (June 1988): 204–11. Chen's account consists of a very detailed analysis and plausible interpretation of what in the last analysis is largely circumstantial evidence. I myself am inclined to attach less central importance than Chen does to the Mao-Li rivalry as a motivating factor in the events surrounding the Futian incident, but the question remains an open one.

59. There are many more detailed accounts of these events in English, including Ronald Suleski, "The Fu-ti'an Incident, December 1930," in Ronald Suleski and Daniel Bays, eds., *Early Communist China: Two Studies* (Ann Arbor: University of Michigan Center for Chinese Studies, 1968). Several Chinese accounts are now available that are considerably more detailed and reliable than Suleski's older version. Among these are Guo Qi and Dong Xia, "Jiangxi suqu chuqi de sufan," 7–8; and Dai Xiangqing, "Luelun 'Futian shibian' de xingzhi jiqi lishi jiaoxun" (A Brief Discussion of the Character of the "Futian incident" and its Historical Lesson), *Jiangxi daxue xuebao*, no. 3 (1979): 15–20 and 78.

Reminiscences by participants include Wang Anguo, "Luetan 'Futian shibian' de jingguo" (A Brief Discussion about the Course of the "Futian Incident"), *Jiangxi wenshi ziliao*, no. 9 (1982): 102–8; and Zeng Shan, "Gan xinan suweiai shiqi geming douzheng lishi de huiyi" (Reminiscences about the Soviet Period Revolutionary Struggle in Southwest Jiangxi), in Chen Yi et al., *Huiyi Zhongyang suqu* (Remembering the Central Soviet Area) (Nanchang: Jiangxi People's Press, 1986), 13–26, especially 17–20.

60. Guo Qi and Dong Xia, "Jiangxi suqu chuqi de sufan," 9; Dai Xiangqing, "Luelun 'Futian shibian' de xingzhi," 16. Chen Yung-fa, "Zhonggong zaoqi sufan de jiantao," 224–34, has by far the fullest discussion of Xiang Ying's activities and the pressures on him.

61. Shen Qinghong and Liu Danian, "Ganxinan de qunzhong lingxiu—Zeng Bingchun" (Zeng Bingchun—A Leader of the Southwest Jiangxi Masses), *Jiangxi dangshi ziliao*, no. 10 (1989): 189.

62. Ibid., 189–90; Dai Xiangqing, "Luelun 'Futian shibian' de xingzhi," 16.

63. The most detailed description and analysis of the entire suppression movement is contained in Chen Yung-fa, "Zhonggong zaoqi sufan de jiantao," which is based on a wide variety of PRC sources and documents. Other accounts include Guo Qi and Dong Xia, "Jiangxi suqu chuqi de sufan," 9–10; Wen Hong, "Guanyu Futian shibian," 109–19; and Dai Xiangqing, "Luelun 'Futian shibian' de xingzhi," 16.

64. For example, Dai Xiangqing, "Luelun 'Futian shibian' de xingzhi," 16, strongly implies that Mao was deeply involved by noting that under the new Wang Ming line "the leading comrades of the General Front Committee" (which Mao dominated) strongly supported the view that the Futian incident had been counterrevolutionary.

65. A detailed examination of the evidence of Mao's activities during this period is undertaken by Chen Yung-fa, "Zhonggong zaoqi sufan de jiantao," 234–50 and passim. I find Chen's summary and interpretation of the evidence (almost all of which I have also examined myself) careful and generally persuasive, though I find him sometimes more daring than I would be in drawing conclusions from circumstantial evidence.

66. Graham Hutchings, "The Troubled Life and After-Life of a Guangxi Communist: Some Notes on Li Mingrui and the Communist Movement in Guangxi Province Before 1949," *China Quarterly*, no. 104 (December 1985): 706–7; Chen Yung-fa, "Zhonggong zaoqi sufan de jiantao," 250.

67. Wen Hong, "Guanyu Futian shibian," 112; Guo Qi and Dong Xia, "Jiangxi suqu chuqi de sufan," 9; Chen Yung-fa, "Zhonggong zaoqi sufan de jiantao," 247.

68. Guo Qi and Dong Xia, "Jiangxi suqu chuqi de sufan," 9.

69. See *Jiangxi dangshi ziliao*, no. 10 (1989): 182–204.

70. Ibid.

71. "Xiao Ke tongzhi tan zhongyang suqu chuqi de sufan yundong," 3. The Social Democratic Party was another non-Communist political group, active mostly in Fujian, that was thought to have infiltrated the CCP.

Chapter 5

Under Arms and Umbrellas: Perspectives on Chinese Communism in Defeat

Gregor Benton

When the Long Marchers set out from Ruijin in October 1934, they left behind a smaller army under Xiang Ying and Chen Yi to harass and tie down the enemy, coordinate with the field armies on their march west, and defend the soviet.[1] Similar armies were left scattered throughout South and Central China. At the end of their Three-Year War and the start of the war against Japan in 1937, their survivors climbed down the mountains to a heroes' welcome from leaders who had given them up for dead. These remnants regrouped as the New Fourth Army (NFA).

For more than half a century Chinese communism has been virtually synonymous with the Long March, which today has become a metaphor for China's economic march toward the year 2000. A study of the Three-Year War permits us to look back on the Long March from the unfamiliar angle of the people it left behind, including the vast majority of the civilian followers of the CCP in the south. This fresh perspective yields startling new insights on the place of the Long March in the Chinese revolution. It also reminds us that the party existed in rich diversity outside the coalition that Mao Zedong accompanied north in 1935.

The Three-Year War has suffered more than most periods in the history of the Chinese revolution at the hands of historians who see their task as supporting the government, apportioning praise and blame, and edifying the public. On the mainland it has been dismissed as a backwater of the revolution polluted by its association with dissidents and traitors, and its history was largely ignored until the 1980s. Historians in Taiwan, as if on cue, award the Three-Year War a contemptible bit part in the drama of communist perfidy. They claim that "the task of extirpating Communists in the twelve pacification zones" had been completed by April 1935, and that thereafter the embers of communism in the south had burned to ash. Nationalist contempt for the "wild men" who "lurked and skulked in the rugged mountains" is echoed in the abuse to which leaders of the Three-Year War were subjected in Mao's Cultural Revolution. Their exploits were bound to be put in shadow by the Long March, which rescued China's Red Army from an impasse and brought Mao Zedong to power. That success explains the general context in which veterans of the Three-Year War could later become targets of vituperation. The specific reason for their ostracism had to do with factional alignments in the CCP. Xiang Ying had early on been cast as a domestic tool of the Moscow-educated "traitor" Wang Ming. But the denigration of the Three-Year War had less to do with the "historical problems" of dead veterans like Xiang Ying than with those of live ones like Chen Yi, whose connection to Xiang was a handy stick with which to beat him in the Cultural Revolution, when he was a source of trouble and annoyance to his "radical" critics. Minor veterans of the Three-Year War, especially those who had worked as communist moles in the *baojia* or militia, were accused of collaborating with the GMD. This campaign against the Three-Year War was not inspired by factional rancor alone: it stemmed from a totalitarian prejudice against any movement that followed its own lights, outside central control.

Despite the odds, the rearguard's achievement, in numerical terms, easily matches that of the Long Marchers, though this fact is rarely acknowledged publicly in China. In late 1934, forty-two thousand troops were left behind in Central and South China, representing one-sixth of the Red Army's total strength. Three years later, this ratio had barely changed. When the Eighth Route Army (ERA) was set up by the Long Marchers in 1937 on the basis of remnants of the two hundred thousand marchers and northern partisans, it claimed a total of forty-seven thousand troops, compared with ten thousand in the NFA. The ten thousand guerrillas who joined the NFA represented about one-quarter of the original rearguard. The main Red Army lost a far greater proportion of its people during the Long March: of the eighty-six thousand who set out in late 1934, a scant four thousand reached Shaanbei (North Shaanxi). Further, by holding out until the end of 1934, the rearguard in Gannan (South Jiangxi) pinned down divisions that could otherwise have joined in chasing the Long March. In keeping up their little war, the southern guerrillas were trying to hold down Chiang Kai-shek's forces and to deplete his resources.

For the purposes of this chapter, I have distilled a set of propositions about the Three-Year War from evaluations of it by communist sources. These serve as loose cues for my own reflections on the guerrillas' strengths and achievements, and on their weaknesses and failures. Before the consensus collapsed, early communist accounts held that the southern guerrillas preserved strategic fulcrums and armed forces for the revolution: that they upheld party policy; that they acted in remote but effective concert with the Long March; and that they held firm because of party leadership and mass support. These claims provide the starting point and framework for my conclusions.

While the Long March helped re-establish the CCP as a force in national political life and became an instant legend, the conditions of those who stayed behind could hardly have been more different. They were physically scattered in dozens of mainly unconnected fragments and cut off from the outside world. For a time, their leaders were imprisoned within useless and discredited dogmas. They lacked an overview of the political processes in China and were often unaware of major crises until after the event.

Theories about Why the Guerrillas Could Survive

Orthodox Communists cite three main reasons why the southern guerrillas survived the hardships of the Three-Year War. First, they upheld the principle of party leadership; second, they upheld party policies; and third, they established roots among the masses. To many, these arguments will seem more like dogma-mongering than explanation, but they appear more rational when their terms are specified.

Xiang Ying and other rearguard leaders had good reason to insist loudly that they had kept party structures essentially intact during their years in the wilderness. According to the GMD, they were degenerate mutants who "killed people and lit fires."[2] These charges outraged Xiang, but many probably believed them. Not all of Xiang's comrades in the south had stayed true to the cause; a minority became outlaws. Even veterans of the Three-Year War referred to themselves half-jokingly as wild men. Rearguard remnants all over South and Central China were chased from the villages into the forests, where they lived as nomads and troglodytes. At first they starved, but gradually they learned to feed themselves, cut spears, thatch huts, and generally survive the rigors of the wild. But though the stone-age analogy is vivid and suggestive, it reveals little of the essence of the Three-Year War. The forest dwellers who darted about the mountains saw themselves not as savages but as the vanguard of society's most advanced form: communist society, the "negation of the negation" of primitive communalism.

Their "three treasures" were the rifle, the umbrella (including the giant umbrella, under which several guerrillas could squat together), and the safety match. The rifle was the tool of their trade, replaced more often than not by the shotgun, the knife, the spear, or the club. The umbrella offered them protection against the sun and rain, but it also symbolized their isolation and self-reliance. The match was both a precious resource and a favorite symbol. It stood for science, industry, and enlightenment; it accorded with the guerrillas' self-symbolizing as "fire-seeds" of the revolution; and it represented the cauterizing power that would one day set the plains alight, just as the Nationalists set fire to the mountains. Books, too, were precious. The printed page represented Marxist learning and the long-term view. Match and book were treasured objects; to carry them and protect them against the elements was a duty and a privilege.

The party, an organizing principle of guerrilla life, often took wayward and unconventional forms, but local leaders rarely strayed far enough from the right path to disqualify themselves altogether as Marxist-Leninists. Aberrations generally resulted from a combination of inexperience and adaptation to circumstance, and they were easily righted once conditions improved. Most regions of the Three-Year War had their sacred calendar of conferences at which old policies were overthrown and new paths charted, and most boasted miniature versions of the main conferences of the Long Marchers in this period: Zunyi, Maoergai, Wayaobao, and Luochuan. Several regions retained at least some party organization at the county, district, and detachment levels. Guerrilla leaders in Ganyue (Jiangxi-Guangdong), Minxi'nan (Southwest Fujian), and elsewhere reacted with statements and manifestos to all major crises in China after 1934. These pronouncements had little impact on events, but they strengthened the leaders' claim to political status, if only in their own eyes.

Party organization in the Three-Year War was characterized by the concentration of power in one or a few individuals and by violent factional struggles. Some guerrillas tried to form collective leaderships like Minxi'nan's Military and Administrative Committee, which produced a torrent of directives as well as several of the party's main later leaders. But many guerrilla bands were under the spell of a powerful individual who dressed and ate better than the rest and was better protected. This retreat into patriarchy was helped by the streamlining of functions and the unification of the army and the party that happened everywhere in the crisis after the start of the Long March.

This concentration of power was partly the result of an extreme shortage of trained leaders, but a strong collective leadership was rare even where no such shortage existed. Sometimes the presence of more than one talented leader led to disagreements and either to a separation of ways or to competition for control over armed forces, followed by purges. Other leaders split up so as to offer a less compact target. Communist patriarchs often turned their tiny fiefs into families of the revolution where widows, orphans, and dependents of Red Army fighters lived in separate caves alongside the guerrillas.

Many losers in factional fights after 1934 had no scruples about joining the counterrevolution. These renegades were the Communists' worst enemy. Where possible, guerrilla leaders stanched the defections by discipline and terror. Hunger and exhaustion tried the resolve of many guerrillas, but defection was also risky, for the Nationalists put defectors to the test by pressing them into dangerous missions against their old comrades.

Factional quarrels developed between proponents of rival strategies and between different generations of guerrillas. For example, some who joined the revolution during the Three-Year War purged veterans who had "passed the gate" in "easier" days.[3] Regional differences became especially important. Many of those in charge of the guerrillas at the start of the Three-Year War were outsiders appointed by higher party authorities. These included Nationalist army officers who had defected to the Communists and found it difficult to switch to guerrilla warfare. Local Communists resented these central plants and frequently turned on them after 1934. These purges were tiny imitations of the purges of the early 1930s; proportionately, they probably did more harm.

Party leaders encouraged the ranks mainly by the promotion of group solidarity and the use of terror against dissidents, but education also played a crucial role in motivating the guerrillas to look beyond their present misery. The guerrillas were scattered along the borders of eight provinces, often ignorant of events and trends and of changes in party policy and under frequent enemy attack. What is surprising is not that they sometimes made wrong decisions but that the overwhelming majority of them accepted the United Front when it was sprung on them. One of the main reasons they held out for so long after 1934 and complied so swiftly with the new policy in 1937 was the schooling they had received in the mountains. Books were scarce there, and few guerrillas could read. But some of the guerrilla leaders were educated and resourceful people who had earlier taught for a living. During periods of quiet after 1934, they wrote literacy textbooks and ran classes in politics.

Most survivors of the initial hecatomb probably continued to identify with the party. They were aware of the advantages of national and regional ties and sought them in different ways, for the most part unavailingly. Guerrillas everywhere closely scanned the local press for news of the party and even fought battles to get newspapers. The news of Chiang Kai-shek's release at Xi'an in December 1936 and of the new moderate policies at first angered many guerrilla leaders, but most of them loyally adjusted to the new line.

In 1937, the Yan'an leaders sent messengers south with secret directives for the guerrillas and assigned cadres to beef them up ideologically. Despite bad communications and continuing harassment, the guerrillas assembled at NFA staging areas in Wannan (South Anhui) within just four months, leaving behind a tiny handful of recusants and rejectionists.

Policy Changes after 1934

It has always been dangerous in the CCP to confess to consulting expediency above principle. In the real world, party activists constantly improvised and fell back on old remedies. But in their reports, they rarely admitted to such practices, instead dressing up impromptu unorthodoxies in conformist garb to escape charges of opportunism, feudal mentality, or worse. During the early stages of the rearguard action, unreflecting "leftism" and failure to adjust military tactics to the new conditions often led to the pursuit of wildly inappropriate political goals. The facade of soviet government, even at the provincial level, was maintained in some regions even beyond the summer of 1935. *Baojia* heads were sometimes killed in large numbers, with the inevitable result that the authorities stepped up their drives against the Communists. But political retreat was as indispensable as military retreat if the stay-behinders were to survive.

The southern guerrillas extemporized on an unprecedented scale, but still they prided themselves on having stuck by party proposals. First, they clung to basic party principles. Policy was never sacrosanct in the Chinese communist movement. Most southern Communists dropped impractical slogans, but they secretly kept the soviet "signboard" and were firmly resolved to start dividing the land again as soon as the new "high tide" came. (They were not, of course, alone in changing names and policies. Even in the north, land revolution was first modified and then suspended after 1935. In this sense, policy evolution in the south was a rough, unheard overture, in a wild flourish of instruments, to the main drama that was to start in Shaanbei in 1936.) Second, most southern Communists promoted the party's policy of resistance to Japan. Third, the policy switches made after 1934 were legitimized by the directives from Zunyi ordering a turn to policies "appropriate to guerrilla areas" and thus absolving the rearguard from impossible obligations.

Not all stay-behinders received these directives, and those who did were not always unanimous about their meaning. In the Chinese communist movement, to switch policies without precise instructions was a gamble that could cost one's head (though failing to switch could also be fatal). Those left behind in the south had little tradition of independent policy-making; at the end of the Three-Year War they reported in fear and trembling on their innovations; it was with great relief that they learned that in the main they had done the right things.

Changes were restricted largely to public policy; the party's internal structures changed less, except insofar as they were simplified. Guerrillas kept up not only party cells and committees wherever possible but also the system of purges. Purges probably thinned the ranks more than any other factor, including enemy attacks. For the obedient core, the Three-Year War was a period of intense bonding, but for dissenters it was a sentence of death or of banishment from the revolution. Even minor differences were often viewed as intolerable; without a soviet state or economy to stabilize loyalties, the only tactic that remained was terror.

Military policy entered a period of experimentation and innovation. In former core soviets and core units of the Red Army, the change was sudden and more or less outright. At first, many such units stuck rigidly to old tactics, but in early 1935, they turned to guerrilla warfare. Some regions had never developed beyond the guerrilla stage and did not need to change. The tactics they adopted were not new, despite Xiang Ying's claim that they had developed tactical principles that were uniquely instructive and a necessary supplementation of earlier guerrilla tactics.[4]

In other areas of policy, leaders of the Three-Year War can claim with greater justification to have perfected useful tactics. Their adoption of new methods in "external work" was neither swift nor uniform. Some changes happened earlier than others; some regions changed sooner than the rest. The new policies and tactics were more flexible, more sensitive to local pressures, and more mindful of the party's limitations. The change in direction was sometimes accompanied by power struggles and defections by the defeated party. Rearguard leaders faced two urgent challenges. They had to redefine their relationship to the outside world now that their organization in the villages was smashed; and they had to devise a milder political program, for while a strong organization can afford aggressive policies, a weak, exhausted one must trim according to expediency.

White Skin, Red Heart

The guerrillas needed new networks of support to replace the ones that had been destroyed. All but a few of their liaison stations had been closed down, and those that remained were in constant danger of discovery. But without a supporting base in the villages, the guerrillas were cut off from intelligence and supplies. Their solution was to subvert existing networks rather than set up new ones. Instead of trying to smash the *baojia*, they developed a "double-edged" policy of isolating reactionaries by winning over those officials who occupied "middle" positions or turning them into double-dealers.

As long as the guerrillas were too weak to restore the soviet, they would strive to "turn the *baojia* into a red joint defense organization." They rebuilt their networks parasitically and even extended their tentacles into the *lianbao* [security network] that linked the *baojia* above village level. At the same time they sapped the foundations of the militias set up against them; in many areas, they either controlled these militias or struck secret pacts with them. Forming such bonds was not difficult, for local office was dangerous and unpopular. Those pressed into it were on the front line of the struggle against communism and were isolated and vulnerable. Many officials were related to Communists by ties of kinship or schooling. Many had themselves been Communists in the past and were susceptible to pressure, especially after the guerrillas softened their stance toward those who had fallen away from the party. Through a mixture of terror, blackmail, and social manipulation, the guerrillas won over many such leaders, or at least fixed them on a neutral course. In some cases, they infiltrated party members into office. Converts or party agents were called inverted radishes or sweet potatoes: people with white skins and red hearts. Double-dealers were called "agents of an intermediate color," and the territory they controlled was called gray or yellow. The old dichromic opposition between red and white gave way to a polychrome through which the chameleonlike guerrillas could move with greater freedom. In some mountain districts, almost the entire *baojia* system came under communist control.

In some regions, the guerrillas worked through Fellow Provincials Associations and exploited distant kinship ties of their supporters in the mountains. Guerrillas in most places formed alliances with marginal or dissident social groups, including bandits (especially "social" bandits), members of Daoist sects, and even monks, all of whom they had tried to destroy in the past. Sipping blood with bandits and "spirit soldiers" increased the guerrillas' security, opened new networks to them in the villages, and even opened channels to Nationalist politicians with criminal or sect ties. But such alliances were risky: some bandits and sect leaders fell out with the Communists and attacked them, and some Communists "changed color," though most kept a safe political distance from their allies.

In the past, "outsider" Communists—usually people from the towns or Red Army professionals—had tended to lord it over the "country bumpkins." After 1934, the balance of power shifted the other way. In some regions, rearguard leaders tried to engineer a change of attitude by calling for the "localization of cadre" and for outsiders to learn from natives. Often the problem was resolved by violence in which local Communists almost invariably bested the cosmopolitans.

The guerrillas had to devise new policies to accord with the new strategy of subversion and alliance, of maximum advantage with minimum friction. Their campaigns were designed to contain the counterrevolution, to win support in classes they had previously attacked, and to restore their base in the mountains by reversing the government's depopulation measures. They were powerless to roll back Chiang Kai-shek's Thermidor, but they tried to retrieve some popularity by campaigning to mitigate its least popular consequences. In Minxi (West Fujian), they campaigned with some success to sustain land reform; elsewhere, they tried to win support by campaigning for lower rents and interest, by seizing grain and secretly distributing it to the peasants, and by opposing government conscription. They were highly successful in combining legal, semi-legal, and illegal actions in support of their campaigns. The Nationalist drive against the guerrillas independently created new issues on which they could campaign. Communists in Minxi campaigned vigorously for an end to the offensive, on the grounds that setting fire to the forests destroyed capitalist industry.

Depopulation was the Nationalists' most effective weapon against the guerrillas. Without a base, the Communists lacked moral support, intelligence, material supplies, and cover. The guerrillas' main concern was to reconstruct a civilian base by mobilizing deportees to petition for the right to return to the mountains. They also tried to befriend any traffickers who slipped through the blockade. Communists in many regions stepped forward as champions of the sojourners and itinerants whose livelihood had suffered as a result of the siege.

The most powerful issue on which guerrillas could win support among the educated classes was resistance to Japan, though this issue was not everywhere equally resonant. However, even where it was not yet a burning political issue, guerrillas often used it as an excuse to squeeze money from the rich. Many guerrillas eventually gave up "fines," outright robbery, and ransoming as ways of raising funds and switched instead to a system of "contributions to the anti-Japanese resistance." Most of them scaled down their financial demands on *tuhao* (local bullies) to "prevent contradictions intensifying."

The Guerrillas and the People

The proudest boast of veterans of the Three-Year War is that they survived because of the "selfless support" of the masses. "We changed all our struggles into struggles of us and the masses," said Xiang Ying. "The masses became our ears, our eyes, our hands, our feet."[5] This claim is, of course, echoed by mainland historians. It is not entirely disingenuous, for the term *masses* has a special meaning in this context. But the evidence speaks against it in all its customary senses. Some guerrillas were less isolated than others, but even in periods of "stabilization" most of them spent months on end flitting between mountain tops in isolation from society, only occasionally descending to kill local reactionaries or collect "contributions."

The Xianggan (Hunan-Jiangxi) case is particularly instructive. According to Xiang Ying, the Three-Year War had a stronger mass base than the Zhu-Mao struggle in Xianggan's Jinggangshan in the late 1920s. But by 1934, Jinggangshan was barred to the guerrillas, not by Nationalists but by the Hakka irregulars who had previously backed Mao. Mountain people may have held the guerrillas in awe, but many also held them at arm's length, for they saw them as fire spirits who either torched the villages themselves or brought Nationalist fire-raisers down onto them. The guerrillas were "constantly moving and . . . unable to build a base anywhere," admitted Xiang in a candid moment; they made their beds in the forests.[6] The flags they raised were not banners of mass support but markers of territory that they had all but lost.

How, then, did the guerrillas manage to survive? At times, they lived almost exclusively off the land and their own resources, but whenever conditions allowed, they tried to "localize" their organization and outlook. To do so, they first had to drop the pretense that they represented a national soviet state. They had to educate themselves to respect local cadres, learn from local people, study local customs, and regard the local area as their home.

"Localization," even where it was successful, cannot be equated with restoring a mass base, which implies a close identity and mutual dependence between the party and a community or class that wants social change and is mobilized to bring it about. Only a small minority of guerrillas achieved ties to society that met these criteria, even by their minimal definition. The great majority were not based on organized mass followings whose interests they represented and elevated into political programs. Instead, they lived on society's margins, stretching out tendrils into it, learning its ways, and studying its social arrangements not to change it but to strike deals with it. Their targets were generally not whole communities but individual power holders, strategically placed networks, and marginal groups. The guerrillas gained food, protection, and intelligence from such deals; the targets won promises of immunity or of support against their enemies. These deals created a vicious circle: they resulted from a lack of popular support, and they made campaigning for such support on radical grounds unnecessary and even undesirable.

Because China in the 1930s was a kinship-based society, it is not surprising that kin ties were a main target of communist manipulation. Many guerrilla leaders were descended from the powerful lineages that stretched like membranes across the provincial backlands. The Nationalists killed relatives of the Communists to intimidate these lineages, but they were rarely able to destroy such ties altogether. Guerrilla leaders were also able to knit other sorts of ties into networks of support. Most had grown up with men who now enjoyed influence in local society. Ever since Chiang Kai-shek's victory in 1927, relations between the rural elite and the new Nationalist administration had been tense and troubled. In the late 1920s, the Communists had tried to profit from these tensions by infiltrating conservative militias in the villages, and they had exploited family and social connections to do so.

At first, their radicalism alienated many of these potential allies. But by 1935, the Communists no longer represented a revolutionary threat in the villages. Moreover, new targets for them had emerged among the many former Communists who had become minor officials. Such people were vulnerable to extortion and appeals. Sometimes the guerrillas created networks by armed force, kidnapping people or holding their relatives for ransom to force them to cooperate. Afterward, the victims, having become the guerrillas' accessories, had little choice but to become their partners.

Secret networks and links of this sort were far more important to the guerrillas' survival than mobilization on class grounds. Official historians describe the Chinese Revolution as a revolution against "feudalism" as well as against capitalism and imperialism. But the links mobilized after 1934 were in many ways strikingly feudal, just as the bonds between communist patriarchs and their guerrilla followers were bonds of feudal loyalty. The strong "feudal" flavor of communism in the Three-Year War contrasted markedly with the bureaucratic-centralist character of the party in the north, and this contrast explains some of the tensions that arose between the two traditions after 1937.

Although most border dwellers had learned to fear the Communists, some continued to believe that the "Red Army will return" and were prepared to risk their lives for it. These people were the true "masses" (or *qunzhong*) of the Three-Year War; but in this case, "masses" meant no more than tiny nests of civilian supporters, which is why writers on the Three-Year War are not embarrassed to record the support that "one *qunzhong*" or "a handful of *qunzhong*" gave to the guerrillas. These masses included young people who had been brought up under the soviet and indoctrinated in its ideology, older people with sons in the Red Army, and women.

Young women played a crucial role in obtaining intelligence and supplies for the guerrillas, carrying messages for them, healing and tending them, and—occasionally—fighting. In Tingrui, some 15 percent of party activists after 1934 were women, compared with something like one in two thousand on the Long March. Many young women who had become confident and "politically aware" under the soviet cherished the rights they had gained through the revolution. Women were therefore more conspicuous in the party in Gannan, Minbei (North Fujian), and Minxi than in Mindong (East Fujian), where there had been no Long March (and thus no shortage of young men) and no strong and rooted soviet to run night schools for young women. Women could move around more freely than men after the worst of the repression was over. Women activists provided an important element of continuity after 1934 and again after 1937: when the majority of men left Tingrui to join the NFA in 1938, all the women activists stayed behind.

If enough individuals, especially important individuals, started working for the Communists in a remote or isolated village, the "color" of the place changed and the Communists hoisted a secret flag over it. Once a village had changed sides, support for the Communists became involuntary and automatic. The party could then move from surreptitious control to an open parade of armed force.

The Long March led to a feminization of the party in the old soviet bases. With the men gone, violent struggle was replaced by milder and subtler tactics, and women's contribution became more important. It also propelled into the front line other people previously on the margins of political life. These groups included outlaws, solitary traders, and religious dissidents: people whom the party in the past had ignored, scorned, or liquidated. The Long March took the Red Army out of Han society and into contact with "tribal" peoples in the remote west. The southern Communists' three-year trek through the wilderness similarly brought some of them into close contact with non-Han peoples on China's internal frontiers in the uplands. The She, with their tightly knit communities, strong ethnic identity, and thick mesh of kinship ties, were an ideal ally for Ye Fei's guerrillas. Once a She village had turned "red," it became an unshakable bastion of the party. But She assistance was not selfless. A red village perched high in the mountains was unlikely to be troubled by rent collectors, tax collectors, or the press-gang. The Mindong guerrillas brought the villagers work, a trickle of loot, a few services (including that of a Red Army doctor), and the chiliastic promise of a society without classes and the state. Here the party did not so much represent an economic interest as create one.

A Comparative Ecology of the Three-Year War

Seas of ink have flowed explaining what causes revolutions and what determines their success. Such explanations are often an exercise in comparison. The scale of comparison is often vast, and the results are correspondingly crude. The Three-Year War permits a more minute comparison of the ecology of revolution. It involved communist movements grappling with similar problems in different regions over a similar span of time, and these common features alleviate some of the problems that bedevil broader studies.

None of these movements escaped the general repression, but some bounced back higher than others. A crude measure of their resilience is the size of the contingent that each delivered to the NFA in early 1938, effectively the differential survival rate. While the numbers that came down the mountains are not a perfect index, they are the most obvious and reliable quantitative measure available. Moreover, they reflect the close relationship in the Chinese revolution between military success and political organization. One might further object that my comparison takes little account of the different starting sizes of the different rearguards, but this omission is broadly justifiable: by 1935 rearguards everywhere had been cut down to roughly the same size.

Veterans of the Three-Year War and communist historians have advanced various theories about why the guerrillas succeeded in outwitting their pursuers. These propositions are asserted rather than argued, and they are cast at a level that is too general to be useful. They have not been tested empirically, for example by measuring their ability to predict regional variance in success. Instead, they are imposed on events and proclaimed incontrovertible. Such an approach is only to be expected, since party history in China embodies general "truths" not subject to empirical investigation. Even so it is interesting to examine these explanations for clues about the conditions that led to success or failure in the Three-Year War. Here I present and test a collection of hypotheses formulated by communist observers. These are not hypotheses entertained by Marxist theoreticians but rather post hoc explanations by party activists (though these two categories overlap). I use them more as a framework of cues on which to hang my own reflections than because I necessarily take them seriously as sociological explanations.

This analysis reveals little or nothing about the origins of the Chinese revolution, for the Three-Year War was a period of massive retreat. Many of its findings are specific to the Three-Year War, which was a unique interlude in the revolution. But there are important parallels between the position of guerrillas in the Three-Year War and that of the party in South China during the War of Resistance against Japan and the civil war of 1946–49 (whose southern campaigns are often called the second Three-Year War). Insofar as my reflections show why some rearguards failed, they will throw light on causes of the communist defeat in 1934. Insofar as they show why some rearguards succeeded, they will throw general light on ways in which mature communist movements can best secure support when under pressure. Guerrilla efforts to re-establish support in areas where the revolution had been repelled in 1934 also have parallels with the NFA's venture into eastern China after 1937, and the same people led both endeavors.

Is it legitimate to treat the Three-Year War as a single and integral episode? The answer must be yes. The course of the war in its main bases was broadly uniform. Most guerrilla units had a common origin in the decisions of 1934, and all but a few eventually came together in the NFA. All the guerrillas were isolated from the party center for long periods; their bases were invaded and broken up into pieces; they lacked ties to guerrillas in other areas; and their links to local society were tenuous at best. Even so, there are striking and important differences between the guerrilla regions in environmental constraints and opportunities and in the strategic choices made by local leaders.

In the past, local historians took pains to stress the orthodox character of movements led by local people, but in the 1980s, they were just as likely to dwell on the special nature and achievements of local movements. In the 1970s, the Three-Year War was described in a monotone. Today, it is revealed as a richly varied episode in party history. Some of its leaders were pragmatists; others were dogmatists, hideaways, or adventurists. Some bases were old, others were young, and a few were new; some were flattened, others contracted. Some guerrillas were active in regions where the soviet had been weak, others where it had been strong. Some movements were home grown and others transplanted before the start of the Long March; still others pulled up their roots after 1934 and sought new sanctuaries. Some stay-behinders had always been guerrillas; others had been regular members of the Red Army. Some units shrank to a few dozen people or even to a handful, others set up independent regiments, and still others died away. The differences were eventually to be ironed out by the NFA, but in the Three-Year War they were paramount.

The geography of the bases varied hugely from north to south and from east to west. These differences bore centrally on guerrilla ecology, many memoirs attest. Guerrillas fought mainly in the wild, with little shelter, medicine, or equipment; the weather had a direct impact on life in their bivouacs. The climate differs markedly between Minxi, Minnan (South Fujian), and Ganyue, on one hand, and the bases further north and further inland, on the other. Winter in the Dabie Mountains can be extremely harsh and lasts for three to four months; in Minxi, Minnan, and Ganyue the winter is raw and damp, but less cold. Guerrillas often lived "like kings" in the gentle mountain climate of the south. Further inland, however, where nature was less clement, they paid a heavy toll in health and life to snow, rain, strong winds, and cloying fogs. Climate strongly affected morale. It was better to sleep rough on a southern mountain than on a northern mountain, and it was easier to find food in the evergreen forests of the subtropical south than in the deciduous forests further north.

The fourteen bases of the Three-Year War can be grouped into three main regions: the bases of the coastal provinces (including the Zhe [Zhejiang], Min, and Yue bases); those in and around Jiangxi and north of Ganyue; and those north of the Yangtze. Political differences between these regions were significant, and national events affected the regions in different ways. The 1936 Liang Guang incident provided a big opening for guerrillas in the coastal provinces, who changed their policies as a result of it and gained in numbers. The Eyu and Eyuwan bases were not directly affected by the Liang Guang incident, but because of their northerly position, they caught reverberations of the Xi'an incident sooner than their comrades in the south. Most of the Jiangxi bases—partly for geopolitical reasons—were not directly affected by either incident. Armed religious sects proliferated in the villages of Fujian and Zhejiang, and in Fujian, some allied with the Communists. Fujian is divided by mountains, and in the 1930s its settlements were scattered and disunited. It was not a normal region of Nationalist control. All these factors benefited the guerrillas. The bases north of the Yangtze, too, were able to draw on a heritage of organized dissent in the villages. Historically, they had enjoyed greater autonomy from the party center than bases south of the river, particularly those in Jiangxi. This independence was a blessing in the Three-Year War, when local roots became all-important. As for Jiangxi, in late 1934 it was a prize and a symbol for Chiang Kai-shek and therefore a special target of his purges. Gannan was a political symbol for the Communists and therefore the focus of Xiang Ying's defensive effort. The bases of the Three-Year War north of the Yangtze and near the Fujian coast were unique in the revolution; they were both old soviet areas and near Japanese forward lines after 1937. They remained party bases from the late 1920s until the end of the civil war in 1949.

Most theories about why revolutions happen focus on origins rather than on what keeps revolutions going after the first surge of enthusiasm has ebbed. These theories have little direct relevance for the Three-Year War, which was primarily defensive. However, propositions abound about the causes of Xiang's "precious victory" in the south. Few try to explain it solely in economic terms, but the theory that class conflict is the ultimate "moving power" of all history is so routine in Chinese social science that it is an obvious starting point in any search for hypotheses. Most other communist explanations of the "victory" look to political, organizational, and strategic factors rather than to the usual social and economic ones.

One common assumption is that places where the communist movement was strongest before October 1934 would more readily support a guerrilla movement. Another is that since the Three-Year War was a defensive war, the further the guerrillas moved from concentrations of Nationalist power and the deeper they ensconced themselves in the rugged mountains and remote forests, the better their chances of survival and revival. They could improve their prospects still further by seeking out regions where there were "contradictions" to exploit. According to a further proposition, even more important for success than these "objective" factors were "subjective" factors like quality of leadership, strength of organization, and degree of unity. Only experienced leaders could "strengthen thought," invent new policies to meet new circumstances, and think out new, flexible fighting tactics. However, links to the party center were (so the theory goes) the surest way of avoiding "subjectivist" mistakes. Class struggle, a revolutionary tradition, geographic isolation, splits in the enemy camp, resourceful leaders, and a line to the CC or the cities—these, then, are the factors to which Communists attribute the southern triumph.

Since none of the guerrillas enjoyed broad support after 1934, the proposition that success correlated with the intensity of class struggle must be false. That assertion does not mean that the Communists failed completely to stimulate class struggle or that they did not occasionally benefit from it. In their three strongest bases (Minxi, Mindong, and Eyuwan) they connected a few isolated settlements with a healthy tissue of communist organization. They mounted spasmodic campaigns on economic issues in all regions of the Three-Year War. In Minxi, they even succeeded in preventing the return of land to the landlords in many villages. Elsewhere, they waged campaigns against rent, tax, and conscription. But these campaigns were often started against the wishes of the masses and without their cooperation, for many peasants feared the consequences of going along with the Communists for a second time. Eventually, the guerrillas worked out ways of binding these people with them in complicity. However, these campaigns were a case not of class struggle producing revolution but of revolution producing class struggle. Class struggle became progressively less conspicuous as guerrillas switched their attention to the more lucrative business of forging links with local power holders.

A Typology of Revolutionary Bases

The second proposition is that guerrillas held out best in areas that had boasted a strong revolutionary tradition before 1935. This hypothesis is more promising than the abstract class-struggle theory, for it concedes that the Communists after 1934 dwelt in a world that they themselves had shaped.

It is easy to show that the mere presence of a revolutionary tradition in a region could not in itself guarantee success after 1934. In the 1930s, several sorts of revolutionary tradition coexisted in China, from the highly centralized to the parochial. It is far from true that the stronger the tradition, the firmer the resistance. On the contrary, deep red bases like the Central Soviet fell almost completely to the Nationalists, while newer ones prospered. To understand the Three-Year War, it is useful to divide both bases and leaders into classes and to see how the resulting typologies interact. These typologies are intended mainly to help explain developments in the Three-Year War, but they are also of wider relevance.

There are two kinds of base that we can call local. A local base was generally remote from the party's central authority. Soviet power in local bases was limited, compromised, and generally responsive to local conditions. The characteristic military style in these bases was irregular, though they were frequently required to contribute levies of men to the party's regular armies elsewhere. The degree of central meddling in such bases is the criterion for a further distinction between autonomous and subordinate local bases.

A good example of an autonomous local base is Mindong, which flourished in relative obscurity and suffered minimal interference. Xianggan, Xiang'egan, and the main Minzhegan base are examples of subordinate local bases that were subjected to a great deal of intervention by the central leaders, who imposed personnel on them and taxed them for soldiers and supplies. For example, local Communists in the Minbei leadership were removed from power and replaced by Jiangxi natives, whereas in Mindong, practically the entire leadership was made up of Mindong natives. Subordinate local bases were sometimes evacuated for a while if they could be preserved only at the cost of more important places. Communist presence in an autonomous local base tended in contrast to be continuous. Eyuwan lies somewhere between these two extremes. Eyuwan's leader, the dissident Zhang Guotao, was appointed by the center, but he left the base's layer of indigenous leaders largely intact. Subordinate local bases like Xiang'egan, Xianggan, and Xiangnan were created largely by outsiders, who imposed red power at gunpoint. The Eyuwan base, like Mindong and Minxi, was native born and bred.

The Gannan and Minxi bases before October 1934 formed interrelated categories that can be described as central and peripheral. Gannan was the hub of soviet life in the early 1930s. Soviet power here was least constrained, mobilization of people and goods was most radical, and the communist elite's local ties were slightest, for centralizers quickly won the upper hand after their arrival in Gannan in 1929; indigenous leaders were neutralized or engulfed.

Ruijin, the soviet capital, was different from other parts of Gannan. In Ruijin, the party had few indigenous roots before 1929, and the Red Army took power there by force of arms. The Minxi base was physically joined to Gannan and was nominally reckoned as part of the Central Soviet, but its origins and character function were distinct. Minxi Communists set up their own guerrillas before the arrival of the Zhu De–Mao Zedong army, and they independently developed their own radical land-reform plan, unlike their more conservative cousins in Gannan. The movement in Minxi kept its local character throughout the soviet period. The same people who set up the party in the 1920s remained in charge until 1938. Minxi Communists generally tried to steer clear of the extreme "commandist" style of the regime in Ruijin. They adjusted their policies pragmatically to local conditions, and their military commanders preferred to fight by guerrilla means. But because Minxi was close to Ruijin, its leaders were inevitably drawn into the affairs of the capital. This involvement diminished their autonomy, but it broadened their political horizons and their range of expertise. Over the years, the communist movement in Minxi evolved into a hybrid between the Central Soviet and local movements outside Gannan.

Not all bases of the Three-Year War had a revolutionary tradition. Some regions, including Zhe'nan (South Zhejiang) and, to a lesser extent, Xiangnan (South Hunan), were relatively blank pages, and Zhexi'nan (Southwest Zhejiang) was altogether blank. All three bases were created by outsiders after 1934. These new bases permit a negative test of the proposition that Communists held out in the Three-Year War because they were able to build on past achievements.

Centralism and Localism in the Three-Year War

The regions that salvaged the most "living forces" for the NFA were Minxi and Eyuwan. The Mindong guerrillas also emerged exceptionally strong from the war. Because of poor communications, Communists in Eyuwan and Mindong had never been closely tied to the center and had long been acting independently. The Minxi party, too, was led by local people whose exposure to the wider movement had not estranged them from their roots. Local bases like Xianggan and Xiang'egan, founded by outsiders and treated as dispensable auxiliaries by the central leaders, emerged less creditably from the Three-Year War, as did locally founded bases like Minbei in which communist outsiders had strongly intervened. The Minzhegan base, founded by local Communists under Fang Zhimin, collapsed entirely, partly because it had been ruthlessly milked by Ruijin and then crushed by the defeat of Fang Zhimin's expedition. Among the weakest bases by 1937 was that in Ganyue under Xiang Ying and Chen Yi. Ganyue was a local base, but it abutted on the Central Soviet and lacked strong and willful local leaders. After the death of Li Letian, its early leader, in 1936, power over the Ganyue guerrillas passed even more surely into the hands of Xiang and Chen, both central leaders, one a dogmatist, the other a pragmatist.

New bases founded by outsiders in 1934 and 1935 either collapsed entirely (in Min'gan and Annanyongde) or only just survived (in Xiangnan, Wanzhegan, and Zhe'nan). In early 1935, the Xiangnan base expanded quickly, and in 1936, the bases in Zhe'nan and Wanzhegan seemed to represent a real threat to the government. In regions with little experience of civil war and soviet power, the Communists could achieve quick breakthroughs but could not translate them into lasting gains. Guerrillas in the old central base in Gannan did about as well as guerrillas in the new base in Xiangnan, but less well than in Zhe'nan.

Minxi apart, the bases that fared best after 1934 were local bases founded by local people and subject to the least central interference. Next best were local bases founded by outsiders and subject before 1935 only to indirect control by the center. The bases that fared worst were new bases and bases previously under direct central control. Minxi was a special case. Although it adjoined the central base, its origins and early history were distinct. Its proximity to Ruijin attuned its leaders to the danger of "leftist" imports and raised barriers that reduced their damage.

Psychologically, politically, and militarily, local leaders were better prepared for the conditions that governed the war than were leaders from stable soviets. They were intuitive adepts of guerrilla warfare and of Minxi's "Luo Ming line," the heresy that sought an end to blanket ordinances. Despite Ruijin's condemnation of Luo Ming, many opponents of extreme centralism continued to follow his approach. Unlike the regular Red Army soldiers scattered across the south after 1934, who could address local people only through interpreters, these Communists spoke local languages. Languages were especially important in the Three-

Year War, when local militias were used in pacification drives and even a wrongly pronounced syllable could betray a guerrilla.

Communists in local and peripheral bases had more experience conciliating their opponents than those in central bases and regular Red Army units, and they were thus better prepared for a period in which they could no longer play the lord. They also had more ties to the market towns and villages, so they could more easily strike alliances with malcontents. Daoist sects had their lodges throughout Fujian and Zhejiang, but it was mainly in Fujian that the party won their support, for most guerrillas in the Min bases were local people with local ties. The guerrillas in Zhejiang were outsiders led by regular Red Army officers with a more orthodox and conventional view of revolution. The alliances in Fujian were crucial to the success of the guerrillas. The Daoists were powerful in the villages, they had channels down into the valleys, and they thought themselves indestructible.

Because "leftism" had been less extreme in local bases in the early 1930s, villagers there were less likely to be disillusioned with communism and alienated from the party. In old "leftist" areas, said Minxi's Lin Jian, erstwhile supporters had become apathetic or downright hostile to the Communists. "But in Yanyonghang [in Minxi] and in other old soviet bases where the 'leftist' line had ruled only briefly, the masses were not only highly aware but . . . understood how to apply different methods of struggle."[7] Xiang Ying's last-ditch stand in Gannan was a final blow to the party's support there. Xiang, a dogmatic centralist, temporized for months before yielding to Chen Yi, who had favored an early switch to guerrilla warfare. Most local bases had made the switch well in advance of the start of the Long March. This tactic paid off, for the Nationalists put most resources into quelling the most obvious trouble spots.

The proposition that regions with a strong revolutionary tradition stood up best in the Three-Year War holds only with important qualifications. A centralist tradition like that in Gannan spelled disaster. In areas where soviet power had been most extensive, counterrevolution was most complete, partly because the Nationalists scoured these areas with particular thoroughness, and partly because disillusion with communism developed in direct proportion to how closely people had experienced the effects of central party rule. Economic crisis caused by war and the commandeering of countless men, animals, and tons of grain, extensive purges, and the final disillusion caused by the Long March and the collapse of the rearguard destroyed morale. Even though the communist movement in Gannan reverted to indigenous leadership after 1934, the damage had been done. Regions like Minxi, Mindong, and Eyuwan with an indigenous tradition in some degree resistant to central meddling weathered the storms best and yielded the richest harvests. Local bases like Xianggan, Xiang'egan, Minbei, and Minzhegan founded by outsiders or subjected to excessive central interference slumped in 1935 and then marked time. New bases without a revolutionary tradition either collapsed entirely or just scraped through. Mindong is an exception. The difference between Mindong and Zhe'nan, the newest base in the Three-Year War, is that Mindong was founded a year earlier than Zhe'nan and by indigenous leaders, whereas the Zhe'nan base was founded by Red Army regulars.

Political Geography

Three of the four remaining propositions about the causes of success in the Three-Year War are best treated collectively, for they are all rooted in political geography. One is that physical isolation was the key to survival. Another is that guerrillas benefited from links to urban party centers. Finally, there is the proposition that guerrillas survived best where they could exploit splits among their enemies.

All guerrilla units fled to the mountains after 1934, but though their natural environments were similar, there were important differences resulting from circumstance and choice. Some regions had more strategic potential than others, and whether this potential was used or not depended on the strategists.

The assumption that safety for stay-behinders lay in maximum seclusion behind rock walls is false. Some insulation was indispensable; too much was suffocating. Guerrillas far from Nationalist garrisons were unlikely to be caught off guard, but they were also unlikely to light on new political opportunities. Strategy is often defined as the art of calculated risk. After 1934, an obsession with security was just as harmful as reckless belligerence. The guerrillas had to strike a balance between hiding and flaunting themselves, between "passive skulking" and "blind activism."

Xianggan and Ganyue, where the guerrillas were most obsessed with security, were among the weakest of the bases that did not actually collapse. Xianggan was physically remote from the scenes of important political events, and its leader's paranoid introversion sealed it even more tightly. The Communists in Ganyue were at the hub of several guerrilla bases and on the border between forces of Chiang Kai-shek and of his rival Chen Jitang, but they remained largely invisible. Xiang Ying and Chen Yi both set greater store by preserving old forces than by developing new ones. Some bases were too secluded; others were not secluded enough. The bases in Minzhewan'gan, particularly the Zhe'nan base, were close to the heartland of the GMD and to the birthplaces of Chiang Kai-shek and his general, Chen Cheng, so they were more likely to become targets of repression.

Not all bases were stuck on the GMD's doorstep or stranded in the outer wilderness. Some were sufficiently insulated to be secure while still keeping tiny windows on the outside world. These openings let in news of major political events that enabled guerrillas to seize new opportunities and stopped them from stagnating or dissolving into their surroundings. On rare occasions, these secret vents and spyholes also allowed the transmission of messages about new directions in party policy. The guerrillas were heartened by the knowledge that communism still survived in the cities and in the north. The outlying soviets had been at the end of the communication chain before 1935. After 1934 intelligence lines from the cities petered out well short of Xiang's headquarters in Ganyue, and these former fringe regions became first rather than last stops on the new, shortened lines of correspondence. Some bases in Fujian and the new base in Zhe'nan were best placed to receive these contacts. Fujian and Zhejiang are coastal provinces with sea links to Shanghai and Hong Kong. Bases in these provinces had secret lines to the big ports along which flowed crucial information. Such contacts were most important in Zhe'nan and Mindong, which had barely got wind of the decisions taken at Zunyi before all radio contact with the center was lost.

The networks run by Fujian bases were quite different in character from those further inland, where guerrilla leaders were lucky if they stayed in touch with their own units, let alone ran lines to the cities or to other bases. Bases in Fujian were linked not only to the ports, which gave them people, provisions, and publications, but also to one another; each reinforced the other in a dialectic of regional cooperation. The Communists in Minxi also used networks created by emigration to spread their message. For example, they made an impact far beyond the mountains by writing to Fellow Provincials Associations in the cities about their proposals for a United Front in 1937. The division between red uplands and white lowlands was clearer cut where "leftism" had been strong than in the old guerrilla areas of Fujian. Communist leaders in Ganyue also used lineage ties to send feelers down onto the plains, but they made little headway.

Accounts differ about the importance of outside party links in shaping the innovations of the Three-Year War. Some say the changes were made in response to directives issued by the party center, for example at Zunyi. Others suggest that the guerrillas worked them out independently. These differences arise partly because some guerrillas received news of Zunyi while others did not, but the differences also have a political explanation. Rearguard veterans like Chen Yi, who supported Mao and welcomed the directives, say that they were crucial; others, like Xiang Ying, caught out by Zunyi, imply that continuity and "native" adjustment were the keys to success. In the 1980s, leaders like Ye Fei also began to claim that they adopted new policies independently after 1934, in accordance with local conditions. Such claims were in part a bid for glory by old men in the twilight of their lives; they were also consonant with the spirit of the 1980s, which valued independent initiative and "seeking truth from facts."

Because remoteness was just as likely as accessibility to inhibit success, the best formula for a strong movement was a middle position. The Annanyongde base, close to Minxi, collapsed because it was too near to the Nationalist garrison at Quanzhou. It was also too near for its own good to the party office in Xiamen, whose proximity left an easy way out for the fainthearted and an easy way in for "leftist" fallacies. The Eyu, Eyuwan, and Mindong bases were all remote from main party centers. Communists from these places say that this remoteness forced them to seek their own solutions to their own problems.[8]

In most cases, it is a tautology to say that the strength of a base was determined mainly by the size of the campaign against it, for the size of the campaign varied with the size of the threat that the base posed. Chiang Kai-shek put most of his effort into pacifying Gannan because Xiang Ying continued to fight large-scale engagements there and refused to concede. Small, inactive bases like Xianggan were less likely to attract attention than large, active ones. Revolutionaries generate their own oppositions by their choice of grounds and tactics. Some bases managed to grow by playing possum. For example, by working secretly and avoiding armed clashes, the relatively successful base in Eyu escaped notice in 1936.[9] All guerrilla leaders sought to minimize opposition and to maximize their chances of survival by retiring to border areas between counties, provinces, and military cliques and by exploiting contradictions among their enemies.

The contradictions that the guerrillas tried to play on ranged from minor tensions in the villages to conflicts among Nationalist armies or between those armies and local elites. These conflicts had a variety of sources: social, economic, political, ethnic, generational, religious, and military. Guerrillas everywhere wiggled the blade of discord in the cracks of rural life and exploited the power vacuum along political borders. But few had the chance to take advantage of bigger schisms. Chiang Kai-shek's campaign against the soviets had not only swept away the Communists but had also extensively undermined Chiang's other regional rivals. The two regions where contradictions gave the Communists most advantage were Eyuwan and Minxi.

In Eyu, Manchurian troops fraternized with communist guerrillas in 1937, and leaders of regional forces opposed to Chiang Kai-shek slipped the Communists money and supplies.[10] In Eyuwan, too, the Communists profited from divisions in the Nationalist camp. In Minxi, they had various contradictions to exploit. Before the Liang Guang incident, they tried to play on anti-Japanese and anti-Chiang sentiment in Minxi's Fujianese garrison. But whatever progress they made came to naught because of the transfer of these Fujianese to Guangdong after the incident (and by the guerrillas' lurch into "leftism"). The Cantonese who took over in Minxi were no well-wishers of Chiang's, and they, too, were susceptible to anti-Japanese agitation. Minxi Communists planted a cell in the Guangdong Army, but their efforts had nowhere near as much effect as those of Communists in Shaanbei on Zhang Xueliang's divisions.

Minxi Communists aimed not only at army targets. The Minxi base was within easy reach of one of southeastern China's main economic centers, around Xiamen and Zhangzhou. Through the local elite ran seams of disaffection at which communist quarriers hacked and blasted in 1936 and 1937. One conflict was between local capitalists and the Guangdong Army, which destroyed profitable bamboo groves in its campaign against the Communists. Another was between local patriots and Japanese soldiers and traders, together with their local or Taiwanese henchmen. Being across the strait from Taiwan, Fujian was vulnerable to Japanese pressure. The Minxi Communists' campaign against Japan won them regard and prepared them better than other guerrillas for the new United Front.

The Quality of Leadership

Subjective factors such as quality of leadership—which according to our final proposition was even more important for victory than objective conditions in the ·different regions—are harder to define and appraise. The Chinese communist definition of good leadership has changed radically over the years. The old belief in forceful and centralized leadership has given way to a more relaxed prescription. Today, a good leader is expected to derive power from esteem rather than from unquestioning obedience. Such a leader prefers rewards to penalties and persuasion to coercion, promotes solidarity over conflict, and consults through established channels before making decisions. Most leaders of the Three-Year War embodied very few of these attributes.

Only a minority were experienced captains of the party. Most had little grounding in theory, and their practical experience was confined to minor posts. Zhe'nan, Ganyue, and Minxi, which were led by experienced leaders, were exceptions. But of the three, only Minxi prospered. One might even conclude that strong leadership fragmented the group, for in Zhe'nan, and, to a lesser extent, in Ganyue, the leadership fell apart amid accusations and counteraccusations. Leaders with less experience—for example, in Mindong and Eyuwan— emerged far stronger from the Three-Year War.

If tolerance is a second measure of good leadership, the results are again inconclusive. Few guerrilla leaders relaxed their internal regimes, and most units were split by struggles between factions. Almost all the winners in these conflicts purged and attacked the losers. Some victims deserted or defected; others died. Confrontations pitted natives against outsiders, guerrillas against Red Army regulars, region against region, "defeatists" against "adventurists," "opportunists" against "leftists," and old Communists against new Communists. Many of these feuds probably involved settling scores that had little to do with politics.

In Ganyue, Chen Yi strove to prevent feuds by urging newcomers to respect local Communists and to learn from them. He took a lenient view of waverers, arguing that it was better to let them go than to hold them against their will. His measures were important for morale. By 1937, the Ganyue remnant was rich in quality (several of its veterans were to have a great influence on China) but poor in number.

Most guerrilla leaders, successful and unsuccessful, purged remorselessly after 1934. Two of the bloodiest purgers, Ye Fei and Gao Jingting, ran two of the best campaigns of the war. Even the Minxi Communists purged one another. Purges resulted in large losses, but, measured in terms of the number of guerrillas, were apparently a stronger cement than the mildness and flexibility advocated by Chen Yi. Some purges coincided with or preceded periods of growth.

According to sociologists, a leader can more easily gain ascendancy over people by courting them than by beating them, for violence and punishment drive followers away; and a cruel and arbitrary leader, according to Machiavelli, engenders paranoia, so the leader is likely to be killed by subordinates. But a leader must first gain a following before he can try to earn its esteem. Chen Yi's authority was unimpeachable: as an adopted son of Ganyue since 1928, he could afford to be magnanimous. Leaders in other regions, who felt less secure, mobilized followers by displaying brute force against their rivals.

The new circumstances after 1934 required new policies; often, the switch involved violent struggles leading to a spiral of terror that welded the survivors of these schisms to the winners. Some people stayed in the mountains, said Ye Fei, "because of the massacre policy of Chiang Kai-shek and especially of local reactionary landlords. . . . They even killed many [communist] traitors, so people had no choice but to continue along the revolutionary road."[11] Would-be defectors also feared the long arm of the party, which, they had been given to believe, stretched everywhere. Though terror may not persuade when it can be avoided, ineluctable terror apparently works only too well. But despite its bonding power, terror devoured talents that the guerrillas sorely needed. It was effective in the short term, but in the long term, Chen Yi's volunteers probably contributed more to the party than the cowed retinues of Gao Jingting or Tan Yubao.

The relative size and complexity of party organization is a third measure of the quality of leadership. The party was best organized in Minxi, where the rearguard's strongest leading team sometimes had logistic help from coastal cities. The Minxi Communists maintained an extensive system of committees and published a steady flow of leaflets, pamphlets, and journals. In Ganyue, too, Xiang Ying and Chen Yi did their best to maintain party organization, though to less effect. However, other bases—particularly those in Mindong, Eyuwan, and Xianggan—were virtual monocracies. Neither the collectives nor the one-man shows had a monopoly on success or failure in the Three-Year War. Neither strong party organization nor leaders' experience and tolerance was the determining factor in the fate of a base.

So far, I have measured success only by numbers, but if we use other criteria, the picture changes. In quantitative terms, Gao Jingting in Eyuwan matched and even surpassed the achievement of the Minxi Communists. But Gao's movement was parochial and self-contained, whereas the Minxi Communists had a broader vision. In 1938, Minxi veterans shot to the top of the NFA and played key roles in the party's rise to power. Eyuwan veterans furnished few figures of any note in party history. In the first few months of 1938, when guerrillas from the southern bases were loyally marching to the front, Gao held back for a while and was criticized as a "mountain-toppist." The conflict between Gao and the NFA command was not resolved even when Gao eventually headed east; and in June 1939, Ye Ting shot him as a "warlord."

The party center mistrusted local loyalties, especially when these were translated into personal loyalties. The Eyuwan leaders were less motivated than were the Minxi leaders to see the revolution through to the end at the national level after 1937. In many bases of the Three-Year War, natives and outsiders fought civil wars within the civil war; the two sides continued to mistrust each other even after 1937. The best prescription for a loyal, competent, and durable movement was neither one-sided "localism" nor a party of cosmopolitans but a leadership like that in Minxi, formed by natives who were knowledgeable about the wider political scene. Here, the distinction between native and professional was less relevant.

I began by formulating some propositions on the basis of Chinese communist theory about the Three-Year War, and I went on to see how far they held good for different regions. The bases that failed were typically those where the party center had previously had the greatest influence, where revolution had been imported, where centralists led the rearguard, or where the party had previously been inactive. The bases that survived best were those founded and led by local pragmatists, defended by guerrillas, neither too secluded nor too exposed, but open to outside influences and opportunities and at the same time secure. There is no consistent correlation between leadership experience and success. Experienced leaders in Ganyue did not do well, whereas experienced leaders in Minxi did extremely well; the most successful campaigns were led by people who made up for their lack of experience by their local ties and knowledge. This is because the Three-Year War involved a switch from the general to the particular, from the center to the periphery, from the valleys to the mountains, from the limelight to the twilight, from being "host" to being "guest."

The Mobilization of All Factors

The southern campaign brings into sharp focus the Chinese Communists' concern in planning their revolution for wider dimensions of time and space. Strategy, the art of marshaling forces over large areas and long periods, is called grand or higher strategy when it correlates closely with national political and other goals. Grand strategy is a good name for the Red Army's disposition of military means over many regions in the mid- to late 1930s. After 1934, the Red Army command achieved no central coordination (not to mention operational management) across its scattered war theaters, but the particular spread of forces in that period was the product of strategic judgment. The strategy depended partly on political and psychological objectives: to signal Nationalist impotence and the invincibility of the revolution, and to drive home the communist claim to represent all China.

We have long been used to fitting the Chinese revolution into geographical slots: the Jiangxi period and the Yan'an period have become so fixed in historical imagination that some even speak of southern and northern phases of the struggle.[12] This view is too simple. Both the Three-Year War and the experience of the NFA show that communist presence in a region was rarely erased even after great defeats. Once the party had sunk roots, it proved remarkably hard to weed out. Nearly everywhere it left some secret marker as evidence for a future claim. The southern bases of the party helped in a small way to relieve pressure on the main Red Army and were the springboards from which Communists vaulted into eastern China in early 1938. Some of these bases remained active throughout the War of Resistance and the subsequent civil war.

This concern to "mobilize all factors" in a grand design is an early example of what later became the hallmark of Maoist strategy. By the mid-1930s, Chinese Communists had trekked from the cities to the mountains and from Gannan to Shaanbei. At each turning point they were loath to relinquish any gain, however small. They were constrained by political considerations to integrate more and more lost battlefields into a "dialectical totality," as they proclaimed each defeat a victory and each retreat an advance. The increasingly military character of the revolution eventually infused strategy into this hopscotch: old bases became subsidiary fronts or future support points in the war.

After 1937, the ERA in the north and the NFA in the east were linked strategically, but the southern leg of the party's strategic tripod bore little weight because too few forces had been left behind in 1934 or 1937, the two turning points in the southern struggle. The Three-Year War bestowed the communist high command with a notion of grand strategy and with the troops, regrouped as the NFA, to realize it. By 1938, the Japanese had created the conditions in central and eastern China for a second communist army to grow apace, beyond the reach of the GMD.

In earlier years, plans for subsidiary fronts to take the heat off the main Red Army had not come to much, mainly because the Communists were unable to commit enough resources to them. In the early 1930s and at the start of the Long March, the transfer of troops from peripheral bases to support concentrated efforts in the main war theaters alienated party supporters in abandoned regions. It even alienated party cadres, who, said Ye Fei, "persevered not for communism but for the local revolution."[13]

Strategists justified the "nationalization" of regional forces by pointing to the interaction between main and ancillary battlefields and the inevitability of defeat at the edges if the center fell, just as party leaders after 1949 justified all-out concentration on steel or grain with the maxim "Once the headrope is pulled up, the meshes of the net will open." But the strategic argument can have convinced few party supporters left behind in the villages, for the headrope was raised too high and the meshes closed.[14]

In late 1937, Mao planned to leave two-fifths of the southern guerrillas behind in the old bases, but he was thwarted by Xiang Ying, who wanted them at the front where he could control them. This case is just one of many in which party leaders strengthened the main force by sacrificing the periphery. As a result, almost all the southern bases fell dormant after 1937, thus failing to fulfill Mao's hopes.

The whittling down of the movement in the south by the evacuations of 1934 and 1937 weakened or destroyed regional traditions of communism and stifled diversity in the party. Communists outside the Red Army's main former garrisons were more likely than those in central bases to moderate their demands on the villages, handle local issues sensitively, and achieve a reciprocal and harmonious relationship with local society. Their transfer north freed them from local constraints and changed their relationship to the villages. On the positive side, it flung the cliques and patriarchs of regional communism into the NFA melting pot.

According to one theory, the CCP's Long March was "dictated by the mandate of political history." The south was too exhausted, physically and mentally, to produce a second revolution; the Communists' historic mission lay in the restless north.[15] This theory, if correct, would justify the abandonment of the south in 1934 and the final withdrawal in 1937. But the record scarcely bears out this apocalyptic view. Parts of southern and central China were still piled high with explosive charge after the main Red Army left. Communists in Fujian and Eyuwan, in particular, preserved thousands of recruits for the NFA. The NFA, far from flocking north after 1937, fought on both banks of the Yangtze and by 1945 had penetrated much further south. The decision in the late 1930s to concentrate the NFA north of the Yangtze was dictated by military strategy, not historical inevitability. Similarly, it was strategic considerations that resolved Chen Yi to strike back south again after setting up a base in Jiangbei in 1940.

The Three-Year War Today

The angle from which Chinese historians view the Three-Year War has changed many times over the last half century. Much of what passes for history in China is important less for itself than for the light it sheds on extrinsic matters of contemporary interest. The party-controlled press devotes huge resources to manufacturing new traditions and updating old ones to match the government's changing goals. Since 1979, the Three-Year War has been spun into a minor legend of the revolution that blends bowdlerized fact and significant fiction, with the aim of producing "pious wonderment and burning ambition" in the Chinese people.[16] Myths and legends are recited to show how things allegedly come to be the way they are and to help keep them so. The expurgated epic of the Three-Year War plays only a humble role in the Chinese communist body of myths and legends, chief among which is the Long March. Some of the virtues celebrated by the major and minor legends—optimism, perseverance, courage, self-sacrifice—are the same. Others, including "heroism in defeat," keeping faith with the masses, and education as an antidote to hard times, are associated mainly with the Three-Year War.

A mythologized Three-Year War has many more potential uses in China now as a counterpoint to the quite different import of the legend of the Long March. Each campaign illustrates an opposite set of aims and values. The Long March symbolizes centralism, homogeneity, and the rise to power of the party's historic leader; the Three-Year War represents polycentrism and regional diversity. The march is celebrated as a new turn after a wrong start; the war exemplifies continuity and loyalty to the victims of party failures. The march was primarily an accomplishment of arms performed by men; the war combined military and civilian forms of struggle and enlisted secret armies of women. The march united the party and brought its different factions into one political line; the war required the creative adjustment of policy to varied circumstance, compromise, improvisation, flexibility, and independent initiative. The march exemplifies urgency and haste, and, as a forced march to safety, has become a symbol of China's hopes for rapid progress toward wealth and power; the war is the tortoise to Mao's hare, the hedgehog to his fox, a symbol of patience and stoical endurance. The march is hailed as an act of immense will that miraculously snatched the Red Army from the jaws of ruin; the virtues of the war were tact, brains, moderation, and its human scale.

Notes

1. This is an interpretative study based on data analyzed in my book *Mountain Fires: The Red Army's Three-Year War in South China, 1934–38* (Berkeley: University of California Press, 1992).

2. Chen Yi, "Nanfang sannian youjizhanzheng" (The Three-Year Guerrilla War in the South), in Museum of the Chinese People's Revolutionary Military History, ed., *Chen Yi yuan shuai fengbei yongcun* (Marshal Chen Yi's Monuments Are Immortal) (Shanghai: People's Press, 1986), 120.

3. Zhang Liren and Ye Jianzhong, "Minbei suqu sufan guangdahuade yixie qingkuang" (Certain Circumstances Concerning the Broadening of the Campaign to Suppress Counterrevolutionaries in the North Fujian Soviet), in *Dangshi ziliao yu yanjiu* (Materials and Research on Party History), no. 4 (1983): 43.

4. Xiang Ying, "Nanfang sannian youjizhanzheng jingyan yu dangqian kangzhande jiaoxun" (The Experience of the Three-Year Guerrilla War in the South and Its Lessons for the Present Resistance War), *Jiefang zhoukan* (Liberation Weekly), 30 October 1937.

5. Ibid.

6. Nym Wales [Helen Foster Snow], *The Chinese Labor Movement* (New York: John Day Company, 1945), 217.

7. Lin Jian, "Lun 'duli zizhu' jiqita" (On "Independence and Initiative" and Other Things), in *Fujian dangshi tongxun* (Fujian Bulletin on Party History), no. 9 (1985): 21.

8. Li Zijian, "Zhonggong Eyu bian dang jianku niandai chuangye jishi" (Record of the CCP's Years of Hardship and Pioneering on the Eyu Border), in *Geming shi ziliao* (Materials on Revolutionary History), no. 9 (1982): 31–32; and Ye Fei, "Zai jiejian Mindong dangshi gongzuozhe shide yici jianghua" (Talk on Receiving Some Mindong Party History Workers), in *Dangshi ziliao yu yanjiu*, no. 8 (1983): 3.

9. Li Zijian, "Zhonggong Eyu bian dang," 32.

10. Ibid., 28–30.

11. Ye Fei, "Huiyi Mindong geming douzheng" (Recalling the Revolutionary Struggle in Mindong), in *Mindong dangshi ziliao yu yanjiu* (Material and Research on Mindong Party History), no. 2 (1983): 5.

12. Bingzhang (Benjamin) Yang, "From Revolution to Politics: The Long March and the Rise of Mao" (Ph.D dissertation, Harvard University, 1986), 339–41.

13. Ye Fei, "Huiyi Mindong geming douzheng," 5.

14. As also happened in 1959, to which Wang Ruoshui was referring when he developed this metaphor. Wang Ruoshui, *Wei rendaozhuyi bianhu* (In Defense of Humanism) (Beijing: Sanlian Press, 1986), 52–53.

15. Yang, "From Revolution to Politics," 349–52.

16. This description of the aim of myths is Erik Erikson's.

Chapter 6

Fits and Starts: The Communist Party in Rural Hebei, 1921–1936

Kathleen Hartford

In the grand overviews of CCP history, our images of the revolution have been shaped by the regional spotlight approach. Historians have woven into their overviews the regionally based experiences that figured either as cases of signal, if temporary success, or as way stations on Mao Zedong's triumphal march to leadership of the party and formulation of a winning strategy. Organizations spring up in one period and one place, are suppressed, and sink out of sight; in the next period, they again spring out of nowhere, in another place, and once more sink out of sight.[1]

The spotlight approach illuminates key actors and events, but leaves in the shadow the action transpiring in the corners of the historical stage. When new actors suddenly step into view, or when the spotlight skips to a new tableau, we have no clue as to where the principals came from, or why, and why we find them striking particular poses. Too often we may assume that actors and events suddenly in the limelight are truly new arrivals, sprung from no place of historical significance.

For the War of Resistance against Japan, the CCP in North China has seemed just such a new arrival in the pageant of CCP history. We have long labored under the assumption that, despite the early flourish of party organizing in cities such as Beijing and Tianjin, virtually nothing of great importance for party history happened in northern cities after 1927, while nothing of *any* importance transpired in rural areas of the north until the Japanese invasion in 1937.[2] Yet to understand not just why the party succeeded in North China during the War of Resistance but also *how* it succeeded, we cannot ignore its prewar antecedents. This chapter reconstructs the history of the prewar communist movement in the rural areas, primarily in Hebei Province, that formed the core of the earliest and most successful of the CCP's bases behind Japanese lines after 1937, the Jin-Cha-Ji (Shanxi-Chahar-Hebei) Border Region.[3]

Some of the most important advantages for the party's growth and influence in Jin-Cha-Ji, and perhaps many of its early problems as well, stemmed from its previous experiences. Hebei was no blank slate for the CCP in 1937. It is well known that party organizations, though weakened and driven underground, persisted in Beijing and Tianjin, as in other major Chinese cities, throughout the 1920s and early 1930s. What is far less acknowledged is that *rural* organization was far from negligible during the same period. The party had a history in the villages of Hebei. It was a history both of radical initiatives on land issues and of uprisings based on community opposition to state encroachments. It was also a history of betrayal, stupidity, ineptness, dashed hopes, suppression, and failure. Such a history of negatives may be every bit as formative for a revolutionary movement as the more positive record of the CCP to the south.

Early Rural Organizing in Hebei: 1921 to 1927

Chinese Communist Party activity in the counties along the Beijing-Hankou railway began well before the start of Chiang Kai-shek's Northern Expedition in 1926. Many of the CCP organizers in Hebei had participated in the May Fourth movement and subsequent nationalist agitations. Most of them were urbanites and intellectuals, and not surprisingly their efforts to extend the revolution to the countryside generally came after, and in service to, their attempts to foment nationalist and proletarian revolutions. The party's peasant efforts thus spread primarily from the metropolises to the smaller cities of Hebei, and only thence to the surrounding countryside.

Although Comintern and CCP policy in this era of the first United Front and preparation for the Northern Expedition placed primary emphasis on urban workers, the peasantry also enjoyed the attention of communist organizers. By late 1923 radical Chinese youth were cognizant of the success of peasant movements such as those in Haifeng and in Hengshan (Hunan). Articles in *Chinese Youth* pointed out that although the peasant movement was still in its infancy, the peasantry could develop into a great revolutionary force, as in Russia and Turkey (*sic*).[4] Party publications throughout 1924 and 1925 continued to provide information on peasant organizing; and of course the founding of the Peasant Movement Training Institute in Guangdong underlined the significance the CCP attributed to the role of the peasantry in the "national revolution" being "led" by the GMD with CCP assistance. In early 1926, a CCP CC Special Conference in Beijing called for making solution of the peasant problem the mainstay of grassroots preparations for the Northern Expedition.[5]

In July 1926, the CC's enlarged second plenum, held in Shanghai, adopted a set of resolutions on the peasant movement that took note of "widespread peasant uprisings" (including some in Hebei), and their significance, and then provided some general guidelines for peasant organizers. Pre-existing village organizations that "truly represented" peasant interests could be used without being required to turn themselves into peasant associations. Peasant associations, in fact, should not have "distinct class color"; rural class relations were very complicated, and only very large landlords and usurers should be excluded. As many people as possible, including small landlords, should be united to challenge a handful of "reactionary big landlords." Organizers were warned to eschew preachy style or vague propaganda, to treat local superstitions and clan relations circumspectly, and to avoid head-on confrontations with the local self-defense organizations (*mintuan*). For entrée into new areas, the document stressed local primary school teachers as key contacts and emphasized the importance of knowledge of local conditions in formulating concrete demands for the peasant movement and in judging the "concrete limits of action."[6]

In Hebei, the party moved into the countryside early on, although most of the initial "rural" organizing was probably limited to the suburbs of Beijing and Tianjin. Almost at its inception, the Shunzhi (Hebei Provincial) Committee planned the formation of "people's schools" (*pingmin xuexiao*) as camouflage for the organization of peasant associations (*xiehui*).[7] Later, students took the movement deeper into the countryside.

Those from Baoding schools proved especially active. During vacations, they began organizing in their native villages. Han Yonglu, one such student activist, was a native of Wan County, from a rich peasant household.[8] In 1922, he enrolled in middle school in Baoding and in 1924 started propagandizing for the party and recruiting members in his home village of West Five-Mile Peak. According to contemporary CCP conceptions of the sources of revolutionary upsurge among the peasantry, West Five-Mile Peak should have been a ripe setting. Eight large landlord families controlled a third of the village's farmland, and the village had experienced sharp enough "struggle" between landlords and peasants to have been characterized as a "model village."

Han used remarkably casual recruitment methods. Shortly after his return to the village, a poor peasant also surnamed Han, a "bosom buddy" of the young intellectual, complained to him about the tax levies. After some conversation, our Han revealed that he was charged with building a party organization in the village, and that his friend should relay this information to other reliable people (apparently his revolutionary activities had left little time for study of the underground organizing principles in *What Is to Be Done?*). Soon the village party organization had grown to about ten members, and Han used the village's adult school to publicize the party program.

The May Thirtieth incident of 1925 provided the catalyst for more concerted efforts at peasant organization throughout North China. But these efforts were still spotty, as lower-level cadres frequently lost contact with all too short-lived upper-level bodies. From 1925 to 1927, the supralocal party organization suffered repeated decimation. Lax security and turncoat betrayals during the May Thirtieth movement led to the destruction of some of the party's urban mass organizations. After warlord Zhang Zuolin's forces entered Hebei in the spring of 1926, CCP organization hit a new low. Party organizations in Baoding, Beijing, and Tianjin were broken in a series of raids, most spectacularly in April 1927, when Zhang seized key CCP leaders, including Li Dazhao, from the Soviet embassy.[9]

Under the circumstances, the amount of rural organizing achieved before the GMD-CCP split in 1927 is impressive. During the summer of 1925, its superiors directed the Shunzhi Committee to organize a peasant association and mobilize a provincewide peasant movement. The times offered auspicious openings: warlord battles raged along the Jing-Han and Jin-Pu railways. The Shunzhi Committee planned to coordinate peasant movements in the three circuits (*dao*) of Jinhai, Baoding, and Daming.[10]

Not all local party bodies responded effectively to this initiative. The organization in Shijiazhuang was notably sluggish.[11] But the Baoding CCP organization responded enthusiastically to the call to go among the peasants. The Baoding city Education Bureau unwittingly assisted by ordering the schools into an early summer vacation, in an attempt to defuse May Thirtieth activism. Activist students carried anti-Japanese propaganda back home with them, while the CCP leadership in Baoding directed their work from behind the scenes.[12]

Thus Han Yonglu returned to Wan County in the summer of 1925 and devoted much of his time to setting up a Wan County Aid Society to conduct propaganda and collect contributions for striking workers.[13] After a few months' hiatus studying at the Guangdong Peasant Training Institute later that year, Han returned to lead the county's peasant movement in 1926.

For cadres, Han drew on Baoding student party members during vacations. Indeed he seems to have sought peasant members primarily to pump up the membership rosters, while he and other students formed the leadership core. Han served as party secretary of the Wan County Special Branch, and party organization reached about twenty villages in the vicinity of West Five-Mile Peak. Some of the Wan County cadres were arrested in Baoding in September 1926, but were later released and returned to Wan County or nearby areas. (Only in Tang County did the party collapse under the wave of repression.) Eventually Wan County formed a full-blown party committee, with Han as secretary.[14] Han's superiors regarded the county as very promising; representatives of the Northern Bureau and the Shunzhi Provincial Committee arrived intermittently to inspect the work and pass on directives.[15]

During the winter of 1926, revolutionary organizing in North China intensified. Several northern cadres, sent to the south earlier in the year to help in the first stage of the Northern Expedition, came back to expand operations in the north. As in South China, their task required not only "organizing" (à la Wan County's previous efforts) but also *activating* peasants. The "banner lands struggle" that developed in East Hebei and the Koubei area in 1926–27 is one example of these efforts.[16]

In 1926 the CCP sent Yang Chunlin, a former Kailan coalminer and member of the Shunzhi Committee, to East Hebei to start up a peasant movement and dispatched another Shunzhi Committee member, Xin Putian, to the Koubei area in northwestern Hebei. These areas figured as prime organizing sites because Zhang Zuolin's underlings were pressing a policy known as "banner lands change to the people's," a euphemism for a new form of squeeze. After the 1911 Revolution, the government had gradually changed rents on the old Manchu banner lands into a kind of land tax. Ever hungry for revenues, the warlord government in northern and eastern Hebei decided to force peasants on banner lands to buy ownership rights at a price of four to ten or more silver dollars per *mu*. If they failed to pay within the time stipulated, they forfeited their rights to lands that had been theirs de facto for years.

In the Koubei area, between August 1926 and August 1927, peasants paid more than two million silver dollars, but many unable to pay faced the loss of their land. Not surprisingly, therefore, Xin Putian's efforts quickly bore fruit. With Yanqing County as a starting point, Xin on 3 May 1927 led an uprising of six thousand peasants from thirty-two villages, moving on the county town. Outside the town, the crowd beat to death six members of the banner lands clearing committee. On the second day, the crowd surrounding the town had swollen in size, and alarmed county authorities issued a proclamation remitting taxes and delaying action on any unredeemed banner lands, thus protecting peasant rights to the two-thirds of the banner lands that remained unpurchased. As news of this victory spread, the peasant movement in the ten-county area grew rapidly. Meanwhile, in East Hebei, Yang Chunlin led the peasant struggles against banner land sales in Yutian and Zunhua counties, and organized peasant associations there and in neighboring Fengrun and Zhi counties. A Jingdong (East of Beijing) Peasant Association was constituted, with Yang at the helm. Although it is unclear whether this group blocked the land sales effectively, it was militant enough to burn one county's government offices and to destroy the county council's headquarters.

If these activities were not the prairie fire the young Mao Zedong predicted for South China, neither were they mere sparks that flickered out quickly. Indeed rural organizing efforts in Hebei continued into the early 1930s, while in South China the peasant movement collapsed under repression after burgeoning so radically and rapidly during the first United Front. Partly because Hebei's peasant movement upsurges were relatively modest and widely scattered, and partly because the GMD's control in North China took so much longer to consolidate, the movement and the *rural* party remained relatively untouched by repression until they later became too troublesome for the authorities to ignore.

Years in the Wilderness: 1927 to 1933

Opportunists and Adventurists: The Struggle over Strategy

In rural Hebei, as in South China, adherence to CC and Comintern policy after the collapse of the first United Front did eventually prove suicidal. But at least on paper, some leading structures survived in the north throughout the 1930s, although they were repeatedly revamped—due as much to battles raging in the CC as to North China's own circumstances. For a while, the Shunzhi Committee functioned in effect as a regional bureau under the CC, supervising party activities in Hebei and Shanxi provinces and Chahar, Manzhou (Manchuria), and Rehe (Chengde). In the summer of 1928, the CC dissolved the Shunzhi Committee, replacing it with separate bodies for each province. In the spring of 1930, the Northern Bureau was established, taking in roughly the same area as the old Shunzhi Committee, but it was dismantled after purges late in the year, and the provincial committees re-established.[17] For the grass roots, however, the most crucial organizational link was probably the subprovincial "special committees" (*teshu weiyuanhui*, or *tewei*), set up to guide the party's work within several counties, usually centering on a major city. The special committees in Hebei eventually included Baoshu (lit., "belonging to Baoding"), Sanhe, Jingdong, and Zhinan (southern Zhili).

The rural organizers found a fairly clear field. In the late 1920s, the GMD government's capacity for maintaining public order in the countryside remained low, and the urban police forces were sometimes little better than Keystone Kops. Nor were many of the local authorities distinguished by their dedication to Communist-hunting.[18] The very capture of activists in the countryside at this point tended to be a matter of happenstance; between October 1928 (the earliest date for which we have some clear record) and June 1930, apparently none of the party's rural organizers was arrested while in rural areas.[19]

But the government gradually developed more sophisticated methods, and police vigilance grew, largely in response to the obstinately adventurist activities dictated by the Comintern and the CC. Most parts of the rural movement in Hebei survived the unrealistic directives of the late 1920s, but many were prodded into foredoomed uprisings in the early 1930s.

The first failure came shortly after the collapse of the first United Front. In the fall of 1927, Cai Hesen reappeared in Tianjin to take command of party work. His first act was to order a peasant uprising in Yutian County. In September, Yu Fangzhou and Yang Chunlin arrived to lead the Yutian peasant movement. They were captured in the subsequent uprising and the movement collapsed.[20] After a period of somewhat greater sobriety in the CC's approach to revolutionary strategy, the application of the "Li Lisan line" in 1929–30, first in response to and then going beyond Comintern directives, pushed the Hebei CCP leadership into trying to ride a new "revolutionary high tide" into "victory in one or several provinces" that would touch off a nationwide revolution. Military mutinies and peasant uprisings were attempted in several locations in West and Central Hebei. The roll of revolutionary martyrs grew. By late 1930, the ascendancy of the "Returned Students group" within the CC led to more devoted toeing of the Comintern line, which, despite periodic amendments and theoretical embellishments, continued to force regional party organizations willy-nilly into foolhardy uprisings.[21]

Despite the demands of democratic centralism, many of the northern cadres recognized that by following the Comintern line of the moment, they were asking of their rank and file nothing but self-immolation. Moreover, they themselves faced the stark threat of prison or execution in very concrete terms. The party leadership based in Tianjin and Beijing suffered high casualty rates all along. In many of the losses at these levels, though, the Comintern line often had to share causal honors with amateurism and rank stupidity. The worst such example was a Provincial Committee–ordered assassination of two of its own members—whose relatives then helped finger their associates for the authorities. Soon the police had rounded up virtually the entire Tianjin city and Hebei provincial CCP leadership, including Peng Zhen and Bo Yibo.[22]

Although the CC and the Comintern played no direct role in these debacles, their indirect responsibility is probably considerable. In the first place, they insisted on a worker-based strategy. By 1928, the GMD controlled most of the region, and Yan Xishan controlled Tianjin. Yellow unions in the factories shut out the communist organizers.[23] In such circumstances, the regional party organizations found themselves deprived of a mass base and strapped for funds. In striving to meet the demands for action that were issued from above, they tended to act desperately.

Conflict over strategy inevitably developed between the CCP in North China and the CC, and the conflict got caught up with ideological differences. Some time in 1930, the CC expelled a leading northern cadre, Zhang Mutao. There is some confusion over the charges against him. Nie Rongzhen claimed that he was removed because of his supposedly Trotskyite tendencies, while the Japanese historian Hatano reported that Zhang fell victim to an anti–Li Lisan purge and was branded as a rightist.[24]

Zhang Mutao did not go quietly—just one example of how the differences between the CC and the northern party might often have exploded into open disputes. Zhang Guotao volunteered in February 1931 to travel to Tianjin and convene an emergency meeting of the Northern Bureau to straighten out the differences. He heard from the meeting's participants about Zhang Mutao's dramatic departure, running off with as many as forty other expelled party members to set up his own organization. But their bitterest complaints were reserved for Li Lisan's "completely disregarding the actual conditions in North China." The Northern Bureau's objections to these policies had been rejected by the CC as "opportunism."[25]

Zhang Guotao urged a fresh start and hammered out an agreement that stressed the Northern Bureau's role in deciding "work procedures" based on the "objective conditions" in the region. Given the ascendancy of the Returned Students by that date, this agreement itself reflected some disregard for objective conditions in the party. Zhang remarked that after his departure from the CC in Shanghai, "doctrinaire repressions" were visited upon the Northern Bureau by the Returned Students group.[26]

Certainly the adventurist actions preceding Zhang's visit and those afterward are hard to distinguish, except that the "Returned Students' line" called for trying them on a grander scale. In May 1932, *Northern Red Flag* published an emergency notice by the Hebei Provincial Committee on the "present political situation and central tasks"—a title that always signaled a renewed trotting out of the bullhorns and banners. The notice clearly indicates consonance with Comintern interests, and the CC's concern for relieving military pressure on the Central Soviet Area in Jiangxi.[27]

The Provincial Committee noted recent evidence of a ripening revolutionary crisis in Hebei: forcible collection of dues by the Kailan mines' yellow union and similar exploitation of other workers had sparked workers' struggles; depression of the agricultural economy and onerous government levies had catalyzed peasant struggles in Tongzhou and the Beijing western suburbs, armed uprisings in southern Hebei, and mass marches on county governments.[28] Beijing students had been politically active on leftist issues, and exiled students from the northeast had been agitating for relief. Even an increase in the price of stamps had fed into mass dissatisfaction with the GMD. The notice went on to list the "central tasks":

> to intensify leading and organizing workers' daily economic and political struggles so that they develop into an ever higher stage, and enlarge allied strikes in several enterprises . . . ; to intensify leading peasants' struggles to resist rent, resist taxes, divide the grain and "eat the big households," and leading soldiers' struggle to demand clearing up the arrears in pay [*faqing qianxiang*] and improving treatment; to develop guerrilla warfare and revolutionary mutinies and land revolution movements, actively prepare for armed uprisings, creating a new soviet area and red army.[29]

In all likelihood, the Hebei committee adopted this position only under duress. With the failure of previous attempts undoubtedly in mind, the Provincial Committee had earlier issued a resolution on the anti-imperialist movement. Noting that the anti-Japanese struggle was far less advanced in the north than in the south, the committee concluded that it would be all the harder to nudge this movement into opposition to the GMD and warlords as well. A blistering criticism of the Provincial Committee's stance, penned by Luo Fu (Zhang Wentian, one of the Returned Students), appeared in the very next issue of *Northern Red Flag*.[30] Denouncing the thesis that a northern soviet was impossible, Luo argued that the intensification of counterrevolutionary white terror and of armed imperialist intervention, viewed dialectically, merely indicated that the counterrevolutionaries and imperialists recognized the challenge posed by the growing revolutionary forces in China. Now was not the time for retreat (Luo made a few nasty asides about those calling for guerrilla tactics of "luring the enemy in deep"), but for further advance. Now the party had to try to link up the several soviets into one large soviet area, seize a couple of important cities, and . . .

The Northern Bureau could not get off the hook by pleading objective conditions, Luo asserted. The northern workers' movement was stronger than those in Guangdong, Hong Kong, and Wuhan, and the peasant movement was stronger than in Jiangsu and Zhejiang. Some northern leaders might have argued that earlier debacles proved the inappropriateness of soviets for the north, but the CC had already ascertained the real reason for these failures: opportunism.

In June, Luo Fu, as representative of the CC, attended an emergency conference of the North China party leadership to establish policy for the north in the wake of the Japanese seizure of Manchuria.[31] Luo used the conference as an occasion to remind northern leaders of their many failings. An article summarizing the conference's findings appeared immediately afterward in *Northern Red Flag*, with the unambiguous title: "Struggle to Create a Northern Soviet." Elaborating at length on the fallacy of "northern backwardness" and on the ideological peccadilloes of the north's various provincial committees, the article echoed the strategic prescriptions of Luo Fu's earlier article, but with enhanced urgency: "[T]he slogan to create a soviet area in the north, at present is definitely not some empty propaganda slogan; it places before the northern party organization a real task for action; it is a war slogan . . . and therefore we must realize it with a fighting spirit."[32]

However much we might fault the Hebei party's judgment, "fighting spirit" was something it never lacked for long. Unfortunately, the spirited attempts to implement the CC's calls for uprisings consistently involved the provincial party organization at all levels in a string of disasters, in abortive military mutinies, "uprisings" of students, and "peasant uprisings" intended for translation into the formation of soviets.

Military Mutinies

Two major attempts at military mutinies touched Hebei.[33] The first, the Tang-shan mutiny, came in March 1930, on the orders of the Northern Bureau (probably under pressure from the CC). It ended, ignominiously, even before it began, because an over-eager conspirator blabbed to the wrong person.

The second mutiny, in Pingding, proved somewhat more successful and culminated in the formation of a short-lived soviet in Fouping County, in West Hebei. This mutiny was ordered by the Shanxi Provincial Committee, for the GMD Army's Eleventh Division stationed in Pingding city. In the summer of 1931, Chiang Kai-shek launched the third Encirclement campaign against the Jiangxi Soviet, and warlords Zhang Xueliang and Shi Yousan were battling for control in Hebei and Shanxi. The Shanxi Provincial CCP Committee decided that the time was ripe to create a revolutionary base in North China. (According to a leading participant in the mutiny, the Provincial Committee came up with this harebrained idea entirely on its own, but got "permission from higher levels.") The new Red Twenty-fourth Army was to march to the Wutai area to form a base. The political commissar was the leader of the Tangshan mutiny, Gu Xiongyi.

Once more the plan of mutiny was discovered in advance, but Gu Xiongyi already had some experience with such misadventures. This time the mutineers moved more rapidly to extricate themselves, but managed to take only about one thousand men. Their route of march took them through Yu and Wutai counties in Shanxi, and eventually to Fouping.

Fouping had a history of radical ferment. In 1919, fifty students of the Normal Study Institute sparked a movement among the county's elementary school teachers to put down a "despotic gentryman." In 1926, peasant associations had formed in various villages in imitation of the Hunan peasant movement. The county boasted many young intellectual CCP or CYL members, and even before the Red Twenty-fourth Army's arrival, some "progressive masses" had already been involved in "Red Army work." The Red Twenty-fourth Army first opened the city granaries to distribute grain to the poor, thus attracting crowds of people into the town. After the municipal granaries were exhausted, the crowd turned to merchant and landlord storehouses. Meanwhile, the party's Fouping County committee and the Twenty-fourth Army Political Bureau convened a mass representative assembly at which they proclaimed the formation of the Fouping County Soviet. The soviet immediately launched a land survey and prepared to mobilize peasants for equal partition of land.

Despite the seesaw battles between warlords in the region, the soviet could not develop unmolested. One local commander who had just gone over to Zhang Xueliang dispatched a force to Fouping. This unit approached the soviet claiming they had wearied of warlord squabbles and wanted to enlist in the Red Army. The soviet and Red Twenty-fourth Army leaders fell for the subterfuge, and nearly all of them were killed or captured and later executed. A few escaped, fleeing through Suiyuan and Shaanxi to become a part of the north Shaanxi Red Army. A handful of underground party members survived in Fouping.[34]

Student Movements and Uprisings

Students and young intellectuals in Hebei were the key carriers of revolutionary agitation into the countryside. They repeatedly proved their feistiness in the late 1920s and early 1930s. After the CCP-GMD split in 1927, the middle schools and normal schools that produced most of the rural teachers provided the hotbeds of revolutionary organizing and continually produced new cadres for urban and rural movements as those who had gone before went down under government repression. If the student movements remained unscathed by repression, they fed organizers into the countryside during vacations; but repression, while it could quench the political fires in the schools, inevitably scattered sparks into the countryside that touched off peasant-based conflagrations.

In some cases, the radical students managed to flex enough muscle to conduct their activities with a fair degree of impunity. In Li County in Central Hebei, for example, the normal school earned the local sobriquet of "red cradle" for the strength of its CYL chapter.[35] Students of the school subsequently fanned out into their home villages to organize peasant struggle. By late 1930, CYL organizers had helped to spark popular defiance of a pig-slaughtering tax declared by the county government, culminating in a mass demonstration at the county offices and frightening the magistrate into canceling the tax.

Similar success accrued to the young communist-inspired students in Wei County in Chahar (formerly part of Zhili's Koubei area).[36] In late 1928, Zhang Xixian (the Zhang Su later to figure prominently in Jin-Cha-Ji) arrived as the new head of the county Education Department. Zhang had been a CCP member for some time and soon revamped the county's normal school curriculum to fit his politics. Zhang himself addressed the students on several occasions, stressing the need for revolution to change the social order. Students drilled in a "student army," marching in uniform.

In March 1930 the students marched on Weixian town during the temple fair, singing the "Internationale." After some dispute with the authorities they gained admission to the town, whereupon they spread out to make speeches to the fairgoing throngs. This provocation prompted the Public Security Bureau to stage a midnight raid on the school in May. Two identifiably leftist teachers and fourteen students were arrested, and all library books with red bindings were confiscated or destroyed. Then students and teachers were herded into the auditorium and harangued by the Public Security chief, brandishing his sword and threatening to hack off the head of anyone who made a peep about the CCP. He then declared the school dissolved and ordered all students to return immediately to their homes.

Student political activism in Wei County stayed at a low simmer until the Japanese seizure of Manchuria in September 1931. In the wake of the student protest demonstrations over this event, the school expelled all the activists. When, in 1932, the Beijing organization sent several cadres to help develop the party in the county, many of these people were recruited into the CCP and promptly set to work recruiting peasants and rural youths in their turn. By the end of the year, the county boasted more than ten branches and nearly one hundred party members. These were able to sustain themselves well enough to foment some tax-resistance movements and anti-Japanese demonstrations in 1933, and indeed persisted right up until the Japanese invasion.

Not so lucky was the most famous student movement of the early 1930s, centered on Baoding Second Normal School. That this school was a revolutionary hotbed is attested to by the fact that many of the leading cadres of the Baoshu CCP Special Committee (including its secretary) were students there. Han Yonglu, of course, hailed from Second Normal; but so did students who had been fomenting revolutionary activity in Yi, Li, Xushui, and Boye counties and in the Baoding suburbs.[37]

The events at Second Normal School in July 1932 bear tribute to the courage of the radical students—matched only by their poor judgment.[38] The Education Department, annoyed by the students' incessant anti-Japanese propaganda, closed down the school and expelled some radicals. Undaunted, the student leaders called on their schoolmates who were home in the countryside to return and occupy the school. After a two-week siege, soldiers stormed the school; eight students died (including the Baoshu Special Committee secretary); thirty-five more were arrested, some of whom were later executed. Those who failed to arrive at the school in time to be besieged, or who evaded capture, remained as a cadre for later underground work. Many of them were to be squandered in the most "successful" and most disastrous peasant uprising attempt of this era.

Peasant Uprisings

The peasant uprising was the disaster of choice for the communist movement in Hebei during the Nanjing decade. Not that disasters were always the result. In some counties, the activity consisted of nothing more than occasional attempts by students on vacation to link up with any discernible local peasant discontent, without building any permanent party structures. Some areas developed numerically significant party organizations that never culminated in any "uprising" attempt. Most notable, however, were the counties whose party organizations were considered strong enough to attempt to launch full-scale uprisings or even (from 1930 on) to form soviets.

Yutian, having demonstrated its revolutionary mettle in the banner lands struggle, became the first sacrificial lamb on the altar of party discipline.[39] The county was chosen for the honor of staging an uprising (led by our old friends Yu Fangzhou and Yang Chunlin) under CC orders in the fall of 1927. After short-lived incursions into two county seats, the uprising was suppressed and its leaders executed.

In West Hebei, martyrdom was postponed for a few more years. Han Yonglu and his cohorts continued to thrive. But Wan County was not left indefinitely to determine its own direction. In July 1930, units of the Red Army attacked Changsha in Hunan, and a wave of "leftist high tide" spread throughout the party. The Northern District and the Shunzhi Provincial Committee created a General Mobilization Committee and directed workers to strike and peasants to rise up. This policy gave rise to suicidal uprisings in Hebei. Wan County was in the front ranks of the lemmings.[40]

The aim for Wan County's peasant uprising was to seize the county town. In the first attempt, on 3 August 1930, a demonstration marched on the county town but turned back when the police shut the town gates. In the second, about five hundred people in West Five-Mile Peak participated in a rising, gathering up some three hundred rifles from landlords and their "dogs' legs" and setting up sentries at the village entrances. This group was then constituted as the Red

Twenty-second Army (the first twenty-one were nowhere in evidence), with Han as the commander. That fall they attacked the county town and captured it after twenty hours' fighting, but fell back the next day, when reinforcements arrived from Baoding. The rebellious army then scattered for the mountains. Village self-defense associations from Yi and Tang counties came out to help the government soldiers. Still in flight and on the defensive, the Twenty-second Army decided to disperse and "conceal the revolutionary forces": each individual was to seek shelter with friends or relatives, and wait for the next opportunity.

They never got one. The government forces launched a campaign of wholesale violence against all identified participants in the uprising. Five were captured in August 1930 and executed on the spot; two were arrested in October and subsequently executed; another was seized in November, decapitated, and his head publicly displayed; and two more were captured in December 1930 and remanded to the Beijing-Tianjin Garrison Headquarters in Beijing. Han himself eluded the dragnet, being transferred to Jin County under a new nom de guerre to organize much the same type of activities. Eventually, however, on the eve of a planned uprising there, he was captured, spent several months in prison, and was executed in the fall of 1931.

It is a familiar story; we know such tragedies occurred time and again in the areas of Hunan and other provinces in South-Central China where peasant organizing had proceeded much further. The successful escape of Mao Zedong's ragtag band into Jinggangshan was a rare exception. In Hebei there were no exceptions, and the attempts to capitalize upon post-1927 progress in rural organizing all ended in much the same sort of disaster. The fact that Han Yonglu had ample company in the Beijing-Tianjin Garrison Command prison attests to the number of debacles: on his arrival there in March 1931 he encountered among his fellow prisoners communist organizers from Yutian, Tangshan, and Tianjin in East Hebei, and Lixian and Gaocheng in Central Hebei.[41]

Only one uprising came any closer to success. The "Gao-Li Uprising" of August–September 1932 threw more of a fright into local authorities than had any of the others.[42] At its height, it threatened public order in four counties and caused anxieties in another nine. Nevertheless, the attempt at an uprising in this plains area was doomed from the start. Of course, higher levels of the CCP, assessing the "objective conditions," found the environment propitious for launching a soviet. The Gaoyang and Li counties' weaving district, where handloom weaving provided a major source of livelihood for many, had been hit especially hard by the depression of the early 1930s. In addition, a government salt monopoly had become a serious irritant to the local inhabitants. Finally, the CCP strategists believed that the "ruling class" in the area was exceptionally weak and that the GMD government's troops, stationed in the nearby area, were "vacillating." That the targeted countryside was highly unpropitious for guerrilla activities (being, in fact, flat as a pancake) and offered convenient communications for the authorities seemed somehow beside the point.

This was one uprising definitely imposed from above. The designated leader, "Xiang Nong" (lit., Hunan peasant), was reportedly a southerner and came into the area via Baoding. (The Hebei provincial government, perhaps too enamored of the outside-agitator explanation, reported participants from Hunan, Henan, and Hubei.) Certainly many former students and teachers from Baoding Second Normal were involved. Before the uprising was launched, CCP organizers agitated throughout Li and Gaoyang counties among the peasants, but not exclusively among peasants; at least one district *baoweituan* [security organization] commander in Gaoyang deliberately colluded with the uprising.

Some of the local party leaders opposed any attempt at uprising. Even before the decision had been made to launch one, the authorities were on the alert: one of the Gaoyang organizers recalled reading in the local newspapers about the preparation of an uprising! On 23 August a meeting of the party committee held in Baoding lasted all day and all night, as a fierce argument raged between those favoring and those opposing the attempt. One of the opponents, "sweating all over," tried desperately to sway the others by using Lenin's theory of "the three conditions," but to no avail. Those attending the meeting had to go back to the countryside and start a "guerrilla war."[43]

On 30 August a soviet government was proclaimed, announcing a program that included confiscation and redistribution of land and food, elimination of high taxes and interest rates, and dissolution of the salt monopoly. The uprising was too large (perhaps fifteen hundred to two thousand active participants) and too well organized for the regular police and *baoweituan* to handle. Flush with the initial victories, the CCP's Hebei Provincial Committee issued a declaration to the "laboring masses," bristling with exclamation marks. It called on workers to go on strike and head out for Lixian and Gaoyang to help out; on peasants, to organize "heroes' armies" struggling for land revolution and expanding guerrilla movements; on soldiers, to mutiny, kill their officers, and take their weapons out to the Gaoyang-Lixian soviet; and on students, to spread out urging workers, peasants, and soldiers to do all of the above.[44]

But the government forces mobilized rapidly, as Linda Grove points out, largely because of the prior attention to extending the *baojia* [militia] system to North China and because of the improvement of provincial communications over the preceding several years. The Lixian and Gaoyang magistrates quickly passed word of the disturbances to provincial authorities and received promises of aid from army commanders in nearby areas. They also alerted their district officials to the danger of rebel attack. Military forces set up blockades at key points and then engaged the rebel units. These attacks split the soviet's forces, following which the government dispatched a garrison army to mop up. As the communist forces split into small groups, the *mintuan* moved into action against them. Most of the military action was over less than a month after the uprising began.

Downward Spiral: 1933 to 1935

By late 1932, the recurrent uprisings had convinced the provincial authorities that effective repression had to be more than serendipitous. The government's analysis of the pattern of uprisings suggested a more systematic approach to identifying the source of the unrest and applying the scalpel there. (It was, of course, inadmissible to posit that the disorders would recur so long as basic socioeconomic ills remained unaddressed.) The pattern identified was seasonal, social, and geographic. According to a January 1933 report, the government believed that "red bandit" activities depended upon students; that the school vacation months of June and January produced the most communist activity (a pattern that, once anticipated, made it easier to eliminate the problem); and that rural activity radiated outward from the key urban centers of Beijing, Baoding, Tangshan, Shijiazhuang, and Daming. Intensified security measures in these locales could help eliminate activity in the outlying areas.[45]

In the countryside, the attempted uprisings had underscored the urgency of the government's larger task of extending state control to the local level. The response to the Gaoyang-Li counties uprising is an extreme but instructive example.[46] Several villages in Gaoyang, Li, and Boye counties were identified as hosts for major CCP organizations, while three villages in Anxin were labeled as "communist bandit lairs" that spread leaflets, attracted *liumang* [hoodlums], and "roused youths with lies." Anxin had not yet hosted an uprising, but its proximity to the Gaoyang County seat (about 10 to 20 *li*) made the government uneasy.

The government's plan for cleaning out the area after the uprising's collapse involved several steps that should be familiar to any student of Chinese history.[47] First, the army occupied a centrally located village, Beixinzhuang, as a base of operations. The defenses were strengthened by the addition of troops to guard the village gates. Especially assiduous attention was to be devoted to investigating and extracting the roots of the CCP strength in the three "red" villages in Anxin. Li County's district heads were ordered to distribute *baoweituan* regulars among the local braves. Merchants in the county town, along with town officials, were to form a defense committee; business firms had to supply ammunition and weapons to set up a "merchant corps" (*shangtuan*) with two hundred men. All these steps were reported as complete early in 1933.

To prevent the recurrence of rural unrest, the provincial government then ordered local authorities to apply *qingxiang* measures. After investigation of all residents of a given village, the village head (*xiangzhang*) and assistant head were responsible for reporting shady characters or suspicious activities to the local security forces. Villagers were held responsible, under the "mutual guarantee" principle, for any unreported activity uncovered by surprise searches. Gaoyang and Li counties' local forces were to coordinate searches to prevent "bandits" from escaping across their common border.

Gaoyang's public security problem was especially acute. Only about 150 assorted and poorly armed guardians of law and order had to police 130-odd villages. The provincial government, in consultation with various voluntary organizations and local gentry, decided to clean up and reorganize the *baoweituan*, and then to group villages "according to custom, geography," and shared interests into "united village associations" (*lianzhuanghui*). The associated villages undertook the obligation to come to each other's defense. A *mintuan* office in the city, embracing local government and merchant and gentry representatives, would oversee security measures. Thus the end result of the uprising, beyond the death of several participants and a few landlords who got in their way, was the intensification of public security controls from above over the countryside, and an attempt at integrating the (now no doubt eager) rural gentry more firmly into the government's social control system.

The intensified rural security measures, coupled with heightened urban suppression, shattered most of the CCP organization in Hebei. By the middle of the decade, upper levels of the party often proved ignorant not only of what lower levels were doing but also of where they were, who they were, and how numerous they were. As late as 1934, the upper levels of the party in Hebei seem to have regained some organizational coherence, but possibly only on paper. One member of the Hebei Provincial Committee recalled a provincewide membership of only about one thousand—most of the leading cadres still being normal school students. Other sources reported the virtual eradication of the party in Tianjin and in West Hebei by 1934–35. To be sure, one important concentration of party activists remained: from 1931 to 1936, more than four hundred were at one time or another incarcerated in Beijing's Caolanzi prison. As of early 1936, fifty to sixty seasoned and fairly senior cadres were still under lock and key. They included Bo Yibo, Liu Lantao, An Ziwen, and Yang Xianzhen, all of whom, with many of their prisonmates, were later to figure prominently in Northern Bureau work and organization of War of Resistance base areas.[48]

Around mid-1935, the Northern Bureau in Tianjin lost contact with the CC. The break meant a hiatus in CC directives—in light of past experience, a blessing in thin disguise indeed—but also the loss of the bureau's major source of funds. Financial hardship drove the few remaining leaders in Tianjin to such desperate straits that the bureau's secretary and his wife sold their four-month-old son and one-year-old daughter for just enough to "maintain the livelihood of the Northern Bureau for three months."[49]

Remarkably, in view of the organizational disarray of the North China party and the intensified state repression, local cadres in many rural areas continued with their organizing efforts from 1933 to 1935. When left to themselves, they engaged in rather modest activities unlikely to attract attention from the authorities. When they heard from higher levels, all too often it was in the form of further prodding for uprisings.

In Wei County, some radical students forced out of the Normal School continued organizing efforts while working as rural teachers.[50] In the autumn of 1933, an envoy of the Beijing committee, who had descended on Wei County in the spring, finally located the local party organization—the time lapse speaks eloquently of the state of communications between lower and higher levels—and seems to have prompted more militant measures. He may have helped to build enthusiasm for plans for coordinated uprisings at the New Year, involving simultaneous tax-resistance uprisings in the county seat and market towns to take advantage of the holiday crowds. The authorities got wind of the scheme, however, and tightened local security. In the end, only one market town saw any action, when several hundred "masses" smashed up the Tax Affairs Bureau's weighing equipment. The county party committee dispatched a few activists to prepare the ground for establishing popular armed forces for guerrilla warfare, but nothing came of this initiative until after the Japanese invasion.

Further east, the Japanese army was encroaching on Hebei. In January 1933, Japanese units occupied Shanhaiguan, and in March they began to attack some of the passes of the Great Wall into East Hebei. The Chinese Twenty-ninth Army, with some assistance from a local "Heroes Army" (which may have included communist activists), put up unsuccessful resistance. By the summer, the eastern portion of East Hebei was already effectively in Japanese hands. In the fall, the party organization in East Hebei sparked a peasant uprising in Qian'an County. The purported aim was to oppose Japanese encroachments and (again, Hebei appears in the service of diversionary actions) to coordinate with the Central Soviet Area's attempts to counter Chiang Kai-shek's fourth Encirclement campaign. The peasant participants, poorly armed and untrained, proved no match for local armed forces led by the rural elite. Many CCP members were captured in the uprising, although a few managed to remain underground in the immediate area.[51]

As such events demonstrate, the strategy of revolution-through-uprising had undergone no creative transformation. The only appreciable difference was that the roster of enemies and the list of potential organizing appeals had grown, with the addition of the ever-encroaching Japanese army. By late 1935, Japan had pried the twenty-two counties of East Hebei away from the Nationalist government and tied them into its own sphere of influence under puppet control, thus heightening the sense of urgency and national crisis spurring Hebei's CCP activists to rural organizing.

The seasoned organizers still looked for the openings for insurgency. A report by a CYL cadre, written after East Hebei was detached from the rest of the province, noted the opportunities afforded by natural disasters, a drop in agricultural prices, the flow of refugees (estimated at 200,000) into Tangshan, and a financial crisis of the provincial government (because of the loss of twenty-two counties' tax base) that resulted in considerable hikes in requisitions and levies on the peasantry.[52]

However, the organizers faced even more serious obstacles than in the early 1930s. The report noted that the GMD had tightened rural security by using *baojia* organizations for mutual surveillance and encouraging the formation of *lianzhuanghui* under the leadership of local elites. Despite the drawbacks, the report estimated that six thousand party and four thousand CYL members could be found in rural Hebei (this was probably a gross overestimate), and that the "mass base" numbered thirty thousand. Poor coordination had left the village movements scattered and ill-organized, but nonetheless a mere three months' activity had involved the CYL in twenty-five rural struggles. The progress manifested in these "struggles" included promotion of the "rural anti-imperialist united front" (e.g., anti-Japanese marches and confiscation of Japanese goods) and "anti-Japanese-imperialism guerrilla warfare." The CYL's demands in the Baoshu area had progressed beyond empty sloganeering to strategic struggles; mass organizations had held representative conferences (indicating organizational improvements); some armed youth groups had formed (Sanhe County had a Youth Self-Defense Army with sixteen members); and the CYL's numerical strength in the villages had grown.

The writer of the report found ample grounds for modesty. The peasant movement in Hebei lacked the organizational strength and "proletarian leadership" necessary to create a northern soviet and red army. The CYL in Hebei, the writer complained, stood outside "the broad peasant youths' struggle" and had failed to "develop to a higher stage" such "anti-imperialist struggles" of the peasant youth as those to "divide the grain" or "seize the grain." Often the struggles consisted of "heroic" (quotation marks in the original) mobilizations launched by "individual comrades" without planning and with poor organizational results. The League had failed to create special organizations for hired-peasant youths. Work in "feudal and reactionary" outfits like the South Hebei Red Spears and the Ding County adult village schools had been completely stymied.

The rural CYL itself betrayed woeful organizational deficiencies. In some villages the League operated openly, making it vulnerable; often only one or two "heroes" handled the work for an entire branch. Higher levels of the League hardly provided more satisfaction. Some county committees failed to hold regular meetings; county and even special committees had lapsed into "one person doing the legwork" and neglected secret work, allowing village branches to "suffer serious losses"—namely, arrests. Added to this, the Provincial Committee had been completely cut off from the counties for a spell.

The report concluded with a section that demonstrates that the CC and the Comintern held no monopoly on lunacy. The writer announced the "present task" of the CYL: to work toward creating a northern soviet that might break the fifth Encirclement campaign against soviet areas in South China.[53] This required developing peasant youths' "struggles for political and economic demands," strengthening their organization and creating a "mass base for the peasant uprising." Every opening had to be exploited: disaster victims' demands for relief, work with existing mass organizations to link the anti-Japanese rising in East Hebei with "peasant demands and land revolution," and development of the Youth Self-Defense Army to oppose Japanese and *baoweituan* armed units.

We have no way of knowing whether this program was seriously attempted, but if it was it got nowhere; no mentions of significant rural uprisings in East, Central, or West Hebei during 1935–36 can be found in published reminiscences or in that most fertile source for information on failed uprisings, *Historical Materials on Hebei Revolutionary Martyrs.*[54] Perhaps the organization's energies were deflected by the outburst of the first significant urban protest since the 1920s and the necessity, from the perspective of the party's long-term goals, of building upon that new movement.

New Blood: 1935 to 1937

The Japanese incursions into North China finally did set a match to the tinder of nationalist sentiments—not in rural but in urban Hebei. Early in the winter of 1935 students in Beijing exploded into the December Ninth movement, spilling into the streets to protest Japanese incursions and the GMD's policy of concilia-tion.[55] From the beginning, some of the most active leaders of this movement were underground CCP members. The initial demonstration in Beijing on 9 December brought out about two thousand participants from Beijing universities and middle schools. Police and soldiers stopped many demonstrators outside the city walls, while other students inside the city broke through police cordons and marched through the city until dispersed by police broadswords and fire hoses. A second demonstration on 16 December attracted nearly eight thousand marchers. The police attacked contingents of demonstrators, wounding hundreds. News of the demonstrations spread to other major cities in China, sparking scores of sympathy demonstrations.[56]

The movement touched off an influx from the CCP's most dependable source of cadres: young intellectuals. Although the party's underground activists did not fully control the movement, hasty organizing efforts after the demonstrations helped both to broaden the party's united front with intellectuals and to groom many of the new youngsters for recruitment into party membership.

This cultivation process was assisted by the authorities' by now standard reaction to student protests: they advanced the winter vacation by a month and ordered all students to leave their schools before 25 December. The party under-ground in Beijing responded with a plan to "go to the people," and the Beijing-Tianjin Student Alliance began urging students to form propaganda teams to take their message to the Hebei countryside. Some 500 students answered the call. Several teams of students marched through Central Hebei in the dead of winter, lodging in citizens' homes and schools in market towns and county seats until, eventually, they were rounded up and sent home by the military police.[57]

The ostensible aim of this latter-day children's crusade was to carry the anti-Japanese message to the countryside. In this respect the mission was hardly successful. The vast majority of the peasants encountered on the route of march seemed more mystified than impressed by the gospel of national salvation. As a former Yanjing University professor reported, one idealistic young lady found "the discovery that peasants cared about nothing but taxes . . . a rude awakening."[58]

Those who had gone out to educate the masses got the education, when they came face to face with the grinding poverty in the countryside. The underground party members on the trek must have anticipated this opportunity. On one stop, they arranged "interviews" between students and peasants, in which students learned the brutal arithmetic of peasants' livelihood: so much went for rent, so much for taxes, so much for interest on grain borrowed to make it to the next harvest. Several students met a mother and her small children who had not eaten for two days; the children were weeping with hunger. Another group of "December 9ers" trooped out to the Mentougou coal mines southwest of Beijing, witnessing the miners crawling "on all fours inside dark mine shafts to excavate coal and when they came out they were paid with a very meager wage according to the weight of the coal they had dug." Such encounters had a sobering effect on the young urban idealists.[59]

For most "December 9ers," this was the only interlude in the countryside before the outbreak of the war.[60] But the rural trek had helped to mold a small core of more committed and more conscious youth. Those who had taken part in the rural march, cooped up in Baoding by the authorities until school reopened, resolved to form a National Liberation Vanguards (NLV) organization. Units of this organization sprang up in cities throughout China. According to Israel and Klein, the NLV eventually became a kind of front organization for the CYL.[61]

Many NLV members may have been unaware of that fact. But undoubtedly the party organization in Beijing had plans for the constitution and employment of the NLV, and, given the muddle usually bedeviling groups (especially groups of intellectuals) that fly into action on the wings of indignation and outrage, steering the NLV discreetly was probably not difficult.

In the ensuing months, police repression against nationalist students rose to intense levels, with raids that netted several activists, although most of the party cadres, forewarned, escaped the dragnet. Many students lapsed into passivity, while others moved further to the left. Those who responded with increased radicalism engaged in confrontational tactics. The zenith of this trend was reached with a "coffin-carrying incident" in late March 1936, when a crowd protesting the death in jail of a "patriotic student" paraded through the streets of Beijing with his coffin. They were met with police force, and some fifty demonstrators were arrested.[62] Apparently this demonstration had been urged by the Beijing party organization. Thus the movement seemed once more to be indulging a penchant for martyrdom and risked dissipating the new momentum provided by the upsurge of student nationalism and the reservoir of potential new cadres.

Sanity was reintroduced with Liu Shaoqi's arrival as CC representative to the Northern Bureau in April 1936.[63] The situation Liu encountered on his arrival would have tried the patience of a saint. The damage done to the organizational apparatus over the preceding several years was glaringly obvious; out of the seven provincial committees that had earlier worked under the Northern Bureau, only the Hebei committee was still functioning—after a fashion—upon Liu's arrival. Only a handful of leading bodies had hung on in cities and villages, and the middle- and lower-level cadres numbered probably only in the scores.

The profligate waste of human resources represented by the coffin-carrying incident was symptomatic of the self-defeating patterns forcibly inculcated in the Hebei CCP organizations over the years. The bizarre adventures dictated by the CC had weeded out most of the less committed, the less lucky, and the less sensible. The few remaining party cadres were very committed, very lucky, and singularly devoid of common sense.

Liu arrived with a brief for straightening out the organizational mess in the northern party and, most importantly, for impressing upon the remaining cadres the new United Front line. The reorganization of the hierarchy, on paper, was simple enough: Liu reconstituted the Northern Bureau with himself as secretary and Peng Zhen as Organization Department head. The uphill battle lay in reversing the bad habits the northern party had gotten into. This took a considerable amount of jawboning and a good deal of writing before Liu's major message began to get through.

Liu endeavored to drive home several points that common sense should already have suggested: (1) that strategic and practical considerations dictated that the strength accumulated through mass mobilization should not be squandered in futile symbolic confrontations, but should be carefully husbanded unless and until it could be unleashed in a manner that was fairly assured of success; (2) that dogmatic approaches to mass organizations and political allies had to end and that the discipline expected of party members could not be forced on the party's allies without risking their alienation; and (3) that all possible opportunities for open work (under the cover of nonparty organizations, affiliations, and publications) should be exploited, that no more cadres should be devoted to secret work than strictly necessary, and that open and secret work (and workers) should be scrupulously separated for reasons of security.

Over time this work bore fruit. The Beijing and Tianjin municipal committees were straightened out; several regional committees were restored; and new provincial bodies for Shandong, Shanxi, and Henan were set up. At least some of these bodies quickly busied themselves with resuscitating grass-roots party organization.[64] To some extent, the message of jettisoning guerrilla escapades for legal methods of organizing even seems to have gotten across at the local level.[65]

Within a year of Liu's arrival, CCP membership in North China had grown to a total of around five thousand. Several "national salvation" organizations, for students, women, and other groups, had been formed with the assistance of underground party members. Numerous smaller organizations and legal or quasi-legal publications spread word of the party's new conciliatory approach to the Nationalist government and of its call for all Chinese to unite in resisting Japan.

Propaganda teams, theatrical and song troupes, and "work teams" ventured into the "countryside" (probably primarily the metropolitan suburban areas) on occasion.[66] By the spring of 1937, when Liu was recalled to Yan'an for a party conference,[67] the organization was well on the road to recovery in both urban and rural Hebei, and preparing itself for the Japanese invasion that it considered imminent. It was by no means the ultimate Bolshevik juggernaut, but it now had seasoned leaders like Peng Zhen at the helm, a clear sense of its appropriate political orientation, a new repertoire of effective methods for approaching and keeping allies, and a program for action when the invasion came: head to the countryside and organize resistance. It was digging in and preparing for the next stage.

Conclusion

Three questions arise in evaluating this history of false starts. First, we must inevitably wonder why the repeated failures occurred. Are these merely the function of human error, or are we watching some ineluctable fate unfold? Second, given the sorry history of attempts at revolution, why did these revolutionaries remain in the fold and obedient to a leadership that had displayed, under fire, an almost invariable talent for choosing the wrong option? Finally, what is the connection between the CCP's experiences in Hebei before the Japanese invasion and its rapid and exemplary success after that historical watershed?

One might argue that the North China CCP failures in the 1920s and early 1930s were a foregone conclusion and that the CC's and Comintern's nudges into uprisings merely hastened the inevitable. Despite the damage wrought by warlords' battles for territory, the economic depression of the early 1930s, and the deterioration of the rural elite into a species of petty local tyrants, so this argument might run, North China lacked the socioeconomic tinder necessary for a revolutionary conflagration.[68]

If success is defined purely in the terms in which the CCP itself defined its goals at the time—setting off a poor peasant-based uprising that could usher in a seizure of power—then, indeed, North China lacked the preconditions for CCP success. But success might be conceived more broadly. The party in Hebei managed repeatedly to organize, motivate, and activate rural people and ruralized intellectuals, despite its dogged persistence in squandering that success and inviting its own extinction. The mere survival of a movement under fire while led by amateurs and adventurists is in itself a signal indicator of success. Moreover, the communist movement in rural Hebei time and again proved capable of growing rapidly when a handy issue presented itself, when it enjoyed a respite from the authorities' attentions, or when the CC could not locate it to hand on the latest breakthrough in tactics for collective self-immolation. Had the North China movement not been pushed into moves that alerted local authorities to its potential strength while it was still small enough and localized enough to nip in the bud, it might well have grown considerably stronger.

The basis for that growth, however, was hardly consonant with the insistent class line of the CC and the Comintern. Time after time, local organizers found issues uniting a local community in struggle against state authorities: resistance to salt monopolies, for example, or outrage against some new warlord levy on the land.[69] Most of the examples discussed above, in fact, pertain to just such issues of new and excessive means of state or quasi-state extraction from the countryside. These touched the interests of rich peasants and smaller landlords (larger ones could use crony ties to evade the levies) as much as, or even more than, the poor and hired peasants toward which communist organizers were supposed to gravitate. The catechism, however, called for attacking both land-lords and rich peasants, and whenever the catechists could get at the faithful, orthodoxy was enforced.[70] Class struggle, uprising, soviet, so the litany ran. And so, in the attempt to set the spark to light a prairie fire, the movement repeatedly sent up columns of smoke that brought in the cavalry.

When its hand was not forced in this fashion, the movement could flourish quietly and attract adherents from diverse backgrounds into antiestablishment activities—often using the script of traditional forms of protests—viewed as right and proper by local communities. The problem with the purely local-issue approach is that it did not answer the needs either of the CCP and Comintern leadership *or* of the local party activists. However impractical and oppressive the local organizers may have found the ukases from on high, they themselves had in mind some future that went well beyond the traditional rural vision of an ideal world in which the state left the village alone. The dilemma of the local activists was thus a deep one: Sharing with the party leadership a vision of a strong China and a transformed society, they nonetheless partook of the short-term priorities and the sense of practicalities of their rural constituents. Most of them at some point realized that the party's strategic program in the late 1920s to the mid-1930s would never bridge the gap between the two, and yet they had to cling to the ultimate goal or lose all reason to act at all. And thus, although from an objective standpoint regaining contact with the center was usually a worse fate than losing it, the local activists cut off from the organization kept hoping for the messenger who would bring them The Word. Only that could renew their con-viction that they were participants in a great and grand cause.

This point helps to explain why they kept trying despite the mounting evi-dence of the futility of the party's strategy. Many, of course, did not keep on: some died; some drifted off into cynicism, frustration, or pursuit of private options. And yet, fresh recruits kept coming in, and seasoned organizers kept going on. The recruits are not perhaps so hard to explain: they were young, idealistic, impressionable, and concerned about China's future; the party recruit-ers were almost as young and articulate and offered a program more appealing to the idealist than anything the establishment had to offer. But after a disaster or two, why stay on? On this it is impossible to get hard evidence, but hints of several factors appear in the historical record. The first was that the "line" and leadership from above changed frequently enough to convey some sense that they were attempting to remedy the faults of past approaches; the hopeful could trust that eventually they would get it right. The tendency to nurture such expectations of the party could only have been intensified by the dearth of credible organized alternatives.

Secondly, the strategic formulations did not promise success in all instances. Some initiatives were sacrifices to benefit the greater cause—thus the importance of the propaganda that emphasized the successes of the southern soviets or the crucial role of diversionary activities. A failure from the local perspective, if a resounding one, could then be claimed, post facto, to have contributed all the more to success elsewhere.

Thirdly, in the climate of intensified repression, there was probably a disproportionate selection of those inclined to self-sacrifice if not to outright martyrdom. Many of the local and regional party writings of the time convey more than a tinge of conviction that the justice and *eventual* chances of success of the cause were in direct proportion to the blood shed by its adherents, presumably because this would convince others of their rectitude, or of the dastardliness of the repressive regime. This belief was not, however, a purely abstract ideological conviction. By the mid-1930s it was probably a rare party activist who had not lost friends, schoolmates, and close colleagues to government suppression; to give up would be to betray them, to betray others in one's primary social group who were continuing the struggle, and to deny the worth not only of one's own actions but also of all those others. There was thus a strong incentive for believing that the blood shed would produce results; it would be surprising if there was not a considerable amount of survivor's guilt driving the remaining cadre as well. Liu Shaoqi appears to have encountered the North China party apparatus on the eve of the Japanese invasion as a group, if not thoroughly socialized into auto-destructive thinking, at least heedless of considerations of self-preservation.

Finally, those deeply involved in the movement rarely had time to step back and think about what they had done, what they were doing, and where it was all going. By the mid-1930s, probably the only reflection going on was taking place among those incarcerated, who experienced for the first time in years a breather from the frenetic pace of trying to whip up mass activism while staying in step with the Comintern line. Nie Rongzhen, transferred out of the area early on, experienced his epiphany while being borne by stretcher on the Long March;[71] Peng Zhen, Liu Lantao, and others conducted a program of study and discussion in Caolanzi prison. It may have been a great stroke of luck for the North China party and for Liu Shaoqi that so much of the leadership had been rounded up and put away for a while, so that they were ready for the new line when it finally arrived. At lower levels, while some of the seasoned activists undoubtedly welcomed the change, others may have been so caught up in the class-struggle ethos as to resist the new message for quite some time.[72]

The wonder, then, is perhaps not that so many stayed under the party's standard during these years but that so many of them survived. Their survival, in fact, provides the key to the Jin-Cha-Ji Border Region's early success and policy leadership during the War of Resistance. True, the Japanese invasion played an important part: removing the *Chinese* agents of state repression, while being too slow to replace them; giving local rural elites a reason to cooperate with the CCP; and propelling large numbers of nationalistic young intellectuals into the countryside. But all these opportunities could and probably would have been lost had it not been for the prewar organizing efforts. On the eve of invasion, there was a small but not negligible potential cadre of leaders spread throughout significant parts of the Hebei countryside, or close to it. These had been steeped in, and tested in, the commitment not only to the party's goals but also to the principles of organizational discipline and had undergone enough disaster and trauma to develop the backbone that could see them through the first reverses under Japanese occupation. At both regional and local levels, there was a core of leaders familiar—sometimes intensely so—with the local environment: Peng Zhen, for example, who became the border region's party secretary early in the war, and numerous former CYL and CCP activists who returned to their home counties and started organizing resistance shortly after the invasion began.[73]

Nor were leaders the only important legacy of the pre-1937 experience. Long-standing or repeated organizing efforts had helped to create a "revolutionary tradition" in certain areas, most notably the Gaoyang-Lixian-Anxin area of Central Hebei, which became the earliest and most famous of "guerrilla bases" in a plains area, and Fouping, which was the heartland of the border region government for most of the war. Other subregional base areas and guerrilla hotbeds during the War of Resistance also corresponded remarkably to the areas of hottest activity during the late 1920s and early 1930s: Wanxian, Yixian, and Xian counties in particular.

Moreover, when the 115th Division of the Eighth Route Army dispatched about two thousand troops into the Shanxi-Hebei border area and beyond, Nie Rongzhen was at their head and knew already where to go to elicit the speediest response. Given his own experience, and Liu Shaoqi's recent reports, the communist forces knew the locations of hotbed counties, knew how to find places where land or other grievances provided relatively easily mobilized citizens, knew with a fair degree of certainty the location of old activists who could be reabsorbed into the movement. In some cases, they found it unnecessary even to initiate action; local activists in several West and Central Hebei locations seized the initiative (and local arms) well before the Eighth Route Army arrived and presented it with a populace already under a United Front dominated by communists and their sympathizers.

These are the more concrete legacies one can trace in the Jin-Cha-Ji area. Another probable legacy is harder to demonstrate, but perhaps no less crucial in forming the success of the border region. The confidence engendered within the Hebei party faithful by their previous experiences and their survival of past disasters, coupled with their hard-won capacity to trust their own judgment of appropriate action in the local environment, must have provided the underpinning for the spirit of creativity and experimentation that made Jin-Cha-Ji the policy and strategy model for guerrilla warfare behind Japanese lines. At times, these same qualities may also have engendered a hubris that got them into trouble. For the most part, however, despite the dismal history of defeat and setback in the prewar era, the legacies carried into the War of Resistance by the Hebei party were largely positive. Without them, it is very doubtful that the Jin-Cha-Ji base would have been an early success; and without the early success of the Jin-Cha-Ji base, the CCP's success in the War of Resistance becomes far from a foregone conclusion.

Notes

I am grateful for the comments made on a draft of this chapter by Parks Coble, Irene Eber, Tony Saich, Hugh Shapiro, Hue-tam Ho Tai, and Yeh Wen-hsing; by participants in the Harvard Fairbank Center's seminar series; and by participants in the conference "New Perspectives on the Chinese Communist Revolution" (particularly Lucien Bianco, discussant for that session) held in Leiden and Amsterdam, January 1990.

1. See, for example, James Pinckney Harrison, *The Long March to Power: A History of the Chinese Communist Party, 1921–1972* (New York: Praeger, 1972); Warren Kuo, *Analytical History of the Chinese Communist Party*, 3rd ed., in 4 vols. (Taibei: Institute of International Relations, 1978). Hatano Ken'ichi's collection of materials on CCP history does include one long sketch of the North China Communist movement from 1918 to 1936. Hatano, *Chugoku kyosanto shi* (History of the CCP) (Tokyo: Jijin tsushinsha, 1961), 8: 847–948.

2. An article by Linda Grove is virtually unique in calling such assumptions into question. Linda Grove, "Creating a Northern Soviet," *Modern China* 1, no. 3 (July 1975): 243–70.

3. The history of the Jin-Cha-Ji Border Region itself during the War of Resistance is traced in Kathleen Hartford, "Step by Step: Reform, Resistance and Revolution in Chin-Ch'a-Chi Border Region," (Ph.D. dissertation, Stanford University, 1980).

4. Deng Zhongxia, "Lun nongmin yundong" (On the Peasant Movement), *Zhongguo qingnian* (Chinese Youth, *ZGQN*), no. 11 (December 1923), reprinted in The Secretariat of the CCPCC, ed., *Liu da yiqian—dang de lishi cailiao* (Before the Sixth Party Congress—Materials for Party History) (Beijing: People's Press, 1980), 91–92; and idem, "Zhongguo nongmin zhuangkuang ji women yundong de fangzhen" (Chinese Peasant Conditions and the Policy for Our Movement), in ibid., 93–96.

5. Zheng Fulin, ed., *Zhonggong dangshi zhishi shouce* (Handbook on CCP History) (Beijing: Beijing Press), 28–29.

6. C. Martin Wilbur and Julie Lien-ying How, eds., *Documents on Communism, Nationalism, and Soviet Advisers in China, 1918–1927* (New York: Columbia University Press, 1956), 296–99 and 301–2.

7. Shao Chi, "Lieshi Yu Fangzhou" (The Martyr Yu Fangzhou), in Hebei Provincial Civil Administration Department, ed., *Hebei geming lieshi shiliao* (Historical Materials on Hebei Revolutionary Martyrs, *HBLS*), in 2 vols. (Tianjin: Hebei People's Press, 1961–62), 2: 19.

8. For background on Han see Luo Fu [Zhang Wentian] et al., "Wan(xian)-Jin(xian)

nongmin qiyi de lingdaozhe—Han Yonglu" (Han Yonglu, leader of the Wan-Jin Peasant Uprisings), *HBLS*, 2: 37–54.

9. Shao Chi, "Lieshi," 20–21; Chen Sizhe, "Guogong hezuo chuqi Baoding jiandang hou de huodong" (Activities after Establishing the Party in Baoding During the Early Period of GMD-CCP Cooperation), Historical Materials and Research National Committee of the CPPCC, ed., *Wenshi ziliao xuanji* (Collected Historical Materials) (n.p.: China Book Company, 1960 [reprinted 1980]), 17: 133; and Harrison, *Long March*, 94.

10. Shao Chi, "Huiyi Xin Putian lieshi" (Remembering the Martyr Xin Putian), *HBLS*, 2: 11–12.

11. Ma Helin, ed., "Gao Keqian lieshi chuanlüe" (A Short Biography of the Martyr Gao Keqian), *HBLS*, 2: 3–5.

12. Chen Sizhe, "Guogong hezuo," 132.

13. Luo Fu, "Wanxian Jinxian," 37–41.

14. One of Han's old school chums, Liu Xiufeng, temporarily served as secretary of a three-county committee. Liu resurfaced in historical records in 1937—as secretary of the CCP for Hebei, in the West Hebei region.

15. Luo Fu, "Wanxian-Jinxian," 37–41.

16. The account that follows is from Zhang Mingyuan, "Yang Chunlin lieshi chuanlüe" (A Short Biography of Martyr Yang Chunlin), *HBLS*, 1: 70–71; and Shao Chi, "Huiyi," 12–13.

17. Hatano, *Chugoku kyosanto shi*, 7: 851–52.

18. Nie Rongzhen, *Nie Rongzhen huiyilu* (Memoirs of Nie Rongzhen) (Beijing: People's Liberation Army Press, 1984), 1: 113.

19. "Hebei sheng chifei tongji gaiyao shuoming" (Outline Explanation of Hebei Red Bandits Statistics), *Hebei yuekan* (Hebei Monthly, *HBYK*), 1: no. 1 (January 1933), appendix table.

20. Shao Chi, "Lieshi," 21; Si Chengxiang, "Canjia Tianjin zaoqi geming huodong de huiyi" (Reminiscences of Participating in Tianjin's Early Revolutionary Activities), The Historical Materials Committee of Tianjin Municipal Committee of the CPPCC, ed., *Tianjin wenshi ziliao xuanji* (Collection of Tianjin Historical Materials, *TJWS*) (Tianjin: Tianjin People's Press, 1978–), 10: 96.

21. On the Li Lisan line, see Harrison, *Long March*, 166–88. On the Returned Students, see Robert C. North, *Moscow and the Chinese Communists*, 2nd ed. (Stanford: Stanford University Press, 1963), 140–46.

22. Si Chengxiang, "Canjia Tianjin zaoqi geming," 94–95, 99; Liu Wenxiu et al., "Huiyi Tianjin wucun nongmin hudian fanba douzheng" (Remembering the Struggle to Support Tenants and Oppose the Despot in Tianjin's Five Villages), *TJWS*, 7: 64–65. Peng, who at the time used the nom de guerre Fu Maogong, was released in 1934. Bo must have been released much earlier, only to be rearrested in 1931. On earlier losses, see also Shao Chi, "Lieshi," 13.

23. Si Chengxiang, "Canjia Tianjin zaoqi geming," 98–99.

24. *Nie Rongzhen huiyilu*, 1: 111–12; Hatano, *Chugoku kyosanto shi*, 7: 853. Zhang Mutao is referred to by different names in different accounts, but the vital details are similar enough to assure us that the names all refer to the same person.

25. Chang Kuo-t'ao (Zhang Guotao), *The Rise of the Chinese Communist Party* (Lawrence: University of Kansas Press, 1971), 2: 161; Hatano, *Chugoku kyosanto shi*, 7: 853.

26. Chang Kuo-t'ao, *Rise of the CCP*, 2: 162–64.

27. "Muqian zhengzhi xingshi di tezheng yu zhongxin renwu" (Characteristics of the Present Political Situation and Central Tasks), emergency notice by the Provincial Committee, *Beifang hongqi* (Northern Red Flag, *BFHQ*), no. 2 (5 May 1932): 1–12.

28. Brief information on the Beijing suburbs is in *BFHQ*, no. 2 (25 May 1932): 39–40.

29. "Muqian zhengzhi xingshi," 8–9.

30. Luo Fu, "Zai zhengqu Zhongguo geming zai yisheng yu shusheng de shouxian shengli zhong Zhongguo gongchandang nei jihui zhuyi de dongyao" (Opportunist Vacillations within the CCP on the Chinese Revolution Winning Initial Victories in One or Several Provinces), *BFHQ*, no. 3 (31 May–5 June 1932): 19–47.

31. Nihon kokusai mondai kenkyuujo Chuugoku bukai, ed., *Chugoku kyosantoshi shiryoshi* (Collection of Materials on Chinese Communist Party History), 6 (February 1932–January 1934): 68. This source reports that the conference took place on 24 to 26 June, possibly until 27 June, and that Shaanxi, Hebei, Henan, Shandong, and "Manchuria" were represented. Three resolutions were passed, relating to the presumably general revolutionary crisis, to the workers' movement, and to the development of the guerrilla movement and the creation of a northern soviet.

32. Chu Jun, "Wei chuangzao beifang suqu er douzheng" (Struggle to Create a Northern Soviet), *BFHQ*, no. 4 (12 June 1932): 3–12. A detailed summary is provided in Grove, "Creating a Northern Soviet," 249–52.

33. Li Zhimin, "Tangshan bingbian, Pingding bingbian di huiyi" (Reminiscences of the Tangshan and Pingding Mutinies), in Shanxi Province PPCC Committee for Historical Materials and Research and Shanxi Province Historical Materials Research Office, eds., *Shanxi wenshi ziliao* (Shanxi Historical Materials) (Taiyuan: Shanxi People's Press, 1979–), 13: 36–44.

34. Chen Ziyi, "Hong ershisi jun de pianduan huiyi" (Fragmentary Reminiscences on the Red Twenty-fourth Army), *Hebei wenshi ziliao xuanji* (Collection of Hebei Historical Materials, *HBWS*), 4: 30–37.

35. Grove, "Creating a Northern Soviet," 245–48.

36. Zhao Zhenzhong, "Weixian jiandang qianhou de huiyi" (Reminiscences of Weixian around the Time of Establishing the Party), *HBWS*, 4: 1–12.

37. "Jia Liangtu deng lieshi chuanlüe" (Short Biographies of Jia Liangtu and Other Martyrs), *HBLS*, 1: 72–77.

38. Zang Boping, "Qiyue de fengbao—Huiyi Baoding Ershifan de hujiao yundong" (July Storm—Remembering the Movement to Support Baoding Second Normal School), *Hongqi piaopiao* (The Red Flag Waves, *HQPP*) (Beijing: China Youth Press, 1957–1958?), 6: 53–79. See also Grove, "Creating a Northern Soviet," 253–55.

39. Zhang Mingyuan, "Yang Chunlin," 70–71; Shao Chi, "Lieshi," 21–22.

40. Luo Fu, "Wanxian Jinxian," 40–42, 47–52. A Hebei government report noted that discoveries of "red bandits," after peaking in mid-1929, dropped drastically from late 1929 through the first half of 1930; but the latter half of 1930 netted numerous captures, a goodly number from Wan County. "Hebeisheng chifei tongji gaiyao shuoming" (Outline Explanation of Hebei Red Bandits Statistics), *HBYK*, 1: no. 1 (January 1933): 1–3 and appendix. The following account comes from these two sources.

41. Luo Fu, "Wanxian Jinxian," 51. Yutian had launched a second party-led uprising in 1930. "Zhou Wenbin deng lieshi chuanlüe" (Short Biographies of Zhou Wenbin and Other Martyrs), *HBLS*, 1: 172.

42. The information that follows is based on several sources: Grove, "Creating a Northern Soviet," 255–67; Shu Ren, "Gaoyang Lixian yuji zhanzheng de geming yiyi ji qi jiaoxun" (Experiences and Lessons of the Baoyang-Lixian Guerrilla War), *BFHQ*, no. 13–14 (15 October 1932): 10–20; Zhai Jiajun, "Huiyi Gao-Li qiyi" (Remembering the Gaoyang-Lixian Uprising), *TJWS*, 14: 64–80; Liao Guang, "Gaoyang Lixian hongjun youjidui shengchan de beijing ji qi jingguo" (Background and Process of the Birth of the Gaoyang-Lixian Red Army Guerrilla Force), *BFHQ*, no. 11 (18 September 1932): 53–55; "Xueping Li-Gao gonghuan ji pohuo Yongnian gongdang'an," *HBYK*, 1: no. 1 (January 1933): 1–17.

43. Zhai Jiajun, "Huiyi Gao-Li qiyi," 68–69.

44. "Zhongguo gongchandang Hebei shengwei haozhao quansheng laoku minzhong yonghu Lixian Gaoyang de hongjun youjidui xuanyan" (Declaration of the CCP Hebei Provincial Committee Calling on the Laboring Masses of the Province to Support the Lixian-Gaoyang Red Army Guerrillas), *BFHQ*, no. 11 (18 September 1932): 5–8.

45. "Hebeisheng chifei," 1–2.

46. The following information is drawn from "Xueping Li-Gao," 4–7.

47. Hsiao Kung-Ch'uan, *Rural China: Imperial Control in the Nineteenth Century* (Seattle: University of Washington Press, 1960); and Philip A. Kuhn, *Rebellion and Its Enemies in Late Imperial China: Militarization and Social Structure* (Cambridge: Harvard University Press, 1970); William Wei, "Law and Order," in Kathleen Hartford and Steven M. Goldstein, eds., *Single Sparks: China's Rural Revolutions* (Armonk, NY: M. E. Sharpe, 1989).

48. Li Qihua, "Yijiusanwunian zhi kangzhan baofa qianhouo dang lingdao xia de Tianjin xuesheng jiuguo yundong" (The Tianjin Student National Salvation Movement under the Party's Leadership in 1935 around the Time of Outbreak of the War of Resistance), *TJWS*, 12: 28; Kokuminto chuyo/soshiki i-inkai [GMD], ed., *Chugoku kyosanto no toshi* (n.p.: Koain seijibu, 1941; a Japanese translation of a 1935 document), 177–78, 290–91; Tai Huaiji, *Tiandi you zhengqi: Caolanzi jianyu yu "liushiyi ren an"* (Heaven and Earth Have an Upright Spirit: The Struggle in Caolanzi Prison and the "61-Person Case") (Beijing: Beijing Press, 1982), 114–15.

49. Gao Wenhua, "Yijiusanwunian qianhou Beifangju de qingkuang" (Circumstances of the Northern Bureau around 1935), in CCPCC Committee for the Collection of Materials on Party History and CCPCC Research Department on Party History, eds., *Zhonggong dangshi ziliao* (Materials on Party History) (Beijing: Central Party School Press, 1982), 1: 184–88.

50. The following is based on Zhao Zhenzhong, "Weixian jiandang qianhon de huiyi," 9–12.

51. Li Yunchang, "Huiyi Ji-Re-Liao kang-Ri genjudi de douzheng" (Remembering the Struggle of the Ji-Re-Liao [Hebei-Rehe-Liaoning] Anti-Japanese Base Area), *TJWS*, 12: 53–55; "Zhongxin genggeng wei geming" (Conscientiously and Uprightly Make Revolution), in *HBLS*, 1: 145.

52. Wen Xuan, "Muqian Hebei nongcun jingji de xianzhuang he Tuan zai nongcun zhong de gongzuo" (Present Circumstances of the Hebei Rural Economy and the League's Work in the Countryside), handcopied report in the Bureau of Investigation Archives (Taibei), BI number 554.49/ 935/ 12020. This report bears only the date 20 November, but from the contents must have been penned in 1935, after the Japanese "puppetized" Northeast Hebei.

53. The Long March had begun a year before this report was written, and the Red Army under Mao had already arrived in Shaanxi. This indication of a serious lapse in communications is not too surprising; as Gregor Benton has shown, even most of those who *remained* in the Central Soviet area after the start of the Long March were slow to grasp that the Red Army was not going to return. *Mountain Fires* (Berkeley: University of California Press, 1993), 18–20.

54. *HBLS*. One is, however, reported for southern Hebei, in the Weixian/ Guangzong/ Nangong counties area, where an "armed uprising" took place in the context of an "equalizing grain" (*junliang*) struggle. Su Buguang and Ma Dafu, "Li Lin tongzhi zhuan" (Biography of Comrade Li Lin), *HBLS*, 1: 147–48.

55. For a detailed history of this movement, see John Israel and Donald W. Klein, *Rebels and Bureaucrats: China's December 9ers* (Berkeley: University of California Press, 1976), chaps. 1–3.

56. Gao Wenhua, "Yijiu sanwu nian," 187; Chen Min, "Treasuring this 'Quiet Desk,' " Foreign Broadcast Information Service, *Daily Report: China*, 12 December 1985, K1–3; Israel and Klein, *Rebels and Bureaucrats*, 87–95.

57. Israel and Klein, ibid., 98–102; Wang Nianji, "Dao nongcun qu" (Going to the Villages), in Li Chang et al., eds., *"Yierjiu" huiyi lu* (Reminiscences of "9 December") (Beijing: Chinese Youth Press, 1961), 141–53.

58. Israel and Klein, *Rebels and Bureaucrats*, 101.

59. Wang Nianji, "Dao nongcun qu," 145, 100; "A Milestone in China's Student Movement," *Beijing Review*, no. 49 (8 December 1980): 23. The quotation is from the latter.

60. There are a few exceptions. A core of underground party members who were students in Tianjin ran a people's school project in the Tianjin suburbs, beginning in the summer of 1936; this was a nodal point both for radical students' interaction with the peasants and for peasant recruitment into the party. Xu Daben, "Huiyi kangzhan qian shenru nongcun kaizhan kang-Ri jiuguo xuanchuan" (Recalling Going Deep into the Villages to Develop Anti-Japanese National Salvation Propaganda before the War of Resistance), *TJWS*, 12: 49–53.

61. Wang Nianji, "Dao nongcun qu," 151; Israel and Klein, *Rebels and Bureaucrats*, 96–97 and 102–4.

62. Israel and Klein, ibid., 104–10; Tai Huaiji, *Tiandi you zhengqi*, 102.

63. The account of Liu's activities here is reconstructed from ibid., 100–105; Ma Huizhi and Liu Chuli, "Huiyi Liu Shaoqi tongzhi zai Beifangqu" (Remembering Comrade Liu Shaoqi in the Northern Bureau), *Renmin ribao* (People's Daily), 14 May 1980, 8; Bo Yibo, "Liu Shaoqi tongzhi de yige lishi gongji" (A Historical Contribution of Comrade Liu Shaoqi), *Renmin ribao*, 5 May 1980, 2; Wang Lin, "Dang zai baiqu gongzuo de kaimo" (A Model of the Party in White Areas Work), *HQPP*, 20: 70–78; Guo Mingqiu, "Yongcun de jiyi" (A Long-lasting Memory), ibid., 79–92; Hatano, *Chugoku kyosanto shi*, 7: 849; Gao Wenhua, "Yijiusanwunian," 188.

64. Tai Huaiji, *Tiandi you zhengqi*, 104; "Zhou Wenbin deng lieshi," 170.

65. See, for example, a remarkable report on the state of party organization in several Central Hebei counties, which almost certainly dates from after Liu's arrival. Anping Central County Committee, ed., *Dingxian gongzuo jiandan baogao* (Simple Report on Dingxian Work) (n.p.: n. pub., n.d.; handcopied document in Bureau of Investigation Archives, Taibei). This report deals with the status of local organizations in Anping, Raoyang, Shenzhe, Shen, and Ding counties and gives one a vivid sense of the shambles that much of the rural apparatus must have fallen into under the guerrilla uprising strategy.

66. Tai Huaiji, *Tiandi you zhengqi*, 104–5; see Hatano, *Chugoku kyosanto shi*, 7: 895–908, for a list of "red" anti-Japanese organizations and publications.

67. This was the National Conference of Party Delegates, attended by some one hundred party luminaries in the north.

68. Chalmers Johnson initiated a hot debate by maintaining that nationalism and not socioeconomic demands underlay peasant support for the CCP. Johnson, *Peasant Nationalism and Communist Power: The Emergence of Revolutionary China, 1937–1945* (Stanford: Stanford University Press, 1962). See also Steven M. Goldstein and Kathleen Hartford, "Introduction," *Single Sparks*, 13–20.

69. Xu Daben, "Huiyi kangzhan," 52–53; Jin Qing, "Beiping xijiao nongmin douzheng di jingguo he jiaoxun" (Experience and Lessons of the Peasant Struggle in Beiping's Western Suburbs), *BFHQ*, no. 4 (12 June 1932): 29–31.

70. Contrast ibid., 31–33; and the blistering criticism of it in "Hebei shengwei dangbao weiyuanhui dui *Beifang hongqi* di jiancha" (Hebei Provincial Committee's Party Publications Committee Investigation of *Northern Red Flag*), *BFHQ*, no. 12 (25 September 1932): 6.

71. *Nie Rongzhen huiyilu,* 1: 241–49.

72. Gregor Benton has provided an example of such reactions in the old Southeast China guerrilla bases, where Chen Yi was nearly shot by one guerrilla group for bringing them news of the CCP-GMD United Front. Benton, "Communist Guerrilla Bases in Southeast China after the Start of the Long March," in *Single Sparks,* 80. I have seen no mention of such incidents in Hebei before 1937, but in the early period of the Jin-Cha-Ji base area, a segment of the party leadership in Central Hebei apparently engaged in anti–United Front agitation and pushed for rural class struggle. Peng Zhen, *Jin-Cha-Ji bianqu hanjian tuopai maiguo zuizhuang* (The Circumstances of the Treasonous Crimes of the Jin-Cha-Ji Border Region Traitor Trotskyites) (n.p.: n. pub., 1938?), speech delivered 7 November 1938.

73. Hartford, "Step by Step," chap. 2.

Chapter 7

Peasant Responses to CCP Mobilization Policies, 1937–1945

Lucien Bianco

The mobilization of peasants in northern and eastern China during and after the second Sino-Japanese War decisively helped the Communists to win their final victory in 1949. This mobilization was no easy task, as Hinton's extraordinary recollection of "revolution in a Chinese village" long ago illustrated.[1] Only recently, however, have historians been able to engage in serious research to unravel the inner workings of CCP-peasant wartime relationships. To accomplish this, historians have "immersed themselves in detailed studies of local revolutionary milieus."[2] In addition to *Single Sparks*, which gathers together a representative sample of that "new generation of scholarship,"[3] one must at least mention Chen Yung-fa's extremely important work on the wartime communist movement in East-Central China.[4] By dealing seriously with "the whole messy business of human affairs" rather than merely "viewing flowers while on horseback,"[5] these base area studies convincingly explain, for the first time, how the Communists learned to overcome the tremendous difficulties entailed in their self-assigned task.

Rather than attempt to do justice to the manifold contents of these recent base area studies, this chapter will merely pick up those of their conclusions that specifically concern peasant responses to CCP mobilization policies and try to show that these findings make much sense in the light of prewar peasant behavioral patterns.

For the sake of clarity, the content of the whole chapter can be summarized in the following eight comments:

• before the anti-Japanese War, noncommunist peasant movements were mostly defensive and parochial, a far cry from revolutionary offensives;
• at the outset of the war, the unresponsiveness of peasant masses to CCP policies compelled the latter to rely on the support of other classes (mostly the elite and *yumin* ["wandering people"] elements);

• few peasants were initially moved by appeals for national defense; more were induced to rally to the communist side by a search for security;

• although more easily motivated by material incentives than by Nationalist appeals, most peasants were initially reluctant, and then slow in rising against economic exploitation;

• when finally stirred or mobilized, peasants did not prove easy to control;

• for the CCP it was just as difficult to maintain as to restrain and channel peasant involvement;

• revolutionary seeds were not found in greater proportion among poorer than among better-off peasants; the late war period predominance of poor peasants among the ranks of civil and military cadres resulted from deliberate CCP policy;

• peasant grudging acquiescence to CCP extractive policies underlines the role of exchange (of benefits for contributions) and even more that of compliance.

Only the first of these eight remarks, which refers to the prewar background, has been inspired by my own research. Needless to say, I assume entire responsibility for my presentation of other scholars' works in the following sets of remarks. Admittedly a few of these remarks, while corroborated by trends observed during one period in one particular anti-Japanese base area, may very well seem to be contradicted by what happened in another base or even in the same base later on, under different circumstances. My answer is that I am trying to figure out the broad pattern of evolving peasant responses to CCP mobilization policies.[6]

1. *"Pin mo dou fu, min mo dou guan"* (the poor do not fight the rich, the people do not fight officials). The first part of this traditional assessment of deferent and law-abiding *laobaixing* (masses) remained basically true during the Republican period. The latter part is admittedly contradicted by the equally venerable *"guan bi min fan"* (oppression by officials compels people to revolt), but even this underlines the purely defensive character of most popular, especially peasant, disturbances. Furthermore, it points to a low level of class consciousness: most peasant riots were directed against tax collectors, local officials, or local bullies, not against the wealthy. In the absence of class consciousness, villagers had at least a sense of belonging to a local community, which often overrode distinctions of class. They sought to protect that socially heterogeneous community against attacks and threats from outside: the parochial and self-defensive features of peasant disturbances are complementary. As a rule, rioters and even rebels aimed merely at redressing some wrongs, ending specific local abuses, or getting rid of what they perceived as encroachments on their traditional rights. Peasants almost never took arms with a view to conquering new rights or bettering their condition. They merely wanted to recover what had been

lost, in other words to restore to them an inimical status quo. More exactly, they aimed at restoring it locally, as they did not care much about the fate of their "brothers" elsewhere.

Such local self-defense is indeed a far cry from revolutionary action, which implies an all-embracing or overarching ambition and an offensive strategy. If my picture of prewar peasant agitation is correct, one can already imagine that given such antecedents wartime communist leaders and agitators must have experienced tremendous difficulties in manufacturing revolutionary fighters out of a material (the "basic peasant masses") that was not prone to revolution.[7]

The following remarks (2–4) refer to the early war period.

2. Early supporters of CCP rule and policies came almost exclusively from the upper and lower strata of the rural population. The rural elite proved more responsive to nationalist appeals than any other social group. In the early days of the war, those who rose against the Japanese were mostly college and high-school students and other young intellectuals or "landlords, small capitalists, and richer peasants, who were better educated and had more to lose to the Japanese invader."[8] At the other end of the social ladder, *yumin* elements and *liumang* (hoodlums) or other village toughs could be easily mobilized against either alien soldiers or local power holders. Most of those who occupied all other rungs except the very lowest and highest—in Peng Zhen's words "the general masses," in everyone's words "the peasants"—maintained a "wait-and-see" attitude.[9]

The initial liabilities of the Communists were compounded by the fact that some of the anti-Japanese leaders belonging to the elite were rivals rather than supporters of CCP rule. Furthermore, only a small minority were likely to participate in a social movement directed against their own "people." As for *yumin*, *liumang*, and the like, who wholeheartedly participated in denunciations of the local elite, they were, as a rule, looking for immediate gains: "if it gives milk, it's Mother" (Peng Zhen).[10] Many of them wavered as soon as a rival power offered the promise of bigger profits. Even though they could not be relied upon as selfless fighters embarking on the long arduous revolutionary path, the party had no other choice than to welcome and recruit many of them during the initial period when peasant support was conspicuously lacking.

The CCP was therefore in the problematic situation of trying to initiate a peasant movement without peasants.

3. At the outset of the war, very few peasants were moved by appeals for national defense. "In the vast areas overrun by the Japanese army the initial reaction of the peasantry was apathy: 'Whatever dynasty it is, we still have to pay taxes.' "[11] Even in those villages where the shock of the invading soldiers was felt directly, "the general masses of peasants were unmoved by appeals for national resistance."[12] "When the New Fourth Army arrived in the Yangtze delta, people sometimes welcomed them for the wrong reasons. Mistaking them

for Japanese soldiers, they greeted them waving Japanese rising-sun flags."[13] Once villagers discovered their blunder, "New Fourth Army troops were shunned, and locals refused to cooperate in providing food, intelligence, and lodging. Militant anti-Japanese exhortations only frightened the local residents."[14]

It was not always the case that the unresponsiveness of most peasants prevented the CCP from winning a degree of support from them. The main reason for the lack of peasant anti-Japanese reaction, namely their concern for security, cut both ways: fear or sheer panic quite often induced peasants to rally to communist or other anti-Japanese leadership.[15] That in such cases peasants looked to protectors rather than to resistants is corroborated by those other examples when panic was caused not by Japanese soldiers but by Chinese roving bands. Whether homegrown or inflicted by foreign invaders, insecurity had the same effect: "bandit depredations served as sufficient impetus for the local population to look to the resistance organizations for protection."[16] Indeed, even before rallying to communist protectors, peasants had often taken the first step of reviving self-defense forces in order to protect themselves from bandit gangs or other outsiders. Such was the case of the venerable *lianzhuanghui* (united village associations) of Northern China, which challenged "the control of *any* outsiders within their own area; they would oppose bandits, other *lianzhuanghui*, the Eighth Route army, or the Japanese. Local self-defense in this case spelled localism and hostility to outsiders, not mobilization on the basis of resistance appeals."[17]

By itself, the protection of hapless peasants did not provide the CCP with gains comparable to those it was to win later through its rural policies: "as soon as the party introduced redistributive economic policies and brought the united front to a high state of tension, its growth quickly outstripped its earlier progress made by using the issue of rural self-defense."[18] Chen Yung-fa is even more outspoken, when he states not only that "nationalism bereft of economic concerns contributed little to building party power" but even more pointedly that "it was primarily redistribution that enabled the CCP to involve peasants in the anti-Japanese resistance."[19]

4. Although more easily moved by material incentives than by appeals for national defense, most peasants were initially reluctant and then slow in rising against economic exploitation. "A combination of factors—fear of reprisal from landlords, uncertainty about the CCP's military future, a desire to avoid confrontation, the persistence of paternalism and fatalism, and emotional bonds of clan and neighborhood—discouraged the majority from taking action against their masters."[20]

It took, for instance, no less than three years to involve a majority of Huaibei tenants in rent reduction. The extremely slow process went through four distinct phases. During the first (1940) and even the second (1941–42) stages, some tenants secretly returned the rent reductions to their landlords. The open split between tenants and landlords occurred only during phase three, in 1943. Rent reduction eventually became a routine procedure in 1944 (phase four), when "the peasant who did not have his rent reduced was a laughing-stock."[21] During the first two phases, the CCP's policy of rent reduction had been confronted by "resistance from both sides":[22] landlords *and* tenants.

Certainly it was easier to mobilize peasants on issues other than changes in tenancy or, for that matter, loan practices.[23] As such practices were sanctioned by tradition, almost no tenant or debtor deemed it possible or fair to abstain from paying land rent or interest. By the same token, a landlord who refused to postpone the remittance of land rent or reduce its amount when the crop was very poor violated community norms, so that his tenant could be more easily mobilized against him. By and large, communist agitators found peasants more responsive when they raised very concrete, specific issues, such as abuses of power, than when they questioned the legitimacy of prevalent land rent and interest.

Each of the factors contributing to the reluctance of a large majority of peasants to attack their landlords was rooted in a long tradition. As Hartford notes, "the Chinese peasant had long been tied into a system of domination-submission, but was tied to it . . . by a network of very personal, individualized face-to-face relations."[24] Before the war, personal relationships between landlords and tenants partly accounted for the overall restraint of the latter and for the fact that antirent disturbances were much less frequent than, say, antitax riots. As a rule, peasants hated much less landlords as such than they did other local power holders who bullied and swindled them in every way, be they district (*qu*) level officials, *xiang*—and village—level subofficials, or other village bosses of the *tuhao* (local bully) variety.

For the CCP, the difficult task of winning over peasants merely represented a first step. The following remarks deal with the next steps: how to restrain and maintain peasant involvement.

5. Once stirred or mobilized, peasants could not be easily controlled. They "often reacted more strongly than the party desired" and the party found it almost as "difficult to restrain (their) spontaneity" as to arouse them in the first place.[25] A struggle meeting had to be carefully planned in advance by mass workers, who assigned a few activists the task of exposing former abuses of the designated target, or of weeping and shouting vengeful slogans in order to arouse the indignation of the audience. The same mass workers were often overwhelmed later on by the success of their tactics and unable to check "an agitated group of hundreds or thousands (of) peasants (who) forgot their vulnerability and moral bondage and acted like totally different people."[26] Indeed, once they had at last taken the stand of publicly attacking their landlords or oppressors, tenants and other peasants frequently became "bold and aggressive," or even enraged and cruel.[27]

The powerful emotions released in the midst of a struggle meeting no doubt account for such behavior, as long-silent victims of injustices and exploitation "suddenly felt unable to restrain their indignation."[28] In other more relaxed circumstances, when peasants were neither angered nor indignant, they nevertheless did not always restrain their exigencies: once they "realized the potential extent of their own power within the villages, they began to press for and to initiate further more radical measures."[29] For example, the same tenants who formerly had secretly remitted to their landlords the whole amount of land rent now refused to pay any rent at all. Border region government cadres therefore experienced difficulties first in preventing tenants from paying more, then from paying less than the reduced amount of land rent legally prescribed. Other tenants insisted on the right to perpetual tenancy. Taking advantage of their control over the majority in village-level organizations, poorer taxpayers sometimes made a handful of well-to-do landowners bear most or all of the tax burden. Claiming hardships or other unforeseen difficulties, peasants sometimes instituted "grain borrowing" movements that deprived landlords and rich peasants of most of their reserves.[30]

6. Peasant mobilization was not only difficult to channel, but fragile and reversible. Not all the peasant excesses and radical claims described in the previous paragraph were unwelcome to the CCP. After all, even "left deviations" could have their utility either in advancing the level of mass activism or in intimidating recalcitrant members of the elite. More often, however, strategic or tactical considerations dictated otherwise, and the CCP had to curb peasant radicalism "in order to avoid alienating the elite."[31] Often, "the price was a decrease in peasants' activism."[32]

A temporary turn to more moderate social policies was frequently linked to the most obvious reason for the recurrence of peasant apathy, namely Japanese or elite repression.[33] The extermination campaigns conducted in the wake of the One Hundred Regiments Campaign succeeded in demobilizing a majority of villagers in the Jin-Cha-Ji Border Region. They did so directly, by "frightening . . . peasants away from the movement," and indirectly, by diminishing peasant confidence in their government.[34] This drop in confidence concerned not only the Red Army and militia's ability to withstand continued Japanese pressure but also the CCP commitment to social reforms, as the party was impelled to moderate its social policies in order to prevent the rural elite from going over to the Japanese or informing against local cadres and activists. Many peasants angrily asked: "why is the party more and more rightist?"[35]

The "truly phenomenal drop in peasants' political, social, and military participation" observed between late 1940 and early 1943 in Jin-Cha-Ji thus resulted from both fear of physical repression and mistrust.[36] The same combination had already accounted for peasant passivity at the outset of the war. The relapse into distrust experienced during the early 1940s underlines the fragility of the confidence peasants had accorded their new (communist) masters.[37] This new elite now appeared intent on colluding with the traditional elite, "as landlords began whittling away at gains peasants had won through the earlier implementation of reforms."[38]

Both increased dissatisfaction and increased risks demoralized "peasant masses" so profoundly that the CCP asked less and less from them, relying instead on a small core of party members and devoted activists to ensure the survival of the base area. During the dark middle years of the war in Jin-Cha-Ji, rather than the water (the masses) protecting the fish, it was the other way around, the security of all depending on very few committed fighters.[39]

Was that inner core of party members, activists, militiamen, and soldiers predominantly of poor peasant stock?[40]

7. Generational rather than class cleavages appear to have been the most decisive criterion in accounting for individual decisions to join the party or the revolution.

From the outset, CCP leaders were eager to analyze rural class structure in order to locate potential friends and enemies. They did not, however, find revolutionary seeds in greater proportion among the poorer peasants than among better-off villagers. While "lack of family ties may have contributed to the responsiveness of some hired hands to the CCP's mass workers," by and large landless laborers "seemed to be neither more 'revolutionary' nor more 'progressive' than poor and middle peasants."[41] Not surprisingly, their reluctance to get involved was dictated by a concern for economic security: "Afraid to make enemies of their employers, some even refused to admit they were hired peasants."[42]

Likewise, poor peasants did not rush in greater proportion than middle peasants into wholehearted cooperation and activism. For tactical purposes the party roughly divided "peasants into four categories: activists, ordinary peasants, backward peasants and landlords' 'dog's legs.' "[43] However, it learned to do so more by assessing individual behavior than on the basis of class *appartenance*. Indeed, factors other than class appartenance, such as marital status and especially age, often fostered adhesion. We have seen that unmarried workers may have been more likely than married ones to take an independent stand. More obvious was the contrast between, on one hand, the readiness of quite a few young peasants of any persuasion (rich, middle, or poor) to stand up in support of CCP policies, and, on the other hand, the cautiousness or skepticism of most of their elders.

By the end of the war, however, poor peasants predominated among cadres of the CCP and mass associations. Such a predominance resulted from deliberate party policy. First, the CCP weeded out many of those early members and supporters who had come from the ranks of either the rural intellectuals or the *liumang*. Once rooted more solidly in an area, the CCP became even more selective and discarded better-off peasants in favor of poorer ones. Furthermore, it often chose among peasant members and activists from a "pure" class background those who would receive special training and be promoted.[44] The high proportion of poor peasants among soldiers and militiamen was even more conspicuous, as the party tried to avoid enlisting many men from a privileged background. In brief, the end result (the 1945 class structure of party membership, military units, and border region government cadredom) owes more to the leaders' caution (taking care not to give arms to potentially unreliable elements) and strategic choices (to rely preferably on the poor) than to the inherent logic of pre-existing class cleavages.

8. Exchange and Compliance

Besides the precious support of a minority of peasants, the CCP obtained from the majority a grudging acquiescence in its extractive policies. Such acquiescence was no doubt helped by the CCP's implicit exchange of favors and benefits for contributions and services.[45] The notion was not altogether new to peasants: however exacting, an exchange governed the bilateral relationship between them and their landlords or lenders. They got land and paid for it with (heavy) rent; they received money or grain when they most needed it and returned a (much) bigger amount later. In a way, CCP-peasant wartime relationships were based on a comparable, but bigger deal (higher benefits, higher costs). As could be expected, consideration of costs came first: the party found it easier to extract grains and services than to enlist men into the army (and less difficult as well to recruit local militiamen than Eighth Route Army or New Fourth Army soldiers).

With respect to conscription, wartime documents criticize two opposite deviations: the "disguised purchase of volunteers" and compulsory conscription.[46] Such deviations were blatant breaches of the ideal of a volunteer army. Cadres who committed them had been assigned a task no easier than that of their distant successors put in charge of birth control policies during the 1980s. Chen Yung-fa's description of wartime recruitment campaigns indeed reminds one of more recent developments brought about by the implementation of the single-child family campaign: "pressure from above and difficulty in filling assigned quotas led some CCP recruiters to resort to deception, coercion, and bribery."[47] Like pregnant women of the 1980s fleeing to the mountains when warned that the birth control work team was drawing near the village, some "youths went into hiding in the Japanese-occupied areas before the recruiter arrived."[48]

I do not claim that such unfortunate incidents were widespread. Neither does Chen Yung-fa, who cautiously indicates where and when his descriptions apply. Suffice it to say that they sometimes occurred. On the whole, the extraction of grain worked somewhat more smoothly than the enlisting of men. In any case, every farmer household had to contribute grain (volunteering may apply to patriotic duty, not to fiscal burden). Furthermore, as suggested above, peasants were less reluctant to contribute material resources than to risk their lives as soldiers or even noncombatant laborers (*minfu*).[49] Finally, tax distribution in the anti-Japanese bases was less inequitable and tax collection less abuse-ridden than in Nationalist areas. This did not prevent but lessened tax resistance.

A more efficient, less unjust tax system amounts to another positive change from what the peasants had experienced before the war. Moreover, at least some wartime peasant behaviors, such as the sudden explosion of rage against landlords or other local exploiters (described above), point to social tensions that had long remained hidden beneath the surface of rural life. The CCP could not have succeeded in exploiting those tensions if there had been none in the first place. Yet, for most peasants, even including poor tenants and agricultural laborers, embracing class struggle and revolution was not a natural, self-evident choice.

At a modest level, contributing grains and services to the border region government did not even result from a free choice. Of the three above-mentioned reasons for the less difficult extraction of grain than of men, the first was the most compelling: peasants had to accommodate the existing regime, they had to agree to pay taxes. While there is no doubt that "the party's 'giving' in terms of economic and political benefits made its 'taking' a much easier job than it otherwise would have been," in the end compliance was more basic than due recognition given to exchange.[50] It was, to be sure, difficult to separate one from the other, as the CCP applied social pressure in order to promote voluntary cooperation. If cooperation was still not forthcoming, the party could supplement social pressure with implied coercion. Ideally, coercion was a last resort, and its use kept at a minimum level; I suspect, however, that while peasants no doubt valued advantages offered by the party, their awareness of its intimidating power and capacity for repression was usually sufficient to settle the matter of whether or not to cooperate.

Readers who deem the above argument far-fetched may also be skeptical about the next paragraph, in which I shall take the argument a step further, relying on Hartford's generalizations. Peasant compliance with CCP extractive policies suggests that compliance may also define the response of a majority of peasants to wartime CCP rule. Since Chalmers Johnson's pioneering work, historians have taken great pains to explain how the CCP won such overwhelming peasant support, thereby implicitly equating communist success with peasant support.[51] By contrast, Hartford has argued that the CCP did *not* attract vast amounts of peasant support and succeeded nonetheless. She contends, and I agree, that widespread and deep-seated popular support was not necessary for CCP success. To explain the latter, one need only explain the growth of its power.[52]

Emphasizing compliance amounts neither to claiming that the CCP expanded its power by sheer brute force nor to negating any peasant or, for that matter, elite support of CCP rule. Indeed, Hartford explicitly states that "the party's ability to obtain compliance from both the elite and peasants rested on three bases: the 'popular support' of a limited number of individuals for the party itself' (in other words, the permanent support of a minority of true believers); "the *ad hoc* support of particular groups or individuals for particular policies" that they deemed beneficial to their interests (here, Migdal's exchange-theory applied best); "and the party's capacity to exert control by direct or, preferably, indirect coercion of those who would not comply on other grounds."[53]

Other scholars who retain the term "support" give it a meaning close to that of compliance. So does Benton, who describes the dramatic effects of a change of "color" in one village or chain of villages. After the place became "red," "the pressure on people was no longer to avoid the Communists but to collaborate with them. . . . Once a village had changed sides, support for Communists became involuntary and automatic."[54]

Concluding Comments

Benton's depiction of an "involuntary support" for the Communists seems consonant with my own description of an "unequal alliance" between peasants and Communists:[55] Let us never overlook the subordinate status of one partner and the pressure or coercion enforced by the senior partner. Yet, the mere job of using the "peasant material to create the rank and file of the revolution" proved a most trying one, as this chapter has attempted to show.[56] This is perhaps best illustrated by the contrast between my favorite—and too often repeated—definition of peasant aims (they "did not question the status quo, but only certain new developments that represented a blow to it") and a central goal of the party as defined by Chen Yung-fa: "peasant confrontation with the status quo."[57] That the CCP eventually succeeded in accomplishing that awesome task, in other words that it learned, "step by step," the trade of "making revolution"[58] rehabilitates the role of the revolutionary actor, as a healthy corrective to the risk of determinism implied by a one-sided reliance on structural theories of revolution.[59] One could object—to whom?—that the communist victory was rather contingent (if there had not been a Japanese invasion!). To me, this is a further argument against determinism, even though imperialism is integrated by structural theories into a world order (or disorder) that produces revolutions.

To come back to Chinese peasants, we cannot evade one last question: were they not transformed at all during the war? Of course they were, by both the opportunities opened to them and the hardships imposed on them. What was striking about prewar, or for that matter traditional, Chinese peasants was not their revolutionary propensity but rather their capacity for endurance. While they once more exhibited the latter during the course of the war, what communist sources call their revolutionary consciousness also grew at the time; we can discuss how widespread that revolutionary consciousness was and analyze the process by which it incorporated traditional behavioral patterns, but the growth itself cannot be denied. The wartime CCP's interaction with rural society undoubtedly changed both of them. My point is simply that it did not change them that much. To be more precise, it did not change them essentially. Whereas the party of the early 1920s as an elitist club of cosmopolitan intellectuals is easy to contrast with the hardened, mass-based party mobilizing villagers and ruling rural bases during the 1940s, it retained throughout its fundamental Leninist outlook and organizational structure. Likewise, the responses of Chinese peasants not only to wartime communist mobilization policies but also to postrevolutionary policies as well (from collectivization during the mid-1950s to communization at the time of the Great Leap Forward [1958–60], and including the partial decollectivization and modernization of the 1980s) exhibit striking continuities with the behavioral patterns of their more traditional parents and grandparents who tilled their tiny bit of "yellow earth" during the 1920s and 1930s. My own reading is that such continuities are more basic than the many obvious changes that have occurred in the meantime.

Notes

1. William Hinton, *Fanshen: A Documentary of Revolution in a Chinese Village* (New York: Monthly Review Press, 1966).

2. Kathleen Hartford and Steven M. Goldstein, "Introduction: Perspectives on the Chinese Communist Revolution," in Kathleen Hartford and Steven Goldstein, eds., *Single Sparks: China's Rural Revolutions* (Armonk, NY: M. E. Sharpe, 1989), 27.

3. Ibid., 3.

4. Chen Yung-fa, *Making Revolution: The Communist Movement in Eastern and Central China, 1937–1945* (Berkeley: University of California Press, 1986).

5. Lyman P. Van Slyke, Foreword to Chen, ibid., xii and xiv.

6. While the main emphasis throughout this chapter will be on wartime peasant responses to CCP policies (1937–45), I shall occasionally refer to the civil war period and use evidence taken from Steven I. Levine, *Anvil of Victory: The Communist Revolution in Manchuria, 1945–1948* (New York: Columbia University Press, 1987). Similarly, I shall also include in the corpus of base area studies Gregor Benton's *Mountain Fires: The Red Army's Three-Year War in South China, 1934–1938* (Berkeley: University of California Press, 1992), even though it deals with the prewar period. Both Levine and Benton contributed to *Single Sparks*.

7. This paragraph summarizes the gist of articles and contributions relating to rural disturbances during the first half of the twentieth century that I have published, mostly in French, since 1968. The most recent are: "Peasant Movement," in John K. Fairbank and Albert Feuerwerker, ed., *The Cambridge History of China* (Cambridge: Cambridge University Press, 1986), 13: 270–328; "Peasant Spontaneous Agitation and Peasant Responses to CCP Mobilization from the Early 1920s to the Late 1940s," in *Proceedings of Conference on Dr. Sun Yat-sen and Modern China* (Taibei: China Cultural Service, 1986), 3: 240–72; "Anhui, Suxian Lingbi xian nongmin kang yanshui touzheng, 1932" (Peasant Uprisings Against Poppy Tax Collection in Su and Lingbi Counties, Anhui, 1932), in *Minguo dang'an yu minguoshi xueshu taolunhui lun wenji* (Proceedings of Conference on Republican Archives and Republican History) (Beijing: Archives Publishing House, 1988), 192–203; "Two Different Kinds of 'Food Riots': Kiangsu, 1930 and 1932," *News-*

letter of Modern Chinese History (Taibei: Academia Sinica, Institute of Modern History), (1991), 33–49. For views close to mine, see Elizabeth J. Perry, *Rebels and Revolutionaries in North China, 1845–1945* (Stanford: Stanford University Press, 1980).

8. Kathleen J. Hartford, "Step by Step: Reform, Resistance, and Revolution in Chin-Ch'a-Chi Border Region, 1937–1945" (Ph.D. dissertation, Stanford University, 1980), 128–29. Except when quoting this work, the "Chin-Ch'a-Chi Border Region" will be referred to as Jin-Cha-Ji.

9. Quoted by Hartford, ibid., 128.

10. Quoted by Hartford, ibid., 571.

11. David Mark Paulson, "War and Revolution in North China: The Shandong Base Area, 1937–1945" (Ph.D. dissertation, Stanford University, 1982), 47.

12. Hartford, "Step by Step,"129.

13. Chen, *Making Revolution*, 34.

14. Ibid.

15. Ibid., 514.

16. Hartford, "Step by Step," 126.

17. Ibid., 119.

18. Paulson, "War and Revolution," 355.

19. Chen, *Making Revolution*, 99.

20. Ibid., 220. Each one of these factors (among which fear of retaliation is the most decisive) is analyzed in ibid., chap. 3, 121–222, which deserves to become the classic treatment of CCP mass mobilization on economic issues.

21. Ibid., 156.

22. Ibid., 157.

23. Ibid., 178.

24. Hartford, "Step by Step," 446. Also see Lucien Bianco, "Peasants and Revolution: The Case of China," *Journal of Peasant Studies* 2, no. 3 (1975): 315.

25. Paulson, "War and Revolution," 85 and 160.

26. Chen, *Making Revolution*, 187.

27. Ibid., 187–88.

28. Ibid., 187.

29. Hartford, "Step by Step," 36.

30. Ibid., 174–75, 178–79, 454–56, and 460. Also see Paulson, "War and Revolution," 85, 87, and 160.

31. Hartford, "Step by Step," 37.

32. Ibid.

33. Kathleen Hartford, "Repression and Communist Success: The Case of Jin-Cha-Ji, 1938–1943," in Hartford and Goldstein, eds., *Single Sparks*, 97–112.

34. Hartford, "Step by Step," 38.

35. Ibid., 491; also 263 and 388.

36. Ibid., 513.

37. After the beginning of the Long March, peasants in western Jiangxi and eastern Hunan who had previously supported the Communists likewise found the party unreliable, because it had "sacrificed the base to wider goals." As a result "guerillas . . . were no longer welcome in the villages" (Benton, *Mountain Fires*, 411 and 391). The same pattern was repeated in 1937–38 and again in 1945 in many other parts of southern, central, and eastern China, with similar long-term consequences: as late as 1949, embittered peasants in the south "looked on in stony silence as the Communists returned to liberate them" (Ibid., 515).

38. Hartford, "Repression and Communist Success," paper delivered to the Workshop of Chinese Communist Rural Bases, Harvard University, East Asian Research Center,

August 1978, 15. Page 112 of the published version of this paper (see n. 33) introduces this idea but does not contain the citation referred to here.

39. Hartford, "Step by Step," 594.

40. In line with the central theme of this chapter, the following discussion is restricted to *peasant* CCP members, army men, etc. The inclusion of other rural classes, such as elementary school teachers, would strengthen the case for sociological cleavages, as many among them joined the party or served in the border region government.

41. Chen, *Making Revolution*, 211.

42. Ibid.

43. Ibid., 183.

44. Hartford, "Step by Step," 496.

45. In an early discussion of peasant responsiveness to organizers, Joel Migdal has distinguished four levels of peasant political action. According to him, each level beyond the first one (to accommodate political institutions wherever necessary) involves a rising scope of exchanges that concern individuals, groups, and finally the entire peasant class. Joel S. Migdal, *Peasants, Politics, and Revolution: Pressures Toward Political and Social Change in the Third World* (Princeton: Princeton University Press, 1974), 218–20.

46. Chen, *Making Revolution*, 398–99; see also 393.

47. Ibid., 385.

48. Ibid.

49. Levine, *Anvil of Victory*, 154–60.

50. Chen, *Making Revolution*, 505; see also Levine, *Anvil of Victory*, 229 and 233–34.

51. Chalmers A. Johnson, *Peasant Nationalism and Communist Power: The Emergence of Revolutionary China, 1937–45* (Stanford: Stanford University Press, 1962). Although Johnson's was an important and fruitful work, its central thesis was wrong and the debate it sparked belongs to a past period of the historiography of the CCP.

52. Hartford, "Step by Step," 13, 29–30, 40–41, 268, and 444.

53. Ibid., 56.

54. Benton, *Mountain Fires*, 487.

55. Bianco, "Peasant Movements," 305.

56. Ibid.

57. Bianco, "Peasants and Revolution," 322; Chen, *Making Revolution*, 597.

58. These expressions are, of course, borrowed from the suggestive titles of Hartford's dissertation and Chen's book.

59. For a recent summary and discussion of these and other comparative theories of revolution, see Hartford and Goldstein, *Single Sparks*, 20–27.

Part III

The Making of Victory

In the 1960s and 1970s, academics based outside the PRC debated whether the Communists had gained power because they had responded as nationalists to the Japanese invasion or because they had proved capable of mobilizing the population through their socioeconomic policies or, inevitably, some vaguely defined combination of the two. Chalmers Johnson in *Peasant Nationalism and Communist Power: The Emergence of Revolutionary China, 1937–1945* (1962) provided the most cogent argument that the Communists used the Japanese invasions essentially to portray the Chinese Communist Party (CCP) as a patriotic party. By contrast, Mark Selden in *The Yenan Way in Revolutionary China* (1971) maintained that it was the Communists' program for socioeconomic transformation, as implemented in the Shaan-Gan-Ning Border Region, that had paved the way for ultimate success. Kataoka Tetsuya in *Resistance and Revolution in China* (1974) was almost alone in arguing that it was the CCP's organizational control that led to its victory.

While confirming some of the earlier findings, more recent research and the newly available sources permit us to present an infinitely more complex picture of the party's policies and its relationship to the different social forces in China. It must be abundantly clear by now that no monocausal explanation for the victory of the Chinese Communists is satisfactory. However, the degree of sophistication and levels of qualification introduced have rendered answering the question of why the Chinese Communists were successful ever more difficult. The answer "because they were" is not entirely satisfactory either.

The focus of much research in the 1980s drew attention away from the CCP either by stressing the *longue durée* of the Chinese revolution and placing it within the long-term context of the profound socioeconomic changes that were taking place or has revealed how diverse the CCP itself was and how much the situation varied between the different base areas. This latter research has had the effect of redirecting attention away from events in the Shaan-Gan-Ning Border Region and Yan'an in particular.

Scholarship has certainly moved beyond a narrow study of power struggles within the party and Mao's rise to power, although even here as Teiwes's chapter demonstrates, there is much new to be said. What we are confronted with is a decentralized revolutionary movement operating in many localities, the ecology of which could greatly influence outcomes.

Despite this, the essays by Apter, Chen, Saich, and Teiwes draw us back to the Shaan-Gan-Ning Border Region and, with the exception of Chen's, to Mao in particular. Cheek, for his part, looks at the issue of intellectual service in the other main border region, Jin-Cha-Ji. In particular, he shows that the CCP not only was successful in co-opting local elites, and striking a delicate balance of support with the peasantry, but also was able to attract and make use of the services of metropolitan intellectuals. Importantly, these intellectuals not only staffed the administration but also propagated the ideology of the CCP's leaders.

The chapters by Apter and Saich deal with the issues of belief and legitimacy. By focusing on Yan'an, they seek to explain what held things together for the party cadres and stopped the movement from being no more than a simple amalgam of local protest movements. They raise the questions of the relationship between power and belief and how so many came to believe in Mao Zedong and what he purported to represent. Saich highlights the importance of the construction of an official history that gave pride of place to Mao and his supporters in China's revolutionary process while denigrating his opponents. Apter takes this line of argumentation further by contending that Yan'an provides a prime example of power generated by an inversionary discourse community that constructed its own language of belief. Mao and his partners set out deliberately and explicitly to change the world by reinterpreting it. In this process, Mao created the necessary "symbolic capital" for both himself and the movement he led. However, both authors are aware of the more brutal nature that lay not far below the surface, and both highlight the case of Wang Shiwei and the "Rescue campaign" as revealing the "darker side" of the Yan'an experience.

This negative side of Yan'an has also received attention recently in the PRC, see for example, the work of Dai Qing.[1] With the benefit of hindsight on Chinese political development after 1949, we can see how the methods developed in the campaigns occurred again and again to become the central disciplining mechanism of the party-state in power. While the spirit of Yan'an production campaigns could be detected in the Great Leap Forward, one could argue that the Cultural Revolution was rectification gone mad. No doubt, it is these and other parallels that explain why the party's central authorities want to prevent too much poking around in the Yan'an period. It is the heroic myth of the revolution, and they do not want it punctured.

Certainly, Chen in his treatment of opium production raises severe questions about one of the key elements of the "Yan'an Way" as outlined by Selden. The economic crisis of 1941–43 was not overcome, in Chen's view, by the "mass line" approach, the mutual aid movements, and the large-scale production campaigns but rather through the controlled production and export of opium from the border region. As Chen points out, in sanctioning this, Mao was "as realistic as he was romantic."

Teiwes, through his charting of the shift from a Leninist to a charismatic party, provides new information on the formation of the pro-Mao leadership in

Yan'an. He reveals a very shrewd Mao who knew that he had to build support within the existing Leninist structures and procedures, to win over a substantial majority of the established party leadership, and to gain the all-important backing of Moscow. He demonstrates that there appeared to be no obvious incompatibility, in the Chinese context, between the new "great leader" and the collective, quasi-democratic procedures within the party. The inherent danger of this situation, which would lead to the devouring of most of the revolution's children after 1949, was perceived only dimly, if at all, in the mid-1940s.

Note

1. Dai Qing, *Wang Shiwei and "Wild Lilies": Rectification and Purges in the Chinese Communist Party, 1942–1944*, edited by David E. Apter and Timothy C. Cheek (Armonk, NY: M.E. Sharpe, 1994).

Chapter 8

Discourse as Power: Yan'an and the Chinese Revolution

David E. Apter

> *Hearing the sound of sobbing increasing in volume, he stood up and brushed past the curtain, thinking, "Karl Marx wrote his Das Kapital while his children were crying around him. He must have been a great man."*
>
> *Lu Xun, "A Happy Family"*

Discourse as Power

China, the first major communist country to move toward liberalization, is now, along with Cuba and North Korea, among the last holdouts against it. Any illusions of a continuing liberalizing political revolution were shattered in Tiananmen Square with the events of June 1989. But the reality had disappeared much earlier despite major changes in economic and social life after the Cultural Revolution. When China became "open" in ways unimaginable during Mao's reign, many hoped that the nature of the political discourse would also change and irretrievably. It is this change that the present leadership continues to resist.

This is so even though what in other spheres appeared to be irreversible change has indeed changed radically. Communism in China has become lifeless, empty, and false. If it is correct to say that the distinguishing feature of revolutions is that they are mainly interesting to the degree that they refashion a moral discourse, or enact what that discourse has already proclaimed as a higher truth, then how they come to an end is even more important. In this respect, in China Tiananmen Square represents that revolutionary benchmark. At Tiananmen the question was posed of what will replace both the prevailing communist discourse and the institutions that represent it.

In this sense China pointedly demonstrates some of the difficulties in filling both the moral and the institutional space left by the decline of socialism. Like a good many other countries where a revolutionary politics prevailed and radical mobilization regimes claimed a privileged role in history, China has seen its earlier political momentum exhausted, and its leaders disagree over what steps to take next.

For the Chinese, the Russian experience has no doubt been terrifying. In Russia not only is the political situation precarious, with no one knowing what to do next, but history—once claimed as the truth emerging from the revolutionary process realized in the October Revolution—has reversed itself. The revolution was an aberration. Leninism and Stalinism, far from being totalizing ruptures, disjunctive in character, were merely extensions of the Asiatic barbarism of a people complicit in their own destruction. ("We Russians don't need to eat; we eat one another and this satisfies us.")[1]

If a good many Russians agree that Russia's revolution and its Great Terror belong to a much longer history, indeed a culture of terror in which the Europeanized Russians, civil and civilized, were victimized under the tsars as well as under Lenin, the same argument can be made for China, including Lu Xun's comment that the Chinese are "maneaters." Even in the heyday of the May Fourth movement, those few "liberals" who proclaimed their faith in science and democracy formed only a veneer, at best a thin and (apparently) insufficiently red line.

In both China and Russia revolution presented itself as the necessary and self-evident condition for forced draft modernization. More than being in tune with history, both represented historical necessity. Both were marked by violence feeding into a transformational discourse—a discourse punctuated by events that represented "irreversible" disjunctive moments. From today's perspective, this was one of those fictional truths characteristic of any revolutionary experience. What appeared to be a disjunctive moment was not. Nothing is irreversible. A political system can be changed. In both cases, revolution was hoisted on the petard of long-standing and persistent cultural characteristics that became resistance, went underground, then penetrated, and finally corrupted the revolutionary process itself.

Perhaps this is too strong. In both the former Soviet Union and China, especially among the older generation, a certain radical sentiment lingers, but only for a very few, and then perhaps only in some quarters, a slight residue of what might be called the myth of the revolution. In Russia today there is a desperate search for a new discourse. The Russian people are struggling to reinvent an appropriately democratic discourse in the face of mounting political and economic difficulties.

In China, however, strenuous efforts are still being made to prop up the old myths, retain official political gospels, and the central role of the party, while the country undergoes drastic economic and social changes. For the keepers of the revolutionary liturgy who use it to hang on to power, it is the myth of Yan'an that continues to stand for the moral moment of a revolution even though few still believe in it.[2] But one ought not forget that those who decided to finish off the demonstrations in Tiananmen Square on 4 June 1989 and abort its short-lived opening toward democracy included many of those for whom Yan'an was a kind of pantheon, including Deng Xiaoping himself, Li Xiannian, Chen Yun, and Yang Shangkun. In Tiananmen Square the last dying moral pretenses of the revolution went, too.

Despite their efforts, an inchoate democratic discourse, liberalistic, if not liberal, lingers in the aftermath of those tragic events. Still lacking in shape and design, it will not go away and will only enlarge. In this larger sense, Tiananmen Square defines a before and after. It remains the event that symbolizes a turning-away from an entire historical and romantic revolutionary political culture; a culture whose nineteenth-century roots began to branch out in the period after World War I when the Russian revolution became the first of those explosions that, in the form of radical mobilizing parties, took charge of the state in the name of the people in order to refashion the latter in the image of some higher truths.[3]

In this larger sense, Tiananmen Square represents a sharp turn toward a new and more appropriate discourse, the search for which goes on in many places in spite of more or less bitter experiences. And, as a specific retrieval of the May Fourth movement (1919), what Tiananmen Square shows among other things is how "irreversible change" reverses itself. Hence, despite the crackdown and subsequent events, it constitutes a fundamental "break" of broad significance. No one realizes this better than the authorities, who continue to do their best to paper it over. The more they try, the more they reveal the moral distance traveled since the revolutionary apogee in Yan'an. For what we are witnessing today is not only an intermediate point in the transition from one political system to another in China but also a striking example of that much larger transformation taking place in many parts of the world where erstwhile revolutionary discourses gave those who had power a monopoly on the interpretation of the meaning of political life. This suggests some of the larger questions that inspire the present essay, as well as the appropriateness of looking back at the recent past to see how that revolutionary discourse was created in the first place and how it was able to generate such power. This in turn raises the question of the connection between discourse and power. What kind of power emerges from certain revelatory and "revealing" texts to create "discourse communities" with a transformational sense of their own difference, messianic, and produced in part by what will be called "exegetical bonding," the result of which is a form of "symbolic capital" with its own forms and terms of social and political exchange? These and similar questions will be explored first by juxtaposing, within the context of the Chinese case, Yan'an and Tiananmen Square, treating China as a "case for comparison" within the larger frame of transitions from what might be called a predemocratic to a democratic politics.[4]

Tiananmen Square, for a moment, and Yan'an for a much longer period of time, define different moral political centers. Each uses a different language of power. So long as the old Yan'anites remain in power, these two will continue to represent mutually adversarial discourses. Moreover, the more adversarial their discourses, the more critically significant the interconnection between events, their interpretation, and their symbolism, and the less likely mediation and reform. In such a struggle, the state can win, but only by reducing its citizens to subjects. For this reason alone, the events in Tiananmen Square continue to define a liberating project. Its student leaders made a conscious effort to convert subjects into citizens with rights and make the state accountable to the people. Displacing and replacing Yan'an, Tiananmen Square has come to represent the politics of the moral moment, both in China and abroad.

Indeed, one can compare the two in precisely in these terms. In both, and in their own time, they became, for at least some of the participants, a moral moment. In Yan'an this moment lasted from 1936 until 1947, a period sufficient to enable it to become what it remains today, the legitimating myth of the Chinese revolution. The events in Tiananmen Square were fleeting. Both retrieved a longer history, and both had consequences, although it may be some time before those of Tiananmen Square become politically manifest in China itself. The essay that follows discusses these two themes in relation to discourse as a form of power and in terms of a process, "exegetical bonding," and a phenomenon, "symbolic capital."

Juxtaposing Yan'an and Tiananmen Square as moral moments and in terms of the political discourses they represent is meaningful because each constitutes a historical and cultural "break." The former marks the point of transition not only from the first round of struggles of the CCP against its enemies but also in welding a party elite committed to the seizure of power—an elite bitterly divided by factional conflicts within the party itself. The latter represents demands for generational change and succession as part of a broader transition in political values including more emphasis on individual rights, a more liberalistic legal framework, pluralism, and political accountability—the validity of all of which were in principle denied in Yan'an, where the emphasis was communal and collective, and democracy defined as a variant of the Rousseauean general will under the control of the party as its synthesizer. Each can be seen as a simulacrum, one for a Chinese *socialism*, the other for a Chinese *democracy*. The one was embodied in a utopian community constructed under conditions of chaos and violence and aimed at transcending both with a new order. The other, an improvised "community," revealed the ultimate conservatism of the "revolution," bringing under public scrutiny the fears of chaos by those in charge of the state and the distrust of the people by the party.

Both events redefined a particular space, marking off the terrain and setting it apart from their customary uses by society. Within that space there occurred a politics of mobilization and confrontation, a semiotics of display, spectacle, and theater, with the leadership extraordinarily sensitive and shrewd about the use of words, images, and symbolic orchestration. In both, orality came before textuality, the discourse of politics occurring within the Agora, a public space, indeed within the sound of the single human voice, the sound itself creating a sense of political intimacy.

My remarks about Yan'an are based on an ethnography of memory, historical events screened by and through survivors of the experience (for whom Yan'an remains an intense personal involvement) as well as documentary materials.[5] The description of Tiananmen Square is based on direct observation. The discussion itself is presented in four rather loosely connected parts. The first applies certain analytical categories to the role of Mao as mythmaker, storyteller, and moral architect, creating both the logic and the text of the revolution. The second describes both Yan'an and Tiananmen Square as symbolic centers and moral moments. The third shifts the ground, describing four critical power struggles that each involved a different dimension of what came to be Mao's monopoly of power, military control, administrative centralization, ideology as praxis, and intellectualism as moral teleology. Each was a necessary ingredient of this monopoly. Together they were insufficient as conditions for power without the final ingredient that concerns us here, symbolic capital.[6] The final part of this analysis discusses the decline of the symbolic capital attaching to Yan'an, its "congealed" form serving as the legitimating myth of the state, and its reappearance in a new form in Tiananmen Square during the people's movement.

After this outline is an analytical procedure that goes from the more abstract to the concrete, while shifting the focus from Mao as storyteller and cosmocrat to Yan'an as a utopian community, indeed, an instructional republic in which the principles derived by Mao were transformed into a special institutional relationship between education, moral principle, justice, and virtue. However, equally important, I want to show that within this moral high ground Mao exercised coercive power so crudely that it reveals the "hard" Yan'an inside the utopian one.[7] Finally, if one can say about Yan'an that its political discourse produced symbolic capital in the form of an independent and Chinese moral synthesis (despite claims and pretenses to Marxism), the ritualization and formalization of that capital and the deception involved in the process of creating the belief eroded it so badly that the moral "space" for a Tiananmen Square was created long before it actually happened.[8]

These comments focus attention on discourse as power, both as a phenomenon and as a problem for analysis. Three different analytical approaches are employed: structural (a mytho-logics), phenomenological (a shared interpretation of experience), and hermeneutical (a collective poring over texts that become hegemonic). From a theoretical point of view, each is more or less free-standing. That is, each has a more or less autonomous pedigree. Applying the structural analysis to Yan'an allows one to examine it as social text which is embodied in three narratives (a long, intermediate, and short story), the events of which can be "read" twice, first as metaphor and second as metonymy.[9] The phenomenological analysis deals with the universe of interpretations and intentions derived from the narrated events as experience. The hermeneutical analysis treats the translation of both into texts, a complete corpus, embodying authority, and logically resolving the inherent tension between assertions of high principle according to a dialectical method and ruthless coercion as a praxis of instrumental action. In effect, in Yan'an the consummatory and the instrumental were so combined that they came to represent a "unity of opposites," a feature of Chinese communism whose relationship has fluctuated according to changes in the party line up to the present.[10]

It was precisely this unity of opposites that was radically separated, indeed, exploded, in Tiananmen Square, and once and for all when the old Yan'anites resorted to ruthless power without even a pretense of principle, just when the students and supporters of the New Democracy movement were appealing to high principles in the absence of other forms of power. What one saw in that miniaturized universe was a society waiting to be born, rather than an alternate model of the state, whereas Yan'an was an alternative model of the state waiting to be born, but not a new societal form.

All three approaches will be applied to Yan'an as it became the nucleus of the Chinese communist movement and the moral moment of the revolution. It, too, is a "break" marking the transition from an earlier clandestine and underground party riddled by factions and internal rivalries to a totally mobilized revolutionary movement. It retrieved the past as a negative pole to be transcended, and redefined the future by means of a logic as well as a praxis of the next stage, among whose objects were the resolution of bitter factional struggles within the CCP (including Chinese versions of the Communist Party of the Soviet Union conflicts). The larger context was the conflict with the Nationalists, presented in terms of "historical truth" working its necessary way from past to present. The more immediate task was the war with Japan. These provided three well-defined objectives: to locate the Marxist truth and the right line, to determine the logic of that truth through the dialectic of class, and to reclaim national sovereignty by means of a single doctrinal method. Each struggle added a necessary dimension of specificity to the ensemble of abstract revolutionary ideas and ideals—a "theory of practice" embodied in strategies combining the passionate intentionality of the Chinese revolution itself with the rationality of survival.

One reason for such an emphasis on the symbolic is that it shows what is necessary to create a political community under conditions of virtual chaos. More usually, and experience elsewhere in China confirms this, circumstances of exceptional risk destroy trust in the future. Each person must survive by acting for himself. Hence mobilizing and collectivizing under such conditions required Mao and his colleagues to transcend randomness and create a logic of order so that the condition of chaos itself became the condition of transition. It was to accomplish this that they improvised what I have called "exegetical bonding."

An instructional method, it cultivated a common interpretation of shared experiences. Projected solutions were culled from conditions of despair, and alternatives identified where people had previously seen none. Converting defeats into lessons and victories into exceptional events, Yan'an shows how in politics (as well as in personal life), the shared illusion of possibilities creates the reality of opportunity.

At first glance, at least, a more miserable place for a utopian community would be hard to find. For one thing, Yan'an was miles from any substantial place other than Xi'an, whose significance was largely historical, redolent of former imperial greatness long since passed. For another, it was racked again and again with drought and famine, its inhabitants scratching a hard existence out of the loess. It was out of this same loess that communist forces carved out caves in which to live, the minimal, primitive forms of abode from which they hoped to recreate the world.

The harsh environment adds to the mythic properties of the Yan'an experience, of course. Together with the Long March, they defined the sheer overcoming of what appear to be absolute physical limitations. They contributed to that narrative of trials and afflictions that helped Yan'an and the communist movement under Mao Zedong become a chosen community, a people of the book, a myth in its own time that, by living it, gave it an intensity and credibility hard to believe in retrospect.

Yet, judging from interviews and re-interviews with well over a hundred survivors of the period, such as Red Army commanders and soldiers, teachers, writers, dramatists, underground workers, and party officials, Yan'an was the total and totalizing experience, the moral moment of the revolution and in their own lives. Even those who did not like a good deal of what they saw, for example, trivialities like Mao's womanizing, or more serious concerns like the hierarchy within the presumed egalitarianism, or suffered in the Rectification and "Rescue" campaigns (the latter led by Kang Sheng in a kind of dress rehearsal for the Cultural Revolution), accepted for the most part what might be called the fictional truths of the moral moment. And, in more practical terms, exegetical bonding enabled Mao to halt the factional killing that had characterized struggle within the party. It offered a genuine opportunity to fight the Japanese. Moreover, it promised to transform China and raise it from its prostrate condition and rescue it from foreign domination and humiliation by changing both economy and society.

These, then, were some of the ingredients of the particular combination of mythic interpretation and instructional logic that made Yan'an the "simulacrum" of the Chinese revolution—one in which occurred a kind of miniaturization and intensification and a moral redefinition of truth. Yan'an was the designated instrument to counter the prevailing environment of negative chance. It offered people the idea that they could think themselves past their predicaments, no matter how hopeless these seemed to be, and by interpretation, unlock history through using a dialectical key, thus resolving the contradictions of history in their own favor. From the start Yan'an was never just a base or a border area sanctuary or a bastion, but a utopian community, an expression of intense political desire, a yearning for political change as much engaged in political learning as in conducting war and revolution.[11]

Mao as Cosmocratic Agent

Before discussing Yan'an itself, I want to indicate the critical role played by Mao in its formation. He created and played the several roles crucial to the analysis undertaken here. In the first instance he is a storyteller, an Odysseus figure, a figure in exile trying to reclaim the lost patrimony. In the second, he is a Socratic agent—teacher, theoretician, and putative descendent of Lenin (with perhaps more than a touch of the first Ming emperor about him). There is also a ruthless, even Stalinist Mao, carefully disguised behind a cosmocratic role. In the end, he achieves an apotheosis as a combination of Lenin and Stalin, which is one reason why de-Maoification has engendered such acute problems. But in the end it is as his own Lenin that Mao is embalmed, a wax dummy in a glass coffin on display, the rooms surrounding him filled with the artifacts of the revolution. During his lifetime and playing these roles, Mao was able both to create and then to symbolize the hegemonic discourse of the Chinese revolution as a unique political culture. Through the selective narration of history, he gave superior weight to the local claims of what began as an external or foreign Marxist intellectual inheritance.[12] Both the immediate claims and the larger Marxist context were embedded in the actual organization of Yan'an, whose structure of military and social life was a drastically altered version of the original Jiangxi base, but with greater emphasis on education and institutions of research, learning, and self-improvement. Hence, from the start, it was Mao who gave Yan'an its wider significance as an extension of his own personality, attractive to aspirants and remarkable in the eyes of its own beholders. It was Mao who created the process of exegetical bonding and who, with a few trusted colleagues, developed the elaborate lexicon that went with it. This was how special meanings were attached to revolutionary insignia, signs, words, which, embodied in myths, stories, and texts, appealed to just the kind of young romantic revolutionaries willing to face agony, wounds, and death. Around Mao as well a Yan'an mandarinate formed, a *Stand* of puritanical revolutionary ascetics who appealed to a good many others who, perhaps lacking in revolutionary hubris, became more willing to commit themselves to the service of the revolution and the anti-Japanese war.[13] In death, Mao's embalmed remains stand for the permanence of his revolution.

What formed in the unpromising terrain high in the loess hills of Yan'an was something of a Platonic republic, a republic of the caves. There a dialectical logic was wedded to the derivation of truths rather than opinions, and an egalitarian social organization disguised functional hierarchies differentiated on the basis of education and party position. There too the distinction was made between permissible and impermissible classes, with virtue embedded in a rising class and justice as a goal in a practice of theory designed to both extend the range, meaning, and orchestration of its code and make the power of words performative. In Yan'an, the CCP presented itself as a state-in-becoming, with Mao its agent, his logic the driving force of change. By redefining the nature of the party and the moral character of the state, it became the accepted view that the forces of production could be redesigned to eliminate the class relations of production, a goal at once logical within the terms of the theory and millenarian in terms of realization.[14]

At the center is Mao Zedong as storyteller, mythmaker, logician, and philosopher-king. He retrieves the past and, by a process of dialectical inversion, converts it to a millenarian projection of truth and virtue. Interpreting concrete experiences screened through an elaborate instructional mechanism enabled Mao to redefine the character of the CCP according to his own purposes. His transcending or "overcoming" revolutionary project had three aims: to overthrow and eliminate internal enemies, to triumph over the GMD, even while in ostensible alliance with it, and to destroy the Japanese. But within these specific objectives many others were embedded. It was Mao the storyteller who enlisted memory on his side by retrieving previous peasant revolts and rebellions. It was Mao the putative Marxist who pressed into service a dialectical logic that seemed to "objectivize" the transformation of history into a revolutionary millennium, and thereby claimed a superior moral vision.

As for the China Mao portrayed, it was a country lost, a story of the fall. He prescribed the conditions for a restoration to a new state of grace, how the patrimonies lost would be redeemed by a double expropriation of the expropriators. The first was to return to the peasant the land lost to landlords (even where it had not been lost). The second was to return to the nation the sovereignty lost to foreigners. Yan'an, then, was not just one among nineteen border area regions. Nor was it a normal "capital." It became the capital because it was the moral center of the revolution, not the moral center because it was the capital. It was the "capital" because the party center was there. There one could find located the CC and Mao, and it was there that the speeches and writings of Mao Zedong Thought were formed into a distinct corpus.

Yan'an was a discourse community whose object was the displacement of conventional Chinese discourse and an inversion of prevailing hierarchies and hegemonies embedded in it.[15] More than anything else, words and language were crucial. Nor would any Marxism do except Mao's own brand. Locked into key texts that took on more or less sacral qualities, the discourse distinguished insiders from outsiders. Like all languages, it separated people in the way the French language separates French people from "others"—say, the Germans. But in addition, Yan'an successfully combined linguistic "otherness" with the notion of revealed truth. Those who entered Yan'an thus enjoyed a certain moral and intellectual privilege. Even the epithets used to describe them by their enemies, "red bandits" for example, took on superior moral Robin Hood virtues, an erstwhile "bandit" like He Long becoming the prototype of the heroic Red Army commander.

What was created and deployed so successfully in Yan'an was "symbolic capital." Embodied in a total discourse, an entire communicative field was established inside the terrain; the sheer physical geography of Yan'an itself. So powerful was it that it enabled the CCP to prevail despite the relative weakness of its force and the odds against its coming to power.

To construct this discourse, Mao created a political grammar, drawing its structure and terminology from many sources, Chinese as well as Marxist, and the logical structure from his own version of the dialectic.[16] He claimed the pedigree of Marx (or better, Leninism and Stalinism) and placed inside the highly rationalistic shell of some of their ideas a highly nonrationalistic kernel— moral, fictive, and evocative. He provided his own notion of rationality, totally distant, different, and disapproving of liberal versions and whose truth claims and dialectical method were applied to events in order to demonstrate necessity. Embodied in a transformational program for developmental socialism, what were improving fables became "truths of history." What came to rest on logic became a form of faith.[17]

As with other variants of Marxism, the starting point is the interpretation of readily recognizable circumstances and events. Maoism shares in common with other forms of Marxism a point of departure as a critical theory. All forms locate obvious structural injustices, providing insight into causes and effects. And Maoism, like the others, had no prescription for state power. Classical Marxism has little to say about socialism. It is precisely here that Marxist political leaders find their discretionary space, namely in the absence of specific socialist political mechanisms of rule and institutions of government. Hence Marxism, where it succeeds, opens a normative space and offers a projected millenarian solution in the absence of more precise prescriptions for rule. In this sense Marxism, which claims to be the ultimate materialism, is in fact the ultimate idealism.

This characterizes Yan'an very well. It begins in concrete events and experiences. It projects idealist projects. But every such project is, in its turn, materialized. Everything mundane is touched with the sacred, including gathering food and shelter, production and consumption, military and civil organization, class conflict and war. Everything is explicitly endowed with principled ethical yearning. Action becomes exemplary. Everyone is an example of *something*.[18]

However, such truths must appear as universals so their articulation cannot appear to have been inspired by Mao. His role is to give voice to an emergent and generalized consciousness that originates with and remains the unique possession of the marginalized class, more peasant than proletariat, including "lumpens" (whom Marx regarded with contempt). In this regard, Maoism appeared to have more in common with anarchism than Marxism.[19] In the cosmology according to Mao, he represented only a spokesman or class agent, not an independent force, the chairman of a party serving as the crucial link between doctrine and class.

In short, what discretionary power Mao actually deployed was based on his ability to make myth appear as logic and acceptable as reality. It can also be explained, less by the quality of Mao's Marxism than by an ingeniousness born of his political restlessness, his desire to reach out to the bottom of society to turn the world upside down. The less theory actually counted, the more it appeared to account for everything. In short, Mao created for himself an independent position in history while at the same time presenting himself merely as its agent. Or, to put it more symbolically, he acted first as a Chinese Odysseus, a wanderer in exile with a redeeming project, a storyteller recounting his trials and gaining wisdom. Wisdom gained, he became a Chinese Socrates applying dialectical logical to the rationality of the millennium.[20] The events of each narrative contain the lessons of that wisdom, lessons to be taught and learned and treasured within the rules of the dialectical method. It is here that the Socratic factor looms large in Mao the teacher, indeed the philosopher-king.[21]

The teacher has a special role in Chinese society as the purveyor and spreader of norms and virtue. So does the storyteller. Mao was one of the great storytellers in a country where story-telling has a long and treasured history. But he disguised his role of storyteller in terms of the theories and tracts he proclaimed. His was the "voice" that expressed what was a relatively conventional understanding of events, and in the guise of praxis and revolutionary interpretation he placed his own imprint on them. He placed his own version of the fall in the familiar Nationalist story of the *longue durée* that begins with the Opium Wars, retrieves the Taiping Rebellion and the history of peasant rebellion, includes the fall of the Qing, and ends in primordial chaos. In the guise of instructions and instructional parables he creates an "intermediate" story out of the struggles between the CCP and the GMD over doctrine, power, and who was to succeed to the legacy of Sun Yat-sen. Finally, this disguised storyteller becomes the chief figure in his own story, the "short one," which is about his ascent, the transcending Mao rising above the bitter internecine conflicts among CCP factions. In the long story, Mao has no role but creates a space for one. In the intermediate one, this role becomes important. In the short story, it is Mao himself who becomes central as the visible cosmocrat.

These stories telescope into one another. The more opened up, the bigger the image and the smaller the field. As the objective magnifies Mao in the sharply focused optic, a symbolic condensation and intensification takes place. Everything excluded from the visual field by the telescope is embodied in that figure in the eye of the telescope. Intensification plus condensation are two of the politically crucial ingredients of symbolic capital.

All this is, of course, fearfully abstract. But in practice it is quite concrete. These stories and narratives are known in advance. They take place in a context of specific struggles that all participants have directly or vicariously experienced. Among the most important are those enabling Mao to box the compass of political power, embodied in a narrative of events including the betrayal of the CCP by the GMD in 1927, the Nanchang Uprising, the Autumn Harvest Uprising, the Long March, not to speak of the conflicts with Zhang Guotao, Liu Zhidan, Wang Shiwei (although Mao does not involve himself directly in this case), and Wang Ming, each a surrogate for larger issues. These are some of the "facts" that entered the syllabus for the Rectification campaigns as mythic facts to be explained by dialectical theories.

It is in this sense that mytho-logics serves as a basis for exegetical bonding, a process establishing Mao Zedong Thought as the way to a superior and more virtuous social existence. It also disguises his ruthless pursuit of power and the hard-boiled morality of the leadership generally. This is particularly worth remembering today, since so many of the senior political leaders still in power are products of this system. The old-time Yan'anites at the top are experienced practitioners. Survivors of doctrinal infighting, torture, and murder within the CCP, as well ancient combatants against the Nationalists and the Japanese, they have few illusions about power.

It was one of Mao's story-telling accomplishments in Yan'an to put an end to the worst such fratricidal and murderous conflicts within the party—which led to the torture and death of thousands of party members who found themselves supporting the wrong party line. By defining and "telling" the correct party line and transforming it into a theory, such incidents—of which the most famous instance was the Futian incident in 1930 but which continued as a common occurrence—were finally brought to an end.[22] As Yan'an became a utopian community, an instructional republic, internal killing stopped. But only on the condition that everyone subscribed to Mao's version of the general will.[23]

To summarize briefly, Marxism is at best a critical theory leading to a hortatory practice rather than remedial solutions. Mao Zedong Thought is a derivative of Marxism that is longer on practice than it is on theory. It is, indeed, a "theory of practice," to use Bourdieu's term, less interesting than Lenin's, utterly pragmatic, like Stalin's, and more "Chinese" than anything else. Mao earmarked certain texts, his own and certain other works including Marxist "classics," to be pored over and studied both by members of the community and senior cadres, all in an appropriately prescribed manner by means of devotional exercises. Organizational principles followed instructional lines. The more general emphasis was on enlightenment, rationality, self-mastery, and collective discipline. This is why one can speak of Yan'an as a utopian community, a simulacrum (rather than a model), whose participants were endowed with almost magical powers by the incantation of the words, and whose function was not only the vigorous prosecution of war and revolution, but to be the chosen instrument of higher truths.[24]

That, indeed, was the momentary accomplishment of Yan'an as a discourse community. To analyze it further requires the use of the three analytical modes described above, applying them to material derived from written records and field interviews. Using the broad rubrics of discourse community, exegetical bonding, and symbolic capital, one can see how in Yan'an new political beliefs were articulated, a new conceptual ordering was superimposed on the prevailing chaos, war, and terror, and with an astonishing freshness and force.

By the same token, such freshness and force is inevitably fragile. The power of meaning is always transitory. Political truths decay with usage. The three methods to prevent this decline are ritualization, re-enactment, and confession. Such qualities turn discourse into sacralistic performatives. Otherwise efforts to prop up the discourse by punitive political means will only hasten the process of decay by opening the door to abuses. Mao recognized this very well, and long before the Cultural Revolution, when he launched the Rectification campaign in Yan'an. It was through a combination of recounting, re-enactment, confession, and ritualization that Mao's version of Marxism burned with a considerable brightness for more than a brief historical moment. Self-consciously constituted by Mao as the "moral moment" of the revolution, he believed that its symbolic capital could serve as both an alternative to economic capital and its functional equivalent.[25]

Using the concepts employed above, I now want to examine the unusual qualities of Yan'an as a moral moment, its dimensionality, and in a context of life as it was lived in its time, place, and manner without imposing the present on the past.[26]

The Republic of the Caves

Structurally, Yan'an also represents a mytho-logics, a utopian community in its own time and for its own members who believed that from Jinggangshan to the Long March the chain of events represented a series of CCP miracles waiting to be explained, truths to be validated by the interpretation of experience. It was a world of well-defined intentions and purposes, ranging from the tactical to the most highly generalized and theoretical. Theory was embodied in praxis, military, administrative, productive, artistic, literary, educational, and applied to a political community very much down to earth, whose inhabitants mostly lived in caves, that is, inside the earth itself.

More concretely, however, Yan'an was a resting place midway between exile and return, defeat and power. An ancient walled trading center on the old Silk Road, it was there that the remnants of the First and Second Front Armies that survived the Long March holed up in caves (the more powerful Fourth Front Army establishing its own base area elsewhere).[27] Among the qualities that made Yan'an unique was the transfer of a certain miraculous quality attaching to the survivors of the Long March to Yan'an itself.[28] Arriving at the end of such a "biblical crossing" they conferred on Yan'an the character of a promised land, a New Jerusalem.[29]

As already suggested it was hardly a land flowing with milk and honey. Indeed, it was one of the poorest and most unpromising environments one could imagine for creating a utopian community. By the same token it was redolent of those "margins" of civilized existence where there were created, often by outlaws and bandits, more "fair" or equitable moral communities in exile.[30] In these, as in Yan'an, it took remarkable feats of will and determination for people to survive and even prosper, despite harsh conditions. Hence the sheer existence of Yan'an would seem miracle enough. To become an instructional republic, a community of communicants, was truly extraordinary.

As used here Yan'an refers to the border area administrative region technically under the authority of the Nationalist government of Chiang Kai-shek. In practical terms it was territorially separate.[31] Comprised of parts of three regions in China's northwest, Shaanxi, Gansu, and Ningxia, it was there that Mao and his shrinking band of survivors retreated after a series of military disasters culminating in the loss of the Jiangxi base and leading to the Long March.[32] Nor did Mao know at the start that he would come to rest in what was originally a local soviet, far from the center, and highly autonomous under the leadership of Liu Zhidan and Gao Gang, two notable guerrilla commanders.

The area itself was impoverished. It was situated at a bend in the Yellow River on a plateau of high loess, 450 kilometers from north to south and 400 east to west. Compared to the original Jiangxi base whence the survivors came, Yan'an was considerably less hard-line and accommodating to the interests of local peasants, particularly in matters of landholdings and such family concerns as divorce.[33]

There were nineteen other CCP border area units. Perhaps the two most important after Yan'an, more properly known as Shaan-Gan-Ning (Shaanxi, Gansu, and Ningxia), were Jin-Cha-Ji (Shanxi, Chahar, and Hebei) and Jin-Ji-Lu-Yu (portions of Shanxi, Hebei, Shandong, and Henan). Shaan-Gan-Ning (which we will refer to as Yan'an) was not necessarily the most militarily significant. But it was the New Jerusalem of the communist movement.

Until 1937 a relatively tolerant political atmosphere prevailed. After that time Mao Zedong became more concerned with rules for governing both the areas directly under CCP control and those elsewhere, behind enemy lines. He recognized the vulnerability of voluntarism and, like others in the party, shared the view that discipline and loyalty were intrinsic to authority in terms of doctrinal consistency and militancy. But within the framework of doctrinal puritanism, he remained highly pragmatic. On the one hand, his ideas became more fully developed in what became Mao Zedong Thought; on the other, they also represented drastic modifications in some of the principles to which he had earlier subscribed. For example, since it was necessary to win over peasants, his notions of class and the definition of class enemies became far less exclusive and more flexible than was the case earlier. The same was true for other matters such as property ownership, divorce, and other family concerns.[34]

Yan'an was established during the most desperate period of the revolution, during which the communist military forces were thoroughly disunited. Party organization was ad hoc and improvised. Soldiers were loyal to different military commanders, not all of whom were loyal to Mao. People followed a generally left line, but more or less idiosyncratically. Spontaneity was important, with people volunteering to build caves and roads, make their own clothes, or grow their own food. Military workshops were built and local arsenals established that could be hidden on a moment's notice in case of Japanese attack. Equipment was so antiquated and the facilities for the production of weapons so primitive that it was necessary to prey on the enemy for supplies. Military tactics had to be adapted to the overwhelmingly superior forces of both the GMD and the Japanese. Hence new principles of organization were developed, army units broken up and reconsolidated, and autonomous guerrilla armies capable of living off the land organized behind enemy lines. In turn, living off the land meant careful, indeed meticulous, relations with the peasants, even exemplary compared to the GMD (the lesson of Jinggangshan). By the same token, it was necessary to allow unit commanders great discretion while preventing them (with their close relations with locals) from challenging party authority at the center. Political programs and local governments were established, seeing to it that people in the villages would remain won over and serve as reliable intelligence posts. This, in turn, meant providing land for peasants without destroying the landlord system root and branch because doing so might bring about economic disaster.

Maintaining discipline was no mean task. Politically, it was the job of the party. Working within the framework of the New Democracy movement, the principle was to locate a "Rousseauean general will" in villages, districts, and larger administrative units, those directly under the control of the CCP as well as those behind enemy lines.

As the original Yan'anites were joined by thousands of students, teachers, artists, writers, journalists, Red Army cadres from elsewhere, and poor peasants, a more ascetic ideal began to emerge, almost Jesuitical in character and doctrinally more severe than had prevailed previously. A high proportion of the new recruits to Yan'an were "intellectuals" (defined as those who had a high school or middle school education).[35] Among them were many with their own radical pretensions and views. Most were more anti-Japanese than ideologically predisposed to Marxism. They regarded the CCP as the main force fighting the Japanese invaders. Hence for many of them "joining the revolution" was more a demonstration of nationalist feeling than a commitment to radical ideals.

Not that people went to Yan'an casually. There was the danger of the trip itself, through GMD or Japanese lines. Each person who went had a story to tell. Part of the chemistry of Yan'an was the blending of these individual stories with the three described above. Each person became a significant part of history. Doing so enabled the mutual embellishment of events with interpretation.

By 1940, it was clear that Yan'an needed an intellectual syllabus, one that could graft important historical episodes to present events to be used to illustrate points of theoretical instruction. People were warned against liberalism and other unapproved doctrines. They were showed how the dialectic could be used as an epistemology of class strategy. Each act took on a wider moral significance than its functions might suggest.

Rules for living were endowed with symbolic density. Hence collective living was essentially learning. New recruits arriving in Yan'an were usually billeted eight to a cave. Married couples were often separated. Larger caves looking out on a common courtyard were reserved for higher-ranking party leaders, who periodically moved their headquarters from one part of Yan'an to another to avoid bombing raids. (Invariably, Mao Zedong had the largest cave with the most beautiful view.) In addition to caves, there were regular buildings. Two were large assembly halls, one on the outskirts of town and the other in the town center. People gathering in these for meetings came face to face with the leading members of the CC. All wore uniforms. Weather permitting, study sessions occurred outside.

Even well before Yan'an was fully established, Mao had begun to consolidate his authority by means of a radical reorganization of military, productive, and political forces. Those formerly under the command of and loyal to army commanders and commissars who at times originally identified with party factions hostile to Mao were reassigned through educational institutions and "universities." In turn, political awareness and doctrinal loyalty were intensified through a total process of re-education. The organization of Yan'an remained "civil-military" within the party (and symbolized by the dual descent of authority to political commissars and commanders), a structure bisected by educational institutions, "universities," institutes, and schools. In this, it enlarged on the precedents established in the Jiangxi base. More liberal in some respects than Jiangxi, Yan'an was nevertheless hardly a college campus, although it reminded some outside observers as having something of the atmosphere of a YMCA encampment. People were earnest and committed. Life was balanced between the volleyball court, military exercises, theatrical performances, the classroom, and productive work, with artists and writers from the Lu Xun Academy of the Arts playing an important role.

After several months in training, people were redeployed. Some went as underground workers to the white areas, others became party workers, soldiers, or commanders in the Eighth Route Army. Still others performed educational roles such as teacher, artist, playwright, or musician. All engaged in growing their own food, and often in making uniforms. (Even Mao, somewhat ostentatiously, cultivated his own tobacco patch.) Because of the intersection or crosshatching of roles, people were easily shifted between organizational positions in a command structure (i.e., unit commander or political commissar) to assignments as teachers, organizers of party organs in villages, and so on. Trained personnel were in very short supply. Those with the appropriate talents might be deployed in operatic troupes, theater groups, or "circuit riding" between militia units and work brigades. A Red Army guerrilla commander might serve as chief executive officer of Yan'an city.

At first, the atmosphere of this instructional republic was relatively tolerant and one could not yet speak of the systematic establishment of a discourse community, or an explicit program of exegetical bonding, or the formation of symbolic capital. But all this began to change as early as 1939. In September 1941, it was decided to mount the Rectification campaign. Its first phase began in February 1942 with the publication of key reports of crucial conferences in the *Liberation Daily*. Twenty-two texts were selected to serve as a core curriculum, including guidelines (for the conduct of party members), not all of them written by Mao. They included, for example Liu Shaoqi's "How to Be a Good Communist" and "On Inner Party Struggle," as well as Chen Yun's "How to Be a Communist Party Member."[36] It included attacks by Mao on the "three evil winds"—subjectivism in study, sectarianism in party work, and formalism in propaganda—as well as his warnings against the "subjectivism" and "dogmatism" of intellectuals, excessive "empiricism" of party workers, the sectarianism and tensions "between the individual and the party, between native cadres and cadres from the outside, between cadres in army services and cadres in civilian work." Other materials included the official, that is, Stalinist, *History of the Communist Party of the Soviet Union (Bolshevik)*.[37]

Ostensibly the object was a higher state of political consciousness, secured by means of a common language, with training provided in logic and literacy. The essential texts embodied the appropriate discourse, and discourse became everything. The actual instructional methods were aimed at the exegesis of these texts and "internalizing" them as independently valued objects containing the principles of the movement. Because the discourse prescribed conduct and procedures for model roles, there was interchangeability of not only persons and roles but roles and functions. Not bureaucracy but flexibility characterized party organizations. Although the party suffered personnel losses, it was never crippled.

Rectification occurred in all units, the most important of which were schools, universities, research centers, and more specialized institutes and training programs. Kangda, the Anti-Japanese Military and Political University, was perhaps the most significant. It had a Yan'an campus as well as twelve outlying branches. All told, it was responsible for training perhaps 100,000 graduates. It was modeled in part on the Whampoa (Huangpu) Military Academy, as well as on the Red Army Academy in Ruijin, the latter making the Long March and re-establishing itself as the Chinese People's Red Army Academy before merging with the Red Army College to become Kangda.[38]

The list of lecturers reads like a *Who's Who* of the communist leadership, including Lin Biao, Zhang Wentian, Ai Siqi, and Zhu De. But it was Mao who emerged as the supreme dialectician. Some of his lectures translating his ideas on strategy and tactics into essays on principle became critical in the corpus of Mao Zedong Thought.[39]

During this period a stream of writings poured forth, virtually all of them interpreting experiences in which everyone had either firsthand experience or knowledge. The raw experience was encoded symbolically within narratives and translated into abstract principles and theories, which were then applied, plunged back into concrete military or production campaigns. Every day was an experience in admonishment. Virtually every matter was dealt with, from the sublime to the ridiculous, from guerrilla and protracted warfare to dealing with peasants and how to improve the use of the hoe in farming. Coexisting within the same text were the most elevated classical allusions and earthy barnyard humor. Narrative myths incorporating uncertainty as the whimsy of natural forces now provided the ground for theories of peasant warfare, production, organization—a logic manifested in dialectical illustrations of conceptual control. During the Rectification campaign, as these texts were studied by everyone, principles were systematically applied to all activities—study and learning, military and production campaigns, the organization of village administration, the establishment of the unit (*danwei*) system, and the establishment of branches of schools and universities in other base areas.

Since Yan'an was relatively small, discussion, speeches, and meetings could be held within everyone's earshot, like the ancient Greek Agora. Some of Mao's most important ideas were first speeches. Sheer orality, voice rhetoric, and the theatrical quality of presentation were crucial. Listeners were thus made complicit in the acts of transposition, speaker to writer, brush and inkpot to gun. To convert orality to textuality was not simply a matter of writing. It was an act of endowment.

In this sense, Yan'an as a discourse community was a place where language, meaning, and understanding were the manipulated objects of conscious action and activity—a design for living out a conceptual inversion; in short, a praxis to be realized within all institutions—army, party, government, university, research institute—and utilizing all kinds of instruments—schoolroom classes, theatrical performances, music and opera, and, of course, newspapers and books. A new ideal of a virtuous state was formed not on the basis of some Confucian order but of a communist mandarinate claiming to represent the rational that was real and the real that was rational.

Veterans still describe with excitement how one could go from the cave to the school, to university or institute, for example from the Shaanxi Public School to the Women's University, to specialist schools like the Motor School, the Lu Xun Academy of the Arts, and the Central Party School. Each person could "evolve" in his or her own way. One could "ascend" from an illiterate original condition to basic literacy to the finer ideological points of Narodism, Legal Marxism, Economism, Leninism, Menshevism, Trotskyism, and Leninism.

As indicated, "communicants" in the rectification process were drawn from a very diverse group ranging from nationalist students drawn to Yan'an to fight the Japanese, to intellectuals (who were every variety of radical, from anarchist to

Moscow-oriented Stalinist), to new cadres created out of peasant families, and to recent GMD converts. To be converted into effective revolutionary cadres, small group learning rituals were employed in the process of exegetical bonding. Successful programs and methods were extended and replicated in other base areas, the curriculum reaching out to embrace those involved in village affairs, national salvation associations, winter schools, and mass literacy campaigns.[40]

For those who "graduated" to programs of higher instruction involving abstract and principled forms of understanding, the hope was that the method of instruction itself would serve as a mutual bond, a reflexive intervention, offering insight into people's lives no matter where they came from in the social spectrum. The purpose was to enable people permanently to break away from the original sin of social distance. So each person was required to give up his or her cultural inheritance, high or low, in favor of a common revolutionary one. Discipline resulted less from hierarchy than from obligation.

Since such worthy objects can never be fully realized, hypocrisy was built into the situation. Dissent became privatized. Precisely because social contact was so intimate, association so face-to-face, people not only did not speak truths that they believed in, they disguised these even to themselves. When certain well-known figures (Ding Ling and Wang Shiwei, for example) publicly criticized what they thought was wrong, reprisals from above were swift, brutal, and punitive.

The Rectification campaign was carefully orchestrated, and within it, for a short period, was a frightening experience that no one could misunderstand. Under the direction of Kang Sheng ("Mao's pistol," whom some survivors refer to as "the dark shadow"), a "Rescue campaign" was initiated, the idea being to rescue people from their innermost thoughts, the very doubts they so deeply disguised, their own false ideas and illusions. Kang Sheng took on the prosecutorial role. He played the part in costume. He dressed in black leather, rode a black horse (Mao's horse was white), and was followed by a ferocious black police dog. As Mao's agent within the Rectification campaign, Kang Sheng symbolized that social and intellectual "cauterizing" necessary to change rectification into purification. He was the necessary evil to enable the good.

The "Rescue campaign" introduced an element of paranoia that came to characterize the later Mao. It represented the element of Stalinism within Maoism. Once Mao became convinced that spies and saboteurs had infiltrated party ranks (for example, members of the GMD AB Corps), it was difficult to dissuade him—especially after Kang Sheng played on his fear that no one was guilt-free—that everyone harbored private reservations about the revolution. Kang Sheng reduced such matters to a problem of method, that is, how to force people to confess to harboring subversive thoughts, how to make them implicate others. The techniques employed were familiar enough. Kang Sheng had learned them during his days with the NKVD (secret police) in the Soviet Union. Although the campaign lasted for only three months, it forever changed the character of Maoism. In time, it would prove a precursor to the Cultural Revolution, in which Kang Sheng played the same role.[41]

Mao brought the "Rescue campaign" to an abrupt end by apologizing for it. But it left an indelible mark even among those most committed to Yan'an principles. Again and again, those interviewed referred to it as the major turning point in Yan'an. Yet there were many who regarded it as necessary. The "Rescue campaign" turned up virtually no traitors. But the beatings and suicides, the interrogations and mock trials, exposed the utterly ruthless side of the process of exegetical bonding.

It would hardly be true to say that before the "Rescue campaign" one could see a genuine innocence in Yan'an, a commitment based more on a genuine sense of personal accomplishment and devotion than a belief in doctrinal purity. But many used these terms to describe the experiences of a collective life totally alternative to Chinese society as it was then (and which they characterized as poisoned, depraved, diseased, weak, deceitful, cruel, and criminal). There was also an excitement of new possibilities after war and revolution, built into which was the long-term agenda just beyond the immediate one. These allowed people to believe that rectification was a valuable experience and the "Rescue campaign" a necessary evil. At the same time, from that time on, no one could ignore the dangers to the movement from its leaders as well as its enemies. Yet to remain a good revolutionary for the rest of one's life one had to accept, and remember, that embodied in the redemptive passion of the Odysseus Mao, and the moral yearning of the Socratic one, was a Mao who was, above all, a monopolist of coercive power—shrewd, manipulative, and if necessary, murderous.

The ultimate object in Yan'an was enlightenment, but of a special kind. It began as a loose overall understanding of methods, goals, and aims, and became a precise program of the rules of the game. Study sessions were carefully monitored. The teachers were remarkably well trained. The syllabus was prepared with surprising meticulousness. Materials were not restricted to how to analyze texts, but to how to write, compose music, and present opera and drama. Some of the principles were applications of Stalinist cultural theories. But there was a conscious effort made to use language and visual imagery as a device for leveling down in order to level up. Those who defined how the leveling ought to be done were by that very act exempted. (The discourse of equality was thus also a discourse of hierarchy precisely in the way Foucault meant it in his studies of prisons and sexuality.) The mass line ensured that a common system of referents prevailed.[42] Most important, the intellectuals had to be leveled down in order that everyone else might level up.[43] The mass line was a crucial ingredient in the methods of exegetical bonding.[44]

Spontaneity went hand in hand with manipulation. Formative ideas were improvised on the spot. Mao, of course, did not become a Socratic figure overnight. As he developed the methods for exegetical bonding in the Rectification campaign, he converted experience to theory and theory into symbolic capital. It was that process which gave him his initial power and changed a relatively accessible person given to folksy expression, who dressed in ordinary clothes eschewing insignia and rank, into the great cosmocrat. What distinguished the Yan'anites from those in other border area regions was the degree to which those who "joined the revolution" in Yan'an became a people of the book, namely the chosen people of the Chinese revolution. It was in Yan'an that the party commandments and the exegetical texts were written, and which, until the end of the Cultural Revolution, continued to serve as the holy writ of the revolution.

What is the cosmos? It is framed by the story of the double loss, loss of patrimony, displacement from place and power. The family patrimony of the peasant is lost to the landlord, the national patrimony to foreigners, the second causing the first. The result is a double marginalization in a double capitalism, to be rectified by revolution in the first instance, in a context of nationalism in the second. The prescriptive corpus includes a dialectical epistemology, a theory of praxis, to provide the redeeming framework. What had been lost could be restored, but only under conditions that transformed the patrimony itself. Hence by taking possession of their patrimony, the marginals and dispossessed also repossess themselves.

In these terms, Yan'an was not only a base, a redoubt, but also a symbolic center or matrix. What the combination of narrative and text established was a set of three concentric circles corresponding to the stories described above, a kind of Tantric mandala, with Mao, Buddha-like, at the center. The first circle illustrates the fall, both before and after the downfall of the Qing dynasty, that is, a primordial chaos and anarchy to be overcome by a redeeming pantheon composed of the members of the CC who, together with Mao, represent the transcending project. The second circle describes the peculiar ferociousness of intimacy, the good and evil that characterized the relations between the CCP and the GMD. The third describes Mao's struggle for power within the party, saving it from the corruptors from within and the seducers from without (including Trotskyites, as well as more domestic breeds). The central optic formed by these three circles is of Mao himself as the seeing eye. Hence the description of Yan'an as a Platonic republic with political hierarchy hidden in the relations between "teacher" and "students" (despite the presumptions to equality).[45] In this sense, one can even speak of it as the venue for a kind of "primitive accumulation" of symbolic capital, or the refashioning of power out of the raw materials of language, signs, and symbols. Here too the ingredients of an entire cosmology, part myth, part theory, were built up out of visual metaphors, whose concrete events stood for other such events resonating one with the other, and with textual metonymies. So events served as representations of Mao's theories.

Here we have a model cosmology, built up of visual metaphors and textual metonymies, each event standing for other events as representations of Mao's theories. The more this version of Chinese communism prevailed, the more effectively factional disputes were extinguished, including those originating in the Soviet Union. Comintern intervention was drastically reduced.

Indeed, this is what makes Yan'an so interesting. For what we witness is a virtual Platonic discourse community in the classical sense of the term (to use the term discourse less in a literary sense than an anthropological one) under the auspices of a party whose head is a single dialectical agent.[46] Forming a single discourse, eliminating others, employing a political language spoken through one voice, and by means of a process of exegetical bonding, all contending languages and alternative interpretations (Wang Ming's, for example) were eliminated. Or, to put it in Bakhtin's terms, the discourse itself was reduced from a pre-rectification state of "heteroglossia" to a post-rectification "monoglossia," from a plurality of beliefs to that kind of monism in which people lose either the desire or the will to speak in any other tongue. Yet this same reduction to a singular discourse is also enriched by metaphor and story, a process in which one logical discourse sustains the three stories or concentric circles, each of which is a mythic experience. If this singularity of the discourse "privileges" Yan'an as a venue, it also makes it into a center for the recreation of the world in its own image, the cave standing for the microorganism, the Ur-unit for deconstructing the world as it is while serving as a simulacrum for a society not yet reconstructed. In its day, Yan'an inverted the world of reality as experienced by outsiders. It revealed the potentiality of the world as visualized by insiders. However, as seen below, underneath such romanticism was the ruthless pursuit of power.

For some of those interviewed, and in spite of a certain regret for lost opportunities, what remains memorable about Yan'an even today is not the hardships (although the memory of these remains sharp enough) but a nostalgia for a lost unification of individual determination with collective action. To many of them, every ordinary act should contain a lesson. Hence Yan'an remains for them a triumph of revolutionary principle, purposefulness, and will. These were qualities that, for some participants and observers, gave the original Yan'an its heroic stamp and impressed outsiders like Anna Louise Strong, Agnes Smedley, and Edgar Snow. What they saw in the Yan'anites was a chosen people living in caves (symbolically an "original" human condition) who were determined to begin the world over again.

Despite all the emphasis on a shared and common view, real differences in perspective remained. Among the radicalized and educated youth who made their way through Japanese lines and who remember their lives as a dedication, an absolute determination in the face of absolute hardship, a triumph of their revolutionary will, not a few bitterly resented the conformity being imposed. For others, exegetical bonding was spirited, even fun. To some of the guerrilla commanders sent there after years of fighting, it was irrelevant. To some of them, the aspect of Yan'an that appealed most was the luxury of peace and quiet.

For all of Yan'an's apparent openness, appearances were deceiving. Outside observers thought the leadership remarkably accessible, leading lives very much the same as those of their followers. Insiders noted that the leaders wore better uniforms, rode horses (instead of marching on foot), ate more refined food, and, most important of all, had access to women in ways not available to the rank and file. Sexual puritanism mostly prevailed, the top elite excepted. To an intellectual like Wang Shiwei, these things represented not only hypocrisy but duplicity on the part of the leadership, an immorality meriting contempt, his persistent criticisms making him a thorn in the side of the leadership.

Four Struggles

The fourth (and more phenomenological) part of this chapter deals with the conditions that had to be met before the process could properly begin. I have discussed how Yan'an was bound up with Mao's role; I now want to show how he systematically went about the business of winning power, gaining the mandate, and placing himself at the cosmological center of the party. To do this I briefly describe what I consider the four main power struggles engaged in by Mao in the process of establishing both his own hegemony in the party and the precondition for the hegemony of his discourse. If, as I have suggested, Mao did indeed transform himself from an Odysseus figure, the leader of a small band in the wilderness seeking to redeem the patrimony into a Socratic one, it happened neither easily nor without bitter resistance. As already suggested, Mao needed to monopolize four different kinds of power, each of which represented one of the cardinal points of his personal cosmos and an irreducible minimum for creating the utopian community. Capturing these commanding heights gave him military dominance, central control, intellectual authority, and party orthodoxy. Each is represented by a conflict: between Mao and Liu Zhidan, commander of the guerrilla unit in Yan'an before Mao arrived there; Zhang Guotao, commander of the powerful Fourth Front Army; Wang Shiwei, one of the few real intellectuals in Yan'an; and Wang Ming, the representative of the Comintern and former party secretary.

The conflict with Liu Zhidan was over centralized versus decentralized authority. The struggle with Zhang Guotao was over military control. But behind it was the even more important issue of political control over the Politburo. The conflict with Wang Shiwei was over Mao's monopoly of intellectual life. Wang Ming's concern was which ideological line would prevail.

In the conflict with Zhang Guotao, Mao was always able to maintain control over the Politburo and control the agenda. By so doing, he fixed the limits within which Zhang Guotao could maneuver. He did this in part by using the "miracle" of sheer survival, represented by the Long March itself as an illustration of the success of his principles, tactics, and strategy. By extending these into a system of appropriate rules, he drew the line between permissible and impermissible military strategy. Despite the much greater military force at his disposal, Zhang—the only person of stature with a sufficient military force to challenge Mao on the ground—was both beguiled and outwitted.

Like Mao, a founding member of the CCP and for a long time much more prominent politically, Zhang led his Fourth Front Army on a long march of its own into Sichuan well before Mao departed on his march (during the fourth rather than the fifth Extermination campaign.) Eventually, in 1935 Zhang Guotao's forces moved across the Jialing River under enemy fire to join up with Mao's First Front Army. When they met, Mao had just emerged from the Zunyi Conference as the most influential CCP leader in China. However, Mao's position was precarious, and he did not know where the Long March would wind up.

The reunion only deepened the existing suspicions between Zhang Guotao and Mao. Zhang favored setting up a northwest federation, a notion resisted by Mao. Indeed, Mao believed that the far stronger Fourth Front Army was only seeking an excuse to replace Mao with Zhang Guotao. The history of their conflict has been written up many times and will not be covered in any detail here. However, one thing became very clear. Not only were the personalities of the two men quite different, but Zhang had no great regard for Mao's capacities, either as military strategist or as leader. In his own words, he considered Mao "imaginative and sensitive; his thinking sometimes became quite bizarre, and he would make mythic utterances. He lacked the ability to organize and was reluctant to make precise calculations when dealing with difficult matters. Sometimes his ideas were not clearly expressed, and he often defended his 'opinions of a genius' in an emotional mood."[47]

But he underestimated Mao, to his later regret. Mao, after a crucial meeting on 20 August 1935, decided to change the direction of the Red Army and move to the northeast. Zhang refused to follow. He argued that the river had become unfordable because of heavy rains and ordered that the army unit guarding the CC be detained. Although Zhou Enlai, Zhang Wentian, Bo Gu, Mao, Xu Xiangqian, Chen Changhao, and Wang Jiaxiang together sent him a telegram, asking him to go north, not south, on 9 September Zhang sent off three telegrams, one to the Left Route Army generals declaring "our goal is to go south," a second to Chen Changhao ordering him to lead his troops south and to "thoroughly launch an inner party struggle," and a third telegram to the CC explaining that the plan to go north had many problems and strongly suggesting they give up the original Xia Tao battle plan.

The next day, Mao literally "escaped" from Zhang, going north and taking the First and Third Armies with him. This left behind the Fourth Front Army, which, under Zhang Guotao, began marching south. Meanwhile the party center, now under Mao's control, was outraged. It continued to call for the entire Red Army to go north. On 12 September it convened an enlarged Politburo meeting at Ejie, Gansu. In response, Zhang broke party discipline and, ignoring the authority of the CC, established his own provisional central committee with himself as secretary.[48] What followed was a long and involved series of maneuvers, eventually resulting in a standoff rapprochement. The legitimate CC set up a Northwest Bureau making Zhang Guotao its secretary and Ren Bishi vice secretary. After a prolonged period of bargaining over the proposed Ningxia Battle Plan, Zhang was persuaded to divide his forces, much against his will. In the ensuing battle, part of his army was defeated. After that, he was no longer a threat to Mao.

The question is, why in the end did Zhang back off and accept (however reluctantly) the authority of the CC after he had already committed what was tantamount to the most severe breach of party etiquette? Worse, he had sent a telegram urging, in effect, the overthrow of Mao Zedong (inner party struggle) and attempted to establish an alternate CC. However, despite Zhang's superior military power, Mao was able to bring Zhang to heel by a combination of logical force and appeals to vanity. He made it clear that the cost of conflict between them would be that both would lose to the enemy. Hence they had to reconcile themselves, at least to the point of accepting the rules of the game. But with Mao in control of the CC, it was a zero-sum situation. Indeed, not only did Mao keep the support of the CC despite Zhu De's sympathy for Zhang, the latter's effort to set up an alternative CC was a severe setback to the legitimacy of his claims. Mao never lost the ability to define the range of feasible options.

Zhang Guotao desperately wanted to maintain the Fourth Front Army power intact and establish his own base. Mao, desperate, needed to divide the Fourth Front Army, split its leadership, and prevent the "great schism" between himself and Zhang from becoming effective. Zhang proposed a joint strategy, a united force to defeat the GMD and establish a unified base. Mao countered that if a united force attacked and lost, everything would be lost. He therefore proposed a divided force attack in which the Fourth Front Army, as the strongest, would bear the main brunt of the fighting. From Zhang's point of view, it was an interesting gamble. If he won, he could establish an enlarged base in the north with a direct link to the Soviet Union. If he lost, however, the First and Second Front Armies would be intact but his Fourth weakened. That risk was unacceptable. Hence Zhang Guotao proposed that no battle take place and that his forces move south and then to the northeast. This was ruled out by the CC. If Zhang had acted against its decision, he would have been violating the rules once again, a course that he regarded as fatal.

Hence the "game" being played by Mao was, above all, one of power and legitimacy. Mao had high political legitimacy and low military power. Zhang had high military power and low political legitimacy. Zhang was also very vain. He accepted the secretaryship of the Northwest Bureau because it provided him with a position of great prestige. Therefore he decided to take the chance that, even if his armies were divided, he might win control over the CC, giving him the legitimacy to challenge Mao. This was a fatal decision. It set up the conditions for the massacre of part of the Fourth Front Army during the two-month Ningxia battle. Even so, it took a while longer before Mao could completely finish him off. On 17 April 1938 he was able to have Zhang Guotao expelled from the party under a CC resolution charging him with Trotskyist activity. Shortly thereafter Zhang, very reluctantly, fled to the GMD.

The second case remains a mystery. Liu Zhidan has always been one of the heroes of the revolution. Snow has written him up as an exemplary figure—as a red partisan, part bandit, part militant Communist, who popped up virtually everywhere in Shaanxi, promoting land reform, executing landlords, attracting followers who followed him with devotion. Eventually, as the leader of an undisciplined band of partisans, he fell afoul of central party authorities. Snow recounts how a shadowy figure nicknamed "Chang the Corpulent" trumped up charges against Liu and, as a result of the internecine party conflict, had him jailed and many of his followers tortured and killed.[49] He describes how Mao had him freed and how Liu Zhidan died, "gazing upon the hills he had roamed and loved as a boy, and among the mountain people he had led along the road he believed, in the road of revolutionary struggle."[50]

According to other sources, Liu Zhidan, as a local partisan leader and Whampoa graduate, collided first with the followers of the Wang Ming line. This was before Mao rose to power. He did not like Wang Ming and did not intend to be told what to do from "the mountain top." He thus posed a challenge to the party in terms of local independence versus central party control. Two political toughs were sent to argue with him, Zhu Lizhi and Guo Hongtao, both from Shanghai. They claimed to represent the CC, but Liu cast doubt on their credentials. He pointed out that the CC was on the Long March and not in Shanghai and demanded evidence that they had consulted it.

By themselves, neither Zhu Lizhi nor Guo Hongtao had any military power. But at that point Xu Haidong and his Red Twenty-fifth Army arrived in Shaanbei. A former "bandit" himself, Xu Haidong (the "red potter" in Snow) was also a follower of the Wang Ming line. His political commissar was Cheng Zihua, well known for having massacred many Communists at the Eyuwan (Hebei-Henan-Anhui) base. Indeed, it was as a result of Cheng's excesses that Xu's army was forced to leave the base, going south in a campaign that resulted in the reckless killing of party members. Arriving in Shaanbei, Xu and Cheng joined forces with Zhu Lizhi and Guo Hongtao.

Xu Haidong wanted to combine his Red Twenty-fifth Army, the Red Twenty-sixth Army, and Liu Zhidan's Red Twenty-seventh Army in order to form the Fifteenth Army Group.[51] He formed a "Central Delegation Group" (which was supposed to be under the auspices of the CC) and began altering the party organization in order to gain control. His main target was the Northwest Military Commission, of whose Front Line Committee Liu Zhidan had been general director. Although Xu accomplished his purpose, Liu Zhidan, because of his brilliance as a military commander, was made chief of staff. Subsequently, in the battle of Laoshan against troops of Zhang Xueliang (the "Young Marshal") in which Liu Zhidan was commander, three thousand prisoners of war were taken. It was a personal triumph for Liu Zhidan. But almost immediately a warrant went out for his arrest, along with that of his top military leaders. A campaign to "eliminate counterrevolutionaries" was mounted. Liu, although aware of the warrant and despite vastly superior military forces loyal to him, did not try to escape. Instead he allowed himself to be arrested.[52]

During his imprisonment Liu Zhidan was tortured but did not break. Despite a "confess one's crimes" campaign, he insisted that he had done no wrong. He pointed out to his captors that he could have destroyed them but firmly believed that a base was more important than those who controlled it. This enraged Xu Haidong. Some of Liu's followers were buried alive. The secretary of the county, Du Wan, was placed in a hole, and buried up to his chest. His head turned purple, and his nose began to bleed. He urged them to shoot him, but they did not. He eventually suffocated and died. There were many other atrocities.

A family member of Liu Zhidan went to see Yang Shangkun and Mao, telling them what had happened. Zhou Enlai was also informed. Zhou knew Liu from their Whampoa days and immediately had him released from prison. Liu was made the vice director of the Northwest Office under Zhou himself. But unlike Gao Gang, his old associate, Liu continued to press for the principle of local autonomy and was no more prepared to knuckle under to Mao than he was to Wang Ming. Too prominent to dismiss, too much the hero to ignore, too good a military commander to employ as an administrative cadre, Mao had him lead the Red Army forces in a battle in which it is said he came under a burst of machine gun fire from a watchtower. Whether he was sacrificed by the CCP or killed by the GMD is not generally known. In his dossier he was labeled a "serious rightist."

We can deal with the last two cases only in an even more cursory way. The real story of Wang Ming remains to be told. His own version of his conflict with Mao (and in which he claims Mao was having him poisoned) was published in Moscow, where he fled and eventually died.[53] It has been said that Wang Ming was a much superior Marxist to Mao. A former student at Sun Yat-sen University in Moscow and leader of the so-called twenty-eight and a half Bolsheviks who were trained under Pavel Mif in the Soviet Union, he replaced Li Lisan as general secretary of the party at age twenty-nine and remained in power from 1931 to 1935. In Moscow during the Long March, he was the Chinese representative of the Comintern and Stalin's favorite. At the Seventh Comintern Congress he gave one of the principal addresses (dealing with revolutionary movements in colonial and semicolonial countries) and was elected to the Presidium of the Executive Committee and chosen one of the three candidates to the seven-member Secretariat. It was at this meeting that the principle of the United Front against the Japanese was laid down by Stalin, aggravating a dispute that, reaching back before 1927, concerned the terms under which the CCP could cooperate with the GMD in fighting the Japanese. From the start, Mao's position had been to associate with the GMD while retaining the autonomy and structure of the party intact, a position that did not coincide with Stalin's. Returning to China, arriving in Yan'an together with Kang Sheng and Chen Yun in 1937, and in the aftermath of the Xi'an incident, Wang Ming redefined the appropriate line. He rejected the "adventurism" of Li Lisan, whose military tactics had been responsible for the unnecessary deaths of many top communist leaders and had almost destroyed the CCP, and also Mao's notion of peasant and guerrilla warfare.

Further, he opposed the principles of peasant revolution as these had been laid down by Mao from early days in Hunan onward. Moreover, in debate Wang Ming displayed much greater knowledge of and facility with Marxism than Mao. More orthodox in the Stalinist sense of the term, he believed that not to consider the proletariat the driving force of the revolution, with the peasantry mobilized behind it, was to miss the essential "motor" force of the revolution. So, despite his opposition to Li Lisan, he supported Moscow's strategy based on the urban proletariat and the reconquest of the cities.[54]

In the debates over a United Front from below versus a United Front from above, Wang Ming favored the Stalinist version of the United Front against Japan, arguing that "the chief weaknesses and shortcomings of our party remain the same; that is, first, we have not understood that the policy of the anti-imperialist united front is the principal and only tactical weapon we can use to put into practice our slogan for a national-revolutionary war; second, we have not yet succeeded in linking up our anti-imperialist united front tactics with our activities in other spheres." These would include milder confiscation policies with respect to rich peasants, craftsmen, and landowners sympathetic to the anti-Japanese war. It meant giving up workers' control of industrial enterprises and allowing noncommunists to fight in the Red Army. He favored a closer association with Chiang Kai-shek (as had Zhang Guotao), and implied that Mao represented a sectarian element in the party.[55]

Mao opposed Wang Ming, of course, while adopting some of his views about how to deal with issues of confiscation, landlords, and so on, but without compromising his basic position on autonomy and the primacy of revolution within the anti-Japanese war. At first, he began to play cat and mouse with Wang Ming. Later he would humiliate him. In any case, with the fall of Wuhan, Wang Ming was finished. This was effectively enshrined at the sixth plenum of October 1938, after Stalin had sent a message stating that Mao should lead the CCP.

The ostensible reason for the 1942 launching of the Rectification campaign was to repudiate the Wang Ming line and break the power of the "twenty-eight and a half Bolsheviks." This was simply an excuse. Not only were the latter doctrinally divided all along, but the most clearly Stalinist figure in practice, Kang Sheng, was also among the most anti-Stalinist. By the time Wang Ming returned to China from Moscow, the influence of the Comintern within the decision-making councils of the Politburo had already waned. Otto Braun's influence had been broken. Stalin was treated warily at best.

In a sense one could say that Wang Ming became Mao's straw man. Not entirely, of course. There was always Moscow's support to contend with. And Wang Ming himself may have been more popular than contemporary accounts suggest. He was, after all, the top Comintern authority on colonial affairs. Moreover, it is said that he returned to China in part to negotiate directly with Chiang Kai-shek on behalf of Stalin. But it soon became clear that he had arrogated the right to speak for the party without official authorization from the CC. As his influence waned, he became ill. Increasingly an object of contempt and relegated to increasingly minor posts, he eventually returned to Moscow.

The last case has been exhumed lately in China largely through the efforts of that remarkable woman journalist, Dai Qing. For many, the case of Wang Shiwei has come to represent the personification of Mao's use and abuse of intellectuals. It has aroused considerable interest among American and French specialists on China.[56]

The case of Wang Shiwei is a good example of multiple codings of the sort we have been concerned with. On one level it shows how one of the few genuine intellectuals in Yan'an (best known as a translator) became a symbol of resistance to Mao's definition of how the intellectual's role should be subordinated to the revolution as laid down in Mao's "Talks at the Yan'an Forum on Literature and Art." Wang Shiwei, stalwartly rejecting subordination, became something of a hero, and the putative representative of the Lu Xun intellectuals. His activities coincided with a preliminary phase of ideological purification, from 1939 to 1941, extending as well into the first phase of the Rectification campaign.

The latter began on 1 February 1942 with Mao's speech and culminated on 23 June 1942 with an anti–Wang Shiwei meeting. This period became known as the "expose one's thoughts" period, or "the exposure phase." Emphasizing openness, encouraging wall posters and bold speaking, this period (like that of the "Hundred Flowers" campaign a little over a decade later) eventually led to a crackdown. For Kang Sheng, "half-heartedness" and "two-heartedness" (a lack of genuine revolutionary fervor and antirevolutionary feelings, respectively) were suddenly revealed, and he moved against both kinds of backsliders as well as spies, enemies, and Trotskyites.

Wang had joined the party in 1926, working mainly in Shanghai. He became involved with some of the Trotskyist opposition, translated some of Trotsky's writing, and thus gave some substance to the later charge that he was a "Trotskyist" (a charge now recognized as an "error" by the CC). He went to Yan'an in 1936 to become a research officer in the Marxist-Leninist Academy (which subsequently became the Central Research Institute), mainly as a translator.

Wang became known in Yan'an as one of the "four eccentrics." A dissenter from the start, he associated himself with Ding Ling and Liu Xuewei, both editors of the Art Column of *Liberation Daily*. Liu Xuewei wrote an article on "Revolutionary Literature," published in June 1942, in which he criticized revolutionary literature as coarse, dull, direct, and inferior and urging a higher artistic level. This article was followed up by another on 7 June, calling for freedom of thought as the basis of the New Democracy. On 22 September, another article argued that too much emphasis on politics lowered the development of the arts.

Shortly after the Rectification campaign began in February 1942, on 9 March Ding Ling published her famous article "Thoughts on 8 March, Women's Day," attacking the party for its treatment of women. Mao was quite upset by the article. A few days later Ding Ling was dismissed as editor of the Art Column and a few days after that Wang Shiwei published "Wild Lilies."

It proved to be a bombshell. Published in two parts on 13 and 23 March in *Liberation Daily*, it was (according to Cheek) modeled after Lu Xun's satirical essay "A Rose Without Blooms."[57] Attacking Mao's taste for beautiful women, it offered as an alternative to Jiang Qing an exemplary model of a woman revolutionary executed in 1928. Wang attacked dancing and the parties for which the leadership became noted. He parodied Mao's style. He implied that the three classes of clothing and five classes of food differentiating people at different levels of rank represented unjustified privilege, indeed class, a charge that struck Mao's rawest nerve.

Coming as it did in the context of other criticisms of party policy in Yan'an, "Wild Lilies" seemed to represent the resistance of the intellectuals by invoking the spirit of Lu Xun, arousing great concern among senior party cadres. It now seemed necessary to establish clear ground rules, all the more so since Wang had already become something of a local hero by having already been thrust into the Rectification campaign in its first phase, that is, during the time when many people put up dissenting wall posters. So alarmed was the party at the time that it proposed establishing a Rectification Campaign Examination Committee to monitor wall posters.

Wang, at that time thirty-six years old, vigorously opposed such a committee. When it became clear that one would be established he insisted that its members be appointed by a vote, and the directors of all departments and the president of the Central Research Institute as well. He also proposed that the writers of wall posters remain anonymous to protect the rights of the writer. Wang's proposals were overwhelmingly supported. Elections were carried out, and while those elected were not favored by Wang Shiwei and his group, the latter were jubilant at this "triumph of democracy." Wang continued to write articles attacking Li Weihan, the director of the institute. He began a wall poster newspaper series called "Arrow and Target," the arrow of dissent being fired directly into the target, the discussions of Marxism-Leninism and the fundamental character of the Chinese revolution. When some of its articles were printed on cloth and put up outside the southern gate of Yan'an city, readers "flocked to read them in the way they flock to a fair." Wang Shiwei became a star in Yan'an.[58]

It did not take long for the party to react. On 27 May 1942 the "struggle session" with Wang Shiwei began. Among the charges were that Wang had associations with Trotskyites, that he claimed Stalin's nature was not "lovable," and that Karl Radek (accused of the Kirov assassination[59]) was a good person. More astounding, he charged that the Comintern itself must be held accountable for the failure of the Chinese revolution of 1927, that the trial of Zinoviev and the accusation that he was a traitor needed to be taken with a grain of salt; that parts of Trotsky's theory were correct. He was also accused of slandering party leaders by calling them corrupt, that he disrupted party unity, and that he used the term *hard bone* (brave) in reference to his friends and *soft bone* (coward) to other comrades. Finally, it was said that Wang's articles slandered the party and that, describing himself as a modern Lu Xun, he had called upon the youth to rally to him.

The results of the attack were mixed. Many sided with Wang Shiwei. To correct the confusion, everyone was instructed by the Standing Committee to read Lenin on "Party Organization and Literature," Lu Xun's speech at the Founding Congress of the Left-Wing Writers Association, Mao's conclusion to the Yan'an Forum on Art and Literature, the first section of the tenth chapter of the *History of the Communist Party of the Soviet Union (Bolshevik)*, and selections from the second volume of Stalin's *Selected Works* (about crushing opposition cliques).

Wang attempted to resign from the party. His request was refused. In his subsequent testimony, he withdrew his request. But he refused to admit mistakes. Kang Sheng, Chen Boda, and others vilified him as a filthy character, elaborating on this theme in great detail. Finally, all the members of the Central Research Institute demanded that Wang Shiwei be expelled from the party. On 11 June, the last day of the proceedings, Ding Ling recanted her thoughts of 8 March and attacked Wang Shiwei for insulting "the literature and arts circle."

Wang Shiwei was put in prison. Mao did not want him killed. He wanted to use Wang Shiwei as the negative model during the Rectification campaign while he was building up the "Yan'an Way" as the obverse. Despite explicit orders that he not be killed (he was weak and sick in prison), when Yan'an was attacked by the Nationalist forces in 1947 and the Communists had to retreat, Xu Haidong (or He Long, there is a dispute over this) had him executed.

The four cases define the immediate context of Mao's politics within Yan'an. The first is a rationalistic calculus, a pure game of power inside the framework of a retrieving myth and projective logic. The second was over power, defining it as top-down, not bottom-up, despite the illusion of democracy. The third was over whose Marxism would prevail and whose texts would become hegemonic. Leading through the Rectification campaign, the basis for exegetical bonding, it established the orthodoxy of Mao Zedong Thought. The fourth established Mao as the sole and proprietary intellectual. In two of the cases the consequence was death, in another exile, in another ignominy. Together, the four "contenders" define alternative principles rejected by Mao and so locate a set of "boundaries" within which Mao emerges as both supreme military figure and cosmocrat. His writings, re-edited into a corpus now referred to as Mao Zedong Thought, universalized what began as specific lectures about particular events. They enabled Mao to situate himself between the rightist and antitheoretical or "pragmatic" line of Zhang Guotao and the more orthodox Stalinist line of Wang Ming;

between the decentralizing pull of Liu Zhidan and the tight central control of the Li Lisan line; and intellectually against the elitism and democratism of Wang Shiwei. As for the discourse itself, it explicitly recognized the crucial importance of culture, text, writing, literature, and the arts as weapons of revolutionary theory and practice.

In the context of these and other disputes and conflicts, we can see Yan'an forming into a "mobilization" or a "semiotic" space. Serving as a revolutionary simulacrum, its symbolic capital radiated outward to communist guerrilla forces and other base areas as a miniaturized version of the revolution to come. Many aspects remain to be discussed. In his conflicts with Zhang Guotao and Liu Zhidan, one sees Mao playing an Odysseus role and rejecting other contenders for the privilege. In the conflicts with Wang Ming and Wang Shiwei, he plays a more Socratic role, that of the supreme dialectician, the cosmocrat, presiding over history while making it.

With the hardening of Mao Zedong Thought into a discourse, a way of thinking, a mode of dialectical truth, each alternative came to be seen not as different views or alternative truths, but rather as alternatives to the truth itself. Moreover, the combination of articulated principle and ruthless struggle is itself part of the story-telling and narrative process and the interpretive experience. Coming early in the Yan'an experience, each struggle leaves a layer of potential doubt and dissent, despite victory. Hence, although unevenly, and particularly in the case of Wang Ming and Wang Shiwei, the Rectification campaign is an attempt not only to develop a hermeneutic by means of exegetical bonding but to make it totally hegemonic as a language separating the enlightened from the unenlightened and segregating a good Communist from backsliders or dissidents. In this sense Yan'an was both a moral high ground and a Machiavellian moment.[60]

Exegetical bonding was in effect Mao's vision, translated by means of his version of the dialectic, convertible to intensely grueling learning sessions following elaborate educational procedures. Its strength (which would become its weakness) was that it could admit no extraneous elements at any level, even though it could be applied with great flexibility and varied to suit local conditions. When the CCP finally won and, in effect, turned the Chinese world upside-down, the next task was not only to universalize this vision and adapt it to new circumstances but also to rout all contrary modes of thought not just in the party but in the country as a whole. But dissent, like sin, when thrown out the front door returns by the back—the hegemonic imposition destroyed symbolic capital itself. Eventually, there was no one else to blame for what went wrong but the party. More recently, the party has come to represent all that went wrong and much that was reprehensible. The re-enactment of Yan'an during the Cultural Revolution is a case in point—the orthodoxy of Mao Zedong Thought turned into a kind of magical realism whose consequences were truly tragic.

The post-1979 reforms weakened the party's monopoly on truth. In doing so, however, it produced a condition for which the party was ill-prepared. Diversities of opinion, the logic of democratization—all posed challenges to dialectical orthodoxy. To square the circle, the authorities accepted the logic of the first without the practice and the orthodoxy of the second without the principle. The party thus got the worst of both possible worlds. And it reasserted its monopoly on truth just as events were moving toward its pluralization.

Historically, Yan'an is of a piece with the radical phases of both the English and French revolutions, succeeding where the others failed. "The ideal was a society of all-round non-specialists helping each other to arrive at truth through the community."[61] It represented an ideal that rejected not only feudalism and capitalism but also individualism, on grounds that the latter would end in anarchy. It offered instead dialectical reason, applied to Chinese conditions, under communitarian circumstances of mutualism, requiring the discipline of the text. In this sense Yan'an, like the other utopian communities elsewhere, was believed by its founders to represent the triumph of collective will over individual competition. To universalize it was to change the nature of social life itself.

In terms of the practical complexities of development, Yan'an had little concrete to offer. Its symbolic capital dissipated despite radical efforts to revive it during the Great Leap Forward and the Cultural Revolution. It became the legitimizing myth of the revolution, but only in ritualized form and devoid of genuine significance.[62] Yan'an was attractive to those who sought to combine radicalism, moral militancy, and political discipline within a rationalistic integument. In contrast to the present, as socialist regimes dwindle and China confronts the void left in the aftermath of Tiananmen Square, the sole and residual significance of Yan'an today is the shadow it casts on both the desire and the need for democratization.

The City in the Square

Nothing, then, could have been more provocative than the events that took place in Tiananmen Square, despite the self-discipline and the peacefulness of the demonstrations. They began, ostensibly, as a memorial to Hu Yaobang, who had defended the New Democracy movement on previous occasions and been forced to resign for his pains. But in fact (and readily perceived by the Yan'anite traditionalists in power) the leadership recognized that something was going on that amounted to much more than provocation. In terms of the present analysis, what the old guard saw was the public expression of the new discourse, not simply a dialogue between intellectuals, and at the most sensitive and symbolic center of power in China. For there in front of the great gate to the Forbidden City, near where the Ming emperors had created a space to refract the heavenly with the imperial mandate, where the May Fourth 1919 demonstrations had occurred, where the People's Republic was proclaimed, where Mao had greeted the Red Guards during the Cultural Revolution, and where the great outburst of mourning for Zhou Enlai had occurred, namely the site of multiple retrievals, a democratic projection was being formed. The object was to recognize politically that a new civil society was taking shape, that it had to be institutionally articulated, and that purification of the elites, greater accountability, pluralism, and institutional change followed a logic of their own. In effect, what the old Yan'anites in power recognized immediately was that in Tiananmen Square in the spring of 1989, a simulacrum had been formed that was capable of generating symbolic capital of its own and mobilizing mass support from within the party and from workers and peasants. What was invoked was an entirely new definition of radicalization, precisely the kind that Mao and virtually all his followers fundamentally opposed and Deng Xiaoping feared.

The Yan'anite old guard flexed its arthritic muscles. As in 1979, 1986, and 1987, its first reaction was to smash the student movement before it gained too much momentum. Despite the limited character of the demands made by the students (who were anxious to discuss democratic reforms with the authorities less in concrete terms than as a process), the old guard knew that dialogue would end the order they represented. Already, although not very systematically, something like exegetical bonding had begun to occur in university dormitories, in eating places, wherever people gathered. Moreover, a "structure" was forming within the vast space of the square as it came alive with students with all the potentiality of a new and democratic revolutionary simulacrum, a miniaturized version of a society that might come into being, a crude and more or less spontaneously organized but functioning democratic society.

The square became a city within a city and a society within the state, not in caves this time but in tents, a sea of tents resembling islands in a sea of red flags and slogans. The public theater and the Agora principle were at work again. Long and hortatory statements blared over loudspeakers, some hand-held, others at the top of the Martyrs Memorial but within visible range of the speakers. Here one saw a repossession of power by an inheriting class of potential elites who refused to wait passively any longer until it arrived at power. It demanded a share in how the power should be defined.

For a few tragically brief weeks, Tiananmen Square became a primitive democracy, indeed, a community. Complete with "streets" and "neighborhoods," it was a semi-autonomous structure of power. Movement within it remained orderly. Different sectors were cordoned off, requiring a pass stamped by someone in "authority" to enter. Each neighborhood had its tents and shelters—each a residential community with a common space and large eating areas. Within, amid a jumble of bedding, pots, and pans, people read, talked, wrote, passed out leaflets, and organized. Like Yan'an, it was structured around universities and schools. Learning became an authorization for opinion.

Some students were representatives of universities and institutes in Beijing. Others came from elsewhere in China taking advantage of the government's remarkable decision to provide free train service and permit privileges, facilitating their travel to the square (privileges that would be withdrawn by the authorities after martial law). Students organized latrines and garbage disposal. Food was donated in large supplies by factory units and rural villages. Support came from town and countryside. Transport—trucks, buses, cars—materialized out of nowhere. Just when it appeared that the movement might falter, the hunger strike began, arousing a great wave of public sympathy. Medical facilities sprang up, and doctors, nurses, and medical assistants rushed to the site dressed in white, wearing surgical masks and caps. "Roads" were made between the encampment areas and kept clear for ambulances. Water was provided in large trucks. Food and soft drinks and bedding of every description were donated by citizens. Funds were collected and distributed, posters printed, newssheets distributed, an internal postal service established, monitors appointed, and tribunals for maintaining law and order, and so on. A people's university was organized, reading material printed and distributed, relations between the "interior" and the "exterior" laid down, and processions orchestrated and choreographed day and night.

The stage was the great obelisk, the monument to the martyrs of the revolution, its tiers of steps leading toward a stone parapet. Anyone was allowed to sit on the lower steps, but to go to the parapet required a pass. At the upper level were representatives of the seven- or eight-member committee representing the top leadership of the student movement and composed of representatives of student committees.

A kind of magnetic field set up around the monument radiated back to each university campus where there was an equivalent public space. In each revolutionary center everyone gathered, surrounded by posters, forests of bicycles, and the inevitable public loudspeaker, each a miniaturized version of Tiananmen Square. Here, too, the loudspeakers interspersed speeches with news from the "front" and organizational announcements. Wall posters could be funny, the calligraphy ferocious. Some were in English. So from Tiananmen Square there radiated out to each university the language and discourse of the new revolution to waiting crowds; it was picked up, received, and from each campus radiated back again. Students themselves moved back and forth continuously, keeping their bicycles ready as they waited for instructions. In the dormitories students hidden from public view and on guard against police agents figured out strategy and tactics and tried to systematize an ever-changing situation. They were joined in their endeavors by young instructors and teachers. Older professors, although in sympathy, remained for the most part aloof.

At the square itself, from the highest parapet of the Martyrs Memorial, speeches and announcements of programs and agendas were within the hearing range and the field of vision of the crowds. People discussed theories of democracy while, over their heads, music played passages from Beethoven's Fifth and Ninth symphonies, the "Internationale," and of course rock and folk music redolent of the 1960s.

Just as Yan'an had become a total community, so too did Tiananmen Square. It became what it was intended to be, a course, a lesson in democracy, and a praxis, an example of how democracy could arise by means of the pluralism of the civic society it claimed to represent. The groups of demonstrators who marched down the main routes and passed though the square followed the lines carefully demarcated by ropes and monitored by students wearing red armbands. Every variety of unit was represented, work, school, institute. Each carried flags and banners. Journalists demanded a free press and the end of censorship. Research workers called for more freedom from control. Workers came from some of the biggest factories in Beijing. There were cadres and members of local branches of the CCP. There were divisions, of course. "Neo-authoritarians" believed in the democratization of the CCP. "Radical democrats" preferred something akin to a nineteenth-century constitutional government. Asked if they accepted the principle of "one person, one vote," people tended to say yes. Asked if they wanted every peasant to have the vote, the same people hesitated. No one had very clear ideas about what kind of democracy might work in China. In fact, they were arguing for intellectual democracy and control over decision-making. All agreed that the process of democratization had to begin.

The tragic events of 4 June are well enough known. The old guard struck the movement down in an exercise of raw power. First, lightly armed units of the army poured out of the gates of the Forbidden City. Then army columns, heavily armed with automatic weapons and tanks, came down from both east and west entry points to the square, along Chang'an Avenue. Out of the Great Hall of the People on one side and the Museum of the Revolution on the other came units of the People's Liberation Army, "liberating" the square from its liberators. The leadership refused those who asked for the power to redefine this space in terms of democracy and violently rejected the claims of the next generation (those who, indeed, were the designated beneficiaries of the communist revolution). Today the square remains heavily guarded, void of that exuberance, vibrancy, spirit, and courage of the many young people who asked their government to begin a process, to start a dialogue, and who were met instead with machine guns and tanks.[63]

If in Tiananmen Square one saw a new discourse community come into being and the beginnings of a new and democratic expression of symbolic capital, one also saw there the final dissolution of that original unity of opposites that for so long was represented in Yan'an, the original contract of power and principle. Yan'an was an instructional republic in which virtually everyone was at some point a student. Now it was the students who sought to teach the instructors that the old social contract was dead and that indeed, communism had become in China much like Mao's remains, a mummy on display in a crypt. Indeed, one could visit the mausoleum and then walk around the corner a few blocks to the largest Kentucky Fried Chicken emporium in the world for lunch. It did a lively business all through the events. Indeed, the two large effigies of Colonel Sanders standing at the entrance matched in rotundness and vacuity of expression the portrait of Mao looking down from its perch on the wall near the entrance to the Forbidden City.

It was toward that portrait that the students placed their Goddess of Democracy. Dressed in white robes of plaster and Styrofoam, holding the torch of freedom in both hands literally under the old man's nose, her large, not ungraceful body slightly turned, as if she could not bear to look at the portrait, she confronted the old man and all that he stood for. Her face was serene, even triumphant, encircled and wreathed by the red flags and painted slogans of the revolution. Below were the tents of those who were her guardians. A magnet for the crowds, she was a first target of the tanks that broke through to the square. But even in the light of the next day, when she lay smashed and in pieces on the ground, all innocence gone, her presence continued to define the space so forcibly evacuated. She remains the absent presence waiting to be filled, despite the guards and the soldiers. No one can walk in that square so redolent of the noise of the tanks and the cries of a lost generation without remembering what was lost.

Despite the strenuous efforts of party and state to brand the movement counterrevolutionary, it remains revolutionary. By proclaiming the need for a fresh start, a demand to begin all over again, Tiananmen Square itself represented an enactment, a new social contract, a powerful normative fiction in an empirical reality, the true occasion for symbolic capital. What the events exposed was how the principles established in Yan'an had been brutalized and corrupted in the political praxis of a state dishonored by abusing its people.

Tiananmen Square "deconstructed" the structure of the state, and the *guanxi* socialism it had come to represent. In its place it sought not a solution but a process, a fifth modernization—democratization—leading toward a normal politics, a self-validating political system, and a new discourse of politics.

Notes

Research for this study was done under a grant from the Committee on Scholarly Exchange with the People's Republic of China, the Department of History, Beijing University, and the Institute of Marxism-Leninism, and Mao Zedong Thought of the Chinese Academy of Social Sciences. I am particularly indebted to Professors Su Shaozhi and Luo Rongqu and my research collaborators, Michelle Chua, Zhang Meng, Song Xiaobing, and Zhao Yi.

For a fuller analysis see David E. Apter and Tony Saich, *Discourse on Power: The Revolutionary Process in Mao's Republic* (Cambridge: Harvard University Press, 1994).

1. See Tatyana Tolstaya, "In Cannibalistic Times," *The New York Review of Books*, 38, no. 7, 3.

2. Evidence of the instrumental value of the myth of Yan'an is demonstrated by the efforts made to revive it along with the discourse of the mass line in order to recapture the rhetorical initiative from critics inside and outside China.

3. China had much the same impact after World War II, especially in the so-called third world, where efforts were made to emulate or refashion the revolutionary experience from above in the form of more or less caricatured replications of Chinese experience in the name of a common liberation struggle against capitalism and colonialism. These

would include such abortive regimes as those of Sékou Touré in Guinea or Kwame Nkrumah in Ghana, not to mention Fidel Castro in Cuba.

4. For the concept of predemocratic politics, see David E. Apter, *The Politics of Modernization* (Chicago: University of Chicago Press, 1972) and *Rethinking Development* (Beverly Hills, Calif.: Sage Publications, 1987).

5. People have become experts at hiding what they prefer not to divulge. In this regard an ethnography of memory is really a kind of historical phenomenology, requiring painstaking and probing interview and re-interviews. Most were conducted with several Chinese colleagues rather than one-on-one with a translator.

We began by dwelling on ordinary details: "How did you happen to join the revolution?" "Did you tell your family of your decision?" "How did you actually get to Yan'an?" "How many times a day and what did you eat?" "Did women prepare the food?" "How many lived in your cave?" "What happened if you were sick to your stomach?" "What did you use money for?" "What happened if you wanted a woman/man?" "What were your most frightening/despairing moments?" "How far were you from a latrine?" And so on, building up to more political questions: "Did you experience rectification?" "What questions were asked?" "Were you 'exposed' during the Rescue Campaign?" "Do remember any spies being discovered during that campaign?" "What were your main doubts?" "Who were your best friends?"

6. The term is taken from Pierre Bourdieu, *Outline of the Theory of Practice* (Cambridge: Cambridge University Press, 1968). Bourdieu uses it to refer to honor, prestige, and the rules of reciprocity and exchange of similar non-economic but highly valued symbolic values. As used here symbolic capital consists of the myths and theories used in retrievals of the past and projections of the future, given density and magnified by means of metaphors and metonymies and embodied in texts and logic, the language and discourses of which have performative consequence.

7. It is not my purpose here to go into organizational details or to describe the political and administrative structure of Yan'an. Although in part dated, the most important single source of such information remains Mark Selden, *The Yenan Way* (Cambridge: Harvard University Press, 1971).

8. See Jean Baudrillard, *Simulacres et simulation* (Paris: Editions Galilée, 1981).

9. See Claude Lévi-Strauss, "The Story of Asdiwal," in E. R. Leach, ed., *The Structural Study of Myth* (London: Tavistock, 1967), 1–48.

10. They reached a second high point during the ideologically intense period of the Cultural Revolution. After that, as symbolic capital waned, principle declined and all pretense of principle was abolished by the events at Tiananmen Square. For a discussion of symbolic revivalism, see Tang Tsou, *The Cultural Revolution and the Post-Mao Reforms* (Chicago: University of Chicago Press, 1986).

11. See Bernard Yack, *The Yearning for Total Revolution* (Princeton: Princeton University Press, 1988).

12. See David E. Apter, "Mao's Republic," *Social Research* 54, no. 4 (winter 1987): 691–729.

13. It was also a movement preoccupied with moral boundaries, geographical and ethnic boundaries, crossings and passages during the Long March, and boundaries of the body (including sexual ones).

14. In part what the present approach aims to do is go beyond the problematics of such historical sociologists as Pareto, Durkheim, and Weber, in whose terms Yan'an might be considered an example of radical and disjunctive change in norms and values, or a transformation in what Pareto referred to as residues and sentiments, emphasizing too as the independent variable a communist functional equivalent for the Protestant ethic. It is, of course, a truism that no society exists without beliefs and cultural systems—moral,

religious, political, etc. The point is to locate those political moments when revolutionary commitments overwhelm the priorities and claims of daily life and impinge decisively on more ordinary calculations, and to try and explain what makes that possible. See Clifford Geertz, *The Interpretation of Cultures* (New York: Basic Books, 1973).

15. Hence the self-conscious efforts made to displace Confucianism and replace it with Maoism. See Joseph R. Levenson, *Confucian China and Its Modern Fate* (Berkeley: University of California Press, 1968); and Jonathan Spence, *The Gate of Heavenly Peace* (London: Penguin Books, 1982). See also David E. Apter, "The New Mytho-logics and the Spectre of Superfluous Man," *Social Research* 52 (summer 1985): 269–307.

16. The "symbolic capital" that concerns us occurred in its own day. We are less interested in Yan'an as the "legitimating myth" of the CCP. We are not trying to understand the immediate circumstances and convulsive events that Mao and his colleagues experienced, understood, and transcended by means of a functional model. Nor is the approach favored here a derivative of modernization theory. We are not contrasting communism with traditionalism, neofeudalism with modernity, nor examining the transformation of norms and values, social structures and classes, and perceptions and motivations in terms of an integrative model.

Rather the view favored here places symbolic capital at the center and emphasizes collective rationality as it was arrived at through the process of "exegetical bonding," in a tradition of analysis that Pareto described as symbol and meaning rather than cause and effect. The focus is not on individual "utilities" but on interpretive understanding, not on self-interested individuals but on their contributions to collective action.

17. While I have relied on the main texts themselves, among the most important interpreters whose works I have consulted, two stand out, Levenson, especially his magisterial work, *Confucian China and Its Modern Fate*, and various writings of Stuart R. Schram, particularly *The Political Thought of Mao Tse-tung* (New York: Praeger, 1969), *The Thought of Mao Tse-tung* (Cambridge: Cambridge University Press, 1989), and his introduction to Li Jui, *The Early Revolutionary Activities of Comrade Mao Tse-tung* (White Plains, NY: M.E. Sharpe, 1977).

18. See Yack, *The Yearning for Total Revolution*.

19. For an earlier field study showing how this process works in a contemporary setting, see David E. Apter and Nagayo Sawa, *Against the State* (Cambridge: Harvard University Press, 1984). For an analysis of the concept of "mobilization system," see David E. Apter, *Choice and the Politics of Allocation* (New Haven: Yale University Press, 1971). See also Apter, *Rethinking Development*.

20. For a preliminary discussion of this matter see Apter, "Mao's Republic," op. cit.

21. What in effect is being examined is how revolutionary commitments overwhelmed the priorities of daily life and powerfully impinged on more ordinary calculations. Of course, as I intend to show, on closer inspection there was plenty of calculation involved among those intent on changing the rules themselves. Hence, while Yan'an represented a normative implosion overturning the normal everyday assumptions about life as it was lived, it happened in a way that first overturned, then recombined and unified rational individual-actor and collective-actor rules.

22. On the Futian incident see Chapter 4 in this volume by Averill.

23. See Boyd Compton, ed., *Mao's China: Party Reform Documents, 1942–44* (Seattle: University of Washington Press, 1952). See also Jane L. Price, *Cadres, Commanders, and Commissars* (Boulder: Westview Press, 1976).

24. See Michel Foucault, *Discipline and Punish* (New York: Vintage Books, 1979).

25. "Symbolic capital," like its more familiar economic counterpart, can be "saved" and "invested." It can be used to define contractual obligations. But politically it differs from economic capital insofar as its significance depends on its ability to mobilize effec-

tively and collectivize a militant band out of a diverse and miscellaneous clientele.

26. See James Clifford, "On Ethnographic Surrealism," *Comparative Studies in Society and History*, 23 (October 1981): 539–64.

27. The walls have since been torn down, partly after being destroyed by Japanese bombing during the war.

28. The events seemed miraculous not only to the Chinese but also to outside observers. Edgar Snow, writing on the Long March, says, "The statistical recapitulation of the Long March is impressive. It shows that there was an average of almost a skirmish a day, somewhere on the line, while altogether fifteen of those were devoted to major battles. Out of a total of 368 days en route, 235 were consumed in marches by day and 18 in marches by night. Of the 100 days of halts—many of which were devoted to skirmishes—56 days were spent in northeastern Szechuan, leaving only 44 days of rest over a distance of about 5,000 miles, or an average of one halt for every 114 miles of marching. The mean daily stage covered was 71 *li*, or nearly 24 miles—a phenomenal pace for a great army and its transport to *average* over some of the most hazardous terrain on earth." See *Red Star over China* (New York: Random House, 1938), 348.

29. Returning to Yan'an today one would find it difficult to recapture what it must have looked like. There are few remains of the period. At the top of the hills overlooking Yan'an city at the bend in the river one can still see the ancient cave of the thousand Buddhas where the Communists set up their printing press. The ancient Pagoda, the symbol of Yan'an embossed on millions of buttons worn by Red Guards during the Cultural Revolution, still stands. Mostly, however, Yan'an city consists of Chinese-Stalinist cement buildings. It is a far cry from the ancient walled city to which Communists retreated.

30. The tradition of semi-autonomous rebel bases is a very old one in China. See the description in Jonathan D. Spence, *The Search for Modern China* (New York: W.W. Norton, 1990), 22–23.

31. Yan'an itself was technically subordinate to the Nationalist government. But after the 1936 accord with Chiang Kai-shek, Yan'an became an autonomous community with its own economy, its own fiscal and monetary system, its own administration and government. Periodically blockaded by the Nationalists (even while engaging in battle against the Japanese), it had to create its own supplies of food, weapons, and materials, especially in 1941. All the more impressive then were its concrete accomplishments. So successful were its efforts to make scrublands into productive farming areas that Mao's ideas of agricultural production were reshaped by what happened. The Nanniwan Brigade, for example, a military unit sent into the bush to clear it and thereby become self-reliant, became part of the Yan'an legend.

32. The smaller the band, the more "purified" it became in its own eyes.

33. See Hua Chang-Ming, *La condition féminine et les communistes chinois en action, Yan'an 1935–1946* (Paris: Editions de l'Ecole des Hautes Etudes en Sciences Sociales, 1981), 19–21.

34. See Selden, *The Yenan Way*.

35. Very few genuine "intellectuals" went to Yan'an; many went instead to Kunming or Chongqing.

36. See Price, *Cadres, Commanders and Commissars*.

37. See Compton, *Mao's China* and Price, *Cadres, Commanders and Commissars*.

38. Price, ibid., 135–72.

39. In the Kangda curriculum Mao taught the Strategy and Tactics of the Red Army, Dialectical Materialism, and, with several others, the course on Dialectics. Ibid., 140.

40. See Martin King Whyte, *Small Groups and Political Rituals in China* (Berkeley: University of California Press, 1974), 32–33, and Chapter 11 in this volume by Tony Saich.

41. After the Cultural Revolution, Kang Sheng become one of the designated villains along with the "Gang of Four."

42. For a detailed analysis of how the methods developed in Yan'an were subsequently employed in a local setting, see Richard Madsen, *Morality and Power in a Chinese Village* (Berkeley: University of California Press, 1986).

43. See Mao Zedong, "Reform Our Study," "Rectify the Party's Style of Work," and "Talks at the Yan'an Forum on Literature and Art," in *Selected Works of Mao Tse-tung*, vol. 3 (Beijing: Foreign Languages Press, 1967).

44. Mao often gave the impression that his ideas were contributed by the people and he only articulated them. For example, when Mao interviewed a well-known and authentically "proletarian" author (who wrote in the tradition of Gladkov) with whom he discussed art and literature for some three weeks, it became clear from her account that Mao had posed questions in such a way as to put words in her mouth. But she firmly believed that through her, Mao's theses on art and literature were derived from the "people."

45. Around Mao were cadres of glossators and commentators representing an elite whose job it was to ensure that the truths and virtues embodied in selected texts were not only studied but uniformly understood, and to which they, like everyone else, had to subscribe. It was precisely the pretentiousness of this elite that Wang Shiwei attacked. See Merle Goldman, *China's Intellectuals* (Cambridge: Harvard University Press, 1981).

46. The pedigree can be variously traced and sometimes uneasily gets put into the category of poststructuralist inquiry associated with figures like Kojeve, Hyppolite, Bachelard, Canguilhem, Foucault, and Barthes to postmodernists like Jameson and Baudrillard. Others who can be associated with discourse theory are Wittgenstein and Austin, even Bakhtin. See Paul A. Bove, "Discourse," in Frank Lentriccia and Thomas McLaughlin, eds., *Critical Terms for Literary Study* (Chicago: University of Chicago Press, 1990).

47. Chang Kuo-t'ao, *The Rise of the Chinese Communist Party* (Lawrence: University of Kansas Press, 1972), 2: 350–60.

48. Ibid., 427.

49. Snow, *Red Star over China*, 210–15.

50. Ibid., 215. Selden gives a more correct version of the attack on and jailing of Liu Zhidan in *The Yenan Way*, 71. See also David Holm, "The Strange Case of Liu Zhidan," *Australian Journal of Chinese Affairs* 27 (January 1992): 77–96.

51. Xu Haidong's Red Twenty-fifth Army was in fact quite small, much smaller than the forces under Liu Zhidan.

52. The story is that the messenger who was supposed to deliver the letter ordering Liu Zhidan's arrest showed it to Liu Zhidan saying, "You are the military leader, so I must give you this letter." Liu looked at the letter (it was in fact the list of people to be arrested) with his name on the top of the list. He then put the letter back in the envelope and gave it to the messenger. He said, "Go ahead and deliver it to Xu Haidong, the general at the front." The letter was written by Zhu Lizhi.

53. See Wang Ming, *Mao's Betrayal* (Moscow: Progress Publishers, 1979).

54. This was particularly clear in his desire to hold Wuhan at all costs in the face of Japanese attacks. For Mao's views see Schram, *The Political Thought of Mao Tse-tung*, 59.

55. McLane, *Soviet Policy and the Chinese Communists*, 1931–1946 (New York: Columbia University Press, 1958), 74–78.

56. See, for example, Goldman, *China's Intellectuals*, 21. See also Timothy Cheek, "The Fading of 'Wild Lilies': Wang Shiwei and Mao Zedong's *Yan'an Talks* in the First CPC Rectification Movement," *Australian Journal of Chinese Affairs*, no. 11 (January 1984): 25–57, and Kyna Rubin, "Writers' Discontent and Party Response in Yan'an Before 'Wild Lily': The Manchurian Writers and Zhou Yang," *Modern Chinese Literature*, 1, no. 1 (September 1984): 79–102. See also Guilhem Fabre, *Genèse de pouvoir et*

de l'opposition en Chine: Le printemps de Yan'an, 1942 (Paris: Editions l'Harmattan, 1990).

57. Cheek, "The Fading of 'Wild Lilies,' " 34

58. I am indebted to Wen Jize and Dai Qing for interviews and materials on the Wang Shiwei affair. See Dai Qing, *Wang Shiwei and "Wild Lilies"* (Armonk, NY: M. E. Sharpe, 1994).

59. The assasination of Sergei M. Kirov on December 1, 1934, served to initiate the Great Purge of 1934–38. Kirov was known as "the darling of the party" and secretary of the Central Committee. Karl Radek, a leading "old Bolshevik" was accused of the crime which was actually committed at Stalin's behest in order to rid himself first of a potential rival, and second, to eliminate an "old Bolshevik" who opposed him.

60. As Snow put it in a later volume, "Mao Zedong did not create or command the forces of Japanese imperialism but his understanding of them enabled him to seize leadership and control over the energies of nationalism and patriotic resistance, to win a sovereign victory for social revolution." See *Red China Today* (New York: Vintage Books, 1971), 69.

61. So writes Christopher Hill of the radical sects in the early phase of the English civil war, *The World Turned Upside Down* (London: Penguin Books, 1972), 272. Much the same could have been said for Robespierre, and even more so those *sansculottes* who became Babouvistes, Dartheans, and other followers of the principle of the Committee on Public Safety. See François Furet and Mona Ozouf, *A Critical Dictionary of the French Revolution* (Cambridge: Harvard University Press, 1989).

62. A political system that confuses the hegemony of its discourse for the effectiveness of its practice will sooner or later come to depend on a rigoristic exercise of state power and nothing dissipates "symbolic capital" more quickly.

63. For the best description and analysis of the events in Tiananmen Square, see Tony Saich, ed., *The Chinese People's Movement* (Armonk, NY: M.E. Sharpe Inc., 1990).

Chapter 9

The Honorable Vocation: Intellectual Service in CCP Propaganda Institutions in Jin-Cha-Ji, 1937–1945

Timothy Cheek

The experiences of the CCP during the anti-Japanese war, especially in the North China base areas, have figured largely in debates over the survival and growth of the party after a decade of nearly constant disasters. Appeals to peasant interests or to anti-Japanese nationalism, moderate reforms and "housecleaning" of the party, inspiring social revolutionary goals, and the ability to co-opt local elites are among the reasons put forward for the party's resilience under terrible wartime conditions and its increasing power thereafter.[1] This chapter draws on newly available sources to assess another factor that contributed to the growth and success of the party: its ability to attract and make use of the services of metropolitan intellectuals. Such people are needed not only to staff higher levels of a modern administration but also to articulate and propagate the ideology of its rulers. The quintessential version of this service is the propaganda department of the CCP, and here the case study is the chief organ of the major North China base area's propaganda department—the *Jin-Cha-Ji Daily*.

Intellectual service in CCP propaganda institutions is also important for our understanding of Chinese society and polity in the twentieth century. The CCP's ability to attract metropolitan intellectuals to the countryside to serve its administration of local areas effectively reconnected urban elites with the countryside. For the first time since the Taiping era in the mid-nineteenth century, CCP administrations like that in Jin-Cha-Ji provided a real government with pretensions to national power that plugged metropolitan intellectuals back into local society in a sustainable (rather than exploitative) fashion, restoring the traditional literati role of scholar-official, mediator between the capital and the locality. The details of the arrangement developed under the CCP in North China around 1940 show no simple continuity from the dynastic period but rather a complex mix of traditional aspirations and social forms interacting with Western, Soviet, and other new influences.

The CCP successfully attracted, motivated, organized, and controlled deviance among many metropolitan intellectuals for service in its revolution by allowing them to view propaganda work as an honorable vocation, work worthy of modern-day literati and aspiring scholar-officials. The nature of the "deal" worked out between the party and intellectuals in Jin-Cha-Ji, as well as Yan'an and other CCP strongholds, set the stage for the successes and failures of the PRC.

Sources and Perspectives

The greatest influence on research on the CCP in the past decade is the "new historiographical period" occasioned by the post-Mao reforms and opening by China to the outside world. Central to this has been the appearance of new source materials and access to Chinese scholars, even to some of the subjects of our studies. Three major categories of new sources inform this research: (1) newly published or available documentary sources, particularly from "*neibu*" (internal circulation) publications, as well as first-time access to other documents (in this case, full runs of the *Jin-Cha-Ji Daily*), (2) newly compiled almanacs and chronologies that organize vast arrays of data unavailable to us before (in this case, the *Chronology of Jin-Cha-Ji Daily* and the *Press Yearbooks*), and (3) personal reminiscences of key actors (in this case, those of General Nie Rongzhen and staff of the *Daily*).[2] All these sources have their limitations (explored case by case, below), but in general, careful comparison between inner party documents, public (*gongkai* or "openly published") documents of the 1930s and 1940s, chronologies and almanacs, and reminiscences can open new vistas of information on propaganda work in North China during the war years. Equally important in influencing new perspectives on the CCP has been our personal access to Chinese scholars and surviving participants of the events we study.[3] Nonetheless, research on CCP history outside China, with a few happy exceptions, has not been able to make use of archival resources in any way similar to developments in Qing historical studies in the past decades.[4]

However, the shift in view that Western scholars present of the CCP base areas during the war years did not begin with the flood of new information in the post-Mao period. Works by Raymond Wylie on Yan'an and Kathleen Hartford on Jin-Cha-Ji supplemented Mark Selden's famous *Yenan Way*—Wylie documenting the bitter political and ideological struggles behind Mao's rise to supreme leadership and Hartford questioning the older "peasant nationalism" thesis of CCP success.[5]

Such studies and the rich new source materials provide a basis for a study of the political culture of the CCP in a way not possible in the 1960s when Lucian

Pye and Richard Solomon made their analyses of "Chinese" political culture.[6] Newer studies of political culture, drawing inspiration from the work of Lynn Hunt and others working on the French revolution, eschew the Freudian reductionism of earlier studies. They call us to study patterns of behavior, values, assumptions, and underlaying epistemologies.[7]

Who were the metropolitan intellectuals attracted to CCP service? By definition, "metropolitan intellectuals" describes people with both advanced education (some equivalent of university training) and an active interest in public affairs and values beyond strict professional concerns. This most closely resembles the current Chinese term "high-level intellectuals" (*gaoji zhishifenzi*). In Jin-Cha-Ji during the war, several generations of such intellectuals were active—from older scholars (such as the poet Hao Qing), to older students or writers, to younger university or secondary-school students in their teens and twenties (such as Deng Tuo). Most had been trained in China's capital or treaty ports, and all but the eldest had received some of their training at new educational institutions—the Western-style universities (set up around the turn of the century) or various technical or military schools or academies. The generational differences among such intellectuals significantly influenced each one's response to conditions offered by the party.

The cohort upon which this chapter focuses was in its teens and twenties during the war and became part of the founding generation of establishment intellectuals in the PRC. Thus, the political experience of these men and women revolved around anti-Japanese nationalism and the destructiveness of fragmented warlord governments.[8] They were also influenced by the New Culture movement or May Fourth movement, which popularized radical Western notions of anti-imperialism, democracy, science, and socialism. The intellectuals who came to the hills of western Hebei and Shanxi in the late 1930s thus carried the dual baggage of traditional scholar-officials (from their parents' generation) and contemporary social critics in search of new creeds (from their own political experiences). Most urgently they carried the frustration of not being able to convince the Nationalist government to fight the Japanese.[9]

The activities and writings of one such intellectual, Deng Tuo, will serve as a case study of intellectual service in Jin-Cha-Ji's propaganda institutions. Deng Tuo (1912–66) was born in Fuzhou, Fujian, to a scholar-official family. He joined the CCP in 1930 while at university in Shanghai. Like many others, he was arrested, jailed, and released and then lost contact with the party during the mid-1930s. He turned up in Wutai, Shanxi, in the autumn of 1937 and was taken aboard by Nie Rongzhen's military press corps. In the PRC Deng Tuo became the first editor of the *People's Daily* and a prominent victim of the Cultural Revolution.[10]

The propaganda system that the CCP developed and staffed was not an original creation; nor was it a repetition of earlier forms. It was largely an import from the Soviet Union. Bolshevik experience and assumptions were particularly amenable to Chinese conditions. The originators of Soviet propaganda systems viewed propaganda as part of education (indeed administering propaganda efforts for a time from the Department of Education). Lenin viewed propaganda as transformative, the needed consciousness to spur the working class on to revolution, and he acknowledged that this propaganda work was the domain of intellectuals. In all, the Bolsheviks created what Peter Kenez calls the "propaganda state," a state-dominated polity that coordinates the education of cadres, the development of a political language, the politicization of ever-larger segments of life, and the substitution of "voluntary" state-controlled societies for independent organizations.[11]

The idea of the "propaganda state" directs us to an obvious aspect of the CCP: it is a revolutionary organization seeking not only power but also the transformation of society. It has, as Lowell Dittmer has emphasized, a "salvationary mission."[12] Since it promotes radical change in order to "save China," the party must communicate its goals and motivate concerted action toward them. This is, after the hot rhetoric is stripped away, the social function of ideology—a set of cultural symbols that represent reality in a persuasive manner to motivate action.[13] Propaganda is applied ideology, and metropolitan intellectuals are needed for its organization and initial dissemination. They weave the "fabric of hegemony" (that series of alliances among social classes that dominates state and society), as Antonio Gramsci suggests, which constitutes the consensual ideology that supports the constraining political enforcement of a state.[14] The opportunity to help weave the fabric of China's new society proved compelling to many Chinese intellectuals at mid-century.

Organization and Institutional Culture

This chapter seeks to outline the "institutional culture" or "organizational culture" of CCP propaganda organs in North China through the case of the *Jin-Cha-Ji Daily*.[15] As such, it is a study of political culture writ small, the political culture of a discrete subsection of the cultures that make up Chinese civilization. It is through such "local studies" that an empirically grounded conception of political culture can be developed to help us understand not only the CCP but China in modern times.

The propaganda organs of the Jin-Cha-Ji Border Region, especially its newspapers, provided a forum in which metropolitan intellectuals could help weave the social fabric together again. In 1937, these were neither august institutions nor propitious times, but they were sufficient to attract intellectual service. Military conflict with the Japanese dominated the history of the Jin-Cha-Ji Border Region from its beginning, which strongly influenced the way in which CCP goals of reform and revolution could proceed. When the fighting was intense, not only the danger of complete chaos but also the need for support from the local elite compelled the communist authorities to seek moderate social reform rather than the radical change the party had pursued in the earlier Jiangxi Soviet. Under its real leader, General Nie Rongzhen, a veteran of the Jiangxi Soviet, Jin-Cha-Ji became the prototype for Mao Zedong's "rural line" in revolution, in contrast to the "urban line" espoused by Wang Ming. In 1939, Mao used the example of Jin-Cha-Ji to promote his point of view in his support of Nie's account of the region, *A Model Anti-Japanese Base Area: The Jin-Cha-Ji Border Region.*[16]

On 7 November 1937, the Jin-Cha-Ji Military District was established in Fuping County, Hebei. The civil administration, the Jin-Cha-Ji Border Region, held its official congress in Fuping in January 1938.[17] The Eighth Route Army had survived the initial Japanese assault but realized it needed to communicate with its public and its often-separated divisions. The CCP had always used the press to propagandize its policies and inform its cadres about them, so Nie's group set about founding a party newspaper. On 11 December 1937, *Resistance News* (Kangdi bao), one of many informal broadsheets, was made the official publication of the Political Department of the Jin-Cha-Ji Military District and offices were set up in Fuping. It was upgraded from a mimeographed sheet to a lithographically printed two-page paper appearing once every three days. By January 1938 it was printing over one thousand copies per issue.[18]

By the summer of 1939, all three major power groups of the Jin-Cha-Ji Border Region had their propaganda organs: the border region government (a United Front institution recognized by the Guomindang [GMD]), the military district, and the local branch of the CCP. After April 1938, *Resistance News* was "publicly" published by the border region government (although in fact controlled by the regional branch of the Central Committee). On 7 July 1939 its editor, Deng Tuo, became the "responsible person" for a new journal published by the Political Department of the Jin-Cha-Ji Military District. At first called *Resistance News Supplement*, it was later entitled *Resistance Weekly.*[19] At the end of July, Deng also became the leading "responsible person" for a new monthly journal, *New Great Wall*, published by the Border Region Party Committee.[20]

Following the Japanese counterattacks to the One Hundred Regiments Campaign, conditions must have improved temporarily for the Jin-Cha-Ji administration by early November, for the *Resistance News* was renamed and expanded on 7 November 1940, becoming the *Jin-Cha-Ji Daily.*[21] Aside from increasing its publication from a once in three days' schedule, the paper increased its size to four pages.

Organization

Jin-Cha-Ji's propaganda periodicals were organized rationally to survive wartime conditions and to achieve the mobilizational goals of the CCP. The *Jin-Cha-Ji Daily* was under strict party leadership but was "held" in a web of other intellectual and cultural organizations sponsored by the party, which attracted intellectuals and promoted and channeled their interests.

The organization of *Jin-Cha-Ji Daily* was carefully arranged to achieve two major goals: (1) to unify leadership—that is, to ensure that the message delivered was both coherent and in line with the desires of the party center and well grounded in local concerns of resistance, reform (for the public), and revolution (for party cadres); and (2) survival through both repeated direct military attacks by the Japanese and puppet forces and the economic deprivations of Japanese "three-all" policies and GMD blockade. Thus, the paper had a clear administrative hierarchy under the local branch of the party center and had dispersed production and distribution networks.

There are several observations to be made from viewing this organization.[22] First, party control is clear: a full-time party branch secretary sits at the top of the organization, along with the director (invariably also a party member). The party branch committee for the paper had been established with the paper itself in the fall of 1937 under the military government and under the party at the first Jin-Cha-Ji Party Congress in April 1938. Hou Xin was the first branch secretary, followed by Liu Ping.[23]

The paper is a typical *jiceng danwei* (basic-level work unit) combining administrative, health, party, and other functions inside the paper's organization—what Dittmer later calls "frames" (and which he says the Chinese call *kuangkuang*).[24] Most of the subsections of the secretariat deal with nonprofessional concerns such as health, housing, and staff questions, though the radio room was responsible for links with Xinhua she (Xinhua news agency), telegram traffic for the CCP leadership, and foreign radio monitoring. This is the social organization that would encourage people in the PRC to become so dependent on their work unit.

It is also a professionally minded organization with a rational division of labor toward the purely professional goals of producing a newspaper on a reliable schedule with reasonable sources of information and a sensible distribution organization. Naturally, the Japanese attacks often wreaked havoc on these goals, but significantly did not shut the paper down. The organization reflects the professionalism expressed by members of the *Daily* in their reminiscences. It also reflects sensible organization in the face of military assault by setting up its printing and production facilities in three separate spots.

The paper was also placed in a web of organizations and associations designed to attract and "organize" educated elites in the border region. A careful study of each organization awaits further study, but a glance at the range of organizations gives a sense of the care that was taken to co-opt intellectuals (in a manner similar to the various other militias, peasant associations, etc.). The first and obvious political organization was the border region government under Song Shaowen. The linkage between meetings of the government and special meetings of intellectuals for artistic and literary purposes, seen in the case of Yanjing University professor Yu Li, who was elected to the leadership, is telling (discussed below). Several other organizations appear. As early as March 1940, the

Jin-Cha-Ji Border Region Students' Anti-Japanese Alliance (Jin-Cha-Ji bianqu xuesheng kang-Ri lianhehui) and the Jin-Cha-Ji branch of the Young Chinese Journalists Society (Zhongguo qingnian xinwenjizhe xuehui) were officially set up. At the journalism meeting, Liu Ping, An Gang, Deng Tuo, and six other party intellectuals addressed the young journalists. The authorities even provided an inspirational drama, "In Guerrilla War" (Zai youji zhong), whose theme was to explain how to publish a newspaper on the run.[25] The drama presentation is a telling indication of the likely low literacy among the Journalist's Society's members. The young journalists met again in September 1943 to hear talks by the same cast of speakers on how to reform the party press.[26] This time, they apparently had no need for inspirational skits.

The first meeting of the Border Region Cultural Circles Anti-Japanese National Salvation Association (Bianqu wenhua jie kang-Ri jiuguo hui) met on 10 October 1940 with such leading party intellectuals as journalist Cheng Fangwu and historian He Ganzhi elected to its standing committee.[27] The Daily, naturally, produced a supporting editorial honoring the meeting on 18 October. In June 1942, four more related associations were officially established (and publicized by the Daily): the border region branch committees for the Philosophy Society, the Natural Science Research Society, the New Educational Research Society, and the New Script Association (Xin wenzi xuehui).[28] All were plausible foci for intellectual energy for less politically minded intellectuals, well under control of the CCP.

Institutional Culture

What was this work like in practice? The details of propaganda work, and the role of metropolitan intellectuals in it, can be seen in the following problem. Even after surmounting the material problems of printing and distribution under war conditions, the Daily's predecessor, Resistance News, had another concern. It was not being taken seriously by its most important audience: experienced party cadres. This was a general problem: Over the years of secretive underground work during the 1930s when the CCP could not publish newspapers and magazines openly, cadres had grown accustomed to ignoring "front organization" publications and developed the habit of paying attention only to secret internal party communications. With the advent of the United Front, the CCP was legally entitled by the Nationalist government to publish openly. Resistance News was one such publication. On 2 April 1938, the party's CC issued a directive addressing the importance of "open" party periodicals in transmitting its wishes and coordinating its work. It set out regulations requiring all party branches to subscribe to its nationwide paper, New China Daily (Xinhua ribao), and to set up correspondent's offices to contribute to the paper. In addition, it stipulated that branch meetings should read and study any articles in the open press by members of the CC Politburo.[29] Deng Tuo explained the directive's application to local cadres in a December 1938 issue of *Battlefront* (Zhanxian), the restricted circulation bimonthly journal edited by the Jin-Cha-Ji branch of the CCP CC.[30]

The article is a classic example of what we may call "internal propaganda"— transmitting party instructions to local cadres. Deng Tuo uses precise wording from the directive, even quoting a few lines directly. His prose is a good deal more lucid than the bureaucratic document, and he fleshes out the directive's points with examples and numerous citations from Lenin. His theme is to use the party's openly published papers to cite Lenin, as the "guide wire" (*yinxian*) by which the party can direct the activities (the "struggle") of the masses. Therefore, in Jin-Cha-Ji all branches and, as far as possible, all party members will subscribe to *Resistance News* and to *Battlefront*. Each branch will set up a sales agent for these publications, as well as organize local reporters for them. Equally, branch meetings will read aloud and study important articles by Jin-Cha-Ji leaders and the reprints from other party papers. Deng especially emphasizes the organization of "reading groups" in which these key articles are to be read by cadres to the citizens of remote villages and discussed. This will not only bind the party more closely to the masses, says Deng, but also will "broadly raise the political and cultural level of the masses."[31] Deng also asks local branches to help distribute copies of the periodicals in Jin-Cha-Ji. Finally, local party members are to organize clandestine distribution networks to sell party papers in Japanese-occupied areas to counteract enemy propaganda. Here we see the footwork that went behind the CCP's famous propaganda machine.[32]

We get a preliminary sense of the "institutional culture" of the paper from its rectification efforts. In May 1941, the *Jin-Cha-Ji Daily* carried out what amounted to a mini-Rectification campaign aimed to "regularize" (*zhengguihua*) thought, rectify work, and increase the quality of the paper. The staff and workers met to commemorate May Day. They resolved to start a movement called the "Red May Assault Program." The study movement was paralleled by authoritative editorials on how to study Marxism-Leninism.[33] For the paper's editor, Deng Tuo, this was ideological rectification. The goal, said Deng, was regularization of the paper, which meant "no matter whether in times of relative stability or change, to be able firmly to maintain a definite system, to uphold a definite order, and to raise the technology of production and the efficiency of work to the highest possible levels." Deng saw the "basic conditions" for this regularization in strengthening the party character (or "discipline," *dang xing*) of their work.[34] This version of rectification was a rather more systematic and professionally concerned version of the model later made famous in Yan'an. Records of other rectification "study" for the paper's staff are not available, though the general picture of Jin-Cha-Ji is that rectification was not pursued with the same vigor as it was in Yan'an.[35] This is not surprising since Nie's programs had been lauded a few years earlier by Mao as part of his competition with Wang Ming and the party "internationalists." Wang Ming's followers were not well represented in

Jin-Cha-Ji, so the factional struggle underlaying the Yan'an rectification was missing. In addition, Jin-Cha-Ji was not the scene of maneuvering for supreme leadership of the party. Several Jin-Cha-Ji leaders, including Nie, were recalled after 1941 to Yan'an to accept promotions in the "rectified" party.[36] There may also be a simpler explanation: the area was under direct attack during the spring of 1942. Although the paper published all the major rectification speeches by Mao and others in a timely fashion in 1942, space in the paper was shared by extensive reports on the campaigns of the spring and summer.[37]

An ideal picture of the rectified *Jin-Cha-Ji Daily* is given in the reminiscences of former workers at the paper. Zhang Fan, a junior editor in the transcription section, recalls life with his editor in the 1940s, when all the members of the paper's staff did a stint of reporting from the front, as well as working as copy editors and printers. This was called the "unity of reporting and editing." This extension of professional training is said to have included helping local people to print their own papers and setting up local branches of the paper. Many other CCP papers were set up with the help of *Jin-Cha-Ji Daily* staff: the *Central Hebei Guide, Boldly Forward News* from the districts west of Beijing (Pingxi), and later the Hebei-Shanxi district's *Ji Jin Daily* and the *Shijiazhuang Daily.*[38]

A sense of what mass line service by the intellectual elite meant to Deng Tuo in practice comes from his relations with the villagers of Malancun, where the *Daily* was housed in 1942. The picture more resembles that of a good-hearted, if informal, Confucian gentleman than a Bolshevik agitator. When the paper moved in, Deng called the villagers to a meeting to explain why everyone should fight Japan. Deng chatted with villagers on his daily rounds, lending a helping hand here and there. The villagers called him by the informal appellation of respect "Old Deng" (*Lao Deng*). The village chief would regularly consult him on local problems and how to resolve them.[39] One can only imagine what satisfaction this respected mandarin role provided for a former frustrated student radical. One can see why Michael Lindsay formed his impression that the Communists in the early war period were largely national patriots bringing hope, fair administration, and defense to a sorely underdeveloped area subject to brutal foreign attack.[40]

The Jin-Cha-Ji Image of the Mass Line

Another way to get at the values that attracted some metropolitan intellectuals to propaganda service in Jin-Cha-Ji is to examine some of the representative propaganda they produced. There had to be not only administrative networks and organizational obedience but also an appealing goal and a unity of purpose. Such values are reflected in the Jin-Cha-Ji propaganda: ideals of public service, harmonious relations among new citizens, and the revival of Chinese culture. These images of the new society help to explain the success of the communist movement in Jin-Cha-Ji, and they also outline the fault lines that would bring the establishment down two decades later: the tension between charismatic and bureaucratic authority styles and between the intellectual roles of "culture bearer" and "cog and screw" in the revolutionary machine.

Propaganda Work

Most fundamentally, the medium, state-sponsored journalism, spoke powerfully to intellectual traditions of public service and propagating the orthodoxy among the common people. Since at least the tenth century, various leading Confucian scholars and various emperors supported the transformation of popular morals through literati-led community compacts (*xiangyue*) or readings of Sacred Edicts (*shengyu*) from the emperor.[41] The Western idea of an independent and critical press, as opposed to an engaged one promoting the orthodoxy, did not take root in CCP areas (though not without some dissent). In the early 1940s, Mao Zedong laid down the function of the news media for New China. The press was to be an active part of (what would become in Yan'an) the party's mass line: propagating the party's policies, gathering information about the grass roots for the leadership, serving as a forum for individual grievances, and supervising the bureaucracy by exposing wrongdoing.[42] Deng Tuo's June 1938 review of the work of *Resistance News* already captured much of this spirit:

> Of course, the production of *Resistance News* also has its mission. It must become the propagandizer and organizer of the border region's mass resistance and salvation movement, it must represent the needs of the broad masses, reflect and pass on the real conditions and experience of the broad masses' struggle, promote various aspects of work, and educate the masses themselves. At the same time, from the promotion and assistance of the broad masses, the paper itself progresses. It is the paper of the masses; it gives impetus to others, and at the same time it also gets impetus from others. It teaches others, and at the same time is taught by others. Only under this mutual promotion and education has it been able to come to today (its 50th issue).[43]

Deng Tuo later clarified that the role of the paper was to be a "guide wire" by which the party directs the people toward revolution. Naturally, the mutual education that Deng mentions here was under the direction of party policy. In an editorial from late 1938, Deng points out that the people get their directions for what to do in war from editorials, articles, and reports in party newspapers, and so these must be carefully written in consultation with the leadership.[44] Thus, what would become Maoist dicta on the party-controlled press—particularly its role as a conduit between state and society—was already for the Jin-Cha-Ji journalists both the standard operating procedure and a matter of painstaking work that included careful listening as well as authoritative goal setting. Deng Tuo's ease with developing Maoist methods underscores a distinction that will be vital in understanding later troubles between Mao and some party intellectuals in the PRC. These mass line methods were familiar and congenial to many party intellectuals—they simply could not abide the abuse of mass line methods, particularly the rules of inner party democracy, in the name of utopian schemes. The kind of mass line that did appeal to intellectuals in Jin-Cha-Ji can be seen in the images of the new charismatic leader, the new-style government, and the new version of Chinese culture given in its own propaganda.

The Charismatic Leader: Nie Rongzhen

The clearest picture of the goals and propaganda style of Jin-Cha-Ji exists in Deng Tuo's paean not to Mao, but to Nie Rongzhen. In July 1942, Deng wrote a lengthy account of "Jin-Cha-Ji's Helmsman, Nie Rongzhen," which fully embodies the new style of idealized leadership emerging out of Yan'an. Deng's article gives the impression that Nie is the "Chairman Mao" of Jin-Cha-Ji. This was less a sign of competition between Mao and Nie for the title of "helmsman" (the actual wording was slightly different) and more an indication of Deng's adherence to the policy of personalizing the party in propaganda in order to give his audience, predominantly peasants, a simple figure to revere. The very fact that the essay's topic is *not* Mao underscores the general use of such charismatic appeals in CCP propaganda and Deng's acceptance of them.

The *Pictorial* itself is an interesting case in the history of CCP journalism. It was originally *Resistance Pictorial*, and like the newspaper changed over to the "Jin-Cha-Ji" masthead. It looked like *Life* magazine. In fact, it was the first major pictorial ever published by the CCP or the Red Army.[45] Full-color cover photographs introduce a professional layout of some one hundred black-and-white photographs. With the exception of Deng's long tribute to Nie, most captions and articles in the journal appear in both English and Chinese. The editors' intent to influence European and American opinion is highlighted by the inclusion of letters praising Jin-Cha-Ji by Michael Lindsay and William Band, along with Lindsay's "Reminiscences of Dr. Bethune," none of which appear in Chinese. Available during the first year of U.S. involvement in the Pacific War, this was an impressive piece of international propaganda. The themes are resolutely nationalist and anti-Japanese, and focus on local self-defense and self-improvement. Naturally, there is no anti-imperialist rhetoric.[46] Deng's article on Nie was not translated, indicating that its personification of the base area in a semi-deified image of Nie was intended to appeal to Chinese audiences, not foreigners.

Deng's glowing account of Jin-Cha-Ji and General Nie appeared as the lead article in the inaugural issue.[47] The piece is ostensibly a brief history of the Jin-Cha-Ji base area from the formation of the military district in November 1937 to the spring of 1942, but the details of military campaigns and administrative programs play second fiddle to descriptions of Nie hard at work and the emotions of his awed followers. Deng builds a picture of the sort of proletarian leader we normally associate with the cult of Mao. This personification of CCP ideals was one onto which the local, mostly peasant, readers (and listeners) could project their loyalty and from whom they could derive inspiration. That is, Nie stood for Jin-Cha-Ji.[48] Despite Deng's punishment later (in 1944) for his excessive praise of Nie, this inspirational hagiography continues in CCP biography. Much of the hagiography on Deng Tuo, and a host of other CCP cadres, written in the recent past follows the same model on the more humble level—how to be a good party journalist, historian, administrator, or whatever.[49] Thus, Deng's piece is also an archetypal example of propaganda that continues in post-Mao China.

Deng is clearly happy with the project. He starts with a poem he sent to Nie in 1937 (and which now appears in Deng's collections of poetry). The text itself flows easily, and sections of the dialogue and description make better reading than most popular short stories written during the Mao period.[50] Deng produces a portrait worthy of revolutionary respect. Nie, a humble man of vision and military genius, leads his troops through the valley of death to victory. Nie has become the hope of millions of people, and though his shadow is cast over twenty years of revolutionary history, he is not a loud or boastful man.[51] The cadre school Nie set up in Fuping in late 1938 reflects the educational methods and spirit of this great revolutionary leader, and however brief the courses, they are helping to train a new generation in his image. Furthermore, the school is not "French style" or "Soviet style" or any foreign model, but is the creation of Nie's own synthesis of his observations and experiences.[52]

Nie is capable of that high Marxist-Leninist art of "synthesis" in his building of the cadre school. He is pictured as equally capable of issuing military plans "that everyone knows will work" based on his revolutionary experience. This talent, however, comes through his long hours of devoted work, late into the night, hearing reports, poring over maps, and consulting with his talented aides: Generals Zuo Quan, Liu Bocheng, He Long, Guan Xiangying, Cheng Zihua, and party stalwart Peng Zhen. He is the picture of the earthy genius, who after a night of planning will breakfast with the troops and crack jokes with them. This is all given in rich and easy detail, such as the picture of Nie, in a raincoat and walking stick in hand, trudging off in the spring rain to consult with Peng Zhen, "his comrade in arms." They walk, chat, and laugh along the banks of the Sha River.[53] Nie, we are reminded, has worked in factories in France, but loves to read and is a competent intellectual. Though a tough-minded general, Nie loves children. He gives candy to two Japanese girls and passes them on to local villagers with admonitions to care well for them. He cried at the death of Norman Bethune. Details of his life with his wife, Zhang Ruihua, round out the picture of the general at home.[54] All in all, Nie is so busy that "he can do the work of five," and his staff officer, Tan Yanjie, is on the telephone all day long.[55]

The accolade reaches a crescendo in the last three pages. In spite of the hyperbole of this genre (role models in propaganda), it is hard not to imagine that

Deng Tuo admired and sought to emulate the leadership qualities he described in Nie as a model for all. Nie was vigorous, well-educated, and a wonderful public speaker. His reports were always complete and clear. When he spoke he used only small notecards with the main points listed out: A, B, C . . . The text was all in his head. He had a marvelous memory. He could remember something about every person he met—enemy or friend—a talent that Deng admires as useful in political work. Most of all, his leadership style was one of "seeking truth from facts" (*shishi qiushi*). In all of this, Nie is a worthy follower of Mao Zedong:

> Jin-Cha-Ji is a vanguard among base areas and Nie Rongzhen is its talented guide [*xiandao*]. This talented creator will have his glorious position in Marxist-Leninist military science, in the realm of Mao Zedong-ism military theory. This shows that comrade Nie Rongzhen is a Mao Zedong-ist proficient in creative Marxism.[56]

Nie is presented as both a highly trained Marxist and a bookish intellectual. However, at a literary conference the general deferred to the specialists, reminding them only that "the weapon of literature and art must complement the development of military struggle."[57] Nie thus shows respect for and appreciation of the talents and contributions of intellectuals. Only on the last page is Song Shaowen, supposed head of the Jin-Cha-Ji Border Region, mentioned as Nie's righthand man.

This essay on Nie Rongzhen provides a vivid picture of the new ideal leader who embodies the goals of resistance and reform (revolution was glossed over in this piece). Deng's medium is his message as well. Deng was happy to paint such role models, and judging from the reminiscences of his colleagues in the newspaper, he sought to practice such ideals, excepting any claims to "synthesize Marxism." Deng Tuo's service to Nie Rongzhen thus serves as a model of an attractive deal between metropolitan intellectuals and the CCP in Jin-Cha-Ji.

New-Style Organization: Peng Zhen's Machine

If Nie Rongzhen was the model of the revolutionary leader in Jin-Cha-Ji, Peng Zhen was an embodiment of its organizational approach, which was to influence many party leaders and intellectuals, such as Liu Ren, Deng Tuo, and (*Central Hebei Guide* editor and later member of the Beijing Party Committee) Fan Jin, through the rest of their careers. This was the organizational side of the emerging CCP orthodoxy, Maoism. Despite the image of a "two-line struggle" given during the Cultural Revolution, Maoism, particularly in its formative, or Yan'an, stage, included both charismatic and bureaucratic styles of authority.[58] Peng Zhen's elaboration of CCP administration not only provided attractive roles for metropolitan intellectuals as "transformational bureaucrats"—an almost priestly function in the revolution—but also contributed to the success of Mao's mass line policies back in Yan'an.[59]

The Jin-Cha-Ji Border Region's internal organization was formalized in 1943. The fifth anniversary of the founding of Jin-Cha-Ji and its survival were celebrated at a major convocation of the Border Region Congress held between 15 and 21 January 1943, at Wentang village in Fuping County. It was actually the first convocation of representatives who had been elected in a 1940 plebiscite, according to the rules of what became known as the "Three Thirds" system. Thus, Nie reports, the 288 representatives gathered for the congress not only represented every geographical unit but included "representatives of the CCP, the GMD, nonparty patriots, forward-looking gentry, scholars from literary circles, scientists and technologists, national minorities, as well as representatives of worker, peasant, women's, youth, and other mass organizations."[60] The congress marked a new stage for the border region, for it was finally able to pass laws in a parliamentary fashion on issues such as rent and tenant relations, taxation, and marriage, and it was able to follow these up with regulations promulgated by a duly elected administrative council. This replaced earlier decrees by the party or military.[61] This also consolidated party control over the institutions of power in the border region—a long-time interest of Peng Zhen, who was the architect of these laws.[62]

Peng Zhen's authoritarian but carefully pragmatic approach to party administration was the version of "mass line" politics Deng Tuo and his colleagues experienced in the base area and praised in the *Jin-Cha-Ji Daily*.[63] The laws passed at the January 1943 Jin-Cha-Ji Congress were based on Peng Zhen's "Double Ten Program" of August 1940. At the congress, Liu Lantao, representing the Northern Branch of the CC Politburo, reminded the participants of the contents of the program.[64] Three aspects of the program and these laws, as Pitman Potter has pointed out, are important for understanding not only Jin-Cha-Ji but also the later history of the PRC. First, the laws were designed to provide the "organizational means of ensuring the party's dominance over popular and governmental organizations."[65] Second, the model of political life embodied in Peng's example is one where issues of personal liberties and statutory rights do not exist. Rather, legal constraints are limited to controlling the abuse of power by officials. This problem, which has become one of central concern in China since the Cultural Revolution, was not a problem in a time of war and moderate reform policies—all of which bred unity. Rather, Peng's model of political life was one of "careful analysis of specific local conditions before introducing policy proposals, revealing a characteristically strong faith in the value of rational objective analysis in the preparation of policy."[66] Third, this approach reveals Peng's view about Chinese society and change. For Peng it was the control of political institutions, rather than engineering basic socioeconomic change (as dictated by orthodox Marxism) that determined historical periods. Thus Peng could conclude that party dominance of politics in Jin-Cha-Ji constituted the overthrow of the feudal system of political power.[67]

The core of the "New Democratic" government proclaimed at the congress

was detailed in a 12 February editorial in the *Jin-Cha-Ji Daily*.[68] The government was based on five principles: democratic elections, the "Three Thirds"
system of corporate representation of CCP and other major social groups, democratic centralism, the rule of law and regulations, and a democratic work style
opposing bureaucratism. Naturally, this was all under the effective control of the
CCP. The result was an intricate web that guaranteed *participation* more than
political *power* to various social groups among the border region's one hundred
counties and population of some twenty million. This was natural, as the party's
goal was to neutralize competitors and mobilize the population. Here was a
government that patriotic intellectuals could serve. And the government was
interested in obtaining those services. As a part of this program, the authorities
set about organizing and keeping their elite intellectuals happy by addressing
their cultural interests.

The New Culture

Deng Tuo's writings on cultural and ideological matters provide us with one set
of rationales for serving the CCP. His is a type of intellectual participation that
contrasts with the image derived from literary suppression in Yan'an. Fundamental to his participation is, on the one hand, an acceptance of party dominance as
outlined by Mao in his now infamous "Yan'an Talks," while, on the other hand,
assuming and inserting into that service a two-track model of intellectual and
cultural life in which intellectuals could maintain a space for their elite pastimes.
Both Deng's version of historical materialism and his reliance on the bureaucratic structure erected by Peng Zhen supported a role for intellectuals as "culture bearers," as the select few with sufficient education to make manifest the
transformational goals of the party.[69] The attraction of this ministering role for
literary intellectuals is not limited to the sons of Confucius. Miklós Haraszti has
made a devastating satire of the lure of "directed culture" for intellectuals in the
Hungarian state socialist regime and George Konrád and Ivan Szelényi include
the temptation to reform society as one of the factors of East European intellectuals "on the road to class power."[70]

The border region administration and Deng addressed the role of literature in
a forum held in February and March 1939. Deng was clearly on what would
become Mao's side in the "Yan'an Talks" on art and literature later in
1942. Deng demanded that literature serve the masses and conform to party
policy needs. Yet he made clear that these requirements should pose no conflict
with the equally important demands of authenticity and historical accuracy. He
favored typical models in literature, but saw this as a challenge to the writer, not
as an encumbrance to artistic freedom. Deng makes his position in the development of China's new literature since the May Fourth movement clear. The new
literature can only come out of a critical acceptance of the old national forms
imbued with new revolutionary content. Ignoring popular interests or vulgariza-

tion won't do. The entryway into "mass literature," says Deng is *language*. The terms and expressions of the working people will allow writers to express their new revolutionary experiences among the masses. "The combination of new content and old national forms is the most pressing question of the current literary movement and is the most important difference between the new enlightenment movement and the old enlightenment movement."[71] This hints at a very important part of Deng's views on literature, a part he leaves unexpressed. He does not support the romantic and spiritual literature of enlightenment based on the individual authority of the artist. This stands in marked contrast to the heart of May Fourth literature and to the values expressed by their representatives in Yan'an.[72] In fact, Deng's speech ignores foreign literature aside from those in the Soviet canon, such as Gogol. Lenin is Deng's literary authority.

Deng, however, was not proposing that writers become docile "cogs and screws" who merely advertise the policies of their party superiors. His definition of national forms differed from that of Mao's disciples in Yan'an who emphasized cutting intellectual snobs down to size. For example, Deng concludes his consideration of the value of working-class language as a vehicle for writers to express new (revolutionary) content by saying:

> Of course, massification [*dazhonghua*] cannot be carried out merely through words; it is not just a matter of simple words (at times new words can be part of massification, such as "imperialism," "traitors," etc. . . .). Also important are: massification of methods, thought, structure, and the representation of the direction and real materials of mass life. Best is to *raise the cultural level of the masses* in the midst of developing the real mass literary and artistic movement.[73]

The grounds for Deng's version of orthodox CCP literary policy become clear in his discussion of poetry. He accepts the leadership's view that poetry and popular songs should be, ultimately, the same thing. And he derides scholars who look down on popular songs as people lacking in patriotic pride and appreciation of China's long culture (a sleight of hand unless one realizes his unnamed target: May Fourth cosmopolitans). Yet Deng declares that under current historical conditions, where class distinctions continue to exist, poetry and popular songs will each have their place. They will realize their basic unity in the future society, not now. Thus Deng allows for an arena of elite culture as a legitimate part of what would soon be called the "New Democracy." By also catering to the masses in other literary arenas, writers will naturally begin the long mutual transformation of elite and popular culture that will ultimately bring them into unity.[74] Deng Tuo maintained this distinction throughout his life. For Deng Tuo popular culture would always be an effort to popularize elite culture for the peasant and worker majority. This contrasts with the peasant-based literature, such as the *yang'ge* drama movement, favored by leaders in Yan'an. Deng's goal was to make every peasant a poet, not every poet a peasant. This difference was a matter of interpretation that would not come to a head until the late 1950s. When Mao would come to insist on the primitivist version of the equation, intellectuals such as Deng Tuo who had found a space inside the CCP came to grief.

The Jin-Cha-Ji model for intellectuals' relations with their superiors and direct subordinates becomes clear in the activities of a poetry society formed immediately after the January 1943 Border Region Congress. The "Yan-Zhao Poetry Society" provides an instructive look at what is normally considered the negative side of the party's cultural policies: constraints on the artistic pastimes of high-level intellectuals.[75] After the congress meetings, a few of the intellectual and political elite of the border region organized a traditional-style poetry society for mutual enjoyment. It was unabashedly elitist. The ability to produce classical regulated verse (particularly *qilü*) was the requirement for membership, and it was peopled by the political elite—those administering the new "mass line." Furthermore, stories about this group and other elite poetry soirées are repeated with great reverence in the post-Mao reminiscence literature, indicating continued approval of them.

The apparent contradiction is this praise of elite cultural pastimes beyond the reach of workers and peasants in the populist culture of Mao's rectified party. Were not writers, even revolutionary writers, suppressed in Yan'an? The answer lies in the traditional nature of the Yan-Zhao Poetry Society. The society's stated goals were literary enjoyment and support of the government. Deng Tuo's very traditional "Record of the Society's Formation" abounds in classical imagery and classical prose (*wenyan*) echoing dynastic loyalists with phrases such as "To serve as a drummer for the three armies with the poetry and song of Yan and Zhao."[76] The society's activities repeated those of the poetry societies to which Deng Tuo had belonged as a teenager in Fuzhou in the 1920s. In this case the elder poet, Hao Qing, produced a set of four regulated verses "to initiate the poetic fraternity." Deng replied in meter and rhyme, and the group was on its way. Such elite cultural pastimes not only harkened to its members' literati origins but clearly were appropriate in Jin-Cha-Ji in 1943. The Yan-Zhao Poetry Society is an example of Deng's two-track policy for poetry and popular songs. In Jin-Cha-Ji, such activities were also considered part of the necessary services the administration should provide for high-level intellectuals to keep them content.[77]

In this way Deng Tuo's work style continued the mind-set of traditional literati and did not reflect the romantic "alienation" expressed by many left-wing writers of the period. Rather, his cultural pastimes became an opportunity for connecting with local society through a paternalistic style of personal education. Deng's love of poetry is a constant theme in the reminiscences of his colleagues in the paper. He would recite poems and explain them to his staff, even when on the run. He struck his subordinates as the scholarly type (*shusheng qi*). He was known in the base area as the author of a book on famine relief, yet his poetic skills were admired and in demand. Chen Chunsen, an editor of the paper, recalls that Deng would often tell them stories from Chinese history, stressing to his listeners that a people with such a long history as the Chinese could not perish. He loved to collect gazetteers and historical artifacts, conducting a search in every town he traveled through.[78] Deng's elite tastes in poetry did not alienate him from his constituency or from his subordinates. Deng's life as a scholar-cadre, blending traditional literati concerns with a new political organization and new goals, formed his approach to work well into the 1960s.

The division between intellectuals and the party apparatus, often so distinct in the case of China's left-wing writers, does not appear among these devotees of traditional poetry. The founding members of the Yan-Zhao Poetry Society included Deng Tuo, Nie Rongzhen, Hao Qing, Ruan Muhan, Liu Dianji, Song Shaowen, Lu Zhengcao, and Yu Li.[79] Here the interests of high-level intellectuals overlapped with those of the leading military (Nie, Lu) and administrative (Song) figures of the border region. In fact, Deng and Yu Li were both leaders in the Jin-Cha-Ji establishment (Yu Li becoming a vice chairman of the Jin-Cha-Ji Consultative Congress). The vitriolic debates over the evils of traditional literature and the indiscipline of left-wing writers that dominated Yan'an in 1942 are not apparent in the current record of Jin-Cha-Ji. The problems of left-wing writers, which have set the impression for Western scholars on intellectual-party relations under the CCP, are highlighted by this contrast with the Yan-Zhao Poetry Society. The left-wing writers were generally out of power, offered a competing strategy in the rectification movement, were unable to harmonize their elite pastimes with popularization work among the peasantry, and were few in number, even among the tiny class of the educated elite.[80] On the other hand, establishment intellectuals like Deng Tuo were in positions of influence, abided by the tenets of rectification policy, were comfortable with the peasant population, were much more numerous, and maintained friendly relations with the military and political leadership.

This is not to say that Maoist cultural policy had no conflict with elite culture—cosmopolitan leftist or traditional—but rather that the version of Maoism at work in Jin-Cha-Ji, which held itself as a vanguard of Maoist policies, was more comfortable with elite culture. The establishment's acceptance of two tracks for elite and popular culture during the long transition to communist society and their managerial approach to party rectification left begging the underlying contradictions between the roles of "culture bearer" and "cog and screw" for intellectuals and the political styles of charisma and routine for the leadership. The Yan-Zhao Poetry Society, and similar intellectual activities, were a privilege, not a right. When Mao turned on elite pastimes and managerial politics en masse in the Cultural Revolution, he was imposing the Yan'an model of cultural affairs upon the Jin-Cha-Ji model—a case of one part of the wartime communist tradition turning on another equally well-pedigreed part. Until that time, the model of intellectual-state relations under Chinese communism on a day-to-day level (leaving aside the very significant periodic campaigns Mao instigated) is perhaps better represented in the Yan-Zhao Poetry Society and the propaganda services of the Jin-Cha-Ji intellectuals than in Wang Shiwei's "Wild Lilies" and the purges of the literary rectification in Yan'an in 1942.[81]

Bureaucratic Maoism

Finally, the bureaucratic values animating propaganda work in Jin-Cha-Ji can be seen in Deng Tuo's application of "Mao's Thought" to journalism work in 1944. He edited the first *Selected Works of Mao Zedong* that May.[82] Since the collection includes Mao's rectification pieces, particularly the "Yan'an Talks," Deng's praise of Mao's work in the "Preface" indicates his satisfaction with the orthodoxy that emerged from the rectification movement, including the dominance of the party in all spheres of intellectual endeavor.

Deng elaborated his praise for the Maoist approach, echoing the application of it that had developed in Jin-Cha-Ji, at a major propaganda work conference held by the Jin-Cha-Ji branch of the Central Propaganda Department in May 1944. After announcement of the new Yan'an rectification policy of "the entire party shall run the press," the Jin-Cha-Ji conference set out to tell journalists how to do this.[83] What Deng said about journalism accorded with what the Yan'an *Liberation Daily* editorialized in August 1942 during the Rectification campaign: "We already know that newspapers do not only report the news, they are also sharp weapons in constructing our nation and party and in reforming our work and our lives."[84] Deng Tuo, too, thought journalism should be used as a form of public education, particularly to mobilize readers to act: "Because real-life struggle is developing, our news reporting methods must be able to reflect and *lead* the whole process of that struggle's development."[85]

The bulk of Deng's speech is on how to write better copy. He covers three aspects of correspondence work and four aspects of news reporting that need to be reformed according to the new party mass line. He directs his listeners to eschew Western grammar and flowery classical Chinese expressions. Reporters are to live among the masses and to encourage ordinary people to write for themselves. More important for the future of socialist journalism in China, Deng Tuo popularizes the concept of "key reporting" (*zhongdian baodao*), in which a key issue, usually an aspect of current policy, forms the guiding theme and central content of all forms of writing in a newspaper—news items, correspondents' reports, essays, and editorials. In this way, Deng says, all the most important aspects of a key issue will be concentrated and therefore better understood by the readers.[86] This style of "key reporting" continues in China today.

Deng Tuo's conclusion to his 1944 speech is an example of the bureaucratic Maoist approach to work:

> In order to reform the correspondence and reporting methods of our party periodicals, every single correspondent and party periodical worker must re-

form his own thought, and, on the basis of Comrade Mao Zedong's speech at the Yan'an forum on literature and art, the Central Propaganda Department's resolutions on literary and art policy, and the directives on military propaganda by the General Political Department, each one of us must link our personal thought and work through deep personal self-examination and reflection.

The frustration one may experience while reading this quotation from Deng Tuo directs our attention to the nature of bureaucratic Maoism. It begins and ends with Mao's dearest concepts—thought reform and reflection—and refers to his "Yan'an Talks," yet Mao's beloved volunteerism, not to mention pretensions to personal leadership of the masses, could hardly survive the labyrinth of bureaucracies Deng lists as guides to implementing Mao's ideas. This list, though, is significant: it reflects the organizational approach to power employed by Peng Zhen to maintain the party in Jin-Cha-Ji—the Propaganda Department representing the civil administration and the General Political Department of the Army representing the military authorities. Deng Tuo and his colleagues believed in the system and its institutions. Mao's genius in the realm of basic principles is real, but distant; it requires mediation through the various departments that will articulate Mao's vision in any given situation. (Naturally, intellectuals would staff or lead many such departments.) This institutional approach to implementing Mao Zedong Thought, while a source of tension in the PRC, was one of the keys to the resilience and success of the CCP during the war years. It was part of the "power management" developed in Jin-Cha-Ji and popularized in Yan'an that successfully resisted the party's adversaries, addressed the needs of localities, and connected some of China's urban elites with rural society. This helps to explain not only the success of the party in the 1940s but also its ability to establish a new nationwide government.

Conclusion

This study has sought to suggest from case studies and partial information how the CCP in North China made successful use of metropolitan intellectuals in the service of a key revolutionary function: propaganda. The Jin-Cha-Ji administration managed to survive Japanese attacks and economic blockade and its major propaganda organ, the *Jin-Cha-Ji Daily*, also survived these threats. It did this through good organization and flexible responses to changing conditions. Thus, it had institutions that could make use of metropolitan intellectuals. The CCP in North China used a range of motivating appeals, which in the case of intellectuals included opportunities to be "culture bearers" in the establishment of a new and just society. They presented propaganda as an honorable vocation. The "institutional culture" of the *Jin-Cha-Ji Daily* reflects a mix of habitual literati attitudes of the metropolitan elite toward society (educating it and transforming it for the good) and voluntary compliance (personal acceptance of the correctness of Marxism-Leninism) in the institutional framework of a classic basic-level work unit of state socialism that would characterize the PRC.

"Institutional culture" is a useful framework for organizing data on CCP propaganda work because it makes this story comparable to the study of political culture in the CCP at other times and places, such as Gilmartin's study of CCP "subculture" in the 1920s (see Chapter 2). It also allows fruitful comparison with later times, such as Andrew Walder's study of the institutional culture of authority in PRC factories (and by extension, society in contemporary China).[87] While the objects of study are quite different (and therefore data in this paper does not address several issues raised by Walder), the questions of consent ("voluntary and habitual compliance") and the personalization of authority (through personal dependence on direct superiors, incarnation of authority in a person, and service to the revolution conflated to loyalty to a superior) bear directly on the roles of metropolitan intellectuals in Jin-Cha-Ji propaganda organs. All this amounts to examining how an institution actually runs and what motivates its members. My conclusion is that the major constituents of the institutional culture that Walder argues makes up "communist neotraditionalism" in China today, and which he suggests are barriers to the achievement of party goals or to reform of the system, were extant by 1944 in Jin-Cha-Ji propaganda institutions. Moreover, this institutional culture did not impede party goals, it promoted them; it did not delay reforms, it advanced them. In short, this political culture worked—then. We must look to changing context over the next forty years to explain how such an institutional culture could shift from promoting party goals to inhibiting them.

A further hypothesis, which lies outside the scope of this paper, is that tensions within this culture helped contribute to the political instability of 1955–75 (in particular, an increasingly erratic personalization of party authority in Mao) and, in turn, this institutional culture responded to repeated assaults on party intellectuals and their key institutions by developing counterproductive defense strategies that look more like what Walder has observed. Thus, what Walder identifies as a Weberian "type"—communist neotraditonalism—I see as one stage of a complex and changing social system, a "political culture," namely parts of Chinese culture as it digests Western influences, from John Dewey, Charles Darwin, and Adam Smith, as well as Marx, Engels, Lenin, and Stalin. If there is a neotraditionalism involved here, it is a *Chinese* rather than a "communist" one, and it is rooted in the *culture* we have seen reproducing and revising itself in Jin-Cha-Ji.[88]

This study leaves as many questions unanswered as answered. Foremost, it remains to be tested how general this picture of intellectual participation was. It has been my goal only to suggest that it may well have been widespread and is worthy of further research. More specifically, the question of how rectification and the "elimination of spies" (the related and controversial "Rescue campaign" purges of 1942–44 now laid, rather ingenuously, at the feet of Kang Sheng) operated in Jin-Cha-Ji remains an enigma.[89] Finally, it remains to be established in concrete fashion how the broader intended audience of Jin-Cha-Ji propaganda received the messages put out by *Jin-Cha-Ji Daily* and similar propaganda organs.

Notes

I would like to thank my colleagues who took the time to read and offer detailed suggestions on this paper, especially the editors of this volume, Steven Averill, David Ownby, Roger Thompson, and Joseph K. S. Yick.

1. This literature is critically reviewed in Kathleen Hartford and Steven M. Goldstein, eds., *Single Sparks: China's Rural Revolutions* (Armonk, NY: M.E. Sharpe, 1989), introduction.

2. For an assessment of these new kinds of sources on party history, see Tony Saich, "Seven Sources on Party History," *CCP Research Newsletter*, no. 4 (fall–winter 1989): 1–12, and Zhang Zhuhong, *Zhongguo xiandai geming shi shiliaoxue* (Historiography of China's Modern Revolutionary History) (Beijing: CCP Party History Materials Press, 1987). Zhang's book is translated in *Chinese Studies in History*, 23, no. 4, and 24, no. 3, and *Chinese Sociology and Anthropology*, 22, nos. 3–4.

3. The impact of such contacts on interpretation of documents is discussed in Timothy Cheek, "Studying Deng Tuo: The Academic Politician," *Republican China*, 15, no. 2 (April 1990): 1–15. This is part of a series of case studies on the topic in this journal.

4. See, for example, Tony Saich, *The Origins of the First United Front in China: The Role of Sneevliet (Alias Maring)* (Leiden: E. J. Brill, 1991), 2 vols.

5. See the base area studies reviewed in Chapter 7 in this volume; Raymond F. Wylie, *The Emergence of Maoism* (Stanford: Stanford University Press, 1980); and Kathleen Hartford, "Step By Step: Resistance, Reform and Revolution in Jin-Cha-Ji" (Ph.D. dissertation, Stanford University, 1981); and Mark Selden, *The Yenan Way in Revolutionary China* (Cambridge: Harvard University Press, 1971).

6. Lucian W. Pye, *The Spirit of Chinese Politics: A Psychocultural Study of the Authority Crisis in Political Development* (Cambridge: MIT Press, 1968), and Richard B. Solomon, *Mao's Revolution and the Chinese Political Culture* (Berkeley: University of California Press, 1971).

7. See Jeffrey Wasserstrom, "Tiananmen: More Lessons for Scholars," *CCP Research Newsletter*, no. 8 (1990): 66–79, and Elizabeth J. Perry, "Chinese Political Culture Revisited" in Jeffrey N. Wasserstrom and E. J. Perry, eds., *Popular Protest and Political Culture in Modern China: Learning from 1989* (Boulder: Westview Press, 1992), 1–11. See in this volume, the study of party "subculture" in the 1920s in Chapter 2.

8. This approach follows the general definition of political generations—based on the formative political experiences of individuals between age 17 and 25—as used by Michael Yahuda, "Political Generations in China," in *China Quarterly*, no. 80 (1979): 796–805, and by Li Zehou and Vera Schwarcz, "Six Generations of Modern Chinese Intellectuals," in *Chinese Studies in History* 17, no. 2 (winter 1983–84): 42–56.

9. The best overview of this history is Jerome B. Grieder, *Intellectuals and the State in Modern China: A Narrative History* (New York: Free Press, 1981), particularly chaps. 6 and 7.

10. The best Chinese biography is: Wang Bisheng, *Deng Tuo pingzhuan* (Evaluative Biography of Deng Tuo) (Beijing: Masses Press, 1986); for a short evaluation in English, see Timothy Cheek, "Deng Tuo: Culture, Leninism, and Alternative Marxism in the Chinese Communist Party," *China Quarterly*, no. 87 (September 1981): 470–91.

11. Peter Kenez, *The Birth of the Propaganda State: Soviet Methods of Mass Mobili-

zation, 1917–1929 (Cambridge: Cambridge University Press, 1985), especially 12–13 and chapter 10. Lenin's views on propaganda and intellectuals come from "What Is to Be Done?" See Kenez, 5–6. See also Chapter 1 in this volume by Hans van de Ven.

12. Lowell Dittmer, *China's Continuous Revolution: The Post-Liberation Epoch 1949–1981* (Berkeley: University of California Press, 1987), 4.

13. Here I explicitly follow the analysis of Clifford Geertz, "Ideology as a Cultural System," in Geertz, *The Interpretation of Cultures* (New York: Basic Books, 1973), particularly 230–31. Thus, my subjects, much like their Bolshevik predecessors as described by Kenez, viewed propaganda (*xuanchuan*) as a good and necessary thing.

14. See Antonio Gramsci, *Selections from the Prison Notebooks, 1929–1935*, edited by Quintin Hoare and Geoffrey Nowell Smith (London: Lawrence & Wishart, 1971), and Joseph Femia, *Gramsci's Political Thought* (Oxford: Oxford University Press, 1981). Propaganda organs, and especially government newspapers, were also used for less noble purposes, such as factional in-fighting. See Kenez, *Birth of the Propaganda State*, 231 and *passim*, and on the vicious fights between Mao and Wang Ming for control of the press in Yan'an, Patricia Stranahan, *Molding the Medium: The Chinese Communist Party and the "Liberation Daily"* (Armonk, NY: M.E. Sharpe, 1990).

15. This useful term is used by Andrew Walder, *Communist Neo-Traditionalism: Work and Authority in Chinese Industry* (Berkeley: University of California Press, 1986). I will return to the implications of the present study for Walder's thesis on "communist neotraditionalism" in my conclusion.

16. Nie Rongzhen, *Kang-Ri mofan genjudi—Jin-Cha-Ji bianqu* (A Model Anti-Japanese Base Area—The Jin-Cha-Ji Border Region) (The Military and Political Press of the Eight Route Army, 1939). Mao wrote the calligraphy for the book (a copy is in the Hoover Institute Library, Stanford) and supported it in other ways, see Tetsuyu Kataoka, *Resistance and Reform in China* (Berkeley: University of California Press, 1974), 92. A similar book with the identical title was issued in Chongqing in March 1939 in the form of notes from a journalist, see Chen Kehan, *Mofan kang-Ri genjudi: Jin-Cha-Ji bianqu* (Chongqing: New China Daily Press, 1939).

17. Nie Rongzhen, *Nie Rongzhen huiyilu* (Reminiscences of Nie Rongzhen) (Beijing, People's Liberation Army Press, 1984), 2: 372 and 380–81. Most accounts draw from Nie Rongzhen, *Kang-Ri mofan genjudi*. The Jin-Cha-Ji Military District, like others operated by the CCP's armies, was a military administrative area whose institutions were a part of and staffed by the military. The Jin-Cha-Ji Border Region was a separate civil administration recognized by the Nationalist government of the GMD and intended to be staffed by elected officials. For most of this period, Nie Rongzhen was leader of the former, Song Shaowen of the latter.

18. *Jin-Cha-Ji ribao dashiji* (Chronology of *Jin-Cha-Ji Daily*) (Beijing: Dazhong Press, 1986), 19–20. Yin Zhou (Deng Tuo), "*Kangdi bao* wushi qi de huigu yu zhanwang" (A Review and the Future of *Resistance News* on Its 50th Issue), in *Kangdi bao*, 27 June 1938, 1; reprinted in *Xinwen shiliao* (Historical Materials on the Press), no. 5 (1983): 9, and *Deng Tuo wenji* (Collected Works of Deng Tuo, *DTWJ*) (Beijing: Beijing Press, 1986), 1: 235–38.

19. *Kangdi bao zengkan* became *Kangdi zhoubao* probably in 1940 when Li Xiaobai took over from Deng Tuo and the journal became a separate entity from the *Resistance News* press. The position "responsible person" seems to be an informal title for editors of small publications.

20. Three other people were listed as "responsible people" on the journal: Li Changqing, Yao Yilin, and Hu Xikui. *Xin chang cheng* was founded on 31 July 1939 in Fuping, where it was printed and distributed by *Resistance News*. See *Zhongguo xinwen nianjian 1984* (Chinese Press Yearbook 1984) (Beijing: People's Daily Press, 1984) (hereafter

Press Yearbook 1984), 627. Hu Xikui later replaced Deng as director of *Jin-Cha-Ji Daily* for most of 1944–45. Yao Yilin, a top party leader today, was general secretary of the North China Bureau and the CCP's Jin-Cha-Ji subbureau between 1937 and 1945. He was in the Ministry of Commerce in the PRC until 1967. He was close to Peng Zhen and purged with him in the Cultural Revolution. See Wolfgang Bartke, *Who's Who in the People's Republic of China* (Armonk, NY: M.E. Sharpe, 1981), 472.

21. This inaugural issue is among the complete set of both papers in the Journalism Department library, People's University, Beijing. *Jin-Cha-Ji ribao dashiji*, 56. Chen Chunsen, in Lio Mosha, ed., *Yi Deng Tuo* (Commemorating Deng Tuo) (Fuzhou: Fujian People's Press, 1980), 30; *Press Yearbook 1984*, 623.

22. Charts are given in *Jin-Cha-Ji ribao dashiji*, 60–61 and 111.

23. Ibid., 20. In May 1940 the CCP CC Northern Bureau under Peng Zhen set up its own Periodicals Committee with Deng Tuo as secretary, and Liu Lantao, Yao Yilin, Li Changqing, and Hu Xikui on the committee; see ibid., 46.

24. Dittmer, *China's Continuous Revolution*, 53.

25. *Jin-Cha-Ji ribao dashiji*, 45.

26. Ibid., 126.

27. Ibid., 55. Other standing committee members named are: Chang Qing, Sha Kefu, Zhou Weizhi, and Tian Jian.

28. Ibid., 74.

29. "Zhonggong zhongyang guanyu dang bao wenti gei difang dang de zhishi" (CCP CC Directive to Local Party Branches Concerning the Question of Party Periodicals), in *Zhongguo gongchandang xinwen gongzuo wenjian huibian* (Collection of Documents on CCP Journalism Work) (Beijing: Xinhua Press, 1980), 1: 86.

30. (Deng Tuo), "Lun dang bao he dang de gongzuo" (On Party Periodicals and Party Work), in *Zhanxian*, 24 December 1938; reprinted in *DTWJ*, 1: 242–46. Discussed in Wang Bisheng, "Deng Tuo—yidai xinwen gongzuozhe de mofan" (Deng Tuo—The Model for a Generation of Journalists), *Xuexi yu sikao* (Study and Thought), no. 2 (1983): 60. Since I have not seen the original I do not know under what pen name it was published. *Zhanxian* was founded on 17 February 1938 and published in Fuping. See *Press Yearbook 1984*, 627.

31. *DTWJ*, 1: 245.

32. Clearly, the propaganda network had not been well established in Jin-Cha-Ji by the end of 1938; it probably wasn't until well into 1940, since Nie Rongzhen complained about this in January 1939; "Zai Zhonggong zhongyang beifang fenju dang daibiao dahui shangde baogao" (Report to the CCP CC Northern Branch Party Congress, January 1939, Nie, "Report'), *Zhonggong dang shi ziliao* (Materials on CCP History), no. 20: 12. A comparison of this piece of "internal propaganda" and the internal party directive also shows the strengths and weaknesses of different levels of documents in the CCP as historical sources. We may assume the directive is accurate, but it is brief and telegraphic. Deng's elaboration of it adds considerable local information but maintains a positive spin that must be interpreted to mean the problem still exists (in this case distribution and a local network of correspondents and reading group leaders).

33. Ibid., 71–72; included among the editorials was "Nawo Makesizhuyi de lilun wuqi" (Grasp the Theoretical Weapon of Marxism), reprinted in *DTWJ*, 1: 38–41. Wang Bisheng, "Fenghuo shinian xie zongheng—Deng Tuo tongzhi zai Jin-Cha-Ji bianqu xinwen xuanchuan huodong jishu" (Writing with Ease Through Ten Years of War—An Account of Comrade Deng Tuo's Journalism and Propaganda Activities in the Jin-Cha-Ji Border Region), *Xinwen shiliao*, no. 5 (1983): 3, and Wang Bisheng, "Deng Tuo—The Model," 60.

34. Quotation from Deng and analysis, Wang Bisheng, "Deng Tuo's Journalism,"

3. Wang suggests that this approach was both the source of the paper's later successes and a model worth deep consideration today.

35. Nie Rongzhen, *Nie Rongzhen huiyilu, 2:* 584–85. *The Central CCP had declared a period of such reform and study at the sixth plenum in 1938.*

36. Peng Zhen had been similarly called in 1941. One of the best accounts of Mao's factional and ideological struggles up to and throughout the 1942–44 rectification movement is in Wylie, *The Emergence of Maoism,* 130–94.

37. *Jin-Cha-Ji ribao dashiji,* 90–105. The Beiyue Party Committee (around Fuping, the capital) did make some efforts at organized rectification study, organizing a Rectification Committee in July 1942 under Liu Lantao and Hu Xikui (ibid., 101).

38. *Jizhong Daobao, Tingjin bao; Zhang Fan* in *Yi Deng Tuo,* 52–54.

39. Zuo Lu, "Deng Tuo shengping, gongzuo pianduan: Xinwen shi shangde qiju" (Fragments of Deng Tuo's Life and Work, no. 4: A Miracle in the History of Journalism), *Xinwen jizhe,* no. 11 (1984): 28.

40. See Lin Maike (Michael Lindsay), "Jin-Cha-Ji yinxiang ji" (Impressions of Jin-Cha-Ji), in *Jiefang ribao* (Liberation Daily), 5 June 1944, 3, and his postscript to *The Unknown War: North China in 1937–45* (London: Bergstrom and Boyle Books, Ltd., 1975).

41. Philip Kuhn, "Local Self Government Under the Republic: Problems of Control, Autonomy, and Mobilization," in Frederick Wakeman, Jr., and Carol Grant, eds., *Conflict and Control in Late Imperial China* (Berkeley: University of California Press, 1975), 261, and Victor Mair, "Language and Ideology in the Written Popularizations of the *Sacred Edicts,*" in David Johnson, Andrew Nathan, and Evelyn S. Rawski, eds., *Popular Culture in Late Imperial China* (Berkeley: University of California Press, 1985), 325–59.

42. Quoted in Laurence Zuckerman "Letter From China," *Columbia Journalism Review* (November-December 1985): 34. These points strike me as accurate, but I have yet to locate Mao saying them in so many words. Nonetheless, the gist is included in a 16 March 1942 *Liberation Daily* editorial, reprinted in *Mao Zedong xinwen gongzuo wenxuan* (Selected Writings by Mao Zedong on Journalism) (Beijing: Xinhua Press, 1983), 91–92. These functions are *precisely* those achieved by the Soviets in the 1920s. See Kenez, *Birth of a Propaganda State,* 224 ff.

43. Yin Zhou (Deng Tuo), "*Kangdi bao* de wushi qi," 8; also in *DTWJ,* 1: 235–38, quotation from 235–36.

44. Zuo Lu, "Deng Tuo shengping, gongzuo pianduan: shi wenchang you shi zhanchang" (Fragments of Deng Tuo's Life and Work Recalled: A Literary and a Battle Field), in *Xinwenjizhe* (The Journalist), no. 10 (1984): 30. Deng's editorial appeared in the temporary *Kangdi waibao,* which was published on the run during the late 1938 Japanese " 'mopping up" campaign in Jin-Cha-Ji under one of his pen names, Wen Zhou, "Zhanshi xuanchuan gudong gongzuo," not in DTWJ.

45. It was published by the Political Department of the Jin-Cha-Ji Military District. See Nie Rongzhen, *Nie Rongzhen huiyilu,* 2: 482. Sha Fei, the former editor of *Resistance News,* was the editor of this pictorial and its predecessor, *Kangdi huabao. Jin-Cha-Ji Pictorial's* inaugural issue is dated: Fuping, 7 July 1942, the fifth anniversary of the start of war with Japan, but it was not published until September 1942. See *Press Yearbook 1984,* 627.

46. This was not to be the case in later issues of the journal, which gave up the use of English, other than on the back cover.

47. Xiao Si [Deng Tuo], "Jin-Cha-Ji's Helmsman Nie Rongzhen—A Model Anti-Japanese Base Behind Enemy Lines and the Life of Its Commander" (Jin-Cha-Ji duoshi Nie Rongzhen—dihou mofan kang-Ri genjudi ji qi chuanzaozhe de shengping), in *Jin-Cha-Ji Huabao,* no. 1 (Jin-Cha-Ji Political Department of the Military District, 7 July 1942):

1–13 (there is no pagination; page citations to this article count from the first page). The text has been subject to some distortion in its post-Mao reprints. In a restricted circulation academic journal, Wang Bisheng, "Deng Tuo—The Model," 60, accurately cites the title without comment. Deng's 1942 article is misleadingly reprinted in significantly edited form as "Nie Rongzhen zai Jin-Cha-Ji," in *Deng Tuo sanwen* (Lyrical Essays of Deng Tuo) (Beijing: People's Daily Press, 1980), 158–79. In line with slightly improved historiographical standards in 1986, *DTWJ*, 4: 266–89, reprints another version of this text with a note indicating that it is the revised 1946 text from *Qunzhong* (The Masses), 9, Nos. 23 and 24, with additions from the 1942 version. For further details, see Timothy Cheek, *Intellectual Service in Mao's China: The Life and Death of Deng Tuo* (forthcoming).

48. It would be worth finding out whether leaders of other base areas were similarly lionized.

49. This tone permeates the very detailed and useful series, *Zhonggong dang shi renwu zhuan* (Personalities in CCP History) (Xi'an: Shaanxi People's Press, 1980). A glaring example of this modern *lie zhuan* (exemplary biography) style is Zuo Lu, "Fragments No. 4," 28–31.

50. It is, as Wang Bisheng, "Deng Tuo's Journalism," 7, notes, a fine example of reportage (*baogao wenxue*).

51. Xiao Si (Deng Tuo), "Jin-Cha-Ji's Helmsman Nie Rongzhen," 3; cut from "Nie Rongzhen in Jin-Cha-Ji" (1980), 162–63.

52. Xiao Si (Deng Tuo), "Jin-Cha-Ji's Helmsman Nie Rongzhen," 4.

53. Ibid., 6–9; some of this has been edited out of the 1980 edition, but not the names of his associates.

54. Ibid., 5 and 10.

55. Ibid., 11.

56. Ibid., 12. None of this appears in the 1980 reprint, and one may wonder why the editors would pass up the chance to show, from an original document of the 1940s, at least Nie's use and Deng's praise of "seeking truth from facts," which is today's slogan.

57. Ibid.

58. An excellent rebuttal of the two-line struggle thesis is given in Frederick C. Teiwes, *Leadership, Legitimacy, and Conflict in China: From a Charismatic Mao to the Politics of Succession* (Armonk, NY: M.E. Sharpe, 1984), 10–42.

59. Peng was recalled to Yan'an in 1941 to join the top leadership, and his administrative policies from Jin-Cha-Ji became those of the famous " 'Yan'an Way" in 1942–44. On the amalgam of charismatic and bureaucratic authority in Maoism and its destructive disassociation in the late 1950s and 1960s, see Timothy Cheek and Carol Lee Hamrin, "Collaboration and Conflict in the Search for a New Order," in Hamrin and Cheek, eds., *China's Establishment Intellectuals* (Armonk, NY: M.E. Sharpe, 1986), 18–19.

60. Nie Rongzhen, *Nie Rongzhen huiyilu*, 2: 550–51.

61. These were duly reported in the *Jin-Cha-Ji Daily* in February, *Jin-Cha-Ji ribao dashiji*, 114–16. For examples, see *Zhongguo xin minzhuzhuyi geming shiqi genju di fazhi wenxian xuanbian* (Selected Base Area Legal Documents from the Period of New Democratic Revolution) (Beijing: Chinese Academy of Social Sciences Press, 1984), 4: 247–59 on rent and 826–28 on marriage, and the follow-ups later in 1943 by the administrative council, 260 ff. on rent and 829 ff. on marriage and inheritance. For laws in vols. 1–3, see note 62 below.

62. See the analysis of the Jin-Cha-Ji legal code in Pitman Potter, "Peng Zhen: Evolving Views on Party Organization and Law," in Hamrin and Cheek, *China's Establishment Intellectuals*, 25–29. Peng's role in developing these programs is made clear in his 1941

Guanyu Jin-Cha-Ji bianqu dangde gongzuo he juti zhengce baogao (Report Concerning Party Work and Specific Policies in the Jin-Cha-Ji Border Region), (Beijing: Central Party School Press, 1981). Extracts of this important report are translated in Tony Saich, ed., *The Rise to Power of the Chinese Communist Party: Documents and Analysis* (Armonk, NY: M.E. Sharpe , 1995).

63. Later, when Mao turned on Deng Tuo in the late 1950s, Peng Zhen (then mayor of Beijing) would give Deng a home in Beijing's municipal administration.

64. Potter, "Peng Zhen," 25–26; Nie Rongzhen, *Nie Rongzhen huiyilu*, 2: 551.

65. Potter, "Peng Zhen," 26–28, shows how this was the intent of the 1940 program and the 1943 legal code. This amounts to the "power management" that Hartford has documented for Jin-Cha-Ji administration over the whole period.

66. Potter, ibid., 27 and 28–29.

67. Ibid., 28.

68. *Jin-Cha-Ji ribao dashiji*, 115.

69. Deng had studied and published on dialectical materialism since 1933, well before Mao enunciated his dogma. For details on this and the issue of "culture bearers" for party intellectuals, see Cheek, *Intellectual Service*.

70. Miklós Haraszti, *The Velvet Prison: Artists Under State Socialism* (New York: Basic Books, 1987), and George Konrád and Ivan Szelényi, *Intellectuals on the Road to Class Power* (New York: Harcourt, Brace, Jovanovich, 1979).

71. *DTWJ*, 1: 373.

72. See Leo Ou-fan Lee, *The Romantic Generation of Modern Chinese Writers* (Cambridge: Harvard University Press, 1973); Vera Schwarcz, *The Chinese Enlightenment: Intellectuals and the Legacy of the May Fourth Movement of 1919* (Berkeley: University of California Press, 1985); and Timothy Cheek, "The Fading of 'Wild Lilies': Wang Shiwei and Mao Zedong's Yan'an Talks in the First CPC Rectification Movement," *Australian Journal of Chinese Affairs*, no. 11 (1984): 26–58.

73. *DTWJ*, 1: 373, emphasis added. For "Maoist" views, see David Holm, *Art and Ideology in Revolutionary China* (Oxford: Oxford University Press, 1991), 43–86.

74. *DTWJ*, 1: 372. He describes it as a dialectical process.

75. Mao's "Yan'an Talks" of May 1942 is the *locus classicus* for his literary policies, though they were prefigured in his January 1940 "On New Democracy." The text of Mao's famous speech with which Deng Tuo and others worked in the 1940s has been translated by Bonnie S. McDougall, *Mao Zedong's "Talks at the Yan'an Conference on Literature and Art": A Translation of the 1943 Text with Commentary* (Ann Arbor: Michigan Papers in Chinese Studies, no. 39, 1980). The positive side to Mao's cultural policies, mass literature, have been covered in Selden, *The Yenan Way*, and in more detail in David Holm's book, *Art and Ideology*, on the *yang'ge* popular drama movement. The negative side has been covered by Merle Goldman, *Literary Dissent In Communist China* (Cambridge: Harvard University Press, 1967), 18–50, and Guilhem Fabre, *Genèse du pouvoir et de l'opposition en Chine: Le printemps de Yan'an, 1942* (Paris: Editions l'Harmattan, 1990).

76. Wang Bisheng, "Deng Tuo's Life," 77; Deng's reply poem to the group's leader, the old poet Hao Qing, and Deng's account of the society are in *Deng Tuo shici xuan* (Selected Poetry of Deng Tuo) (Beijing: People's Literature Press, 1979), 22–24; quotation from 24 and *DTWJ*, 4: 38–39. Yan is the ancient name for the northwest Hebei region and Zhao the name for western Hebei and eastern Shanxi, the same areas occupied by Jin-Cha-Ji.

77. Lou Ningxian, in *Yi Deng Tuo*, 39.

78. Various authors in ibid., 33, 37–39, 49, and 56–57.

79. *Deng Tuo shici xuan*, 23–24. Deng had a similar evening of wine and poetry with

Nie and General Chen Yi in 1947; see Wang Bisheng, "Deng Tuo's Life," 77, and *Deng Tuo shici xuan*, 35.

80. This is what I argue in "The Fading of 'Wild Lilies,' " 26–58.

81. Susanne Weigelin-Schwiedrzik has found a similar pattern among some party historiographers—an appreciation of Mao, organization, and the opportunity to save Chinese culture by serving the CCP while disliking utopian futurism. See Weieglin-Schwiedrzik, *Parteigeschichtsschreibung in der VR China: Typen, Methoden, Themen und Funktionen* (Weisbaden, 1984).

82. *Mao Zedong xuanji* (n.p.: Jin-Cha-Ji Daily Publishers, 1944). It appears in two versions: a single hardback, which I viewed at Ding Yilan's, and five separate volumes in blue mimeograph ink, which I viewed at the Toyo Bunko, Tokyo, and the Fairbank Center Library at Harvard. On this and other editions of Mao's collected works, see Timothy Cheek, "Textually Speaking: An Assessment of Newly Available Mao Texts," in Roderick MacFarquhar, Timothy Cheek, and Eugene Wu, eds., *The Secret Speeches of Chairman Mao: From the Hundred Flowers to the Great Leap Forward* (Cambridge: Harvard Council on East Asian Studies, 1989), 84–90.

83. "Gaizao women de tongxun yu baodao fangfa" (Reform Our Correspondents' and Reporting Methods), given May 1944 with subtitle: "Excerpts from the May 1944 Speech at the Subbureau's Propaganda Department News Workers Forum," *Xinwen gongzuo zhinan* (Guide to Journalist Work), no. 1 (Kalgan: Jin-Cha-Ji Xinhua Bookstore, 1946), 49–56. Photocopy of the original pamphlet is available through Center for Chinese Research Materials, Oakton, Virginia. Reprinted in *DTWJ*, 1: 261–68.

84. Reprinted in *Xinwen gongzuo zhinan*, 57.

85. Ibid., 54; emphasis added.

86. Ibid., 50–51 and 53–54.

87. Walder, *Communist Neo-Traditionalism*.

88. A comparison of this local study with the political culture on the ground for other social actors (peasants, nonmetropolitan intellectuals or elites, soldiers, etc.) as well as other base areas is needed before an empirically based conception of CCP political culture can be put forward. In the meantime, I prefer Tom Gold's analysis of related social patterns among post-Mao youth, which occurred unintentionally in response to political abuses over the past twenty years. See Thomas B. Gold, "After Comradeship: Personal Relations in China Since the Cultural Revolution," *China Quarterly*, no. 104 (December 1985): 657–75.

89. The intimate link between the "salvation" of rectification doctrine and the "inquisition" of the rescue movement purges in Yan'an in 1942–44 is supported by documentary evidence collected by Dai Qing in *Wang Shiwei and "Wild Lilies": Rectification and Purges in the Chinese Communist Party, 1942–44* (Armonk, NY: M.E. Sharpe, 1994).

Chapter 10

The Blooming Poppy under the Red Sun: The Yan'an Way and the Opium Trade

Chen Yung-fa

During the Cultural Revolution, hundreds of people flooded into Dazhai every day to learn from the local farmers how to create new men and women through ideological struggle, how to produce economic miracles through the mass line, how to change terrain through human efforts, and how to overcome poverty through community endeavors. In a word, they came to learn what Mark Selden calls the Yan'an (Yenan) Way from the experience of Dazhai.

Inspired by the Dazhai miracle, Selden chose the Shaan-Gan-Ning (Shaanxi-Gansu-Ningxia) base area as the focus of his study of the wartime communist movement.[1] He found that the base area suffered a deadly crisis from 1941 to 1943, when the Nationalist government tightened its economic blockade and the Japanese army launched relentless attacks on the party's rear base areas. To overcome the crisis, the party developed a mass line approach in lieu of bureaucratic command and initiated new policies such as rent and interest reduction, rustification of cadres, mutual aid movements, and large-scale production campaigns. As a result, the Shaan-Gan-Ning base area went through a dramatic change and lifted itself from extreme poverty and backwardness.

In the 1960s and 1970s, the Maoists celebrated the Dazhai experience as a resurrection of the Yan'an Way that had revived Shaan-Gan-Ning and proclaimed it to be the key to economic emancipation of the third world. Of course, soon after the era of the Cultural Revolution ended, the Dazhai model was discredited. Today, everyone familiar with PRC politics knows that huge state subsidies underlay the economic miracle of Dazhai. But until now, no one has ever re-examined the history of Shaan-Gan-Ning to see whether Mark Selden's account holds true in light of the recent revelations.

I have discovered that profits from opium production and sales by the CCP made a substantial contribution to the economic development of the Shaan-Gan-

Ning base area and the financing of its government. Documentation of this finding and an account of the CCP's evolving policies toward the opium trade are provided in the pages that follow. In this chapter, I make no attempt to deny entirely the validity of Mark Selden's account of the "Yan'an Way," but I do argue that omission of the opium revenues from accounts of the Yan'an Way is a serious mistake. For without the opium trade, the economic improvements Mark Selden found in Shaan-Gan-Ning would have been simply impossible. In studying the problem of economic development, Selden stressed dedication, voluntarism, and the human spirit, but failed to realize how important financial subsidies were to the production campaigns and other economic ventures of the time. The party considered various options in handling the fiscal problems of the base area, but in the end opium revenues emerged as its most important financial resource. After the civil war of the late 1940s, when the opium trade ended and the CCP refocused its attention on the Beijing-centered nationwide economy, the Shaan-Gan-Ning economy stagnated and even began to lose ground because of the lack of development capital formerly supplied by opium revenues.

While showing the importance of the opium trade, this chapter also addresses the following questions. First, what was the nature of the communist financial crisis from 1941 to 1943 and how should we account for its severity? Can the crisis be attributed solely to the Nationalist economic blockade and Japanese "three-all" offensives? Second, how did the communist leaders come to think of the opium trade as a way out? The CCP had claimed to be the most fervent champion of Chinese national interests and loudly condemned the Western powers for their opium traffic. How did the party justify fostering this infamous trade to garner revenues? Third, the traditional opium trade in northern Shaanxi was mired in crime and corruption. How could the party minimize these dangers and still exploit the trade?

Before answering these questions, I should emphasize that the statistical evidence used is far from precise. That evidence is drawn primarily from a documentary study of the Shaan-Gan-Ning economy published in the political atmosphere of post-Mao liberalization. I have no way of checking the accuracy of these materials. But from my own experience in handling original party documents collected by the Nationalist intelligence apparatus, I have no reason to doubt the authenticity of these Communist-compiled documents. Insufficient training and carelessness by transcribers largely explain the inconsistencies I found in the statistics of those handwritten or mimeographed party documents held in libraries on Taiwan. In the materials used in this chapter, these problems are compounded. In addition to careless proofreading, an economy of high inflation, many different currencies, and numbers of eight or nine digits all account for the numerical contradictions careful readers should find in the statistics presented in this essay. Fortunately, the statistical inconsistencies uncovered cast no serious doubts on my sketch of the border region economy or challenge my conclusions with respect to the importance of the opium trade.

The Three-Year Crisis and Its Roots

In 1941, millet prices in Yan'an soared 36 percent over the previous year. This was an improvement over the 50 percent year-on-year jump the previous year, but not compared to an 8 percent increase in 1939. More alarming was the increase in the following two years. In 1942, the price jumped 129 percent and in 1943, 107 percent. The problem of skyrocketing prices was much more serious than in Nationalist-controlled Xi'an.[2] In explaining the inflation, Mark Selden emphasized two external factors: the Nationalist economic blockade and the Japanese military offensive. Such an explanation has its merits, but does not take into account other constraints on attempts to develop the Shaan-Gan-Ning economy. The CCP, despite the land revolution it had carried out, had failed to establish a sound financial base and financially depended first on confiscation of the properties of enemy classes, and later on outside help to maintain its solvency from 1933 to 1941. It was this heavy dependency and lack of an independent revenue base that accounted for the severity of the economic problems faced by the party during the three difficult years. Failure to appreciate the internal financial weakness of the party has led us to underestimate the party's desperation during the three-year crisis and overestimate the accomplishments of a Yan'an Way that in fact depended on opium revenues.

After setting up a soviet government in Shaan-Gan-Ning in 1934, the local party immediately began the land revolution, confiscating the grain, livestock, landholdings, and other properties of the landlord class and redistributing the rich peasants' land according to the two principles of quantitative and qualitative equality. Unquestionably, such a radical policy helped ameliorate the misery of many rural poor and attracted them to the communist revolution.[3] However, the emancipation of the forces of production as promised by the land revolution did not quickly come true. Of course, this failure might be attributed to the war environment and the party's resultant inability to invest in the rural sector. But whatever the reason, the party still faced a peasantry unable to support a revolution financially; the party depended almost completely on fines, confiscations, and the extralegal method of "attacking local gentry" for revenue and left the "emancipated" peasants largely to themselves.[4]

In October 1935, Mao Zedong led six thousand to seven thousand Red Army soldiers to the Shaan-Gan-Ning border area. Exhausted from crossing the snow-capped mountains, the troops brought with them only hungry stomachs and insufficient clothing, and soon found impoverished northern Shaanxi unable to provide for them. During the Muslim rebellion a century earlier, General Zuo Zongtang had deliberately forced the rebels to retreat into northern Shaanxi, where the harsh environment caused a natural demise of the rebel army. Whether or not Chiang Kai-shek had the same idea in mind, Mao Zedong and his followers soon realized that their arrival had strained the northern Shaanxi economy to the point of total breakdown.

Table 10.1

CCP Finances in Shaan-Gan-Ning, 1935–36

		Revenue		
	Total (yuan)	Confiscation (yuan [percent])	Bank credit (yuan)	Salt tax and state enterprises (yuan)
Dec. 1935	1,686,948	87,364 (51.79)	—	—
Dec. 1936	1,187,227	652,858 (55)	1,194,016	57,775

		Expenditure		
	Total (yuan)	Military expenses (yuan [percent])	Grain (yuan [percent])	Administrative expenses (yuan)
Dec. 1935	146,150	−133,172 (91.12)	—	—
Dec. 1936	2,321,606	1,343,680 (57.86)	105,663 (4.5)	75,281

Sources: Xingguang and Zhang Yang, ed., 27 and 31; *SGNBQ*, 5:5.

Note: Some figures are clearly wrong. For example, the total revenue for 1936 should be 1,904,649 if the three other figures are correct. The currency unit for yuan is *supiao* and the exchange rate of supiao to *fabi* is 6:1.

Less than two months later, the party found that 87,364 yuan, or 51.8 percent of its total monthly income of 168,694 yuan, came from confiscations, fines and "attacking local gentry." The percentage derived from extralegal income increased slightly over the next twelve months, but the total deficit grew more than twelve-fold. Table 10.1 gives us some details of the party's financial situation.

The party found it necessary to supplement income from confiscation with revenue from taxation and bank loans. Why couldn't it look to the commercial and industrial sector for help? Northern Shaanxi had neither modern industry nor large businesses other than opium. In fact, land redistribution, hostility toward merchants, and the initial ban on the opium trade had depressed the local economy. To revive local commerce, the party even reduced and abolished "customs" and business taxes. Thus printing paper money through the state bank was the main solution to the budget deficit in this period. To reduce expenditures, the party unified the confiscation agencies and called for additional frugality measures.[5]

Yet a population of roughly 600,000 could hardly produce enough to provide for an army of 10,000, including the units operating there before Mao Zedong's arrival. The Nationalist economic blockade began to tighten in 1936. As domestic confiscation failed to meet revenue needs and domestic self-sufficiency was still only a remote possibility, the party had to extend to neighboring areas its extralegal methods. In the spring of 1936, the Red Army invaded Yan Xishan's Shanxi, nominally to fight Japanese aggression but actually to attack the local gentry in order to acquire grain and other supplies. The arrival of about 20,000 Red Army soldiers in October 1936 further complicated grain-supply problems.[6]

As the part of Inner Mongolia north of the Shaan-Gan-Ning base area became the site of action against the Japanese invasion, the party moved its troops northward. The declared goal was to fight the intruders. But secretly the party was planning a surprise attack on the Nationalist garrison in a nearby town. Grain was what the party really sought. As the town was poor, the party also considered an expedition to southern Shaanxi. However, before any plan was put into effect, the Xi'an incident occurred. The party had to scratch the project and seek other means to provide for its fast-growing army and government.[7]

About eight months before the Xi'an incident, the party had already reached secret agreements with both General Yang Hucheng and Zhang Xueliang, creating large holes in the Nationalist economic blockade.[8] After the incident, the embargo was formally lifted and the CCP immediately restored contacts with the outside world. In the spring of 1937, the Comintern contributed an unspecified "large sum" (jukuan) to the party. To convert it into Nationalist currency and truck the amount to Yan'an, the party had to send Mao Zedong's brother to Shanghai and mobilize almost the whole underground apparatus in Xi'an.[9] Russian aid and remittances from the families of the anti-Japanese students who had flooded into northern Shaanxi since the spring of 1936 also benefited the party tremendously.[10]

Far more important aid, however, came from the formation of the second United Front in late 1937, when fast-moving events forced the Nationalist government to accept the nominal incorporation of the communist army and government into the Nationalist hierarchies. In exchange for nominal concessions, the Nationalists allowed communist troops to join Yan Xishan's troops defending neighboring Shanxi and promised to appropriate funds for the operation of both the reorganized communist army and the renamed communist government, respectively 6 million yuan and 1.2 million yuan (fabi) a year. Whether or not the GMD meant to foster a communist dependence on them, the compromise temporarily worked to the advantage of their erstwhile foes. In combat areas, the reorganized communist army simply disregarded Nationalist wishes, forming its own government and collecting taxes from the local population for the CCP's own operations. As a result, the Shaan-Gan-Ning government acquired larger revenues than the Nationalist government realized. Nationalist funds plus other outside help enabled the CCP to continue a policy of light taxation on its own constituents in the Yan'an area.[11]

Lin Boqu, the chairman of the Shaan-Gan-Ning Border Region government, once commented that from 1937 to 1939 the base area needed annually 120,000 dan of grain and 13 million yuan in fabi but because of outside aid, his government felt no need to increase taxes within its jurisdiction. Let us take the case of "national salvation public grain." Lin Boqu's border government began to collect this grain tax from 1937, but until 1940 tax grain was no more than 5 percent of local production.[12] It was collected according to a progressive schedule, and the impoverished were exempted. But since the tax demand was so minimal, the

Table 10.2

Communist Income in Shann-Gan-Ning, 1937–40 (in yuan *fabi*)

	Nationalist appropriation	Outside (primarily overseas Chinese) contributions	Commercial taxes	Others	Total
Oct. 1937– Sept. 1938	[411,000]	?	591,000	180,000	1,182,000
1939	7,900,000+	?	?	?	8,800,000+
1940	7,260,000	300,000+	?	?	15,120,000

Source: SGNBQ, 1: 73–74 and 94–95; and 6: 22.
Note: The question marks are this author's, indicating the lack of relevant materials. The bracketed figure means total outside aid.

peasants responded to the collection enthusiastically. The tax cadres usually collected their quota ahead of time; some needed only five or six days to finish their duties. Many of the exempted peasants insisted on paying grain to show their gratitude to the communist government.[13]

Outside financial help, especially Nationalist appropriations, accounted for the continuation of the Yan'an government's light extraction policy. Mark Selden mentions the Nationalist contribution, but he never fully realized the financial implications for the poor Shaan-Gan-Ning base area. The statistics produced by communist authors are inconsistent concerning details, but they all point to the same conclusion: the border region government depended heavily on outside aid for its operation. Even after the GMD-CCP United Front began to show signs of stress in late 1938, the heavy communist dependence continued; only after the New Fourth Army incident (in early 1941) did this financial transfusion come to a complete end. Thereafter, circumstances forced the party to move toward genuine self-reliance.

In 1944, the communist authorities produced the above statistics to show the degree of their dependence on outside help for maintaining a state within a state in the Yan'an area (see Table 10.2).

This party document reveals that the Nationalist appropriation of 1939 accounted for 89.66 percent of the total base area budget, and if other outside contributions are included, the percentage rises to 89.89 percent. In 1940, even though the party accused the Nationalist government of withholding the appropriation, the Nationalist subsidy still accounted for 73.53 percent of the yearly budget.[14]

Two other sources challenge the accuracy of the above statistics, though not the implication of financial dependency. I cite these materials here to show my awareness of the statistical disparities. The first source was issued in 1948; its major concern was to document the percentage of outside aid in the whole Yan'an budget:

	Total revenue	Outside aid	Aid/Revenue (percent)
1937	526,302.45	456,390.01	77.20
1938	907,943.31	468,500.00	51.69
1939	6,602,909.88	5,644,667.34	85.79
1940	9,750,995.31	7,550,855.04	70.50

Source: SGNBQ, 6: 13 and 427. All figures are in yuan *fabi*.

Though ambiguous in meaning, the term *outside aid* should include the Nationalist appropriation. The percentages are generally lower than the earlier ones, but they also document the great importance of outside subsidies.

The second set of statistics was circulated within the party in 1946. It supposedly gives us the precise figures of the Nationalist appropriation and other external contributions to the communist cause:

	Nationalist appropriation	Domestic and foreign donations	Total
July–Dec. 1937	1,927,672.84	36,254.20	1,963,927.04
1938	4,480,157.16	1,973,870.97	6,454,028.13
1939	5,000,436.10	604,207.53	5,604,643.63
1940	4,997,074.11	5,505,901.69	10,502,975.80
1941	0.00	779,106.20	779,106.20

Source: SGNBQ, 6: 428. All figures are in yuan *fabi*.

What the party shows here contradicts our earlier statistics. While the Nationalist appropriation appears much lower, the domestic and foreign donations from outside Shaan-Gan-Ning appear much higher. These figures may reflect the party's desire to show that the Nationalists withheld the appropriations at the party's request and to rally further domestic and foreign support for the Communists. Beyond this speculation, I cannot offer any explanation for the discrepancy with other statistics. Given this limitation, nevertheless, these statistics document that outside subsidies were substantial. I can safely argue that the Shaan-Gan-Ning border area depended heavily on outside support for the maintenance of a state within a state.

The New Fourth Army incident of 1941 ended any communist hope of further Nationalist appropriations. In addition, the Nationalist government deployed its troops in several consecutive zones to barricade the communist territory. An unprecedented economic blockade was formally imposed. As a result, normal trade between communist and Nationalist territories dropped to almost zero. Although immense profits still lured merchants into smuggling, the price for their imports, primarily industrial goods, soared. And no matter how much the party lowered prices of its exports (primarily agricultural products), these goods were unattractive to profit-minded smugglers.

To make matters worse, the Japanese army began its "three-all" offensive almost at the same time, in retaliation for the One Hundred Regiments Campaign of 1940. This large-scale attack reduced the communist territory and population behind Japanese lines. If these base areas had been able to use their surplus to help Shaan-Gan-Ning earlier, the Japanese attack now ended this possibility completely. Instead, the policy of maintaining "crack troops" and simplified government in these contested areas meant that many cadres were sent back to the Yan'an region. Adding the soldiers withdrawn to Shaan-Gan-Ning for local defense, the large number of evacuated cadres severely strained the party's already shrinking financial resources. The party began to tax the local population heavily, but the new taxes were unable to compensate for the lost revenue. In 1941, the border region government declared a deficit of 5,672,699 yuan in *bianbi*.[15]

During that lean year, the party issued its own currency called *bianbi*. As the border region suffered a heavy trade deficit, the currency soon had to be devalued. The deficit amounted to 15 million yuan in *fabi*, pushing up the *bianbi* prices of commodities much faster than *fabi* prices. Let us take the Yan'an case as an example. Assuming the price index of December 1940 was 100, the figure one year later would be 884.2. In other words, commodity prices rose 784 percent. The price jump undermined confidence in the communist currency. By demanding more Nationalist currency, the border region residents forced the communist authorities to depreciate their paper notes further.[16]

In the next two years, the situation improved but inflation continued. In Yan'an, the index of commodity prices increased threefold in both 1942 and 1943.[17] Concerning these financial difficulties, Mao Zedong had the following to say in 1942: "[In the worst times, we] have neither clothes to wear, nor oil for cooking, nor paper to write on, nor vegetables to eat. Soldiers have no stockings and shoes and cadres have no quilts in the [harsh] winter."[18]

How did the party overcome its financial difficulty and survive the economic crisis? Among soldiers, voices were heard saying that the whole army should learn from the Long March. In other words, they argued for the abandonment of the Shaan-Gan-Ning border area and the establishment of a new base area elsewhere. Mao Zedong criticized this view and insisted on staying.[19] To solve the problem, he advocated self-reliance and launched a bold production campaign throughout the border area, using various means to increase agricultural production and revive rural handicraft industry. He also urged soldiers and cadres to produce for their own needs. Realizing the low return of agricultural production,

Table 10.3

The Finances of Shaan-Gan-Ning in 1943

Total expenditures	501,900,000	100.00%
Tax Revenues	170,000,000	33.90
Shortfall	331,900,000	66.1
Production campaigns	100,000,000	19.9
Frugality campaigns	79,250,000	15.8
Deficit	252,650,000	40.4
	(152,650,000)	(30.4)

Source: SGNBQ, 6: 18–19. All figures are in *bianbi.*

he even encouraged all state units to engage in commerce. This caused a great debate within the party leadership. Some pleaded for a conservative production plan on the grounds that the necessary capital was far beyond the party's means, but Mao and his followers were determined and refused to allow the revenue problem to bother them.[20] Yet the problem of raising the capital needed for the production plans could not be wished away. What was Mao's answer?

Overcoming the Crisis

How did the CCP overcome the financial crisis? The current scholarly literature gives only one answer: the "Yan'an Way." By the "Yan'an Way," Mark Selden meant the mass line and the policies embodying that political principle. New evidence enables us to move beyond this magic formula. First, let me cite a set of 1943 statistics (see Table 10.3) to facilitate our discussion of possible answers. I cite it only because of the lack of similar materials for the two other years.

Assuming the correctness of the first five lines above, the last line evidently contains a simple typographical error and should be changed as indicated by the parentheses. The text accompanying these statistics also reveals the insufficiency of Selden's "Yan'an Way" as an answer. First, the famous production campaign, which peaked in 1943, still fell short of expectations, although many state units did produce enough to meet their daily needs other than grain. Second, the frugality campaign, including the much-praised policy of "crack forces and simplified administration," helped offset the deficit, but the party was still left with a sizable deficit amounting to at least 30.4 percent of the base area's annual budget.[21] Where could the party find the resources to fill the gap?

The party tried three other means: taxation, printing money, and expanding "foreign trade." In the end, considerable extra endeavor was needed to make all the efforts worthwhile.

The Yan'an authorities intensified their extraction efforts drastically. The "national salvation public grain" previously amounted to no more than 100,000 *dan*; in 1941, the quota was doubled. A detailed study found that the tax burden was unevenly distributed. In newly occupied areas such as Suide and Mizhi, the peasants had to send 8.63 percent to 12.2 percent of their grain production to the authorities, despite suffering from poor harvests. The major burden fell on the peasants in the consolidated communist territory. As a result, the average burden for Yan'an County amounted to 35.03 percent of the annual yield, at least five times the tax burden imposed on Nationalist Huainan. Since the peasants of Qinghua district paid an average 43.7 percent of their harvest to the party, we can imagine that their discontent increased.[22]

To indicate the mood of the discontented peasants, one need only refer to a story widely circulated around this time. In a storm, a cadre was "struck" by lightning and killed. On hearing the news, peasants were overheard to have wondered why the lightning did not strike Chairman Mao. In the face of such discontent, the party reduced the quota for the grain tax in 1942, but the next year it had to raise the quota again. The party took even more in actual collection.[23] Communist investigators therefore found that peasants in such counties as Qingjian, Huachi, and Quzi bore a tax burden amounting to 18.2 percent to 40 percent of the harvest.[24] Only in 1944 could the party reduce the extraction significantly. Under these circumstances, the party had to try other solutions.

The printing machine of the communist state bank also helped tremendously. But unless the party could assure the supply of commodities in the domestic market, issuing unbacked currency would inevitably reignite inflation. This is exactly what happened in 1943, when the party pumped an additional 276 million yuan (*bianbi*) without solid backing into the economy. The bold effort helped the party underwrite many aspects of the production campaigns. However since the return was not immediate, the *bianbi* immediately depreciated and fierce competition from *fabi* drove the *bianbi* out of circulation. In terms of price, millet rose 1,400 percent in a year, cotton textiles 1,900 percent, and the *fabi* 1,000 percent. As a result, the party eventually gave up its attack on the conservative money policy and decided to stop further printing and tighten the money supply.[25]

To expand the "foreign trade" (i.e., export earnings) of the base area was a sensible answer to the problem of inflation, but to expand it at a time of economic blockade was surely an uphill struggle. However, the party did not spare on the attempt. The Shaan-Gan-Ning Border Region was famous for "three treasures" (*sanbao*) in the late Qing and early Republican periods. The first was an herb called *gancao*. The export of the herb in large quantity required cheap transportation, which was impossible in the loess plateau. The second treasure was leather, but the influx of outsiders had already reduced the exportable quantity to near zero. So the only hope hinged on salt, which could be mined in great quantities along the Ningxia-Shaanxi border. Salt had been mined in the area for hundreds of years, but because of high transportation costs, it could not compete with sea salt. The Japanese occupation of the coastal areas eliminated this competition; the Nationalist territory of eastern Gansu and central Shaanxi needed a new source of salt.[26]

Indeed the party placed high hopes on salt production and trade. It enlisted peasants to transport the salt, but as they saw no profit in the work, they began to complain loudly and eventually forced the party to commute the corvée into taxes. The party also mobilized soldiers for production. In any case, in 1943, the party exported 727.09 million yuan (*bianbi*) of salt. Though the total value (not the total profit) exceeded the party's budget for the year, salt accounted for only 13.59 percent of total trade.[27] I cannot explain the basis on which the party calculated the value of the salt trade, but feel quite safe in concluding that the export of local products could not solve the deficit of the Shaan-Gan-Ning government.

Yet I might be wrong in drawing such a quick conclusion, because in communist materials we find constant allusions to a "special product" (*techan*) that tipped the trade balance. Even the much talked-about salt could not compare in terms of trade value; the "special product" helped the border government survive the financial crisis. In fact, in 1943, the communist state bank printed paper notes on the backing of a large holding of this "special product." Unfortunately for the party, the peasants did not share the bank's faith in the commodity; unless the bank could sell it, the unusual deposit inspired no confidence. The communist bank somehow understood this, but the Nationalists' outbidding in a secret "trade war" forced it to hoard the commodity. Poor quality and high price gave the bank no other alternative, unless it lowered the price.[28]

The Local Product Company, which was founded to handle the sale of the "special product," encountered powerful opposition to price cutting. It proposed a 20 percent reduction in price, but its stockholders, who were all state units, were vehemently opposed. Accustomed to super-profits, these units accused the company of mismanaging the business and ignoring their interests.[29] Party leaders eventually allowed the company to have its way in the debate. Indeed, thanks to the price reduction, the company was able to make a profit of 350 million yuan (*bianbi*) in a slack season.[30]

The chief manager of the Local Product Company, Yu Jie, has left us a record of "special product" sales for all of 1943: January, 76,712 boxes; February, 138,696; March, 68,598; April, 74,718; May, 61,968; June, 81,749; July, 112,749; August, 99,033; September, 87,543; October, 56,360; November, 55,263; December, 58,807.[31]

Take notice of the unit "boxes" (*xiang*). A total of 972,196 boxes of this "special product" was sold, their cash value being 2,071,640,000 yuan (*bianbi*). According to a communist author, the total value was 2.8 times more than that of salt in 1943. Without the successful marketing of these boxes of "special product," the border region government would have seen a doubling of its trade deficit. From Table 10.4, we can also see the contribution the "special product" made in 1944 and 1945. Almost singlehandedly, the "special product" tipped the trade balance in the party's favor.

Table 10.4

"Special Product" in Shaan-Gan-Ning Trade

Year	Import value	Exports minus "special product"	Balance	Export value of "Special product"	New Balance
1943[1]	6,474,640,000	2,524,850,000	−3,949,790,000	2,071,640,000	−1,878,150,000
1944[1]	15,960,163,959	9,170,389,985	−6,789,773,964	22,421,065,704	15,631,291,340
1945[2]	2,027,318,453	1,066,552,739	−960,765,714	3,991,368,484	3,030,602,770

Source: SGNBQ, 4: 67–68.
[1]In *yuan bianbi*
[2]In *yuan biquan*

These statistics are full of minor inconsistencies, but the importance of the trade in the "special product" is not contradicted by other communist materials. One other source reports that the trade deficit for the border area in 1943 was 1,107,920,000 yuan (*bianbi*), but if one excludes the "special product," the deficit triples, climbing to 4,791,170,000 yuan.[32] The "special product" accounted for 68.86 percent of the total trade for the year. In the following two years, it engineered a trade coup for the CCP; in 1944, exports exceeded imports by 40.5 percent and in 1945, by 94.8 percent (by my calculation, 96.9).

In terms of public finance, profits from the "special product" accounted for 40.82 percent total revenues in 1942. The figure was slightly higher than that for 1941. Afterward, the party gave the percentages only in terms of yearly expenditures, 26.63 percent and 40.07 percent for 1944 and 1945, respectively. Again, despite our reservations about the imprecision of these statistics, we can safely conclude that the "special product" was miraculous.

Year	Profits from "special product"	
1942	139,623,000 yuan *bianbi*	40.00 percent of total revenue
1943	65,347,927 yuan *juanbi*	40.82 percent of total revenue
1944	135,388,778 yuan *juanbi*	26.63 percent of total spending
1945	757,995,348 yuan *juanbi*	40.07 percent of total spending

Source: SGNBQ, 6: 17, 59, and 426–27.33

The question is, What is the "special product"? We can only be sure that it was not one of the three treasures of northern Shaanxi. But what could attract merchants from both the Nationalist and Japanese territories to risk their lives in illegal smuggling? Why did the communist author use the adjective "distorted" (*jixing*) to describe the favorable trade balance brought about by the trade of "special product"?[34] Why did the party call the "special product"–centered finance "special [*teshu*] finance"?[35]

Xie Juezai's diary provides us with some clues. Xie was one of the five elders in the CCP in the 1950s. He was the president of the Shaan-Gan-Ning Border Region Council in the 1940s. During the Cultural Revolution, he was paralyzed by a stroke. In order to protect his diary, he hid it in a sofabed and lay on it day and night.[36] In the 1980s, the government published the diary posthumously. In his private writings, Xie mentioned Mao Zedong's self-criticism around 15 January 1945. According to Xie, Mao confessed that the CCP had committed two grave mistakes in its history that could be excused only by circumstances. The first was taking Tibetan barley without consent during the Long March. If the party had stuck to its rule of military discipline, the whole Red Army would have perished. The second forgivable mistake was planting "a certain thing" (*mouwu*).[37]

Xie gave no explanation for his euphemism in the secret diary. Why was planting a certain thing as heinous a crime as seizing a minority people's grain? Evidently, Xie was referring to growing opium. This is no wild guess. In his diary, Xie gives further clues, of which the following is the most pertinent. On 12 March 1944, he wrote down six interesting and humorous comments (*quyu*) he heard in an official discussion. The fourth comment reads "*tehuo duo, bianbi shao, jianglai budeliao*." Xie's interpretation is this: "if we tighten the money [*bianbi*] and allow the price of the 'special' goods to drop, we will have a problem controlling the buyers." This explanation does not help much. It is widely known, however, that in Republican China "special goods" was a euphemism for opium. The sixth comment reads "*yu tu gong cunwang*," a fashionable usage during the anti-Japanese war. Yet if we choose to interpret this comment literally, as a humorous comment it would evoke no response whatsoever. It literally means "live or die with our land." But if we know the term *tu* also meant raw opium, then the comment becomes very funny.[38] Given our discussion of the "special product," we can interpret the fourth comment in the following way: if the party refuses to cut the price for opium and pushes for sales, then the party will perish together with its stockpile of opium.

The most convincing evidence, however, comes from the publication of source materials on the finance and economy of the border region. This multivolume documented study is supposed to be circulated only within mainland China, but fortunately several copies have made it overseas. In this compilation, one constantly comes across the terms "special product" and "local products" (*tuchan*). Both terms have distinct meanings, the former usually referring to the three treasures discussed earlier and the latter denoting anything produced locally. But in many contexts, we know they were as often as not code names for opium. The compilers knew the special meaning of these two terms, so in discussing the three monopolies—salt, "special product," and "tobacco and alcohol"—they omitted the middle term but not the other two. Yet in the conclusion, they reveal that the "special product" was exported by means of smuggling and many "underground shops" (*mimidian*) were set up for that purpose.[39] Much more revealing was a comment by a bank expert of the border area. He said the border area depended on four things for revenue. Ranked by importance, they were black "special product," yellow "public grain," green paper notes, and white salt.[40] Our question thus becomes the following: What "special product" can we find in the border area that was black in color, sold in boxes, handled by underground shops, and smuggled out of the communist territory? The inescapable answer is opium.

Return to the Old Days, but with an Important Change

What historical memory did Mao Zedong have in making the provocative decision to grow opium? No later than the Long March, he had learned the enormous cash value of opium. On his way to northern Shaanxi, his army constantly attacked local gentry and among the confiscated property opium stood out for its high exchange value; the party used it to buy grain and weapons.[41] Concerning the northern Shaanxi opium industry, he might have known very little. But no matter how much he knew, his decision to plant opium differed significantly from that of his predecessors, although opium as a source of easy revenue had never changed.

By the mid-nineteenth century, Shaanxi ranked only after the three southwestern provinces (Sichuan, Guizhou, and Yunnan) in opium growing; it had an extensive market and became a pillar of the local economy and finance. Attempts to suppress its production were short-lived at best, and hard-pressed local officials or warlords were often tempted to use its revenues. Even the Christian general and model warlord Feng Yuxiang compromised his principles to take advantage of the revenues that opium could provide.

The CCP was opposed to the opium production in Shaanxi. In both 1937 and 1938, the party reiterated its injunction against growing and trading opium; it also urged various agencies to hand over their confiscated opium.[42] In 1940, border region government chairman Lin Boqu reported that in the two previous years, the court system handled a total of 2,166 cases, of which about one-quarter were opium-related.[43] In addition to these court cases, the party sought to reform the opium addicts through campaigns to rehabilitate the "good-for-nothings" in 1939. The goal was to change these wastrels into diligent workers.[44] In 1941, the party even followed the Nationalists' example, setting up an opium prohibition bureau and entrusting it with full power to handle opium addicts and confiscated goods.[45]

Obviously the fight against opium smoking was an uphill battle. Thus, every year when the party launched a production campaign, there was always a simultaneous campaign to reform the "good-for-nothings," who were mostly opium addicts. In 1943, the production campaign peaked in its intensity; so did the campaign to reform the "lazybones." Xie Juezai found the method of orchestrated persuasion and compulsion quite effective in achieving these goals, and he himself drafted a one-year plan to eradicate opium smoking from the border region.[46] But in the second half of the year, the party found it was unable to export as much opium as it would have liked. Thus some leading cadres advocated marketing the opium domestically. Xie said Mao Zedong believed in "benevolent rule" (*renzheng guandian*) and therefore vetoed the proposal.[47] This suggests that within communist territory, there was still a market for the domestic sale of opium. But given this fact, we can still safely conclude that the CCP succeeded in combating opium within the border region.

As suggested earlier, the CCP began to grow opium in 1941, but except for the brief mention by Xie Juezai, we have little information to go on. Two Nationalist intelligence reports offer some clues. Both suggest that the party depended heavily on imports for its sale of opium, as it did not grow much opium in the Yan'an area. The first report says the opium came through the Yellow River ports from Qikou and Linxian. The second gives more details. The opium came from the Japanese-occupied areas of Jiaochen, Lanxian, Xingxian, Linxian, and Lishi; the party obtained its supplies by purchase or looting. The contraband was first carried back to the Yan'an area across the Yellow River and then, in conjunction with local products, smuggled along various land routes into the Nationalist and Japanese-occupied areas. In 1941, the party gave instructions for growing opium at least in Fuxian and Yanchuan. But even Chiang Kai-shek had doubts about the reliability of this information, and he urged his underlings to produce better evidence.[48]

The Nationalists had better intelligence for 1942. According to their investigation, the Communists planted opium in nine counties of the Jinsui (western Shanxi and southern Suiyuan) base area: Hequ, Baode, Pianguan, Shenchi, Ningwu, Wuzhai, Pinglu, Shouxian, and Kelan.[49] Strategically, this area was part of the Yan'an area, and Mao Zedong's staunch supporter He Long was then in charge of the joint defense of the two base areas, with Liu Shaoqi's protégé Lin Feng as his political commissar. Within the Shaan-Gan-Ning Border Region, far more acreage was devoted to opium growing. In eastern Gansu, the planting centered on the river lands of Heshui; in Central Shaanxi, in Liulin and Yaojin of Chun(hua)-Yao(xian); in northeastern Shaanxi, in Wubao and Jiaxian; and in the Ningxia-Shaanxi border, in Dingbian and the nearby Mongol lands.[50] If we assume each *mu* produced 50 *liang* of opium, then Nationalist intelligence suggests that the party devoted only 2,000 to 3,000 *mu* of land to its cultivation; if we assume the party produced all the 31,200 *jin* of opium it exported, in 1943, then the party used 9,984 *mu* of land in both the Jinsui and Yan'an base areas.[51]

In 1942, the weather was excellent; the better-than-average spring rain forecast a good harvest of opium. The party sought poppy seeds from local peasants, but found it necessary to import them in large quantities from Japanese-occupied Shanxi. To encourage peasants to cooperate, the party allowed them to use the poppy seeds they had hidden away to pay their grain taxes. The seeds were distributed by the authorities according to a certain formula. In many cases, the party just followed a traditional practice, asking the peasants to plant seeds on public land and dividing the harvest later by fixed proportion. However, peasants were not allowed to market any portion of the harvest; they had to sell to the authorities at fixed prices. To help solve technical problems, the party recruited experienced peasants from Wubao and Jiaxian and sent them around as agricultural extension agents. In addition to peasants, soldiers also engaged in growing opium; but no details are available on their involvement.[52]

Nationalist intelligence suggests that the party decided to stop planting opium after the three years of financial crisis. In fact, in 1943, 60 percent of the opium exported came from the Jin-Sui base area nearby; the party apparently decided to reduce the area planted that year. In 1944, the Shaan-Gan-Ning Border Region government depended completely on Jin-Sui for the contraband. The shift of the opium-growing area notwithstanding, the party produced 3 million *liang* of opium in 1943, estimated to be worth in 6 billion *fabi*.[53] Nationalist intelligence also reported that by 1943 the growers were primarily army and government employees; peasant participation was insignificant.[54]

As mentioned above, party elder Xie Juezai notes that Mao Zedong gave permission for growing opium in 1941 but vetoed the domestic sale of the hoarded opium in 1943. Following his belief in "benevolent rule," Mao lodged his veto and seems to have decided against opium growing after the economic crisis receded. Regrettably, Xie Juezai never tells us when Mao considered the crisis to have ended. According to Nationalist intelligence, the party center instructed the "local product company" to end its opium business in late 1945 and strenuously refuted Nationalist charges of growing and selling opium.[55] Clearly, the party decided to phase out opium cultivation in Shaan-Gan-Ning with its eyes simultaneously on the shift of the Japanese war priority from rear areas to the Nationalist fronts and on the importance of wooing anti-Nationalist public opinion—both domestic and foreign, but especially American—for the ensuing civil war.

Nationalist intelligence in 1946 also reported communist opium growing in both the Shaan-Gan-Ning and Jin-Sui areas and their importation of opium from the northeast. As the Nationalists just collected intelligence and made no attempt to analyze it, I cannot make much sense of the fragmentary materials. A recent PRC publication, however, shows that the party continued the opium traffic at least until 1948. That year, the management of the Northwest Trade Company asked the party center for permission to use "soap [sic] as foreign currency to import goods." The worsening war situation even forced the party to order the surrender of savings from all economic, military, and political units. In compliance with this injunction, many units registered their savings and these savings turned out to be "illegal commodities (black, white, and yellow) [sic]." A list of what the units actually handed over includes soap as well as gold, silver, and paper notes. As the quantity and cash value of the "soap" were enormous, I believe the "soap" here referred to is actually opium.[56] On this, I will say more later.

Now let me describe briefly the harvesting and processing of raw opium. In 1942, when the harvest season came, the opium prohibition bureau would send its agents around to assess the harvest, the fee being 2 percent of the harvest. Afterward, the mutual aid cooperatives would come and buy at a fixed price; in order to encourage sales, the cooperatives often made special efforts to increase the variety of goods available for purchase. The collected opium then went to government-appointed factories for classification and packaging.[57] Unless necessary, the workshops would not cook the raw opium. On the processing plants, I have no hard data. We know only that the Local Product Company provided materials and bought their products from factories affiliated with such intelligence apparatuses as the Central Praetorian Regiment, the Social Affairs (Investigation) Department of the party center, the Commission on Work Toward the Japanese Enemy in the party center, and the Garrison Command of the border region. These factories were highly secret so no public materials are available on them, but I surmise that they handled a large amount of the collected opium harvest.[58]

Other factories that depended on the Local Product Company for materials were the Supply and Sales Department, the Weihua Textile Factory, the Match Factory, the Xinhua Chemical Plant, and the Daguang Soap Factory. I have no information about the Supply and Sales Department. Weihua Textiles was affiliated with the border region government, but I have no further information about it other than the fact that it wove woolen cloth. The Match Factory did have something to do with opium; its management had raised capital through opium sales.[59] There are plenty of materials on the Xinhua Chemical Plant, the largest soap-making factory in the Yan'an area, but again I can find no clues about its precise relationship with the Local Product Company.

The materials on the Daguang Soap Factory are suggestive, however. It was formed in Suide in 1939 by the 359th Brigade. The commander of this unit was the famous production hero of Nanniwan, Wang Zhen, a staunch supporter of Mao Zedong.[60] The party never published statistics on this factory's soap production, but it did give figures combined with those of Xinhua Chemical Plant. If we deduct the production figures of the Xinhua Chemical Plant, which we know from a different source, we can determine that the Daguang Factory produced no soap at all:

Year	Daguang employees	Production (including Xinhua)	Xinhua employees	Xinhua production
1939	78	22,405 bars	$ (24)	(22,405)
1940	?	118,703	48 (31)	118,703
1941	?	147,602	76 (61)	147,602
1942	?	310,659	124 (77)	310,659
1943	?	482,855	67 (61)	482,855

Source: SGNBQ, 3:237–38, 242, and 245.
Note: The figures in parentheses are from a 1946 source; the others, from 1943. I cannot explain the discrepancy between the two sources.

What can we make of this statistical oddity? Mao Zedong once highly praised the Daguang-produced soap. Strangely, when the Bureau of Commodity Supply reported on its exports of soap, it mentioned only Xinhua Chemicals and three other smaller factories.[61] I suspect that the "soap" produced by Daguang was in fact raw opium. My reasons are outlined below.

Merchants bought the opium from the factories or Local Product Company, and the Red Army, like the warlord troops, collected a protection fee. Nationalist intelligence reported that the Rearguard Office of the Eighth Route Army transferred to the border region government part of its opium income, about 1.5 million yuan (fabi) each month. The tax rate was 90 yuan per liang of opium. In addition, the merchants had to pay a registration fee of 75 yuan and customs of 20 yuan for every liang of opium. Nationalist intelligence also reported that communist officials and military officers sometimes transported opium themselves. The Special Commissioner of eastern Gansu, Wang Weizhou, the deputy chairman of the border region government, Li Dingming, the deputy head of the Educational Department, He Lianchen, and Wang Zhen's aide-de-camp Liu Chenghai were the best known among them.[62] The Rearguard Office commander Xiao Jingguang wrote in his memoirs that he sent his men to work in the Local Product Company but neither explained the nature of the company nor confirmed the Nationalist charge mentioned above.[63]

In general, the Communists used three routes to export their opium. The first route was the Yellow River; the party shipped the opium southward into the garrison area of the warlord General Yan Xishan, who still held parts of southwestern Shanxi. The second route was via the Luo and Jing rivers; the opium moved southward from the Yan'an area to the Wei River valley, where Nationalist general Hu Zongnan ruled as "the Northwest King." Sometimes merchants would ship the goods upriver along the Wei. The third route was in eastern Gansu, where the Nationalist general Zhu Shaoliang maintained a precarious hegemony over local warlords.[64] I have little information about the opium policies in the three Nationalist areas. It seems that the three Nationalist generals all prohibited the planting of opium, but compromised themselves on the issue of opium smoking. In 1942, the Nationalist authorities even sought to compete with the communist opium by importing opium from Suide and Yulin of northern Shaanxi, where other Nationalist warlords governed. The decision then forced the Communists to cut opium prices in order to stay in the market.[65]

Opium Trade Policy: From Decentralized to Centralized Management

The available data on communist opium trade policy only reveal that the party started the opium trade when it decentralized control over production and commerce to the various units of party, army, government, and mass associations. But it quickly moved to centralize control over the opium trade. The early 1940s can be divided into beginning, transitional, and mature periods according to the agencies handling the opium trade for the CCP. In terms of timing, the three periods overlap to some extent; the periodization, however, enables us to trace the communist attempt to develop a comprehensive state monopoly over the opium trade.

The First Phase (1941–February 1942)

By the winter of 1940, the CCP was already feeling the pressure of the Nationalist blockade; the party could no longer import any cotton from Nationalist Xi'an. The party had to depend on the Yellow River port of Qikou for industrial products. Dingbian, in the Shaanxi-Ningxia border region, helped import the needed goods, but not much. In order to meet the coming trouble, the party set up new agencies to coordinate trade matters, while providing all the state units with very limited capital and urging them to produce for their own needs.

In early 1941, the Japanese decided to impose a blockade at Qikou. This complication then forced the party to realize the limits of its self-help program.[66] The returns on agricultural production were extremely small; unless the party allowed the various units to engage in trade, it would be unable to overcome the financial crisis. As a result, publicly owned businesses (*gongying shangdian*) proliferated in late 1941 and early 1942. The majority were new transportation, brokerage, and other service businesses, though some also engaged in trade.[67] The party claimed that their appearance had stimulated the export of local products. Here the term *local products* was not specified. Later the party revealed that only the publicly owned shops of the regional government did not sell opium;[68] I therefore infer that most of the publicly owned shops unaffiliated to the government probably engaged in the opium trade.

There are no materials explicitly referring to involvement in opium trade, but available data cast heavy suspicion on the Daguang business. It was initially a cooperative and became an army-run enterprise in 1941. Its managers reported their accomplishments as follows:

	Capital	Profit	Profit/Capital
1940	31,000	191,700	6.18
1941	400,000	2,982,000	7.15
1942 (Jan.–Sept.)	2,000,000	6,720,000	3.36

Source: SGNBQ, 4: 268–71.

The Daguang enterprise supposedly devoted itself to "promoting local products and resisting outside products." Could the sale of genuine "local products" make such large profits? According to the party's investigation, Yan'an had forty-six publicly owned shops in 1941. Their total combined capital amounted to 2.738 million yuan; the profits for half a year, after expenses, were 1.103 million yuan.[69] Even if all forty-six shops made the same profits in the second half of the year, these shops could not make profits comparable to those of the Daguang enterprise. Mao Zedong seemed to suggest that the chief earner for the enterprise was the "soap" produced by Daguang Chemicals, the "soap" I suspect to be opium. In fact, the soap business of Xinhua Chemicals supports my speculation. In 1943, Xinhua Chemicals incurred a heavy loss in its soap business. It is hard to imagine the Daguang enterprise making large profits by selling real soap at the same time. Besides, the materials indicate that Daguang depended on the Jin-Sui base area for commodity supplies. What commodities could the base area export? It produced little salt. Even if it produced as much as the Yan'an area, Daguang could not have made much profit because it sold salt at lower-than-usual prices.[70] Besides, we can find in this region no commodity as profitable as opium. As a matter of fact, a responsible official accused Daguang of engaging in "special product business" even after the party centralized the opium trade in 1944.[71]

This accusation charges that Daguang and seven other state businesses sold a total of 1,781 *jin* of "special product" in 1944. It seems that they simply continued the opium trade they had begun during the period of decentralization.

The Second Phase (February–December 1942)

Early in 1941, the party set up a trade bureau and began to centralize control over the publicly owned businesses. Initially the trade bureau functioned as an affiliate of the border region bank, but later the party placed it under the Economic Construction Department of the border region government to strengthen its power. The head bureau had branches in big cities, and each branch bureau also had its own trade centers in less important cities and towns. Its charter stipulated that the bureau should collect "local products," promote their trade and stimulate their production. Here the "local products" included genuine local products. In August 1941, the bureau set up the Northwestern Local Product Company. The "local product" in the name of the company refers primarily to opium.[72]

The Local Product Company had six branches and twenty-two shops throughout the border region. With capital of 10.97 million yuan (*bianbi*), it started to trade in opium. In 1942, it handled a total of 9,260.5 *jin* of opium, supplied in the following ways:

Sources	Amount
Opium as investment	1,212.8 *jin*
Entrusted for sale	2,850.7
Army's tax-free opium	4,099.1
Company's purchase	1,010.9
Confiscation	87.0
Total	9,260.5

Source: SGNBQ, 4: 94–95.

The opium price rose from 8,000 yuan per *jin* to 24,000 yuan in 1943. Assuming an average price of 16,000 yuan per *jin*, the company had 148,172,490 yuan (*bianbi*) worth of opium on hand. The company used 40 percent of it to import goods and sold the rest for much-needed *fabi* currency.[73]

Theoretically, the company should have controlled all the publicly owned enterprises and shops. But, being accustomed to their previous ways, these publicly owned enterprises and shops mostly continued their sale of opium, this time against communist laws. The civilians also resisted the monopoly and engaged in smuggling opium. Because of these illegal activities, the Local Product Company only sold 10,000 *jin* of special product in 1941; other businesses exported an estimated 15,000 *jin*. The situation was better the next year. The border region should have been able to export 50,000 *jin* of opium, but the Local Product Company actually sold only 36,000 *jin*.[74] The reasons were complicated. One reason was the separate existence of the opium prohibition bureau. The Trade Bureau could not combat opium smuggling itself, and the opium prohibition bureau had its own interests to guard. Besides, the Local Product Company was short of both capital and labor. For these reasons, the Trade Bureau appeared to be no more than a large publicly owned enterprise, although one given the authority to monopolize the opium trade.[75]

The Third Phase (February 1943 onward)

After the Northwest Party Bureau Conference of Senior Cadres in late 1942, the party bureau called a separate meeting to overhaul the financial system of the border region. It decided to combine the Guanghua Enterprise, the Salt Company, the Trade Bureau, and the Local Product Company and set up a Bureau of Commodity Supply.[76] At this time, the opium prohibition bureau was abolished, its functions absorbed by the new bureau.[77] The new bureau theoretically affiliated itself with the Shaan-Gan-Ning Border Region government, but actually took orders directly from the party center. It had authority over both the Shaan-Gan-Ning and Jin-Sui base areas.[78] In 1944, the Salt and Local Product Companies became independent of the bureau, but after the Japanese surrender, the two independent companies again joined the Bureau of Commodity Supply and became its branches.[79]

The Bureau of Commodity Supply supervised through five subbureaus, ten registration offices, and two checkpoints in all the important trade cities and towns in Shaan-Gan-Ning. Merchants were required to come to these registration offices or checkpoints to pay taxes; even if the commodities were tax-free, they still had to register. Only with the tax receipts or registration papers could they sell their commodities and convert their earnings into *fabi* currency, which was necessary to purchase local products, including opium. Local merchants could buy opium after paying a certain fee, but they could not sell it on the domestic market. Whether the buyer was a local or an outsider, he was entitled to protection of his opium, of course, after paying certain fees.[80]

Under the bureau, Shaan-Gan-Ning exported 5,364,720,000 yuan (*bianbi*) worth of commodities and imported 6,472,640,000 yuan (*bianbi*) worth of cotton goods and other products in 1943. Opium earned for the border region 3,683,250,000 yuan (*bianbi*), accounting for 68.66 percent of the exports. Assuming the average price was 127,432 yuan per *jin*, a communist expert suggested that the bureau sold 28,900 *jin* of opium from its own stocks. Added to the opium entrusted by other units and the opium imported from Shanxi by the army and government, the bureau sold a total of 34,000 *jin*.[81]

Each of the four subbureaus claimed the following share of the opium trade:

Central Shanxi	31.86%
Eastern Gansu	26.90
Yan'an subregion	21.74
Shanxi-Ningxia	19.50
Total	100.00

Source: *SGNBQ*, 4: 58.

For unclear reasons, the situation in Suide does not figure in the above calculation. We only know that the Suide subbureau sold 1,310 *jin* of opium for other units. In the Yan'an subregion, the local branch of the Local Product Company sold primarily for export. All the other subbureaus aimed exclusively at external markets. The Nationalist territory of Central Shaanxi and Gansu appear to have been the major markets. The bureau exchanged the opium for cotton textiles. If it was unable to do this, it would sell the opium for *fabi* and transport the currency to Yan'an, Suide, and Dingbian to buy cotton, cloth, matches, and other daily necessities.[82] As the Nationalist authority would connive at smuggling as long as the merchants made no purchase from the bureau, the bureau set up many underground shops to sell the opium as if they were managed by private smugglers.[83]

In late 1943, the party had already exhausted its opium stocks and decided to stop growing opium in the Shaan-Gan-Ning area. As a result, the border region became a mere trader, importing opium from the nearby Jin-Sui base area and the Japanese-controlled area and transshipping it to the Nationalist territories in Central Shaanxi, eastern Gansu, and Suiyuan. The profits for the trade fell by 50 percent under the new circumstances. Assuming it could sell 31,200 *jin* of opium at a higher average price, 240,000 yuan (*bianbi* after inflation) per *jin*, the bureau estimated the total sale at the value of 7.488 billion yuan. So the profit would have been 3.744 billion yuan.[84] Actually, as mentioned earlier, the bureau sold three times more opium by value the next year.

In 1944, the Nationalists tightened their blockade in the Suide area. The Central Shaanxi and eastern Gansu subbureaus had to spend all their earnings on the spot. But the party seems to have met little difficulty in making the adjustment. The border region profited so much from the opium trade that its currency eventually won autonomy, ceasing to fluctuate in value relative to the unstable Nationalist currency.[85]

At the lower levels, the opium trade was conducted differently in different phases. First, let me review the trade practices in the prohibition days for the light they shed on later practices.

When the Communists occupied the city of Yan'an in 1935, a local merchant from neighboring Shanxi decided to flee, closing his sundry goods shop and converting his stocks into opium and cash. But because of the party's tight security, he was unable to leave and thus started an opium business within the city. The opium was worth 16 yuan (*fabi*) a *jin* within the city walls. After it was smuggled out, its price doubled. So this merchant made a small fortune. Within a month, his capital grew from a meager 300 to 400 yuan to 15,000 yuan. In 1936, the Nationalist (Northeast) army retook the walled city. The merchant closed his business. Forced by family problems, however, he soon restarted his opium business, but to avoid official detection, he asked someone else to run it for him. When the Red Army returned to the city during the Xi'an incident, he had already again doubled his initial capital. The communist prohibition of opium then forced him to concentrate on legal business.[86] This case indicates how profitable the opium business was.

The communist authorities seem to have rooted out the opium business in Yan'an by imposing severe laws and punishments. But the situation in the border city of Suide was different. Under warlord rule, there were two opium businesses in the city; in terms of capital, they were second only to the sundry goods stores.[87] They closed after the Communists occupied the city in 1940. But according to party investigations, the big Suide merchants were mostly local landlords; some of them, forced by the party's policy of rent and interest reduction, diverted their capital to the opium business.[88] So long as they did not openly violate the communist law and so long as they sold their opium only outside communist territory, the party made no attempt to suppress their businesses. When the party began to grow and trade in opium, this policy of acquiescence enabled the party to enlist the landlord-merchants for investment and expertise. In 1942, the party set up the Yongchang Company and appointed a prominent local gentry-merchant its chief manager. Under him were four assistant managers, of whom two were reported to be opium addicts. I have no evidence that the company engaged in the opium trade, but we should not ignore the fact that the city depended on the opium trade for prosperity that year. The next year, the party decided to centralize the monopoly on opium trade; it then accused one opium addict manager of engaging in "special product business" and dismissed him.[89] These bits of evidence, though fragmentary, suggest that the party had acquiesced in the opium trade by local gentry-merchants and used these people as important channels for promoting its own opium trade.

How did the outside merchants acquire their opium in such cities as Yan'an, Suide, and Dingbian? The sources allow us to sketch the following scenario. Whenever an outside merchant arrived, he would choose a hotel-*cum*-brokerage as a place to stay. The hotel charged him a 20 percent commission, in addition to room and board, after it found a buyer for the goods he had brought with him. With the earnings and Nationalist currency, the outside merchants then bought their opium from the government company. According to communist investigations, the largest hotels in these big cities were run primarily by Shanxi merchants, who had extensive connections with opium merchants elsewhere.[90] The party inherited this relationship and used it to its own advantage.

The Communists believed that the outside opium merchants mostly had extensive ties with Nationalist and puppet intelligence, making windfall profits under their protection and with their collusion.[91] The party provided no concrete evidence, but the charge fits with our understanding of the opium trade in both the Nationalist and Japanese-occupied areas, where opium businesses could not operate "openly" unless they received protection from the concerned authorities.

As suggested earlier, the publicly owned shops proliferated in 1940 under the slogan of self-reliance. The majority of them were hotels-*cum*-brokerages. I surmise that these publicly owned hotels mostly continued the previous business practices and that some even engaged in opium transactions. I have no evidence to go on for this discussion. Fortunately, however, we have some materials on the operation of the companies under the supervision of the Bureau of Commodity Supply after it was formed, which show clearly that both the Local Product and Nanchang companies engaged in the opium trade.

Nanchang Company

In August 1943, the party decided to unify all publicly owned businesses in Yan'an. Carrying out the decision, the bureau formed the Nanchang Company. The owners of the participant businesses handed over their assets and personnel in exchange for company shares. Together with the salt and special product companies, it formed a tripartite business under the bureau's supervision. According to its profit report from October to December 1943, the company had capital of 84,429,000 yuan (bianbi) and earned profits of 16,609,422 yuan. Of these earnings, the "special product" accounted for 26.5 percent; it earned 4,402,107 yuan. The company owned three hotels-cum-brokerages; so after earning the commission, it could promote the sale of opium. It had transportation teams, so if necessary, it could carry the goods for the buyer. It also had branches in Suide, Anzhai, and Ganguyi, so if merchants could not come to Yan'an, it could sell the opium there.[92]

The Local Product Company

The company was formed in late 1942 to promote the sale of local product. Located in Yan'an, it had branches in all the other important cities and towns in the Shaan-Gan-Ning border region. Under the branches, offices were set up in all the riverports and trade centers in the area. It raised capital from almost all the state "units." A short list would include the CCP Central Committee Office, the Central Party School, the Military Commission Office, the Northwest Sub-bureau, the Subregional Committee, Wang Zhen's 359th Brigade, Zhang Zongxun's 358th Brigade, and Wang Weizhou's 385th Brigade, the Liberation Daily, the Suide Normal School, the Garrison Command, and the Social Affairs Department. Total capital was valued at 2.1 billion yuan (bianbi).[93]

The Local Product Company traded such local products as wool, cotton yardage, and tobacco, but the most important business was "soap." So in his business report, Chief Manager Yu Jie devoted much more attention to the latter than the former, and his underlings made no serious effort to supply information on local products other than "soap." Strangely enough, the section on the ordinary local products also contains some materials on soap. According to it, the Local Company sold 57,000 bars of soap and the supply came from Xinhua Chemicals and three other smaller factories. Distinct from these bars of soap, the "soap" on which Yu Jie focused his attention appears to have been something else. He reported that the company had marketed about a million boxes of this special kind of "soap." Since at Xinhua Chemicals each box contained a hundred bars of soap, Yu Jie's figure should mean that the company sold 100 million bars of special soap.[94] This supply would require an enormous market to absorb, especially since northwesterners of the border region and nearby were famous for their stinginess in using water.[95] In terms of production, this supply would also require an industrial capability far beyond that of the wartime Yan'an area.

As mentioned earlier, Xinhua was the largest soap producer in the Yan'an area. In 1943, it only produced 480,000 bars of soap. Even though the other three soap factories could manufacture as much as Xinhua, the Local Product Company could not take as many as 2 million bars of soap for its business. Moreover, in 1943, Xinhua Chemicals produced two kinds of soap, one at the market price of 66 yuan *bianbi* and the other at 42 yuan. Therefore a box of soap could only sell for 4,200 to 6,600 yuan.[96] Yu Jie told us, however, that his special soap sold for 23,000 yuan per box. How can we account for all these incongruities?

If we remember that Xinhua incurred heavy losses in selling soap, we will be even more surprised. In 1943, the company lost a total of 6,593,825 yuan (*bianbi*). If this was the loss after the sale of 480,000 bars of soap, how could the Local Product Company absorb the loss that would result from marketing 100 million bars of special soap? Yet Yu Jie told us the Local Product Company made an astronomical profit by selling the special soap. Given all the evidence, I believe that what he referred to as special soap was, in fact, opium.

Yu Jie reported that in 1943 the Local Product company had 1,312,092.5 boxes of special soap, of which 304,730.5 boxes came from the inventory of the previous year. Of the 1,007,362 boxes procured in 1943, 795,365 boxes came from the Jin-Sui base area. In other words, only 39.4 percent of opium was produced locally; the rest came from the neighboring base area. Since quite a large amount was entrusted for sale, I surmise that the processing of opium was still decentralized, though the party had already begun to monopolize the "special product" trade. Among the marketed opium, there were 1,660 boxes that Yu Jie described as "cooked soap." If the cooked soap referred to cooked opium, the implication is that the Local Product also sold a small quantity of opium for domestic consumption; no opium merchants would sell cooked opium to a remote market.

The Local Product Company and its five branches all sold the special soap, and their business achievements give us clues as to the distribution of its potential customers:

	Stocks (boxes)	Sold (boxes)	Unsold (boxes)
Head company	325,145.5	97,125	?
Central Shaanxi	?	405,813	?
Eastern Gansu	?	363,351	?
Yan'an subregion	?	55,364	?
Gu-Yan	?	28,900	?
Fuxian	?	21,418	?
Subtotal	986,947	874,846	?
Total	1,312,092.5	971,973	340,119.5
	(1,311,892.5)	(971,971)	(339,919.5)

As indicated by the corrections, the statistics contain minor inaccuracies. But a fundamental point remains incontestable: the quantity of opium marketed was enormous. And as suggested earlier, the majority of the party's opium customers were residents in Nationalist territory.

The average price for a box of special soap was 23,067.6 yuan (*bianbi*). The company sold 22,421,065,704.3 yuan worth of the commodity. In reality, the company used the special soap to exchange for the following items:

Silver dollars	145,253 yuan
Silverware	2,672 *liang*
Gold	8,397 *liang*
Guangjinjuan (Nationalist currency)	136,967 yuan
Fabi (Nationalist currency)	1,002,765,823 yuan
Bianbi	8,729,730.224 yuan
Commodities (textiles, cotton, stationery, medicine, yarn, military equipment) in *bianbi*	827,211,148 yuan

The Local Product Company sold the imported goods at lower than market prices; despite this business practice, it still made a huge profit:

Income		
Special soap	10,721,929,909 yuan	61.45 %
Other commodities	3,677,181,409	21.07
Investment return	217,366,556	1.25
Other (including loans)	2,832,705,072	16.23
Total	17,449,182,946	100.00
Expenditure		
Packaging and processing	606,531,940 yuan	
Miscellaneous taxes	400,930,046	
Damage	2,500,089,500	
Business taxes	4,757,254,423	
Profits	9,187,567,037	
Shareholders' profits	1,241,777,100	

The company paid its shareholders beforehand by season. In the first season, it paid 150 percent of the investment; in the second, 100 percent; in the third, 150 percent; and in the fourth, 200 percent. How could any company afford to pay benefits this way? The Local Product Company not only asked for investment, it sought to centralize the opium trade. Unless assured of a handsome return, no publicly owned businesses were willing to cooperate with the Local Product Company.

The enormous return on investment actually underwrote all the investing units' production projects. Besides, the Local Product Company also provided materials for the projects and even marketed their products for them. So in evaluating the production campaign of 1943, we simply cannot ignore the role played by the company's opium trade.

The Opium Trade and Corruption

In 1941, the party urged all units to engage in profit-making businesses in order to pull through the period of economic difficulty. To meet the party's expectations, many state units found it necessary to engage in smuggling. Needless to say, greed also accounted for this phenomenon. Many smuggled salt in and cotton out, but others were bold enough to smuggle opium. In fact, smuggling by these publicly owned businesses overshadowed smuggling by private citizens. For example, the transportation team of the Third Garrison Brigade was caught trading "special product" in Inner Mongolia and Shanxi. For another example, the transportation team of the First Garrison Brigade went to Dingbian, nominally to carry salt but actually to trade in opium.[97] To combat the contraband trade, the party therefore set up the Bureau of Trade first and the Bureau of Commodity Supply later.

Concerning opium smuggling in Shaan-Gan-Ning, we have only the fragmentary materials noted above. The case of Huainan might help us imagine it. In 1941, the central China base area followed the example of Yan'an and encouraged the army, government, and other organizational units to form cooperatives and engage in commerce. These publicly owned ventures immediately began to smuggle contraband, including opium.[98] The seriousness of the problem even forced a newly appointed commissar to call a meeting, in which the commander of the local garrison faced charges of corruption. The commander, a Long March veteran, had joined Mao's Red Army immediately after the collapse of the first United Front in 1927. He was accused of allowing the cooperative of the garrison command to engage in opium smuggling and dividing the high profits among members. Yet even faced with the accusation, he refused to reveal any details. The charge against the local public security office was more concrete; it engaged in "attacking local gentry," but kept no detailed records of confiscated opium. The cooperative of this unit also smuggled opium. It even burned the accounting book after learning of the charge and denied any wrongdoing during the interrogation.[99]

Other than publicly owned shops, the Local Product Company itself might have been a hotbed of corruption. One-time chief of the Commodity Supply Bureau Ye Jizhuang disclosed in a discussion with his underlings the party view on how to maximize opium exports. He said that while "making friends" with the Nationalist officials responsible for the blockade, the cadres should cultivate friendships with all other related people, including merchants, soldiers, and ordinary people. Ye also advised his underlings that in "making friends," they should disregard both political differences and moral considerations. As long as the sale could be maximized, bribery in any form was acceptable. To collect trade information, Ye even offered some cadres the privilege of special accounts.[100] Directives along the above lines might have been issued by party leaders outside northern Shaanxi. Whether my speculation is borne out or not, Ye's talk reminds us that cadres in charge of the opium trade were subject to unusual temptation because of the unique position they were put in by the party.

At any rate, the corruption problem brought about by opium seemed less serious in Yan'an than in Huaian. Compared to the situation in Nationalist areas, it also seemed under control. In Nationalist territory, the bureau of opium prohibition was legendary for its corruption; in the Yan'an region, I have found one case of opium-related corruption. A district-level party cadre of eastern Gansu was found in 1945 to have been an opium addict; he had been ordered to go to the countryside to handle a murder case, but instead he used the opportunity to obtain the drug. He was therefore transferred to the county government and instructed to make self-criticism there. This cadre had joined the communist revolution in 1938 and became a party member the following year. Yet the party's punishment did him no good. In 1946, he was again found purchasing opium and trading in contraband. As a result, he was dismissed from the party.[101]

There is also the strange case of He Weide, the head of the financial department of the border region government. He had joined the CCP in the early 1930s and for this reason was considered an elder in local party politics. In 1942, he fell sick and became addicted to opium. By his own confession, he not only smoked himself but also gave opium to other people. Among those given the opium were Bai Qian (for her sick child), Zhang Aimin (for his bedridden mother), Xu Fanting, Liu Shaoting, and Liu Jiesan.[102] Bai Qian was a high party cadre; Zhang Aimin's identity is unknown; the last three were United Front targets. Xu was a member of Sun Yat-sen's Revolutionary Alliance. In the early 1930s, he cut his stomach in Sun's mausoleum to protest Chiang Kai-shek's "appeasement" of Japanese aggression. In the 1940s, he led his troops to join the Communists after his superior, Yan Xishan, had initiated a purge of radicals from the Shaanxi army. He apparently used opium to alleviate the pain caused by tuberculosis and an old wound. Liu Jieshan went back and forth between the Communists and their northern neighbor, warlord Deng Baoshan. He was evidently an opium addict for pleasure.[103] We have no idea who the other Liu was. He Weide's generosity had some justification, but his other ventures were much less excusable. He helped his mother-in-law to undertake the opium trade, and without permission from above he cooperated with private merchants to invest in the opium trade. His confession shows how power could corrupt an old revolutionary, but it also testified to the effects of the Rectification campaign in checking deviant behavior during this period. In contrast to the Nationalists' evasion of the problem, the party at least seemed able to deal with the corruption brought about by opium traffic.

Conclusion

During the New Fourth Army incident of early 1941, the second United Front between the GMD and CCP suffered an irrevocable split. After 1941, the Nationalist government constantly accused its foes of growing opium in the Yan'an area and elsewhere. But the charge stirred up little emotional response. In sharp contrast to the effective communist propaganda, the Nationalists' accusation was dismissed mostly as exaggeration, if not complete fabrication. Forty years later, the Communists' own data force us to accept the Nationalist charge as a fact. How can we explain the lengthy disbelief? Here I would like to propose two plausible explanations. First, the Nationalist government had by this time lost credibility. The Nationalist government had started to prohibit opium ever since the launching of the Northern Expedition, but its successes had been meager. The bureaus of opium prohibition, set up to combat the opium trade, largely degenerated into proxies of drug syndicates. With such a record of opium prohibition, the Nationalists could expect few people to believe in their charge against the Communists, especially on the matter of opium trading. Second, the Communists were very effective in eradicating opium smoking in areas under their rule. Unable to find an opium den in the communist areas, observers naturally believed the communist insistence on innocence. Furthermore, the party matched its propaganda with deeds. When it decided to open the Shaan-Gan-Ning territory to outside scrutiny, it first moved the opium fields to the neighboring Jin-Sui base area, so that outsiders could not find opium fields in the Yan'an area after they actually arrived en masse in 1944.

Put in historical context, what Mark Selden calls the Yan'an Way appears problematic. No one can deny the Communists' achievement in developing the Shaan-Gan-Ning Border Region through the mass line in the 1940s. But ignorance of the role played by opium revenues led Selden to exaggerate the economic accomplishments and overlook the internal constraints imposed by the poverty and backwardness of the border region. In fact, self-reliance was both a myth and an ideal. It was a myth because the border region could never have survived without external trade. It was an ideal because in its pursuit, the party succeeded in increasing agricultural production and creating some light industry. But as the size of opium trade testifies, the border region never achieved the goal of genuine self-reliance.

In fact, the war environment, rather than political aspiration, dictated self-reliance. The Nationalist and Japanese blockades cut the Communists' supply of cotton cloth. So unless it encouraged peasants to grow cotton and weave cloth, the party simply had no other way to keep its cadres and soldiers warm. But once the blockade ended after the war, the Yan'an region could not compete with the cotton produced elsewhere. Salt provides another example. Large-scale salt mining was made profitable in the Yan'an region only during wartime. Afterward, local salt could not compete with cheap supplies from the coastal areas. But what

I want to emphasize here is the internal weakness of the Shaan-Gan-Ning economy; unless it could find financing for its self-reliance campaigns, the party could do little with its production projects no matter how well it planned them. This explains Mao Zedong's later discarding of the Yan'an model of economic development in the 1950s; if there was an alternative, he preferred other choices.

Some questions remain unanswered. The CCP had always been virulent in its attack on imperialism. In its historiography, it insisted on calling the British war with China in the 1840s the First Opium War and the British-French aggression in 1850s the Second Opium War. Few Chinese intellectuals could forgive the British for selling opium. The CCP inherited the banner of anti-imperialism and made nationalism its chief cause. In fact, it had always criticized the Nationalists for their failure to put the opium ban into practice, and whenever it formed a counter-government its own policy of opium prohibition had been effective. But in Yan'an the party gave up its honorable record and resorted to trading in opium to overcome the economic blockades imposed by the Nationalist government and the Japanese army. How did it justify this policy retreat? What did it tell its nationalistically inspired cadres and officers?

These are hard questions that I cannot answer at present. I can only detect a pragmatism in Mao Zedong's decision to grow opium. If anyone in the party raised moral objections to growing opium, Mao must have overruled them, which would confirm that Mao's primary concern was the success of the communist revolution rather than abstract moral principle. When his communist revolution required it, he challenged common notions of morality. The revolution, not morality, dictated his behavior. Of course, he never regarded opium trade as moral, but his view of the revolution required making opium traffic a necessary evil. Mao occupied a pivotal role in interpreting the needs of the communist revolution. As long as he occupied this pivotal role, he could himself define any "necessary evil," if not morality.

In reviving the opium trade, however, Mao Zedong never allowed himself to degenerate to the level of the warlords. He insisted on banning opium smoking within his jurisdiction and on the use of opium profits for the development of the Shaan-Gan-Ning economy. Although we are doubtful of the lasting effect of his economic policy in the 1940s, we cannot deny that he used the opium trade revenues to build a viable and integrated program of economic development. Moreover, unlike his warlord predecessors, he had a firm grip over the cadres and officers and, through rectification, developed an effective mechanism of behavior control, in which ideological commitment played a vital role. Mao's problem lay in his inability to make idealism work over the long term, but idealism was precisely what made his rectification program effective in the short run.

The predicament in which Mao Zedong found himself in the 1940s should alert us to the need for reassessing the Maoist emphasis on such values as dedication, sacrifice, and voluntarism. Regardless of the means he used to mobilize the peasants and intellectuals through the mass line, Mao also understood the necessity of financing his development projects. In this sense, he was as realistic as he was romantic. And no matter how much he believed in human perfectibility, he also understood the necessity of fighting against the lure of corruption. We should not overlook this realism in characterizing Maoism as a belief in human transcendence.

Notes

1. Mark Selden, *The Yenan Way in Revolutionary China* (Cambridge: Harvard University Press, 1971).

2. Ibid., 181. In 1941, the commodity index jumped by a factor of 4 in Yan'an, but only by 2.7 in Xi'an. In the following year, the index jumped by a factor of 14 in Yan'an but only by 6.8 in Xi'an. See The Editorial and Writing Group of the Finance and Economics Departments of the Shaan-Gan-Ning Border Region and the Shaanxi Provincial Archives, ed., *Kang-Ri zhanzheng shiqi Shaan-Gan-Ning bianqu caizheng jingji shiliao zhaibian* (Selected Historical Documents on the Finance and Economics of the Shaan-Gan-Ning Border Region During the Anti-Japanese War, *SGNBQ*) (Shaanxi: People's Press, 1981), 5: 124. Also see *SGNBQ*, 4: 437, for more details. The statistics on this page contain some obvious errors that I cannot explain.

3. Xingguang and Zhang Yang, eds., *Kang-Ri zhanzheng shiqi Shaan-Gan-Ning bianqu caizheng jingji shigao* (Draft History of the Finance and Economy of the Shaan-Gan-Ning Border Region During the Anti-Japanese War) (Xi'an: Northwest University Press, 1988), 17–18, 20.

4. Ibid., 28.

5. Xingguang and Zhang Yang, eds., *Kang-Ri zhanzheng shiqi*, 31, and *SGNBQ*, 5: 6–9.

6. Xingguang and Zhang Yang, eds., *Kang-Ri zhanzheng shiqi*, 29–30.

7. Li Weihan, *Huiyi yu yanjiu* (Memories and Research) (Beijing: CCP Party Historical Materials Press, 1986), 380–81. In mid-July 1936, only seven communist counties in northern Shaanxi could be declared free from Nationalist attacks. All these counties depended on the party center for finance. See *SGNBQ*, 5: 6–7. On the military situation and the evolvement of the CCP's policy toward the Guominchang (GMD), see the Department of Military History of the Academy of Military Sciences, ed., *Zhongguo renmin jiefangjun zhanshi* (The War History of the Chinese People's Liberation Army) (Beijing: Sciences Press, 1987), 1: 333–69; Gan Tangshou et al., *Shaan-Gan Ning geming genjudi shi yanjiu* (Study on the History of the Revolutionary Shaan-Gan-Ning Base Area) (Xi'an: Sanqin Press, 1988), 162–67; Guo Hualun (Warren Kuo), *Zhonggong shilun* (The Analytical History of the CCP) (Taibei: The Institute of International Relations and the Institute of Eastern Asia, National Zhengzhi University, revised ed., 1973), 3: 148–58; and Yang Kuisong, "Guanyu gongchan guoji yu Zhongguo gongchandang 'lian Jiang kang-Ri' fangzhende guanxi wenti" (On the Relationship Between the Comintern and the CCP's Policy of "Uniting with Chiang to Resist Japan"), in *Zhonggong dangshi yanjiu* (Research on CCP History), no. 4, 55, 1989.

8. The History of the Xi'an incident Leading Group, *Xi'an shibian jianshi* (A Brief History of the Xi'an incident) (Beijing: Chinese Historical Documents Press, 1986), 20–21 and 26–27.

9. Research Committee on Biographies of CCP Personages, ed., *Zhonggong dangshi renwu zhuan* (Biographies of CCP Personages) (Shaanxi: People's Press, 1988), 39: 252.

10. *SGNBQ*, 6:, 428–29.

11. *SGNBQ*, 1: 66–67 and 123, Selden, *Yenan Way*, 139–40. Selden's figures for the

Nationalist appropriations come from Nationalist intelligence. He emphasizes the frugality of the CCP and its ability to operate with minimum Nationalist subsidies.

12. *SGNBQ*, 1: 73–74, 94–95, 123; 4: 13, 152; and 9: 31.

Year	Hulled millet (piculs)	Grain tax (piculs)	Tax as a percent of production
1937	1,260,000	10,000	0.79
1938	1,270,000	10,000	0.78
1939	1,370,000	50,000	3.63
1940	1,430,000	90,000	6.29
1941	1,470,000	200,000	13.33
1942	1,500,000	160,000	10.69
1943	1,600,000	180,000	11.25
1944	1,750,000	160,000	9.00
1945	1,600,000	125,000	7.80

Source: Selden, *Yenan Way*, 182.

As Mark Selden notes, the above table substantially underreports the actual collection of the grain taxes before 1940. The actual collection exceeded the above figure by 30–50 percent in 1937 and 1938, by 4–8 percent in 1939 and 1940. Selden believes that the figures for 1941 to 1945 are close to the actual collection. One point he fails to notice is that the border region population seemed to have doubled (from 600,000 to 1.3 million) through natural growth, territorial expansion, and immigration. In this case, the percentage above does not really reflect the communist burden on the peasants.

13. Xingguang and Zhang Yang, eds., *Kang-Ri zhanzheng shiqi*, 136–37; and *SGBBQ*, 6: 42, 95.

14. *SGNBQ*, 6: 40–41 and 44–45.

15. Ibid., 6: 49.

16. Ibid., 4: 172; 5: 33.

17. Ibid., 4: 172.

18. Ibid., 1: 1.

19. Ibid., 1: 2–3; 4: 9.

20. Ibid., 1: 2; and He Ganzhi, *Zhonggong xiandai gemingshi* (The Revolutionary History of Modern China) (Beijing: Higher Education Press, 2nd ed., 1956), 255.

21. Concerning the party's view on the production and frugality campaigns, see He Ganzhi, *Zhonggong xiandai gemingshi*, 255.

22. Cai Shufan et al., *Suide Mizhi tudi wenti chubu yanjiu* (Preliminary Study on the Land Problem of Suide and Mizhi) (Beijing: People's Press, 1979), 122–30; and Chen Yungfa, *Making Revolution: The Communist Movement in Eastern and Central China, 1936–1946* (Berkeley: University of California Press, 1986), 370–72.

23. Xie Juezai, *Xie Juezai riji* (Xue Juezui's Diary) (Beijing: People's Press, 1984), 579. On the story of the lightning strike, see Li Weihan, *Huiyi yu yanjiu*, 540–41.

24. *SGNBQ*, 6: 19, 152; 5: 356.

25. Ibid., 5: 63–64, 108, 138–42, 197, and 199.

26. Ibid., 4: 11–12, and 430; and 5: 26. Nan Hanchen was the party's most important economic expert. He said in 1947 that the border region could not export *gancao* (an herb) and leather.

27. Ibid., 4: 50. The Salt Company was responsible for the monopoly on salt. Its capital mostly came from the Local Product Company. See ibid., 4: 129 and 140.

28. Ibid., 6: 19; and 5: 64.

29. Ibid., 4: 431–32.

30. Ibid., 4: 172–74.

31. Ibid., 4: 209–10.

32. Ibid., 4: 50.

33. One other source says that the "special product" revenue amounted to 110 million yuan *bianbi* and accounted for 42 percent of the government's income. See *SGNBQ*, 1: 171. But according to another source, the opium trade generated 40.82 percent of the government's revenue and enabled the party to meet the financial needs of the next spring. See *SGNBQ*, 6: 19–20.

34. Ibid., 4: 64–68.

35. Ibid., 6: 18.

36. The Editorial and Writing Group of the Biography of Xie Juezai, *Xie Juezai zhuan* (Biography of Xie Juezai) (Beijing: People's Press, 1984), 296–97.

37. *Xie Juezai riji*, 734.

38. Ibid., 586–87, 600.

39. Ibid., 4: table of contents, 3, 8, 11, 150, and 154–56.

40. Ibid., 5: 351.

41. Harrison Salisbury, *The Long March: The Untold Story* (New York: Harper and Row, 1985), 108, 181 and 247. According to a communist bank official, the party's bank had 90,000 yuan (*fabi*) worth of "special product" in its treasury in 1940. If the "special product" here refers to opium, the opium should have come from confiscation and it was treated like a bank deposit. See *SGNBQ*, 5: 18–19 and 85.

42. *SGNBQ*, 6: 38–39.

43. Zhang Houde, "Zhonggong bianqu genjudi lishi wenjian xuanji" (Selected Documents on the History of the Border Regions of the CCP), in *Gongdang wenti yanjiu* (Research on the Problem of the Communist Party), 11, no. 8 (1985): 89.

44. *SGNBQ*, 2: 687–89.

45. The Institute of History of the Gansu Provincial Academy of Social Sciences, ed., *Shaan-Gan-Ning geming genjudi shiliao xuanji* (Selected Documents on the Revolutionary Shaan-Gan-Ning Base Area) (Gansu: Gansu People's Press, 1980), 1: 146–50; *SGNBQ*, 4: 167; Xingguang and Zhang Yang, eds., *Kang-Ri zhanzheng shiqi*, 398–99.

46. *Xie Juezai riji*, 485.

47. Ibid., 734.

48. Wang Jianmin, *Zhongguo gongchandang shigao* (Draft History of the CCP) (Taibei: Chinese Book Publishing Company, 1974), 3: 307.

49. Ibid., 305–6. Wang's materials receive some confirmation from party publications. A communist expert revealed in his discussion of the relationship between monetary policy and commodity prices that the Shaan-Gan-Ning government imported "a large quantity of special products" from outside. See *SGNBQ*, 5: 131.

50. Zhang Houde, "Zhonggong bianqu genjudi," 133; Lu Xizhi, *Shaanbei tequ pohuai jinzheng qingxing ji banli jingguo qingxing* (The Violation of the Opium Prohibition in the Special Region of Northern Shaanxi and the Handling of the Problem), handwritten copy, 1943.

51. Lin Manhong, "Qing mo shehui liuxing xishi yapain yanjiu—gongjimiande fexi" (Study on the Spread of Opium Smoking in the Late Qing—Supply Side Analysis) (Ph.D. dissertation, Taiwan Normal University, 1985), 245 and 267; The Unity Press, ed., *Zhonggong xianzhuang zhi yanjiu* (Study of the Current Situation of the CCP) (Chongqing: n.p., 1944), 33.

52. Wang Jianmin, *Zhonguo gongchandang shigao*, 305–6; Zhang Houde,

"Zhonggong bianqu genjudi," 133; Lu Xizhi, *Shaanbei tequ*. A collection of CCP materials lends some support to the charge that the Red Army was involved in opium production and sale. See the Shaanxi Provincial Archives and the Shaanxi Provincial Academy of Social Sciences, ed., *Shaan-Gan-Ning bianqu zhengfu wenjian xuan bian* (Selected Documents of the Shaan-Gan-Ning Border Region Government) (Beijing: Archives Press, 1988), 5: 314–15; and 6: 200–01. In the two cases mentioned here, the Red Army soldier was found selling opium to unauthorized merchants and local residents.

53. *Bannianlai Zhonggong zhongyao dongtai* (The Important Events of the CCP in the Last Half Year) (n.p.: n.p., 1944), 14–15. In 1944, four merchants of Xing County, the capital of the communist Jin-Sui base area, went against the party's advice to Linxian to trade in opium. They were arrested together with their contraband and severely punished. This episode suggests that before 1944 the Jin-Sui party allowed the merchants to trade opium. See Editorial and Writing Group of the Xing County Revolutionary Base, *Xingxian gemingshi* (The Revolutionary History of Xing County) (Taiyuan: Shanxi People's Press, 1985), 204.

54. *Bianqu caijing suowen* (Intelligence on the Finance and Economy of the Border Area), Internal Publication of the Central Bureau of Investigation and Statistics, the National Government, nos. 31 and 32. (Published during the 1940s.)

55. Ibid., nos., 31–37.

56. The Editorial and Writing Group on Financial and Economic History of the Shaan-Gan-Ning Border Region et al., ed., *Jiefang zhanzheng shiqi Shaan-Gan-Ning bianqu caizheng jingji shiliao xuanbian* (Selected Materials on the Financial and Economic History of the Shaan-Gan-Ning Border Region During the War of Liberation) (Shaanxi: Sanqin Press, 1988), 2: 66–67 and 440–48. Even the Industrial Cooperative that was run with foreign help handed over "soap."

57. Lu Xizhi, *Shaanbei tequ*.

58. *SGNBQ*, 4: 215.

59. Ibid., 4: 215; 3: 157, 199, 207, and 276.

60. Ibid., 3: 237–38.

61. Ibid., 4: 208; 8: 154, 164, and 557.

62. Lu Xizhi, *Shaanbei tequ*; Zhang Houde, "Zhonggong bianqu genjudi," 133. For a rare example of CCP evidence, see the Shaanxi Provincial Archives and the Shaanxi Provincial Academy of Social Sciences, *Shaan-Gan-Ning bianqu*, 7: 2–6.

63. Xiao Jingguang, *Xiao Jingguang huiyilu* (Memories of Xiao Jingguang) (Beijing: People's Liberation Army Press, 1987), 306.

64. Wang Jianmin, *Zhongguo gongchandang shigao*, 3: 306–07.

65. *SGNBQ*, 4: 121.

66. Ibid., 4: 39.

67. Ibid., 4: 242–46.

68. Ibid., 4: 246, 256.

69. Ibid., 4: 44.

70. Ibid., 4: 268–71; the Shaanxi Provincial Archives and the Shaanxi Provincial Academy of Social Science, *Shaan-Gen-Ning bianqu*, 7: 2–6.

71. *SGNBQ*, 4: 82.

72. Ibid., 4: 167, 169, 178; and 5: 76.

73. Ibid., 4: 94–95.

74. Ibid., 4: 90–91, 94–95, 171, and 183.

75. Ibid., 4: 75, 166–67, and 171.

76. Ibid., 4: 108–9; Xingguang and Zhang Yang, ed., *Kang-Ri zhanzheng shiqi*, 397.

77. Xingguang and Zhang Yang, ed., ibid., 398–99; *SGNBQ*, 4: 167, 180–81, and 183. The opium prohibition bureau exported 22 million yuan (*bianbi*) worth of "local

product" in the first half of 1943. Of the trade, 70 percent was conducted on the basis of barter. See *SGNBQ*, 4: 173.

78. Xingguang and Zhang Yang, ed., *Kang-Ri zhanzheng shiqi*, 399; *SGNBQ*, 4: 167.

79. *SGNBQ*, 4: 167.

80. Ibid., 4: 179–86; and *Bannianlai Zhonggong zhongyao dongtai*, 15.

81. *SGNBQ*, 4: 50 and 53.

82. Ibid., 4: 428.

83. Ibid., 4: 115 and 155.

84. Ibid., 4: 174.

85. Ibid., 4: 50 and 427–28.

86. Ibid., 4: 307–8.

87. Ibid., 4: 31, 343, and 349. There were 155 shops in Suide. Of the nine largest stores there, six were sundry goods stores, but only one was in the opium business. Of the 19 second-largest stores there, 13 were sundry goods stores, but still only one traded in opium.

88. Ibid., 4: 355; Cai Shufan et al., *Suide Mizhi tudi wenti*, 112.

89. The other had resigned earlier. *SGNBQ*, 4: 239–41, 347–48, and 368.

90. Ibid., 4: 340–41.

91. Ibid., 4: 156.

92. Ibid., 4: 226–32. In 1943, the party also unified the publicly owned enterprises in the Jin-Sui base into the Xinye Company. With a department of "local product," this company set up secret purchase and transport points in the Japanese-occupied areas; one duty of these secret points was to promote the sale of local and "special products." I suspect this company to be the counterpart of the Nanchang Company in the Jin-Sui base area. See Editorial and Writing Group of the Xing County Revolutionary Base, *Xingxian gemingshi*, 202.

93. *SGNBQ*, 4: 207–8. This section draws its materials primarily from ibid., 68 and 207–17.

94. Ibid., 3: 243.

95. Zhang Pengyuan, Lin Quan, and Zhang Junhong, *Yu Da xiansheng fangwen jilu* (Interview with Mr. Yu Da) (Taibei: Modern History Research Institute of the Central Research Academy, 1989), 77; Zhang Wentian, *Shenfu Xingxian nongcun diaocha* (Investigation of Villages in Shenfu and Xing Counties) (Beijing: People's Press, 1986), 74.

96. *SGNBQ*, 3: 252–53.

97. Ibid., 3: 782 and 784.

98. Zheng Weisan, "Guanyu dangqian Huainan dangnei zhuyao buliang qingxiang ge qudangweide xin" (A Letter to the Regional Party Committee Concerning Major Undesirable Tendencies Within the Party), in *Huainan dangkan* (Huainan Party Journal), no. 12 (1943); 9; and Xiao Wangdong, "Ershi dierci zhengfeng chubu zongjie" (Preliminary Summary of the Second Rectification of the Second Division), in *Huainan dangkan*, no. 15 (1943): 13.

99. Tan Zhenlin, "Huainan shanggan huiyide renwu ji zongjie" (Summary and Duties of the Huainan Senior Cadres Conference), *Huainan dangkan*, no. 13 (1943): 17–18.

100. *SGNBQ*, 4: 116–17.

101. CCP CC, "Longdong diwei zuzhibu dui Zhao Tingjie tongzhide chufen jueding" (Decision Concerning Comrade Zhao Tingjie's Punishment by the Organization Department of the Subregional Party Committee of Eastern Gansu), in *Gongfei dangwu jueding* (Decisions on Party Affairs by the Communist Bandits) (n.p.: n.p., 1946).

102. "Xibeiju guanyu He Weide tongzhi de cuowu jueding" (Decision on He Weide's Mistakes by the Northwest Party Bureau), in *Dangnei tongxun* (Internal Party Bulletin), no. 5 (1947): 2–5.

103. Wang Jing, *Deng Baoshan zhuan* (Biography of Deng Baoshan) (Lanzhou: Lanzhou University Press, 1988), 139 and 165–68.

Chapter 11

Writing or Rewriting History? The Construction of the Maoist Resolution on Party History

Tony Saich

History is made up of facts that become lies; legends are lies that finally become history.

—*Jean Cocteau*

The Rectification campaign launched by Mao Zedong in Yan'an between 1941 and 1944 has long been recognized as the key period in which a new orthodoxy was defined for party members.[1] The campaign clarified organizational goals and created a loyalty based on a Maoist interpretation of the past and present. Crucial to this process was the establishment of the supremacy of Mao Zedong and his thought within the CCP. This was achieved through the construction of a party history that placed Mao Zedong at the center of the revolutionary movement, with other key figures portrayed as either complementary to Mao (for example, Liu Shaoqi) or as having obstructed the implementation of Mao's "correct" policy line (Wang Ming). Thus, positive contributions by Wang Ming to the correction of Li Lisan's policies and to the formulation of the second United Front were eradicated from the official party history.

This chapter focuses on this crucial aspect of the creation of the Maoist discourse. The study of party history by senior cadres preceded the more broadly based Rectification campaign and, in October 1943, the Politburo made it clear that returning to the study of party history and "line" was the logical culmination of the Rectification campaign.[2] The summary phase was completed with the adoption by the CCP CC in April 1945 of the "Resolution on Some Historical Questions" ("Resolution").[3] The chapter examines the role of party history within the Rectification campaign, how the Maoist history was constructed, and how this history was popularized through the use of specific materials and study sessions before the campaign entered its phase of summing up.

Party History and the Rectification Movement

> The Yan'an Rectification campaign began with party senior cadres discussing
> the question of the party's line, in the middle phase it turned into a widespread
> Rectification campaign covering the entire party, sweeping away the influ-
> ences of subjectivism, sectarianism, and formalism among the broad ranks of
> cadres. Further, it raised the Marxist and Leninist ideological level of all
> cadres. Finally, the Rectification campaign once again turned to the study by
> party senior cadres of line.
>
> —Wang Zhongqing[4]

The communist movement was in a desperate state when Mao Zedong and the
survivors of the Long March arrived in Yan'an to link up with the local partisans. Not only were they pursued by the GMD but they were also bitterly divided
internally. Mere survival seemed to be the overwhelming priority. Yet within a
short time Mao Zedong had embarked on an exercise to create a sense of order
and logic from the seeming disorder and chaos. He saw clearly that the party
needed a guiding framework of reference to rally the allegiance of most party
members and give a purpose to their actions that was greater than mere survival.
This allegiance would ensure that most party members would behave in a pre-
dictable way most of the time despite the enormously varied environments in
which they operated. One did not have to be a "true believer" to propagate the
new orthodoxy. At worst, it simply provided the new "rules of the game" that
were not to be infringed.

Various factors must have convinced Mao of the need for this cohesive
framework. First, with the exception of the Shaan-Gan-Ning (Shaanxi-Gansu-
Ningxia) base area, the other Communist-held base areas were coming under
increasing pressure from the Japanese invaders. To resist this pressure and to
protect against GMD encroachment in subsequent years, it was necessary to
make sure that the party and its army would fight as a coherent force. Second,
the expansion of party membership since the start of the Sino-Japanese War
(1937) and the presence of Yan'an as a center of resistance to the Japanese
brought with it problems. Many intellectuals and patriots had come to Yan'an to
wage war against Japan rather than because they were attracted by the theories of
Marx and Lenin and the communist organizational form. Many new recruits had
joined the party without proper screening during the "storm membership drives"
in the early years of the anti-Japanese war. Mao Zedong and his supporters felt
that many of these recruits were not well-versed in Marxism-Leninism in its
"sinified" form or clear about the party's ultimate aims. This strengthened their
perception that if the CCP was to remain a coherent, fighting force a certain
degree of ideological orthodoxy was necessary.

Third, the history of the CCP during the 1930s had been marked by bitter
internal struggles that had on occasion spilled over into fratricide.[5] Adherence to
the correct ideological line came to legitimize policy, and understanding of the

"line" became a necessary condition for leadership after the dismissal of Chen Duxiu and the 7 August Emergency Conference (1927).[6] Debate in the party became governed by the manipulation of ideological symbols, with the result that genuine debate about policy disputes declined. Policy difference became synonymous with line struggle.[7] If party members could be persuaded to rally behind the new orthodoxy, the risk of such violent inner-party struggle would be substantially diminished. This was clearly desired by many veteran party members and lay behind their acceptance of the judgment that the party had suffered from "leftism" in the later years of the Jiangxi Soviet period. Some had been imprisoned, and many knew fellow comrades who had suffered from the imposition of strict ideological criteria to judge work in the base areas. However, as is discussed below, initially this was not sufficient reason for them also to reject the validity of the fourth plenum (January 1931).

Yet these factors do not explain fully why the definition of a "correct" party history was such an important component of this process. A necessary explanation is found both in the form of legitimation to rule in the CCP and more particularly in Mao Zedong's power struggle with Wang Ming. Wang's demise coincided with Mao's desire to place himself as the unchallenged interpreter of China's revolutionary experience. When senior cadres began to study revolutionary history in 1939 and when Mao later launched the Rectification campaign in late 1941, Wang Ming had already been defeated politically. In fact, Wang's position had been precarious ever since his return to China in November 1937. He enjoyed great prestige because of his work with the Comintern, his capacity for theoretical analysis, and his contribution to the development of the second United Front. However, his long stay in Moscow had cut him off from a practical involvement in the Chinese revolution and deprived him of the ability to form the kind of alliances with other party leaders and military commanders that had been forged by Mao Zedong. His speeches full of Marxist rhetoric and abstract analysis must have had a hollow ring for his audience. While Wang has often been thought of as the "Comintern's man," the Comintern itself was aware of local sensibilities and, by implying that Mao should take the senior position in the party, perhaps unwittingly played into his hands. In September 1938, the Comintern informed the CCP that it approved of the United Front policy during the previous year while Georgy Dimitrov, the Comintern member responsible for Chinese affairs, let it be known that Mao Zedong should be the party's senior leader.[8] Wang's position was undermined further by the failure of his approach to expanding communist influence through legal means. His prestige suffered a final blow when Wuhan, a city that he had pledged to defend to the end, fell to the Japanese in October 1938.

Thus, when Mao Zedong sought to discredit Wang Ming and his policy line of the early 1930s, Wang was effectively finished as a genuine rival in the CCP. The construction of a Maoist party history had a more far-reaching objective. It would provide a source of allegiance for party members by linking their precarious situation to China's degradation at the hands of the imperialist invaders and the warlords who were products of China's feudal system. Their redemption would come through following the "correct" policies of the party.

This history was intended to do more than simply order and retell the past. By placing himself in the central role of the party's revolutionary history, Mao was providing himself with the legitimacy necessary to secure an unchallengeable leadership position. In Orwellian logic, Mao as supreme leader and correct interpreter of the past would become the ideological authority defining present policy and the future orientation of the revolution.

One of the indispensable qualifications for leadership of a communist movement, as Schram has noted, has been a reputation as a Marxist theoretician and philosopher.[9] It was precisely on these grounds that Wang Ming presented a threat to Mao. Wang had received a solid training in Bolshevik theory while in Moscow and was generally regarded as a theoretician of greater significance than Mao or anyone else in the Chinese movement. Indeed, until Mao began the process of reassessing party history, Wang Ming's *The Two Lines* was the most substantial review of the party's history.[10] It was no coincidence that Wang republished this book when discussions of party history began in Yan'an.

Mao needed to attack Wang at the level of theory and to discredit his view of CCP history in order to establish his own right to leadership. Mao combined these two exercises by constructing a party history designed to show that Mao's correct leadership of the Chinese revolution was intrinsically linked to his correct thought that had guided the revolutionary process while at the same time being a product of it.[11]

Mao neatly undercut Wang Ming's theoretical pretensions by labeling him a "dogmatist" who derived his Marxist theory from books and not from the practice of the Chinese revolution. This stress on a theory so closely linked to revolutionary practice not only derived from Mao's own experiences but also was probably increased by Mao's none too successful excursion into theory in the winter of 1936–37. Mao devoted time to the study of Marxist philosophy, resulting in a series of lectures on dialectical materialism. As Schram has noted, much of these lectures and writings was little more than plagiarism of Soviet sources with a result that was often very crude.[12]

Soon after this experience, Mao concentrated on promoting himself as a theorist who had fully understood the course of the Chinese revolution. In his speech to the sixth plenum in October 1938, Mao claimed that there was no such thing as abstract Marxism and that it had to take on a national form.[13] Marxism-Leninism was to be "sinified." Mao rounded off his comments by calling for an end to copying foreign styles of writing and for empty, abstract talk and dogmatism to be replaced by a new lively Chinese style. Mao believed that this would be well received by the ordinary Chinese people.[14]

The written word has always been important in traditional Chinese political culture as a form of legitimation, as has adherence to an idealistic belief system.

The ethical system that underpinned the Confucian state formed an important part of the institutions of government, and the correct explanation of the world was an important part of the legitimacy to rule. In this context, the CCP was able to supply an ideology that provided an "entire cosmology that summed up all of human history on a cosmopolitan, supra-national basis."[15]

Standard dynastic histories have formed an important part of the structure of, and right to, rule. Each dynasty would sum up the past to suit its present interpretations. A commentary on the dynasty's progress was often maintained. The task of these histories and commentaries was moral, and it was their duty to apportion "praise and blame" in ethical terms.[16] They would provide the essential guidance for leaders and led with the leaders attempting to show that the present was a harmonious continuation of the past. While the CCP's revolution was a conscious break with the past, the use of the written word in the form of an official history was distinctly traditional. The Maoist history resembled the veritable records of the Ming. Neither purported to be academic summations of the past but were consciously political in their objectives. As the historian W. Franke has noted, the grand secretaries who supervised the compilation of the records had often been involved in the political controversies and constructed the histories to reflect their own, rather than opposing, views.[17] However, unlike the veritable histories, which were not intended for publication but rather for the compilation of a standard history by later generations, Mao's history was intended expressly for immediate consumption by party members.

If this traditional predilection was not enough, the publication of the official Stalinist history of the Communist Party of the Soviet Union in 1938 must have convinced Mao Zedong that it was the correct thing for a ruler to compile. Mao praised the Stalinist history, and it was used for study by cadres with the "Conclusion" being included among the twenty-two documents that formed the core reading for the Rectification campaign.

By creating the terms of the discourse for analyzing the Chinese revolution, Mao constructed the necessary "symbolic capital" to enhance his own status as the revolution's supreme leader and interpreter.[18] His capacity to interpret what seemed to be a defeat as merely a setback in a process of history that was moving inexorably forward and his capacity to make sense of the rapidly changing world must have been reassuring to party cadres. It appeared to offer a logic and order that, if accepted, would end the fratricide in the CCP. Moreover, Mao Zedong not only seemed to make sense of the various disparate elements confronting those in Yan'an, but he was successful.

However, there was more to the construction of a "correct" party history than providing a framework for party members to relate to. It was intended to end alternative discourses within the movement. The creation of this single discourse eliminated the pluralism of ideas that had temporarily replaced the monism that is common in the Chinese polity. Disagreement with the Maoist view of party history would be tantamount to committing a mistake in "line." Rectification was not just a peaceful proselytizing event but entailed the eradication of alternative intellectual responses to party rule, regardless of whether the challenge came from Wang Ming and his supporters or from those intellectuals who represented the cosmopolitan trend of the May Fourth movement within the CCP. The construction of a "correct" party history and the presentation of Mao Zedong Thought based upon it disguised the ruthless Mao who pursued his ultimate vision.

Two events in Yan'an made this quite clear. Mao Zedong, in his talks on literature and art, pointed out that the independent critical role of the intellectual as had developed from the May Fourth movement onward would no longer be tolerated within his republic. In case anyone had missed the message, the humiliation of Wang Shiwei served as a warning.[19] Secondly, in 1943 the campaign to "screen" cadres ("Rescue campaign") was linked to rectification, making the threat of the use of terror apparent to errant cadres.[20] Ostensibly, the "screenings" that took place were to protect the party against presumed GMD and Japanese supporters who had infiltrated the party and the base areas. However, Kang Sheng, the organizer of the campaign, admitted that less than 10 percent of those who had "confessed" were actually spies or enemies.[21] This campaign would certainly have caused anyone who might have thought of openly challenging Mao and the party center to think twice for fear of being accused of being a traitor or a spy. It certainly would explain why the Maoist version of history as reintroduced in the later phase of rectification was more readily received than it had been in Mao's first attempt in 1939–40.

The major reassessment of party history that senior cadres had to accept concerned the fourth plenum of the Sixth CC (January 1931) and the Zunyi Conference (January 1935). Until Mao began to reconstruct party history, Zunyi had been, by and large, ignored.[22] In Yan'an, it began to assume the reputation as the meeting at which finally the party began to listen to Mao's "correct" policy line. Gaining acceptance of this assessment proved relatively simple. This was not the case, however, with Mao's re-evaluation of the fourth plenum. Before looking at the construction of this reassessment and its popularization, it is necessary to provide some information on the two meetings as background.

The Fourth Plenum (January 1931) and the Zunyi Conference (January 1935)

> the Fourth Plenum . . . was convened under circumstances in which pressure was being applied from all directions by the "left" dogmatist and sectarian elements headed by Wang Ming and in which some comrades in the central leading organs who had committed empiricist errors were compromising with the elements supporting them. The convening of the session played no positive or constructive role. . . . The Zunyi Conference was entirely correct in concentrating all its efforts on rectifying the military and organizational errors, which at that time were of decisive significance. The meeting inaugurated a new

central leadership, headed by Comrade Mao Zedong—a historic change of paramount importance in the CCP.

—Resolution

The "Resolution" concentrated its critique on party history until the Zunyi Conference and more especially on the period from the fourth plenum of the Sixth CC. According to the "Resolution," this was the period dominated by the third "left" line pursued by Wang Ming and Bo Gu. Yet, as is argued below, it took Mao Zedong some time to reach this conclusion, and when he did, it had more to do with his later disagreements with Wang Ming and his desire to place himself at the center of party history. The reassessment was designed to bolster Mao's position in Yan'an as supreme leader. While not necessarily reliable, Wang Ming's account of a discussion with Mao on 1 April 1944 is interesting. Wang claims that Mao stated that his intention was to rewrite party history as his own history.[23]

The fourth plenum was convened in the wake of the failure of Li Lisan's insurrectionist policies. Although the Comintern refrained from criticism of Li Lisan while the strategy was in operation, as soon as it failed harsh condemnation followed. Between the third plenum (September 1930), when Li had been initially criticized, and the fourth plenum, factional conflicts and power struggles within the CCP increased. Li Lisan's strongest opponents were Wang Ming and the "Returned Students group," who enjoyed the patronage of Pavel Mif, the Comintern representative in China.[24] However, Wang Ming had earlier shown himself to be in essential agreement with Li Lisan's assessment and thus initially the struggle was not seen in terms of rectifying a "left" line.

This changed as the Comintern began to toughen its stance when Pavel Mif and his supporters in the Comintern became dissatisfied with the decisions of the third plenum. In October 1930, the ECCI sent members of the CC a letter stating that Li Lisan's mistakes were ones of line.[25] It labeled Li Lisan "anti-Comintern" and a "semi-Trotskyite." Mif himself arrived in China in mid-December 1930 and proposed that the fourth plenum be convened as soon as possible. The plenum was held in Shanghai on 7 January and was dominated by Mif and his protégé, Wang Ming.

The plenum was harsh in its condemnation of Li Lisan, who was accused of betraying the correct instructions of the Comintern and wreaking havoc on the party. This positive view of the fourth plenum persisted until the very end of the Rectification campaign. It appears that it was only at the very last, when senior cadres returned to the study of party history in late 1943 and 1944, that Mao Zedong was able to shift this judgment. For its new leadership in China, the Comintern did not turn to Mao Zedong and the soviet areas but to the Returned Students, with real power in the hands of Wang Ming.

The later Maoist history was to cite this plenum as the origin of the third "left" line, which was corrected only with Mao Zedong's assumption of power at Zunyi. According to the "Resolution":

a number of party comrades who were inexperienced in practical revolutionary struggle and guilty of "left" dogmatist errors came forward, with Comrade Chen Shaoyu [Wang Ming] at their head, and fought against the central leadership . . . [their program] continued, revived, or developed the Li Lisan line and other "left" ideas and policies in a new guise. Thus, there was a further growth of "left" ideas in the party which took the form of a new "left" line.[26]

However, during the period itself, the differences were not so sharp and there was even a degree of mutual respect between the two men.[27] Mao was considered favorably by the Wang Ming leadership and was praised in Wang's appendix to the *Two Lines*. Further, while there may have been conflict by the fifth plenum (January 1934), Mao Zedong was not dropped from the Politburo as some studies have suggested.[28]

Mao Zedong, speaking to the Second All-China Soviet Congress held in January–February 1934, followed in broad outline the decisions of the fifth plenum. The plenum had provided an upbeat view of the revolutionary situation and stressed that the party's major task was simply to continue the fight against the "right opportunists" who refused to see this excellent situation. Mao's assessment of the plenum stands in stark contrast to his judgment in the 1945 "Resolution." In 1945, Mao criticized the fifth plenum for its bad judgment of the current situation. In 1934, Mao's speech supported the Returned Students' contention that currently the crucial factor in the Chinese revolution was the life-and-death struggle between revolution and counterrevolution. Again this counters Mao's 1945 judgment that they had ignored the needs of the intermediate classes.[29] However, Mao did stress that the socialist revolution could not be achieved until the bourgeois democratic revolution had been completed throughout China. This was in contrast to the views of the Returned Students.[30]

Rightly, Mao's rise to power is traced back to the Zunyi Conference. This meeting also saw the origins of the criticism of the previous period, but only in the military sphere. Even after Zunyi, it was not until after the sixth plenum (1938), when Wang Ming had been defeated, that Mao began to attack him for pursuing an incorrect line. In the summer of 1936, Mao Zedong did not talk of a "left" line under Wang Ming and praised the defeat of Li Lisan's line in January 1931 as marking a vital contribution to the defeat of the GMD's first Encirclement campaign.[31] Zhu De informed Agnes Smedley that the fourth plenum marked the affirmation of our "line" and the final repudiation of the Li Lisan line.[32] Even in October 1939, Mao provided an essentially positive assessment of the fourth plenum as having combated Li Lisan's "left" line and referred to it and Zunyi as historic meetings.[33]

This persistent positive interpretation of the fourth plenum was, of course, well known by senior cadres when they began to study party history in Yan'an. While many seem to have readily accepted that the "line" had been "left" since 18 September 1931, there seems to have been resistance to dating its origins to the fourth plenum.[34] This derived from the widely accepted belief that Wang

Ming and his supporters had indeed played a positive role in putting an end to Li Lisan's "adventurism" and from the view that the plenum had faithfully represented the Comintern's line. A premature attack on the fourth plenum could have been interpreted as an attack on the Comintern, and this could have backfired on Mao. When the Comintern was dissolved in May 1943, this obstacle was removed.

The criticisms of Wang Ming's ideas that were later promulgated in Yan'an amounted, on occasions, to a misleading characterization of his actual writings.[35] Wang was by no means an opponent, as accused, of guerrilla warfare per se, and the blame for failure during the GMD's fifth Encirclement campaign lay more correctly with Bo Gu and the Comintern adviser, Otto Braun. In fact, in December 1934 and January 1935, Wang Ming criticized mistakes in military leadership as having led to the loss of the Jiangxi Soviet, an assessment remarkably similar to that adopted at Zunyi. However, while criticizing "positional warfare" he did not endorse fully the continued use of guerrilla tactics either, as he felt that the GMD had grown accustomed to them.[36] At the September 1941 Politburo meeting that discussed party history and marked the prelude to the Rectification campaign, Wang claimed that he had opposed Bo Gu's mistakes and that it was Bo who had been responsible for the "leftist" mistakes that were made in the Soviet areas.[37]

It was at Zunyi that the critique of the earlier period began, but, as we shall see below, it was given its form by Liu Shaoqi, not Mao Zedong.[38] The Enlarged Meeting of the Politburo turned into a major review of past military policy and heralded a shift in the party leadership. The resolutions adopted contained a compromise approving the party's political line, while ascribing the military failure during the fifth Encirclement campaign to the erroneous military line of "pure positional defense" pursued by Bo Gu and Braun. Bo and Braun are mentioned by name in the "Outline Resolution" adopted by the CC's Secretariat on 8 February 1935.[39] Chen Yun noted that the political line was "generally correct" but because military command constituted a major part of this general line, the base area could not be defended and the fifth Encirclement could not be broken up.[40]

Although Mao did not become the dominant figure in the party and army immediately, the Zunyi Conference provided a decisive step in Mao's move to supreme power. He was appointed to the five-person Secretariat together with Zhang Wentian (general secretary), Zhou Enlai, Chen Yun, and Bo Gu. Together with Zhou Enlai and Wang Jiaxiang, he was to serve on the CCP Central Military Leadership Group. While Zhou was to be the chief decision-maker, Mao was to be his chief assistant. This broke up Bo Gu's and Braun's control over military affairs. At Zunyi, Mao did not become chairman of the Military Council or of the Politburo, as some historians have suggested, but he did become one of the five top leaders of the party and had the right to be involved in all party and army decisions.

Further, as the Maoist history would later claim, Mao was the one leader present who had represented the "correct" political line in the past. This assessment begs two interrelated questions that need to be touched on briefly. First, why was the question of political line not raised at the Zunyi Conference and, second, did Mao pursue a clearly distinct policy line before Zunyi?

It seems that during the Rectification campaign, senior cadres also required an explanation as to why only criticisms of the military line had been raised at Zunyi. In a 1944 speech, Lu Dingyi outlined the official reasoning: it was logical that the political line had not been discussed because the party was in flight and in a war situation. Thus, primacy had to be given to sorting out the military line in order to ensure the party's survival. However, Lu added that the "basic character" of the meeting was that of "combating opportunism" and that the acknowledgment of the correctness of the political line was wrong. According to Lu, even though participants might not have realized it they were opposing the "current Wang Ming line."[41]

Apart from certain tactical considerations, it is difficult to discern a distinct Mao "line" during this period. Mao's relationship to Li Lisan's policy is more complex than either slavish adherence or consistent opposition.[42] It seems that the only time that there was direct confrontation was from April to June 1930, when Li Lisan tried directly to control the operations of Mao Zedong's troops. For the remainder, it appears that Mao, acting in line with his perception of the local situation, generally pursued a policy in line with the Li Lisan–dominated party center.

After Li Lisan's removal, differences between Mao Zedong's policies and what was later referred to as Wang Ming's "left" line were not so clear-cut as was claimed in the "Resolution" and, as was noted above, there was a mutual admiration between the two men. However, Mao did have differences with the party center run by Bo Gu, and these were exacerbated after Bo moved to the Jiangxi Soviet in early 1933. While arrival in Jiangxi clearly indicated that it was the center of revolutionary activities, members from the party center also felt that it was natural that they should be accorded key leadership positions, thus impinging on Mao. Further, having worked underground in conditions of secrecy and with a stress on ideological orthodoxy, they seemed to have been shocked by what they saw as the compromises and ideological laxness in the base areas. The "revolutionary idealism" of the party center came into sharp conflict with the political realism represented by the "local" cadres. The anti–Luo Ming campaign at the elite level and the land investigation movement at the base levels created great uncertainty within the base areas and led to the arrest of many local leaders. These problems that affected all the base areas were, perhaps, sufficient to convince many veteran cadres later that there had indeed been "line struggle," especially in the later period of the Jiangxi Soviet.

The Development of the Maoist Party History

The methods of struggle within the party during and after the fourth plenum meeting contained similar errors [of "leftism"]. There were excessive mistakes of factionalism. Many cadres, especially veteran cadres, were scorned and persecuted. This was wrong. At the same time, the fourth plenum was originally designed to oppose "leftism," but the struggle against "leftism" soon stopped while the fire was concentrated on fighting rightism. That was also wrong, because the main mistake at that time was still "leftism." But we let "leftism" escape.

—Liu Shaoqi, 4 March 1937
Letter to Party Center

Criticism of a "left" line after the fourth plenum was started by Liu Shaoqi based on his experiences in the white areas and within the context of the newly evolving policy of the United Front.[43] Liu launched a major critique of CCP policy during the early 1930s. His views were strongly refuted at the time, but they provided the framework for the line of analysis that would be worked out during the rewriting of party history in Yan'an. In late February and early March 1937, Liu Shaoqi wrote four letters to the CC expressing his concern about past and present party work.

In a letter of 4 March 1937, Liu attacked the political line of the party as suffering from "leftism" ever since the 7 August Emergency Conference of 1927.[44] According to Liu, the failure to clear up properly the mistakes of "left adventurism" meant that they had now become a habit in the party. This, together with "factionalism," Liu saw as more important than "objective" factors such as GMD suppression in preventing the party from doing its work properly in the white areas. However, Liu did not limit his criticism to work in the white areas. "Leftist" mistakes had also been made in the soviets on issues such as the land question, mass work, and inner-party struggle. Liu felt that the party had missed the chance provided by the Japanese conquest of Manchuria in 1931 for building a broad United Front both to isolate Chiang Kai-shek and to resist the Japanese incursions into Chinese territory. The party, according to Liu, should have shifted the focus of its work from the class to the national struggle, and he criticized what he saw as a serious strategic mistake in dealing with the Fujian Rebellion.

Rounding off his letter, Liu stressed again that the mistakes in the previous ten years had been consistently "leftist." Within the party, Liu claimed that the methods in ideological struggle had been excessive to the point that "absolutely no freedom of calm discussion" existed within the party. Later, Mao and his supporters, including Liu, attributed this "leftist" line to Wang Ming, but here Liu blamed the party leadership in China for not following Comintern instructions. In fact, there was an element of truth in Liu's assessment.

The party leadership rejected Liu's opinion that "leftist" errors had been committed during the early 1930s. This was not surprising given that contemporary leaders such as Bo Gu and Zhang Wentian had been key figures during those years. In May and June 1937, the party held two important meetings where this and other issues concerning the United Front were discussed. From 2 to 14 May, a national conference of party delegates was held in Yan'an. While Mao summed up the current state of affairs in the United Front, much of the remaining discussion focused on the points raised by Liu.

Zhang Wentian, in his opening comments to the conference, made it clear that Liu's attack on the party line as a whole having suffered from "leftism" was unacceptable.[45] Zhang claimed that one could not conclude that the political line of the previous ten years had been mistaken just because of recent changes in the United Front policy. On the contrary, Zhang saw the history of the previous decade as glorious. He admitted that some mistakes had been made but claimed that the party center's line had been basically correct and had followed the Comintern's. However, he was willing to concede that mistakes in work had been made in the white areas. In particular, he referred to the existence of "closed doorism" over a long period of time and military adventurism and conservatism (!) in the civil war. Rejecting Liu's views, a report drafted by Zhang Wentian was adopted that defended the political line of the party center during the period. This document blamed the "white" terror, and the nationalists' military attacks and the disruption caused by "Trotskyism" for the failure of work in the white areas.[46] Mao Zedong was willing to accept this assessment, perhaps recognizing that it was a debate he could not control at the time. In fact, Mao sent American journalist Nym Wales to talk to Zhang Wentian because he was the "official communist historian." Zhang, while critical of Li Lisan, made no mention of Wang Ming's "left" line when talking to Wales. Further, neither he nor Mao mentioned the Zunyi Conference.[47]

After this meeting, a party conference was held on work in the white areas. Zhang Wentian gave the main address, and Liu Shaoqi delivered a major report.[48] Noticeably, Liu dropped his criticism of the party center's political line during the early 1930s. However, he continued his criticism of mistakes such as "closed doorism," "sectarianism," and "adventurism" that had dominated party work since the 7 August Emergency Conference. Further, he claimed that the party suffered from "subjectivism" and "formalism" in mechanically mouthing Marxist phrases and support for the Comintern's line while often opposing it in practice.[49] Perhaps unknowingly, Liu was providing Mao Zedong with the framework for his later criticism of Wang Ming.[50]

This challenges Raymond Wylie's view that it was Chen Boda who played the dominant role in developing the criticisms laid down in the "Resolution." According to Wylie, an article by Chen Boda published on 1 July 1938 formed the genesis of the "Resolution" and even suggests that it was Chen who drafted it. As we shall see below, this was not the case. In broad outline, Chen's July 1938 article was in line with the general view held in the party: he denounced Chen Duxiu's "right opportunism," the subsequent adventurism, and Li Lisan's "leftism." His criticism of "leftism" after the fourth plenum is no harsher than that of Liu Shaoqi's earlier denunciation; similarly, he does not mention Mao's correct line even by allusion. Interesting in his analysis is his stress on the "struggle between two lines" ever since the party's founding—a method of analysis that would become a standard feature of Maoist historical analyses.[51]

After Mao had defeated Wang Ming politically at the sixth plenum, he set about staking his own claim to power. An important step in this was to establish his credentials as the theoretician of the Chinese revolution, the person who could link the general theses of Marxism-Leninism to the concrete situation in China. This meant that he had to establish himself as the sole correct interpreter of the CCP's history. He set out to show that his correct theory had been generated by a proper understanding of revolutionary practice that, in turn, led to correct guidance for the CCP. In this sense, Wang Ming became Mao's "whipping boy" to establish his own credentials as the correct interpreter of the Chinese revolution.

Mao Zedong, in his report to the sixth plenum, made an appeal to develop a national form of Marxism that would appeal to the Chinese people. An important part of its creation was to be the study of China's historical heritage and the use of the "Marxist method" to sum it up critically.[52] In his summary of recent party history, Mao Zedong mentioned the Zunyi Conference as having corrected "serious errors" of a " 'left' opportunistic character" during the fifth Encirclement campaign. Importantly, Mao referred to them as errors of principle and did not specifically reaffirm that the political line had been correct.[53]

In October 1939, Mao made the thrust of his criticism clearer. He reviewed the history of the party as a prelude to putting forward his new policies. In this review, Mao declared that the Zunyi Conference had set the party on the road to Bolshevization and laid the foundations for forming the United Front against Japan. This marked the beginning of the attacks on Wang Ming and his supporters through a reinterpretation of party history. The official party view had remained that it was Wang Ming and his supporters who had brought about the Bolshevization of the party as a result of the fourth plenum. This marked the start of the process that would result in the plenum's being discredited. Mao Zedong now publicly accepted Liu Shaoqi's criticisms that there had been problems with "left" opportunism in the revolutionary war and in work in the white areas. The usefulness of such a position was clear to Mao, but he had to ensure that it was the party center that was blamed and not his "local" leadership in the Jiangxi Soviet. Liu himself followed up his earlier criticisms in a speech on 20 October 1939.[54] In a wide-ranging speech on the questions of open and secret work, Liu criticized those who, after 1927, had pursued "leftist" policies and failed to protect the party's strength. The mistakes made had devastated the organization and had created a feeling of pessimism within the party. The alliance between Mao as leader of the party in the soviet areas and Liu as leader in the white areas had been formed.

On 25 December 1940, Mao drafted an inner-party directive summarizing current policy in which he repeated more forcefully his criticisms of leftist mistakes during the later Jiangxi period. He highlighted the mistaken policies toward landlords, rich peasants, and capitalists, attacks on intellectuals, and monopolizing of organs of political power by Communists. He characterized the policy as "all struggle and no alliance."[55] Clearly, a major part of Mao's purpose in pointing out these problems was to prevent them from recurring during the renewed phase of collaboration with the GMD. However, it was also useful to him in his struggle to discredit Wang Ming and to install himself as the correct interpreter of the CCP's revolutionary history. The draft directive was passed by the CC but the view that Wang Ming's "political line" was wrong met opposition, indicating cadres' resistance to a shift in interpretation.[56]

On 19 May 1941, Mao addressed senior cadres on the question of study pointing out that the party still suffered from "very great shortcomings" that had to be redressed.[57] Mao highlighted three areas that needed study: current affairs, history, and the practical application of Marxism-Leninism in revolutionary work. The last area posed the greatest problems. According to Mao, especially with respect to the application of theory, the Returned Students and middle and senior cadres were the most susceptible to a "subjective attitude." This criticism was clearly directed at Wang Ming and his supporters. Yet opposition remained to Mao's ideas and the speech was not published until 27 March 1942. However, the speech was not without effect, as it set the political terrain for the ensuing period. To celebrate the twentieth anniversary of the party's founding (July 1941), *Liberation Daily* published an editorial on the subject of combining the theories of Marxism-Leninism with the realities of China's situation. Further, Mao Zedong's undaunted leadership over the previous twenty years was praised.[58]

The strands of this drive for intensified study and the construction of a new party history were drawn together at an Enlarged Politburo meeting that began on 10 September 1941. The meeting marked the effective launching of the Rectification campaign.[59] The question of how genuine party unity could be achieved was discussed through debate of two major issues. First, how could cadres understand the link between Marxist-Leninist theory and the concrete situation in China? Secondly, what was the correct interpretation of party history and "political line" during the 1927–37 period? Concerning the latter, discussion focused on the issue of whether mistakes in "line" had been made after the fourth plenum. At the beginning of the meeting, many participants were not convinced by this argument. However, the party's "big guns" (Mao Zedong, Wang Jiaxiang, and Ren Bishi) were mobilized and all stated that errors in "line" had been made. This had the effect of swaying those present.

Mao opened his talk by referring to the Li Lisan line and the "left" opportunism of the later soviet period as representing examples of subjectivism. Mao claimed that the latter of these two was the most dangerous and had dominated longer because its proponents claimed that they represented the "Internationalist line." The damage had been all the greater because, unlike the Li Lisan line, the "left" opportunism totally embraced the Soviets and had "caused a great defeat for the Red Army." Mao placed the question of party line from 1932 (not the fourth plenum, January 1931) until December 1935 onto the discussion agenda (extending beyond Zunyi to the Wayaobao Conference), calling for its clarification by the Seventh Party Congress.

Mao claimed that, while the Zunyi Conference had modified the political line, subjectivism in the realm of ideology remained and that this still influenced work in Yan'an. Mao traced the origins of this subjectivism to three factors: first, "leftism" within China's tradition; second, the influence of people such as Nikolai Bukharin and Grigory Yeuseyvich Zinoviev in the Comintern; and third, that China was a broadly petty bourgeois country because its science was not well developed. He rounded off his comments by outlining the methods to overcome this incorrect work style. These included recognizing the seriousness of subjectiveness, clarifying the difference between Marxism and dogmatic Marxism, and exposing the qualifications of those whose theory was divorced from practice and dealing with sectarianism. Ideological education was to be at the heart of the movement, and the recently translated soviet *History of the Communist Party of the Soviet Union (Bolshevik). Short Course* was to form the core of the study, and CC decisions between the Sixth and Seventh Party Congresses were to be researched. In organizational terms, the movement was to be run by the Central Study Group under Mao and Wang Jiaxiang and an Education Committee under Zhang Wentian. A mobilization meeting in Yan'an at which all Politburo members were to speak was to mark the launch of the movement. According to Mao, the purpose of this movement was to destroy subjectivism and sectarianism and thereby save the party's cadres.[60]

Wang Jiaxiang put forward the view that Mao Zedong had, in the past, upheld the dialectical materialist viewpoint in the party at large while Liu Shaoqi had done so in the white areas. This cemented Mao and Liu's alliance and predicted the evaluation adopted in the "Resolution." Further, Wang echoed Mao's criticisms of "subjectivism" in the party, blaming it on those who had "studied a bit of theory" but who had no practical work experience. He especially singled out people who had returned from Comintern work. For Wang, "dogmatism" or "narrow empiricism" was less likely to occur among those with practical work experience.[61]

The meeting made three decisions relating to the early 1930s, but they were not publicized. First, from the fourth plenum until 18 September 1931 the political line of the party center was basically correct although there had been serious mistakes. Second, from 18 September until the Zunyi Conference, the party center had pursued an incorrect line, whereas, third, after Zunyi, the line had been correct.[62] It was decided that Wang Ming had made many mistakes in his work with the party's Yangtze Bureau during the anti-Japanese war period.[63] Not surprisingly, Wang opposed this assessment and continued to claim that the line of the fourth plenum had been correct. Where there had been mistakes in work, particularly in the latter phase of the Jiangxi Soviet, Wang claimed that Bo Gu was to blame.[64]

The meeting ducked the key question of the role of the fourth plenum itself, the focus of the wrath in the "Resolution." At this stage, neither Mao nor Wang appear to have publicly called for a reassessment of the plenum, with Mao calling for reassessment from 1932 onward and the draft decision fixing the point of origin of "leftism" from 18 September 1931 with the Japanese invasion of Manchuria. Even should Mao have wished it, it is unlikely that veteran party members would have accepted wholesale denunciation of the fourth plenum. The plenum was still widely regarded as legitimate and as having played a crucial role in terminating the Li Lisan line. Indeed, many senior cadres had probably read the republished version of Wang Ming's *The Two Lines for the Further Bolshevization of the CCP*, which still represented general party wisdom on this period. Many senior cadres had been involved in the events and may have been unhappy to see their own positions potentially undermined by criticism of the plenum. Finally, there were the sensibilities of the Comintern. The fourth plenum had been convened under the auspices of the Comintern, and its decisions and leadership were said to have been in line with the Comintern's wishes. By contrast, many senior leaders were aware of the serious mistakes that had been made in the politics of the United Front after the Japanese invasion of Manchuria and that excessive "leftism" had taken its toll on the soviet areas in the later period. However, it seems that a sufficient number of senior cadres were unsure whether this actually amounted to errors in "line." Given this, it is perhaps not surprising that the decisions of the meeting were not made generally known within the party.

The Popularization of the Maoist Party History

> Senior cadres above the level of prefecture need to concentrate their study on the theories of, and the history of, the CCP. They should gradually read properly the thirty to forty Marxist-Leninist works assigned by Chairman Mao. Ordinary middle-level cadres must learn to apply policies. Thus, in the main, they should study the government program of the border region and should apply it in their own work. All cadres with insufficient education should make plans, and be determined to become educated first and then to study theory. Ordinary cadres who are intellectuals must first go down to the grass roots to get some training in practical work and gain experience in all kinds of practical work.
> —Gao Gang, 14 January 1943,
> Summary Speech to Northwest Senior Cadres' Conference

Having taken up the issue of party line and having begun the work of constructing a Maoist party history, there remained the question of its popularization and of convincing senior cadres of its veracity and of Wang Ming's mistakes. This was not so easily achieved, as many of the cadres had participated in this history and felt themselves to be under threat by any redefinition of political line in the early 1930s. As a result, rectification was extended to the party as a whole, and incorrect tendencies in thought were identified for criticism. After this task had been completed, the specific issue of party history was returned to.

The techniques for popularizing the newly emergent Maoist party history became the hallmark of later CCP campaigns. First, the "correct" version of events and the contents of the campaign were identified by senior leaders. Second, a corpus of texts and materials was chosen for study. These materials contained both positive and negative examples and were geared toward reinforcing the thrust of the leadership's views. Third, the study itself had to be organized and the phasing of its stages decided upon. Small groups for discussion of the texts formed the backbone of the study system. This study was accompanied by lectures by key figures and publications in party journals explaining the correct interpretation of the texts. People in the study groups were called on to think of concrete examples from their own experiences to illustrate the thrust of the campaign's message. On this basis, individuals were to evaluate their own past behavior, and that of others. Acceptance of the new orthodoxy would provide a sense both of relief at having "passed the test" and of admittance into the new order. Finally, the campaign would enter a summary phase in which particular targets (already decided upon by the leadership at the beginning) would be identified. The rewards for those who accepted "unity of thought" were accompanied by the threat of terror or exile for those who refused to accept the new line.

The party's Northwest Bureau under Gao Gang played a crucial role in developing and promoting the new party history. The bureau provided Mao with an institutional support base, and as the campaign entered its summary phase Gao Gang outlined an official history of the Shaan-Gan-Ning Border Region. This history drew on Liu Shaoqi's earlier critique and extended it to the history of one soviet area in the early 1930s. This provided the crucial stepping-stone to the evaluation adopted in the "Resolution."

The first major source for the study by senior cadres was the *History of the Communist Party of the Soviet Union (Bolshevik). Short Course*; its dissemination was followed by edited collections of documents covering CCP history from its foundation to the present. The *Short Course* gave impetus to the idea of compiling an official party history. While the publication of this work marked the triumph of Stalin in the soviet political system, its translation into Chinese was used by Mao Zedong to assume ideological hegemony based on a "correct" history of the party's past. The *Short Course* was held up as a fine example of linking Marxist theory to the particular road of the Russian revolution. In this sense, it was interpreted as an attack on the tendency to be dogmatic. The book served as a model for the study of party history, and in May 1941, Mao Zedong praised the work as the "highest synthesis of the world communist movement in the last 100 years, a model for the union of theory and practice; in the whole world, this is still the one comprehensive model."[65]

Translation work began quickly, and in November 1938 Chapter 7 and the conclusion were published in the weekly *Jiefang* (Liberation). Thereafter, three translations of the complete work were done. In Chongqing, it was translated in two volumes for dissemination in areas under GMD rule; a translation was done in Shanghai that was also intended for the areas where the New Fourth Army was active; and a third translation was done in Moscow and published by the Foreign Workers' Press for distribution in the anti-Japanese bases in North China as well as in Shaan-Gan-Ning. It is claimed that by March 1941 some 100,000 volumes were in circulation.[66] Ren Bishi, who was later to head the committee to draft the "Resolution," played an active role in the work of translation and promotion. In particular, Ren was responsible for translating Chapter 4, on Dialectical and Historical Materialism.[67]

Mao Zedong himself took an active role in editing the Chinese study materials. His first work was to supervise the editing of a collection of documents covering party history from its origins until the present. This collection was to form the basis for "clarifying" the political, organizational, and ideological line after the fourth plenum.[68] Research was to focus on specific meetings or events and senior cadres were called on to summarize their own experiences.[69]

The two publications *Before the Sixth Party Congress* and *After the Sixth Party Congress* contained the most important materials for study.[70] Compilation began in July to mid-August 1941 following a Politburo decision that put Mao Zedong in charge of the work.[71] Informal circulation of these materials provided important preparatory work for the September 1941 Politburo meeting, and one CCP historian has claimed that discussions could not have proceeded so smoothly without the materials, as they disarmed various senior cadres and "helped them realize their mistakes."[72]

After the Politburo meeting, responsibility for editing was placed under the Committee for Clarification of Party History (set up by the Secretariat in October 1941) with Mao Zedong still possessing final responsibility. According to Mao, this study of party history was intended to improve current policy and to ensure that the line was correct.[73] *After the Sixth Party Congress*, formally published in December 1941, contained some 550 documents covering the period from July 1928 until November 1941. The materials were drawn from CC resolutions, directives, announcements, telegrams, articles, and speeches by various leaders.

On 11 February 1942, the Politburo discussed and approved a suggestion by Chen Yun to publish a companion volume covering the period before the Sixth Party Congress. The plan for the new volume was approved by the Secretariat on 27 March, and it was also decided that Mao should use this occasion to report on the development of the party's history.[74] Mao's comments implicitly supported Chen's suggestion by calling for broad study of the Chinese revolution from 1911 onward so that party members could understand the general context within which the party had its origins.[75] Wang Shoudao and Hu Qiaomu were Mao's chief aides in the work of editing, and the volume was published in October 1942. It contained some two hundred documents covering the period from March 1922 to June 1928. Essentially, the materials contained in the two collections affirmed the correctness of the emerging Maoist party history. However, the materials covered a wide range of issues, and thus when the movement entered its final phase in late 1943, a more tightly focused selection of 170 documents was published under the title *The Two Lines* (Liangtiao luxian).

Small groups were organized to study these materials. Mao had begun to pay attention to the education of senior cadres shortly after the sixth plenum. On 13 December 1938, Mao, on behalf of the Secretariat, stated that it was necessary to step up the study of Marxism-Leninism and China's revolutionary history and that preparatory work should be finished by 25 January 1939.[76] Subsequently, on 17 February 1939, the CC established a Cadre Education Department with Zhang Wentian as head and Li Weihan as his deputy.[77] The task of this department was to mobilize cadres for the study of Marxism-Leninism and revolutionary history and to discuss methods of study.[78]

Serious study by senior cadres began in May 1939 with consideration of the *Short Course*; this was basically completed by March 1941.[79] In June 1940, middle-level cadres began their study, also finishing in March 1941; in all, 2,118 people participated in study in Yan'an.[80] On 15 March, a three-month period of cadre training began, with study broadened to include the questions of "line" and "rectification."

The program of "educating" senior cadres was regularized further after the September Politburo meeting. On 26 September 1941, the Secretariat published a decision on organizing study for senior cadres.[81] The decision outlined the objectives of study, the scope and number of those who should participate, the method of study and the contents, and the relationship between the central and the local study groups. Some three hundred cadres drawn from the CC, central departments and bureaus, the regional or provincial party committees, and leaders of the Eighth Route Army and the New Fourth Army were to participate. One-third of those engaged in study were to be from the Yan'an area. Mao Zedong headed the central study group, with Wang Jiaxiang as his deputy; all the other study organizations came under the jurisdiction of this central group.

On 4 October 1941, Mao Zedong and Wang Jiaxiang called for small groups to be organized within the senior study groups to study Leninist theory and the political line since the Sixth Party Congress. By the end of 1941, these groups were expected to have studied Dimitrov's report to the Seventh Congress of the Comintern (1935) and the documents in the collection *Since the Sixth Party Congress*. This preliminary study was to prepare cadres for deeper research in the coming spring. In fact, rectification of the party as a whole was launched in the spring. Mao and Wang recognized that not all areas might be able to obtain the relevant documents. If documents could not be found, people could report on them from memory. However, Mao and Wang stressed that during this initial phase of discussing the past, the question of particular individuals was not to be brought up.[82] In fact, this would come in the last phase of the campaign in late 1943.

On 13 October 1941, the Secretariat set up a Committee to "Clarify Party History" consisting of Wang Jiaxiang, Ren Bishi, Kang Sheng, and Peng Zhen, and Mao Zedong as its head. The target of rewriting history was becoming clearer. The committee entrusted Wang Jiaxiang with drafting a document on the question of leadership and line since the fourth plenum. This document passed through numerous revisions, and it is said that many of its assessments were included in the final "Resolution."[83]

Study groups at the center and in the localities used similar methods. The study of the document was combined with the consideration of specific events or meetings. Thus, for example, on 13 April 1942, the Northwest Bureau of the party organized a meeting to report on party history; such meetings were intended to be held twice a week. The first report was by Li Hebang on the Jinbei region; this was followed by reports on Yanhe, Longdang, Guanzhong, Sanbian, Lu, Ganquan, and Yan'an.[84] This detailed reporting and discussions laid the foundations for Gao Gang's important report summarizing the history of the Shaan-Gan-Ning Border Region.

The study contained regular periods for summing up and the use of written or oral examinations to monitor progress. In late July 1942, the Northwest Bureau held a meeting to draw conclusions from the Rectification campaign. It asked the middle- and lower-level study groups to examine three questions. First, participants were asked whether study of the rectification documents had led them to recognize any shortcomings in their own work. Participants were asked, second, if they had encountered subjectivism in their work, and, third, how they thought shortcomings in their own study or that of their study group could be overcome. This summary and examination took place between 1 and 15 August. At the same time, the bureau asked for reports to be compiled and sent on. It was specifically asked that these reports point out who were the best and worst participants in the study, as well as the best and worst organizations.[85] Earlier, the bureau had announced that the notes and speeches of participants would form the basis for understanding "each comrade's" thought and his transformation.[86]

The same method was used when the time came for summing up the study of party history. In mid-May 1943, *Jiefang ribao* reported that cadres in the Suide district were devoting three weeks to a thorough study of the documents on the history of the party in the Northwest.[87] Two-line struggle was stressed in this process of study, and cadres were expected to review their own work in light of this. They were asked whether they had committed errors of "line," particularly in the period since the United Front against Japan had been launched. *Jiefang ribao* claimed that this soul-searching had led to some cadres reporting to the party problems in their history or thought that they had never told anyone else before.

Study of Party History Broadens
to Include Party Rectification

Marxism-Leninism is the theory of Marx, Engels, Lenin, and Stalin created on the basis of actual facts, and it consists of general conclusions derived from historical and revolutionary experiences. If we only read this theory, but have not used it as a basis to study historical reality and revolutionary reality, have not created our own and specific theory in accordance with China's practical needs, then it would be irresponsible to call ourselves Marxist theorists.

—Mao Zedong, 1 February 1942,
Rectification of Study, Party Style, and the Style of Writing.

Mao Zedong's new view of party history was not immediately accepted by senior cadres. The knowledge for some of what had happened in Soviet Russia to those who were defined out of a positive role in history must have caused them concern that the rewriting of party history might lead to a witch hunt. Such opposition may have contributed to Mao's decision to widen the campaign to look at faulty work style as a whole.

Party history was not entirely forgotten as a subject in the small groups, and on 30 March 1942, Mao delivered an important report to the Central Study Group in Yan'an on how it should be studied.[88] Mao made it clear that study of party history and line was crucial to an understanding of the present. He proposed dividing party history into three periods, although he made it clear that this was his own view and did not amount to a CC decision. The first period went up to 1927 and was distinguished by opposition to the "Northern Warlords," the second period was marked by opposition to the GMD, while the third was hallmarked by opposition to the Japanese and Wang Jingwei. His brief comments on these periods echoed the decisions of the September 1941 Politburo meeting. Chen Duxiu had been guilty of right opportunism in the latter phase of the first United Front and the period between 18 September 1931 and the Zunyi Conference had been marked by "leftism." When alliance was necessary, the CCP had continued to put struggle first. In his comments, Mao linked the study of party history to the themes of the newly launched Rectification campaign. The study was to have China at its core, which, according to Mao, would avoid the problems of subjectivism, sectarianism, and formalism. In Mao's words the "backside had to be attached to China's body."

The signal for widening the movement to rectification of work style within the party as a whole was given in two speeches by Mao on 1 and 8 February 1942 to the Central Party School in Yan'an.[89] These two speeches identified three mistaken tendencies within the party; subjectivism, sectarianism, and formalism. Mao's comments were critical of two groups in Yan'an. First, the intellectuals who had recently come to Yan'an and lacked practical revolutionary experience and, second, and initially more important, Wang Ming and the Returned Students. This movement combined Mao Zedong's attempts to present himself as the revolution's foremost source of theoretical wisdom with a drive to end the intellectual diversity in Yan'an by proposing obedience to a new orthodoxy. The party under Mao would provide the direction for the revolution, and the role of its intellectuals would not be to examine it critically but to proselytize it faithfully.

On 1 February, Mao asserted that recently the party's general line had been correct but that problems remained because "progress" on the theoretical front had been "extremely inadequate." Mao saw subjectivism as the core of the problems, and he defined two types: dogmatism and empiricism, dogmatism being worse. Mao clearly did not wish to be accused of rejecting theory, and he acknowledged that one's "immediate perception" was limited and thus only through theoretical study could experiences be raised to "the level of reason and synthesis, the level of theory."

This line of attack was clearly directed against Wang Ming and his supporters. In the same talk, Mao claimed that it would be irresponsible to call oneself a Marxist if one had only studied the Marxist classics and had not used them as the basis for understanding China's specific conditions and to "create our own specific theory in accordance with China's practical needs." China needed the kind of theorist who could apply the standpoints, concepts, and methods of Marxism-Leninism to China's actual problems. "The arrow of Marxism-Leninism," to use Mao's classic phrase, "must be used to hit the target of the Chinese revolution."

In the second part of the talk, Mao turned to the problem of sectarianism. He criticized those party members who put their own particular interests above the party's. Subjugation of one's own interests to those of the party would ensure unity of action and help the party achieve its "fighting objectives." This view led Mao to argue that while the party needed democracy, it needed centralism even more urgently. For Mao, the spirit of unity was necessary for "the people of the entire nation." Only if this were achieved would it be possible to defeat the enemy.

Finally, Mao put forward the principles to be observed when attacking erroneous tendencies. Criticism of the past was to serve as a warning for future actions. Mao likened the process to a doctor curing a disease: The objective was not to kill the patient but to cure the symptoms so that the diseased party member would be able to become a good comrade once again. This would have helped reassure senior cadres who were wary of the adverse consequences of rewriting party history.

In his talk on 8 February, Mao took up the issue of party formalism in a clear attack on Wang Ming and the Returned Students. According to Mao, those guilty of subjectivism and sectarianism used party formalism as their propaganda tool and form of expression. The three incorrect tendencies within the party Mao traced to a petty bourgeois mentality that had penetrated the party from society at large. In his attack on party formalism, Mao highlighted the problem of "foreign formalism." He claimed that although the eradication of "foreign formalism" and "dogmatism" were called for at the sixth plenum of the Sixth CC, "some comrades" were still advocating them.

The identification of non-acceptance of Mao Zedong's viewpoint with incorrect thought made it easier for him to gain acceptance of his and his supporters' view of party history once this topic was returned to in the summary phase of the campaign. Further, the treatment of Wang Shiwei and the "rescue" campaign pursued in 1943 under Kang Sheng's direction must have made it clear that those who did not accept the new orthodoxy could suffer penalties.

The Final Phase of the Creation of
a Maoist Party History

> The history of the CCP should be the history of the development of Marxism-Leninism in China; it should also be the history of the struggle of Marxist-Leninists with all groups of opportunists. Objectively, this history has developed with Comrade Mao Zedong as its center.
>
> —Liu Shaoqi, 1 July 1943

During the critical years while preparing and launching rectification, Mao received strong institutional support from the Northwest Bureau of the CCP and personal support from its key figure, Gao Gang. Mao had already spoken favorably of Gao Gang's knowledge of local conditions when he launched the Rectification movement.[90] From 19 October 1942 to 14 January 1943, the bureau convened an important meeting for some 267 leading cadres from various organizations. The ground had been well prepared, and as Gao Gang's summary report showed, the conference made decisions that reinforced Mao's view of party history, exerted his supremacy over Wang Ming, and supported his view of economic and administrative affairs. The meeting consciously adopted the method of discussing and "clarifying" party history as a way of correcting current problems in work, and Gao's report paved the way for the construction of a "correct" party history for the party as a whole.[91] At its conclusion, *Liberation Daily* devoted its front page to praise of the meeting and highlighted that it had resolved the question of party history in the border region.[92] During the meeting some seventy people summed up past practice using the method of "criticism and self-criticism." This historical review was completed in the second month, and in the third month time was devoted to the issues of current policy and its direction. In fact, the meeting was addressed by nearly all the CCP's top leaders except Wang Ming and his supporters.

On 11 November, Xi Zhongxun and Ma Wenrui spoke on party history and outlined the questions that had to be clarified in Shaan-Gan-Ning's history and again stressed the importance of understanding past history.[93] Gao Gang in his speech of 17 and 18 November outlined the answers to these questions.[94] The conclusions drawn vindicated Mao's position over Wang Ming's, and Gao's approach served as a model for the general task of revising party history.[95] An important part of Mao's "revision" of party history was to establish that errors of political line had been committed before the Zunyi Conference, a point first made by Liu Shaoqi.

During the early and mid-1930s, Gao Gang, Liu Zhidan, the head of the local movement, and the other local party "comrades" had found themselves in a position similar to Mao's in Jiangxi. Gao and Liu had clashed with the emissaries from the party center, Guo Hongtao and Zhu Lizhi, who had tried to force on them a change in their guerrilla tactics and to submit them more tightly to party center control. This clash came to a head in the summer of 1935, when the local party and military organizations were shaken up and the local comrades excluded from top leadership positions. In the ensuing arguments, one hundred locals were purged and many were imprisoned, including Liu and Gao. When Mao and the other Long March survivors arrived, an investigation was ordered into the situation.

In his speech, Gao sought to vindicate his previous policies and to denigrate those of the representatives from the party center. The charges made by Gao were almost identical to those that Mao would level against Wang Ming and his supporters. Gao accused Guo and Zhu of committing the mistake of "left deviation" before 1935 and then "right opportunism" after the United Front policies went into effect. Gao thus forged an identification of interest between the history of the Shaan-Gan-Ning Border Region and Mao's own experiences in Jiangxi. With the Northwest Bureau as a powerful organizational base in the party, Mao could push ahead with his rectification policies.

The twenty-second anniversary of the CCP's founding provided the opportunity to launch two initiatives that would dominate the ensuing period. These were the public building up of the person of Mao Zedong and the revision of party history to show the central and correct role Mao had played in that history. These two initiatives were signaled by Liu Shaoqi in an article published on 6 July 1943.[96]

Liu attacked what he termed "false Marxists" ("Mensheviks") and praised "true Marxists" ("Bolsheviks") and called for an eradication of the influence of the first group through the provision of a "correct" Marxist-Leninist interpretation of CCP history. Liu criticized the tendency of some only to "learn the lessons of the revolutionary experience of comparatively distant foreign countries." As bad examples in the past Liu lists Chen Duxiu, Peng Shuzhi, the Chinese Trotskyites, the Li Lisan line, the "left" opportunism of the civil war period, and dogmatism. To replace this, he called for a Marxist-Leninist summary of China's own revolutionary experiences. Central to this process was Mao Zedong, whose "guidance" was to "penetrate into all working sections and departments." The future task was to "take stock of the party's historical experiences, especially of the struggle between two lines to teach our cadres and comrades." In a eulogy that placed Mao at the center of China's party history, Liu stated that all party members should "diligently study and master Comrade Mao Zedong's doctrines of the Chinese revolution and other subjects. They should arm themselves with Mao Zedong's thought and use Mao Zedong's system of thought to liquidate Menshevik thought in the party." Now that Mao had been placed center stage in CCP history, it remained to lay down exactly what the history had been.

The final phase of the movement to construct a new party history began with a Politburo meeting, or series of meetings, held from early September 1943 to October or November 1943.[97] Now there was a clearly defined focus for criticism—Wang Ming and Bo Gu. The meetings criticized Wang Ming's "right capitulationism" during the early phase of the anti-Japanese war, and as the meetings progressed the criticisms became harsher. The meetings also marked the return to study of party history for senior cadres.[98]

On 21 September 1943, Liu Shaoqi produced a detailed critique of the republished version of Wang Ming's book *The Two Lines*. Liu stated that, as far as line was concerned, there was little difference between the struggles against Li Lisan and Wang Ming and that, in many respects, Wang Ming's words were even more "leftist." Liu even accused Wang of contravening Bolshevik guidelines in his struggle against Li Lisan by employing the method of small group factionalism. In Liu's view, the fourth plenum itself was prepared, manipulated, and presided over by Wang Ming and his agents, who had pursued their own objectives while using the name of the Comintern. For Liu, the plenum was the source of a crisis within the party.[99]

On 10 October 1943, the party center decided that senior cadres should renew the study of party history and party line. Study was to begin with the period of the anti-Japanese war and would then move backward in time to reviewing the late 1920s and early 1930s. In the final phase, the anti-Japanese war period would be returned to. This was a sound tactic for Mao, as he was generally held to be successful and correct during this period. The pressures of the Rectification campaign ensured that people would also accept his view of the past as correct. The conscious intention was to create a link between a correct view of party history and current policy direction.

To support this intensified phase of study, a shorter, more sharply focused version of the two collections before and after the Sixth Party Congress was edited by the Secretariat and circulated in October 1943. It contained 137 documents covering party history from May 1922 to October 1943 and concentrated more specifically on the question of "line" as the title *The Two Lines* (Liangtiao luxian) indicates.[100] The dissemination of this collection was accompanied by writings of specific individuals summarizing the "correct" view of various phases of party history and the use of discussion forums to "unify thought."

Key figures, apart from Liu Shaoqi, began to make speeches outlining the bare bones of the "Resolution" while stressing their differences with Wang Ming and Bo Gu. Zhou Enlai primarily contributed to clarifying issues of "line" and correct policy in the 1920s, in two main speeches. In the spring of 1943, he spoke on relations between the CCP and the GMD in the period from 1924 to 1926 and on 3–4 April 1944 he delivered a major talk on the Sixth Party Congress.[101]

Zhou stressed the "opportunism" of Chen Duxiu in his account of relations with the GMD and suggested that it first allowed Chiang Kai-shek to consolidate his political and military position and later prevented the CCP from retrieving the initiative in the United Front. The identification of Mao Zedong with correct policy options was apparent in Zhou's talk. Mao Zedong was already highlighted as the "representative" in the party who realized that as a result of the May Thirtieth movement, the revolution was turning into a revolutionary peasant war. According to Zhou Enlai, over the previous six months there had been heated disputes about how to evaluate the Sixth Party Congress. Zhou's talk was intended to clarify key issues. He affirmed that the resolutions of the congress were basically correct although they contained mistakes on specific and practical questions. Again Mao is singled out for praise. Zhou contrasted the failure of the congress to recognize the importance of armed struggle, to build up the party, and to establish its own regimes with the correct development of Mao's thought on these issues. Zhou proceeded to note that the congress decisions carried more weight because Mao "had not yet become leader of the party as a whole," a fact that was the "party's misfortune." Zhou also took up the rectification criticism of dogmatism and formalism in analyzing views in the party around the time of the Sixth Party Congress. For example, he criticized as too tight the parallel drawn between China's current situation and that of Russia in 1905. Further, he stated that copying the Soviet Union's experience by stressing the establishment of soviets in the cities amounted to dogmatism.

Wang Ruofei also spoke on the period from 1924 to 1927.[102] Lu Dingyi reported on the decisions of the Zunyi Conference, while, at Zhang Wentian's suggestion, materials concerning the conference were circulated so that people could be won over by seeing the difference in views between Bo Gu and Otto Braun, and Mao Zedong, Zhang himself, and Wang Jiaxiang.[103] As noted above, Lu's report justified why the issue of political line had not been discussed explicitly at Zunyi and provided a thorough introduction to the decisions made at Zunyi. To undermine previous and later contributions by Wang Ming in developing the idea of a second United Front, Lu suggested that the meeting had also resolved the issue of the "Oppose Chiang–Anti-Japan United Front." Later in his report, Lu qualified this by noting that this issue was of secondary importance to a discussion of military line and that it had not been thoroughly discussed.[104]

The discussion forums focused on the period from 1931 to 1935. Forums were organized for all the previous base areas and for those working in the army. A meeting was called for each district and regiment. The objective of these forums was to link the general decisions being made at the center to each locality, thus enabling the cadres to move from the realms of personal experience to general acceptance of a new party history. For example, from 10 March 1944 the Seventh Red Army held a forum with the key summary speech delivered by Deng Fa on 17 March, a speech that was said to have followed Mao's methods and views.[105]

During the summary phase, it was made clear that the targets for reassessment of party history were indeed Wang Ming and Bo Gu. On 1 December 1943, the General Study Committee of the party center issued an announcement calling for the study of writings from 1935 by various Comintern leaders such as Dimitrov and Maniulsky that were bundled together under the title "On Opportunism in the United Front." This was used to support Mao by showing how such opportunism deviated from Marxism-Leninism and from Comintern strategy and policy.[106]

On 28 December 1943, the party center issued a directive on the study of Wang Ming and Bo Gu's "sectarian, opportunist mistakes of line."[107] Study was to be restricted to an optimal number of between 100 and 200 in each region under a subbureau. The precise name lists were to be decided upon by the Central Bureaus and subbureaus. Documents for study were to be taken from *The Two Lines*, although there were not to be too many. The committees of the Central Bureaus or subbureaus were to make preparations, both practical and ideological, before cadres began their study. The round of study was defined as marking the "deepest and highest of rectification" and was seen as the necessary ideological preparation for the resolutions of the Seventh Party Congress.

The same day, the Politburo issued a directive making the specific objectives of the study clear.[108] It stated that in 1941 "Bolshevization" of the party had begun with the express intention of criticizing the "left" and right opportunist sectarianism of Wang Ming and Bo Gu and other opportunists. It criticized their usurpation of power at the fourth plenum and claimed that their influence had only been overcome at the Zunyi Conference. Before the resolutions of the Seventh Party Congress were published, senior cadres in leading organs in the Central Bureaus down to the regional party committees should discuss Wang Ming's and Bo Gu's sectarian faults of "left" opportunism during the early 1930s and the heavy damage that had been caused. The directive claimed that the damage had been total in the white areas and 90 percent in the soviet areas.

It is important to note that official documents had now pushed the origins of Wang Ming's "leftism" back to the fourth plenum rather than adhering to the previously accepted date of 18 September 1931. As is noted above, as late as January 1943, even as crucial a figure as Ren Bishi was still using the latter date. How easily this new assessment was received by veteran cadres is difficult to assess. However, those veteran cadres who may have harbored doubts would have learned through rectification that it was best to keep them to themselves. For the large number of cadres who had joined the party since the beginning of the Second United Front, it was, in a sense, prehistory. Having undergone the Rectification campaign, they were probably quite willing to accept Mao Zedong's guidance on historical matters. The dissolution of the Comintern in May 1943 aided this reassessment. There was no longer an organ in Moscow that could object to such a reassessment or to which dissenting party members could address an appeal.[109]

The December directive also dealt with the "mistakes" of Wang Ming in the later period. Wang and his supporters were criticized for having used the Yangtze Bureau of the party to carry out their "antiparty" activities between December 1937 and the sixth plenum in October 1938. The directive specified the "heavy damage" caused by Wang Ming's "antiparty right opportunist line (capitulationism)" in the anti-Japanese front. Wang Ming was criticized for opposition to protracted struggle and his theory that rapid victory was possible, for his opposition to independence in the United Front and blind faith in the GMD, and for his opposition to guerrilla warfare and the promotion of mobile warfare. Further, he was accused of ruining inner-party discipline by setting up a second CC in Wuhan. This blatant reassessment of history did not figure in the "Resolution."

The name of the now disbanded Comintern was used to discredit Wang Ming. Wang and Bo were accused of opposing the Comintern's line, and cadres who were opposed to propagating the new orthodoxy were instructed to study the essays contained in "Oppose Opportunism in the United Front." According to the directive, this would show them that under Mao Zedong's leadership, the CC had pursued an entirely correct line since Zunyi. Opposition to this view was declared incorrect. Those who might still be wavering were informed of their isolation. The directive ended by stating that, except Wang Ming and Bo Gu, the leading comrades were all "unified" and had rallied around Mao Zedong as the head of the party. Instructions went out the same day, informing senior leaders of the directive and calling on them to put their energies into its study. Again, it was stressed that not too many cadres should be involved at the present time.[110]

Not surprisingly, this process of naming names was accompanied by certain key leaders' keeping their distance from Bo Gu and Wang Ming. For example, Zhou Enlai, who had been closely embroiled with Bo, was at pains during a Politburo meeting on 17 November 1943 to outline his differences with Bo at Zunyi.[111] Zhang Wentian explained how he had linked up with Mao and Wang Jiaxiang to oppose the three-member military group (Bo Gu, Otto Braun, and Zhou Enlai). Zhang noted that "contradictions" with Bo Gu had led to his gradually being squeezed out, a process that accelerated after the fifth plenum. While Zhang noted that he was quickly converted to Mao's view during the Long March, he admitted that he had not fully appreciated that the political line was incorrect.[112]

Bo Gu and Wang Ming tried to resist the tide as best they could, but it must have been clear to them that they were fighting a losing battle. At a Politburo meeting on 13 November 1943, Bo acknowledged that the military plan for the Long March had been incorrect and that it was not discussed in the Politburo. Further, he accepted that Mao Zedong had saved the party and the army at the Zunyi Conference. However, it appears that Bo did not refer explicitly to any mistake in political line.[113] While Bo was showing signs of surrender, Wang Ming, according to his own account, refused to accept the newly emerging Maoist party history.[114]

On 12 April 1944, Mao summarized the winter discussions among senior party cadres, and his comments provided the basis for the "Resolution" adopted at the seventh plenum.[115] While critical of Wang Ming and his supporters, Mao accepted that their leadership at the fourth plenum had been legally established. This seemed to counter the thrust of the December 1943 directive, offering them the assurance that they would not be punished for criminal or antiparty activities. Mao was careful not to emphasize individual responsibility for "mistakes."[116] This must have reassured those who had been criticized, in view of what had happened to Stalin's defeated enemies in the Soviet Union. Mao reaffirmed that the party had taken the correct path since the Zunyi Conference and that, at present, there were no major deviations from the party line. Mao noted that the Politburo was concerned primarily with reviewing party history before Zunyi. In fact, the "Resolution" adopted at the seventh plenum concerned only the pre-1935 period and stated that decisions on post-Zunyi history would be decided at an appropriate time.

On 26 April, Li Fuchun confirmed that assessment of the anti-Japanese war was not on the immediate agenda. Five or six months of extra study would be necessary for this because most party members had participated in the war and because there were so many documents. Whereas only one group had begun study of the documents for the anti-Japanese war period, senior cadres in the majority of study groups had finished the documents on the period 1927 to 1937.[117]

On 10 May 1944, the Secretariat organized a committee to prepare a resolution on the question of party history. It appointed Liu Shaoqi, Kang Sheng, Zhou Enlai, Zhang Wentian, Peng Zhen, Gao Gang, and Ren Bishi, who bore primary responsibility for the work of the committee.[118] On 19 May, Bo Gu was added; Hu Qiaomu also helped in the work of preparation.[119] Presumably this is the committee appointed formally at the opening session of the seventh plenum that was charged with drafting the "Resolution" and taking care of any necessary revisions.[120] The addition of Bo Gu was significant since he was one of the two key leaders singled out for criticism. Bo had already indicated that he was willing to renounce his former views, and his involvement in the drafting process would have made it extremely difficult for any other party member, apart from Wang Ming, to oppose the resolution's assessments.

Under Ren Bishi's guidance the draft was revised some fourteen times during the second half of 1944.[121] Vladimirov confirms that Ren played a major role in the drafting process and that it brought him to the verge of physical exhaustion. He notes that the "Resolution" was based on the draft report by Ren to the plenum titled "On the Political Line of the Party Between 1931 and 1935." Vladimirov suggests that this report sparked off a major debate and that although the "Resolution" was based on the report, there were significant differences between it and the final version.[122]

Addressing the Seventh Party Congress, Mao Zedong acknowledged that the draft "Resolution" had caused considerable debate and called on the new CC to look it over with care as it might "still contain flaws." Indeed, it was deliberately kept off the agenda of the Seventh Party Congress and was handled at the preceding plenum so that the congress portrayal of the meeting as one of "unity and victory" would not be upset.[123]

The precise contents of the "Resolution" adopted by the seventh plenum on 20 April 1945 remain unclear, and it appears that several key elements were changed even after its official acceptance. The Russian China scholar Shevelyoff has seen three versions of the "Resolution" and has confirmed that important changes were made.[124] The version officially published in 1953, while clearly profiling Mao as the supreme interpreter of the Chinese revolution, paid due deference to Marxism-Leninism, the Comintern, and Stalin. However, it appears that the version adopted by the plenum referred only to "Mao Zedong Thought" as the sole guiding force of the Chinese revolution.[125] Thus, there was no mention of Stalin or the Comintern. According to Shevelyoff, the text circulated on 12 August denied completely any positive role played by the Comintern, attributing all the achievements to Mao Zedong himself. Finally, according to Shevelyoff, the names Wang Ming and Bo Gu appear only in the final version published in 1953. However, they had already been cited in earlier party documents during the phase of summation, and it seems strange that this was not one of the changes in the final "Resolution" pointed out by Wang Ming himself in his memoirs. This is a question that deserves our further attention.

The "Resolution," as officially published in 1953, provided an analysis of party history until Zunyi but, unlike Mao's speech of 12 April, did not venture any opinion on affairs after that date.[126] While the "Resolution" identified three "left lines" in the period from 1927 to Zunyi, it is clear that the major focus of attack was the third "left" line said to be in operation from the fourth plenum until the Zunyi Conference. For the first time in such an official document, Wang Ming and Bo Gu were named as the "two dogmatists" leading the mistaken line.

After a historical review, the remainder of the "Resolution" is devoted to a criticism of the political, military, organizational, and ideological line of Wang and his supporters. The errors outlined are contrasted with the correct line developed by Mao Zedong. Their mistakes in political, military, and organizational lines were deemed to derive from ideological errors based on their subjectivism and formalism and in the even more pronounced form of dogmatism. Politically, they were said to have been confused about the different stages of the democratic and socialist revolution. This meant that they underestimated the role to be played by the peasantry and often proposed an attack on the whole bourgeoisie, including the petty bourgeoisie. In fact, the third "left line" was even said to put the struggle against the bourgeoisie on a par with the struggle against imperialism and feudalism. In military affairs, they were said to have rejected guerrilla warfare as the correct form of struggle in favor of positional warfare. In general, the "left" lines were said to have created a sectarianism that alienated the masses inside and outside the party.

The "Resolution" thus demonstrated the correctness of Mao's principles and line over those of his opponents throughout the crucial years of the early 1930s.

It also cemented the alliance between Mao and Liu Shaoqi.[127] While Mao was praised generally and specifically for his line developed in the base areas, Liu Shaoqi's line was hailed as the model for work in the white areas, marking the vindication of Liu's criticisms of eight years earlier.

In the interests of unity, both Wang Ming and Bo Gu had to agree to the contents of the "Resolution" before its formal adoption. While Bo's support was readily forthcoming, Wang's was ambivalent, to say the least. Bo had joined the drafting committee and was thus bound to its findings. Bo's speech to the Seventh Party Congress amounted to a self-criticism, although, perhaps in a small act of defiance at the beginning of his speech, Bo referred to the "third left line" as running from 18 September 1931 to the Zunyi Conference. However, later in his speech, Bo referred to the tendencies of dogmatism and sectarianism as having come together around the time of the fourth plenum. He highlighted policy in the white areas as being opposed to Liu Shaoqi's correct line and the campaign against Luo Ming as having been directed against Mao's correct policy in the soviet areas. As for himself, he claimed that he did not realize his faults as far as political line was concerned at Zunyi and persisted in the mistaken line until the end of the year.[128]

Gaining Wang Ming's positive approval was more difficult. He had not participated in discussions because of illness but on three occasions was sent drafts for his perusal. In addition, members of the Presidium discussed the issue of his "mistakes" with him.[129] Finally, Wang Ming wrote a letter to the plenum accepting the "Resolution," stating that he recognized his errors, that he was responsible for the policies of the "left" line, and that he accepted the criticism that his work *The Two Lines* contained "leftist" errors.[130] This acceptance was important to show Mao's total triumph and to let other party members see that there was indeed unity within the party. This unity was based entirely on the terms set by Mao Zedong and his supporters. Wang Ming's reward was Mao's support to ensure that he be elected together with Bo Gu to the CC of the Seventh Party Congress.

Concluding Comments

This chapter has argued that the construction of a Maoist party history was a crucial element of the Rectification campaign in Yan'an. The elaboration of a party history, with Mao at its core, formed a key component in the creation of his legitimacy to rule the party. The history itself did not originate with Mao, but he saw the value of it once he set out to create a new orthodoxy in Yan'an. The writing of the "Resolution" was a political process that was designed to undercut the position of any potential rivals and that cemented the alliance between Mao Zedong, Liu Shaoqi, Ren Bishi, and Gao Gang. Unlike the *Short Course*, the Maoist history did not cover the entire period of the party's history and it did not place Mao at the center of every event in the party's history. Presumably too many party members were still around who had participated in the events themselves to make this feasible. It was sufficient that Wang Ming and Bo Gu publicly accepted the decisions of the "Resolution." This prevented the necessity of a witch hunt in the party. The promotion of the new party history contained elements that were to become a set feature of later Maoist campaigns, wherein intense study was followed by a phase of summation, during which each individual's attitude and behavior is evaluated.

Rectification and the writing of the party's official leadership provided the basis for the creation of a stable and unified leadership, something that was essential for a vanguard Leninist party. This unity was no longer based on an abstract theory but on one that Mao felt suited Chinese realities and that could provide party cadres with a guide to action. Mao's central role as the correct interpreter of the past ensured that the party would accept him as the person most qualified to outline policy for the future.

Notes

This chapter was first delivered as a paper to the conference "Policy and Popularization in China" held in Leiden between 8 and 12 July 1990. The conference was sponsored by the Sinological Institute, Leiden, and National Taiwan University. I would like to thank Frederick Teiwes for his perceptive comments on an earlier draft. In addition, I would like to thank Timothy Cheek, Michael Hunt, and Hans van de Ven for their comments on an earlier draft.

1. For the first analysis and translation of key documents studied in the campaign, see Boyd Compton, *Mao's China: Party Reform Documents, 1942–44* (Seattle: University of Washington Press, 1952).

2. The Yan'an Rectification Campaign Writing Group, ed., *Yan'an zhengfeng yundong jishi* (Chronology of the Yan'an Rectification Campaign) (Zhangjiakou: Seek Truth Press, 1982), 432.

3. "Zhongguo gongchandang zhongyang weiyuanhui guanyu ruogan lishi wenti de jueyi," in The Secretariat of the CCP CC, ed., *Liuda yilai: Dangnei mimi wenjian* (Since the Sixth Party Congress: Secret Internal Party Documents) (Beijing: People's Press, 1952), 1: 1179–1200.

4. Wang Zhongqing, "Yan'an zhengfeng yundong de fazhan guocheng" (The Process of the Development of the Yan'an Rectification Campaign), in Jian Zhong, ed., *Yan'an zhengfeng he Zhongguo gongchandang* (The Yan'an Rectification Campaign and the CCP) (Gansu: Gansu People's Press, 1982), 102.

5. The worst example of this inner-party fighting was the Futian incident of 1930 and the subsequent violent movement to "suppress counterrevolutionaries" within the CCP. For an excellent account of this affair see Chapter 4 in this volume.

6. On this point see Chapter 1 in this volume.

7. For a critique of this phenomenon and the "leftism" it caused within the party see Liu Shaoqi, "Guanyu guoqu baiqu gongzuo gei zhongyang de yifengxin" (A Letter to the Party Center Concerning Past Work in the White Areas), 4 March 1937, in The Secretariat of the CCP CC, ed., *Liuda yilai*, 1: 803–12.

8. Wang Jiaxiang relayed this information to a Politburo meeting held on 14 September. After receiving this news Mao decided to convene the sixth plenum of the Sixth CC (September–November 1938). See "Gongchan guoji zhixing weiyuanhui zhuxituan de

jueding" (Decision of the Presidium of the ECCI), September 1938, in The Central Committee Archives, ed., *Zhonggong zhongyang wenjian xuanji* (Selected Documents of the CC of the CCP) (Beijing: Central Party School Press, 1985), 10: 574–75. See also Zhao Shenghui, *Zhongguo gongchandang zuzhishi gangyao* (An Outline Organizational History of the CCP) (Anhui: Anhui People's Publishing House, 1987), 145.

9. Stuart R. Schram, *The Political Thought of Mao Tse-Tung* (Cambridge: Cambridge University Press, 1989), 62.

10. This pamphlet of Wang Ming's was originally published in February 1931 and was reprinted in Moscow in 1932 under the same title. During the campaign to study party history, Wang Ming republished his pamphlet in Yan'an (March 1940) under the title *Wei Zhonggong gengjia buersaiweikehua er douzheng* (The Struggle for the Further Bolshevization of the CCP). The full text can be found in Hsiao Tso-liang, *Power Relations Within the Chinese Communist Movement, 1930–34. The Chinese Documents* (Seattle: University of Washington Press, 1967), 2: 499–609.

11. On this point see Raymond F. Wylie, *The Emergence of Maoism: Mao Tse-tung, Ch'en Po-ta, and the Search for Chinese Theory 1935–1945* (Stanford: Stanford University Press, 1980), 226–27.

12. Schram, *Political Thought*, 62.

13. This could be interpreted as being in line with Comintern policy. The Comintern had decided at its Seventh Congress in 1935 to loosen its direct control over national parties. It called for problems to be settled on the basis of the concrete conditions and situation in the individual countries.

14. Mao Zedong, "The Role of the Chinese Communist Party in the National War," in *Selected Works of Mao Tse-tung* (Beijing: Foreign Languages Press, 1965), 2: 259–60.

15. John K. Fairbank, *The Great Chinese Revolution 1880–1985* (New York: Harper & Row, 1986), 226.

16. See E. G. Pulleyblank and W. G. Beasley, Introduction to Beasley and Pulleyblank, ed., *Historians of China and Japan* (London: Oxford University Press, 1961), 2. For the origins of this form of moralistic historiography, see P. van der Loon, "The Ancient Chinese Chronicles and the Growth of Historical Ideals," in ibid., 24–30.

17. W. Franke, "Historical Writing During the Ming," in Frederick W. Mote and Dennis Twitchett, ed., *Cambridge History of China*, Vol. 17, part 1, *The Ming Dynasty 1368–1644* (Cambridge: Cambridge University Press, 1988), 743–44.

18. For the concept of symbolic capital, see Pierre Bourdieu, *Outline of a Theory of Practice* (Cambridge: Cambridge University Press, 1977), and Pierre Bourdieu, *In Other Words: Essays Towards a Reflective Sociology* (Cambridge: Polity Press, 1990), 123–39 and *passim*. For its application to Mao Zedong and Yan'an, see Chapter 8 in this volume.

19. The talks are translated in Bonnie S. MacDougall, *Mao Zedong's "Talks at the Yan'an Conference on Literature and Art": A Translation of the 1943 Text with Commentary*, Michigan Papers in Chinese Studies No. 39 (Ann Arbor: Center for Chinese Studies, 1980). Mao delivered these talks on 2 and 23 May 1942. For an account of Wang Shiwei's view and the party's attack on him see Timothy C. Cheek, "The Fading of 'Wild Lilies': Wang Shiwei and Mao Zedong's *Yan'an Talks* in the First CPC Rectification Movement," *Australian Journal of Chinese Affairs*, no. 11 (1984): 25–58.

20. For the argument that moves further to assert that "terror" was a necessary component of rectification in Yan'an, see Peter J. Seybolt, "Terror and Conformity, Counterespionage Campaigns, Rectification, and Mass Movements, 1942–1943," *Modern China*, 12, no. 1 (1986): 39–73.

21. This was in a report by Kang Sheng delivered on 29 March 1944 at a senior cadres' conference in the Northwest Bureau. It is extracted in Warren Kuo, *Analytical*

History of the Chinese Communist Party (Taibei: Institute of International Relations, 1971), 4: 421.

22. Wang Ming claims that when he asked Chen Yun, one of the main participants at Zunyi, why he had not mentioned the meeting at the time, Chen replied, "[i]t was neither a party congress nor a CC plenum—only one of many meetings of the Politburo, nothing more. What special need was there to write about it?" Wang Ming, *Mao's Betrayal* (Moscow: Progress Publishers, 1975), 30. Indeed, in the Comintern's journal in early 1936, Chen Yun was still praising the fourth plenum. See *The Communist International*, nos. 1 and 2 (1936).

23. Wang Ming, *Mao's Betrayal*, 61.

24. The "Returned Students group" (or "Twenty-eight Bolsheviks") refers to those who had come back to China from studies in Soviet Russia. Western and Chinese writing has presumed that they formed a group under the leadership of Wang Ming, Bo Gu, and Zhang Wentian. In reality, the group was very loosely organized and it fragmented after its members returned to China.

25. This letter is often referred to as the letter of 16 November 1930 because of the date of its arrival in China. It is reprinted in the Translation Group of the Institute of Modern History of the Chinese Academy of Social Sciences, ed., *Gongchan guoji youguan Zhongguo geming de wenxian ziliao* (Documentary Materials Concerning the Comintern and the Chinese Revolution) (Beijing: Chinese Academy of Social Sciences Press, 1982), 103–12.

26. Based on the translation in *Selected Works of Mao Tse-tung*, 4:180–81. As the Taiwan historian Warren Kuo has pointed out, the Maoist critique bore resemblances to that of Luo Zhanglong that was advanced at the time of the fourth plenum. Luo and his supporters concluded that the new leadership appointed at the plenum continued Li Lisan's policies. In particular, Luo criticized Wang Ming not only for his inexperience but also for making "Lisan-type mistakes." See "Lizheng zhaokai jinji huiyi fandui sizhong quanhui baogao dagang" (Program for an Emergency Session to Oppose the Report of the Fourth Plenum), January 1931, in the Central Committee Archives, ed., *Zhonggong zhongyang wenjian xuanji (neibu ben)* (Selected Documents of the CCP CC [internal volume]) (Beijing: Central Party School Press), 7: 51–61, translated in Tony Saich, *The Rise to Power of the Chinese Communist Party: Documents and Analysis, 1920–1949* (Armonk, NY: M.E. Sharpe, forthcoming). In the resolution expelling Luo from the party, the simple defense used was that as the fourth plenum had been convened by the Comintern, anyone who opposed its decisions was anti-Comintern and antiparty. Certainly, until the Comintern was dissolved in 1943, the legitimacy and correctness of the fourth plenum was not openly questioned.

27. This contradicts the standard view that Wang Ming's rise was detrimental to Mao Zedong. For this view see Hsiao Tso-liang, *Power Relations Within the Chinese Communist Movement, 1930–34* (Seattle: University of Washington Press, 1961); John E. Rue, *Mao Tse-tung in Opposition, 1927–1935* (Stanford: Stanford University Press, 1966); and Benjamin I. Schwartz, *Chinese Communism and the Rise of Mao* (Cambridge: Harvard University Press, rev. ed., 1979).

28. See Wang Jianying, *Zhongguo gongchandang zuzhishi ziliao huibian* (Collected Materials on the Organizational History of the CCP) (Beijing: Red Flag Press, 1983), 190. I am grateful to Benjamin Yang for pointing this out to me.

29. For a discussion of this and other differences of interpretation with the 1945 "Resolution" see Hsiao, *Power Relations Within the Communist Movement*, 271–72.

30. "Zhonghua suweiai gongheguo zhongyang zhixing weiyuanhui yu renmin weiyuanhui dui erci quanguo suweiai daibiao dahui de baogao" (Report of the CEC and the Council of People's Commissars of the Chinese Soviet Republic to the Second All-China Soviet Congress), in Hsiao, 2: 702–27.

31. Edgar Snow, *Red Star Over China* (London: Victor Gollancz, 1973; originally published by Random House Inc., 1938), 177.

32. Agnes Smedley, *The Great Road: The Life and Times of Chu Teh* (New York: Monthly Review Press, 1956), 294.

33. Mao Zedong, " 'Gongchandangren' fakanci" (Introduction to "The Communist"), 4 October 1939, in *Gongchandang ren* (The Communist), no. 1 (October 1939). On this point see William F. Dorril, "Transfer of Legitimacy in the Chinese Communist Party: Origins of the Maoist Myth," *China Quarterly*, no. 36 (1968): 55. On the fourth plenum see 52–56.

34. For example, in January 1943, Ren Bishi was still referring to the political line as having been wrong from 18 September until Zunyi while inferring that the leadership inaugurated at the fourth plenum was valid. Quoted in Warren Kuo, *Analytical History*, 4: 690–91.

35. For a reassessment of Wang's views in the early 1930s, see Kristina A. Schultz, "Wang Ming's Vision: 1930–1935" (master's thesis, Harvard University, 1989)

36. See the two articles, Wan[g] Ming, "The New Situation and the New Tactics in Soviet China," *The International Press Correspondence*, 14, no. 62 (8 December 1934), and "The Struggle of the Chinese Red Army Against Chiang Kai-shek's Sixth Drive," *The Communist International*, 12, no. 1 (5 January 1935).

37. The Party Historical Materials and Research Department of the Central Party Archives, "Yan'an zhengfeng zhong de Wang Ming" (Wang Ming During the Yan'an Rectification), in *Dangshi tongxun* (Bulletin on Party History), no. 7 (1987): 6.

38. For the fullest recent account of Zunyi, see Benjamin Yang, "The Zunyi Conference as One Step in Mao's Rise to Power: A Survey of Historical Studies of the Chinese Communist Party," *China Quarterly*, no. 106 (1986): 236–39. Mao Zedong did not, as Wilson suggests, criticize the political as well as military line at Zunyi. Dick Wilson, *The Long March* (Harmondsworth: Penguin Books, 1977), 135. According to Warren Kuo's sources, Liu Shaoqi had proposed a thorough review of policy at Zunyi and had criticized "left adventurism" in the white areas since the fourth plenum. This was rebuffed by Chen Yun and Bo Gu. Warren Kuo, *Analytical History*, 3: 17–19 and 42. While this was the thrust of Liu Shaoqi's later critique, recently available materials give no support to this view, and none of the memoirs refer to such an attack. See The Committee for the Collection of Materials on Party History and the Central Committee Archives, ed., *Zunyi huiyi wenxian* (Documents on the Zunyi Conference) (Beijing: People's Publishing Press, 1985); *Zunyi huiyide guangming* (The Bright Rays of the Zunyi Conference) (Beijing: Liberation Army Press, 1984); and the Memorial Hall of the Zunyi Conference, ed., *Zhang Wentian yu Zunyi huiyi* (Zhang Wentian and the Zunyi Conference) (Beijing: Materials on CCP History Press, 1990).

39. "The Outline Resolution of the Enlarged Politburo Meeting on Summing up Experiences and Lessons in Smashing the Fifth 'Encirclement' Campaign," in Yang, "Zunyi Conference," 262–65.

40. This was in his account of the meeting drafted to inform the lower rank party cadres and army officers. Chen Yun, "Notes for Communicating the Enlarged Politburo Conference at Zunyi," February–March 1935, in Yang, ibid., 267.

41. Lu Dingyi, "Guanyu Zunyi huiyi de baogao" (Report on the Decision of the Zunyi Conference), 1944, in *Wenxian he yanjiu* (Documents and Research), 1985, 240 and 249. In his memoirs published some fifty years later, Li Weihan followed the same line of reasoning. He stressed that to have raised the question of political line at Zunyi would have undermined unity. According to Li, many CC and military leading cadres had not yet realized the errors of Wang's ways and that raising the issue could have led to much unnecessary argumentation. As a result, Mao and others did not raise the issue and they

decided that it could be left until later. However, as has been indicated, there is no evidence to suggest that Mao Zedong had already decided that Wang Ming's "line" was incorrect. Li Weihan, *Huiyi yu yanjiu* (Reminiscences and Research) (Beijing: CCP Party History Materials Press, 1986), 1: 355.

42. These comments are based on Benjamin Yang, "Complexity and Reasonability: Reassessment of the Li Lisan Adventure," *Australian Journal of Chinese Affairs*, no. 21 (January 1989): 133–38.

43. It should be pointed out that it was Wang Ming who was crucial in formulating the shift in CCP policy via a "United Front from below" to cooperation with the GMD.

44. Liu Shaoqi, "Guanyu guoqu baiqu gongzuo gei zhongyang de yifengxin" (A Letter to the Party Center Concerning Past Work in the White Areas), in the Secretariat of the CCP CC, ed., *Liuda yilai*, 1: 803–12; an English translation can be found in Saich, *The Rise to Power of the Chinese Communist Party*.

45. Zhang Wentian, "Zhongguo gongchandang suqu daibiao huiyi renwu (tigang)" (Tasks of the Meeting of Delegates from the CCP Soviet Areas [Draft]), 2 May 1937, in The Central Committee Archives, ed., *Zhonggong zhongyang wenjian xuanji*, 10: 201–5.

46. Luo Fu (Zhang Wentian), "Shinian lai de Zhongguo gongchandang" (The CCP During the Last Ten Years), 20 June 1937, in Luo Fu, *Shinian lai de Zhongguo gongchandang* (n.p., n.d.), 1–21.

47. Helen Foster Snow (Nym Wales), *Inside Red China* (New York: Da Capa Press, 1979), 220 and 227–41. Originally published by Doubleday and Company in 1939.

48. For part of Zhang Wentian's speech see "Baiqu dang muqian de zhongxin renwu" (The Central Task of the Party in the White Areas), 6 June 1935, in The Secretariat of the CCP CC, ed., *Liuda yilai*, 2: 126–44.

49. The whole of Liu Shaoqi's speech "Guanyu baiqu de dang yu qunzhong gongzuo" (Concerning Party and Mass Work in the White Areas), May 1937, can be found in The Secretariat of the CCP CC,, ed., *Liuda yilai*, 2: 107–25. Four of the eleven parts of the speech are translated in *Selected Works of Liu Shaoqi*, 1: 65–81.

50. Wang Ming later claimed that in 1948, Mao Zedong had said to him that the mistakes of the fourth plenum were Liu's invention rather than his own. Wang Ming, *Mao's Betrayal*, 71.

51. Chen Boda in *Jiefang* (Liberation), nos. 43–44 (1 July 1938). See Wylie, *Emergence of Maoism*, 73–75.

52. Mao Zedong, "The Role of the Chinese Communist Party in the National War," 259.

53. Ibid., 256.

54. Liu Shaoqi, "Lun gongkai gongzuo yu mimi gongzuo" (On Overt and Covert Work), in The Secretariat of the CCP CC, ed., *Liuda yilai*, 2: 215–27.

55. Mao Zedong, "On Policy," 25 December 1940, *Selected Works*, 2: 441–42.

56. The Yan'an Rectification Writing Group, ed., *Yan'an zhengfeng yundong jishi*, 28.

57. Mao Zedong, "Reform Our Study," in Compton, *Mao's China*, 59–68. Wylie has provided an interesting analysis of this speech on which this draws. Wylie, *Emergence of Maoism*, 151–54.

58. "Jinian Zhongguo gongchandang ershinian zhounian" (Commemorate the Twentieth Anniversary of the CCP), *Jiefang ribao* (Liberation Daily), 1 July 1941.

59. The Yan'an Rectification Campaign Writing Group, *Yan'an zhengfeng yundong jishi*, 41; and The Teaching and Research Department of the Central Party School, *Zhongguo gongchandang shigao* (A Draft History of the CCP) (Beijing: People's Press, 1983), 3: 145. The meeting or series of meetings lasted until 22 October 1941.

60. Mao Zedong, "Fandui zhuguan zhuyi he zongpai zhuyi" (Oppose Subjectivism and Sectarianism), in *Wenxian he yanjiu*, 1985, 1–7.

61. Wang Jiaxiang, "Zhengzhiju yao yi sixiang lingdao wei zhongxin" (The Politburo Must Take Ideological Leadership as Its Core), in *Wang Jiaxiang xuanji* (Selected Works of Wang Jiaxiang) (Beijing: People's Press, 1989), 326.

62. See the telegram of 21 February 1942 from Mao Zedong and Wang Jiaxiang to Zhou Enlai in *Wenxian he yanjiu*, 1984, 19. See also Zhang Jingru et al., *Zhonggong dangshi xueshi* (Historiography of CCP Party History) (Beijing: Chinese People's University Press, 1990), 67, and Zhao Shenghui, *Zhongguo gongchandang zuzhishi gangyao*, 171–72, and The Yan'an Rectification Campaign Writing Group, ed., *Yan'an zhengfeng yundong jishi*, 41.

63. The Party Historical Materials and Research Department of the Central Party Archives, "Yan'an zhengfeng zhong de Wang Ming," 7.

64. Wang even claimed that he had opposed Bo Gu's mistakes while he was still in the Soviet Union. This was in his comments to the meeting of 12 September. Zhou Guoquan et al., *Wang Ming pingzhuan* (A Critical Biography of Wang Ming) (Hefei: Anhui People's Press, 1989), 385–86 and 391.

65. Mao Zedong, "Reform Our Studies," in Compton, *Mao's China*, 68.

66. Zhang Jingru et al., *Zhonggong dangshi xueshi*, 63–64.

67. The Comprehensive Research Group of the Document Research Department of the CCP CC, ed., *Ren Bishi yanjiu wenji* (Selected Studies on Ren Bishi) (Beijing: CCP Party History Materials Press, 1989), 184. In May 1938, Ren had gone to Moscow to report on the progress of the CCP's United Front policy. In so doing, he is credited by CCP historians with undermining Wang Ming's influence in Moscow.

68. See telegram from Wang Jiaxiang and Mao Zedong to Zhou Enlai and Dong Biwu, 17 November 1941, *Wenxian he yanjiu*, 1984, 107.

69. Zhang Jingru et al., *Zhonggong dangshi xueshi*, 68.

70. Both were published under the imprimatur of the Secretariat of the CCP CC. *Liuda yiqian: Dang de lishi cailiao* (Before the Sixth Party Congress: Materials for Party History) and *Liuda yilai: Dangnei mimi wenjian*.

71. Zhao Pu, " 'Liuda yilai' he 'Liuda yiqian' liangshu jianjie" (A Short Introduction to the Two Books "Since the Sixth Party Congress" and "Before the Sixth Party Congress"), *Dangshi yanjiu* (Research on Party History), no. 1 (1987): 7.

72. Pang Xianzhi, "Guanyu dang de wenxian bianji gongzuo de jige wenti" (On Several Problems in the Editing of Party Documents), *Wenxian he yanjiu*, no. 3 (1986).

73. Mao Zedong, "Ruhe yanjiu Zhonggong dangshi" (How to Study CCP History), 30 March 1942, *Dangshi ziliao zhengji tongxun* (Bulletin on the Collection of Materials on Party History), no. 1 (1985): 1.

74. Zhao Pu, "Liuda yilai," 7.

75. Mao Zedong, "Ruhe yanjiu Zhonggong dangshi," 4–5.

76. The Yan'an Rectification Campaign Writing Group, ed., *Yan'an zhengfeng yundong jishi*, 10.

77. Ibid., 12.

78. "Zhonggong zhongyang ganbu jiaoyubu zhaokai xuexi dangyuan dahui" (The Cadre Education Department of the CCP CC Convenes a Meeting for Party Members), *Xin Zhonghua bao* (New China News), 26 May 1939.

79. Thus, on 2 June 1939, it was announced that the study movement in the Shaan-Gan-Ning Border Region government had already begun the study of party history (*Xin Zhonghua bao*). On 6 June the Chinese People's Anti-Japanese Military and Political University began study of the *Short Course* (The Yan'an Rectification Campaign Writing Group, *Yan'an zhengfeng yundong jishi*, 16).

80. Zhang Jingru et al., *Zhonggong dangshi xueshi*, 64–65.

81. "Zhongyang guanyu gaoji xuexizu de jueding," in The Central Committee Archives, ed., *Zhonggong zhongyang wenjian xuanji*, 11: 743.

82. Mao Zedong and Wang Jiaxiang telegram to Zhou Enlai, 21 February 1942.

83. Zhang Jingru et al., *Zhonggong dangshi xueshi*, 67. The draft was titled "Guanyu sizhong quanhui yilai zhongyang lingdao luxian wenti jielun cao'an" (A Draft Summary of Problems in the CC's Leadership Line Since the Fourth Plenum). A copy is held by the Central Committee Archives in Beijing.

84. The Yan'an Rectification Campaign Writing Group, ed., *Yan'an zhengfeng yundong jishi*, 102.

85. Ibid., 232–34.

86. Ibid., 193. This was decided by the party committee on 11 June 1942.

87. *Jiefang ribao*, 12 May 1943.

88. Mao Zedong, "Ruhe yanjiu Zhonggong dangshi," 1–8.

89. Mao Zedong, "Zhengdun xuefeng dangfeng wenfeng" (Rectification of Study, Party Style and the Style of Writing), 1 February 1942, *Zhengfeng wenxian* (Harbin: Liberation Society, 1948), 6–22, translated in Compton, *Mao's China*, 9–32, and "Fandui dang bagu" (Oppose the Party's Eight-Legged Essay [Party Formalism]), in *Zhengfeng wenxian*, 23–27, translated in Compton, ibid., 33–53.

90. See Mao Zedong's speech of 1 February 1942.

91. The Yan'an Rectification Campaign Writing Group, ed., *Yan'an zhengfeng yundong jishi*, 299.

92. *Jiefang ribao*, 31 January 1943.

93. The Yan'an Rectification Campaign Writing Group, ed., *Yan'an zhengfeng yundong jishi*, 316.

94. Gao Gang, "Bianqu de lishi wenti jiantai" (Examination of the Question of the History of the Border Region), 17 and 18 November 1942 (Yan'an: Northwest Bureau, 1943), 1–50.

95. On this point, see Wylie, *Emergence of Maoism*, 228–31.

96. Liu Shaoqi, "Qingsuan dangnei de Mengsaiweizhuyi sixiang" (Expose and Criticize Menshevik Thought in the Party), *Jiefang ribao*, 6 July 1945, translated in Compton, *Mao's China*, 255–68.

97. Chen Kang mentions September to November while Zhou Guoquan et al. refer to the meetings as taking place from early September to early October. See Chen Kang, "Kangzhan chuqi Huabei wojun zhanlüe fangzhen tantao" (An Inquiry into Our Army's Strategy and Policies in Northern China in the Early Period of the War of Resistance), in *Jindaishi yanjiu* (Research on Modern History), no. 1 (1982): 87, and Zhou Guoquan et al., *Wang Ming pingzhuan*, 410.

98. Peter Vladimirov, who was in Yan'an for the Comintern, noted that Wang Ming had been isolated politically and spiritually at the meeting. His entry for 28 October 1943 claimed that Wang had been accused of every conceivable sin, such as wallowing in opportunism and following a capitalist line: on 15 November, he noted that Wang had been named as a Trotskyite who was seeking to undermine the anti-Japanese United Front. Vladimirov noted that this criticism went hand-in-hand with a " "hasty" revision of party history. P. Vladimirov, *The Vladimirov Diaries: Yenan, China, 1942–45* (New York: Doubleday, 1975), 150, 162, and 178.

99. The Yan'an Rectification Campaign Writing Group, ed., *Yan'an zhengfeng yundong jishi*, 422–23.

100. Vladimirov noted that the choice of documents in this work was clearly devoted to the struggle between Mao and Wang. According to Vladimirov, the collection was divided into three sections: the Great Revolution, the Civil War, and the Anti-Japanese War. Vladimirov, *Vladimirov Diaries*, 180 and 182.

101. Zhou Enlai, "On the Relations Between the Chinese Communist Party and the Kuomintang from 1924 to 1926," spring 1943, in *Selected Works of Zhou Enlai* (Beijing:

Foreign Languages Press, 1981), 1: 130–43, and "On the Sixth Congress of the Party," in ibid., 177–210.

102. Wang Ruofei, "Da geming shiqi de gongchandang" (The CCP in the Period of the Great Revolution), mentioned in Zhang Jingru et al., *Zhonggong dangshi xueshi*, 70.

103. Ibid.

104. Lu Dingyi, "Guanyu Zunyi huiyi de baogao," *passim*. The report was delivered at the Yan'an Central Party School to students of the second and fourth departments.

105. The Yan'an Rectification Campaign Writing Group, ed., *Yan'an zhengfeng yundong jishi*, 445. Similar meetings were held in this phase of summation by, among others, the Xiangegan, Xiangan, and Eyuwan border regions, the Chaomei, Fujian, and Minxi districts, and the Fifth Red Army.

106. "Zhonggong zhongyang zongxuewei guanyu 'fandui tongyi zhanxianzhong de jihui' wenjian de tongzhi" (Circular of the General Study Group of the CCP CC Concerning the Study of the Document "Oppose Opportunism in the United Front"), in *Yan'an zhengfeng yundong (ziliao xuanji)* (The Yan'an Rectification Campaign [Selected Materials]) (Beijing: The Central Party School Press, 1984), 122–23.

107. "Zhonggong zhongyang shujichu guanyu yanjiu Wang Ming, Bo Gu zongpai jihui zhuyi luxian cuowu de zhishi" (Directive of the Secretariat of the CCP CC on Studying Wang Ming's and Bo Gu's Sectarian, Opportunist Mistakes of Line), 28 December 1943, in ibid., 123–24.

108. "Guanyu 'fandui tongyi zhanxianzhong de jihui zhuyi' yiwen de zhishi" (Directive Concerning the Document "Oppose Opportunism in the United Front"), 28 December 1943, in ibid., 124–26.

109. In a letter of 22 December 1943, Dimitrov did, however, complain to Mao about the criticism of Wang Ming. Yet without the organizational authority, it could easily be dismissed. Zhou Guoquan et al., *Wang Ming pingzhuan*, 414. Vladimirov, in his entry for 3 January 1944, mentions a telegram from Dimitrov in which he expressed his concern over relations with the GMD and policy toward the "Moscow group." Vladimirov, *Vladimirov Diaries*, 190.

110. See telegram from Mao Zedong on behalf of the Secretariat to, among others, Nie Rongzhen, Deng Xiaoping, Deng Zihua, and Lin Feng, 28 December 1943, *Wenxian he yanjiu*, 1984, 25–26.

111. Zhou Enlai, "Zai Yan'an zhong zhongyang zhengzhiju huiyishang de fayan (jielu)" (Speech at Yan'an Politburo Meeting [Extracts]), in *Zunyi huiyi wenxian*, 64–65.

112. Zhang Wentian, "Cong Fujian shibian dao Zunyi huiyi" (From the Fujian Incident to the Zunyi Conference), in *Zunyi huiyi wenxian*, 78–80.

113. Bo Gu, "Zai zhongyang zhengzhiju huiyishang de fayan (jielu)" (Speech at Politburo Meeting [Extracts]), 13 November 1943, in *Zunyi huiyi wenxian*, 103.

114. See Wang's account of his discussion with Mao Zedong in April 1944. Wang Ming, *Mao's Betrayal*, 61–62.

115. Mao Zedong, "Our Study and the Current Situation," 12 April 1944 in *Selected Works*, 3: 163–76. This was a speech to senior cadres in Yan'an.

116. Zhou Enlai, in his talk on the Sixth Party Congress, had criticized the practice of personal attack on a couple of key leaders and believed that their removal amounted to the resolution of the problem. See "On the Sixth Congress of the Party," 193.

117. The Yan'an Rectification Campaign Writing Group, ed., *Yan'an zhengfeng yundong jishi*, 450.

118. Wylie's suggestion that the real author was Mao's "alter ego," Chen Boda, is not borne out by the current evidence.

119. Feng Hui, "Mao Zedong lingdao qicao 'guanyu ruogan lishi wenti de jueyi' de jingguo" (The Process of Mao Zedong's Leadership in Drafting the "Resolution on Certain Questions in the History of Our Party"), *Dangshi tongxun*, March 1986.

120. The Teaching and Research Department of the Central Party School, *Zhongguo gongchandang shigao*, 3: 218.

121. The Yan'an Rectification Campaign Writing Group, ed., *Yan'an zhengfeng yundong jishi*, 455.

122. Vladimirov, *Vladimirov Diaries*, 374, 389–95.

123. Mao Zedong, " 'Qida' gongzuo fangzhen" (Policy on Work Methods for the "Seventh Party Congress"), in Takeuchi Minoru, ed., *Mao Zedongji pujuan* (Supplements to the Collected Writings of Mao Zedong) (Tokyo: Sososha, 1985), 7: 264–65. See also Vladimirov, *Vladimirov Diaries*, 385–86.

124. Shevelyoff has seen the draft of 15 April that was adopted in principle on 20 April 1945; the text approved on 9 August and issued as an inner-party document on 12 August and the version officially published in 1953. I am grateful to Dr. Shevelyoff for sharing this information with me, and I look forward to seeing his study of the differences between the texts. It was presumably during this period of redrafting that Hu Qiaomu played a major role.

125. This point was also noted by Wang Ming, *Mao's Betrayal*, 153. Wang also referred to a draft in which the term *Maoism* is used instead of the thought of Mao Zedong, ibid., 152.

126. Wylie interprets this as a definite decision of the CC to play down the Maoist interpretation of history. Wylie, *Emergence of Maoism*, 268. This might not necessarily be the case. It had already been accepted that it was more difficult to come to a decision on the complexities of the second United Front and that this decision would have to wait until later. Moreover, what was most important for Mao was the discrediting of Wang Ming and this he achieved with the denunciation of the fourth plenum. If it was accepted that Mao had pushed the "correct line" before Zunyi and that after Zunyi his "correct line" had been implemented, it was not necessary to spell out the details. Mao and his supporters might have been afraid of being deflected from their primary purpose by becoming bogged down in details.

127. Vladimirov in his entry for 21 August 1943 made the interesting observation that Liu was the direct conductor of Mao's ideas while Ren Bishi was their technical executor. For Kang Sheng, Vladimirov reserved the role of "reprisals man." Vladimirov, *Vladimirov Diaries*, 144.

128. Bo Gu, "Zai Zhongguo gongchandang diqici quanguo daibiao dahuishang de fayan (jielu)" (Speech to the Seventh Congress of the CCP), 3 May 1945, in *Zunyi huiyi wenxian*, 104–07.

129. The members of the Presidium were Mao Zedong, Zhu De, Liu Shaoqi, Ren Bishi, and Zhou Enlai. See also Wang Ming, *Mao's Betrayal*, 145.

130. Party Historical Materials and Research Department of the Central Party Archives, "Yan'an zhengfeng zhong de Wang Ming," 11. He sent the letter to Ren Bishi to pass on to Mao Zedong and participants at the plenum. For lengthy excerpts see Zhou Guoquan et al., *Wang Ming pingzhuan*, 419–23. According to Wang himself, he initially refused to write a statement acknowledging the "Resolution" and repenting his mistakes. Eventually, after discussions with friends, Wang claims that he wrote the letter so that he could preserve his position for a future struggle against Mao Zedong. Ibid., 145.

Chapter 12

From a Leninist to a Charismatic Party: The CCP's Changing Leadership, 1937–1945

Frederick C. Teiwes
with Warren Sun

By the Seventh Party Congress in 1945 Mao Zedong's position as the pre-eminent—indeed dominant—leader of the CCP had been fully consolidated. Not only was he reconfirmed as the number one figure in both party and military hierarchies, but he was also the beneficiary of a major personality cult, a "Resolution on Some Historical Questions" had declared him the consistent source of the "correct line" within the CCP since the late 1920s, and the "Thought of Mao Zedong" was enshrined in the new party constitution as an integral part of the official ideology.[1] It is less clear precisely when Mao attained such dominance; it has long been recognized that the official view of the Zunyi conference in January 1935 as marking Mao's ascent to leadership of the whole party is greatly overstated.[2] Indeed, from the latter part of 1937 and throughout most of 1938 Mao was involved in a major struggle with the Returned Student leader Wang Ming after Wang's return from the Soviet Union. This chapter elaborates on the growth of Mao's authority and power in the late 1930s and early 1940s and analyzes the key factors involved in this process.

The study is also concerned with a broader phenomenon, however. That is, it examines the formation of the entire Maoist leadership that emerged at the Seventh Congress and continued to rule the CCP with relatively few disruptions over the next twenty years.[3] It asks why various individuals were included in this leadership core and others excluded or marginalized. In particular, why did Liu Shaoqi emerge as the number two leader in the party and as Mao's accepted successor? Why was Zhou Enlai's position under threat in 1943, only to recover dramatically within a year? Why did Wang Jiaxiang, a crucial figure in Mao's rise, fade into relative obscurity at the Seventh Congress? And why did the position of Kang Sheng, who had clearly aligned himself with Mao and who held operational control of the security apparatus, decline significantly after his reelection to the Politburo after the congress? The focus on such key individuals is intended to illuminate the processes and forces involved in the creation of the new leadership.

The years in question were clearly a period of transition in CCP leadership. This transition went deeper than the change in Mao's personal status from *primus inter pares* to unchallenged leader, or that of the leadership as a whole, which was transformed from a somewhat uneasy coalition of different factions (*zongpai*) into a genuinely cohesive group—various "factional" (*shantou*) allegiances not withstanding—which adhered closely to the policies and person of Mao Zedong.[4] More broadly, this transition encompassed a shift from a leadership mode that in many respects corresponded, albeit loosely, to an orthodox Leninist organization to a decidedly more leader-oriented party. The Leninist "model" called for an institution where authority was vested in the organization itself, where the power of individual leaders was restricted by collective quasi-democratic procedures, where civilian party officials controlled the organization's coercive machinery, and (particularly significant for the CCP in the 1930s) where the national party was a subordinate branch of the world party, the Comintern, it was duty-bound to obey, and these features were in evidence for much of the period and especially between 1937 and 1941.[5] But, particularly after 1942, a more leader-oriented structure was increasingly apparent reflecting the charismatic authority acquired by Mao over the entire period, a deep cultural attachment to the "leader principle," and, ironically, the Comintern's own tradition of highly concentrated leadership.[6]

While tension arose between the institutional and personalized modes of leadership throughout pre-1949 party history, in the 1937–45 period it was blurred in the eyes of the participants in high-level party politics for reasons examined below. Moreover, as we shall see, by the end of the period the transition was far from complete: institutionalized procedures, quasi-democratic decision-making, and a circumscribed political role for the security forces were all prominent features of the new Maoist leadership structure confirmed at the Seventh Congress.

The analysis offered here is based on a wide variety of sources. Substantial documentary research has been undertaken, particularly into party history accounts, new collections of documents from the period, and participant memoirs that have appeared in the post-Mao era. In addition, important information and insights have been gained from discussions with party historians who have been candid and willing to go beyond both past orthodoxies and present taboos. Using these and other sources, we begin with an overview of the period from Wang Ming's return in late 1937 to the Seventh Congress. The on-again off-again process of steps toward the congress that began with Wang Ming's arrival, together with the major meetings advancing Mao's cause, provide one framework for this overview. A second framework is formed by the various personnel changes over this period, the question of who was going up and who down. The key events in organizational terms before the congress itself were the reorganization of the Secretariat in March 1943 and then the formation of a Presidium to take over daily party work in May 1944. In the course of this overview, some general propositions concerning the criteria for inclusion in and exclusion from the new leadership are put forward.

Towards the Seventh Congress: An Overview of Events, Late 1937–June 1945

The Zunyi conference marked a major turning point in Mao's career, but it was a turning point initially limited largely to military affairs. Mao only raised military and not political issues at the conference, only the military line of the Returned Student leadership was repudiated, and Mao's authority was established only in the military sphere.[7] Even here some ambiguity existed with Mao's being but one, albeit the most influential, member of the three-man military affairs group together with Zhou Enlai, who formally held supreme command, and Wang Jiaxiang; soon thereafter, moreover, Mao faced pressure from some long-time followers to loosen his detailed control of Red Army operations.[8] Within the party structure Mao now became a member of the Politburo Standing Committee, but the top post of party secretary in charge of overall CCP affairs went to Zhang Wentian, who continued as the CCP's chief administrative officer until the end of 1938.[9] While the relationship between Mao and Zhang, who was largely disinterested in competing for ultimate power, was basically cooperative, it was not without tension and was vague as to authority.[10] More broadly, the leadership situation within the party reflected the absence of a political consensus. Zunyi necessarily focused on military issues during the desperate days of the Long March, but in not raising political issues Mao was undoubtedly aware of this absence of consensus that particularly applied to the just-ended Jiangxi period, and he apparently chose to avoid those deeply divisive matters.[11]

Over the next three years Mao survived a challenge from Zhang Guotao and achieved enhanced stature once the Long Marchers were safely established in northern Shaanxi.[12] His voice was still only one of many, however, and the interpretation of the past remained as controversial as ever. Mao offered some tentative criticisms of the "leftist" tendencies affecting United Front tactics that had typified the "Returned Student group" at the Wayaobao conference in December 1935,[13] while Liu Shaoqi developed a more extensive and wide-ranging critique particularly in the spring and summer of 1937, but widely differing views on the earlier period remained.[14] Yet overall, Mao's position as the *de facto* leader of the CCP had gradually consolidated by the time Wang Ming arrived in Yan'an in late 1937.

Wang Ming's return from the Soviet Union together with two other party leaders, Chen Yun and Kang Sheng, changed the situation. Wang represented a challenge to Mao although, as seen below, he did not openly seek the top party ranking. Wang brought with him the high prestige of his position as the Comintern official responsible for the East, while the "leftist" policies of the Returned Students during the Jiangxi period were still seen as correct by a substantial section of the party. Ironically, moreover, in 1935–37 he was more responsible than was Mao for the evolution of the United Front policies that were so essential for the CCP's enhanced strategic position.[15] And not least, unlike Zhang Wentian, he was determined in his views and drive for power and unwilling to subordinate himself to Mao then or later.

The CCP leadership as a whole had to accommodate both Wang Ming as a Politburo member and former pre-eminent leader and the Comintern authority he implicitly represented. Very quickly Wang became the party's *de facto* number two leader. In organizational terms, Wang, together with Chen Yun and Kang Sheng, now occupied seats on a revamped Politburo selected by "the December Politburo conference" (see Table 12.4, p. 353). Even more graphic was the reorganized Party Secretariat shown in Table 12.1:[16]

Table 12.1

CCP Secretariat Changes, December 1937

Before December	After December
Zhang Wentian (secretary in overall charge)	Zhang Wentian
Mao Zedong	Mao Zedong
Zhou Enlai	Wang Ming
Wang Jiaxiang	Chen Yun
Bo Gu	Kang Sheng

Apart from the dramatic shake-up of personnel in this key operational body as a result of the inclusion of all three of the recent arrivals from Moscow,[17] change in the previous Mao-Zhang Wentian leadership arrangement and the significance of Wang Ming's new role was further indicated by a decision to carry out "collective leadership" within the Secretariat, which seemingly reduced Zhang's status.[18] The room made for the new arrivals was clear-cut in the case of Wang Jiaxiang, who had already left for Moscow to join the CCP delegation to the Comintern as well as for medical treatment. Bo Gu's stepping down to a lesser post as head of the CC's organization department is also understandable in that he, as the leading Returned Student actually in China before Zunyi, had been held responsible for the military failures of that period. In addition, Bo had opposed the criticisms of "leftist" United Front tactics at Wayaobao, a position that put him in conflict with both Mao and Wang Ming.[19] Zhou Enlai's demotion to head of the CC's committee for work in enemy areas is somewhat more difficult to understand given his contributions on the Long March and more recently during the Xi'an incident, but he too had been judged responsible for the military "errors" of the Jiangxi period at the Zunyi conference. Whatever the reason, it was a clear indication of a decline in Zhou's position as the new Returned Students—who, like their predecessors, were by no means a unified bloc—assumed critical positions in the reorganized party hierarchy.[20]

Wang Ming also brought with him the Comintern's desire for convening the Seventh Congress. This was a natural step in several senses; it had been nine years since the Sixth Congress and the CCP had clearly entered a new stage with the outbreak of the anti-Japanese war and the formation of the second United Front with the GMD. The December Politburo meeting formally decided to convene the congress and laid down the following agenda: (1) drawing a conclusion on the previous ten years of struggle and basic policy; (2) determining how to organize victory in the anti-Japanese struggle; (3) laying down policy for mobilizing the working class; (4) determining a program for party construction; and (5) electing leading party organs.[21] A twenty-five-member preparatory committee was set up with Mao as chairman but with Wang Ming as secretary and in actual charge of preparatory work.[22] Thus the Congress would deal with the contentious issue of past errors, the future course of policy at a critical juncture in CCP history, and the distribution of power. According to an authoritative interview source, while Wang understood that he could not challenge Mao as pre-eminent leader, he apparently hoped to grasp real power as general secretary in the new leadership selected at the congress while restricting Mao to an empty position as party chairman. In any case, holding a party congress at that juncture surely would have confirmed Wang in a very powerful position within the CCP.

Conflict soon manifested itself on both the policy and organizational fronts. At the December conference, Wang criticized Mao as being too "left" on the key issue of the United Front and pushed for greater cooperation with the GMD; Mao held his ground but avoided a confrontation. Some party leaders—notably Zhou Enlai—were attracted to Wang's approach, and all had to come to terms with the discordant views of the CCP's two most influential figures. Indicative of the situation was the puzzled reaction of Peng Dehuai, who did not know whom to listen to; when subsequently reporting on the meeting Peng would say only that Mao had said this and Wang had said that.[23] Organizationally, Mao resisted the push for the Seventh Congress on the grounds that the party's forces were too scattered in various base areas and the time was not yet right. Indeed, as party historians observe today, there were objective reasons for delaying the congress caused by the demands of war and difficulty of gathering delegates in Yan'an, a situation of particular significance during the heated battles of 1938. But there were also subjective reasons, as manifested in Mao's distrust of Wang at this juncture and later in his desire to "unify thought" before convening the congress. As 1938 unfolded, the policy differences between Mao and Wang also took on organizational form as Wang took charge of the party's Yangtze Bureau in Wuhan. Now two distinct sets of party leaders existed, each following its own version of the United Front. In Wuhan three Politburo members, Wang

Ming, Zhou Enlai, and Bo Gu, emphasized cooperation with the GMD to "safe-guard Wuhan" from the Japanese. In Yan'an Mao, Zhang Wentian, Chen Yun, and Kang Sheng emphasized the development of communist forces and base areas. The lack of consensus in the leadership was clearly reflected in Wang Ming's argument that neither group should claim to be the CC.[24] For Mao's part, he later looked back on the period and claimed that while the party line had been correct since the Zunyi conference, there were twists and turns "especially at the December Politburo meeting," and, rather overdramatically, that after Wang Ming's return "my authority didn't extend beyond my cave."[25]

This situation was transformed by the sixth plenum of the Sixth CC in September–November 1938. The significance of this meeting in Mao's rise has long been noted but perhaps not fully appreciated.[26] Chinese scholars today describe the plenum as marking a radical change in Mao's position. The change was based on two factors: first, the collapse of Wang's United Front approach with the GMD closing down the CCP's Wuhan operations shortly before the city fell to the Japanese while Mao's base area strategy continued to reap dividends; and, second, the Comintern's explicit endorsement of Mao's leadership as reported by Wang Jiaxiang on his return from Moscow shortly before the meeting. Moscow's endorsement was crucial. Party historians today emphasize the high prestige of the Comintern and Stalin within the CCP in the late 1930s, and in 1938 many leaders who had previously backed Wang Ming came over to Mao's side in view of this international recognition. Mao himself acknowledged this at the Seventh Congress by observing that "if it had not been for the Comintern's instruction it would have been very difficult to solve the problem [of his leader-ship]."[27] In organizational terms the concrete results of the sixth plenum included Mao's now being formally ranked first in the party Secretariat and placed in charge of its daily work, while Wang lost control of preparatory work for the Seventh Congress to the party center under Mao. Moreover, the Yangtze Bureau was disbanded, with the pieces going to the Central Plains and Southern Bureaus under Liu Shaoqi and Zhou Enlai respectively, and the plenum adopted a resolu-tion on party discipline critical, in fact if not name, of the independent tendencies of the Yangtze Bureau. Wang retained his seat on the Secretariat but was now ranked fifth and last on the body. With regard to policy, the plenum approved Mao's critique of Wang's United Front approach, and party historians now, as in the past, regard the meeting as having basically eliminated Wang's line. This, however, rather oversimplifies a complex situation wherein the Comintern and various party leaders still had a different understanding of the United Front, a situation reflected in the fact that Mao waited until Wang Ming had left the plenum before launching a systematic attack on his policies and securing CC endorsement. Finally, Mao also used the occasion to propose the "sinification of Marxism"—an emphasis on linking theory to Chinese reality that, over the next few years, would evolve into "Mao Zedong Thought"—and to raise the issue of past errors in party policy.[28]

The last two matters suggest the limits on Mao's victory. The "sinification of Marxism" did not find its way into the plenum's political resolution perhaps in deference to presumed Soviet sensibilities, while the question of past mistakes was also not dealt with thoroughly again most likely with an eye to Moscow.[29] Thus while Mao's leadership had been widely accepted,[30] significant resistance remained to some of his ideas, and Wang Ming was still an important if diminished figure within the CCP.[31] Perhaps the best way to view this situation is that his position was secure barring two possible developments—a dramatic collapse of the CCP's revolutionary gains or a withdrawal of Comintern support—but to make Mao's ideas fully accepted within the leadership and internalized as a basis for action in the party as a whole required building on the leverage provided by his new status. In this, Mao was both prudent and relentless, developing a pattern of promoting his political program at every opportunity but avoiding fracturing the carefully nurtured consensus that would mark his actions before the Seventh Congress. Although constrained by Comintern reluctance to deal with past errors, Mao was again lobbying concerning historical questions early in 1939 and in December 1940 issued a CC directive formally attacking for the first time the "ultraleftist policies" of the Jiangxi period. Here again, however, Mao revealed his prudence. In a context in which the Jiangxi policies were directly relevant as a negative example to combat current "leftist" attitudes toward the United Front resulting from growing CCP-GMD tensions, some Politburo members, notably including Liu Shaoqi, wanted to designate those policies as reflecting a mistake in line, but Mao proposed to drop the term "line" from the document in the interest of unity.[32] Meanwhile, Mao continued to push his ideas on "sinification" while theorists and other party leaders began praising Mao's theoretical contributions, and by 1941 early formulations of "Mao's Thought" had already appeared.[33]

Throughout this building momentum Mao demonstrated considerable circumspection and remarkable patience in other ways besides sidestepping the issue of line mistakes as he sought the substance of full authority rather than the form of a prematurely enhanced status. Thus in October 1938 during the sixth plenum, Zhang Wentian proposed that Mao assume the position of general secretary, but Mao declined seemingly because he realized that he was already the number one leader and without the full acceptance of his ideas such additional titles would only be nominal.[34] Similarly, when the sixth plenum resolved to convene the Seventh Congress with the process, unlike the period following the December 1937 Politburo conference, now under Mao's control, he did not rush to hold the conclave that would surely have affirmed his new status. Again a mix of "objective" and "subjective" factors was at play. Delegate selection was under way in 1939 and some delegates reached Yan'an in 1940, but many could not get through because of the worsening battlefield situation. Subsequently, further plans for a congress in 1942 were also aborted in the face of a Japanese offensive and GMD blockade, and an August 1943 decision to hold the congress by the end of the year was foiled by a new round of Japanese attacks. But while the objective consequences of the war had an undoubted impact on the delays, before 1943 the postponements clearly fit well with Mao's desire to "unify thought" behind his programs before a new party congress.[35] The key turning point in this regard was the enlarged Politburo and Secretariat conference of September–October 1941.

The September–October 1941 meeting, which began as an enlarged Politburo conference but was converted into a Secretariat meeting in early October, has been a relatively neglected event in accounts of Mao's rise. Mao himself, however, recognized the meeting as one of five key steps in the process and the next major benchmark after the sixth plenum.[36] The importance of the occasion can be seen in the developments that emerged from it: the establishment of a senior cadres study group within the center led by Mao and Wang Jiaxiang, a measure normally regarded as the beginning of the Rectification campaign; the reorganization of the Central Party School with Mao, Ren Bishi, and Peng Zhen now taking control; the establishment of a committee to "clarify past history," the start of the three and a half year process culminating in the "Resolution"; the subsequent publication of *Since the Sixth Congress*, the basic materials for the high-level cadre study of party history during rectification; the convening of a "white area work review committee" under Mao to review historical experience in underground work; and (most likely) the creation of a "cadre screening committee" under Kang Sheng.[37] Taken together, these measures represented a formidable launching pad for further organizational changes, the rewriting of party history, and, most importantly, Mao's project of "unifying thought" through rectification.

The September–October conference was more than a launching pad, however. Party history accounts claim that around the time of the conference, that is, before the Rectification campaign, a basic unanimity had *already* been achieved on key theoretical and historical issues.[38] This, as we shall see, may overstate the situation, but party historians specializing on the period claim to have no clear evidence of opposition to Mao's ideas on rectification or the emerging concept of Mao's Thought at this juncture, although the situation was somewhat different with regard to historical issues. Some resistance, of course, may be inferred from the very fact that organizational changes such as the revamped leadership of the Central Party School were deemed necessary. An interview source, moreover, reported that in the opinion of Li Weihan, the January 1942 decision of Zhang Wentian, who had made a serious self-criticism at the September–October meeting, to undertake grass-roots study was a sign of passive opposition to rectification and an attempt to avoid the process, a view hotly contested by others who were historically connected to Zhang.[39] In any case, little open opposition was expressed on the eve of the launching of rectification. But this was a situation at some variance with that four months before the September–October conference. Why?

An indication of less than total unanimity earlier in 1941 came when Mao's earliest rectification statement, his May address on "Reform Our Studies" to a senior cadre study conference, was not reprinted in the official *Liberation Daily*, a development that has led one party historian to note a "great difference" in the situation when compared to the fall conference. In attempting to explain the change from May to September, this historian pointed to the heightened awareness resulting from the senior cadre rectification study already under way by mid-1941, an awareness culminating in broad acceptance of Mao's arguments at the September–October meeting as various leaders, in a comparatively low-key atmosphere, began to relate his ideological themes to their own past performance and to engage voluntarily in self-criticism.[40] It is, of course, difficult to evaluate such a claim, yet it is important to note its similarity to the reasons offered by party historians for the success of rectification after it was formally launched in early 1942. In various discussions such historians claimed the remaining process of accepting Mao's views during the Rectification campaign, especially on historical issues, was primarily the result of persuasion. In particular, the examination of the historical evidence in the collection *Since the Sixth Party Congress*, a collection that included the positions of all party leaders during the "leftist" early 1930s, reportedly demonstrated that Mao, and Liu Shaoqi, had been far more correct in their views than were any other leaders. In this view, Mao's slogan of "seeking truth from facts" was indeed the key to "unifying thought."

Of course, as party historians admit, the story was more complicated than this. They freely acknowledge the pressure that built up in the course of rectification, pressure that is examined in greater detail below. Some note that this pressure meant people with different views did not dare to speak, although others believe that such a phenomenon, which was particularly intense during the "Rescue campaign" in 1943, largely affected low-ranking cadres while their higher-ranking comrades were generally convinced by argument. This, however, ignores the political pressure various leaders, for example, Zhou Enlai, were under, and the need to jump onto Mao's bandwagon if their careers were to prosper. For all this, the main thrust of the party historians' argument retains considerable force. Not only was there much factual basis for Mao's policy preferences, particularly in the context of the CCP's improved position under his leadership, but the whole ethos of the revolutionary movement contributed to the persuasiveness of his message. The aim of such a movement was, naturally, revolutionary success, and while ultimate victory was still distant in the early 1940s, it was at least a real possibility, which stood in sharp contrast to the failures of the Jiangxi period under the "Wang Ming line." While historical events beyond Mao's control contributed significantly to the changed situation, in a movement weaned on the notion of ideological correctness, the apparent correlation between party successes and Mao's ideas was powerful persuasion indeed. In the process, not surprisingly, the personal authority of the leader was considerably enhanced.

But to return to the September–October 1941 conference itself, everything did not go completely Mao's way. Despite significant advances, the historical issue was not totally solved to Mao's liking. In the discussions during the meeting, agreement was reached that a "leftist" mistake of political line had taken place during the early 1930s and that Wang Ming and Bo Gu were principally responsible. No consensus emerged on precisely when it began, however. In Mao's view, the erroneous line dated from the fourth plenum in January 1931, that is, from the meeting which placed Wang Ming in overall charge of the party. Wang, however, hotly contested this view and was not without support at the conference. The "draft conclusion" on the historical issues drawn up by Wang Jiaxiang declared that the fourth plenum's line had been basically correct and the "leftist" mistakes began in September 1931, after the GMD's third Encirclement campaign had been defeated, that is, after Wang Ming had left for Moscow and Bo Gu was in charge of party affairs in China. In these circumstances, in yet another example of Mao's patience and realism, the discussion of the fourth plenum was stopped and plans to submit the "draft conclusion" to the Politburo for approval were put on hold. On the historical question generally, as one party historian put it, part of the problem had been solved. The rest of the problem, however, would await the Rectification campaign and especially the northwest senior cadres conference in October 1942–January 1943 and the ongoing discussions of party history by senior cadres from October 1943 to the approval of the "Resolution" in April 1945. In those meetings and discussions, a combination of persuasion, the pressure created by the campaign atmosphere, and undoubtedly at least some political calculation produced the virtually total consensus that had eluded Mao in 1941.[41]

The preceding discussion emphasizes both Mao's persistence and restraint. The analysis also points to various instances of resistance to specific ideas of Mao's while indicating the lack of evidence of major opposition to the very far-reaching reshaping of official ideology, party history, and leadership authority under way in 1941–42. In retrospect, this process seems much smoother and less conflictual than has generally been assumed.[42] We shall subsequently address claims of doubts and hesitation on the part of those like Liu Shaoqi who were unquestionably on Mao's side by the time of the Rectification campaign. Here the focus is on the group with presumably and, as things turned out, actually the most to lose, the Returned Students. Zhang Wentian and, especially, Wang Jiaxiang were on Mao's side from an early stage. Wang's case is examined in detail below. As for Zhang, his October 1938 proposal that Mao become general secretary reflected not only a longer term disposition to play second fiddle to Mao but also a recognition of Mao's importance to the party's cause, some tensions between them notwithstanding.[43] Shortly after the sixth plenum, moreover, Zhang criticized Wang Ming's "rightist" views on the United Front at length. And whether Zhang's decision to go to the grass roots in early 1942 reflected agreement with or an unspoken protest against rectification, when he returned over a year later he fully accepted Mao's program and rebuffed Wang Ming's argument that the campaign was "directed against us."[44] Bo Gu, the leading representative of the "left" line in Jiangxi during Wang Ming's absence, took longer to come around, but the evidence suggests that by 1942 Bo was offering little resistance to Mao, and by 1943 he had rejected the "left line" openly and engaged in limited self-criticism. Bo's full submission to Mao, however, only came in 1945, when he carried out a self-criticism so severe as to be viewed by party historians today as excessive.[45] Meanwhile, a non–Returned Student who had recently sided with Wang at the Yangtze Bureau, Zhou Enlai, fully committed himself to Mao by mid-1939.[46]

In all this Wang Ming was something of the odd man out. This was apparent in his objections to Mao's 1940 treatise "On New Democracy" and the republishing in the same year of Wang's own 1931 pamphlet *For the Further Bolshevization of the CCP* in order to defend the policies carried out in Jiangxi.[47] But the most important instance of Wang's dissent from the emerging consensus came at the fall 1941 Politburo and Secretariat conference, a meeting where he reportedly was "quite isolated." The first part of the conference in September, while affirming the fourth plenum, still declared that a "leftist" line had occurred and that Wang had been one of those chiefly responsible. The Secretariat meeting in October again declared that Wang had committed a "rightist" error in Wuhan in 1938. This, together with the various decisions concerning rectification and an outpouring of praise for Mao by other high-ranking figures in attendance, surely marked Wang's final defeat.[48] Yet Wang Ming remained largely defiant throughout this conference. Most dramatic was a bitter all-night argument with Mao, Wang Jiaxiang, and Ren Bishi in which he asserted that the party was now deviating to the "left" and called for putting the issue before the Comintern. Apart from this spectacular row, Wang's resistance was manifested in his willingness to admit only "individual mistakes" rather than errors of "line" and in his withdrawal from the conference on the alleged pretext of illness.[49]

Wang's behavior at the fall 1941 meeting reflected an ongoing pattern of defiance, one that can be summed up as an unwillingness to abide by the emerging rules of the game and participate in the increasingly leader-oriented rituals of inner-party life. Apart from rebuffing various other leaders, who were sometimes emissaries from Mao, and rejecting their advice to accept his views, of particular note was Wang's refusal to undertake a deep self-criticism. While Wang did make several offerings to Mao in the 1943–45 period,[50] party historians view these as superficial and insincere, and certainly in contrast to the "excessive" self-criticisms of people like Zhou Enlai and Bo Gu.[51] Basically Wang declined to participate in the Rectification campaign. He was clearly on sick leave during the year-long seventh plenum in 1944–45 and apparently did not attend the Seventh Congress itself. Wang's resistance continued after the Seventh Congress involving another colorful argument with Mao over the "Resolution on Historical Questions" in 1948 and finally culminating in his departure to reside in the Soviet Union in the mid-1950s.[52] Well before that time Wang had been left behind by virtually all other leaders, including the bulk of the Returned Students who had joined in the full-throated praise of Mao in most cases by 1943, when his authority was confirmed beyond all doubt.

If the sixth plenum had been the decisive moment in Mao's achievement of the unambiguous position of number one in the CCP, 1943 marked the culmination of all the measures that had been set in train after the plenum to enlarge his status and power. In circumstances so ably analyzed by Raymond Wylie—the dissolution of the Comintern, the publication of Chiang Kai-shek's *China's Destiny*, and a new GMD anticommunist upsurge—the CCP extended the burgeoning praise of the preceding years into a full-scale glorification of Mao and his "Thought," while key party leaders undertook ever more penetrating self-criticisms of their own past errors.[53] With rectification continuing to expand, the year also saw an intensification of coercive methods within the party in form of the cadre investigation and "rescue" movements—a step that arguably put further muscle behind Mao's rising status but in fact, as argued below, was one of the few blights on Mao's progress in this period. Organizationally, Mao's position was further bolstered by the establishment in March 1943 of a new Secretariat, which now excluded Wang Ming, and by the formal granting to Mao of final authority over day-to-day decisions in this body and the new titles of chairman of the Politburo and of the Secretariat. To be sure, these arrangements still contained various collective elements. The Politburo as a whole was to consider "all important problems" and provide guidelines for the Secretariat, while clearly collegial discussion was expected within the Secretariat itself. But as party historian Liao Gailong would put it many years later, "The 'one-voice rule' was . . . written into a resolution," with the result that "final decision-making power rested with one man alone." Yet since collective aspects were present in the decision and, even more significantly, Mao's political style in this period remained broadly consultative, Liao could still conclude that well beyond these years up until 1957 "Comrade Mao [Zedong] gave full play to democracy." It is hardly surprising, then, that party leaders in 1943 did not see clearly the latent contradiction in the March measures.[54]

This new Secretariat and the associated organs established under it (see Table 12.2) marked a major if still incomplete step in the formation of the Maoist leadership. Perhaps the most striking feature of this new arrangement was the assumption by Liu Shaoqi of key leadership posts at the party center for the first time. Liu was further bolstered by his addition to the party's Central Revolutionary Military Commission (CRMC) at this time;[55] all told he was now clearly the CCP's second-ranking figure. In addition, Ren Bishi's rise was confirmed in the new arrangement. Also of note is the prominent role of Wang Jiaxing, the only leader to serve on both the propaganda and organization committees as well as retaining his seat on the CRMC. Of interest too is the continued absence of Zhou Enlai from top central organs notwithstanding his confirmation as a Politburo member along with all other sitting members. Finally, the appointment to these bodies of Returned Students Bo Gu, Kai Feng, and Yang Shangkun (in addition to Wang Jiaxing and Zhang Wentian) suggests both the gradual nature of the process of leadership change and the apparent willingness of these leaders to support the Maoist cause.

Table 12.2

Reorganized Central Leadership

Secretariat
Mao Zedong (chairman)
Liu Shaoqi
Ren Bishi

Central Propaganda Committee
Mao Zedong (secretary)
Wang Jiaxiang (deputy secretary)
Bo Gu
Kai Feng

Central Organization Committee
Liu Shaoqi (secretary)
Kang Sheng (deputy secretary)
Wang Jiaxiang
Chen Yun
Zhang Wentian
Deng Fa
Yang Shangkun (secretary-*mishu*)
Ren Bishi

As significant as the new Secretariat was, its leading function was short-lived. When the seventh plenum was convened in May 1944 to prepare in earnest for the Seventh Congress (the plenum was formally a drawn-out affair lasting to the eve of the Congress in April 1945), a Presidium (*zhuxituan*) was selected that assumed the full powers of the party center while both the Politburo and Secretariat ceased to function.[56] This powerful five-man body had the same composition as the new Secretariat to be elected following the Seventh Congress, although in different order (see Table 12.3).[57] Clearly the most remarkable facet of this arrangement is the reappearance of Zhou Enlai in a key central post, a development analyzed below. It also marked a complete changeover of the membership of the most authoritative body in charge of daily activities—only Mao remained from the December 1937 Secretariat.

Table 12.3

Highest Party Leadership, 1944–45

Presidium (5/44–4/45)	*Secretariat (6/45)*
Mao Zedong (chairman)	Mao Zedong (chairman)
Zhu De	Zhu De
Liu Shaoqi	Liu Shaoqi
Ren Bishi	Zhou Enlai
Zhou Enlai	Ren Bishi

Meanwhile, in policy terms, perhaps the most significant development at the seventh plenum was the drafting and approval of the "Resolution on Historical Questions." With the results of rectification clearly playing an important role, the plenum finally adopted a version fully in accord with Mao's wishes—the January 1931 fourth plenum was now declared totally wrong and the start of Wang Ming's "left" line. This conclusion emerged from both wide consultation and changes on the basis of the opinions expressed and a clear directing role on the part of Mao, who contributed six sets of revisions to the document. The process thus involved both "democratic" procedures and the leader principle, the kind of intermingling of the two organizational approaches, which blurred the distinction in the perceptions of the participants.[58]

At the Seventh Congress itself and its first plenum immediately thereafter a broader leadership was selected, including a new CC and Politburo. While Mao's hand was evident, so, again, was a quasi-democratic process. The voting procedures for the CC adopted at the congress allowed for genuine input from the delegates. It is, however, necessary to understand the context. Delegates were drawn from the scattered base areas and organizations of the CCP and thus often had limited knowledge of party leaders from outside their areas, including those at the center. Much of their knowledge, moreover, had been filtered through the discussions of past errors and the self-criticisms of concerned officials.

The procedures themselves operated as follows. First, the congress was divided into eight large delegations representing various regions and central organs, and these in turn were broken down into fifty-odd small groups.[59] The groups proposed candidates and sent their names directly to the congress Presidium—a larger body than the May 1944–April 1945 Presidium, but one led by the same individuals. On the basis of these proposals the Presidium drafted a list of prospective CC members and sent it to the large delegations for discussion and voting by secret ballot. The results of this process were known as the preliminary election from which the Presidium drew up a new list with more candidates than places that was sent to the congress as a whole for voting, once again, by secret ballot. This formal election was divided into two segments, first for full CC membership, and finally for alternate membership where those who had failed in the ballot for full membership were added to the list of candidates.

While Mao and other party leaders clearly intervened through lobbying to secure desired results in various cases—although not always with complete success as the strange case of Wang Jiaxing would show—even at the formal election stage delegates had the right to alter the lists and insert candidates not included by the Presidium. Moreover, and more crucially, the procedures adopted apparently prevented the Presidium from including on its revised lists candidates who did not receive a set proportion of delegate votes at the preceding stage or excluding those with the requisite number.[60]

The "democratic" input of delegates notwithstanding, the leadership selected can be taken to reflect the preferences of Mao and his ranking colleagues to a

Table 12.4

CCP Politburo Members

December 1937	June 1945	1945 CC rank
Mao Zedong	Mao Zedong	1
Zhang Wentian	Zhu De—conflict with Mao over party-army relations, 1929	2
Zhou Enlai		
Zhu De	Liu Shaoqi	3
Zhang Guotao—fled to GMD, 1938	Zhou Enlai—cooperated with RS, 1932–34, 1938	23
Wang Jiaxiang—RS, omitted 6/45		
Bo Gu—RS, omitted 6/45	Ren Bishi—presided at stripping of Mao's party and military power, 1931–32	4
Ren Bishi		
Chen Yun		
Peng Dehuai	Chen Yun	8
Xiang Ying—RS supporter, died 1941	Kang Sheng	17
Liu Shaoqi	<u>Gao Gang</u>—first contact with Mao, 1935	12
Kang Sheng		
Wang Ming—RS, omitted 6/45	<u>Peng Zhen</u>—close ties to Liu Shaoqi	18
Deng Fa—RS supporter, omitted 6/45		
Kai Feng—RS, omitted 6/45	<u>Dong Biwu</u>—party elder, supported Wang Ming, 1938	7
	<u>Lin Boqu</u>—party elder, supported Wang Ming, 1938	
	Zhang Wentian—RS, opposed Mao, early 1930s	26
	Peng Dehuai—various arguments with Mao since late 1920s	33

RS = Returned Student group
Italics = not on 1945 Politburo
Underlining = new member 1945

considerable extent. Not only did Mao secure the election of Wang Ming and Bo Gu to the last two places on the full CC against strong sentiment to the contrary among the delegates, but his wishes were particularly reflected in the Politburo chosen after the congress, which departed significantly from the number of votes gained in the CC balloting. Here, according to interview sources, Mao played a more forceful role concerning personnel selections than he had at the congress itself. This and other aspects of the new leadership are indicated in Table 12.4 comparing the December 1937 Politburo, which had remained unchanged except for the defection of Zhang Guotao and death of Xiang Ying, to the new 1945 body.[61]

In the cases of those whose CC ranking did not entitle them to a Politburo seat, an apparent pattern emerges. First, in the cases of Zhou Enlai, Zhang Wentian, and Peng Dehuai, extensive criticism of past errors had taken place. In

Zhou's case this was amplified by his own zealous self-criticisms, which may have enhanced the delegates' perceptions of his mistakes; Peng, in contrast, may have been harmed by his obvious distaste for the excesses of the criticism he suffered at the early 1945 North China rectification meeting.[62] Second, the less dramatic cases of Kang Sheng and Peng Zhen seemingly were affected by unpopularity due to their roles in the 1943 "Rescue campaign"; according to an authoritative interview source it took Mao's intervention to secure their relatively high standing in the congress vote.[63] The case of Kang Sheng will be examined in detail below.

But what does this new Politburo tell us about Mao's preferences and leadership style? Most fundamentally, it demonstrates Mao's basic objective of unifying the party's diverse revolutionary forces. To this end, Mao distinguished between the leader who had seriously challenged his power after 1935—Wang Ming—and those who opposed him on policy or even organizational issues at various junctures but had not competed for power after the Zunyi conference. As indicated in Table 12.4, more than half his colleagues on the new body had stood on different sides of important issues from the party's newly confirmed chairman. Yet Mao seemingly valued both the individual talents of these men and the broader constituencies they represented more than strict personal loyalty in the past. Thus even where the congress voting gave Mao scope to include close followers—specifically Lin Biao (sixth on the CC) and Li Fuchun (thirteenth)—he refrained in order to make room for wider sections of the party. The exclusions of previous Politburo members, however, were not limited to those who had threatened Mao's power; he did not stop with Wang Ming but instead swept out the entire Returned Student group and their supporters with the symbolic exception of Zhang Wentian.[64] Here Mao's preoccupation with theoretical correctness came into play. Since Mao was in deadly earnest about unifying thought, rejecting the dogmatic copying of foreign models that the Returned Students epitomized in his eyes, and correcting past errors, it was only logical that those responsible be removed from the top policy body. But unity argued for limiting such dismissals to that group.

Finally, as already suggested, Mao sought unity by giving representation to as wide a group of constituencies within the party as possible. To this end Mao recognized the importance of status and seniority in Chinese culture and the CCP itself. Not only were two party elders, Dong Biwu and Lin Boqu, added to the Politburo, but apart from the Returned Students and their associates all who had achieved Politburo status before Mao's consolidation of power—and, in most cases, before the Zunyi conference—were retained. Mao did not want to cause resentment by removing people who had long served the CCP: historical position was to be respected in the name of solidarity. Also, in bringing in new members Mao sought to recognize diverse constituencies that had not previously been included. At the congress itself, he explicitly noted the need to acknowledge such "factional" constituencies, or *shantou*, in the election process, and to eliminate them only gradually as the larger party unity solidified. Cases in point were Gao Gang, a key figure of the northwest revolutionary movement whose leaders had not figured in earlier Politburos dominated by veterans of the southern revolution, and Peng Zhen, a leader of the northern underground struggle, who became new members. Significantly, although Mao had declined to bring his own close supporters such as Lin Biao into the Politburo, in Peng Zhen he endorsed a close political associate of Liu Shaoqi largely because of the underrepresentation of northern underground leaders. Such appointments further demonstrate that Mao attached greater importance to such considerations than to any comfort that might have been gained by adding loyal followers. The impulse for unity dominated, so the Maoist leadership emerging from the Seventh Congress was broadly based and able to focus its energies on completing the revolutionary task.[65]

Liu Shaoqi—Mao's Natural Successor

The May 1943 reorganization clearly placed Liu Shaoqi in the number two position in the CCP, and shortly after the Seventh Congress at the latest Liu was recognized as Mao's successor.[66] Liu's new prominence and alliance with Mao Zedong in the mid-1940s have long puzzled observers in significant respects. Mao and Liu have been seen as representing two distinct constituencies in the party—Mao the base areas and Liu the underground or "white areas." This has been an oversimplification but not without some basis in fact.[67] Less valid have been interpretations seeing Liu as urban-oriented in contrast to the peasant mobilizer Mao. Such differences, both real and imagined, have led analysts to think that the Mao-Liu arrangement of the 1940s was something of a factional alliance, even, as one foreign observer speculated, "a dirty political deal."[68]

In contrast to such sentiments, Chinese scholars see Liu's emergence as Mao's number two as a natural historical development.[69] They emphasize Liu's theoretical contributions, his practical achievements, and his loyalty to Mao's cause *throughout* the years under examination in this study. An earlier analysis of the Mao-Liu relationship has focused on these factors with particular attention to Liu's political will in both theoretical and practical matters.[70] Here we will expand on that analysis and elaborate on related matters. But while there is every reason to believe that Mao wholeheartedly supported Liu as his successor and that he certainly had the power to prevent Liu from attaining such a status, the very fact that Liu's rise was in some sense "natural" makes it feasible that Mao's direct role in Liu's elevation was relatively low key. None of the party historians consulted knew the precise circumstances of Liu's appointment in 1943 or who nominated him for the successor role. Much as a consensus had emerged on Mao's leadership four and a half years earlier with the decisive contribution of the Comintern, a similar consensus may well have emerged on Liu by the later date.

Although they had known each other since the 1920s, Mao and Liu were not particularly close before the Long March. Although Liu had supported Mao on the Long March, his role was less significant than that of others, and the epic journey was not without tension between the two.[71] Nevertheless, by this time a fateful parallelism had already developed between the careers of the two men. Simply put, both had crossed swords with the "Wang Ming line" albeit in different areas of work. Various aspects of Mao's base area program had been overturned by the "leftist" policies of the Comintern-backed Returned Students; Liu's policies for white area work similarly had been rejected by the same leadership. While his career in these years did not suffer to the same degree as did Mao's, Liu lost several posts and was rebuked by the Comintern.[72] Moreover, while both Mao and Liu considered themselves theorists, their theories were rooted in practical work and reflected a disdain for the kind of "dogmatism" they believed the Returned Students represented. Thus even before active support began, there was a strong circumstantial basis for Mao-Liu cooperation.

Party historians emphasize that Liu was a firm supporter of Mao's beginning in the latter part of the agrarian war period (1927–37), especially in theory, and especially after the December 1935 Wayaobao Conference. Even earlier, at the Zunyi conference, Liu raised political issues that Mao, it has been said, "cleverly avoided." In April 1936 Liu took over as head of the CCP's Northern Bureau and began to implement his own program for white area work in contrast to the failed policies of the Returned Students. In the same month, Liu developed the themes of the Wayaobao Conference and wrote a critique of "leftist" errors in underground struggle ostensibly committed by Li Lisan but in fact by the Returned Students.[73] In this as at Zunyi he was actually out in front of Mao, who was cautiously biding his time before engaging Wang Ming's followers on political issues. A year later, in early 1937, Liu went to Yan'an from the front to attend a party conference and presented to the CC a series of letters criticizing in more systematic and direct fashion the white area work of the Returned Students. This was not a popular view and was rejected; Mao, moreover, apparently did not feel the moment ripe and offered Liu only mild support. According to party historians, however, it was during this period that Mao began to look highly on Liu.[74]

As we have seen, the year from Wang Ming's return to the sixth plenum was crucial. During this year, Liu stood four-square behind Mao. Liu showed his "Maoist" credentials in carrying out guerrilla warfare and mass mobilization according to Mao's precepts in the base areas under the Northern Bureau. More than that, Liu threw his support directly behind Mao in the struggle with Wang Ming. According to the memoirs of Wang Shoudao, at that time Liu declared, "Our Northern Bureau has not only become an anti-Japanese base area, it is also a base area for supporting Comrade Mao Zedong's struggle against Wang Ming's right opportunism." When the sixth plenum was held, Liu was again in the forefront of Mao's cause, articulating a particularly scathing attack on Wang Ming's policy of "everything through the United Front" as amounting to "everything through Chiang Kai-shek and Yan Xishan," to which Mao commented, "well said."[75]

Such firmness was not without its rewards. When Wang's Yangtze Bureau was disbanded at the end of the plenum, part of its territory was taken over by the newly established Central Plains Bureau under Liu Shaoqi. But a broader point should be made. Not only did Liu both support Mao politically against Wang Ming and back his policies of guerrilla warfare and mass mobilization, he was also eminently successful in implementing these Maoist policies. This was the case in both the Northern and Central Plains Bureaus, then in East China, where Liu rebuilt the New Fourth Army after the GMD attack of January 1941. As a result of this, interview sources emphasize, Liu had developed a track record of success in the northern, central, and eastern areas, and his reputation as both a capable leader and as a Mao loyalist was firmly established among the party *and military* leaders in each of these important CCP constituencies. While undoubtedly Liu's most intimate ties were to those who had served under him in the white areas before 1937, his support extended beyond this group.

Interview sources also give great weight to Mao's appreciation of Liu's unwavering support in the "final battle" against Wang Ming during the Rectification campaign. Liu's support in this regard came very easily, even before rectification as such. At the time "How to Be a Good Communist" was delivered in mid-1939, Liu told Wang Shoudao that the need was to study Mao, not Wang Ming. Mao, for his part, was much impressed with Liu's speech and referred to it as a "correct wind."[76] During the movement itself, "How to Be a Good Communist" became one of several important documents by Liu under study, which made him the second most important contributor to the rectification curriculum.[77] Liu's concern with rejecting dogmatism and emphasizing sinification fit perfectly with Mao's agenda, as, of course, did his own long-standing desire to revise party history. Indeed, it was precisely in the area of theory that Mao and Liu were so close. Ironically, given Western interpretations to the contrary, a case in point is Liu's July 1941 letter to Song Liang complaining about the CCP's inadequacies in Marxist theoretical achievement. Far from being an oblique criticism of Mao as suggested by some analysts, Liu's comments were directed squarely at the problem of theoretical underdevelopment in the party as a whole given the pressing nature of practical work—a viewpoint mirroring that expressed by Mao at the sixth plenum and a concern addressed by him during precisely the same period as Liu's letter.[78] Finally, in 1943 Liu developed the most systematic formulation of "Mao Zedong Thought." While others had been playing with various versions of "Mao's Thought" or been more extreme in public praise of Mao earlier, there is nothing in the overall record of the 1936–42 period to suggest that Liu was anything other than a fervent supporter of Mao.[79] In 1943, he took the final step and, in the view of one high-ranking party historian, became the most prominent architect of the Mao cult.[80]

Thus by 1943 Liu was inextricably linked to Mao's cause. The emphasis on reviewing party history, which reached new heights, also enhanced those links *and* Liu's new status as number two, as the review of past history showed that Mao and Liu had made fewer mistakes than any other leader.[81] There was, however, one little-known by-product of this development. While Liu was playing his part in building up the cult of Mao, which party historians today see as the first step in undermining party democracy, he was at the same time engaging in a similar, if necessarily paler, transformation himself. If "correct thought" produced leadership prerogatives, then Liu too had reason to act with a certain imperiousness. Even before his elevation in 1943, Liu demonstrated this trait. According to an interview source present on the occasion, Liu came to the Northern Bureau, which was then under Peng Dehuai, on his way to Yan'an in mid-1942 after major CCP losses stemming from the May 1942 Japanese attack on the Taihang region. He delivered a report to the bureau critical of Peng's performance, particularly with regard to inadequate attention to mass mobilization and rent reduction. While this source was very impressed with Liu's report at the time, in looking back, he believes it had a major flaw—the claim that Liu himself had always been correct. With regard to the Northern Bureau, Liu contrasted the achievements during his earlier stewardship with "the mess" that had been made since he left. Liu went on to say that when he arrived in East China he discovered similar shortcomings had developed under the leadership of Returned Student supporter Xiang Ying, but that he rectified the situation and built up the North Jiangsu base area. Liu apparently was indeed full of himself, convinced of his correct policy orientation, and, no doubt, confident in his alignment with the ever more dominant figure in the CCP—Mao Zedong.

But the real evidence of Liu's arrogance came in the crucial year of 1943. Party historians are unaware of any self-criticism by Liu during that year or in the period through the Seventh Congress, something that left him in limited (and uncomfortable) company.[82] Even Mao himself, in the one restricted case of the "Rescue campaign" for which Liu also bore some responsibility, made several self-critical offerings (see below). But the highlight of this tendency of Liu's came in a 24 October 1943 speech during the re-examination of party history, a speech viewed today by Chinese scholars as a "Cultural Revolution style report." According to these scholars, in this speech Liu systematically criticized Wang Ming for mistakes from the agrarian war period through to his stewardship of the Yangtze Bureau. Liu was particularly harsh concerning the performance of the bureau, claiming that it had made no contributions whatsoever and its organ, the *New China Daily*, was a paper of capitulation. Even more significantly, Liu's attack ranged well beyond Wang Ming himself or even his Returned Student associates such as Bo Gu. He even went beyond other members of the Yangtze Bureau such as Zhou Enlai and Ye Jianying to lambaste such key contemporary players, and Mao supporters, as Ren Bishi and Wang Jiaxiang. And although avoiding names, he took a swipe at Zhu De and Peng Dehuai for militarism. The only top leaders to avoid Liu's sharp criticism, according to these sources, were Mao and Liu himself.

In explaining this speech, a speech that contrasts with a much more balanced offering by Liu at the time of his elevation to the number two post in March that distinguished between good and bad points in all party work, party historians point to both a personal psychological weakness on Liu's part and the overheated atmosphere of the time associated with the developing Mao cult. They refer to a "psychology of being number two," of wanting to demonstrate the firmness of his commitment to Mao. This, of course, dovetailed with his already demonstrated confidence in his own correctness in carrying out Mao-style policies. Moreover, excesses in analysis were fed by the attitude common during rectification that the more severe the criticism, the better, that "left is better than right," in this case "left" being not the policy orientation of the Returned Students, but, rather the expression of fervor for the leader. Of course, one further issue is Mao's role in the 24 October speech. The party historians consulted have no evidence on this point but conclude that Mao must have approved because Liu "would not have dared to criticize so broadly" otherwise. In the end, Liu's report was not publicized within the party. Perhaps Mao, or Mao and Liu, felt on reflection that it had gone too far and damaged the overarching drive for party unity as well as "democratic" norms. In any case, Liu's report indicated a willingness to go to extremes, whether that willingness was fueled by the self-righteousness of one who shared the "correct" theory that promised revolutionary success or by the desire to ingratiate oneself further with the leader.[83] But the bitter irony in view of events more than two decades later was the development of a situation where the leader was beyond question, where party leaders of the highest rank could be severely criticized without, apparently, any effective avenue of reply, and where a second-ranking leader could share in the reflected glory of Mao at his discretion.

Rising and Falling Stars: Ren Bishi, Zhou Enlai and Wang Jiaxiang

Undoubtedly there are as many reasons for the inclusion or exclusion of particular figures in the new Maoist leadership as there are relevant leaders. More generally, some key factors already have been suggested. Continuity of membership in the top bodies, the representation of various constituencies within the CCP as a whole, and a willingness to accept Mao's ultimate power were undoubtedly crucial considerations for holding or gaining a place at the top at the Seventh Congress. In contrast, dogged resistance to Mao's power, especially after the Zunyi conference, and perceived theoretical inadequacies did not put individuals in good standing for a position in the new leadership. These observations are refined by examining the contrasting fortunes of three key figures of the late 1930s and early 1940s—Ren Bishi, who seemingly moved smoothly into one of the top handful of powerful posts; Zhou Enlai, whose position weakened at the end of 1937 and was seemingly precarious in 1943, but who nevertheless recovered spectacularly by 1944–45, and Wang

Jiaxiang, who despite immeasurable services to Mao found himself reduced to an alternate CC member at the Seventh Congress.

Ren Bishi

While Ren and Mao may have had some contact when Ren was young, the interaction of the two men as major party leaders began inauspiciously.[84] From a Maoist point of view, Ren's rise to Politburo status came at a particularly unfortunate juncture, the famous fourth plenum of January 1931, which installed the Wang Ming leadership and marked the start of the "third left line." Shortly thereafter, Ren was dispatched to the central soviet area together with Wang Jiaxiang, whose career was to parallel his own in so many ways. Although not himself a Returned Student, once in the soviet areas Ren not only implemented the "left" policies of the new party leadership but came into direct conflict with Mao. Of particular significance was Ren's role at the Gannan and Ningdu conferences in 1931–32. On these occasions Ren presided over the stripping of Mao's party and military power and the criticism of Mao for conservatism and guerrillaism. Subsequently, in early 1933, Ren played a major role in the sharp attacks on the "Luo Ming line," an attack that in fact was aimed at Mao's policies and removed many of his supporters from their party posts. These developments were hardly promising for the relations between Mao and Ren.[85]

Ren Bishi, like Wang Jiaxiang, was more flexible than the closer followers of Wang Ming, however. Because of the deterioration of the situation in the soviet areas, Ren began to take serious heed of Mao's opinions. Although he had been transferred from the central soviet to the Hunan-Jiangxi border region in 1933 and subsequently moved west ahead of the main Long Marchers, thus missing the historic Zunyi meeting, Ren seemingly became more partial to Mao's views. Several key developments with major implications for Ren's relations with Mao occurred from mid-1934 to late 1936. First, Ren became one of the leading figures of a major emerging inner-party constituency. In October 1934, Ren's forces linked up with those of He Long, and out of this union came the Second Front Army with Ren as political commissar and He as commander. What was arguably crucial for Ren's subsequent rise was the role this combined force was to play in Mao's struggle against Zhang Guotao. The Second Front Army linked up with Zhang's Fourth Front Army in June 1936 in the far southwest. An argument ensued over where this force should go, not unlike that between Mao and Zhang over the destination of the Long Marchers a year earlier, with the decision finally made to head north to join Mao's forces in Shaanxi. Official histories credit Ren with a particularly significant part in the struggle to overcome Zhang's objections and persuading both armies to move north together. Once in Shaanxi, Ren was rewarded with major military posts, becoming in July 1937 the head of the general political department of the renamed Red Army, the Eighth Route Army.[86]

Ren subsequently served Mao faithfully in the struggle against Wang Ming. Given the critical importance of the Comintern's endorsement of his leadership, Mao must have been especially pleased with the lobbying efforts Ren undertook on his behalf as head of the CCP delegation to the Comintern in 1938. When Ren returned to China in March 1940, he was soon assigned to work in the Secretariat, and in July or August of the same year he was appointed to the significant post of CCP secretary general (*mishuzhang*). Thus Ren's selection as a member of the new three-man Secretariat in March 1943 was the culmination of three years' work in the crucial operational body, work that saw him deeply involved in some of Mao's most important projects. Both before and after his elevation to the Secretariat, Ren played a major role in assisting Mao with the Rectification campaign and the rewriting of party history: at the fall 1941 Politburo conference he strongly supported Mao's version of the "leftist" errors of the early 1930s; in April 1942 he was placed in charge of rectification in the Shaan-Gan-Ning area and subsequently was a key figure at the critical northwest senior cadres conference; and in 1944 he became the convener of the drafting committee for the "Resolution on Historical Questions" at the same time as assuming his seat on the Presidium, which took charge of all party work. Ren's closeness to Mao apparently involved more than just pushing through Mao's ideas, he was able to deal with delicate issues as well. Thus in the summer of 1943, when the issue of the "Rescue campaign" heated up (see the discussion of Zhou Enlai below), Ren's investigations uncovered Kang Sheng's use of torture, and his report led Mao to take the first step to bring the movement under control. Thus, it was no surprise that at the Seventh Congress itself Ren was one of the most prominent figures as congress secretary general, and when he received a 100 percent vote in the CC elections, Mao stood and applauded. Ren's selection to both the Politburo and Secretariat immediately after the congress was a foregone conclusion.[87]

In one sense, Ren's rise is a fairly straightforward story of rewards for services rendered in the two key post-Zunyi struggles for power, where Mao bested first Zhang Guotao and then Wang Ming. The value of this support to Mao, moreover, was magnified by Ren's standing as an established Politburo member and as a leading figure of the Second Front Army—factors that fit perfectly with Mao's larger project of building party unity. Yet Mao's willingness to place so much trust in Ren remains intriguing. Ren, after all, had been directly involved in the destruction of Mao's power in the period of the "Wang Ming line." He had come to the top of the party with the hated Wang Ming and followed his line for over two years, and there is little to suggest that he softened the blows against Mao, at least not to the extent that Zhou Enlai did.[88] It is also relevant that Ren was not at the Zunyi Conference, where Zhou, Wang Jiaxiang, and Zhang Wentian, among others, made such major contributions to Mao's cause at what still must be regarded as the *most* critical juncture in his career. And Ren's role in the struggle with Zhang Guotao, while clearly appreciated, nevertheless was far less significant to Mao's ultimate victory than the destruction of Zhang's forces by Muslim troops after they had broken away from the Ren–He Long army on the trek north. Finally, Ren's contributions to the anti–Wang Ming effort, however valuable, were no more so than those of others, most particularly, Wang Jiaxiang.

Speculatively, Ren's rapid rise may have reflected the fact that, in addition to his unstinting support for Mao since 1936, he possessed a combination of qualities few others in the leadership could match. He had seniority on the Politburo, which undoubtedly was essential for a position at the very top. He represented an important constituency in the party, more important than any represented by, say, Chen Yun. He was a political rather than a military figure, as befit Leninist principles, but one with strong military links. And he was not a Returned Student, his cooperation with that group in 1931–33 notwithstanding. Of all the other sitting Politburo members on the eve of the Seventh Congress, only Liu Shaoqi had a superior curriculum vitae in these terms. Yet when the Seventh Congress had concluded and the new Politburo and Secretariat were selected, Ren somewhat surprisingly slipped below another key figure—Zhou Enlai.

Zhou Enlai

In terms of many of the criteria discussed with regard to Ren Bishi, Zhou's key position by 1944–45 is easy to understand. Zhou had greater seniority in the party than virtually any other figure except Mao himself: he joined the CCP in 1921 and became a Politburo member in 1927. While not identified with a specific constituency such as Ren Bishi's Second Front Army, Zhou had from the very earliest days developed extensive ties within the CCP as a whole and particularly with its military wing. In the 1920s, as political commissar of the Whampoa (Huangpu) Academy he was the first party leader placed in charge of military affairs, and in 1927 he was one of the key leaders of the Nanchang Uprising, which came to be regarded as the founding of the Red Army. And, of course, he played a leading role in guiding military affairs on the Long March, both helping to shift support to Mao initially and then implementing Mao's policies after the Zunyi conference. These accomplishments and contacts were further enhanced by the widespread recognition within the elite of Zhou's great organizational talents, his capacity for hard work, cordial relations with a wide range of people within the party, and a mediating style and unthreatening posture toward others. All told, Zhou's experience and qualities generated substantial respect and even personal affection within the party leadership.[89]

From the point of view of Mao's personal interests, placing Zhou in a high leadership position also made sense. Apart from providing valuable support at Zunyi, Zhou's posture toward Mao even as he carried out the policies of the Returned Students in the early 1930s had much to recommend him. Zhou was solicitous of Mao's feelings and indicated support for Mao under those most awkward circumstances. Thus in 1932, after Ren Bishi presided over stripping

Mao of his military posts at the Ningdu conference and Zhou was named to replace him as general political commissar of the Red Army, Zhou attached a dissenting opinion to the report sent to the CC in Shanghai. In the end, Zhou did accept the post, but he continued to sign both Mao's name and his own as *acting* commissar on documents, and on seeing Mao off from the Red Army, he expressed the hope that Mao would someday return.[90] From the perspective of the mid-1940s, moreover, a broader tendency on Zhou's part of subservience to higher-ranking party leaders was a decided plus for Mao. Zhou's famous lack of ambition and willingness to serve his superiors might be a questionable quality when Wang Ming was the superior in question, but by 1939 such tendencies could only work to Mao's advantage. While Zhou's failure to stand up to Wang Ming and his lack of a clear theoretical perspective made him clearly less suitable than Liu Shaoqi as a successor, the qualities Zhou did possess made him eminently useful in his self-proclaimed role as Mao's loyal and trusted assistant.[91]

Yet the period 1937–43 was clearly a difficult one for Zhou, in terms of both his overall position in the CCP and his relations with Mao. As we have seen, Zhou's position suffered at the time of Wang Ming's return in late 1937 as he lost his place on the Secretariat. Perhaps this reflected no more than the circumstances that if the Secretariat was to remain a five-man body and if the three new arrivals had to be accommodated, then Zhou had to go as both Mao and Zhang Wentian had superior claims to retain their seats. But it may also be the case that Mao, despite Zhou's services in the Long March and obvious abilities, made no particular effort to retain Zhou. Even before Wang's return, Mao and Zhou had policy differences. While party historians view it as a minor disagreement, at the Luochuan conference in August 1937, Zhou and Peng Dehuai had advocated mobile war as the party's main military strategy, in contrast to Mao's emphasis on guerrilla warfare. Thus, a combination of the pressures created by the return of Wang Ming and company and Mao's dissatisfaction with Zhou's policy views may well account for Zhou's loss of status at the end of 1937.[92]

The real problem for Zhou *vis-à-vis* Mao, of course, came directly from Zhou's support of Wang Ming in 1938. To a significant degree, the Wang-Zhou cooperation at this juncture is probably explained in terms of the organizational discipline of being under Wang in the Yangtze Bureau as well as Zhou's personal proclivity for getting along with his superiors. Nevertheless, there is reason to believe that Zhou was genuinely attracted to Wang's version of the United Front. When the sixth plenum met in conditions wherein the Wuhan experiment had failed and the Comintern had endorsed Mao's leadership, Zhou's views still reflected those of Wang Ming. Later, during his 1943 self-criticism, Zhou looked back over his past errors and observed that it was from May 1939 that his line was in full accord with the center—namely, a full half-year after Wang's defeat on the United Front question. It may have taken the GMD's January 1939 plenum, which attacked the CCP as an "alien party," to convince Zhou completely of the wisdom of Mao's approach.[93] Whatever the case, Mao would not have been impressed with either Zhou's theoretical grasp or his firmness in dealing with Wang Ming.

It is understandable, then, that from the sixth plenum to mid-1943, Zhou's role, while still significant particularly in handling delicate relations with the GMD in Chongqing, was somewhat secondary to the main areas of CCP policy and accomplishments. When not in the Soviet Union for medical treatment, Zhou spent most of his time heading the Southern Bureau in Chongqing. Although still retaining his position as vice chairman of the party's Military Commission, from 1938 his functions seemingly were taken over by Wang Jiaxiang.[94] Despite his self-proclaimed total commitment to Mao's cause from mid-1939, Zhou's position seemed particularly shaky in early 1943. No place was found for Zhou in any of the central bodies reorganized in March. Later in the same year, Comintern head Georgy Dimitrov believed it necessary to telegraph the CCP with a plea that Zhou and Wang Ming be retained in the leadership, a plea that one leading party historian, undoubtedly overdramatically, feels "saved" Zhou.[95] Further complicating Zhou's position in mid-1943 was the launching of the "Rescue campaign." During this movement, Kang Sheng claimed to have uncovered so-called red banner parties in the underground organizations under Zhou's ultimate leadership at the Southern Bureau—namely, party organizations that allegedly had been deeply penetrated by enemy agents. Thus, a major contemporary issue, as well as the legacy of past errors, hung over Zhou's head when he arrived in Yan'an in July 1943 for policy meetings connected with the dissolution of the Comintern in May and to participate in rectification.[96] Yet within ten months of his arrival at the communist capital, Zhou emerged as one of the top five figures in the leadership. Why?

Zhou dealt with his predicament by using two bold strategies.[97] The first was an absolute declaration of support for Mao and zealous, indeed, in the view of party historians, overzealous, self-criticisms of past mistakes. The second was to deny Kang Sheng's accusations against the "red banner parties" and defend the reputation of the underground Communists under his stewardship. Zhou put his first strategy into operation shortly after his arrival. At a welcoming meeting organized by the office of the CC, Zhou took the opportunity to lavish praise on Mao, declaring that Mao's orientation was the party's orientation and his line was the true Bolshevik line. Zhou followed this up with extensive self-criticisms during the re-examination of party history in the following months. These self-criticisms, which exceeded twenty thousand words, summed up his personal experience over the previous two decades and divided his performance into positive and negative aspects. On the positive side, Zhou claimed never to have been discouraged or timid in front of the enemy and to have been loyal, honest, and patient in his inner-party relations. But the negative aspects were wide-ranging and emphasized long periods of following Wang Ming. They included adopting a "leftist" approach when criticizing the "Li Lisan line" in 1930, sharing a "certain responsibility" for the military errors of Bo Gu and Comintern military adviser Otto Braun during the fifth Encirclement campaign in Jiangxi, and sharing responsibility for the errors of the Yangtze Bureau particularly in watering down Mao's principle of independence and initiative in the United Front and making concessions to Wang Ming.[98] It was in this context that Zhou declared that from May 1939, he wholeheartedly accepted Mao's line, which had been confirmed by practice. In addition to outlining his own faults, Zhou's criticisms involved a thorough analysis of the "left" errors of the 1930s as producing the defeat of the CCP in the period, thus providing a major affirmation of the emerging Maoist historical orthodoxy by one of the key executors of the "Wang Ming line." Zhou's performance seemingly had the desired effect of winning Mao's confidence; several party historians believe this was the crucial factor in the turnaround of Zhou's fortunes by the end of 1943.

The second strategy, rebutting the charges against the "red banner parties," also had its effect. In early August, Zhou denied such allegations to Li Weihan, and this may have led to Ren Bishi's investigations uncovering Kang Sheng's use of torture to produce false confessions. As seen below, Ren's intervention produced several policy reversals concerning the "Rescue campaign," and by December a re-examination of the cadres affected by the campaign led to the conclusion that 90 percent had been wrongfully dealt with; subsequently these cadres were duly rehabilitated. Zhou Enlai had been proved correct in his protestations while Kang Sheng's methods had been exposed as excessive and his claims as unwarranted. It would be a turning point in the careers of both men.[99]

By this time Mao could see in Zhou someone who was pledging personal loyalty and articulating the correct theoretical line. Together with the widespread respect for Zhou in the party, his past contributions to the revolution and Mao, and his great work capabilities, this was apparently enough for Mao to put aside Zhou's waverings in 1938. As we have seen, by May 1944, Zhou was formally number five in the leadership. The following year, however, the Seventh Congress provided the somewhat incongruous spectacle of electing Zhou to only the twenty-third place on the CC, well below not only Ren Bishi but even a past purveyor of wrong policies with no recent accomplishments to his credit, Li Lisan.[100] As party historians believe, the extensive criticism and self-criticism of his responsibility for the Wang Ming line primarily explain Zhou's low vote, and, according to these interview sources, Mao was apparently caught by surprise at the outcome, something that occurred in even more striking fashion in the case of Wang Jiaxiang. Nevertheless, at the plenum immediately after the congress, Mao overrode the delegates' reservations and elevated Zhou again to the very top, this time over Ren Bishi to the formal number four, and in fact number three, position.[101] Zhou's talents and status—and his crucial demonstration of loyalty to Mao in 1943—had won the day. "Democracy" was clearly present at the congress, but in the end the leader's wishes prevailed. The situation would be even more complicated with regard to Wang Jiaxiang.

Wang Jiaxiang

Of all the leaders affected by the formation of the new Maoist leadership, the case of Wang Jiaxiang remains the most puzzling. Mao arguably owed more to Wang than any other individual, a fact Mao went a long way toward acknowledging in a speech to the Seventh Congress.[102] Wang's support for Mao was more crucial than that of Ren Bishi, and both more crucial and constant than that of Zhou Enlai. Yet while Zhou and Ren were among the "five big secretaries"[103] selected in 1945, Wang could achieve no more than the second position on the list of CC alternates—and that only after Mao's intervention on his behalf. What explains this strange turn of events?

The answer lies largely in Wang's early career. Although he would later deny that he was a member of the Returned Student faction, Wang in fact had all the credentials to be considered a member of that group.[104] From late 1925 to early 1930, he studied in Moscow, including at Sun Yat-sen University, where Wang Ming had been based, and after returning to China in early 1930, he worked in the party's central propaganda organs, as did Wang Ming. Wang Jiaxiang's star rose with the January 1931 fourth plenum although, unlike Ren Bishi, he had to wait until 1934 before gaining Politburo status, in his case, as an alternate member. Mao would later say that Wang's mistakes were particularly significant with regard to the fourth plenum. Shortly after the plenum, he was dispatched to the central soviet area, where he carried out the "left" line, with perceived dire consequences in the military struggle against the GMD Encirclement campaigns. It was also during this period that he assisted Ren Bishi in attacking Mao at the Gannan conference, but he opposed the decision to strip Mao of his military posts at the Ningdu conference, over which Ren presided.[105]

Thus even before Ren, Wang had begun to take increasing note of Mao's opinions as the CCP's situation worsened. This was to be particularly fateful in Wang's case as he swung around to back Mao's views during the early stage of the Long March and began to agitate for a major party meeting.[106] This turned out to be the critical Zunyi conference, where Wang played an essential role in supporting Mao. As Mao put it at the Seventh Congress, "[We] absolutely cannot forget these two people [Wang and Zhang Wentian]," whose roles were especially crucial because they were from the dominant "left" faction and split from it.[107] Wang's role was reflected in his new status after Zunyi: he was a full Politburo member, a member of the Secretariat, and a member of the three-man military leadership group with Mao and Zhou. For the remainder of the Long March, he worked closely with Mao and steadfastly supported him in the struggle with Zhang Guotao. Once in North Shaanxi, he continued to play a key role in various posts providing political oversight of the military. He was clearly one of the CCP's most important figures before he left for the Soviet Union in June 1937 largely for health reasons.[108]

Wang's second great service to Mao was, like Ren Bishi, lobbying for his cause in Moscow and then bringing back to China the decisive message of Comintern support in time for the sixth plenum. Once having played his critical role at the plenum, he again assumed key posts at the center particularly as before in military affairs, where he worked extremely closely with Mao. In 1945, Mao spoke of Wang's shortcomings after the sixth plenum, including big short-comings in [army] political work and defects in his dealings with people, but there is little to suggest any significant tension between the two men at the time. In fact, like Ren, Wang was deeply involved in some of Mao's most important political projects in the post–sixth plenum period. It was Wang, along with Ren Bishi, who supported Mao during the all-night row with Wang Ming in the fall of 1941 and who authored the first draft of the "Resolution on Historical Questions" at that time, albeit a version that did not completely endorse Mao's views, a position apparently less enthusiastic than that of Ren. Nevertheless, it was Wang who in July 1943 coined "Mao Zedong Thought" as the formulation to express the CCP's China-oriented version of Marxism-Leninism. In these circumstances, it is hardly surprising that Wang assumed key posts on the propaganda and organization committees, the only leader to be represented on both, when these were set up during the reorganization of March 1943.[109]

By 1943, however, Wang's health problems had caught up with him, and he went on sick leave until mid-1946. As a result, he seemed unable to participate in the continuing rectification process, offer public self-criticisms, and express his attitude toward Wang Ming, or attend the Seventh Congress although he did send Mao a brief letter during the congress, which made a self-criticism and expressed agreement with the "Resolution" on history.[110] In the context of the times, it is quite understandable that Wang's ill health kept him off the 1944 Presidium responsible for all party work and similarly prevented him from being one of the "five big secretaries" chosen after the Seventh Congress. But Wang's drop from the Politburo to a mere CC alternate caused great surprise, even embarrassment. Senior leaders Zhu De, Peng Dehuai, Chen Yun, and Li Fuchun visited Wang after the congress to offer condolences. Wang's wife, after over-coming her shock, discussed the matter with various people, but no one could figure out what had happened. And to this day party historians and senior leaders can only speculate about the turn of events.[111]

Any explanation of Wang's fate must take account of the "democratic" process used to elect the CC. Wang, like Zhou Enlai, had to share the blame for the errors of the "Wang Ming line," and Wang, after all, actually qualified as a Returned Student. Party historians believe that, as was the case with Zhou Enlai, Wang's low vote primarily reflected the delegates' extensive exposure to attacks on the "left line" and the deep feelings it created. Wang's illness, moreover, meant that delegates did not experience Zhou Enlai–style self-criticisms, self-criticisms that, on the one hand, may have lost Zhou some votes but, on the other, were palpable evidence of his current commitment to Mao's cause. Wang may also have been disadvantaged by his almost continuous posting at the center; he would not have been well known among the various regional constituencies of the party as, for example, Liu Shaoqi was. According to his wife, many delegates only heard of his name but did not understand him as a person. Clearly Wang's aloof personality, which gave the impression of coldness, had something to do with the lack of support, as did the fact that he had a reputation for being very strict in his relations with subordinates. Yet such factors did not prevent others who were far less significant in Mao's rise from securing election to the full CC. Various cases demonstrated that health was certainly no bar to high status, nor was being absent from the congress or being merely a name to most delegates, as shown by the case of Li Lisan, who had been in the Soviet Union since 1930. Past mistakes were no obstacle either, as the extreme examples of Wang Ming's and Bo Gu's receiving the last two slots demonstrate. And as Wang's wife discovered when taking her postelection soundings, his personality was not regarded as a credible explanation since quite a few leaders with similar personal characteristics attained high station.[112]

At the core of the mystery, of course, stands Mao. Mao had proved himself quite willing and able to save the CC seats of Kang Sheng and Peng Zhen, who were unpopular for their roles in the "Rescue campaign," not to mention that of Wang Ming himself. And indeed he became active in Wang Jiaxiang's case with his speech on Wang's crucial contributions, but only after the full CC members had been chosen. Mao asked the delegates to make Wang the first CC alternate, yet even his intervention could secure only the second alternate ranking. But what Mao's intervention highlights is that any earlier efforts he undertook to secure Wang's position during the elaborate process for electing the full CC were inadequate. As we have seen, the congress Presidium headed by Mao, with Ren Bishi responsible for routine work, was well positioned to know delegate sentiment through compiling the election lists. There was also the opportunity to indicate the preferences of the top leaders, particularly by visiting and lobbying various delegations and smaller groups, as Ren was known to do on at least one occasion.[113] Questions therefore arise as to why Mao was ineffective in this case, why he apparently neglected the interests of the comrade who, above all others, had aided his cause even though he could arouse himself in the name of party unity to guarantee a place for his most tenacious enemy, Wang Ming. What can explain Mao's failure to act in a decisive fashion until it was too late?

In attempting to explain the puzzle one line of speculation centers on Mao's political and personal calculations. In terms of unifying the factions that made up the party, there was little to recommend Wang Jiaxiang. Rather than representing an important constituency like Ren Bishi's Second Front Army, the faction he was identified with, the Returned Students, was being phased out and sufficient recognition was given to them through the retention of Zhang Wentian on the Politburo and the inclusion of Wang Ming and Bo Gu on the new CC. Wang, moreover, did not have a large personal following; he seemingly did not build up a group of admirers, as Zhou Enlai had done. And for all the support Wang offered Mao from the Long March on, he was not, as Liu Shaoqi had been, initially convinced that the "Wang Ming line" was wrong in politics, and in 1941 he had different views from Mao concerning the origins of that line.[114] Finally, at the end of the period, presumably for health reasons, he did not participate in the ritual denunciations of the "left line" or his own role in it. Given inner-party opinion in 1945, if Mao harbored any hidden resentment over either Wang's role in the early 1930s or his failure to recant fully, he had only to do nothing to give expression to such complex feelings.

On balance, however, the answer probably lies less in Mao's calculations than in the "democratic" process providing a result at variance with what Mao expected. Mao was attempting to reconcile two objectives: he sought both to reject decisively any remnant influence of the "left" errors of the Returned Students, yet at the same time, to retain some symbolic representation of that group on the top party bodies. Thus, he called for the election of some representatives of past wrong lines. In talks to the delegates, Mao apparently named Wang Ming, Bo Gu, Wang Jiaxiang, and Kai Feng as well as non–Returned Student Li Lisan as people who should be elected to full committee membership in the name of unity,[115] but opposition to the Returned Students in particular soon made it clear that not all of these could be successful.[116] In these circumstances it would seem Mao believed that, given Wang Jiaxiang's prominence as part of the Maoist coalition since the Zunyi conference, his election would pose no problem; thus his efforts were focused on Wang Ming, Bo Gu, and Li Lisan as the major representatives of erroneous lines. This was perhaps demonstrated in Mao's behavior during the counting of votes during the formal election for the full CC. According to congress procedures, a candidate had to receive half the votes in order to be elected, and Mao, reportedly worried that Wang Ming would not be chosen, stayed for the ballot count until Wang Ming obtained the necessary 50 percent and then left.[117] He apparently learned later to his surprise and embarrassment that Wang Jiaxiang had failed to pass the same threshold; only then did he focus on his old comrade's problem.

Several things stand out from the oral accounts of party historians and participants in the Seventh Congress. One is the general belief—perplexity over exactly what happened notwithstanding—that Mao wanted Wang Jiaxiang on the full CC. The suggestion that a link existed between the Mao-Wang differences over historical issues in 1941 and the result in 1945 was repeatedly rejected. A second factor is the great weight the delegates gave ideological and historical correctness as defined by Mao during the Rectification campaign. The resentment against past erroneous lines genuinely ran deep. But if this reflected the growing adulation of the leader, such adulation contradicted the "democratic" features of the congress. Party historians see the Seventh Congress as very democratic, as an embodiment of the Yan'an spirit. While the latter view clearly clashes with some of their own observations about the Rectification campaign in particular, they point to the limits of the newly confirmed chairman's influence on the Wang

Jiaxiang case as proof. As one historian put it, the delegates were ready to answer Mao's call but not to endorse every single suggestion. On balance, Mao's charisma and the preoccupation with correct theory predominated at the Seventh Congress, but the "democratic" aspects were real. Ironically, a combination of both factors saw Wang Jiaxiang's failure to achieve full CC status, apparently against the wishes of the great leader.

Kang Sheng and the Coercive Apparatus: A Debit to Mao's Cause

The explicit reform philosophy of rectification for many years resulted in inadequate scholarly attention to the role of coercion in the party's political processes in the 1940s. Some scholars virtually denied that any inner-party coercive measures were used,[118] while even studies calling attention to the role of force perhaps understated it.[119] Recently, however, in a reasoned if circumstantial argument, Peter Seybolt has not only focused on the coercive, indeed terrorist, element of CCP politics during rectification but has also argued that the introduction of such measures in 1942–43 was a conscious effort not to prevent espionage as claimed but to create widespread fear within both the party and population in order to enforce conformity with both Mao's policies and his leadership.[120] Yet while the tension and fear Seybolt analyzes were real, the asserted motivation is unlikely in the most extreme case of the "Rescue (qiangjiu) campaign" in mid-1943. Moreover, whatever the motivation, this was virtually the only major issue of the entire period after 1938 on which Mao suffered a significant loss of prestige.

The realities of revolutionary struggle required the establishment of secret police organs to protect the CCP against the espionage and sabotage activities of more powerful enemies. Enemy agents had penetrated the party in the past, making necessary harsh countermeasures. Such an environment of struggle, however, led to excesses in inner-party life, with disputes over power and policy frequently distorted into struggles against counterrevolutionaries. Such struggles were often settled by violent means and caused considerable resentment within party ranks. This was dramatically manifested at the Seventh Congress with the demotion of the party's security chief during the early 1930s, Deng Fa, from the Politburo and his removal from the CC altogether. Deng's descent was directly linked to his responsibility for the killing of large numbers of cadres during earlier movements to suppress counterrevolutionaries; according to a well-placed interview source Deng was the most hated of all the leaders up for re-election in 1945. Mao had long been acutely aware of such sentiment and indeed addressed it directly in attacking "Wang Ming's organizational line." Thus in addition to his critique of Wang's political, military, and ideological errors, Mao also blamed the Returned Students for an intolerant and coercive approach to party discipline—the method of "ruthless struggles and merciless blows." Part of

Mao's platform as he built support within the party was the promise that such excesses were a thing of the past, that under his leadership patient persuasion would be used to handle political problems. While Mao's own past impetuosity and excesses, particularly concerning the Futian incident in 1930,[121] most likely raised some doubts about his promises, it is clear that the appeal was popular.[122]

The promise of a persuasive approach to inner-party differences did not, of course, obviate the need for a CCP secret service or attention to infiltration of the party by enemy agents. By the summer or fall of 1939 responsibility for these matters had fallen to Kang Sheng. Although allegedly sycophantic toward Wang Ming in Moscow, Kang became one of the Politburo members working with Mao in Yan'an while Wang was in Wuhan in 1938. After the decisive sixth plenum, Kang apparently managed to align himself even more closely to Mao. In addition to his direct security responsibilities as head of the center's social affairs (investigation) department, Kang's support was rewarded with a major leadership role in the Rectification campaign. In the fall of 1941, he was made chairman of the new committee for cadre screening (*shencha ganbu*), which would be conducted in conjunction with rectification. And when a General Study Committee with Mao as chairman was established in June 1942 to provide overall guidance for the movement, Kang was placed in charge of daily operations. It was from this position that Kang exercised great power over both rectification and the related cadre investigation campaign; ultimately both the authority of this post and his control over the security apparatus became involved in the "rescue" effort.[123]

Rectification, of course, had its coercive aspects early on, as evinced by the harsh treatment of intellectuals who had used the opportunity to be critical of life in Yan'an. Beginning in May 1942 harsh methods were applied to these intellectuals, the most famous case being that of Wang Shiwei, who was denounced as a Trotskyite, arrested, and five years later executed under different circumstances.[124] Later in the year, during a senior cadres meeting held from October 1942 to January 1943, which assessed the effects of rectification, a decision was made to launch a cadre screening movement in the context of rectification. Such a movement, while understandable in terms of the need to verify the credentials and commitment of party members and cadres, inevitably meant a purge of some proportions and thus generated considerable tension among ordinary cadres. In a December speech to the meeting, Kang Sheng increased the tension by introducing the topic of "traitor weeding," thus linking the previous focus on deviations in thought to traitorous activities. At the same time concern over the need to increase vigilance "against spies," which had been raised by Mao at a July 1942 meeting of the General Study Committee, led to the development of a counterespionage movement targeted at the entire population in Communist-held areas.[125]

As a result of these events, considerable momentum had developed in the effort to weed out subversives from both the ranks of cadres and the general population by mid-1943. By that time, new circumstances arose to raise further

CCP anxiety about enemy activities. These circumstances were fundamentally the same as those contributing to the upsurge of the Mao cult in the same period: the dissolution of the Comintern and the new aggressiveness of the GMD in political struggle against the CCP. The two factors were intimately linked. The local GMD commander, Hu Zongnan, used the dissolution of the Comintern to organize some nominally Communist writers to call for abolishing the CCP itself at the very time his forces surrounding the Yan'an area intensified their pressure. It was at this point that Kang Sheng "discovered" large numbers of spies within the base areas, particularly among students and intellectuals who had come from the "white areas." Kang's activities will be further examined below, but here it is important to emphasize that his alarmist views had ample support at the very top. Mao had been expressing concern over subversion for at least a year, and now he adopted a posture described by party historians as "very leftist," concluding that "spies were as thick as fur."[126] Apart from Mao's undoubted responsibility, full concurrence with the dire prognosis was given by Liu Shaoqi, who, in the view of these historians, must share responsibility for this error notwithstanding official efforts decades later to place the blame solely on Kang Sheng. Moreover, one of Liu's closest associates, Peng Zhen, also bears major responsibility. Not only was Peng an active figure at the late 1942 senior cadres meeting that introduced the theme of "traitor weeding" into the cadre investigation discussions, but some of the worst excesses in inner-party struggle in 1942–43 occurred under his stewardship at the Central Party School.[127]

The incident causing the launching of the intense "rescue" effort in July 1943 concerned a young nineteen-year-old student at the Northwest Public School, Zhang Keqin. Zhang's father had been both a former underground party worker and a low-level GMD official, and Zhang himself had also worked in the CCP underground. Apparently some humorous remarks caused suspicion to fall on Zhang, and, using the methods of arrest and torture for which Kang Sheng became famous, the school authorities forced him to make a confession. In this confession, Zhang fabricated a story that his father had been sent by the GMD to join the CCP as a special agent and that the entire party underground in Gansu was controlled by the GMD. Kang learned of the case and used it to paint his picture of severely compromised "red banner" underground parties. Shortly after Zhang's confession, Kang organized a large conference, where Zhang discussed his "experience" and Kang reported on the need to "rescue" cadres from the type of mud hole Zhang had fallen into. Kang exhorted cadres with problems to confess, and over the next several months an intense movement involving torture unfolded. As noted earlier, particular pressure was brought to bear on those from the underground parties under Zhou Enlai, not only in Gansu but especially in Sichuan and Henan. Kang's methods resulted in fifty to sixty deaths, including suicides, according to party historians. Among those affected were the secretary of the Sichuan party organization, Zou Fengping, an official who was working directly under the Chongqing-based Zhou Enlai and who committed suicide, and

Guo Xiaotang, the propaganda chief in Henan, who was arrested. As indicated, Kang already had Mao's, and Liu Shaoqi's, support for launching the movement, if not necessarily for his methods.[128]

As we have seen, upon arriving in Yan'an, Zhou Enlai challenged Kang Sheng's assertions concerning "red banner parties." Kang indeed had virtually equated underground work with unreliability and severely criticized Zhou for his responsibility in this area. Zhou was not the only person to take exception to what was going on and complaints over the excesses and injustices of the "rescue" effort grew within the party. Many of those adversely affected were delegates from the white areas who had been selected for the Seventh Congress then scheduled for the end of the year. This may perhaps explain Ren Bishi's involvement since, as the chief congress organizer, he would be responsible for delegate credentials. In any case, Ren began to look into the "Rescue campaign," discovered widespread abuses, and reported to Mao, who responded with a nine-point CC decision on 15 August.[129] This decision marked a retreat from the "Rescue campaign" by emphasizing leniency and reform, and it called for careful investigation and research when conducting cadre screening. It also strictly forbade all illegal methods and rejected indiscriminate arrests and killing. A further step came on 9 October, when Mao noted on materials concerning the movement that "we shouldn't kill anyone, most people shouldn't be arrested, and this is the policy we should stick to." This had the effect of ending the "Rescue campaign," and the cases already handled were re-examined. In December the conclusion was reached that 90 percent had been wrongfully treated and these, including posthumous cases, accordingly were to be rehabilitated. Zhou Enlai was fully vindicated, while Kang Sheng was left with the task of criticizing the excesses he, and others, were responsible for and overseeing the rehabilitation of those who had suffered at his hands. While Kang attempted to treat such excesses as an "unavoidable phenomenon," he clearly had lost face as a result of how things had turned out.[130]

What were the broader ramifications of this episode? First, the great unpopularity of the "rescue" effort not only led Mao to backtrack on the anti-spy measures of 1943 but apparently contributed to a re-emphasis on the "persuasive" discipline plank of his larger platform. Thus in 1944 during discussions on the "Resolution on Historical Questions," when attention turned to the suppression of counterrevolution under the "third left line," calls were made for the rehabilitation of party members who had been wrongly persecuted, and this was duly included in the document.[131] At the same time, it was apparent that Mao had been deeply embarrassed by the whole affair. At a time when Mao was being hailed as a virtual god, the chairman apologized for the excesses of the "Rescue campaign" on at least five occasions. The first of these, during a 12 April 1944 address to a Yan'an higher party cadres conference, was apparently when Mao bowed to the audience as a sign of remorse. According to party historians, resentment over the events of the previous year ran so deep felt that the audience was unmoved, forcing Mao to bow two more times until applause signified that the apology was accepted.[132] Subsequently, at the Central Party School in early 1945 and just before the Seventh Congress Mao again apologized. During what was otherwise a very formal and unprobing self-criticism at the congress itself, in which he acknowledged only that merit did not belong to him alone and that he too had made errors, Mao addressed the concrete issue of the mistakes committed during cadre screening, admitted that many had been wrongfully dealt with, maintained that the center should be held responsible, and personally apologized to those who had been mistreated. Finally, a similar exercise was reportedly repeated shortly after the congress in August 1945.[133]

But what of Kang Sheng and the coercive apparatus? By all accounts, Kang did not make any deep self-criticism for the events of 1943 despite the clamor of Seventh Congress delegates for an accounting, but instead emphasized the accomplishments of the "Rescue campaign," glossing over its excesses, and claimed that he had only followed Mao's line.[134] Kang was to suffer for this recalcitrance, but it was not immediately apparent to outsiders. As we have seen, Kang was re-elected to the CC and Politburo as a result of Mao's intervention, but within a year or so of the congress his actual position had plummeted. By 1947, at the latest, he had lost all his key operational posts at the center, including control of the security organs.[135] He was sent to conduct land reform in East China, where he assertedly made new "leftist" mistakes, and when the new East China party and government organs were set up in 1949, he was passed over for the leading positions by a lower-ranking, non-Politburo figure, Rao Shushi. Kang then withdrew from active politics in apparent bitterness and went on a fake sick leave, only to re-emerge in 1955 after Rao's fall as part of the Gao Gang affair.[136]

What explains this sudden turnaround? If Mao was willing to support Kang at the Seventh Congress, why did he allow his subsequent humiliation? According to party historians, Kang's re-election to the CC and Politburo was a way of handling Mao's embarrassment over the "Rescue campaign." Since Mao was so clearly identified with that movement, and indeed had openly apologized for it, to remove his key operational lieutenant would have meant a loss of face for the chairman. These sources assert that the delegates knew Kang's influence was on the wane but were still very angry, yet they went along because they knew Mao's prestige was on the line.[137] The handling of the affair suggests that while the charismatic leader could be embarrassed at the hands of his constituency, that constituency was nevertheless committed to protecting the leader's prestige.

More broadly, the results of the Seventh Congress indicate the low standing of the security apparatus as a whole. Not only was the security chief of the 1930s, Deng Fa, ignominiously dropped from the CC, but those who had served under Kang after 1939, Pan Hannian and, especially, Li Kenong, who took over the social affairs department from Kang after the congress, failed to attain even alternate CC status. Perhaps the most significant individual with a security background, but other qualifications as well, who achieved significant recognition at the congress was Luo Ruiqing, and he ranked only eighth from last in the list of CC alternates.[138] In sum, the Seventh Congress reflected a broad attitude within the top ranks of the party since at least 1943. While party leaders recognized the need for coercion in dealing with enemy forces and equally, if not more significantly, contributed to an excessive *ideological* climate within the CCP, which produced great pressure for conformity, they were largely opposed to introducing coercive measures too baldly into the operations of the party itself, and certainly not at the leadership level. The basic Leninist principle of the superiority of the party organization was strongly affirmed. Those most clearly identified with coercion, whether Deng Fa under the "Wang Ming line" or Kang Sheng under Mao's direct leadership, suffered politically in the period surrounding the Seventh Congress. Mao himself, of course, was too central to the entire revolutionary enterprise to suffer any lasting damage from these events, but they did nothing to enhance his cause.

Conclusions

This chapter has addressed broad issues concerning the processes of CCP elite politics during consolidation of Mao's power. It has attempted to illuminate not only the key factors in Mao's rise to the undisputed position of party leader, but also those factors influencing the selection of the other top CCP officials who coalesced around the chairman in the new Maoist leadership. The analysis has focused on major changes in the mode of party leadership from a fairly orthodox Leninist approach to one increasingly, if incompletely, charismatic in nature. The following conclusions have been reached:

1. Despite his emergence as the most influential CCP leader after the Zunyi conference, Mao's authority was still limited and suffered a major setback with the arrival of Wang Ming in Yan'an in late 1937. Over the next year, a deep conflict developed between Mao and Wang over power, policy, and organizational arrangements, but this was settled decisively, albeit not finally in Mao's favor, at the sixth plenum in September–November 1938. Mao's victory was due to the backing of the Comintern and the success of his interpretation of the United Front in comparison to the failure of Wang's approach. After the sixth plenum, Mao's position as the number one party leader was secure, and could have been overturned only by massive failures of Mao's revolutionary strategy or possibly a Comintern change of heart. However, full agreement on Mao's theoretical orientation and interpretation of past party history, particularly for the period of the "Wang Ming line" in 1931–34, was still lacking, and Mao moved patiently and gradually over the next few years to build support for his positions on these matters. Notwithstanding some reservations among sections of the party, and particularly among the Returned Students, in the context of continuing success for Mao's revolutionary program there was overall remarkably little opposition to substantial changes in party ideology and history. Mao's patience

reflected a shrewd awareness of the need to build support within existing Leninist structures and procedures, to win over a large majority of the established party leadership, and to gain the backing, or at least to avoid the wrath, of Moscow. By 1943 Mao's triumph had become irreversible. A new, completely Maoist Secretariat was formed, Mao's position and authority was heightened yet again, the "Thought of Mao Zedong" was systematically articulated as an integral part of the official ideology, and party leaders began to make increasingly extensive self-criticisms of their own past errors as part of rectification and the rewriting of party history according to Mao's precepts. The Seventh Congress was only the final formal recognition of this new situation.

2. Liu Shaoqi emerged as the number two leader of the CCP and putative successor to Mao in what party historians refer to as a natural process. Although not close to Mao at the time, Liu had experiences largely parallel to Mao's during the Returned Students' leadership of the party in the early 1930s: both pushed more cautious policies than the "leftist" approach of the CC leadership, and both suffered as a result. From 1936 on, Liu began to articulate a systematic critique of the Returned Students' errors, often in advance of Mao, and consistently supported Mao in policy and theory. He staunchly supported Mao against Wang Ming in 1938, referring to his Northern Bureau as a base area for Mao's struggle against Wang. Although slower than some others to heap lavish public praise on Mao, Liu played a crucial role in rewriting theory and history and developing the cult of Mao after the sixth plenum. All told, he had supported Mao longer and more consistently on key political-theoretical issues than had any other CCP leader. Given the preoccupation of rectification with "correct theory," it was all but inevitable that Liu would emerge as number two. It was perhaps less inevitable, but ironically human, that Liu's new status led to manifestations of the kind of hubris that were to become so typical of Mao as time wore on.

3. The larger Maoist leadership selected around Mao and Liu at the Seventh Congress was based on considerations of party seniority, talent, representation of important inner-party constituencies, and loyal support for Mao's leadership and programs. While opposition to Mao before the Zunyi conference did not rule anyone out, support after Zunyi was a critical if not absolute criterion. Also important was a rejection of the theoretical and political errors of the "Wang Ming line" of 1931–34, the period of Mao's greatest political setbacks. In this context, the fate of several of the party's key leaders is particularly noteworthy. Ren Bishi, who was confirmed as number five in the leadership in 1945, had been a major figure in stripping Mao of his military power in 1931–32, but he consistently supported Mao in the post-Zunyi struggles against Zhang Guotao and Wang Ming. He was also a Politburo member of long standing and represented the key inner-party constituency of the Second Front Army. Thus, despite his transgressions of the early 1930s, Ren represented a package of highly desirable qualities. The case of Zhou Enlai was more complex. Although he also

"opposed" Mao in the early 1930s, Zhou handled the situation with great tact. Yet, from Mao's perspective, he blundered by supporting Wang Ming's version of the United Front in 1938. Before 1943 Zhou was outside the core Maoist leadership, in spite of his own fervent support of Mao since 1939. By 1943, he appeared to be in considerable trouble, but during the latter part of that year he seemed to win Mao's confidence with extensive self-criticisms of his own past and systematic critiques of the "Wang Ming line." This, together with Zhou's obvious talent and wide support in the party, placed him among the top five leaders in 1944–45. The most perplexing case is that of Wang Jiaxiang, the man to whom Mao arguably owed more than any other CCP leader. Although a Returned Student, Wang played a critical role in supporting Mao first at Zunyi and then in arguing Mao's case in Moscow and bringing back the Comintern's endorsement. Wang continued to play a vital role in support of Mao through 1943, but by then he was ill, went on sick leave, and missed the Seventh Congress. Still it was a shock when Wang was demoted to CC alternate status at the congress; none of the explanations expressed at the time are completely convincing. But it seems that the fact that Wang was a Returned Student and, in the context of his illness in 1944–45, apparently did not offer a Zhou Enlai–style critique of the 1931–34 period was the key to his decline. In a congress atmosphere charged with hostility toward the purveyors of the "third left line" after rectification, the "democratic" sentiments of the delegates apparently overrode the preferences of the leader in denying Wang full CC status.

4. Although the rectification effort of 1942–43, and particularly in the context of the GMD's new 1943 anticommunist upsurge, produced considerable coercive pressures within the party, it is unlikely that the major aspects of this, the cadre investigations and mid-1943 "Rescue campaign," were designed to bolster Mao's personal power. Even if this had been the case to some degree, these developments did not enhance Mao's position but instead were perhaps the only major loss of prestige he suffered in the entire 1939–45 period. The excesses of the "rescue" effort went directly against an important plank of Mao's overall program, a more persuasive approach to inner-party differences in contrast to the Returned Students' "ruthless struggles and merciless blows." Moreover, Mao, who had been ultimately responsible for this campaign, felt constrained to offer apologies on at least five different occasions in 1944–45. Resentment within the party was widespread and focused on the main figure in carrying out the movement: security chief Kang Sheng. Although Kang was formally re-elected to the Politburo after the Seventh Congress in order to protect Mao's prestige, shortly afterward his status was severely diminished. The role of the security apparatus more generally also suffered at the congress, with hardly anyone from this potentially potent instrument receiving a place on the CCP's top representative bodies. These measures, then, served to re-emphasize the authority of the party's political leadership over its coercive instruments.

At the start of the period examined in this study, Mao Zedong faced several constraints linked in various ways to Leninist organizational precepts. Although tendencies toward personalized leadership had appeared in the earlier history of the CCP, no leader had established anything remotely like the personal dominance of Stalin or indeed Lenin, and authority rested more in the "center" than in individuals. Collective leadership processes were particularly in evidence on the Long March and subsequently, as Mao painstakingly built his power through the skilled use of these procedures.[139] These collective processes placed a further constraint on Mao since many of the individuals on the legitimate leading bodies of the party had been deeply involved in the failed policies of the early 1930s and were slow to see or admit errors in those policies outside the military realm.

Another limitation on a potential great leader, although in Mao's case a limitation more in theory than practice given both his goals and political skill, was the subordination of the CCP's coercive apparatus to civilian party authority. Despite bloody excesses in the earlier history of the CCP, the security forces had not been a major avenue to power and Mao used resentment over their excesses as part of his political program;[140] moreover, after new abuses appeared under his leadership in 1943, he beat a hasty retreat and reined in those forces. Perhaps the most difficult "Leninist" constraint on Mao was the subordination of the CCP as an organization to the Comintern, but here too Mao acted with the necessary patience and respect of official norms and was rewarded with Moscow's endorsement in mid-1938.

After the sixth plenum, Mao steadily acquired the status and authority of a great leader. While this was to a large extent based on Mao's conscious efforts to rewrite party history, enshrine his "Thought" as official ideology, and eliminate conflicting ideas through rectification, Mao's success was based fundamentally on another part of the Leninist tradition that ultimately always was more potent than organizational prescriptions—the primacy attached to correct political strategies in producing revolutionary success. As the party's fortunes waxed during these years, Mao accumulated genuine charisma as the chief architect of the successful program. Another "tradition," in this case Stalin's perversion of Leninist norms to create one-man rule, also bolstered Mao by reinforcing the culturally based leader principle.

Yet in the Chinese context of the mid-1940s, there was no obvious incompatibility of the new great leader and collective, quasi-democratic procedures within the party. This derived mostly from Mao's style and program, a style involving broad consultation within the leadership and "democratic" mechanisms at the Seventh Congress, and a program that kept the coercive apparatus subordinate to civilian control. Thus, for those attached to notions of inner-party democracy there was no inherent bar to Mao's new status, a status confirmed unanimously by one of the most "democratic" congresses in the CCP's history. In fact, the contradiction was profound and would grow, at first gradually, after Mao's charisma received the massive infusion of the victory of 1949, and then profoundly over the last twenty years of the chairman's life. But in 1945 it was perceived only dimly, if at all, by the celebrants of Mao's elevation.

Notes

Thanks are due to David Goodman, Bruce Jacobs, Felix Patrikeeff, K. K. Shum, and the participants in the conference on "New Perspectives on the Chinese Communist Revolution," particularly K. V. Shevelyoff and Susanne Weigelen-Schwiedrzik, for their comments on an earlier draft. We also gratefully acknowledge the financial support of the Australian Research Council, and the Ian Potter Foundation. An expanded version of this study appears as *The Formation of the Maoist Leadership: From the Return of Wang Ming to the Seventh Party Congress* (London: Contemporary China Institute, 1994).

1. For the politics that went into the drafting of the "Resolution," see Chapter 11 in this volume.

2. For an argument to this effect, see Benjamin Yang, "The Zunyi Conference as One Step in Mao's Rise to Power: A Survey of Historical Studies of the Chinese Communist Party," *China Quarterly*, no. 106 (1986): 235–71.

3. The major disruptions at the Politburo level, of course, were the purge of Gao Gang in 1954 and the dismissal of Peng Dehuai in 1959.

4. As indicated by the different Chinese terms, "faction" is being used here in a somewhat different sense from that in the immediately preceding part of the sentence. The earlier reference, *zongpai*, is to political groupings within the leadership with their own particular programs or power goals that brought them into conflict with other leadership groupings. The "factions," *shantou*, within the unified Maoist leadership refer to party constituencies formed around similar career patterns and revolutionary experiences. While these constituencies may have had their own policies or power goals, by the early 1940s these were subordinated to the larger Maoist program.

5. This model, of course, was never fully implemented in the Soviet Union. Even under Lenin, adherence to Leninist norms was checkered at best, while Stalin totally subverted organizational principles. For an extensive analysis, see Graeme Gill, *The Origins of the Stalinist Political System* (Cambridge: University Press, 1990), especially 86–110, 172–98, 242–55, and 297–306.

6. In attempting to explain Mao's increasingly erratic one-person rule during the Cultural Revolution, the 1981 "Resolution on Certain Questions in the History of Our Party Since the Founding of the People's Republic of China," in *Beijing Review*, no. 27 (1981): 24–26, cited not only "certain grievous deviations . . . in the history of the international communist movement [concerning] the relationship between the Party and its leader" and the "very long history" of "feudalism" in China, but also Mao's high "prestige" albeit in a somewhat different sense than used here. These factors were all clearly operative in the developments of the early and mid-1940s. For an overview of the tension between institutional norms and the leader principle in the pre-1949 period, see Lawrence R. Sullivan, "The Evolution of Chinese Communist Party Organization and Leadership Doctrine, 1921–1945," paper delivered to the conference on "New Perspectives on the Chinese Communist Revolution," Leiden and Amsterdam, 1990.

7. *Mao Zedong yiwenlu* (Record of Mao Zedong Anecdotes) (Beijing: Legal Press, 1989), 93; and interview sources.

8. See Wang Jianying, ed., *Zhongguo Gongchandang zuzhishi ziliao huibian* (Compilation of Materials on CCP Organizational History, *ZGZZH*) (Beijing: Red Flag Press, 1983), 235; and Frederick C. Teiwes, "Peng Dehuai and Mao Zedong," *Australian Journal of Chinese Affairs*, no. 16 (1986): 85. Mao's formal military role was determined in the period immediately after Zunyi, and his *de facto* pre-eminence quickly became apparent.

9. Wang Jianying, *ZGZZH*, 235, 297, 331. Wang Jianying refers to Zhang Wentian as general secretary in the period up to the December 1937 Politburo meeting. Although the matter is contentious among party historians, on balance this appears to be technically

in error as the title of general secretary seemingly was never formally conferred. In fact, however, Zhang performed the role of general secretary until his duties were redefined at the December 1937 meeting (see below), and he was often colloquially referred to as general secretary. After December 1937, Zhang continued as the party's main administrative officer until the September–November 1938 sixth plenum, when Mao formally took over responsibility for daily party affairs, but he went out of his way to deny that he filled the general secretary role. *Dangshi yanjiu* (Research on Party History), no. 2 (1980): 79; and interview sources.

10. In Yan'an Mao observed that Zhang "never scrambled for power"; see Frederick C. Teiwes, "Mao and His Lieutenants," *Australian Journal of Chinese Affairs*, nos. 19–20 (1988): 30.

11. Although the issue of a mistake in political line was raised at Zunyi by Liu Shaoqi, Mao reportedly "cleverly avoided" the issue. See *Wenxian he yanjiu* (Documents and Research), no. 4 (1987): 43; and Liao Gailong, ed., *Zhonggong dangshi wenzhai niankan 1982* (1982 Annual CCP History Abstracts) (Beijing: CCP Party Materials Press, 1984), 558. In any case, the conference resolution declared that the party's political line was correct; *Hongqi* (Red Flag), no. 3 (1985): 14.

12. See Harrison E. Salisbury, *The Long March: The Untold Story* (New York: Harper and Row, 1985), chaps. 23–24, 26.

13. *Selected Works of Mao Tse-tung* (Beijing: Foreign Languages Press, 1965), 1: 156 and 163–65. Ironically, the pre-eminent Returned Student, Wang Ming, as a Comintern official in Moscow was the first to address these errors; see below, note 15.

14. See Teiwes, "Mao and His Lieutenants," 59.

15. See the analysis of Wang's contributions to the development of the United Front by Li Liangzhi in *Shixue yuekan* (Historiography Monthly), no. 2 (1989): 64–72, translated and with an introduction by K.K. Shum, in *CCP Research Newsletter*, no. 5 (1990): 21–35; no. 6 and 7 (1990): 23–31.

16. Wang Jianying, *ZGZZH*, 296–97. Although Zhang Wentian is listed first here, interview sources believe he ranked third in fact. One such source, citing Zhang's rank of sixth on the committee set up by the conference to prepare for the Seventh Congress (ibid., 296), believes even this is overstated.

17. Unlike Wang and Kang, Chen did not come directly from the Soviet Union but was picked up in Xinjiang, where he had been stranded after leaving Moscow the previous year.

18. Wang Jianying, *ZGZZH*, 297; and above, note 9.

19. Interview sources give these reasons for Bo's demotion. Also, at the December Politburo conference Wang Ming acknowledged the mistakes of the January 1934 fifth plenum, which was held under the leadership of Bo Gu well after Wang had left China for the Soviet Union. Zhou Guoquan et al., *Wang Ming pingzhuan* (Critical Biography of Wang Ming) (Anhui: Anhui People's Press, 1989), 303.

20. Chen Yun and Kang Sheng remained with Mao in Yan'an when Wang Ming went to Wuhan in 1938 and soon clearly adopted pro-Mao postures, while earlier the defection of Wang Jiaxiang and Zhang Wentian from the leading Returned Student on the scene in China, Bo Gu, was crucial for Mao's victory at Zunyi. See below, 344 and 366.

21. *Dang de wenxian* (Party Documents), no. 3 (1988): 60.

22. Wang Jianying, *ZGZZH*, 296; and *Zhongguo gongchandang lici daibiao dahui* (Previous CCP Congresses) (Beijing: People's Press, 1982), 146.

23. *Memoirs of a Chinese Marshal—The Autobiographical Notes of Peng Dehuai* (Beijing: Foreign Languages Press, 1984), 418–19.

24. Shum Kui-Kwong, *The Chinese Communists' Road to Power: The Anti-Japanese United Front (1935–45)* (Hong Kong: Oxford University Press, 1988), 118–37; *Hongqi*,

no. 12 (1981): 34; and interview source. For further details on Yan'an-Wuhan tensions in 1938, see Zhou Guoquan, *Wang Ming pingzhuan*, 340–44.

25. *Wenxian he yanjiu*, no. 4 (1986): 32; Li Weihan, *Huiyi yu yanjiu* (Reminiscences and Research) (Beijing: CCP Party Materials Press, 1986), 1: 443; and interview source.

26. See, for example, the brief discussion in Raymond F. Wylie, *The Emergence of Maoism: Mao Tse-tung, Ch'en Po-ta, and the Search for Chinese Theory 1935–1945* (Stanford: Stanford University Press, 1980), 71–72.

27. *Wenxian he yanjiu*, no. 4 (1986): 32–33.

28. Wylie, *Emergence of Maoism*, 88–95; *Selected Works of Mao Tse-tung*, 2: 195–96n, and 205–7; Shum, *Chinese Communists' Road to Power*, 138–46; Wang Jianying, *ZGZZH*, 331, 337–38; Jin Chongji, *Zhou Enlai zhuan (1898–1949)* (Biography of Zhou Enlai (1898–1949) (Beijing: Central Documents Press, 1989), 424–25; *Hongqi*, no. 17 (1985): 14; *Zhongguo Gongchandang lici daibiao dahui*, 147; and interview sources.

29. Wylie, *Emergence of Maoism*, 96–97; and *Hongqi*, no. 23 (1983): 2.

30. According to *Zhongguo gongchandang lici daibiao dahui*, 292, at the time of the sixth plenum the whole party recognized Mao's status as leader.

31. Organizationally, Wang's position was shored up by a sixth plenum decision that there would be no changes in the Politburo or Secretariat before the Seventh Congress; *Zhonggong dangshi yanjiu* (Research on CCP History), no. 1 (1988): 94. Politically, Wang retained important regional support in East China before the death of Xiang Ying in 1941 and the Northeast, which was under the direct leadership of the CCP delegation to the Comintern in Moscow. These two regions, in the opinion of the Soviet specialist K. V. Shevelyoff, were Wang's "military fists."

32. See *Wang Shoudao huiyilu* (Memoirs of Wang Shoudao) (Beijing: Liberation Army Press, 1987), 200; *Selected Works of Mao Tse-tung*, 2: 441–42 and 445; Shum, *Chinese Communists' Road to Power*, 182; and interview sources.

33. *Wenxian he yanjiu*, no. 1 (1982): 11; and Wylie, *Emergence of Maoism*, 154–58.

34. Interview source specializing on Zhang Wentian. The full implications of this story are somewhat unclear given that the general secretary post did not exist in 1938 and Mao did assume responsibility for the party's daily affairs at the plenum (see above, note 9), but the source is well placed to know that such a proposal was made by Zhang and rejected by Mao.

35. *Dang de wenxian*, no. 3 (1988): 60–61; and interview sources. The written source places greater emphasis on "objective" obstacles, while interview sources give greater attention to "subjective" factors.

36. According to Mao's assessment of April 1944, the other critical "inner-party struggles" were the Zunyi conference, the sixth plenum, the 1942 Rectification campaign, and the campaign beginning in winter 1943 for the study of past line struggles. *Selected Works of Mao Tse-tung*, 3: 165–66.

37. Li Weihan, *Huiyi yu yanjiu*, 2: 487; Central Party School, ed., *Zhongguo gongchandang lishi* (History of the CCP) (Beijing: People's Press, 1990), 2: 147; Zhao Shenghui, *Zhongguo Gongchandang zuzhishi gangyao* (Outline History of CCP Organization) (Hefei: Anhui People's Press, 1987), 189; *Dangshi yanjiu*, no. 1 (1981): 71–72; CCP Central Party History Research Office, ed., *Zhonggong dangshi dashi nianbiao shuoming* (Explanation of Chronology of Major Events in CCP History) (n.p.: CCP Central Party School Press, 1983), 98–99; *Wenxian he yanjiu*, no. 2 (1986): 10; and Wang Jianying, *ZGZZH*, 380.

38. *Hongqi*, no. 23 (1983): 3; and *Dangshi yanjiu ziliao* (Research Materials on Party History), no. 4 (1988): 28.

39. *Zhang Wentian xuanji* (Selected works of Zhang Wentian) (Beijing: People's Press, 1985), 313–15; and interview sources. The dissenters from Li Weihan's view claim that Zhang's decision to go to the grass roots was precisely to acknowledge his acceptance

of Mao's principles of combining theory and practice. In any case, even those believing Zhang's act reflected his discontent accept that while spending a year in the countryside Zhang became a firm believer in Mao's ideological line.

40. Wang Yifan, in *Dangshi yanjiu ziliao*, no. 4 (1988): 29; and interview source. According to the interview source, the 1941 senior cadre study, which involved 120 key base area and army leaders, should be seen as part of an ongoing process consisting of Mao's efforts to propagate his views since 1937 and the year-long Marxist study movement launched in May 1939.

41. *Hongqi*, no. 13 (1986): 8–9; Zhou Guoquan, *Wang Ming pingzhuan*, 385 and 390; *Selected Works of Mao Tse-tung*, 3: 163–64n; and interview sources. The Northwest senior cadres conference was a crucial meeting at which the past history of the Shaan-Gan-Ning area was taken as a model for analyzing historical questions generally. On this meeting see Mark Selden, *The Yenan Way in Revolutionary China* (Cambridge: Harvard University Press, 1971), 200–7. During the discussions of high-ranking cadres starting in October 1943 officials from different regions were organized into groups to consider the historical problems of their own areas.

42. For example, Wylie's sensitive study, *Emergence of Maoism*, 4–6, 158, 193, and *passim*, gives considerable attention to "ambivalence," "misgivings," and "reluctance" on the part of high-level party leaders toward Mao in this period. Without denying that such phenomena existed *on specific matters*, the results of this research suggest rather a strong and growing acceptance of Mao's leadership and related claims after the sixth plenum.

43. According to an interview source specializing on Zhang, such tensions were more the result of differing personal and leadership styles than major differences over policy.

44. *Hongqi*, no. 16 (1985):24; Zhou Guoquan, *Wang Ming pingzhuan*, 409; and above, 346 and note 39.

45. *Dangshi yanjiu yu jiaoxue* (Party History Research and Teaching), no. 1 (1988): 36; *Hongqi*, no. 24 (1983): 3–4; *Dangshi tongxun* (Bulletin on Party History), no. 1 (1985): 17; interview sources; and Patricia Stranahan, "The Last Battle: Mao and the Internationalists' Fight for the *Liberation Daily*," *China Quarterly*, no. 123 (1990): 522, 532, 534, and 536. As the title suggests, Stranahan emphasizes conflict between Mao and the Internationalists on the *Liberation Daily* staff, yet she observes that although "lack[ing] zeal" they "never actively opposed Mao's program[s] and policies" (522). She also notes the view of a former staff member, Li Rui, that Bo Gu's spring 1942 self-criticism concerning the paper was sincere (532). On balance, Bo's resistance seems to have largely ended by early 1942 although his apparently restrained attitude still saw him officially bracketed with Wang Ming in December 1943 as the only leading comrades not "unified" around Mao. See *Wenxian he yanjiu (1984 huibianben)* (Documents and Research, 1984 Collected Edition) (Beijing: People's Press, 1986), 25–26; and below, note 48.

46. See below, 363.

47. Shum, *Chinese Communists' Road to Power*, 170–71, and 213–14; and Wylie, *Emergence of Maoism*, 132–33.

48. It is, of course, always difficult to date someone's "final" defeat, and the formal denunciation of Wang Ming and Bo Gu by name in December 1943 might be viewed as having greater finality; see *Yan'an zhengfeng yundong (ziliao xuanji)* (The Yan'an Rectification Campaign [Collected Materials]) (Beijing: CCP Central Party School Press, 1984), 123–25. After the September–October meeting, however, while Wang remained personally defiant he apparently made no further serious efforts to oppose Mao politically.

49. Liao Gailong, ed., *1986 nian Zhonggong dangshi wenzhai niankan* (1986 Annual CCP History Abstracts) (Beijing: CCP Party Materials Press, 1988), 337; Zhou Guoquan, *Wang Ming pingzhuan*, 390–91; *Dangshi xinxi* (Party History News), 1 June 1986, 1; and interview source.

50. Between 1942 and 1945 various leaders, including Liu Shaoqi, Zhou Enlai, Ren Bishi, Li Fuchun, Zhu De and Mao himself visited Wang to urge self-criticism or acceptance of the "Resolution on Historical Questions," but generally these encounters ended without full satisfaction if not outright hostility. Zhou Guoquan, *Wang Ming pingzhuan*, 407–9, 412 and 418; and interview sources.

51. On at least two occasions, in December 1943 and April 1945, Wang wrote letters of self-criticism to Mao; Zhou Guoquan, *Wang Ming pingzhuan*, 413 and 419–23.

52. Li Weihan, *Huiyi yu yanjiu*, 2: 478; Quan Yanchi, *Zouxia shentande Mao Zedong* (Mao Zedong Down to Earth) (Beijing: Chinese–Foreign Cultures Press, 1989), 107–9; and interview sources.

53. Wylie, *Emergence of Maoism*, chap. 8.

54. Wang Jianying, *ZGZZH*, 424–25; and Sullivan, "Evolution of Leadership Doctrine," 65 and 136; and Liao Kai-lung (Liao Gailong), "Historical Experiences and Our Road of Development" (25 October 1980), part II, in *Issues and Studies* (November 1981): 91–92.

55. Wang Jianying, *ZGZZH*, 428.

56. Ibid., 479.

57. Ibid., 479 and 481. These listings distort the actual situation in that Zhu De, as leader of the communist armies, is listed in a higher position than was in fact the case. The real rank order of the 1945 Secretariat, which was well understood within the CCP, was Mao, Liu, Zhou, Zhu, and Ren; interview source.

58. *Hongqi*, no. 12 (1981): 45–51; ibid., no. 13 (1986): 12–21; and interview source.

59. The eight large delegations were: organs directly under the party center and the military headquarters, the Shaan-Gan-Ning Border Region, the Shanxi-Suiyuan area, the Jin-Cha-Ji (Shanxi-Chahar-Hebei) Border Region, the Jin-Ji-Lu-Yu (Shanxi-Hebei-Shandong-Henan) Border Region, Shandong, Central China, and the great rear areas (*dahoufang*). *Dangshi yanjiu*, no. 2 (1982): 59.

60. Zhao Shenghui, *Zhongguo gongchandang zuzhishi gangyao*, 195; Central Committee Archives, ed., *Zhonggong zhongyang wenjian xuanji* (Selected Documents of the CCP CC) (Beijing: CCP Central Party School Press, 1987), 13: 50–51; Hu Hua, ed., *Zhongguo xinminzhuzhuyi gemingshi cankao ziliao* (Reference Materials on China's New Democratic Revolution) (Beijing: China Books Press, 1951), 398 and 492; *Hongqi*, no. 13 (1981): 46; Gan Zhengwen, *Ren Bishi* (Ren Bishi) (Hunan: Hunan People's Press, 1979), 232; interview sources; and below, 367–70.

61. See Wang Jianying, *ZGZZH*, 296 and 481.

62. *Renmin ribao* (People's Daily), 23 October 1988, 4; and interview source. Also see Teiwes, "Peng and Mao," 86.

63. See below, 374. A documentary source, *Dangshi yanjiu ziliao*, no. 10 (1982): 19, presents Peng Zhen as someone who curbed the excesses of the movement in the Central Party School, but the interview source is well positioned to know the facts of the case.

64. In the case of Deng Fa, who had supported the Returned Students in the early 1930s, the failure to be re-elected even to the CC probably had more to do with Deng's excesses in killing many cadres during movements to suppress counterrevolutionaries. See Hu Hua, ed., *Zhonggong dangshi renwu zhuan* (Biographies of Personalities in CCP History, *ZDRZ*) (Xi'an: Shanxi People's Press, 1980), 1: 356–58. Also see below, 370.

Of course, strictly speaking, Mao may not have had many options since, apart from Wang Ming, only Bo Gu had full CC status and presumably eligibility for Politburo membership. Bo, however, both had long-standing service on the Politburo and by 1945 had engaged extensively in rectification, yet he was passed over.

65. The preceding paragraphs are based on Teiwes, "Mao and His Lieutenants," 38–40.

For Mao's comments on *shantou*, see *Weidade licheng* (The Great Course) (Beijing: People's Press, 1977), 219.

66. See Teiwes, "Mao and His Lieutenants," 8–9.

67. See the identification by the 1945 "Resolution on Historical Questions" of Mao and Liu as representing the correct line in the base areas and white areas respectively; *Selected Works of Mao Tse-tung*, 3: 198. See also Chapter 11 in this volume. On the legacy of this distinction in post-1949 political conflict, see Frederick C. Teiwes, *Politics at Mao's Court: Gao Gang and Party Factionalism in the Early 1950s* (Armonk, NY: M.E. Sharpe, 1990), chap. 4.

68. Krishna Prakash Gupta, "Mao's Uncertain Legacy," *Problems of Communism* (January–February 1982): 50.

69. This was a consistent theme of interviews with various party historians conducted over a four-year period from 1986 to 1990.

70. See Teiwes, "Mao and His Lieutenants," 59–60.

71. Liu as well as Peng Dehuai and Lin Biao expressed reservations about the course of military developments under Mao's leadership in early 1935; see Peng's *Memoirs of a Chinese Marshal*, 365–70.

72. See Teiwes, "Mao and His Lieutenants," 54, on Liu's travails in Moscow. In this period Liu lost the positions of head of the center's labor department and party secretary of the national trade union organization. Wang Jianying, *ZGZZH*, 150; Liao Gailong, *Dangshi niankan 1982*, 557; and *Mianhuai Liu Shaoqi* (Remember Fondly Liu Shaoqi) (Beijing: Central Documents Press, 1988), 5 and 17.

73. *Selected Works of Liu Shaoqi* (Beijing: Foreign Languages Press, 1984), 1: 34–44. On Liu's role at Zunyi, see above, note 11.

74. *Wenxian he yanjiu*, no. 5 (1987): 33–35; *Zhongguo xiandaishi ziliao xuanbian* (Selected Materials on Modern Chinese History) (Harbin: Heilongjiang People's Press, 1981), 3: 445–50; and interview sources.

75. *Wang Shoudao huiyilu*, 212–13.

76. Ibid., 215–16.

77. See the collection of rectification documents in Boyd Compton, *Mao's China: Party Reform Documents, 1942–1944* (Seattle: University of Washington Press, 1952/1966).

78. Compare Liu's letter in *Selected Works of Liu Shaoqi*, 1: 217–21, to Mao's sixth plenum views in *Selected Works of Mao Tse-tung*, 2: 208–9. In mid-1941, Mao also promoted the theoretical level of senior cadres, especially by forming study groups that, at his direction, studied Soviet materials; *Hongqi*, no. 24 (1983): 3 and 6. It is true that Liu's letter, which was written in response to a query about the state of theoretical studies, had a different emphasis than Mao's May 1941 "Reform Our Studies" (*Selected Works of Mao Tse-tung*, 3: 17–28), but in the context, both views should be seen as opposite sides of the same coin. For a view of Liu's letter as reflecting reservations concerning Mao's theoretical accomplishments, see Wylie, *Emergence of Maoism*, 158–59. Interview sources, however, deny that any such purpose existed.

79. See Wylie, ibid., 158–60, 168, and 192–94.

80. A decade and a half after the event; Liu himself expressed a similar view; see Liu's 1959 comments on his enthusiasm in promoting the personality cult in *Lilun daokan* (Theoretical Guidance) (Xi'an), no. 7 (1988): 40–43.

81. Interview source. Note that all Liu's "historical errors" used by Gao Gang in his 1953 effort to undermine Liu came after the Seventh Congress; see Teiwes, *Politics at Mao's Court*, chap. 2.

82. According to these sources, only Wang Ming refused to make a self-criticism, if one excludes several letters to Mao (see above, note 51), while Kang Sheng's was superficial in the extreme (see below, 374). Wang Jiaxiang (see below, 367) also did not participate in rectification because of illness.

83. Party historians, however, distinguish Liu from "flatterers" such as Lin Biao and the "Gang of Four" on the grounds that he was "sincere" in his praise of Mao.

84. Ren was associated with various organizations in Changsha during 1915–20 where Mao had connections, most notably the "Russian Study Club," and in 1920 he was recommended by the club to be received in Shanghai for the purpose of arranging his study in Moscow. *Wenxian he yanjiu*, no. 4 (1984): 27.

85. Donald W. Klein and Anne B. Clark, *Biographic Dictionary of Chinese Communism* (Cambridge: Harvard University Press, 1971), 1: 412–13; Wang Jianying, *Hongjun renwu zhi* (Red Army Personnel Records) (Beijing: Liberation Army Press, 1988), 402; and interview source.

86. Klein and Clark, *Biographic Dictionary*, 1: 413–14; Wang Jianying, *Hongjun renwu zhi*, 402; and *Hongqi*, no. 8 (1984): 8.

87. Gan Zhengwen, *Ren Bishi*, 224, 230–30 and 233; Wang Jianying, *Hongjun renwu zhi*, 403; Wang Jianying, *ZGZZH*, 380; *Dangshi yanjiu*, no. 6 (1980): 56; *Zhongguo gongchandang lici zhongyao huiyiji*, 1: 224; and interview source.

88. Ren may have made some effort to temper the blow, however. In November 1931, Ren invited Mao to give a lecture at the first representative congress of the soviet areas; Gan Zhengwen, *Ren Bishi*, 99.

89. Wang Jianying, *Hongjun renwu zhi*, 717; Salisbury, *Long March*, 130–33 and *passim*; and interview sources.

90. Hu Hua, *ZDRZ*, 8 (1983): 18–19; and interview source.

91. See Teiwes, "Mao and His Lieutenants," 52–53.

92. Interview sources.

93. Jin Chongji, *Zhou Enlai zhuan*, 563; and interview source.

94. Wang Jianying, *ZGZZH*, 299, 334–35, and 380–81; and Klein and Clark, *Biographic Dictionary*, 1: 210–11.

95. *Kommunisticheskii Internatsional i Kitaiskaya Revoliutsiya: Dokumenty i Materialy* (The Communist International and the Chinese Revolution: Documents and Materials) (Moscow: Science Press, 1986), 295–96.

96. Jin Chongji, *Zhou Enlai zhuan*, 552, 554–55; and interview sources.

97. The following is based on discussions with party historians.

98. The texts of Zhou's self-criticisms are not available, but his self-critical remarks at the Seventh Congress can be found in *Selected Works of Zhou Enlai*, 1: 220 and 242–44.

99. Interview source; and below, 373.

100. Li ranked sixteenth on the new CC even though he had long been absent in the Soviet Union, and in fact, was unaware that the Seventh Congress was being held. As in other cases, Mao's intervention seems decisive. See Hu Hua, *ZDRZ*, 16 (1984): 79–80; and *Zhonggong dangshi jiaoxue cankao ziliao* (CCP History Teaching Reference Materials), (n.p.: Chinese People's Liberation Army Political Academy's Party History Teaching and Research Office, 1986), 17: 375.

101. See above, note 57.

102. *Wenxian he yanjiu*, no. 4 (1986): 32–33.

103. This was colloquial usage among party cadres; interview source.

104. *Renmin ribao*, 27 December 1979, 2.

105. Wang Jianying, *Hongjun renwu zhi*, 472–73; *Wenxian he yanjiu*, no. 4 (1986): 32; Jin Chongji, *Zhou Enlai zhuan*, 254–57; CCP History Teaching and Research Office of the Political Academy, *Zhongguo Gongchandang liushinian dashi jianjie* (Brief Introduction to Major Events in the CCP's Sixty Years) (Beijing: Chinese People's Liberation Army Political Academy Press, 1985), 143–44 and 149–50.

106. Salisbury, *Long March*, 70–71; and Wang Jianying, *Hongjun renwu zhi*, 473.

107. *Wenxian he yanjiu*, no. 4 (1986): 32.

108. Wang Jianying, *ZGZZH*, 234–35; Wang Jianying, *Hongjun renwu zhi*, 473; and Salisbury, *Long March*, 277 and 295–96.

109. *Wenxian he yanjiu*, no. 2 (1986): 11, and no. 4 (1986): 33; *Dangshi wenhui*, no. 2 (1987): 66; Wang Jianying, *Hongjun renwu zhi*, 473; and interview sources.

110. *Wenxian he yanjiu*, no. 4 (1986): 31; and interview sources. Mao reportedly was quite happy with Wang's letter and had it circulated to the congress delegates. However, according to interview sources, it was only at the second plenum in early 1949 that Wang made a significant self-criticism. It is also of interest that Wang was not included on the new committee set up in 1944 for drafting the "Resolution on Historical Questions." While explainable in terms of his illness, it is still surprising he was not given a nominal position in view of his role in 1941.

111. Zhu Zhongli, *Wang Jiaxiang wenxue zhuanji* (Literary Biography of Wang Jiaxiang) (Beijing: Liberation Army Press, 1986), 337–39; and interview sources.

112. Zhu Zhongli, ibid., 339; interview sources; *Hongqi*, no. 12 (1981): 45–51; ibid., no. 13 (1986): 12–21; interview sources; and above, note 100.

113. Gan Zhengwen, *Ren Bishi*, 232.

114. Interview source.

115. P.P. Vladimirov, *China's Special Area 1942–1945* (Bombay: Allied Publishers, 1974), 423–26, 430, 448–50; and interview sources.

116. In the event, of the Returned Students only Zhang Wentian, Wang Ming, and Bo Gu were elected full CC members, while Wang Jiaxiang attained alternate status. Previous Politburo member Kai Feng was dropped altogether, while even such a significant figure as Yang Shangkun failed to achieve alternate status.

117. *Nanwang de huiyi—Huainian Mao Zedong tongzhi* (Unforgettable Memories—Remembering Comrade Mao Zedong) (Beijing: China Youth Press, 1985), 24; interview sources; and above, 352.

118. See Mark Selden, "The Yenan Legacy: The Mass Line," in A. Doak Barnett, ed., *Chinese Communist Politics in Action* (Seattle: University of Washington Press, 1969), 107.

119. See Frederick C. Teiwes, *Politics and Purges in China: Rectification and the Decline of Party Norms 1950–1965*, 2nd ed. (Armonk, NY: M.E. Sharpe, 1993), 56–57.

120. Peter J. Seybolt, "Terror and Conformity: Counterespionage Campaigns, Rectification, and Mass Movements, 1942–1943," *Modern China* (January 1986): 39–73.

121. Teiwes, *Politics and Purges*, 49; and interview source.

122. See Teiwes, *Politics and Purges*, 48–51.

123. Zhong Kan, *Kang Sheng pingzhuan* (Critical Biography of Kang Sheng) (Beijing: Red Flag Press, 1982), chap. 7, and 10–11; Wang Jianying, *ZGZZH*, 380; Seybolt, "Terror and Conformity," 46; and interview sources.

124. Seybolt, "Terror and Conformity," 47–50; Teiwes, *Politics and Purges*, 58–60; and Timothy C. Cheek, "The Fading of the 'Wild Lilies': Wang Shiwei and Mao Zedong's 'Yan'an Talks' in the First CPC Rectification Movement," *Australian Journal of Chinese Affairs*, no. 11 (1984): 25–58.

125. Seybolt, "Terror and Conformity," 51–54; Teiwes, *Politics and Purges*, 56–57; and *Dangshi yanjiu*, no. 6 (1980): 61.

126. A 1944 document criticized the phrase "spies are as thick as sesame," apparently attributing it to Kang Sheng; *Zhonggong dangshi jiaoxue cankao ziliao*, 17: 137. An interview source, however, clearly remembers reading the "thick as fur" comment in a statement by Mao early in the cadre screening movement. For documentary evidence suggesting Mao's responsibility, see CCP Central Party History Research Office, ed., *Zhongguo gongchandang lishi dashiji (1919.5–1987.12)* (Chronology of Major Events in CCP History, May 1919-December 1987) (Beijing: People's Press, 1989), 131.

127. Seybolt, "Terror and Conformity," 50, 54; interview sources; and above, 354 and note 63.

128. Hu Hua, *ZDRZ*, 14 (1984): 311–12; *Dangshi yanjiu*, no. 6 (1980): 62; and interview sources.

129. *Zhonggong dangshi dashi nianbiao* (Chronology of Major Events in CCP History) (Beijing: People's Press, 1987), 164; and interview sources. Seybolt, "Terror and Conformity," 55, incorrectly places the CC decision in April 1943 on the basis of Taiwan sources.

130. Zhong Kan, *Kang Sheng pingzhuan*, 93–94; Seybolt, "Terror and Conformity," 65–68; *Dangshi yanjiu*, no. 6 (1980): 62–63; and interview sources.

131. *Hongqi*, no. 13 (1986): 13; and interview source.

132. *Zhonggong dangshi dashi nianbiao*, 167; and interview sources. Teiwes, "Mao and His Lieutenants," 43, states that the bowing incident took place at the Seventh Congress, but this appears to be in error.

133. Zhao Shenghui, *Zhongguo Gongchandang zuzhishi gangyao*, 183; Li Weihan, *Huiyi yu yanjiu*, 2: 514; Liao Gailong, *Dangshi niankan 1982*, 279; and interview sources.

134. *Dangshi ziliao tongxun* (Party History Materials Bulletin), 1981 combined volume (Beijing: CCP Central Party School Press, 1982), 196; Vladimirov, *China's Special Area*, 357–58 and 447; and interview sources.

135. Wang Jianying, *ZGZZH*, 487–88; Zhong Kan, *Kang Sheng pingzhuan*, 96; and interview sources.

136. Zhong Kan, *Kang Sheng pingzhuan*, chaps. 12–13; and interview sources.

137. Interview sources specializing in the period.

138. See Wang Jianying, *ZGZZH*, 332 and 480–81.

139. See Sullivan, "Evolution of Leadership Doctrine," 17–19, 25–27, 81–82, for a discussion of earlier tendencies to personalized leadership. According to an oral source specializing in Zhang Wentian, once Zhang became the leading party secretary at Zunyi he consistently emphasized collective decision making procedures.

140. While various party leaders including Mao (see above, 371) were guilty of using force in inner-party conflict during the late 1920s and early 1930s, operational control of the security forces seemingly did not make one a contender for party leadership. According to a well-informed interview source, early 1930s security chief Deng Fa was an obedient servant of the dominant party leadership lacking in cunning rather than an ambitious politician, while as we have seen the ambitious Kang Sheng suffered a major loss of power as a result of the excesses of 1943; above, 374.

Chapter 13

Conclusion

John Dunn

To judge what caused the Chinese revolution, it is first necessary to decide what the Chinese revolution really was: what exactly it consisted in. Which aspects of the history of China and its population, and over what period of time, plainly form part of the revolution, and which merely coincide with it in time or overlap with it in space? When, for example, did the revolution begin? When did it end? Has it, indeed, ended yet?

The most skeptical interpreters of French or Russian history today must concede that their two great revolutions are now at long last firmly concluded—the French by laying the ghost of Jacobinism and stabilizing, at the fifth attempt, the bourgeois liberal republic, the Russian thus far by destroying the residual political capacity of the Communist Party of the Soviet Union, if as yet by stabilizing scarcely anything at all.[1] Even this degree of clarity, to be sure, is a product of rather recent experience. The Jacobins are no longer with us. The Terror is firmly over. The Communists, admittedly, struggle gamely on. But, in Russia at least, they palpably lack either the appeal or the conviction to recapture power for themselves; and, even in the postcommunist regimes of Eastern Europe, where they do at times float back on the electoral tide, they do so in a guise that is so etiolated compared to their former selves, and so plainly shaped principally by alien political and economic agendas, as to render any personal continuity in identity politically more misleading than it is illuminating. In China, however, matters remain otherwise. The economic agenda of the People's Republic, too, is certainly very different today from what it was in the days of the "Gang of Four." But there is no mistaking the continuity in identity among the personnel who rule it. Nor is this simply a demographic matter—the geriatric residue of the leadership of an army victorious long ago. It is a continuity also and, altogether more importantly, in ultimate legitimation, in the asserted basis of the title to rule. There is, therefore, a close and ineluctable tie between the assessment of the validity of that claim and an assessment of how it is most illuminating to conceive China's long revolution, and a close tie, again, between that assessment itself and the prior judgment of what the concept of revolution really implies and what the category of revolution appropriately refers to.

388

From the beginning the modern political concept of revolution has been an ideological category, as much so for its friends and advocates as for its bitterest critics. Recent attempts to convert it into a noncommittal analytic tool for would-be dispassionate social science were foredoomed to failure from the start. At the center of every revolution, as the chapters of this book remind us, is an intense and deadly struggle for power (personal and impersonal, imaginative and economic, organizational and coercive): an internecine war *à l'outrance* between enemies whose allegiance can never be confidently predicted and for control that can never be conclusively secured. This is not how the exponents of the Rights of Man expected it to be in the early months of the French revolution.[2] However, it is how Edmund Burke warned that it was bound to turn out, almost from the beginning: and Burke, not Paine, has proved to be right.[3] The Chinese revolution is probably harder to characterize convincingly (and therefore harder also to explain) than any other historical revolution: vast in scope, bemusingly protracted in time, enduringly diffuse in focus, politically still very much unresolved, and formidably occluded and opaque throughout. It is also, palpably, of immense political and historical importance—very possibly, now that the cold war has ended without unleashing full-scale thermonuclear war, the single most important historical event of the twentieth century.

Taken together, these attributes pose an intimidating challenge to explanatory hope and drastically reinforce what is already today in the social sciences a comfortably conventional acceptance of the prudence of epistemic modesty. Yet in at least one way the Chinese revolution has been charitable, even generous, to its students. In contrast to any of the great revolutions, whether of the twentieth or of earlier centuries, the Chinese revolutionary experience, and the public political culture of the government and party that revolution brought to power, has highlighted insistently the centrality and significance of the bitter struggle for power itself. In the face of its formidable opacity, and its lengthy passages of purposeful and brutal closure, it would be ironic to suggest that the Chinese revolution was the most self-aware of all the great revolutions. No one could accuse the CCP, at any point in the last seven decades, of naked honesty. But virtually throughout that long history the party has in fact remained remarkably explicit politically: about its goals, about its enemies, even about many of the expedients that it proposed to utilize. Selective and self-serving though its own version of that story has plainly always been, its career has also formed throughout a key element in the story of the revolution as a whole. There is very much else to specify and explain in the history of the Chinese revolution. But even its most obtuse student could hardly fail to register the indispensability of establishing and explaining the history of the party that in the end made it (and which may—or may not—be now unmaking it, bringing it to an abrupt end, completing it, or merely prolonging it for an indefinite period of time). Hence the focus of this book.

Modern revolutions (of which the Chinese revolution is clearly an example) unite two very different components: a passage of relatively decisive social and political destruction and a passage, seldom or never as decisive and usually far less rapid, of social, economic, and political re-creation.[4] Ideologically, what they claim to have done (and been) is usually rather simple: the end of something bad and old, and the birth of something new and good. But if that claim itself is simple to the point of ingenuousness, the grounds espoused for supposing it valid are often (perhaps always) tortured, sophisticated, and highly unstable over time. To present any given revolution as an ideological totality in this way is always likely to appear to detached and critical observers as either distastefully brazen or mildly imbecile. But it is not hard to recognize that conceptions of this kind may be easier to defend as political choices (irrespective of political taste) than they can hope to prove as purely analytical assessments.[5] The claim to comprehensive renovation has always been disquieting: too complete, too benign, and too conclusive to be finally credible. But it would be ingenuous to suppose that it has been the effrontery of that promise that prompted most participants to fight for, rather than against, a revolution.

After a certain stage in the political creation of the new, the remaining political options for individual agents (or often for entire social categories) become either very narrow or else dismayingly bleak: choices between strenuous complicity, pure opportunism, silent impotence, or a brief and rapidly strangled voicing of categorical dissent. For much of the period between October 1917 and 1989, the prevaricatory resources of Marxism enabled many to shroud the harshness of these options in a more or less fluent and intellectually poised tradition of apologetics. But the last few years have exposed to full view just how threadbare these resources always were, and how hard it really is to reconcile the political imagination to history's unyielding choices.

The easy response today is a retreat into more prepossessing modesty (professional, epistemic, political): a brusque narrowing in explanatory ambitions, a refusal to apply evaluative predicates at all, a nominalist repudiation of shape or meaning in the history of societies, an unideological and deconstructed recording of episodes frankly acknowledged as too confusing or too disquieting to take in—too alien, too obscure, or too elaborate to dare even to try to understand.

Modesty is seldom a vice, and perhaps not often even an imprudence. But as the essays in this volume show, it is far from easy to sustain. Inside the CCP, and above all within the ranks of its present leadership, it remains impossible to distinguish historical interpretation of the revolution's causes, character, and trajectory from the ongoing struggle for power: to tell where one stops and the other starts. But for its enemies also, in Taiwan, in Hong Kong, in the Chinese diaspora across the world, and above all in the People's Republic itself, interpreting the revolution, identifying its causes, and explaining its trajectory are all inseparable from the current political task of defining and vindicating their own allegiance and stigmatizing the allegiances of those who choose to stand against them.

It is possible to define the Chinese revolution rather narrowly—in terms of the political triumph and consequences of a single political agency, the CCP. (This is essentially how it is defined in the present volume.) But this narrow definition has an important analytical disadvantage, since it sets aside the fundamental question of what exactly the victorious party triumphed over. The champion, in its own eyes, of the good and new is the regime built by the party. But what exactly was the bad and old array of political and social forces over which that triumph was secured? In purely political terms, this may not seem a difficult question to answer. However it began and altered along the way, the struggle ended up as a civil war between two political and military organizations, the CCP and the GMD. One won; the other lost. What could be clearer or simpler than that? Along the way the CCP fought many battles, and against a wide variety of enemies. But, in the end, it won one war. The historically given (still actually existing) explanatory task is to explain why it won and the GMD lost. But even so defined, as many chapters of this book show, this is not at all an easy task. Several contributors, indeed, plainly believe it not even to be a possible one. Yet no serious participant in Chinese politics from 1921 to today could conceivably be content with seeing the explanatory problem merely in this way. What matters politically, today as for many decades in the past, is the significance of the victory of one organization and the defeat of the other—what this outcome shows about the reality of China's society and economy before and afterward, and about the relations between that society and economy and the states, societies, and economies that, throughout, have acted upon it from the outside.

In China's long revolution both the GMD and CCP were, in their own self-conceptions, revolutionary parties: historically accredited protagonists of the good and new against the bad and old, builders of the future that China needed and deserved. In evicting the GMD from the mainland, the CCP supplanted a rival only a little older than itself, and no more avowedly committed to perpetu-ating the society, economy, or polity of China's millennially (if somewhat mythi-cally) continuous past than the Communists themselves professed to be. In its own eyes the CCP was able to carry through this ejection because it, unlike the GMD, was authentically committed to the future that China needed, while the latter was disabled by more or less compulsive commitment not merely overtly to an inferior (and, on a world scale, historically superannuated) version of that future, but also covertly to the millennially oppressive, if ever-changing, eco-nomic and social basis that had long crippled China in face of the expanding power of Western imperialism.

As several chapters of this book show, this is too impacted a conception of what really occurred in the long-drawn-out and messy struggle between the armies of the two parties to be at all convincing.[6] Each was contending, in the vast and bewilderingly variegated Chinese countryside, as an essentially external agency in arenas neither perforce understood with any precision and that neither was really equipped to control at all securely (still less to meet most of even the more urgent economic and social needs of their denizens).[7] In the struggle for military domination and political support, the Communists had much less to lose, and nowhere else much to which to retreat. They were more alert to the need to win and hold political support, less inhibited in where they chose to look for it, and, it now turns out, just as ideologically relaxed in how they were willing to finance its retention.[8] There is far more of the struggle about which we still know virtually nothing (and about which it must by now be likely that we shall never really know) than there is about which we are reasonably vividly and intimately informed. But even within what we already do know, it is clear enough that the expedients that worked in one setting, and at one time, frequently failed to work in others or at other times, and that, even where they did work, they often did so in ways and as a result of causes quite unapprehended by those who espoused them. At no point in the sequence as we now understand this does the Communist Party, under any of its leaders or lines, appear as clairvoyant interpreter of the properties of Chinese society or economy, or clairvoyant judge of the strategic military requirements for defending the needs of that society. Yet what it does, of course, still emerge as, in these brutal processes of attrition, is a more robust and defter military and political combatant in the end than its GMD adversary. We know that, because we know who won in 1949. In the late 1960s and early 1970s, in the course of the Vietnam war, many scholars found it natural to attribute this conspicuous combative superiority to the special political prowess of the CCP.[9] But with the advantages of hindsight, and in the light of the research reported in this volume, it seems distinctly more likely that a sharper explanation might be achieved by focusing instead upon the comparative debilities of the GMD.[10] It is at least as easy to lose a war as it is to win one.

To explain the Chinese communist revolution (a decisively narrower and less challenging task than explaining the Chinese revolution in its entirety), it is therefore necessary above all to explain the comparative political appeal and coercive potency of the CCP and GMD in the course of the protracted war that they fought against each other (along, in each case, with so many other antagonists), and which residually continues virtually up to the present day. In one view of social and political explanation the only valid explanation of the outcome of that war is (or will be) the full narrative of its course from beginning to end. If it has yet to end, therefore, we cannot even now be confident of having explained it correctly.[11] In a second view, narrative as such can never explain social or political outcomes (though it can readily be employed, of course, to convey explanation of them). What explains must be structure: a fundamental balance of social, economic, and political forces that compels a given human grouping to persist or change as and when it does.[12] Narrative highlights agency—the reasons that human beings have for acting as they do within their own historical world. But while it is unmistakably agency that constitutes and implements revolutions, only structure, in this view, can hope to carry the weight of explaining either their occurrence or their outcomes.

Even in relation to the initiation of revolutions, this is a less clear contention than it initially sounds, though it does at least capture a distinct analytical orientation toward the incidence of revolution. If the fundamental balance of social, political, and economic forces was always given territorially, revolution would be a purely endogenous process; and each society's history would be caused exclusively by its own prior properties. But by the seventeenth century it had come to be true in Europe—and has remained so with steadily greater insistence and on an ever wider scale ever since—that the fundamental balance of social, political, and economic forces within a given territory depended largely on the external impact of other societies.[13] Since the most condensed and decisive form of this impact is full-scale warfare (a peculiarly concrete and hectic spasm of agency), the model of structural determination prior to (and somehow external to) human agency has become very hard to sustain. Structure may sometimes determine who wins a war (the Persian Gulf War, for example).[14] But it can scarcely hope to explain with much conviction exactly why wars break out as and when they do, why particular political actors prepare, or fail to prepare, for them, risk them deliberately in the last instance, capitulate, or struggle to the death. How, for example, could there be a fully structural explanation of the situation in which Stalin left the Soviet air force on the day when Hitler unleashed the German invasion of Russia?[15] How could there be a fully structural explanation of why in the end Saddam Hussein chose to invade Kuwait? And if the preferred explanation is less than fully structural, how can it still be true that only structure can explain, while agency at most can serve to specify or fill out the explicandum in question?

Both the GMD and CCP premised their political agency on a model of the Chinese revolution as a whole: a picture of how China could and should be transformed from its now superannuated past to face its inescapable future, how it could move from the bad and old to the new and good. Both, in effect, still do so, even if their account of the character of the new and good society that they have hoped to construct has wavered considerably over the decades and is not at present in either instance in one of its more explicit phases.[16] It might seem, on initial consideration, that comparison of their purely military potency over time would not need to linger over this larger framework of perception of self and other. But in fact it is hard, as several chapters of this book make clear, to distinguish where the military potency began and the political capacity to recruit and sustain support ended.[17] Fear is overwhelmingly important in armed struggle; but it cannot itself determine either what there is to fear, or what resources or opportunities are open to human agents to confront and face down the objects of their fear. The political construction of the CCP armies, as many chapters again show, depended throughout to no small degree on intimidation and even terror (as, of course, did that of the GMD armies or those of their warlord rivals).[18] In the case of the CCP, as the chapters by Teiwes, Saich, and Apter all make clear, such intimidation sometimes degenerated into the most regressive and politically profligate brutality. But even an interpretation of these struggles that privileged the part played by terror to the maximum, which saw the essence of the struggle itself in the eagerness to use terror to the utmost, would still in the end have to explain the process of recruitment in very different terms. The students who left Beiping to join the red armies in the hinterland certainly did not do so out of masochistic yearning. They did so because on balance they wished the Communists to win and, more confidently whether with good or bad reason, they were increasingly convinced that the GMD deserved to lose. At this point (and in ways that the chapters of this book perhaps do not wholly succeed in bringing into focus) the history of the Chinese communist revolution plainly merges into the history of the Chinese revolution in its widest dimensions, into the long, slow, painful struggle in the minds and lives of Chinese intellectuals and would-be political leaders to identify and implement the policies and institutional agencies needed to rescue China from its ruined past and build for it a future commensurate with its historical grandeur.

Historiographical dispute over the determinants of Chinese communist triumph has isolated many different components that might reasonably be judged to have entered into that triumph. There are at present four main candidates: (1) an unsteadily tightening grasp of the class dynamics of the Chinese countryside, and of how those dynamics could best be harnessed by the presumptive representative agency of a party in arms; (2) a firmer and more readily credible adoption of the burden of national liberation in the face of intensifying Japanese pressure; (3) a cleverer (or simply more fortunate) exploitation of the purely spatial coordinates for building and sustaining military capacity in face of their multifarious enemies; and (4) a hardening organizational code and deepening ideological subjection of those whom they recruited to their ranks. If the triumph itself is seen as a historical sequence, ending in 1949 with military victory over the mainland as a whole, there is, on the evidence of this volume, no good case at present for excluding any of these four elements, and little case either for claiming firm priority of one over the others. Each figures prominently in the narrative of military struggle and armed conquest. The military triumph was a sufficient condition, at least as of 1949, for political triumph too; but military triumph in its turn clearly built on, and needed to build on, a prior range of more interstitial and provisional political ascendancies. There is no convincing way of reading these ascendancies out of the prior social and economic structures of China in 1898 or 1911 or 1921, and little reason to see them in any case as a sufficient condition in themselves even for the military triumph itself. But this lacuna may be partly a result of the failure to analyze the history of the CCP throughout in close enough conjunction with that of its principal and far from ghostly twin enemy. This remains of some political importance. If it is sometimes far easier to explain why a particular political agency lost a war than to explain why its immediate enemy won that war, it may show an ill-considered analytic (and even political) indolence to give up the explanatory task at the point by which it has become reasonably clear that no very shapely and conclusive explanation for victory is going to be forthcoming.

An endogenous secular structural explanation for revolutionary triumph offers a secular equivalent to providence. It vindicates the merit of the victory which it claims to explain by attributing the latter in its entirety to the most fundamental features of the historical entity within which it occurs.[19] Even a structural explanation with a large exogenous component can at least dissipate domestic political culpability. But a pure narrative, articulated with the skeptical nominal sensibility characteristic of much contemporary social science, may be insufficiently explanatory to be at all instructive politically. If the facts themselves are essentially as described, there need not necessarily be anything wrong with it; but it may nevertheless, and just as necessarily, fail to illuminate many questions that require an answer, and do so both practically and imaginatively. This is not a criticism of the validity of such an account, so much as an acknowledgment of its inherent limitations. History needs to be true. It does not need to be politically illuminating.[20] But there is appreciably more need (and therefore decidedly more demand) for political illumination than there is for truth as such. In this respect one criticism that might be leveled at this volume is the limited integration of its two halves, its comparative failure to highlight connections between the initial shaping of the CCP (what it originally was, where its personnel and imaginative appeals came from, what their principal preoccupations really were) and the political and military force into which it was molded in the course of the 1930s. To highlight such connections need not collapse agency back into structure. (As Apter's chapter underlines effectively, no one who took the trouble to consider it with any intimacy could readily miss the frenetic activism at the core of that process of fashioning.) But highlighting such connections would make it far easier to see the history of the party in these crucial years, as it plainly was, as a segment of the larger, still blinder, and even more cruelly driven, history of China as a whole, a China still predominantly made up of a past much of which had to die, but with a future still bewilderingly hard to define and struggling (for the most part, apparently unavailingly) to be born. Besides the intense and deadly struggle for power at its core, every revolution is also a more or less baffled exercise in learning how to begin again, to construct a new and endurable order out of the old, chaotic and increasingly intolerable.[21]

Because in the Chinese case this learning has been so protracted and so erratic, and because of the sheer savagery of so many episodes of the party's history, both before[22] and after winning state power, it is hard to keep historical patience with its heuristic vagaries, hard not to homogenize these into a single stupendous error of political judgment, a vast cruel detour, without ultimate profit or enduring point.[23] Such a perspective is all the more natural today because of the geopolitical and military accident of the survival of the GMD, as a kind of Jacobite Republic over the Water, along with the marked recent success of its economy and the apparent abandonment of any distinctively communist approach to economic development in the People's Republic itself. Certainly comparison between the heritages of the CCP and the GMD today is less embarrassing to the latter or flattering to the former than it appeared to be a quarter of a century ago.[24] It would be unwise, however, to assume that the appearances of today are any more dependable than the semblances of twenty-five years ago. Judging the heuristic felicity of strategies for transforming huge impoverished societies in the twentieth century has proved extraordinarily difficult. There is little reason to assume that it is any easier now than it was in earlier decades. Whatever the comparative felicity of their approaches to building the Chinese future, nothing can hide the historical fact that the CCP in the 1940s won the civil war against its Republican enemies and swept the latter from the mainland.

Explaining that victory will have to remain at the center of any account of what the Chinese revolution really was and why and how it came about. In that explanation the meticulous case studies in this volume—of local military dominance and disruption, of career-building and political elimination within the ranks of the party, of the painstaking specification and relentless imposition of a shared vision of what the party was and represented and how it had taken shape—will be indispensable components. But so too, *mutatis mutandis*, will studies of the corresponding processes in their vanquished rival. So too will more elaborate and systematic tracking of the social and imaginative sources of the party's recruitment and self-understanding in its opening decade (for which the present volume whets rather than satiates the appetite).[25] So too will more historically protracted and open-ended explorations of the changing agrarian economy over time and space, or of the subtle, oblique but remarkably obstinate reproduction of the moral and political *weltanschauung* of a millennially continuous intellectual culture proudly sufficient unto itself.[26] In the end explaining the Chinese communist revolution blends into (and depends upon) an explanation of the broader history of China's revolutionary transformation from the Middle Kingdom into whatever the next century proves to hold for it. The most nominalist and skeptical modern interpreters will find themselves grappling with structures of meaning and imaginative force in which they have been carefully educated to disbelieve: to see as categories of more or less raw superstition. The demand for political illumination will swamp even the most assiduously inculcated professional *pudeur*.

Thinking about revolution has been both politically discomfiting and politically indispensable ever since revolution was first isolated as a distinct subject for reflection.[27] The heady events of 1989 in Europe and across the U.S.S.R. (to say nothing of China itself), the dispiriting recent intellectual history of the social sciences, and the extraordinary dynamism of the Chinese economy over the last decade, taken together, have made the Chinese communist revolution as urgent and recalcitrant to understand, and as uncomfortable to contemplate politically, as anything in modern history. It cannot be true that these events have made it any harder to understand. But what they palpably have done, along with the careful processes of historical inquiry reflected in this volume, is to bring out more starkly just how far we still remain from understanding it, and how disabling to political judgment that limited comprehension is likely to remain, unless and until it can be drastically deepened.

Revolution is not a topic for those who crave rapid and dependable intellectual results. Those who yearn for successfully routinized understanding should pick, insofar as they can, well-established routines for their study. But there is no better setting than revolution for taking the measure of the faltering progress of academic social and political inquiry or of our persistently hazy comprehension of what is really going on and what is genuinely at stake in the politics of the modern world.[28] No one who reads the present volume from one end to the other with any intellectual attention could expect us to fathom for many decades to come either what has given China's long revolution its shape thus far or what will determine its eventual outcome. To see why is not to explain the Chinese communist revolution. But it is certainly to grasp something of the greatest intellectual and practical importance, and not just for us, but also for the people of China themselves.

Notes

1. François Furet, *Inventing the French Revolution*, trans. Elborg Forster (Cambridge: Cambridge University Press, 1981); Sunil Khilnani, *Arguing Revolution* (London and New Haven: Yale University Press, 1994); John Dunn, "The Identity of the Bourgeois Liberal Republic," in Biancamaria Fontana, ed., *The Invention of the Modern Republic* (Cambridge: Cambridge University Press, 1994), 206–25.

2. Emmanuel Joseph Sieyes, *What Is the Third Estate?* trans. M. Blondel (London: Pall Mall, 1961); and compare later Thomas Paine, *The Rights of Man* (London: J. M. Dent, 1915).

3. Edmund Burke, *Reflections on the Revolution in France*, in Edmund Burke, *Writings and Speeches*, Vol. 8, ed. L. G. Mitchell (Oxford: Clarendon Press, 1989).

4. For the particularity of modern revolutions see John Dunn, *Modern Revolutions: An Introduction to the Analysis of a Political Phenomenon*, 2nd ed. (Cambridge: Cambridge University Press 1989), esp. introduction to the 2nd edition; and "The Success and Failure of Modern Revolutions," in John Dunn, *Political Obligation in Its Historical Context* (Cambridge: Cambridge University Press 1980), Chapter 9. The claim that the destructive and the (presumptively) creative elements are in any genuine manner yoked to one another is always and necessarily politically controversial, as is the presumption that the first element (the destruction of the old, whether bad or not) has been effectively completed. In the case of China, in part simply because of the prodigious historical depth of its prerevolutionary culture, skepticism today is especially acute over this latter judgment.

5. See Burke's path-breaking analysis of the grim counterrevolutionary options opened up by the debacle of the French ancien régime. Edmund Burke, *Writings and Speeches*, Vols. 8 and 9, ed. R. B. McDowell (Oxford: Clarendon Press, 1991); and compare the reading in John Dunn, "Against Vanity," *Times Literary Supplement*, 29 July 1990, 691–92.

6. See Chapters 4–8 and 11–12.

7. For the historical and geographical dimensions of this variety see, inter alia, Evelyn Sakakida Rawski, *Agricultural Change and the Peasant Economy of South China* (Cambridge: Harvard University Press, 1972); Peter C. Perdue, *Exhausting the Earth: State and*

Peasantry in Hunan 1500–1850 (Cambridge: Harvard University Press, 1987); Philip C.C. Huang, *The Peasant Economy and Social Change in North China* (Stanford: Stanford University Press, 1985); Ramon H. Myers, *The Chinese Peasant Economy: Agricultural Development in Hopei and Shantung 1890–1949* (Cambridge: Harvard University Press, 1970), and especially the masterly summary by Lucien Bianco in the present volume. Compare the interesting attempt to interpret political alignment in the English Civil War in terms of ecologically based variations in the culture of different localities in David Underdown, *Revel, Riot and Rebellion:Popular Politics and Culture in England 1603–1660* (Oxford: Oxford University Press, 1986).

8. See especially the compelling argument of Chen Yung-fa, Chapter 10.

9. See Mark Selden, *The Yenan Way in Revolutionary China* (Cambridge: Harvard University Press, 1971); and earlier, classically, Edgar Snow, *Red Star over China* (London: Gollancz, 1937), and William Hinton, *Fanshen: A Documentary of Revolution in a Chinese Village* (New York: Monthly Review Press, 1966). Compare the careful analysis of the first phase of the CCP's rural campaign in Roy Hofheinz, Jr., *The Broken Wave: the Chinese Communist Peasant Movement 1922–1928* (Cambridge: Harvard University Press, 1977).

10. These have been studied less intensively in the last few decades than the sources of the CCP's strength. But see Lloyd E. Eastman, *The Abortive Revolution: China under Nationalist Rule 1927–1937* (Cambridge: Harvard University Press, 1974), and *Seeds of Destruction: Nationalist China in War and Revolution 1937–1949* (Stanford: Stanford University Press, 1984).

11. See Arthur Danto, *Analytical Philosophy of History* (Cambridge: Cambridge University Press, 1965). For the eminently practical implications of this point in the case of China, see Edward Friedman, "A Failed Chinese Modernity," *Daedalus* 122 (spring 1993): 1–17.

12. See in relation to revolutions more particularly, Theda Skocpol, *States and Social Revolutions* (Cambridge: Cambridge University Press, 1979), and John Dunn, *Rethinking Modern Political Theory* (Cambridge: Cambridge University Press, 1985), Chapter 4.

13. Istvan Hont, "Free Trade and the Economic Limits to National Politics: Neo-Machiavellian Political Economy Reconsidered," in John Dunn, ed., *The Economic Limits to Modern Politics* (Cambridge: Cambridge University Press), 41–120; and compare Robert Brenner, *Merchants and Revolution* (Cambridge: Cambridge University Press, 1990), and Perry Anderson, "Maurice Thomson's War," *London Review of Books*, 4 November 1993, 13–17.

14. See Lawrence Freedman and Efraim Karsh, *The Gulf War 1990–91* (London: Faber, 1993).

15. John Erickson, *The Road to Stalingrad* (London: Panther Books, 1985), Chapters 2–4.

16. See Ramon H. Myers, ed., *Two Societies in Opposition: The Republic of China and the People's Republic of China after Forty Years* (Stanford: Hoover Institution Press, 1991). For a particularly drastic index of the ideological discontinuity in the case of the CCP, see the objection by Lu Ping, director of the Hong Kong and Macao Affairs Office, over the 1993 negotiations with the governor of Hong Kong, Chris Patten, to democratizing the functional constituencies for membership of the Legislative Council: "What he envisages is that all the workers will have a vote. For instance, we're going to have a functional constituency for the textile industry. . . . According to his proposal it might be quite possible for somebody who is an ordinary worker, maybe a cleaner, to be elected. . . . That's what I asked him: 'Do you think a cleaner, an ordinary worker in the textile industry, can represent the textile industry?' I don't think so." Simon Holberton, "Hong Kong," *Financial Times*, 17 December 1993, 6. And contrast the virulent hostility to a division of political labor based on class and occupational privilege in the classic texts of

Marx himself (*The Civil War in France*) and Lenin (*The State and Revolution*), to say nothing of the privileging of redness over expertise in the Cultural revolution, see Franz Schurmann, *Ideology and Organization in Communist China* (Berkeley: University of California Press, 1966).

17. See Chapters 4–8, 11, and 12 in this volume.

18. See especially Chapters 8 and 9 in this volume.

19. For the political significance of these categorizations and its historical impact upon attempts to understand the character of modern revolutions, see John Dunn, "Revolution," in *Interpreting Political Responsibility* (Cambridge, England: Polity, 1990), Chapter 6.

20. See John Dunn, "The Identity of the History of Ideas," in Dunn, *Political Obligation*, Chapter 2.

21. Dunn, "Success and Failure"; and compare Roberto Mangabeira Unger, *False Necessity* (Cambridge: Cambridge University Press, 1987). As Unger himself insists, it is quite unwarranted to expect revolutions in general to prove successful in this feat of reconstruction.

22. See, in particular, Chapters 9 and 12 in this volume.

23. See in the Russian case Neil Harding, "The Marxist-Leninist Detour," in John Dunn, ed., *Democracy: The Unfinished Journey* (Oxford: Oxford University Press, 1992), 155–87. For the fundamental shift in economic and political judgment behind the intellectual acknowledgment of this debacle, see, for example, Wlodzimierz Brus and Kasimierz Laski, *From Marx to the Market* (Oxford: Clarendon Press 1989), and John Dunn, *The Politics of Socialism* (Cambridge: Cambridge University Press, 1984).

24. See Friedman, "A Failed Chinese Modernity"; George T. Crane, "China and Taiwan: Not Yet 'Greater China,'" *International Affairs* 19 (October 1993): 705–23.

25. But see Hans J. van de Ven, *From Friend to Comrade: The Founding of the Chinese Communist Party 1920–1927* (Berkeley: University of California Press, 1991).

26. See, for example, the oeuvre of Thomas A. Metzger, especially his contribution to Myers, ed., *Two Societies in Opposition* and his *Escape from Predicament: Neo-Confucianism and China's Evolving Political Culture* (New York: Columbia University Press, 1977). The theme is, of course, prominent in a slightly less explicit form throughout the rich literature on China's modern intellectual history.

27. See John Dunn, "Revolution," in *Interpreting Political Responsibility*, Chapter 6, and "Against Vanity," *Times Literary Supplement*, 1990, 691–92.

28. See John Dunn, *Western Political Theory in the Face of the Future*, 2nd ed. (Cambridge: Cambridge University Press, 1993), especially "Conclusion."

Index